Struggle on the High Plains

An Economic History of Eastern Colorado

Wilson D. Kendall

HUGO HOUSE PUBLISHERS, LTD.

Struggle on the High Plains: An Economic History of Eastern Colorado

©2023 Wilson D. Kendall. All rights reserved.

No part of this book may be reproduced or transmitted in any form or by any means, electronic or mechanical, including photocopying, recording, or by an information storage and retrieval system without written permission of the publisher.

ISBN: 978-1-948261-45-6

Library of Congress Control Number: 2022906646

Cover Design & Interior Layout: Ronda Taylor, www.heartworkcreative.com

Hugo House Publishers, Ltd.
Austin, TX • Denver, CO
www.HugoHousePublishers.com

Dedication

To my father, Charles Kendall,
who devoted his talents and efforts to better his plains community.

Contents

Dedication iii

Preface xiii

    Overview xvi

    Preface Exhibits. xx

CHAPTER 1

Indians, Traders, Ranchers and Railroads: Eastern Colorado Through the Middle 1880s 1

    Native Peoples and Early Exploration 1

    The Traders and Bent's Fort 2

    The Cattle Kingdom 4

    Other Livestock. 15

    Railroads Through the Plains. 16

    The Plains in 1885 23

    Chapter 1 Exhibits 24

CHAPTER 2

Early Farming: Middle 1880s Through 1900 27

    The First Wave of Homesteaders 28

    End of the First Homestead Boom 35

    The Introduction of Irrigation in the Arkansas and South Platte Valleys 38

        Need for New Water Law. 39

        Irrigation Projects. 41

    Early Irrigated Farming 47

    Plains Agriculture in 1900. 48

Chapter 2 Exhibits 50

CHAPTER 3

The Golden Age of Agriculture:
1900 through Twenties. 55

The Agricultural Environment 55
The Second Wave of Homesteaders. 57
A Revolution in Agricultural Technology and Farming Techniques 61
Crops. 64
    Sugar Beets 64
    Wheat 72
    Corn and Other Dryland Crops 75
    Alfalfa. 76
    Cantaloupe and Other Vegetable and Fruits 78
Livestock. 78
Plains Agriculture in 1920. 81
Chapter 3 Exhibits 82

CHAPTER 4

The Non-Farm Economy, Population and Labor Force Through 1930 85

Non-agricultural Industries 85
Demographics and the Labor Force 1870-1930 91
Education and Literacy 93
Early Towns. 95
Foreign Immigrants 97
The Plains Region in 1930 104
Chapter 4 Exhibits 105

CHAPTER 5

Depression and Drought: the 1920s and 1930s 111

The Farm Depression of the 1920s 111
The 1930s 113
The Federal Government's Response to the Depression 115

    Drought and Depression on the Eastern Plains 118

    Eastern Plains Farming and Ranching in the 1930s 121

    The Non-farm Economy 126

    Banking 128

    Emigration 132

    The Plains Region in 1940 133

    Chapter 5 Exhibits 134

CHAPTER 6

The Dust Bowl 139

    Drought in Southeast Colorado 139

    Government Response to the Dust Bowl 145

    Causes of the Dust Bowl 150

    Legacy of the Dust Bowl 153

    Chapter 6 Exhibits 155

CHAPTER 7

War and Postwar: The 1940s 159

    Wartime 159

    Plains Agriculture in Wartime 163

    Plains Agriculture in the 1940s 165

    Another Wheat Boom 168

    The Nonfarm Economy in the Forties 171

    Population and Labor Force 173

    Eastern Colorado in 1950 176

    Chapter 7 Exhibits 177

CHAPTER 8

Post-War Exuberance Fades: 1950-1970 181

    Return of the Dust Bowl 181

    The Agricultural Environment in the 1950s and 1960s 186

    Impacts on Regional Farmers 187

    Irrigation 191

Oil Boom in the Denver-Julesburg Basin 195
Other Key Industries. 198
Population and Incomes 202
The Eastern Plains Economy in 1970. 204
Chapter 8 Exhibits 205

CHAPTER 9

Boom and Bust Once More: The 1970s and 1980s 209

Agricultural Prosperity in the Early 1970s 209
The End of the Boom. 212
The Return of Farm Populism 215
Challenges for Plains Bankers. 218
Surface Irrigation Threatened. 221
The Nonfarm Economy 223
Interstate Highways and Railroads. 225
Manufacturing in the Seventies and Eighties 227
Population and Labor Force. 233
The Plains Economy in 1990 235
Chapter 9 Exhibits 236

CHAPTER 10

Coping with the New Economy: 1990-2015 239

Agriculture 1990-2011 240
Destructive Weather 241
Another Farm Boom. 244
Agriculture Consolidation Continued 244
Hog Farms. 246
Further Threats to Irrigation 248
The Non-farm Economy. 250
Prisons: A New Economic Driver for Rural Communities 253
The Arkansas Valley Economy Slumped in the 2000s 256
Population and Labor Force. 258

  Regional Incomes. 261
  The Surging Latino Population 263
  The High Plains in the Twenty-First Century. 266
  Chapter 10 Exhibits 267

CHAPTER 11

The Prairie Towns **273**
  Evolution of the Plains Towns. 273
  The Larger Towns. 276
    Fort Morgan 277
    La Junta 280
    Lamar. 284
    Sterling 287
  Other Economically Important Towns 291
    Brush 291
    Burlington 293
    Las Animas. 294
    Limon 296
    Rocky Ford 297
    Springfield 298
    Yuma 299
  The Smaller Towns 300
  Chapter 11 Exhibits 304

CHAPTER 12

The Eastern Plains Today. **307**
  The Structure of Plains Economies. 307
  Agriculture 308
  The Non-Farm Economy 309
  Future Population Trends 313
  Challenges Facing Plains Economies. 314
  Issues Confronting Agriculture. 315

    Transportation and Communication 316
    Labor Availability and Quality 317
    Financing Local Businesses 319
    Social and Cultural Issues 320
    The High Plains: Looking Back 321
    Chapter 12 Exhibits 323

Appendix **327**
    Description of Data Sources 327

Endnotes **331**

Bibliography **387**
    Books 387
    Articles and Pamphlets 393
    Newspapers and Periodicals 399
    Government Reports and Data Sources 400

Index **405**

About the Author **431**

The author with mannequins of his two great aunts, Stella and May. The two women settled in Prowers County in the 1880's. This picture was taken by Susan Kendall at Big Timbers Museum in Lamar.

Preface

This book was inspired by my lifetime involvement with the economy and history of eastern Colorado. I was born and spent my childhood and teenage years in Lamar where my family lived for over a century. My two great aunts, pictured above, were among the early settlers in the town. A few years later in the early twentieth century, my recently widowed paternal grandmother moved to Lamar with her two sons, my father and his brother, to join her sisters. At about the same time my maternal grandfather established his alfalfa milling company in Hartman, a small town in eastern Prowers County. He and my grandmother, who came from a pioneer family in the San Luis Valley, made their home there where my mother was born, later moving both the company and their home to Lamar.

Growing up in the forties and fifties, I was entranced by family stories about the early days. I heard how the townspeople wanted Aunt Stella to be the district school superintendent, but since women were not eligible for that post, her husband was appointed to the position with the understanding that Stella would run the district. I recall stories from my grandfather about the early days of alfalfa milling in the Arkansas Valley. My father told of the struggles of the local economy during the depression, and my mother often talked of the travails of the Dust Bowl. During my later teen-age summers, I delivered bakery products to grocery stores and restaurants throughout southeast Colorado. I saw the euphoria produced by a good wheat harvest. I felt keenly the struggles of small-town businesses as they lost customers to the larger trading centers.

My father was deeply involved in economic development efforts for his community. After I began my study of economics in college, we had many fascinating conversations about prospects for the local economy. During the eighties I served on the board of directors of First National Bank in Lamar. The bank had been bailed out during the depression by my grandfather and other local businessmen and, as a result, our family had substantial stock holdings and felt that we should be represented on the board. It was a challenging time for agricultural lenders, and I was exposed to some real-world economics. I learned a lot from my fellow board members, a knowledgeable collection of businessmen, farmers, ranchers, and feedlot operators.

Throughout the seventies and early eighties, I worked as an economist at the Colorado's Governor's Budget office where I monitored and forecast the state's economy. My dealings with the different government departments and politicians from all over the state led to an awareness of diverse economic issues facing different parts of Colorado. I soon became aware that while the state economy was dominated by the urban areas on the state's Front Range, the outlying areas including the eastern plains with vastly different economic structures, were often neglected. For the next thirty years, I worked at a small economic consulting firm that I cofounded. Among my projects was developing, with state demographer Jim Westkott, a forecasting model for economies of all the state's counties. We were forced to examine the different factors that affected the local economies throughout the state.

I long wished to delve more deeply into Colorado's economic history when I had more time. I initially planned to write a history of each of the state's regional economies and decided to start with the eastern plains, but soon found that task more than enough to occupy my retirement years. I have tried to bring together information from a variety of sources for a comprehensive picture of the region's economic history. I have drawn upon numerous books, articles, memoirs, and local newspapers about such subjects as the open range era, settlement by homesteaders, the Dust Bowl, the sugar beet industry, the fifties oil boom, farm unrest in the 1980s, and the siting of prisons in rural communities.

Several sources of information have proved invaluable. The Western History Collection at Denver Public Library contains an exhaustive compilation of publications, documents, photographs, and archives on the plains region. The Hart Research Library at the Colorado History Museum has a similar collection as well as historical newspapers from many of the region's towns. The Business Research Division at the University of Colorado's Leeds School of Business has recent and historical reports on the State's regional economies. The Colorado State Demography Office (SDO) maintains an extensive collection of historical and current data on the region, and the SDO staff have been a valuable source of information about recent developments in plains communities. The staffs at all these organizations have been extremely helpful to me in my efforts.

As this is an economic history, I have tried to limit it to developments affecting the economy. For example, discussion of the Sand Creek Massacre, surely one the most noteworthy events in the region's history, is limited to noting that it resulted in land grants to members of the affected tribes, many of which were later acquired by the region's large ranchers. Since the narrative is primarily a work of history, I have chosen to end it in roughly the middle teens. I have noted some more recent major developments such as the closing of the Kit Carson Correctional Center in 2016 and have incorporated data from the 2017 Census of Agriculture. But I have not attempted a comprehensive description of the regional economy after about 2015. I was completing

Preface

the book as the Covid-19 pandemic raged and have not included any information about its effect on the region nor have I speculated about its future impacts.

Colorado's eastern plains region covered here includes the 16 counties east of the urban settlements along the Front Range. This definition is largely a matter of convenience due to the nature of data, much of which are not available for finer gradations than the county level. Colorado's eastern plains region as an economic entity extends somewhat to the west of these counties. The irrigated farming land along the two river valleys includes parts of Weld, Boulder and Larimer Counties in the north and Pueblo County in the south. The short-grass prairie encompasses the eastern portions of Adams, Arapahoe, El Paso and Las Animas Counties. However, the economies of these counties are dominated by their western urban cores. It could be argued that western Elbert County and parts of Morgan County no longer belong to the plains economy as they became bedroom communities for the Front Range, but they were primarily agricultural until the late twentieth century.

In this work I cite many economic statistics from a variety of sources. The more important data sources are listed and described in the Appendix. In the text I have often chosen to round the figures. In part this reflects my stylistic preference, round numbers seem less technical and formal. Furthermore, most economic data are not that precise, and I do not wish to give a false sense of precision. It is unlikely, for example, that the 1890 population of Kiowa County was exactly 1243 as the Census reported. In the text I describe the entire sixteen counties as the region, the plains, the high plains or eastern Colorado at various points. I also refer to irrigated and non-irrigated parts of the region based on irrigated acreage in a county prior to the 1950s when some dryland properties were irrigated from the Ogallala Aquifer. In later chapters counties are grouped into Baca County, the Arkansas Valley, the Central Plains except Elbert County, the South Platte Valley and the Northeast Plains. This sorting is useful as counties in each group have common characteristics, particularly in their agriculture.

I have described the plains Hispanic population as "Mexican" in the chapters covering the early twentieth century and as "Latino" in later chapters. This is consistent with terminology in use at the time and is accurate as most of these early migrant workers were of Mexican descent. I have incorporated personal memories where I felt they might provide background to events in the region.

I hope this volume will be of interest to those like me who have roots in the region or are curious about it, and that it will be useful as a reference and resource for anyone wanting to learn more about the plains economy and its history. If the book seems pessimistic in places, it reflects what I consider an accurate picture of the plains economy. It does not indicate any lessening of my real and deep fondness for the region and its people. Creating this work has been a labor of love for me, and I hope that it brings knowledge and pleasure to the reader. I take responsibility and apologize for errors in the text, tables, or charts.

Overview

It is harsh country, confronting residents and visitors with a brutal and unforgiving environment. The plains of Colorado stretching east from the Rockies is an arid land subject to fierce winter blizzards, scorching summer heat, and high winds that can bring dust storms in dry years. As the nation looked west in the nineteenth century, the plains were often dismissed as part of the Great American Desert, a term that is said to have originated with a label on a map from Major Stephen Long's 1820 expedition up the South Platte to the Rockies and back along the Arkansas.[1] Greg Hobbs, former Colorado Supreme Court Justice and state water-law guru, pointed out that Long came during the driest season of the year when the rivers had slowed to trickles.[2] Had he visited during spring runoff his assessment might have been more sanguine. Indeed, John C. Fremont, whose expedition explored northeast Colorado in June 1843, wrote, "The valley of the Platte looked like a garden, so rich was the verdure of the grasses, and so luxurious the bloom of abundant flowers."[3] Nonetheless, the bleak "desert" appellation was not inappropriate. The high plains lacked abundant rainfall and were unsuitable for the kind of agriculture practiced elsewhere in the US in the nineteenth century. Since there were no commercially exploitable mineral deposits or navigable rivers, economic value was limited to fur trading and open range cattle century until most of the rest of the nation had been settled.

The region's continental climate is characterized by extreme temperatures, a short growing season, recurrent drought and persistent wind.[4] Most of the land is shortgrass prairie at altitudes ranging from 3,300 to over 6,000 feet and annual rainfall averaging well under twenty inches per year. Two major rivers, the South Platte in the north and the Arkansas in the south, flow east from the mountains with the largest population centers found along their valleys. The economy has depended upon farming and ranching despite geographical and climatological limitations. The economic history of the region is dominated by the rise and relative decline of agriculture in the American economy.

The high plains' aridity meant that early settlers attempting to farm had to cope with conditions vastly different from their previous experiences. They were forced to develop new techniques and new institutions. The preeminent historian of America's plains region was Walter Prescott Webb who grew up on the parched prairie of west Texas. In his magisterial work *The Great Plains* he stressed the transformation brought about by the regional settlers' struggles for survival.[5] In Webb's telling: "the Plains destroyed the old formula of living and demanded a new one."[6] Eastern Colorado epitomized both this destruction and the efforts toward creation of a new way of life. From the time of its earliest settlement, Colorado's plains have made great demands on its people. They have not always met them successfully, but the story of their efforts is a fascinating and inspiring one.

The economic prospects of the region have been denigrated for two centuries. A chronicler on Long's expedition described the region as "unfit for residence for any but a nomad population. The traveler who shall at any time have traversed its desolate sands will, we think, join us in the wish that this region may forever remain the unmolested haunt of the native hunter, the bison, the prairie wolf."[7] In the 1870s John Wesley Powell in his *Report on the Lands of the Arid Region* catalogued the many impediments to farming in the arid west.[8] Planners in the New Deal's Resettlement Administration viewed the southern plains as having limited agricultural potential and advocated moving many of its farmers to more suitable land elsewhere. In the 1980s Rutgers University academicians, Deborah and Frank Popper, proposed abandoning much of the arid plains, restoring them to their pre-Columbian state in what they called a "Buffalo Commons."[9] In 2015 a *Denver Post* reporter described the area around Lamar as "a savage country. Tornadoes, hail and blizzards can hit without warning. A prolonged drought has pummeled the economy, with dust storms so severe the schools have closed early twice so buses wouldn't be dropping off kids in blackout conditions."[10]

But if there were detractors, the region also had its boosters. Geographer John Allen argued that conflicting visions of the Great Plains, "The Great American Desert" and the "New World Garden," competed throughout the nineteenth century.[11] In 1868, William Gilpin, Colorado's first territorial governor, described the plains as a "pastoral Canaan"[12] although, as Christopher Schnell pointed out, "His consistent praise for the continent's interior coincided conspicuously with his personal economic interests."[13] Railroad companies and land speculators, also reflecting pecuniary motivations, lauded the region's potential. A 1910 promotional pamphlet effused: "The great agricultural possibilities of the unirrigated plains of Eastern Colorado have not been understood or appreciated until within the last few years." It went on to describe northeast Colorado's Yuma and Washington Counties as "the healthiest country in the world…. the air is pure, bracing and invigorating."[14] In 1975 the Colorado Division of Commerce and Development released economic reports on Colorado's regions lauding the plains region as offering "unparalleled advantages to the prospective employer," providing an "unprecedented new home for your thriving enterprise," promising "a fine place to locate your business."[15]

In the early years of penetration by Europeans, fur traders and open range cattlemen exploited the abundant grasslands. Further economic development awaited infrastructure investment and new farming techniques and technologies. The construction of railroads and large-scale irrigation projects along with the introduction of barbed wire, farm machinery, and innovations in farming spurred a growing economy and population in the late nineteenth and early twentieth centuries. Both government and private action served as stimuli for burgeoning economic activity. The region enjoyed robust agriculture-based growth until the farm recession in the early 1920s and the drought and national depression of the 1930s. As farming and ranching grew, agricultural processing industries sprang up along with trade and service businesses for farmers and their families. Population in the "original" Bent County,[16] made up of six current counties in southeastern Colorado and part of southern Lincoln County, increased from fewer than one thousand in 1870 to almost 62,000 in the 1930 Census.

Over the next eighty some years, the economic importance of agriculture dwindled. Farming and ranching became less labor intensive, and the rural population declined. Local businesses suffered a parallel reduction. Firms processing farm products consolidated to take advantage of economies of scale or relocated to other regions abandoning facilities in many plains towns. Improved transportation and communication allowed much trade and service to shift to large metropolitan areas. Government interventions, which helped fuel the expansion, tempered the decline. Federal farm support programs ensured the survival of wheat and corn growers and mitigated the effects of the worst declines in livestock markets. State and federal government facilities provided critical jobs and income for many plains communities. With the expansion of federal entitlement programs, transfer payments to an aging and increasingly impoverished plains population assumed ever greater importance in the economic base. The private sector also contributed to growth. Large manufacturing plants sustained local economies, but often their eventual closures led to losses of jobs and population.

But government programs, along with modest increases in light manufacturing, were insufficient to replace agricultural losses in much of the region. Since the 1920s, economic activity and population have declined except in the bedroom communities adjoining the Front Range metropolitan areas and in parts of the South Platte Valley where a thriving complex of feed grain production, livestock feeding, and meat packing has flourished. By the 2015 population in the original Bent County had fallen by more than one quarter from its peak and by over one-third if the four thousand inmates in state penal institutions were not counted.[17] Of the sixteen counties in Colorado's eastern plains, twelve reached their maximum Census populations in 1920 or 1930 with several reporting declines of more than fifty percent over the ensuing decades.

Throughout its history the eastern plains farmers and businesses were buffeted by forces beyond their control. The region saw cyclical booms and busts along with the longer-term economic trajectories of growth and decline. Weather patterns generated both prosperity and depression. Severe droughts in the 1930s and again in the 1950s brought sizable losses to farmers and ranchers as did winter storms in the middle 1880s, in 1946, and in 2002. Abundant rainfall in the 1880s and the 1940s contributed to verdant crops and pastures. World markets became another source of vulnerability. Demand for farm and ranch products mushroomed during and after each of the world wars as well as in the early 1970s and the 2010s. But the booms were followed by prices so depressed that producers struggled to survive.

Preface

Today many eastern Colorado communities must deal with an aging population, an influx of immigrant workers, and a declining tax base. The region's agriculture still suffers from the vicissitudes of world markets and an undependable climate. Farmers and businessmen must put up with the capriciousness of Federal farm policy and unpredictable actions of a state government dominated by Front Range urban voters. Farmers face potentially severe water shortages as irrigated farmers' water rights are being transferred to Front Range urban areas where they have greater value in domestic or industrial use. The underground aquifers are also being depleted. Household incomes are well below the national mean, and job growth is insufficient to provide employment for young people entering the workforce. The region offers moderate land and labor costs, but the industries attracted are often those most vulnerable to technological change and foreign competition. Plains residents are resilient and resourceful and have overcome many trials since the Bent brothers built their trading fort on the Arkansas in the 1830s. To continue to do so, they must cope with a demanding and unpredictable modern world along with the plains' isolation and climatic adversity.

The warning from the Long expedition two centuries ago may yet prove precient.

Preface Exhibits

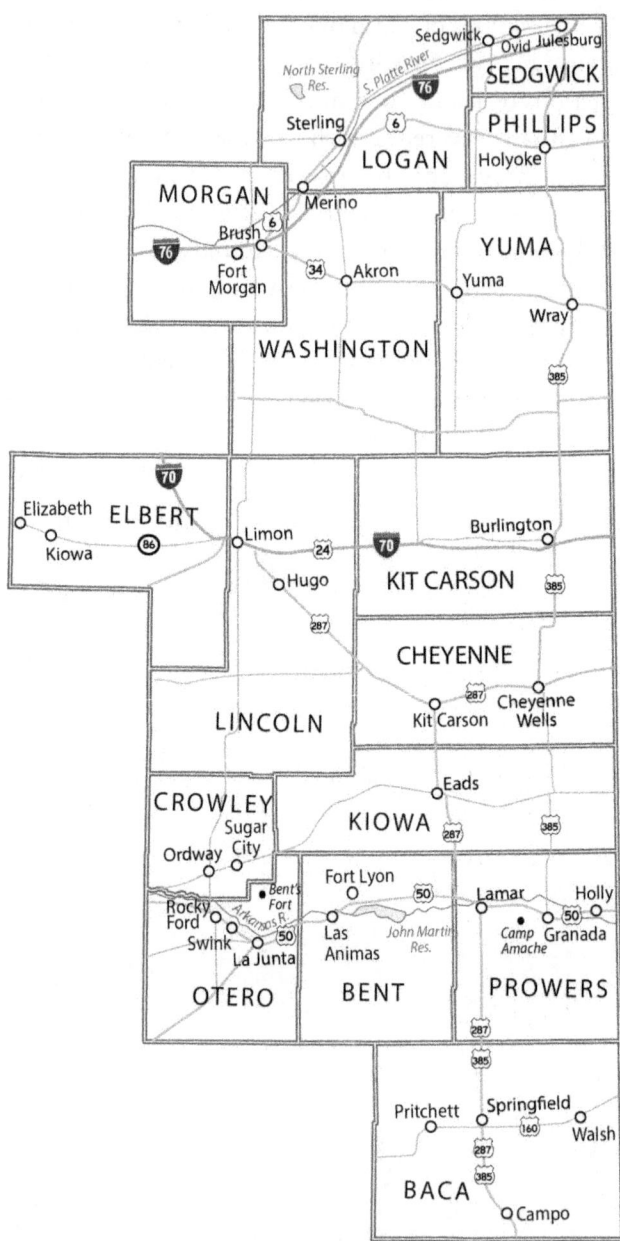

Colorado's eastern plains region consists of the sixteen counties shown in the map. Two major rivers, the South Platte in the north and the Arkansas in the south, run through the region. The larger population centers are found in the two valleys and in western Elbert County adjacent to the urban areas of the Front Range.

Average Annual Precipitation

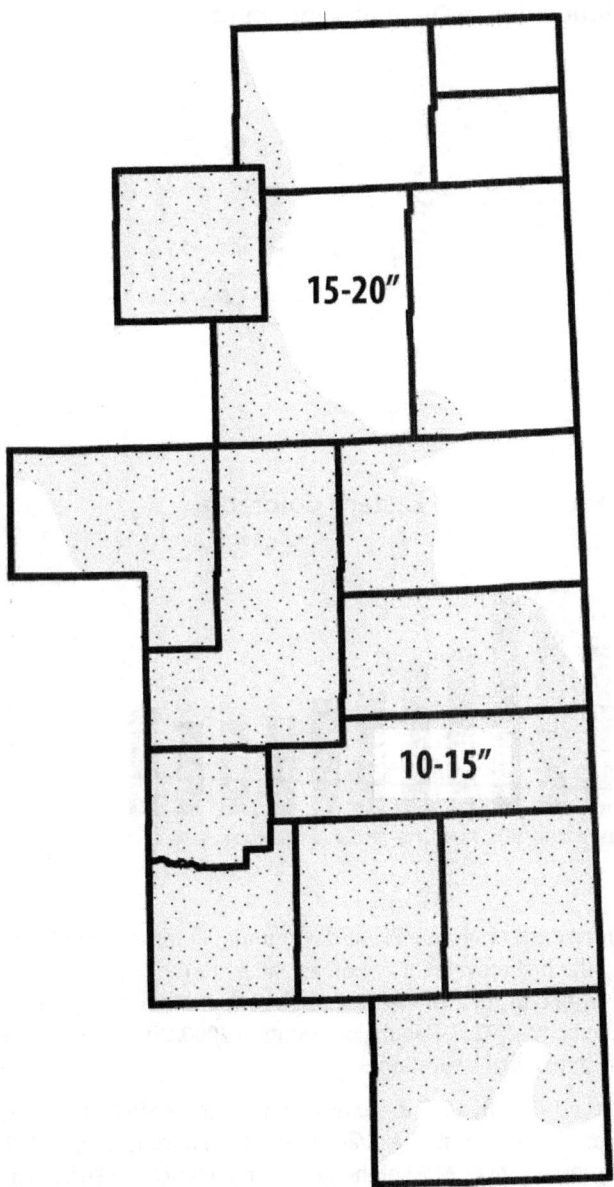

The plains climate is a continental one, characterized by hot summers and cold winters, extreme temperatures, a relatively short growing season, recurrent drought, and strong and persistent winds. The dominant climatic feature of the high plains is its aridity. Precipitation falls short of twenty inches per year for the entire region with weather becoming drier as one moves further west. The map shows average annual precipitation between 1961 and 1990.

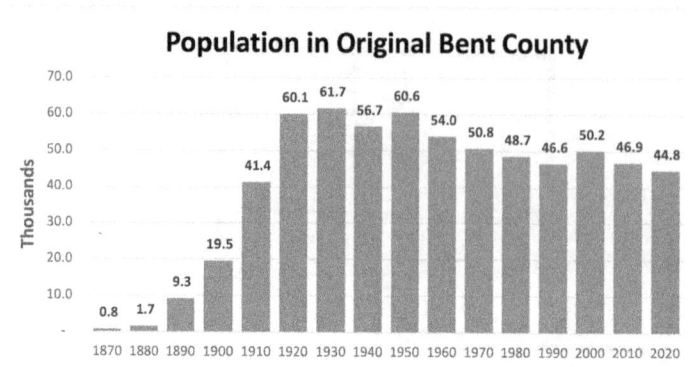

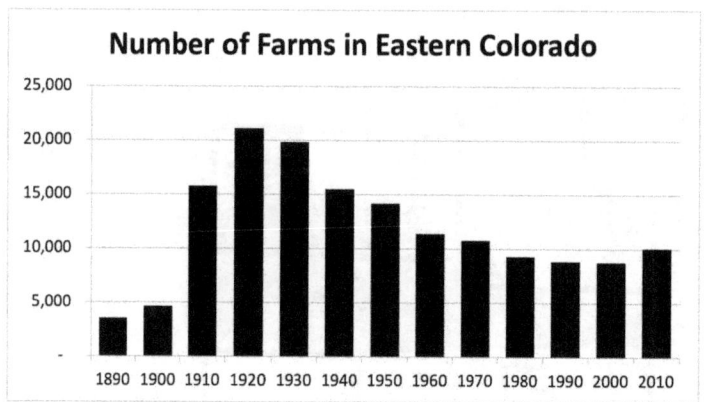

The "original" Bent County included parts of seven present-day counties in southeast Colorado. The population grew rapidly during the first movement of homesteaders to the region in the 1880's. Another growth surge occurred during the first two decades of the twentieth century with population reaching an all-time high during the 1920's. Population counts in 2000, 2010 and 2020 include nearly four thousand inmates in state penal institutions.

The number of farms peaked in the 1920s. By 1980 it had dropped by more than half although the acreage in farms and ranches had grown almost one quarter. The sharp decline in the 1930's was the result of the drought and depressed prices. Most of the subsequent reduction can be explained by consolidation. The increase after 2000 was a result of growing numbers of very small "hobby" farms without which the declined would have continued.

Source: Census. 2020 projection from SDO. Estimate for original Bent County for 1870 includes Bent and one half of population in Greenwood County. Estimates for 1890 and following years include Bent, Cheyenne, Crowley (beginning 1920), Kiowa, Otero and Prowers Counties. The original Bent County also included a sparsely populated part of today's Lincoln County. Farm numbers from Census of Agriculture. After 1950 estimates of the number of farms are based on interpolation of Census estimates to decennial years.

CHAPTER 1

Indians, Traders, Ranchers and Railroads: Eastern Colorado Through the Middle 1880s

UNTIL THE LATE NINETEENTH CENTURY, DIM PROSPECTS FOR CONVENTIONAL farming on the high plains meant that the vast expanse of open grassland was the only readily exploitable resource. The indigenous peoples depended on native plants and animals for survival. Those who followed the early explorers trapped and traded with the Indians for buffalo skins and beaver pelts. After the Civil War, ranchers grazed cattle on the open grass lands. The age of open grasslands ended with the construction of railroads through the largely uninhabited country, helping bring the demise of the cattle kingdom but providing a foundation for future growth.

Native Peoples and Early Exploration

One thousand years ago, the plains enjoyed precipitation well above recent levels. The natives lived in villages along the river valleys where ample precipitation nourished an economy based on farming supplemented by hunting and gathering. By around 1200 the climate became markedly drier forcing the tribes to migrate.[18] The now-arid plains attracted nomadic peoples. The climate was unsuitable for the agriculture of the day, and the plains Indians did not develop the sophisticated settlements of some other native peoples in the Americas. The buffalo, according to Webb, was "life, food, raiment and shelter to the Indians."[19] The introduction of the horse by the Spanish in the sixteenth century improved their lot, a rare instance when American aboriginals received some benefit from contact with Europeans. Horses increased their hunting and war-making capability and expanded their range, but the plains Indians' economic activity was still largely confined to hunting and foraging. By the early nineteenth century, Comanche and Kiowa occupied the lands south of the Arkansas while Arapaho and Cheyenne ranged north of the river.[20]

The first Europeans came to the region in 1601 when the Spanish conquistador Juan de Oñate y Salazar passed through what would become southeast Colorado in an attempt to find the legendary silver of Quivira.[21] The early explorers were disappointed and abandoned the region since, according to Webb, "there was almost nothing in the area that the Spanish desired sufficiently to make them pay the price to obtain it. [There were] no precious stones or gold, not servants or slaves."[22] The Spanish left no lasting imprint other than a few place names such as that of the town of Las Animas, Spanish for the spirits, which local legend attributes to the fate of a party of conquistadores who died without benefit of last rites and were condemned to purgatory. Later, French trappers worked the Great Plains; in 1793 Peter and Paul Mallet traveled up the South Platte and down the Arkansas, but their imprints on the region were also fleeting. At the beginning of the nineteenth century, US Army Major Zebulon Pike traveled up the Arkansas toward its source in 1806 and the Long expedition, mentioned earlier, explored the South Platte and the Arkansas in 1820. Trappers and fur traders established the first permanent European presence on Colorado's high plains in the 1830s.

The Traders and Bent's Fort

The fur trade had grown to a substantial American industry by the early nineteenth century. The nation's richest man, John Jacob Astor, made his fortune acquiring beaver pelts from Indians and trappers in the west and selling them to easterners and Europeans. By 1830 Astor's American Fur Company and other large firms were engaged in bitter struggles to control trade on the upper Missouri. Excessive trapping had depleted the beaver population while changing fashions reduced demand for beaver pelts and boosted that for buffalo robes.[23] The Arkansas was largely virgin territory and Charles Bent and Ceran St. Vrain saw an opportunity to gain control of trade with the tribes near the river. The trading firm, Bent and St. Vrain, what would become the region's first significant commercial enterprise, was formed in 1830. Both principals were St. Louis natives; St. Vrain had been trading with Mexicans and Indians in Taos and Santa Fe while Charles Bent was trapping on the upper Missouri and its tributaries. Charles's younger brother William, who had accompanied Charles on several western expeditions, soon joined the firm. In 1832 Bent and St. Vrain began constructing a trading post on the north bank of the Arkansas near today's La Junta that became known as Bent's Old Fort. Trading commenced the following year. The Arkansas was then the border between the US and Mexico. What is now eastern Colorado, north of the Arkansas, was part of the Louisiana Purchase. Mexican territory extending to the Rio Grande was later claimed by the Republic of Texas and then the state with the same name. As a result of the Compromise of the 1850, today's eastern Colorado south of the Arkansas was removed from Texas and became a part of what would be designated as the newly created Colorado Territory in 1861.

CHAPTER 1

William Bent assumed control of the Fort's operation as St. Vrain remained in New Mexico and Charles spent much of his time in Santa Fe or Taos where he was killed in an 1846 uprising. The Fort's business model was based on acquisition of beaver and buffalo pelts from the Indians and shipping them east for sale. The firm purchased manufactured goods in St. Louis or Independence, Missouri that were then transported to the Fort via oxen or mule-drawn wagons for trade with the natives. William Boggs, who at eighteen joined a trading party crossing the plains led by William Bent, listed in his memoir: "red cloth, beads, tobacco, brass wire for bracelets, loop iron for arrow points, butcher knives, small axes or tomahawks, vermillion, powder and bullets" as popular with natives. Abalone shells were especially prized as were Navaho blanket which were "procured from the Navahoes (*sic*) at great expense by the Company."[24] The Indians also craved whiskey and guns although trade in these items was forbidden by the Federal government, a rule frequently ignored by many traders. The Fort's traders were reportedly more restrained than most in this regard although they traded the forbidden goods when necessary.[25] Establishing good relationships with the Indian tribes was critical to traders' success. William Bent took a large step in that direction in 1837 when he married Owl Woman, the daughter of a high-ranking Cheyenne holy man. Boggs related how Bent spent the winter of 1844-45 in a Cheyenne Village in a tepee with his wife who was described "an influential person among her tribe."[26]

Bent's Fort employed a large and varied labor force. Thomas Farnham, who visited the Fort in 1839, listed the diverse tasks of the approximately sixty workers:

> Fifteen or twenty of them in the charge of one of the owners, are employed in taking to market the buffalo robes &c., which are gathered at the fort, and in bringing back with them new stocks of goods for future purchases. Another party is employed in hunting buffalo meat in the neighboring plains; and another in guarding the animals while they cut their daily food on the banks of the river. Others, under command of an experienced trader, goes (*sic*) into some distant Indian camp to trade. One or more of the owners, and one or another of these parties which chances to be at the post, defend it and trade, keep the books of the company, &c.[27]

Boggs' memoir provided a detailed description of the Fort's operation. The prime season for buffalo robes was winter. At the beginning of that season, William Bent or a senior employee laid out plans with the traders. As described by Boggs, "The Company would entrust them with thousands of dollars' worth of goods and send them to distant tribes of Indians to barter for robes, furs, and peltries."[28] The traders were a colorful lot including such individuals as Mexican Sol Silver, named for his huge sliver earrings. Sol had been captured by the Comanches and sold to the Kiowa. After escaping he joined the Osages for a raid on the Kiowa where he killed his former owner. The traders remained away from Fort for months before returning with the robes and pelts. The trade in buffalo robes could be quite profitable. In *The Fur Trade in Colorado,* William

Butler[29] wrote that robes could be obtained from the Indians for merchandise worth $1.35 and sold in St. Louis for $3 to $6. However, expenses were high as was the risk to both life and property. Continuing good relations with the Indians were critical, so when Bent's wife died in childbirth, he married her sister.

Along with its fur trading, the firm hauled freight to settlements in New Mexico and sold provisions to the military and to government exploration parties. The company's reach was vast. According to David Lavender in his 1954 history of the Fort, it extended "from the Panhandle of Texas on the south, northward through Colorado and western Kansas into Wyoming, Nebraska and the fringes of South Dakota."[30] But its trading business became less profitable by the late 1840s due to greater competition and depletion of the wildlife. William Bent and St. Vrain dissolved their partnership in 1848.

Dealing with the Indians became more difficult. As western historian William Cronon and his co-authors pointed out, "Peaceful trade relations between Indians and Europeans persisted only so long as European demand for commodities did not interfere with Indian subsistence."[31] But gold discoveries in California and later in the central Rockies brought more Europeans into the region, disturbing the delicate bonds between traders and Indians that made their commerce possible. William Bent attempted to negotiate a sale of the Fort to the Army but was frustrated in his efforts and blew it up. He later built another fort called "Big Timbers" some forty miles downstream near today's Lamar and continued his trading and freighting business, but the halcyon days for Bent's Fort had ended. Bent sold his newer fort to the army in 1860 and moved to the bottomlands at the mouth of the Purgatoire in Bent County near the present town of Las Animas. Bents new fort became the Army's Fort Wise, later renamed Fort Lyon. It was destroyed by flooding in 1867 and was relocated to its present location east of today's Las Animas.[32] Following the slaughter of defenseless Cheyenne and Arapaho at the 1864 Sand Creek Massacre, Bent and his friend, Kit Carson, worked with the US government and the Indians attempting to deal with the natives' grievances and improve relations with white settlers.[33] These efforts turned out to be fruitless. Although Bent sympathized with the Indians, he was deeply grieved when two of his mixed-race sons sided with their mother's people in the plains battles following the Civil War.[34] William Bent died in 1869 in what was to become his namesake County.

The Cattle Kingdom

By the outbreak of Civil War trading furs and pelts was no longer profitable and farming was not yet feasible on the arid plains. The next two decades were the heyday for what Webb labeled "The Cattle Kingdom," and ranching dominated eastern Colorado's economy. In the early years, sizable cattle herds were driven north by Texas ranchers, initially to be sold to the mining camps. Later the animals were fattened on the high plains for resale in Colorado's Front Range or mountain regions or shipped via rail to eastern or Midwestern markets. Soon Colorado ranchers started their own operations fattening cattle from Texas and other states and later acquiring their own herds. By the middle 1870s, eastern and foreign capitalists, observing the success of local ranchers, invested in their own ranching operations. The open range cattle kingdom soon fell victim to overinvestment, falling prices, and some harsh winters. The influx of homesteaders brought about its end by the late 1880s.

Successful ranching depended upon land with ample grass, water, livestock and men to work the herds. Land was readily available. During the early open-range era, cattle grazed unencumbered by land titles but access to surface water was critical before the introduction of the windmill, and flourishing ranches depended on control of the streams. Livestock accounted for the bulk of ranchers' capital outlays. The initial herds were purchased from Texas and later augmented by breeding stock from the Midwest. An itinerant army of cowhands provided the manpower needed to manage the herds. The work was grueling, and the cowboys' lives were difficult and often dangerous. As Christopher Knowlton wrote in his 2017 history of the era:

> The job of a cowboy entailed an astonishing number of ways to get hurt or killed. You could fall from your horse, you could get kicked in the head while roping a steer, you could be gored by a horn, you could get drowned while crossing a river, you could be caught in quicksand, you could be scalped by an Indian, you could be shot by a rustler, or you could be involved in a barroom brawl. And this list overlooks the less than fatal but uncomfortable perils of the job, such as the torment of mosquitoes and horseflies and many untreatable maladies, such as sunstroke in the summer and sun blindness in the winter, infections, sprains, food poisoning and piles.[35]

Work was seasonal for many cowboys and they drifted from ranch to ranch with their own horses, saddles and equipment. The average cowhand received $40 to $50 per month.[36] During the 1930s several men who had worked on the early ranches were interviewed by local writers employed by the New Deal's Civil Works Administration.[37] The long-retired cowboys looked back on a life of hard work and meager rewards. Charles J. Farr, who worked on a ranch on the Arkansas in what was to become Otero County, recalled being "out in all kinds of weather" including a severe thunderstorm which stampeded the herd. He felt the "food was rather poor and at times we got tired of the bacon and salt 'sow-belly' they fed us."[38] J. L. Tanner, who worked in the future Baca County, reminisced, "For amusement we went to dances or got drunk."[39]

Early attempts to profit from cattle included that of William Bent, who kept a small herd near his fort for sale and feeding his workers, and "road ranchers" along the Overland and Santa Fe Trails who exchanged fresh oxen for worn-out animals from wagon trains. They then restored the animals on their pastures and sold them to later travelers.[40] The first sizable cattle herds in Colorado were from Texas where large-scale

US cattle ranching began during the decades preceding the Civil War. The first herds were driven north to meet new demand from the gold and silver miners who came to the Colorado mountains in the late 1850s. Cattle traffic increased after the North seized control of the Mississippi closing much of the Confederacy to Texas cattle. This left the only markets for Texas cattle with the wartime enemy in the North and Midwest. These markets were accessed by driving the cattle into Colorado.[41]

Texas cattlemen soon realized the value of letting their herds fatten on Colorado prairie grasses before being sold. The early Texas ranchers raised Longhorns, a breed that thrived under the harsh conditions of the plains. But Longhorns had two costly flaws in addition to the lack of flavor of their meat. Their weight gains on the Texas plains were meager and the critters harbored protozoa which caused a disease called Texas Fever. Longhorns usually developed enough resistance so that the disease caused them little long-term harm. But the malady was spread by ticks so that other breeds encountering the Longhorns on the trail or in stockyards sickened and died. This made moving and marketing the Longhorns difficult. Pasturing the Longhorns in eastern Colorado or other grasslands further north ameliorated both shortcomings. Grazing cattle were able to put on more weight than in Texas, and the colder winters killed most of the ticks that spread Texas Fever.

Perhaps the most famous of the trail masters who organized and managed the cattle drives from Texas was Charles Goodnight. He grew up in Texas and in his youth worked as a jockey, a teamster, and a freighter. As demand for beef in the mining camps swelled, Goodnight and Oliver Loving formed a partnership moving cattle from Texas to the camps. Herds were assembled in west Texas and driven through that state's panhandle and part of New Mexico into southeast Colorado along what came to be known as the Goodnight-Loving Trail. They were then moved on to the mining camps and the Front Range cities as well as to the railheads where they were shipped to markets in the Midwest. The routes of the Goodnight-Loving Trail were varied according to dangers from Indians and rustlers and the location of railheads. After the Santa Fe line reached Granada, Colorado in 1873, the town became the preferred terminus.[42]

The herds left Texas in March and reached their Colorado pastures in June or July. Cattle towns, including Bovina in Lincoln County and Trail City in Prowers County, sprouted along the trails where the cattle were sold and shipped by rail to their final markets or driven onto the prairies for fattening. The latter town came into existence as result of laws in both Kansas and Colorado prohibiting Texas ranchers from grazing herds in their states due to the risk of Texas Fever. As a result of either a survey error or dispensation from the Federal government, Texas herds were permitted along a three-mile strip on the Colorado-Kansas border known as the National Cattle Trail.[43] This trail reached the Santa Fe line in Trail City on the Arkansas between the present towns of Holly, Colorado and Coolidge, Kansas. The Railroad built a siding, stockyards, and loading chutes. The town's location on the state line encouraged defiance of the law as offenders could move from Kansas to Colorado or vice versa when confronted by lawmen. As the town was the end of the cattle drives, cowboys often received their first pay since leaving Texas. The community attracted gamblers, prostitutes, and other purveyors of vice eager to prey on the anxious-to-spend cowhands. The town's population swelled to 500 during the cattle driving season. Ora Brooks Peake in his history of Colorado's open-range cattle era wrote that between June 9 and 26, 1886, fifty-seven herds of cattle ranging from 3,300 to 70 head, a total of 126,951 animals, crossed the Arkansas at Trail City.[44] The town's heyday was short-lived. The practice of driving Texas cattle north declined, and by 1890 the town had withered away.

Although Colorado ranchers continued to supplement their herds with Texas cattle well into the 1880s, Texans' dominance of Colorado plains ranching was being challenged by the late 1860s. The withdrawal of Federal troops during the Civil War increased the danger from hostile Indians and discouraged raising cattle on the plains, but within a few years much of the region's Native American population had been killed, relocated to reservations, or had moved north to take part in the final chapters of the Plains Indian wars. As large-scale settlement by homesteaders was still a decade and a half in the future, massive tracts of eastern Colorado grass land were available for grazing. At about the same time, the demand for beef from the western prairies surged. Herds in the South had been destroyed by Civil War fighting and a mid-century European anthrax epidemic reduced the continental supply. A market for beef was emerging along Colorado's Front Range and in the mountains. By the end of the Civil war, marketing and slaughter of cattle and the meat packing industry was concentrated in Chicago with its massive stockyards and confluence of railroads.[45] And Chicago would soon have rail connections to eastern Colorado.

At first Colorado ranchers purchased Texas stock that they fattened for the remainder of the season. Sometimes they would keep the stock until the next year. Eastern Colorado cattleman Joseph Bowles recalled that he and his father would buy some three thousand Texas yearlings in Trail City at around $8 per head. After two winters on the range, at no cost, they could be sold as fattened steers for as much as $40.[46] Under the difficult conditions of the early Colorado cattle industry, the Longhorns' resilience led ranchers to rely on the breed. As eastern and European customers demanded meatier and tenderer beef, ranchers shifted to less hearty but more marketable breeds such as Herefords and Shorthorns. Ranchers retained cows and heifers for breeding and often purchased bulls from midwestern breeders to improve their herds. However, many still supplemented the income by purchasing and fattening Texas cattle.

Early ranchers owned relatively few acres of land, but the land they chose often ran along rivers or creeks. Such ownership gave them effective control of adjacent territory, often extending for vast distances. These claims were recognized by other ranchers if not by law. Herds roamed freely over wide expanses and were gathered in roundups in the spring and fall. Area ranchers pooled labor and selected the routes, winter camps, and time of the roundups of cattle. The spring roundup, conducted by a consortium of ranches, sorted out the different ranchers' herds, branded the calves and castrated the young males. The fall roundup, a smaller affair with single ranch or maybe two or three, separated the fat steers for market. Joe Dillon, who homesteaded in Logan County in the 1880s, described spring roundups which began in Nebraska and ended in Greeley. These roundups featured ten to twelve mess wagons with ten to fifteen men per wagon and a total of a thousand to twelve hundred horses.[47] J. L. Tanner, quoted earlier when he described his entertainment preferences as dancing and drinking, talked about a spring roundup beginning on the Kansas line on May 25 and ending at Trinidad around the first of July, a distance of nearly 150 miles.[48]

The first formal organization in Colorado formed to coordinate these efforts was the Bent County Stock Association, founded in 1870. Later renamed the Bent-Prowers Cattle and Horse Growers Association, it is still in existence in the twenty-first century. Rufus Phillips who hired on as a cowboy at a ranch operated by a relative near Rocky Ford recalled the Association's spring roundups consisting of more than five hundred men, three to four thousand horses and fifty chuckwagons.[49] The roundups moved from east to west, starting in eastern Kansas and working west as far as present-day Manzanola.[50] A parallel roundup began on the Cimarron River in Oklahoma panhandle a month earlier to retrieve cattle that had wandered south of their normal territory. The activities of the Association soon expanded beyond organizing roundups. Early records show it pressuring the railroads for better service and lower fares. The Association also paid a bounty on predators.[51] Perhaps the most pressing issue was cattle rustling. The Association considered the formation of "a vigilance committee, a trial by cattlemen…. the penalty for stealing cattle was to be death." Although this draconian policy was not adopted, the Association succeeded in getting eight persons sent to prison in Cañon City for stealing horses and cattle.[52] Other stock associations were soon formed throughout the region. The political weight of these organization brought an 1879 state brand inspection law with inspectors employed by the Colorado government.

Among the most successful of the early eastern Colorado cattle barons were John Wesley Prowers, who ranched along the Arkansas, and John Wesley Iliff with holdings in the South Platte watershed. Prowers was born in Westport, Missouri and in 1856, at age eighteen, he crossed the plains with Robert Miller, the Indian Agent for the upper Arkansas.[53] For several years the young man worked for William Bent trading with the Indians and hauling freight. He made ten trips across the plains in charge of wagon trains. In the winter of 1859, he observed that a small herd of surplus cattle turned loose for lack of feed survived the winter in good health and remained near the Fort. Inspired, Prowers set a goal of owning his own ranching operation. Leaving Bent's employment, he established an independent freighting operation and accumulated enough capital for his ranch. In 1861 Prowers purchased a hundred head of cattle in

Missouri, grazing them on open range between the Arkansas and Purgatoire Rivers near the present town of Las Animas. He built a home and ranch headquarters on Caddoa Creek south of the Arkansas and, like his mentor Bent, developed a good working relationship with the regional Indians aided by his marriage to Amache, the daughter of a Southern Cheyenne Chief. According to P.G. Scott, who worked for Prowers as a young man, he had "cordial relations with his wife's people."[54]

Prowers recognized that control of water allowed him to pasture cattle on adjacent open land and acquired additional property along the Arkansas over the next two decades, some of which had been deeded to Indians in a settlement following the Sand Creek Massacre where Prowers' father-in-law had been killed. This means of land acquisition was not uncommon among early southeast Colorado ranchers. Prowers County pioneer George Merrill, writing in 1930, noted that large ranchers had acquired lands along the Arkansas either through purchases from or marriages to Indians who had obtained it through claims growing out of post-massacre settlements.[55] In 1984 a Las Animas surveyor and amateur historian researching old Bent County land deeds found that the federal government deeded 640 acres to each of thirty-two blood relatives of persons killed at Sand Creek. Recipients included John Prowers's wife and two of his children.[56]

Prowers improved his cattle with breeding animals from the Midwest developing stock highly rated throughout the nation. In 1874 the *Rocky Mountain News* reported that "J. W. Prowers, of West Las Animas, has sold the finest Short Horn cow in Colorado, to Ben. B. Groom, of Kentucky. So the scales are turning. Colorado used to purchase blooded cattle from Kentucky. Now the latter state comes to this territory to improve its stock."[57] Another article described his animals "as the choicest and best herd of short-horn grade American cattle and crosses on Texas females in southern Colorado."[58] In addition to his ranching activities, he operated a successful mercantile business in West Las Animas and was a partner in an early Arkansas Valley irrigation project. He introduced barbed wire to Colorado ranching. In the winters of 1874 and 1875 Prowers and several partners including Charles Goodnight built a meat packing plant at the West Las Animas rail terminus. The results of this effort were disappointing as warm winters caused the meat to spoil.[59] His warehouse and merchandise store advertised in the *Las Animas Leader* as a "Wholesale Grocer and dealer in Dry Goods, Clothing, General Merchandise, Wagons and Farm Implements."[60] He represented Bent County in the territorial legislature and later in the Colorado General Assembly. He also served as county commissioner and ran unsuccessfully for Lieutenant Governor of Colorado. At the time of his death in 1884 he owned about forty miles of fenced river front extending from east of present-day Lamar to west of today's Las Animas, controlling over four-hundred thousand acres of range land.[61]

John W. Iliff grew up in Ohio, the son of a prosperous farmer and stock raiser. After college he obtained funds from his family and opened a store in Kansas. Seeing an opportunity in the Colorado mining boom, he sold his business and moved to Denver where he set up a firm outfitting miners. Soon he expanded his operation to purchasing draft animals from newly arrived settlers and fattening them on the prairies east of Denver for eventual sale to the mining camps. By 1865 profits from the cattle portion of his business had grown to the point where he became a full-time rancher. He regularly purchased several thousand Longhorns from Texas, often from Charles Goodnight, at a price of $10 to $15 a head. He grazed them on grass for a year or two and then sold them for $30 to $37.[62] He soon acquired his own breeding herd of six to seven thousand Shorthorns selling his steers each year and retaining cows and heifers. He developed extensive markets for his beef including Denver merchants, military posts, and mining camps. Like Prowers, Iliff realized the importance of controlling access to water. He owned more than one-hundred separate parcels of land along the South Platte watershed, all either including or bordering rivers or streams. By the mid-1870s his range extended from the South Platte north into Wyoming and from the eastern border of the state west to near Greeley with Iliff's headquarters near the present-day eponymous town in Logan County.[63] He was said to be able to "travel from Julesburg to Greeley and always be able to eat and sleep on one of his own ranches."[64]

In 1877 Iliff's operation was visited by James Macdonald of *The Scotsman,* a publication for British investors in American cattle business, who described it in an article entitled "Food from the Far West."[65] According to the article, Iliff owned 35,000 cattle on 9 ranches. He had title to 15,000 acres but another 650,000 acres were directly controlled. His breeding herd consisted of 6,000 to 7,000 cows serviced only by high-grade Shorthorn bulls. Along with his own herd he fattened 10,000 to 15,000 Texas steers trailed up from the south and finished on grass in one or two seasons. His steers weighed 1,100 to 1,200 pounds and sold for $38 to $50. He employed forty men all summer and a dozen during the winter paying them $25 to $30 a month plus providing board. According to Macdonald, "Occasionally in a severe storm the cattle get a little hay, but never tasted corn." Upon his death in 1878, an obituary in his native Ohio described Iliff as "The Wealthiest Herder of the Western Plains" and stated that he "was known in the business centers of the east as the great cattle-grower and dealer of the west."[66]

Prowers and Iliff were not alone in achieving success in high plains ranching. Other large operators included Jared Brush, who shared the South Platte with Iliff, and Tilghman P. Hersperger with ranch headquarters in Karval in Lincoln County. German immigrant Conrad Schafer and a partner founded a ranch near Boyero in Lincoln County that subsequent generations of the family continued to operate in the twenty-first century.[67] Large ranchers in the south included the Jones brothers who brought a herd of 1,100 from Texas in the fall of 1869 and wintered on the Purgatoire. They remained in southern Colorado and by 1881 their "JJ" brand owned 30,000 head of cattle and 16,000 acres south of the Arkansas.[68] The SS ranch on the north side of

CHAPTER 1

the Arkansas founded by Hiram Holly and partners in 1871 owned as many as 35,000 cattle and employed about thirty cowboys.[69]

By the late 1870s, surging cattle prices and a seemingly endless availability of "free" grassland appeared to promise high and relatively risk-free returns. The Bureau of Agricultural Economics estimated that the value per head of "Cattle on farms other than milk cows" for the nation rose from $15.38 in 1879 to $23.52 in 1884.[70] Prices may have risen even faster on the plains; according to Webb, cattle there sold for $7 – 8 per head in 1878-79 and rose to $30 – 35 by 1882.[71] The extension of the railroads through the plains and the introduction of refrigerated steamships opened markets in Europe, particularly in England. James Brisbin's *The Beef Bonanza, or How to Get Rich off the Plains,* distributed by the Union Pacific, enticed aspiring cattle barons with can't-miss schemes. It laid out a tempting scenario for a prospective venture in plains cattle. An initial stake promised to more than triple. "If $250,000 were invested in ten ranches and ranges, placing 2000 head on each range, by selling the beeves as fast as they mature, and all the cows as soon as they were too old to breed well, and investing the receipts in young cattle, at the end of five years there would be at least 45,000 head on ten ranges worth at least $18 per head, or $810,000." [72] Other promoters of plains cattle investment included Baron von Richtofen, uncle of the famed World War I ace and builder of an extravagant castle in east Denver, who wrote an effusive volume entitled *Raising Cattle on the Plains.*[73]

The prospect of quick riches attracted eastern and foreign capitalists, most knowing little of cattle operations and many never seeing their properties. These investors formed cattle companies that were usually run by on-site managers who reported to a board representing the owners. Investment in cattle companies was particularly popular in England and Scotland. As Knowlton[74] pointed out, the repeal of the Corn Laws in 1846 subjected grain grown on British estates to foreign competition driving down its price. This rendered once profitable English farmland an unreliable producer of revenue and forced landowners to seek other sources of income. Accounts of opportunities in American cattle herds found an eager audience. The American west also promised adventure and new experiences, particularly for the younger sons of landed families cut off from inheritance of the family estate by primogeniture. The opportunity for adventure also appealed to sons of wealthy eastern-US families such as the young Theodore Roosevelt who acquired a ranch in Montana. Foreign capitalists usually purchased existing operations, sometimes assembling several into massive holdings. The Prairie Cattle Company, an English corporation, bought the JJ ranch in 1881 for $625,000, nearly $18 million in today's dollars.[75] The firm acquired other ranches, and its Colorado holdings exceeded two million acres and covered 350 square miles extending east and south of the Arkansas and Purgatoire to the Cimarron. The Company also owned other similar sized operations in New Mexico and Texas. Nearly 54,000 cattle grazed on the Company's ranches in the early 1880s and, according to

Steinel's *History of Agriculture in Colorado,* the Company "furnished probably more cattle to the Kansas City market than any other single brand used on the western range."[76] Among the Company's managers was the legendary Murdo Mackenzie, a Scot described as "one of the real cattlemen of the great southwest."[77] Other investors included The Pawnee Cattle Company that bought much of Iliff's ranch properties after his death. The Arkansas Valley Land and Cattle Company, another English firm, acquired Hiram Holly's SS ranch in Bent County.

Resident ranchers were often quite willing to sell to outsiders as meeting their growing capital requirements was becoming increasingly difficult. Cattlemen held their wealth in land and livestock but lacked access to cash. A general scarcity of credit, the result of government policies to correct for the effects of the Civil War monetary expansion, meant high interest rates. Maurice Frink and his co-authors in their history of the range cattle industry concluded that "in 1880s, the rate was usually 1 percent a month plus commissions,"[78] a punitive rate in that deflationary era. As bankers grew more aware of the cattle firms' conditions, they became reticent to originate or extend loans making ranchers more willing to sell. According to Harmon Motherhead, "partnerships between cattlemen and bankers was usually not satisfactory. The banker-investor wanted a guaranteed annual return on his investment. Cattlemen could seldom provide this, particularly at the time they were building their herd. The next step for cattlemen was to sell their land and cattle to companies or corporations and become holders of stock certificates instead of livestock. The previous owner usually remained on the range as a resident manager, foreman or some other functionary of the company."[79]

The plains cattle industry achieved new heights in the eighties, fulfilling the hopes of the new owners even as their prospects became more perilous. By the late 1870s, many were highly leveraged, making them vulnerable to market fluctuations or unfavorable weather conditions. An 1884 article in *The London Economist* noted healthy dividends paid by British-owned cattle but warned future investors that these companies had acquired their land and cattle before recent price appreciation.[80] The high plains ranching model, labeled "Anglo-Texan" by Terry Jordan[81] would not survive changes in the late nineteenth century. The system had developed in more moderate and humid climates and a succession of relatively wet years beginning in 1860 helped sustain it through the 1880s, but these favorable conditions did not last. Letting the stock run freely without supplemental feed or protection did not work so well when faced with the harsh winters and droughts of the Great Plains. Operating expenses and capital requirements had risen since the early open-range days. The introduction of barbed wire and windmills meant that a rancher could no longer control tens or hundreds of thousands of acres of grazing land through ownership of relatively small holdings along streams.

CHAPTER 1

Homesteaders became yet another threat as the government in Washington enacted measures to encourage populating the western prairies. Along with sheep ranchers, they competed with the cattlemen for land. Homesteaders often disrupted the operations of the large ranches. The cattlemen's view of the new settlers was expressed in Webb's quotation from an old trail boss in the 1870s that "They are the ruin of the country, and have everlastingly, eternally, now and forever, destroyed the best grazing-land in the world."[82]

At times homesteader-rancher disputes escalated to violence. In 1875 Bud Jones, the nephew of the founders of the JJ, shot and killed a settler after a dispute over ownership of a calf. Jones was arrested and acquitted to the dismay of the settler's friends[83]. A. H. Baxter, a long-time southeast Colorado cattleman, recalled that in 1886 settlers "russeled (sic) so many calves and butchered so many young cattle to eat"[84] that the Prairie Cattle Company decided to handle only steers on their Colorado ranges. Issac Messenger of Kit Carson County recounted a settler-rancher dispute where "one of the foremen of the Bar-T ranch tried to make a settler by the name of Munsinger move off his homestead, and they tried various ways, but the settler stayed. Then the foreman and one of his cowboys went to Munsinger's home and was going to run him out. [Munsinger] met these two men with a shotgun and gave them fair warning to get off his land and stay off. The foreman would not heed this warning, so Munsinger shot him dead."[85] The shooter was acquitted of a murder charge but was later shot and killed by a neighbor in a dispute over a stolen pig.[86] If the conflict between ranchers and homesteaders can be characterized as a war, the homesteaders won. As more settlers arrived, the cattlemen's resistance proved futile. Federal law favored the homesteaders and so did local law once farmers had achieved a majority in the county.

Cattle barons strove to increase their legally recognized holdings by exploiting measures designed to encourage settlement by independent farmers. Legislation limited claims by single owners and required settlers to prove their claims through occupying the land and such actions as cultivation, planting trees, or developing irrigation systems. But regulations were often poorly enforced and large ranching companies circumvented them through such subterfuges as having their hired hands file claims or bribing enforcement officials. Some ranchers attempted to protect their pastures by fencing public land. Laying barbed wire fences across disputed range land led to sometimes violent confrontations between ranchers. An 1885 Presidential order forbade this practice although enforcement was not always consistent. In 1888 the J.W. Prowers ranch was forced to remove fencing that enclosed 75,000 acres.[87]

According to extension agent J. E. Payne, the number of cattle on the books of eastern Colorado, which included all land east of the Rockies, in the 1880s totaled "nearly half a million head."[88] Knowlton cited 1884 as marking "the apex of the cattle boom. [But] as is often the case in a speculative bubble, few saw what was actually happening: the industry had peaked."[89] In many areas the number of cattle grazing exceeded the capacity of the land and the density and quality of the grass was diminished.[90] Foreign demand for American beef plunged when Britain restricted imports for health reasons in 1879. The latter stages of the cattle boom exhibited the pattern typical of such fits of economic exuberance including inflated claims, fraud, and ultimate collapse. By the middle 1880s many cattle operations resembled Ponzi-schemes with payouts financed by money from new investors. Livestock reported on a firm's books for investors and as collateral for lenders often vastly outnumbered those actually on the range. The fragility of the plains cattle industry was exposed. A market glut pushed prices down.

A severe winter in 1885-86 and another bad winter the following year may have delivered the final blow to many of the nineteenth century cattle empires. Record cold, snow and wind decimated herds from the Texas panhandle to the Canadian border in what became known as the "Big Die-Up." A *New York Times* story described a January 1886 blizzard: "The worst phase of the storm is the disastrous effect it will have on the cattle interest. It is thought that the storm will cause a high death rate in Southern Colorado because of the intensely cold weather and high winds. Along the Arkansas Valley, the herds are drifting to the river and showing unmistakable evidence of exposure and fatigue."[91] The Holly Chieftain described Prowers County ranchland following an 1886 blizzard: "Big fat bulls that were kept at the headquarters of the ranch were found frozen dead in the pastures. Jackrabbits were frozen stiff and were found dead just as they sat behind a clump of sage brush."[92] A blizzard the following year was even more destructive: "The river was frozen solid, and the ice was so strong that the cow-punchers galloped across it in a body. …. The cattle from the north drifted in in such quantities that the fences had to be cut, and to save their lives they had to be drifted south to be permitted to go with the storm. As many as 50,000 were trailed over the river."[93] Ranchers suffered destruction of much of their herds although many reported cattle deaths represented a removal of nonexistent animals from the cattle companies' records. According to Wallace Stegner, "British companies, taking advantage of the disaster to correct their inflated 'book count' of cattle, reported as much as 65 percent loss of their herds."[94]

The harsh winters were soon followed by drought in the late 1880s. The limited data on rainfall in eastern Colorado suggest the severity of the late 1880s drought. Rainfall in Las Animas from 1888 to 1890 was just over half that of the previous four years. Prices continued to fall through the remainder of the decade.[95] The last big roundup in Yuma County took place in the fall of 1887 as the large tracts of grazing land were mostly gone. All the region's large ranchers joined forces herding their cattle together and driving them to Haigler, Nebraska. There they were separated and shipped by train to New Mexico, Texas, Arizona, or Wyoming.[96] Many cattle companies went bankrupt and western banks with a high proportion of cattle loans frequently failed in 1886-7 and again in 1891-2.[97] Future cattle operation on the plains would need a different business model and a more modest scale.

CHAPTER 1

Other Livestock

Cattle were not the only domestic livestock on the plains. Sheep grazed south of the Arkansas early in the nineteenth century. The herders were mostly Mexicans as the land was part of Mexico prior to Texas independence. After the Texas annexation in 1845 and the Mexican War of 1846-48, these herds could move north of the river and some Anglo settlers took up sheep raising. Initially the animals were mostly Mexican breeds that, like Longhorn cattle, were able to survive under unfavorable conditions but did not produce much meat. Early sheep ranching in eastern Colorado, like the cattle industry, was largely an open range operation, concentrated in the plains north of the Arkansas extending to the Platte-Arkansas divide. The sheep population north of the Arkansas increased rapidly in the 1870s as the newly completed railroads provided access to markets in eastern cities and Europe.[98] The 1880 Census reported that Bent and Elbert Counties combined had a population of almost 130,000 sheep and, in these areas, sheep ranchers held title to much of the land with access to water. Steinel's 1926 *History of Agriculture in Colorado* estimates the statewide sheep population increased from 110,000 in the early 1870s to two million in 1886.[99] Steinel's figure might have been exaggerated as the 1890 Census of Agriculture reported 717,000 sheep in the state although harsh winters certainly culled the flocks. The Census reported sizable sheep losses in several winters during the 1880s. Wool was the major export although mutton was sold to the mining camps and Front Range cities. Like the cattlemen, sheep ranchers later improved their flocks by bringing in purebred stock such as Merinos.

Sheep were cheaper to purchase and to feed. The value of single sheep was roughly one-fifth that of a cow, and its grazing-land needs were smaller by about the same ratio.[100] Sheep could survive on poorer pasture than cattle but were more vulnerable to severe weather as well as to attacks by predators. The sheep were turned to their summer pastures around July 1 in flocks of 1,500 to 2,000 under control of a sheepherder with a dog. By late November they were moved to winter pasture with shelters and stored feed for emergencies. Rams were turned with the ewes between mid-December and mid-January. Lambing began in early May with some shelter frequently necessary. Shearing got underway in June and upon its completion the sheep returned to their summer pastures. According to Steinel, sheep ranching was largely a profitable undertaking until the panic of 1893 brought a sharp decline in prices for both mutton and wool.[101]

The political dominance of cattle interests and their opposition to sheep grazing on the grasslands limited expansion into major cattle ranching areas. Sheep ate grass closer to the roots and, in ranchers' views, damaged pasture. Sheep ranchers sometimes encountered hostility from cattlemen. Some two hundred head of sheep were killed by riflemen in northwestern Logan County,[102] and Prairie Cattle Company cowboys slaughtered four thousand sheep grazing on what they viewed as cattle pasture.[103] A Bent County French Canadian sheep rancher named Tarbox was reportedly threatened and shot at by cowboys until he left with his family.[104] However, disputes between the two in eastern Colorado did not reach the intensity of those in some other parts of the west. Indeed, some high plains cattle ranchers also raised sheep.[105]

Although the cattle industry dominated the eastern Colorado economy between the Civil War and the mid-1880s, it was relatively small. Webb noted that the entire Great Plains cattle population at its peak accounted for about one-fourth of all cattle in the US.[106] The number on Colorado's high plains during the cattle kingdom era was well short of what it would be twenty years later. But its influence on the region was pervasive and lasting. It was the first permanent industry in the region; the trappers and traders were transitory, exploiting the regions wildlife and then moving on. The cattlemen, by contrast, made major contributions to the formation of towns and counties and became active in other businesses and in politics. Eastern Colorado's two cattle kings were memorialized in the names of Prowers County and in Iliff Avenue and the Iliff School of Theology in Denver. The ranchers and their children continued to play major roles in the region even as the cattle kingdom receded. Many young men who got their start as cowboys went on to become substantial members of their communities. Two one-time cowboys, whose memoirs of youthful ranching jobs were described earlier, rose to presidencies of community banks. Rufus Phillips, headed the First National Bank of La Junta[107] and C.B. Scott achieved a similar position at the Bent County Bank of Las Animas.[108]

Railroads Through the Plains

The economic historian Robert Fogel argued that US railroad development in the nineteenth century had little overall effect on national growth as substitute means of transportation, notably canals and waterways, were readily available.[109] But there were no realistic alternatives on Colorado's eastern plains and without railroads any significant settlement would likely have been delayed for several decades. Before the railroads were laid, moving people and goods relied on slow-moving animal-drawn wagons traveling primitive and dangerous trails. When the rail lines were completed, many early settlers arrived by train and most depended on rail to ship their products to market. In the absence of the railroads, it is improbable that the region's economy would have evolved much beyond open-range cattle and sheep ranching until the introduction of motor vehicles and highways.

The plains' sparse population offered few potential railroad customers. According to Webb, proposed railroads on the plains faced "nothing to support them—no population to travel on them, few supplies and little produce to be sent to market."[110] The lines' destinations along Colorado's Front Range had greater promise but probably not enough to justify the required investment. Potential financiers faced limited revenues in the years following construction and consequently needed government subsidies to whet their interest. The early western railroads were given rights to substantial land with possession granted as the lines were completed. They were granted more than 171 million acres throughout the west of which they secured 131 million.[111] These lands could be sold to settlers or used as collateral to finance construction. Graft and insider dealings by the railroad companies led to public opposition and government land grants were discontinued in 1871. As a result, the Kansas Pacific was the only line with eastern Colorado land holdings. A nineteenth century map[112] shows a twenty-mile-wide strips of land in checkerboard patterns on both sides of the line from the Kansas border through Hugo and Kit Carson to Denver. The Santa Fe received land grants for completion of its line through Kansas but none in Colorado, and other railroads through Colorado's plains were built too late to obtain them.

But subsidies to railroads were not limited to land. According to historian William Greever, "The national government donated free rights-of-way and especially assisted with a loan to the three lines forming the pioneer transcontinental. States, counties, towns, private corporations, and individual citizens helped with gifts of material, labor, equipment, rights-of-way, city lots, negotiable paper, cash, tax exemptions, and guarantees of company bonds. They also invested in railroad securities."[113] Contributions from locals were often extracted under some duress. The Kansas Pacific attempted to wrest $2 million from the City of Denver in exchange for rail service.[114] Abner Baker, often described as the "father of Fort Morgan," turned over sizable land holdings to Burlington executives to persuade them to locate a station in his town.[115] Rail supporters justified these early instances of corporate welfare, contending that the railroad added value to the land which could be recouped either in higher prices when public land was sold or benefits accruing to the settlers and the public. This argument was undoubtedly valid for some of the lines. Economist Lloyd Mercer analyzed costs, returns, and social benefits from the Union Pacific and Central Pacific railroads in California and concluded that land grants to railroads produced a net social benefit by raising expected profits and causing the lines to be built sooner than they otherwise would have.[116] Whether a similar examination of the lines built across less populated eastern Colorado would yield the same result is uncertain.

Not surprisingly, such public largess gave rise to scandals involving prominent politicians and businessmen. A Congressional committee investigating the Kansas Pacific found that construction, including that in eastern Colorado, cost almost $25 million compared to a replacement cost of only $12 million. The difference was largely accounted for by company insiders awarding inflated construction contracts to firms they owned.[117] A similar insider-owned construction company, the Credit Mobilier, surfaced in 1873 as a major scandal in the Grant administration. Despite generous subsidies the western railroads typically disappointed investors. Most were not generating enough revenue to meet their fixed costs including debt service. In 1874 Poor's Manual of Railroads warned investors about the western roads, advising stockholders to "put a stop to a policy that is suicidal—a policy that is working more mischief to the railroad interests of the country than all other causes combined."[118] The Kansas Pacific was one of the more troubled lines, described by historian Richard White as besieged by "numerous, contentious, and divided claimants whose financial paper promised them assets and dividends that did not exist and who could not agree how to divide what did exist." The railroad's creditors included German holders who had "a first mortgage on 245 miles of Kansas Pacific track that ran into Denver, a mortgage on half the company's land and a third mortgage on the rest of the road."[119] Infamous gilded-age financier Jay Gould, who controlled the Union Pacific engineered an acquisition of the Kansas Pacific and merged the two railroads in 1880. The rapid expansion of the Santa Fe, fueled by debt and stock issuance, caused losses in late eighties and forced reorganization by the line's bankers in 1888. The railroad went into receivership in December 1893.[120]

Railroads in the East and Midwest were laid out to serve existing populations, but the paths of the western railroads were designed to minimize mileage subject to topographic limitations. The first railroad to penetrate eastern Colorado was the Union Pacific, the eastern half of the first transcontinental link, which passed through the far northeast corner of the state near Julesburg in 1867 before crossing the continental divide in Wyoming. Despite tempting markets in Denver and the mountain mining camps, the easier northern route was chosen to avoid the cost of laying track through Colorado mountains and to complete the line on schedule, necessary to claim land grants. Denver business interests, bypassed by the UP, lobbied for a rail connection to the city. In 1870 the Kansas Pacific[121] extended its line toward that city from western Kansas through Kit Carson and Hugo. The Santa Fe pushed westward from Kansas, reaching Granada, about 3 miles east of today's town of that name, in 1873. The line carried relatively little traffic west of Dodge City but the Santa Fe's agreement with the state of Kansas required it to reach the western border of that state to qualify for subsidies.[122] Granada remained the terminus of the line for two years and goods shipped to the town by rail were loaded onto wagons to be hauled to the city of Santa Fe. The Kansas Pacific constructed a line from Kit Carson to West Las Animas, later renamed Las Animas, to compete for the Santa Fe traffic. Further construction was delayed by lack of funds due to the panic of '73 precipitated by rail investor Jay Cooke.

By 1875 both the Kansas Pacific and Santa Fe had extended their lines to La Junta and the town became a major rail hub although the Kansas Pacific removed its Kit Carson spur in 1878. The town served as the most important transshipment point to the southwest. The wagon-borne freight traffic provided a substantial economic base for the new town. Ralph Taylor, a historian of southern Colorado, described the transshipment activity in La Junta's early heyday. "All the freight for New Mexico and as far as Tucson, Ariz. was unloaded from the railroad cars at La Junta and taken by wagons across the plains and mountains. Sometimes there were as many as fifteen wagon trains in La Junta at one time, with twenty to twenty-five wagons in each outfit."[123] Transshipments came to an end when the Rio Grande constructed a line from Pueblo to near the Colorado-New Mexico border.[124] Although the loss of freight business dealt a serious blow to La Junta's economy, the Railroad soon extended its own line over Raton Pass into New Mexico and eventually provided the basis for the town's future growth. Over the next two decades the Santa Fe built a depot and roundhouse and railroad repair shops along with housing for employees. La Junta was chosen as the site of the Railroad's Colorado administrative offices and its Harvey hotel and restaurant.[125]

By the end of the century other railroads had built lines through eastern Colorado to reach Denver, Pueblo or Colorado Springs. The Union Pacific constructed a spur from Julesburg to Denver in 1881 through Sterling and Fort Morgan. The Chicago, Burlington, and Quincy completed tracks from McCook Nebraska to Fort Morgan and then to Denver in 1882 and continued a westbound line through Sterling to Cheyenne, Wyoming in 1887. In the same year the Missouri Pacific crossed into today's Kiowa and Crowley Counties though Sheridan Lake, Eads and Ordway, and the Chicago, Rock Island and Pacific line through Burlington, Flagler and Limon with branches to Colorado Springs and Denver was built.[126]

The railroads were a boon to the cattle industry. Long drives to markets were eliminated encouraging the improvement of herds as the quality and quantity of meat became more important and the ability to withstand weeks or months on the trail less so. Open range cattle could be driven to Granada, Limon, or Brush instead of Denver, Omaha, or Kansas City. The introduction of refrigerated rail cars accelerated the emphasis on meat quality.

Faced with the paucity of population along their lines, the rail companies eagerly sought new customers. According to Greever, "the rail roads used all techniques of publicity and salesmanship then generally known to attract farmers into the West."[127] They offered farmers in the eastern US and in Europe incentives such as free or inexpensive passage, reduced shipping costs, generous credit and free or reduced-price land. An 1873 marketing brochure for the Kansas Pacific advertised nearly thirteen thousand acres of land per mile of mainline track.[128]

An early 1900s promotional brochure from the Union Pacific Land Company, which had gained the Kansas Pacific's land when it acquired the company, offered settlers land from these holdings[129] that could be purchased at $3.50 to $6.50 per acre with the buyer having the option of paying cash or taking a 5-year loan at 6 percent interest.[130] By the 1880s recruitment offices were opened throughout northern and eastern Europe and the railroads established subsidiary land companies. Farmers and their families, along with their furniture, equipment, and livestock, were transported to their new homes—one way—at little or no cost. The railroads also offered advice to prospective high-plains famers. The Burlington line hired Hardy W. Campbell, widely known for developing and promoting the dryland farming techniques that bore his name, to tout western farmland.[131] The recruitment efforts were successful so long as the region enjoyed at-least-average precipitation and were important contributors to the influx of homesteaders in the mid and late eighties described in the next chapter.[132]

The railroads not only attracted settlers to the plains but influenced development patterns within the region. Bruce Garver's examination of early Great Plains settlement patterns highlighted their critical role. "No technological innovation more profoundly determined patterns of urban and rural settlement in the Great Plains states from North Dakota to Texas than did the railways."[133] Population and new towns began to be located along the rail lines. Setting up towns was part of the railroads' strategy to populate and control the territories along their lines. Farmers expected trade centers and businessmen needed farmer as customers; the railroads promoted both.

When construction paused, activity burgeoned at the point where the line ended. An 1875 article in *Harper's Magazine* observed that as the western railroads were being built "every temporary terminus of track laying became a city, wicked, wonderful and short-lived."[134] Even the transcontinental railroad's slight penetration of Colorado's northeast corner gave birth to a short-lived boom town in Julesburg. Murray Klein's history of the early Union Pacific describes the town in the summer of 1867. "In June the population of Julesburg was forty men and one woman; by the end of July, it swelled to four thousand. The old stage station had become 'The Wickedest City in America', its dusty streets choked with stores, saloons, warehouses, gambling dives and a theater."[135] According to Journalist Henry M. Stanley, who was later to achieve fame by finding Dr. Livingston in Africa, "Women appeared to be the most reckless and the men seemed bent on debauchery and dissipation."[136] Klein wrote that the town's wild days came to an end when local gamblers refused to pay for lots purchased from Union Pacific, and the company responded with a posse of two hundred hired gunmen who restored order.[137] It is more likely that tranquility resulted from completion of the line to Cheyenne which became the new end-of-the-track town and therefore a new "wicked city."[138]

Later railroad towns enjoyed similar bursts of exuberance. During the two-year hiatus before the Santa Fe extended its line to West Las Animas and La Junta, the town of Granada enjoyed perhaps its most prosperous period, fueled by cattle driven from Texas and teamsters hauling cargo to the southwest. In July 1873, the Granada correspondent for the *Las Animas Leader* enthused, "I find Granada contains forty-two houses completed and several others in course of construction. This for a town not two months old…From reliable authority I understand over two hundred and forty wagons are on their way to this place to get freight for New Mexico."[139] By 1874 the community boasted two hotels, a grocery-hardware store, a drug store, numerous cafes, and a public school. Other businesses included several livery stables and Ham Bell's dance hall. Granada may have reached its maximum population, perhaps as many as 1,500 persons, during this period.[140] But the line was eventually extended to West Las Animas where, according to historian David Dary, substantial building of both businesses and homes was soon underway "Within days of the railroad's arrival."[141] When both the Santa Fe and Kansas Pacific lines were completed to that town the local paper gushed, "With two great competing lines of railroad—the Kansas Pacific and the Atchison, Topeka & Santa Fe—completed and terminating within her borders, Bent County can boast of the best and most direct eastern connections of any part of Colorado."[142] The town briefly became the new center for transshipments to the southwest until the lines were extended to La Junta. Charles W. Bowman in the 1881 *Las Animas Leader* described the activity in the mid-seventies town where "Wagons were constantly in sight in the summer. The entire bottom around West Las Animas was at times covered with camping trains."[143]

Western historian Robert Athearn described a similar pattern of boom followed by decline in the town of Kit Carson in today's Cheyenne County:

> Just as soon as the Kansas Pacific was built farther west, the new town of Kit Carson, Colorado, sprang forth to claim prairie commerce and to threaten even Denver. Within a few months, the namesake of the famous western scout had more than a thousand residents and town lots were selling for seven hundred dollars each. Then the Kansas Pacific moved on to Denver, the city that so eagerly awaited its rails. Kit Carson, struck by economic paralysis, became another small Colorado town.[144]

Even the prospect of a rail line, however uncertain, could give birth to a new town. The discovery of coal deposit near Trinidad in the late 1880s led to the siting of a rail line and the incorporation of several small towns along the proposed route in southern Prowers and northern Baca Counties. The line was never built, and the towns soon disappeared.[145]

More than a century later, most towns of any size are still found along the early rail lines. Kit Carson was founded at the temporary terminus of the Kansas Pacific. As the line extended further west, the KP established a division point and built a depot in Hugo in 1879. Granada, West Las Animas and La Junta were successive end points for the Santa Fe, and La Junta remained an administrative and service center for the line. Rail access was also crucial to the location of several other towns along the Arkansas which parallels the Santa Fe line. Sterling was incorporated in 1881 along the Union Pacific's line from Julesburg to Denver. The Burlington later extended another line through that city. Fort Morgan's growth was spurred by its proximity to both the UP and the Burlington. In 1888 the Rock Island established a division point in Lincoln County where it intersected the Union Pacific's line. The site became the town of Limon. The Rock Island built a two-stall roundhouse, a two-pocket coal chute, an eating house and a section house in the new town.[146] However, a railroad did not guarantee future municipal prosperity. When the Missouri Pacific pushed into Kiowa County in 1887, the towns of Arden, Brandon, Chivington, Diston, Eads, Fergus, Galatea, Haswell, Inman, Joliet, and Kilburn appeared along its line west from Sheridan Lake, each up to ten miles distant from the last, that being the distance between watering points for the trains' engines. The names in sequential alphabetical order were reportedly the contribution of the daughter of the Missouri Pacific president.[147] Of these towns Brandon, Chivington, and Haswell grew into what could generously be described as hamlets. Eads achieved a peak population of just over a thousand in 1950 and the rest soon disappeared.

Entrepreneurs who possessed the judgment, timing, and luck to profit from the railroads arrival became leaders of the new communities. They can be viewed as exemplars of the railroad period in the plains' development much as William Bent epitomized the trapper and trader era and Iliff and Prowers the cattle kingdom. Don Miguel Antonio Otero was the son of a prominent family in what was then Mexico. He received his early education in St. Louis and New York state and later studied law. After his admission to the bar, he returned to what had become New Mexico Territory where he served as a territorial delegate to the US Congress at age twenty-four. He established a mercantile business in Kansas at the end of the Civil War. As the railroads moved west, he expanded his business, Otero-Sellars Company, opening his first Colorado facility in Kit Carson when that town was the terminus of the Kansas Pacific Railroad. When rail lines reached La Junta, he was one of the principal organizers of the town and moved his warehouses there. His firm served as a wholesaler for many eastern firms, receiving goods via rail and transferring them to New Mexico-bound wagons. One of the new counties created from Bent County in 1889 was named for him, honoring a leading early businessman and contributor.[148]

The experience of the plains railroads provides ammunition for both critics and supporters of government industrial policy. Railroad financing and construction gave rise to massive waste, graft, corruption, and misallocation of resources. While connecting midwestern population centers with those at the base of the Rockies and on the west coast was a worthy goal, the number of lines built across Colorado's eastern plains was almost certainly an overinvestment and a waste of resources. Richard White's history of the western railroads characterized the Santa Fe and the Kansas Pacific as "utterly extraneous as transcontinentals when they even managed to complete their lines."[149] However, without the railroads, the arid plains would have been settled much later, if ever. And populating the plains, along with linking up sections of the nation, was the public vision which, in the eyes of politicos and advocates for national expansion, justified the subsidies. The settlement patterns determined by the railroads would persist through the next century and beyond.

CHAPTER 1

The Plains in 1885

The Cattle Kingdom was in its death throes and Colorado's eastern plains were still largely undeveloped and sparsely populated. The completion of the railroads set the stage for new settlement. A lack of good affordable farmland further east and a few years of favorable weather would soon bring a surge of aspiring farmers to the region.

Chapter 1 Exhibits

Bent's Fort was the first major commercial enterprise on Colorado's eastern plains. Located on the north bank of the Arkansas River near today's La Junta, the Fort served as a place of commerce, temporary respite for travelers along the Santa Fe Trail and a relatively safe environment in a sometimes-hostile territory. It was constructed in 1833 and for almost two decades was a hub of activity, usually full of traders, trappers, soldiers, Indians and travelers. It served as a focal point for Bent, St. Vrain & Company's trade in beaver pelts and buffalo hides with the native tribes. The picture above is a copy of an 1845 painting. The Fort has been reconstructed at its original location and is a National Historic Site.

Source: The Denver Public Library, Western History Collection, call number c74-4

CHAPTER 1

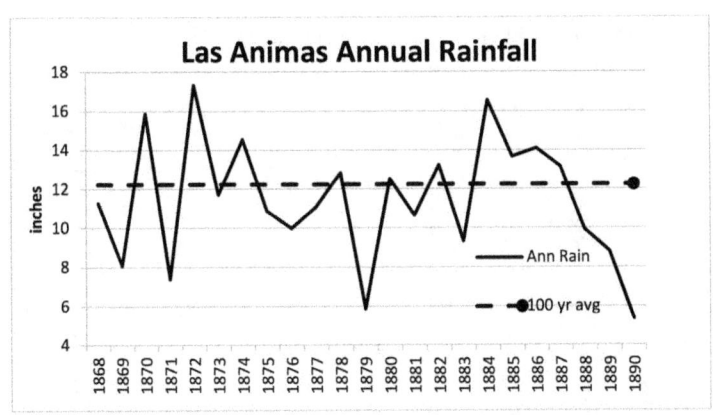

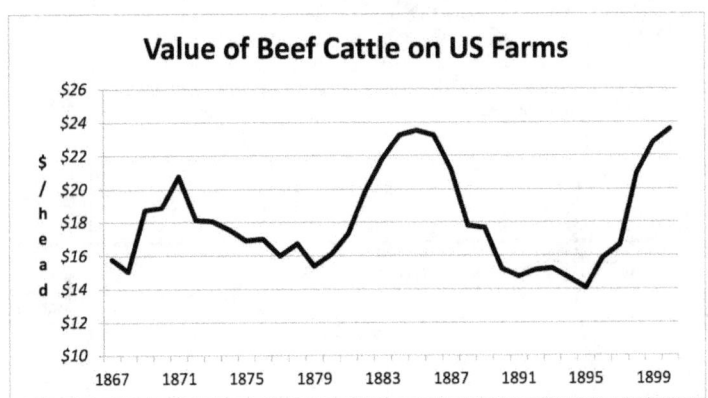

Rainfall had been above or near normal through most of the 1870's and early 1880's nourishing verdant pastures. But a major drought struck in the late eighties compounded the difficulties facing cattlemen.

Drought and falling prices, along with overinvestment and harsh winters, helped bring an end to the "cattle kingdom," an era characterized by large ranches and open range. Cattle prices, represented in the chart by the average value of beef cattle of US farms, surged in the early 1880's. The high price stimulated herd expansion bringing about a virtual collapse in the cattle market. By the late eighties many large ranches were reduced to insolvency.

Source: Bent County Soil Conservation District, from *History of Bent County*; US Department of Agriculture, 1930 Agricultural Yearbook

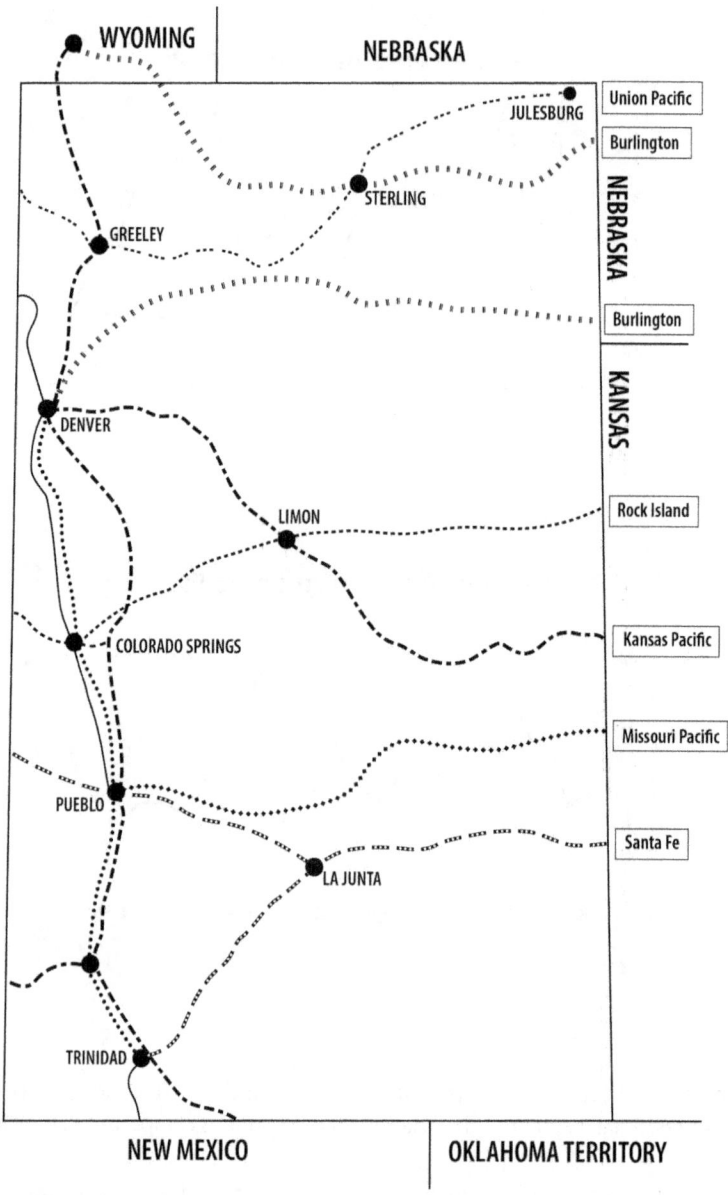

The above map shows eastern Colorado railroads in late nineteenth century. By 1890 most major rail lines through Colorado's eastern plains had been completed. The labels in the boxes correspond to those used in the text. Reorganizations and acquisitions of failing lines gave rise to frequent name changes. For example, by 1890 the Kansas Pacific had been acquired by the Union Pacific.

CHAPTER 2

Early Farming: Middle 1880s Through 1900

MIGRANTS TO THE AMERICAN WEST USUALLY PLANNED TO FARM. MOST AMERicans lived and worked on the land in the late nineteenth century. Farmers and agricultural workers made up 49 percent of the national work force in 1880.[150] But the high plains presented multiple challenges to prospective agriculturalists. Cultivation techniques that brought bountiful crops in the Midwest often failed on the arid plains. Insufficient precipitation made it difficult to sustain agriculture as practiced in the American Midwest. Small scale farming dependent on rainfall usually did not return enough to support a family. Fencing the land was challenging. In the eastern and mid-western United States, farms were demarcated with stone or rail fences, but the plains lacked both trees and readily available boulders. Even if the farm was productive, transporting crops and livestock to markets in major population centers was nearly impossible before completion of the railroads. It is hardly surprising that the plains region between the hundredth meridian, a little over a hundred miles east of the Colorado-Kansas border and roughly the western boundary of the zone of twenty-plus inches of annual precipitation, and the Rockies was among the last areas in the nation to be settled.

But most of these obstacles were eventually overcome or at least managed. By the mid-1880s several railroads crossed Colorado's plains. Investment in irrigation projects became more attractive when the number of potential farmer-customers increased, providing access to water for crops that enabled higher-yield farming in the river valleys. Barbed wire, commercially available beginning in the 1870s, enabled fencing at a low cost. Acquiring land became easier. Federal legislation, albeit often ill-designed for high-plains conditions, encouraged settlement of the empty lands. Railroads, needing customers, recruited immigrants from the rest of the nation and from abroad. The open-range cattle kingdom gave way to small farmers and less expansive ranches. Thousands of settlers came by train and wagon. But the uncharacteristically benign climate of the middle eighties soon turned cruel and large numbers of homesteads on the unirrigated prairie were abandoned.

The First Wave of Homesteaders

Post-Civil War America was undergoing dramatic changes. US prosperity and unsettled conditions in Europe attracted waves of immigrants with the number of Americans doubling from thirty-one million to sixty-three million between 1860 and 1890. Burgeoning national population meant soaring demand for food and fiber in eastern and midwestern cities. It also gave rise to pressures encouraging migration to less crowded locations. Politicians and social philosophers envisioned the west as an outlet for the teeming urban masses, relieving the conflicts between labor and capital then plaguing old Europe. In what must seem a precursor to current themes in US politics, federal support for plains settlers encouraged an outlet for a threatened white middle class squeezed between rapacious capitalists and immigrants eager to work at meager wages. As Horace Greeley opined in his newspaper, "When employment fails, or wages are inadequate, they may pack up and strike westward to enter upon the possession and culture of their own lands on the banks of the Wisconsin, the Des Moines or the Platte, which have been awaiting their advent since creation. Strikes to stand still will be glaringly absurd when every citizen is offered the alternative to work for others or for himself, as to him shall seem most advantageous."[151]

In late 1850s the new Republican Party embraced the idea of distributing land to small farmers, invoking the Jeffersonian vision of the virtuous rural yeoman, a policy that promised to generate support in the upcoming 1860 election. That year's party platform demanded free homesteads for settlers and the party's victory insured passage of the Homestead Act in 1862. An earlier piece of legislation, The Preemption Act of 1842, allowed a claimant to secure title to 160 acres of public land at $1.25 per acre and "preemption" under the terms of the act remained an option for settlers through 1891. But the drafters of the 1862 act made land settlement more attractive for the motivated but destitute settler by permitting a homesteader to acquire title to 160 acres of public land after living on it and cultivating it for five years with military veterans given credit for their years of service. The only out-of-pocket costs were nominal patent and survey fees. The claimant was required to make "substantial improvements." To claim title to the land, the settler's habitation and improvements had to be sworn by two witnesses at the land office.

Often these requirements were interpreted rather loosely by officials on the scene. Katherine Harris, who turned her University of Colorado doctoral dissertation into a book on northeast Colorado homesteaders, quoted a woman whose family homesteaded in Washington County as remembering that "a visit of once in six months to the land was considered legal residence for unmarried people."[152] Homestead claims were limited to heads of households, which meant that a wife was unable to file if her husband had previously done so, although the husband, considered head of the household, could claim if the roles were reversed. Even so, allowing single women to file claims represented an expansion of women's rights as the 1846 Preemption Act limited women's claims to widows and heads of households, excluding unmarried women.

Later homestead legislation was even more generous. It was soon recognized that 160 acres were insufficient for an economically viable farm on the arid plains. The Timber Culture Act of 1873 allowed a settler to claim an additional quarter-section by growing forty acres of trees for ten years. The Act was later amended to require only ten acres. The Desert Land Act of 1877 permitted claiming an entire section, or 640 acres, by demonstrating reclamation through irrigation. These two later acts were not terribly helpful to potential plains settlers as irrigation was only feasible on land adjacent the rivers prior to the development of large dams and canals, and cultivating trees on the high plains presented a challenge. Ava Betz in her history of Prowers County reported only limited use of timber claims.[153]

The *Wray Republican* in 1889 summarized for its readers the procedures for claiming government land. Potential claimants had "three rights to public land. One timber-culture, one pre-emption, and one homestead right." Each could be used only once. Since both homestead and pre-emption required residence, "A person who wishes to use his three rights, should first take a timber claim and a pre-emption, and after six months' residence, prove up by paying $1.25 per acre for the [pre-emption], and then take a homestead. This plan gives one person 480 acres of land at a cash outlay of about 50 cents an acre."[154] Settlers had other options for acquiring land. The railroads offered plots from their grants. As noted earlier, Union Pacific held substantial holdings in Colorado. Settlers could purchase homesteads from their original claimants through relinquishments. Despite shortcomings and inequities in the various land distribution schemes, they played a vital role in attracting immigrants to the high plains even if many of the homesteaders were ultimately unsuccessful.

The ingenuity of the settlers in navigating the intricacies of federal land legislation was illustrated by the McMillin family who settled in what is now Prowers County. Family members took advantage of the several homestead provisions to put together the core of what became one of the largest ranches in the region and one that continued under family ownership into the twenty-first century. James M. McMillin arrived in 1876 from Beaver County, Pennsylvania and took out a homestead. In March 1878, his wife Margaret and son Marsena arrived in Colorado. Margaret established a home on the ranch and both she and her son took out homesteads. As a married woman, Margaret was not eligible for a homestead claim, but the local land office may well have overlooked this restriction. Marsena also proved up a timber claim. He had to replant the trees each year for ten years before they finally took root and lived. Mary Craig arrived at Coolidge, Kansas in October 1887, filed a homestead claim and married Marsena. Later Thomas Craig, Mary's father and John F. Craig, her brother, came to area and established homesteads which were later purchased by Marsena and became part of his ranch. More lands were acquired through purchases in the following years, and at Marsena's death in 1931 the family ranch contained more than 6,600 acres of deeded land and several thousand more acres of school lease and open land.[155]

The dream of the citizen-farmer acquiring ownership of his small farm through his own labors may have precluded a more realistic settlement policy that would have allowed settlers to claim larger plots. In any event, the homestead legislation fell somewhat short of providing free land to the masses. As Henry Nash Smith noted, Federal land policy, "did not lead to the settlement of large numbers of farmers on lands which they themselves owned and tilled. Vast land grants to railways, failure to repeal the existing laws that played into the hands of speculators by allowing purchase of government lands and cynical evasion of the law determined the actual workings of the public land system. Between the passage of the Homestead Act in 1862 and 1890, only 372,659 entries were perfected."[156] As noted earlier, large ranchers were able to exploit the various programs to enhance their holdings.

By 1880 most land east of the hundredth meridian was already settled. That left the Great American Desert, including Colorado's eastern plains, not the most promising for cultivation on quarter-section plots. The lands were the domain of the cattle and sheep ranchers, but the mid-eighties collapse of the cattle kingdom and the political ethos of the time called for the ranchers' displacement by small farmers, even if the territory was better suited to its earlier occupants. As University of Nebraska geographer David Wishart observed in his history of settlement of the western Great Plains:

> The Cattlemen's plan for the western High Plains was more realistic than that of the Rainbelters. In early days of settlement parts of western Great Plains were optimistically referred to as "the rainbelt." (See below.) But it could not possibly prevail at the time because of the national ideology, which promoted the small farmer over the large landowner, or in this case, the large land occupier. It was the same rationale that was used to dispossess the Indians—the cattlemen were not using the land to its fullest, God-given potential. The fact that the cattle business was increasingly controlled by foreign interests, especially English and Scottish, was another strike against it.[157]

Despite the region's reputation, would-be plains farmers were attracted by the availability of relatively cheap acreage and were enticed to settle on the high plains by speculators and railroads propagating a somewhat fanciful vision of a verdant and fruitful land. These sales pitches were supported by the then popular belief that "rain follows the plow," that cultivation gives rise to atmospheric conditions that bring forth increased precipitation.

CHAPTER 2

Several damp years that coincided with early farming in parts of eastern Nebraska and Kansas appeared to support the theory. It was endorsed by prominent climatologists, notably Samuel Aughey, a professor of natural science at the University of Nebraska and the State Geologist. The currency of this belief was reflected in the common use of the term "rainbelt" to describe the region. According to David Wishart, this appellation was applied to Western Kansas and Nebraska along with eastern Colorado.[158] Henry Wells who homesteaded eight miles south of Wray in Yuma County recalled that "This section of Colorado was called the rainbelt of the west."[159] Not surprisingly, this rosy view of farming on the plains was embraced by Colorado's booster politicians as well as those with a pecuniary interest in land sales.[160] According to David Emmons in his history of Great Plains promotional efforts, Colorado's State Board of Immigration in 1899, "assured incoming settlers that within the previous five years the rainbelt had extended far enough to reduce the need for irrigation in the eastern part of the state."[161] The Syndicate Land and Irrigation Company claimed that on its land offerings in Baca County, "successful farming without irrigation is an established fact."[162]

At the time of Colorado statehood in 1876, much of the land in eastern part of the state was in the public domain. Privately held acreage included parts of the Vigil and St. Vrain Mexican land grant which extended west of the Purgatoire and south of the Arkansas. Ranchers had established some claims, most of it along rivers or streams. The Kansas Pacific Railroad, then in the process of being incorporated into the Union Pacific, held land granted along its tracks that could be marketed to settlers. Finally, some property had been deeded to Indians. The remainder was available to the federal government, with most of it eligible for distribution under the Homestead Act and subsequent legislation. Boosters saw a surfeit of available land and a favorable climate for agriculture, and government officials encouraged settlement. Colorado's Territorial Legislature established the Territorial Board of Immigration in 1872, "to promote Colorado as an attractive and desirable locality for those seeking homes, to supply immigrants with full and authoritative information, and to aid and facilitate their journey to the territory."[163] The Board was not re-authorized but similar agencies were established by the state in 1889 and 1909.

Relatively few farmers came to eastern Colorado's plains in the 1870s. The 1880 Census reported that tilled land, including that lying fallow, totaled just over 5,000 acres in Bent and Elbert Counties which, at that time, included most of today's counties in the central plains and the Arkansas Valley.[164] By the middle 1880s, adequate precipitation raised hopes that the vision of the rainbelt might be realized and attracted large numbers of hopeful homesteaders. The number of farms and ranches in the original Bent and Elbert Counties increased from fewer than two hundred to more than thirteen hundred over the decade of the eighties. The acreage in farms and ranches went up fivefold and the amount of improved land more than tripled.[165] This probably understates the extent of settlement as many homesteaders abandoned their land when drought came late in the decade. The influx of homesteaders in other parts of the region, where 1880 comparisons cannot be made because these areas were parts of larger counties, was likely even greater. The 1890 Census suggests extensive new settlement in several dryland counties. At the time of the Census, Baca, Phillips, Washington and Yuma Counties had the largest number of farms among the counties in the region. Anecdotal information also indicates substantial migration into dryland counties. J. E. Payne, Superintendent of the Plains Sub-station at Cheyenne Wells observed, perhaps with some exaggeration, that "Almost the whole of eastern Colorado was settled quite thickly during the years from 1886 to 1889."[166]

New settlers often came quickly and in large numbers. In 1889 The *Bent County Leader* reported that "5 to 10 claims are taken out around Lamar daily."[167] Wallace Wilcox, who homesteaded in Kit Carson County in 1887, remembered "When I first came to my claim there was not a thing in sight and one could see ten miles away." Wilcox left to bring his wife and baby and when he returned, he "counted sixty shacks and dugouts from the high point on my land."[168] The 1890 Census reported around 2,500 residents each in Kit Carson, Washington and Yuma Counties even though many left before the Census was taken.

Most new settlers were farmers from the Midwest. Based on an analysis of family histories of Washington and Logan County homesteaders entering claims before 1900, Katherine Harris estimated that more than half previously lived in Nebraska and another 30 percent in Iowa or Illinois.[169] Most had farming experience. Either their earlier farms had not been successful and free land in Colorado offered an opportunity to start over, or they were sons of farmers whose family did not have enough land for all its offspring. The new settlers arrived either by rail or oxen-drawn wagon. The head of household usually had scouted the area and filed a claim before bringing family and animals. Wagon trips were usually cheaper, but the railroads, eager for new customers, frequently discounted fares. Settlers' livestock and farm equipment were shipped in "immigrant cars," boxcars with a family member along with furniture and farm equipment at one end and livestock at the other. The rest of the family was supposed to pay fares and ride in passenger cars, although some attempted to save money by putting the whole family in the boxcar. The boxcar was often parked on a siding and served as a temporary home until a more permanent residence could be built.

The first home was often constructed from bricks of sod cut from the prairie. While the "soddies" were smelly, leaked and were plagued by insects and rodents, they were a step up from "dugouts" which were essentially caves dug in the sides of hills often with concrete or wooden walls. Dryland farmers depended on precipitation for their crops, but they needed water for livestock and home use. Until the family could dig their own well, it had to be hauled from a distant stream or a neighbor's well. Wallace Wilcox reported hauling water for three and a half years to his Kit Carson County acreage.[170] Angelina Fuller who homesteaded in Kit Carson County in 1888 recalled

CHAPTER 2

"When we first located on our homestead the greatest problem was to get water. There was a well about four miles east of us, and we hauled water from there, but so many others hauled it too that my husband had to get up at two o'clock in the morning and get in line so he would get home before night."[171]

Although most settlers planned to remain on their land, some hoped to resell their claimed land for a profit. Such selling one's right to an unpatented homestead was termed "relinquishment." The buyer did not have to prove ownership and could file another homestead entry elsewhere. Katherine Harris argued that the availability of land to the masses extended an opportunity earlier granted to railroads and state governments. She wrote "the Homestead Act simply democratized speculation by allowing small-scale capitalists to claim quarter sections of the federal domain."[172] Lizzie Gordon Buchanan filed a preemption claim at the present site of the town of Holyoke in 1886. The next year the railroad needed the land for the town site and paid her $6,000.[173]

The persistence of the homesteaders is exemplified by M.D. Johnston who, at age twenty-one, arrived from central Illinois in Cheyenne Wells by UP train in September 1887. He traveled fifty miles by wagon to the Lamar land office to file a claim on land eighteen miles south of present-day Burlington. Johnston initially lived in a tent kept warm by a sheet iron stove that burned dry cow or buffalo chips. Unsuccessful in his attempts to grow corn, he taught school in Nebraska six months of the year and worked on the construction of the Rock Island Railroad. Resuming farming, he leased an adjoining school section for grazing and purchased a small herd of Shorthorn cows and calves in Lincoln, Nebraska. To get them to his homestead, he drove the cattle along a road at ten to twelve miles per day, a process that took a month.[174]

Many of the immigrants had crossed the ocean as well as the prairie. Johannes Lutz, a German from South Russia, filed a claim on land in present day Kit Carson County in 1886. He borrowed $235 and bought a plow, farm wagon, harness, two horses and household goods. He built a sod house with a board and sod roof, a stovepipe and chimney and two windows, probably traveling at least seventy miles on primitive trails to purchase necessarily building materials. He moved in with his wife and five children in 1887. He plowed fifteen acres in 1887 and thirty-seven acres in 1888 and planted corn, oats and a garden.[175] Lutz was the first of many German Russians to settle in Kit Carson County.

Most homesteaders were couples of modest means viewing the farm as necessary for a living. Harris reported that 79 percent of homesteaders in Washington County and Logan Counties were couples, 14 percent were single men and 7 percent unmarried women.[176] The latter were intrepid single women, willing to face the dangers and uncertainties. Alzada Lotz, who grew up in a prosperous Ohio family, moved west when faced with threatening health issues. At age seventeen her doctor diagnosed tuberculosis, pronouncing her health too poor to marry her fiancée and raise a family and suggested that she move west for a less threatening climate.[177] In 1887 she took the train to Granada where she settled with an uncle. Her health improved, and she was able to assist her uncle by delivering mail via buckboard to a town thirty miles away. When she filed a claim on 160 acres by paying $200 under the Preemption Act at the Lamar Land Office, the local paper described her as a "true representative of western perseverance, grit and enterprise. …. She can hand a pistol or gun skillfully and is intelligent and pretty."[178] She married her Ohio fiancée who filed a claim on a quarter section adjacent to hers, and the couple was later able to claim more land as the homestead laws were liberalized. Because of her family wealth and her husband's jobs in the community, their property became a source of pleasure rather than a necessary means of support.[179]

Minnie Palmer from Manhattan, Kansas, another single-woman settler, filed a pre-emption claim on 160 acres southeast of Sterling. After constructing a small house, digging a well and fencing part of her land, she left to work a few months in Denver to earn funds for spring planting. Upon returning she found her house occupied by large man attempting to usurp her claim. She confronted him with a .22-caliber pistol and shot him in the shoulder and hip. When the intruder begged for mercy, she dressed his wounds and sent him on his way.[180]

Settlers heading west to file their initial claims viewed the land as their salvation, a means to the American dream, but reality often turned out to be far harsher. When confronted with the struggle for survival on their newly claimed property, homesteaders' outlooks frequently darkened. To John Bergson, the father of the homesteading family in Willa Cather's *O Pioneers!*, the land became a demon, an enemy to be tamed: "This land was an enigma. It was like a horse that no one knows how to break to harness, that runs wild and kicks things to pieces."[181] For Charles Morgan and his brother Wendell in Marshall County Iowa, "Land in Iowa was getting scarce and high priced and at that time rumors of rich land in Colorado that could be had for the taking had reached their ears. [The Morgans] had visions of a cozy farmhouse set in a grove of trees like that of his father and a barn big enough to house their stock and feed."[182] But they soon faced disappointment. Their first corn crop was beginning to tassel out, promising a bountiful harvest as in Iowa fields they left behind. Charlie was offered $1,200 for his claim which he rejected. But the next day, a hot searing wind came up and the corn and other crops were hopelessly ruined.[183] Many homesteaders failed and abandoned their plots. But many others gave it another try.

Farming was not always the primary occupation of homestead claimants. Owning a piece of land could provide a nest egg for town-dwellers. Two of my great aunts who taught school in Lamar in the late nineteenth century perfected a claim on a quarter section west of town. M.N. Wagner moved to Fort Morgan with his wife and infant daughter and filed a homestead claim. But Wagner soon developed other interests. When not on the homestead, the family resided in a rented home in Fort Morgan while Mr.

Wagner operated an implement business. When the homestead claim was perfected, he built a large home in town. Later, along with a partner, he owned the local grain elevator and a seed store but retained possession of his rural property.[184]

The settlers' choices of crops, particularly corn, were often not well suited for the high plains climate. However, growing corn was a part of American farmers' DNA. It provided a staple for farm families in such dishes as hominy, corn bread, or corn meal pudding. According to Thomas Schaeffer's analysis of nineteenth century farming in southwest Kansas, "corn was far more than just another crop—it was a symbol of civilization and of American patriotism.... a veritable 'corn cult' existed in the United States during the nineteenth century. The attachment of American farmers to this crop was profound."[185] Colorado homesteaders brought their affection for corn to their new homes. The 1890 Census reported that more acres of corn were planted by famers on Colorado's eastern plains than any other crop. In 1944, Robert Dunbar, a professor at what was then Colorado A&M, described the farming of early settlers in Kit Carson County. "They proceeded to plant and to cultivate as they had back East. Using oxen or horses, they plowed from ten to twenty acres the first year and planted corn, the traditional sod crop of the American frontier. Of the 35,429 [acres] reported planted in Kit Carson County in 1889, 24,406 were planted in corn. Everyone used the seed which he had brought with him."[186] But concentration on corn served dryland farmers poorly. Varieties that produced healthy yields in the Midwest languished without irrigation in their new locations. Timothy Burns, an Irish immigrant who settled in Yuma County, planted corn in both 1893 and 1894 and was unable to harvest a single bushel either year.[187]

Along with a selection of crops more appropriate to the arid plains, settlers also needed new methods of cultivation and farm management. While the new plains farmer was learning what worked, yields were often meager, and his family lived at near subsistence. The successful dryland grower adapted his schedule for working the land, plowing deeply after the infrequent rains so that the soil retained moisture. Profitable farming on the dryland usually required additional investment in equipment and acquiring or leasing more land. Homesteaders were generally short of funds but were sometimes able to raise capital by mortgaging their property. Often husbands made ends meet by taking off-farm jobs in the towns, on ranches, or with the railroads, leaving wives and children to work the land. Recognizing the difficulty of making a living on 160 acres of dryland, some young couples filed for two quarter-section homesteads before getting married.

End of the First Homestead Boom

Plains farming would soon become even more challenging. Conditions in the late eighties and early nineties shattered homesteaders' illusions about the rainbelt as they faced the onset of a drought as severe as any yet recorded. Las Animas received less than ten inches of rain in six of seven years beginning in 1888.[188] In the winter of 1890-91, harsh blizzards took a heavy toll on livestock. A.W. McHendrie, then thirteen, settled with his family in Baca County in 1887. He recalled excellent crops in 1888 due to moisture retained in soil. But drought forced many settlers out by the summer of 1890, and a severe blizzard the following fall ruined many of the survivors.[189] Similar narratives of settlement and abandonment were chronicled by the 1890 Census:

Baca County "an influx of farmers [in 1887] but many of those left during succeeding years on account of drouth."

Kit Carson County "Most of settlers came into the county about 1886 or 1887 and tried to make homes. ....Some succeeded in adapting themselves to conditions, while other have failed on account of the prevailing drouths."

Phillips County "Many farmers were induced to settle here upon representations that the drouths were diminishing, but after four- or five-years' ineffectual struggle a number have been compelled to abandon their claims."

Prowers County "....during the years 1886 and 1887 settlers poured into the county and after struggling against drought became discouraged to a greater or lesser extent, many leaving their home and possessions to avoid starvation."

Sedgwick County "Lack of farming success caused population to steadily decrease between 1887 and 1890."

Yuma County "Many of the settlers not being able to make a living by agriculture have had to abandon their claims and leave the county." [190]

By early 1891, a succession of dry years had left many east-central Colorado settlers destitute. The *Rocky Mountain News* published a series of articles depicting this tragedy. These dispatches convey the desperate condition of the homesteaders including a Yuma County official's description of the plight of John Eckman who settled northeast of Yuma. "He took up his claim in 1886 when he possessed in money only $7. He had a wife and a daughter 16 years old. He has put in a crop every year since but has succeeded in raising only a little fodder. One year he raised a very small quantity of wheat. One year ago his daughter died. He is at the present time paying 3 per cent per month interest upon what stock he has. The land company has sold out his land, but he is still living on it."[191] The *News* correspondent noted than many of the farms were run by wives and children as the men had left to take off-farm work. Some of the homesteaders were only hanging on until they could secure title to their land. Then they planned to take out a mortgage and abandon their property. But many remained determined. The reporter praised the perseverance of the settlers noting that "A very large majority of the people wish to remain in this 'rain belt' section. All they have is there and they wish to prove up on their homesteads. They cannot bring themselves to desert their homes even if they are devoid of comforts, the cupboard bare, the children half-clothed and debt and starvation staring them in the face."[192] Citizen groups in Denver and Colorado Springs organized relief efforts for the beleaguered settlers and appealed for further help from state and federal governments. Publicity about dire conditions did not sit well with promoters who were hyping the region's agricultural and economic potential. According to Robert Dunbar, the Burlington Development and Improvement Company forced the editor of the local paper to retract earlier stories about difficulties in Kit Carson County.[193]

Widespread failures among homesteaders reverberated beyond the prairies. According to Wishart "the failure of the western High Plains in the 1890s had national, not just regional, implications. It was part of the wider 'frontier anxiety', the uneasy perception that the era of free land was at an end, and with it everything that had made the United States exceptional."[194] Frederick Jackson Turner in his 1893 paper, "The Significance of the Frontier in American History," famously cited readily available land as the key to American culture and character, and abandoned farms were a blow to the national psyche. The unhappy experiences of dryland settlers called into question American's belief in their nation's supposedly unique ability to provide second chances.

The drought persisted into the early 1890s[195] and the depression following the panic of 1893 drove down farm prices adding further to the burdens of the beleaguered dryland farmers. The national price of corn fell from 58 cents a bushel in 1890 to 26 cents in 1895.[196] Bank failures made obtaining farm credit more difficult. More homesteaders were forced to abandon their land. In 1894 Lelia Walters wrote her grandmother from Burlington that "A good many people have left the country, in fact nearly all that could get away, for there are many mortgages that compel people to stay; a few families left in the night."[197] Between 1890 and 1900 the number of farms in Baca County fell by 56 percent and by more than one-third in Phillips, Washington and Yuma Counties. The dryland counties lost almost a quarter of their population during the nineties, a net loss of 3,600 people. All but three of the dozen towns in Baca County disappeared and the population, perhaps more than 3,000 at its peak in the middle eighties, fell to 1,479 in the 1890 Census and 759 ten years later.[198]

As conditions worsened farmers reacted with frustration and anger, frequently directed toward the railroads and bankers and other powerful interest that held power over their lives. The ire of plains homesteaders formed part of a wave of dissatisfaction on the part of workers, intellectuals and agriculturists that drove the populist movement of the 1890s. Robert McMath, in his chronical of American populism, described the mounting rural discontent: "By the end of the 1880s, farmers from the tragically misnamed rain belt of Colorado's eastern high plains, as well as those from the irrigated lands to the north and south, were focusing their anger on absentee capitalists who controlled access to transportation and water."[199] Grievances about wages, prices for farm produce, lack of political power, combined in the populist political movements.

In Colorado, farmers and workers formed an unlikely alliance with mine owners. Both favored restoration of silver to the currency base, which would not only benefit the mine owners but inflate prices and lessen farmers' debt burdens that had risen with deflation. This coalition was energized by the 1896 presidential election that pitted William McKinley, a sound money Republican, against Democrat William Jennings Bryan, who advocated populist positions and an inflationary "free silver" policy. Although McKinley won the national election convincingly, Bryan carried Colorado overwhelmingly, winning nearly 85 percent of the popular vote in the state and receiving a majority in thirteen of the then fifteen counties on the eastern plains.

With homesteading in retreat, cattle and sheep ranching enjoyed a resurgence. By the end of the nineteenth century the cattle industry had evolved into what geographer Terry Jordan called a "Midwestern" system of ranching that was more capital and labor intensive than its predecessor.[200] With the elimination of the long cattle drives, ranchers were able to raise cattle that were less hardy but produced more and better beef. Herds became smaller and cattle more expensive. Barbed wire, introduced in Colorado by John Prowers, allowed the rancher to keep his stock separate from that of other ranchers and eliminated the need for big spring roundups. Windmills provided water for stock away from streams, so owning land along a creek or river was no longer necessary. Winter sustenance for the herds increasingly came from farm-raised hay or other forage. Many ranchers included feedlots as part of their operation, either raising their own feed or purchasing it, and the first commercial feedlots opened.

Livestock prices rebounded in the late 1890s. The Department of Agriculture estimated that the value per head of cattle on farms rose from $16.56 in 1895 to $26.50 in 1900. The open range was gone, but ranchers were able to acquire abandoned homesteads. As the number of farms shrank, cattle and sheep populations increased. Charlie Morgan who, as described earlier, had abandoned his Sedgwick County homestead, returned and succeeded in the cattle business. In 1893, after several years working odd jobs in Denver, he purchased land which he thought had irrigation potential and helped develop one of the County's early irrigation ditches. But he discovered that raising livestock on his land was more profitable than raising crops. Instead of leaving cattle on the range through winter where they often died in spring storms, he kept fewer cattle than old time ranchers and fed them through months of cold weather. Morgan found irrigated land excellent for raising wild hay and alfalfa. It would yield 3 crops per season and provide ample feed for horses and cattle through winter.[201]

The Introduction of Irrigation in the Arkansas and South Platte Valleys

The effect of irrigation on plains agriculture and settlement patterns was profound. I was stuck by the contrast between irrigated and dry acreage when driving from Denver to Lamar in the 1970s and 1980s to visit family or on business. Heading south on highway 287 from Eads, the dryland landscape featured short-grass prairie dotted with sagebrush and yucca interrupted by a few large fields of wheat or occasionally corn. The farms and ranches enclosed by barbed wire fences were large, consisting of hundreds or thousands of acres. A few cattle grazed on the grassland. Several miles north of the Arkansas River the highway crossed the Fort Lyon Canal. The change in the landscape was striking. Green alfalfa or other irrigated crops grew in well-tended quarter-section plots. Dairy cattle and hogs occupied pastures or pens. Most farms included attractive residences. A similar transition could be seen on many north-south roads into the South Platte or Arkansas Valleys vividly demonstrating the transformation brought by reservoirs and canals.

While throngs of farmers on the dryland abandoned their land in nineties, settlement continued in the river valleys as early irrigation projects allowed settlers to survive the drought years. Farmland in the valleys generated higher yields and was more valuable. Dryland acreage, on the other hand, was more vulnerable to climate fluctuations and required different farming strategies and techniques. To illustrate these differences, discussions and statistics in the early chapters will sometimes distinguish between "irrigated counties" and "dryland counties". The irrigated counties are those along the valleys of the two major rivers: Bent, Otero, Crowley and Prowers Counties in the Arkansas Valley and Morgan, Logan and Sedgwick Counties along the South Platte. While almost all farming of the "dryland counties" depended on rainfall until the Ogallala Aquifer was accessed for irrigation in the late twentieth century, much of the land in the "irrigated counties" was not in fact irrigated. But data are not available at the sub-county level. Presenting information in this form suggests the differences between the two types of farms although the actual differences between irrigated and dryland operations are usually larger than reflected in the county comparisons.

Need for New Water Law

It soon became apparent that normal precipitation was often insufficient for raising successful crops on a consistent basis, suggesting rainfall should be supplemented where possible with man-made irrigation. Hopes were raised that construction of dams and canals might meet some the goals that early homesteading had failed to achieve, notably supporting a sizable population of small farmers. Proponents of the western lands as "safety valves" pressed for Federal assistance for irrigation projects. Among these was William Ellsworth Smythe, a Nebraska journalist, who despaired of the failures of small dryland farmers and held high hopes for irrigation's potential.[202] A speaker at the 1882 Kansas state fair envisioned irrigating along the Arkansas River bringing to its valley an opulence comparable to that which the Nile provided ancient Egypt.[203]

But if the rivers of the plains were to furnish water to more farms, the methods of organizing and regulating water use in the eastern two-thirds of the US were unworkable. John Wesley Powell's *Report on the Lands of the Arid* Region released in 1878 stressed the incongruities of agricultural water distribution and use in the east and

Midwest with conditions in the arid west. Powell was a soldier, geologist, and explorer of the American west. He held high government posts in the late 1870s, giving him an opportunity to apply his knowledge of the west to issues of settlement and water law. Powell had high hopes for irrigated farming in the west. He wrote that "It may be anticipated that all the lands redeemed by irrigation in the Arid Region will be highly cultivated and abundantly productive, and agriculture will be but slightly subject to the vicissitudes of scant and excessive rainfall."[204] But he felt that the prevailing basis for allocating water was incompatible with needs in the newly settled lands.

American water law in the mid-nineteenth century was based on English Common Law, a series of court decisions some having roots in the Justinian Code of the Roman Empire. Labeled the Riparian Doctrine, it developed when water consumption was mostly confined to personal use or running small grist mills. The term "riparian" refers to a river or stream, and the Riparian Doctrine tied water use to ownership of land bordering its source. Water use for crop irrigation was severely limited as the user was prohibited from altering the course or reducing the volume of the stream to the extent that downstream users were imperiled. Riparian owners did not hold title to specific quantities of water, but their rights to water from the stream were inseparable from other rights associated with the land and could not be detached from its ownership. Some flexibility was introduced as larger water use became more common. As applied in the eastern United States in the nineteenth century, the doctrine had been modified to allow "significant impoundments if they were 'reasonable' in relation to the needs of other riparians on the stream."[205]

Powell advocated replacing the Riparian Doctrine with an allocation system modeled on the Mormon communities he had observed in Utah. The connection between water use and land ownership would be retained but the size of farms would be controlled. "Within the Arid Region only a small portion of the country is irrigable. Theses irrigable tracts are lowlands lying along the streams."[206] Irrigated farms with rights to water would be limited to eighty acres, and dryland farms would be allowed 2,560 acres. Water delivery systems would be developed and managed on a communal basis.

But Powell's advice was mostly ignored. Land speculators and politicians feared that his vision of the west would interfere with rapid settlement.[207] But the legal basis of allocating water needed to be changed since much of the land that could benefit from irrigation lay at some distance from the stream, and withdrawing the amount of water needed for larger farms would substantially reduce the stream's flow. A different method of allocation had already come into common use in much of the west although not incorporated into law. It first appeared in the goldfields of California. The land on which the miners sought gold was largely owned by the government, and the water needed to separate the gold ore was frequently some distance from the mine. The miners applied the same principle for allocating water as for gold; it belonged to the one who found and extracted it. A similar set of practices grew up in Colorado's mountains after the 1859 discovery of gold and, as the plains were cultivated, was also adopted by early farmers. This practice became the doctrine of "Prior Appropriation" that replaced riparian common law in Colorado and other western states. It was recognized by the Colorado territorial legislature as early as 1861 and in the 1876 state constitution.[208] The doctrine, sometimes described as "first in time, first in right," allowed the first appropriator to divert whatever water he needed for "beneficial use" leaving the remainder for later arrivals. Retention of the right depended on continued beneficial use. The statutory definition of beneficial use was "use of that amount of water that is reasonable and appropriate under reasonably efficient practices to accomplish without waste the purpose for which the appropriation is lawfully made."[209] Prior appropriation made possible the development of large commercial or mutual irrigation projects that delivered water to farms often miles from the stream from which it was drawn. It made water a tradable commodity. Appropriation rights could be transferred to other users, a provision that grew in importance over the next century.

Irrigation Projects

Early efforts at irrigated farming in eastern Colorado were not terribly successful. According to Colorado water lawyer A.W. McHendrie,[210] whose childhood experience with drought in Baca County was described earlier, the Bent brothers attempted irrigation on a small scale in the 1830s. Their undertaking was soon abandoned as the crops were destroyed by Indian ponies. In 1861 Arapaho leader Little Raven and Cheyenne leaders Black Kettle and White Antelope, believing that buffalo could no longer provide a livelihood for their tribes and that an agricultural settlement was the only option, negotiated the Fort Wise Treaty with the resident Indian agent. This agreement provided for a triangular-shaped reservation north of the Arkansas. Although few Indians were interested in settling there, the government expedited construction of the Fosdick Irrigation Ditch to be used by the natives. Between fifty and sixty acres of irrigable land were planted in corn in 1864. But Arapaho raiding parties attacked the farm, government support was halted, and the farming effort was abandoned. The Cheyenne leaders again met with government officials, but negotiations were unsuccessful and the Sand Creek Massacre later that year destroyed any hope for further agreement. The ditch was sold to a rancher who used it to water livestock and for limited crop irrigation.[211] Over the next twenty years, other small-scale irrigation projects were attempted. Most of the land served by these projects lay in the bottom lands of the river valleys. The first irrigation ditch in Logan County, the South Platte Ditch, was built in 1872.[212] By 1880 much of the land adjacent to the Arkansas was already under irrigation.[213]

Larger projects for irrigating land beyond the bottomlands got underway when enough potential users had settled to justify the necessary investment. The transformation of the high plains agriculture effected by man-made irrigation began in the 1880s and continued over the next thirty odd years. In 1884 eight ditches between the

Bessemer headgate in Pueblo County and the state line appropriated 331 second feet of water from the Arkansas. By 1893, the appropriation had risen to 5,815 second feet.[214] Federal assistance was soon forthcoming. The Newland Reclamation Act of 1902 allocated funds in the form of loans for dams to provide irrigation water for small farmers. Irrigated land area increased by more than 150,000 acres in the 1890s and by roughly the same amount in the 1900s. By 1910 the six counties along the river valleys had 202 main ditches totaling 1,696 miles in length and with a capacity of 29,000 second feet. Ninety-six reservoirs had been built with a total capacity of 868,000 acre-feet. In the teens an additional 187,000 irrigated acres were added. The 1920 Census estimated that the cost of "irrigation enterprises" in the sixteen counties at more than $18 million.[215] By then the systems of canals and ditches were virtually completed. Further additions awaited the massive storage and diversion projects of the late New Deal and post-war years.

Irrigation is a capital-intensive enterprise, requiring sizable initial investment in headgates, ditches, and reservoirs for storage, the costs of which had to be spread over many users. In 1881 the state of Colorado enacted legislation permitting the establishment of water districts under which private firms or groups of farmers could organize, build the necessary infrastructure, provide for its maintenance, and allocate water among users. The Arkansas and South Platte Valleys saw a boom in ditch companies enabled under this legislation. The companies were organized either as mutual stock companies, owned by the water users, or as private firms. In the former case, the farmers often took on the debt of the developers in exchange for shares of the water. But to realize these returns, the early promoters needed to be able to raise funds from investors and convince farmers to sign up for water.

Construction of irrigation canals along with the supporting reservoirs and other structures was a massive and costly undertaking. James Sherow in his history of Arkansas Valley irrigation describes how "Several hundred teams of horses and sometimes several thousand men might be employed."[216] Workmen were typically brought in for the duration of the project and lived in construction camps. Katherine Harris characterized the camps in Logan County as having "much the same wide-open atmosphere as camps spawned by western mining and railroad booms. Wages amounted to $3 a day, less charges taken out for room and board. But if the men preferred, they could receive their pay at the end of each day in liquor, drugs, or poker chips. Drunken carousing reverberated through the nights."[217]

Recouping the investment in such projects was challenging. Debt had to be serviced and the canals and dams needed to be maintained. Litigation over contested water rights was an ongoing expense. Most developers did not recover their costs from farmers' assessments but hoped to profit from sales of land. But promoting farmland under the new ditches was expensive, and often the receipts from assessments and land sales were insufficient to cover costs. This led to perilous financial conditions for the newly formed companies, and the early boom in privately financed irrigation projects was followed by the almost inevitable busts. As Pisani wrote in his history of water policy in the late nineteenth century West, "By the mid-nineties, most large irrigation companies had collapsed, and the rest tottered on the edge of bankruptcy. Stockholders lost everything and bondholders were asked to pay assessments to help their company survive."[218] At the 1907 National Irrigation Congress, Samuel Fortier, an agricultural economist, estimated that "95 percent of the capital invested in canal enterprises from 1885 to 1895 paid no dividends and much of it was entirely lost."[219] The failed private companies were typically reorganized as mutual companies with farmers under the ditch as stockholders. They were described by James Sherow as "non-profit canal compan[ies] that provided division of river flow, levied assessment for upkeep, and allowed a vote in policy formation in proportion to each stockholder's stake in the enterprise."[220]

The promised benefits to farmers were not always realized. The flow in the Arkansas and South Platte Rivers varied widely depending upon winter snowpack. The 1890 Census described the South Platte in Logan County as "at one time a broad swift stream, at another almost dry."[221] As more projects were completed the capacity of the irrigation systems and commitments to irrigators in both the South Platte and Arkansas Valleys exceeded the amount of water available in most years, resulting in conflict between farmers and ditch operators as early as the late 1880s. The 1890 Census reported:

> It is stated that the ditch companies operating in the Arkansas valley of eastern Colorado have sold more water rights than can be made good by supply available and have misled settlers by statements regarding probable crops and prices. Many of the farmers have mortgaged their land to the companies and must pay the interest and part of the principal at stated periods. There is no penalty imposed on the company for failure to furnish water, and thus the farmers state that they are left in the position where, not receiving the water paid for, they cannot raise crops and pay off the mortgages. The feeling against the speculators or capitalists who have organized these schemes has been especially bitter.[222]

The developers of the irrigation projects were worthy heirs to the cattle and railroad promoters. Prominent among such individuals in eastern Colorado was Theodore C. Henry whom Stenzel and Cech labeled the "Irrigation King of Colorado."[223] Henry came to the State in 1883, already wealthy from wheat, cattle, and other investments in Kansas. He constructed irrigation canals in eastern Colorado as well as in the San Luis Valley and on the Western Slope. In 1884 he developed the Pawnee canal on the South Platte River near Sterling[224] and was later responsible for the Bob Creek and Fort Lyon canals on the Arkansas.[225] He envisioned a utopia of small farmers prospering under his ditches. According to his family genealogy, "He planned to irrigate an empire as other men planned to irrigate a farm."[226] Henry claimed that an irrigated farmer could make a successful living on twenty-five acres of land. He borrowed heavily to finance his projects, which, in many cases did not produce enough funds to service the debt, leading to their eventual failure. According to Stenzel and Cech, "Some saw Henry as an enlightened town builder and redeemer of the Great American Desert. Others saw him as a shameless promoter, manipulator, and reckless developer."[227] Arthur C. Gordon, a Lamar lawyer who served over thirty years as attorney for the Fort Lyon, summarized Henry's legacy. "Unfortunately, most of his early promotions were failures which eventually passed into other hands, but no man in Colorado's history can be named who had a greater and more vital interest in irrigation for farming than Henry."[228]

Henry's involvement in the saga of the Fort Lyon canal illustrates the tumultuous early history of irrigation in the region. The canal evolved from the unsuccessful farming efforts of the Cheyenne and Arapaho described earlier. In 1883 a group of investors incorporated as the Arkansas River Land and Canal Company purchased this ditch's water rights and began construction of a seventeen-mile canal. Irrigation from the new venture was limited and it was taken over by a Denver investor from whom Henry purchased all stock and property and most of its water rights in 1887. He expanded both the capacity and length of the canal and acquired additional land and water rights that provided collateral for financing further construction.

The late 1880s saw a surge of new farms north of Lamar. In response to potential new demand and with the encouragement of the Santa Fe railroad, Henry extended the canal to near its present size. The project included more than 110 miles in the main ditch along with two reservoirs. But the Canal's water rights were junior to several irrigators further up the river and, according to Sherow, "proved inadequate for growing cereals and alfalfa on the land under such a long ditch."[229] Additional construction and the acquisition of more water rights led the company to sell access to more irrigation water and to take on additional debt. When it could not meet its financial obligations, the canal was sold by the sheriff to a local bank and several investors. It was later resold to Henry's brother-in-law who reorganized the company, with Henry still involved in its operation, but inconsistent flow in the Arkansas continued to plague the Fort Lyon. The promised water frequently could not be delivered, and several floods damaged the infrastructure. Irrigators were often cut off for extended periods. Angry farmers sued, asking for a receiver to manage the canal and the distribution of water. The court ruled in favor of the farmers appointing William C. Burke as receiver, and the judgment was sustained by the Colorado Supreme Court. But the canal continued to suffer from further flood damage and insufficient water. The farmers, still unhappy, pressed for cooperative ownership. The Colorado Supreme Court in 1903 gave the farmers control of the ditch through a mutual stock company, the Fort Lyon Canal Company. But conflicts over the Fort Lyon would continue through most of the next century.[230]

Abner Sylvester Baker was another irrigation pioneer. He was born in Ohio in 1841 and moved with his family to Wisconsin where he enlisted in the army at the onset of the Civil War. In 1870 he came to Colorado settling in the Union Colony near Greeley.[231] Baker's first impression of the eastern plains was decidedly mixed. He commented at the time that "There is nothing in the dry sterile looking plains to awaken enthusiasm in anyone" but "so far as the lay of the country is concerned nothing could be finer."[232] Later, while hunting buffalo east of present-day Fort Morgan, he was inspired by a vision of the land's agricultural potential if canals could be built to bring water.[233] His involvement in irrigation projects in the San Luis Valley and near Greeley and in contract grading for railroads earned him a modest fortune as well as construction experience allowing him to undertake the development of irrigation in Morgan County. In partnership with a Scottish nobleman, he formed a company that issued stock to finance the Fort Morgan Canal that was completed in 1884. He urged users to take as much water as possible to establish a priority of water rights, furnishing the water without charge in exchange for notes which were then canceled.[234] Baker later developed plans for yet another project, the fifty-mile-long Bijou Canal. George W. Willis, a boyhood friend of Baker in Wisconsin and his partner in irrigation and land development projects, prepared a brochure entitled "OASIS IN THE DESERT" lauding the regions' agricultural potential.[235] But the Bijou became a casualty of the depressed mid-nineties economy. It failed despite expenditures of more than $100,000. Local leaders were unable to attract funds for reviving the project, and it was finally completed with outside dollars. As described by the *Fort Morgan* Times, "This ditch was built by the farmers of the region before the business depression came and when they had to abandon it. The Jarvis Conklin Company, which had made a loan upon the ditch, took charge of it."[236] The completion of the Bijou Ditch in 1900 opened some forty thousand to fifty thousand acres of land to irrigation[237] and brought a new surge of economic activity to Morgan County.

Other contributors to plains irrigation included George Swink whose small ditch in Otero County evolved into the sixteen-mile-long Rocky Ford Ditch. As the canal was expanded, the Rocky Ford Ditch Company secured water rights senior to nearly any others in the Valley. The company provided reliable water for its users and was, according to Sherow, "the most stable and envied irrigation enterprise in the valley."[238] Another was Peter Peterson, a German immigrant, who came to Julesburg in 1885. He took advantage of the strong economy fueled by an influx of homesteaders and built a successful grocery and dry goods store. After struggling through the dry years in the late eighties and early nineties, he developed a plan for an irrigation ditch that would alleviate future droughts in Sedgwick County. In 1895, with funds from local businessmen and labor furnished by some of his customers who owed him money, Peterson Canal and Reservoir Company filed on 184 cu. ft. of water. But the project encountered difficulties. Mark Burke, his young surveyor, was frequently ordered off land at gun point by owners opposed to the project. Costs exceeded estimates. Peterson and his partners raised more money by selling water rights and were able to complete the project by persuading Julesburg's leaders to issue $5,000 in town bonds to provide water when available for lawns and gardens. The ditch was finished in the spring of 1896, but the river was dry. It finally rained on May 1 and demand for water rights surged. In 1897 the ditch was enlarged, and a second filing was made for an additional 35 cu. ft. [239]

The growth of the sugar beet industry in the South Platte and Arkansas Valleys, described in chapter 3, provided incentive for more irrigation projects. Beet farming required substantial amounts of water, and growers provided customers for the ditches. The Twin Lakes Reservoir just east of the continental divide stored irrigation water for what is now Crowley County but lacked customers. In 1899 Twin Lakes investors financed a sugar beet plant in Sugar City, the first such facility in eastern Colorado. [240] Jackson Reservoir near Brush was built in 1904 to persuade Great Western to locate a plant there. Soon thereafter the Brush plant was built. [241]

Irrigation in the Sterling area was limited to a few thousand acres along the South Platte River before the Great Western plant was built in 1905 although attempts to build a major project had been underway since 1893. Great Western financed the Prewitt Reservoir that provided a supplemental water supply for thirty-thousand acres. [242] The sugar beet plant also served as the impetus for forming the North Sterling Irrigation District, which authorized a bond issue to conduct a survey and develop plans from constructing the reservoir, canals, and other elements of the two-million-dollar North Sterling Reservoir project. [243] Construction employed more than a thousand men and four-hundred horse teams. [244] Dynamite blasting was required to dig the seventy-mile intake ditch. When completed in 1911, the project boasted a five-thousand-foot-long dam backed by a reservoir that could hold more than eighty-thousand acre-feet of water. When the project was completed, the *Sterling Democrat* boasted of "Eighty thousand acres of cheap grazing land, by the public spirit of a few faithful men, lifted into the miracle working realm of irrigation." [245]

Irrigation in eastern Colorado affected relatively little land. Surface irrigation was, and still is, concentrated in Bent, Crowley, Otero and Prowers Counties along the Arkansas River and in Logan, Morgan and Sedgwick Counties on the South Platte. (Beginning in the 1950s irrigation using ground water from sedimentary aquifers became important in several dryland counties.) In 1920, only 14 percent of all farmland in the seven "irrigated" counties was in fact irrigated but yields per acre in these counties were markedly greater than in the others. [246] The 1910 Census reported that Colorado corn production in counties with substantial irrigation exceeded that in the remaining counties by almost eight bushels per acres or more than 50 percent and the alfalfa yield was 40 percent higher. [247]

Irrigation transformed both the economy and the landscape of the eastern plains. But watering the river valleys was not without cost. As noted earlier, financial failures were common, and damages were not limited to those on balance sheets. The early developers had little concern or comprehension of the sustainability of their creations as, in Sherow's rendition, they "sought to force water to fulfill their economic and social ambitions, rather than developing a sense for the ecology of the valley and adjusting their lives to the seasons of the High Plains."[248] They were often oblivious to the constraints of climate and terrain. Losses through transpiration and evaporation reduced river flows by as much as 40 percent. Irrigation eroded farmland increasing sedimentation clogging ditches and laterals, and alkaline salts leached from the soil increased the salinity of the water.[249]

Early Irrigated Farming

Although the chronicle of the dryland homesteader is often presented as the defining story of the era, early settlers in the river valleys experienced earlier and more extensive agricultural development. With enough water, the land and climate were favorable to farming although the often-meager flow of the rivers meant the land that could be irrigated was limited.

The first farmers along the Arkansas and South Platte Valleys, other than the Indians or traders who occasionally cultivated small plots, settled in the 1860s. M. E. Sizer filed a claim on 320 acres on the Purgatoire south of the Arkansas in 1865. He was able to grow wheat, corn, and fruit trees irrigated with water from the river and is credited with introducing alfalfa to Bent County.[250] One of the most successful early irrigators was George Swink. Upon arriving in the Arkansas Valley in the early 1870s he established a general store near today's Rocky Ford. His choice of location was prescient as the "rocky ford" was one of the few places on the lower Arkansas that provided firm footing for crossing the river. Traffic was heavy, and the store did a booming business with travelers fording the stream as well as with nearby ranchers.[251] Swink also applied his energies to agriculture. He filed preemption, timber, and homestead claims and raised cattle and crops. Upon examining the operation of his store, he saw an opportunity to profit from growing his own vegetables rather than buying from local truck farmers. He experimented with a wide range of grains, vegetables, and hays and began irrigating on a small scale with water hand-drawn from the Arkansas. Impressed by the yield of irrigated crops, he organized a cooperative effort to construct a ditch so other farmers could benefit from watering their fields that eventually became the Rocky Ford Ditch. He imported bees to speed pollination and developed the famous Rocky Ford Cantaloupe. After the turn of the century, he was instrumental in promoting the sugar beet industry in the Arkansas Valley. Swink is memorialized by a plaque in Rocky Ford stating, "He developed Rocky Ford's two main cash crops, melons and sugar beets; courted the town's largest corporation, the American Beet Sugar Company; and helped build the Rocky Ford Ditch, the spine of an extensive irrigation network. Swink's formula—land, transportation, industry, and water—represented prairie town-building at its best."[252]

William Aukland was one of the beneficiaries of Swink's efforts. A native of Scotland, he arrived in penniless in the US in 1882. Through saving and trading land, he accumulated enough money in 1889 to buy a 1,500-acre site along the Arkansas River in what was to become Crowley County. The farm had ample water rights and he grew wheat, corn, and oats and raised Hereford cattle, Poland China hogs, Shropshire sheep, and turkeys. When the sugar factory was built in Sugar City, he began growing beets. He built a drying and grinding mill for his alfalfa. Auckland operated his farm until 1933 when he retired and distributed the farm among his children.[253]

Most irrigated farmers weathered the late eighties and early eighties drought. All counties with substantial irrigated farming except Sedgwick attracted settlers during the nineties while the dryland counties were losing population. The number of farms in the irrigated counties increased by 1,470 in the nineties with Prowers County adding 370 and Otero County more than 600. By contrast, only Elbert among the dryland counties saw a significant gain in the number of farms. The leading crop on irrigated land in the nineties was alfalfa which provided forage for cattle and sometimes for sheep. In 1900 the alfalfa acreage in the six counties in the Arkansas and South Platte Valleys, not all of which was irrigated, was nearly three times that of wheat and corn combined.[254]

In the absence of irrigated agriculture, pessimists' forebodings about the great American desert likely would have come to pass. Most of the region's growth occurred where irrigation supported large numbers of smaller farms. The six irrigated counties added more than twelve thousand people between 1890 and 1900, nearly doubling their population. In 1900, two-thirds of the population in the region lived in the six counties along the Arkansas or South Platte Valleys. Both agricultural production and other economic activity were similarly concentrated. Upon his retirement in 1903, John Vroman, the first president of the Catlin Canal in Otero County, wrote:

> When I first came to this country some 30 years ago, the general appearance of the landscape was all but inviting to prospective farmers, who now are located on beautiful homes. There was nothing but a vast expanse of hill and dale thickly covered with sagebrush and greasewood for habitation for the coyote, the rabbit and the rattlesnakes. Thus, it has been for countless ages and thus it seemed doomed forever to remain and thus in fact it would have remained, but for the dauntless courage, foresight and of the few hearty pioneers who, realizing the enormous possibilities of the soil when plentifully supplied with water, began the building of canals to convey the water from the river to these lands.[255]

Plains Agriculture in 1900

The aspirations of the early homesteaders were frequently unrealized. The nineties were a trying time for many of the region's settlers, especially those trying to farm

CHAPTER 2

dryland. But, as the new century drew near, promises of better times were beginning to appear. Farm prices improved and the drought seemed over. The stage was being set for two decades of the most robust growth in the region's history.

STRUGGLE ON THE HIGH PLAINS

Chapter 2 Exhibits

Selected Economic Statistics
Combined 1880 Bent & Elbert Counties

	Population	Number of Farms	Number of Farms less than 500 acres	Number of Farms Cultivated by Owner	Pct Cult. By Owner	Land In Farms acres	Improved Land acres
1880	3,456	195	159	186	95%	86,260	30,106
1890	14,259	1,323	1,191	1,222	92%	421,518	104,270

	Value Per Acre	Number Cattle Except Milk Cows	Number of Swine	Number of Sheep	Acres Wheat	Acres Corn	Acres Hay *
1880	$ 14.77	27,491	262	128,643	148	1,486	5,657
1890	$ 11.51	83,121	5,233	186,842	499	3,324	12,743

* Mostly Alfalfa

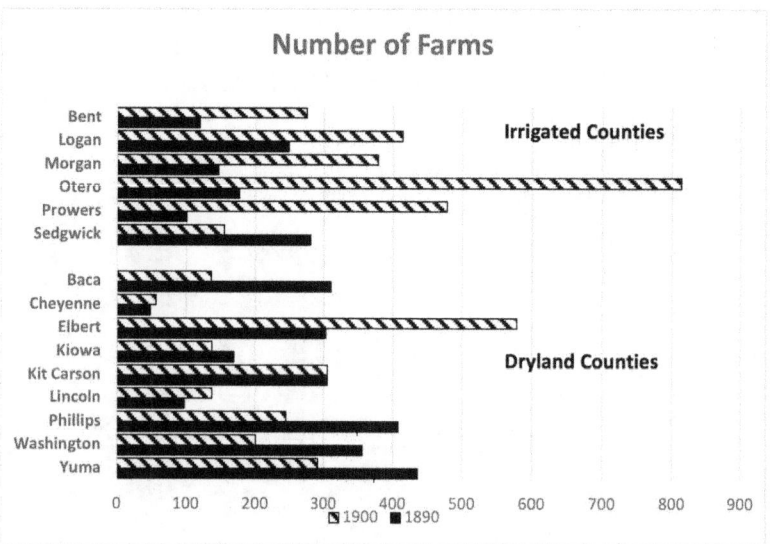

The first wave of homesteaders in the 1880s brought a dramatic increase in population and economic activity. The upper table shows the extent of settlement and agriculture between 1880 and 1890. The 1890 figures include the new counties created in the 1880's that were earlier part of Bent or Elbert County.

Drought and deflation in the late 1880s and early 1890s caused many homesteaders to abandon their farms. Dryland counties showed a decline in the number of farms while the less vulnerable irrigated counties continued to attract new settlers.

Source: Census

CHAPTER 2

Irrigated Farming in Eastern Colorado

	Number of Farms Irrigated				
	1890	**1900**	**1910**	**1920**	**1930**
Bent	83	223	404	438	518
Logan	73	226	272	397	617
Morgan	97	306	561	777	845
Otero *	139	762	1,310	1,604	1,572
Prowers	18	377	546	660	729
Sedgwick	-	81	141	130	161
Other	45	131	128	127	173
Total	455	2,106	3,362	4,133	4,615

	Acres Irrigated				
	1890	**1900**	**1910**	**1920**	**1930**
Bent	422	33,039	59,497	128,712	64,338
Logan	8,970	8,913	63,166	85,079	111,378
Morgan	16,443	37,012	97,849	132,231	105,277
Otero *	16,431	62,268	122,457	177,987	144,452
Prowers	1,808	46,091	71,684	76,322	111,643
Sedgwick	-	4,779	22,023	21,510	22,375
Other	4,103	10,004	19,639	21,469	20,256
Total	48,177	202,106	456,315	643,310	579,719

* Otero in 1920 and 1930 includes Crowley

Most of the large irrigation projects in the South Platte and Arkansas Valleys were completed between 1890 and 1920 and were undertaken by private developers. As many of these ran into financial difficulties, they were converted to mutual ditch companies.

Source: Census, based on county level data with irrigated county statistics covering entire county.

Irrigated Farmland in Eastern Colorado-1920

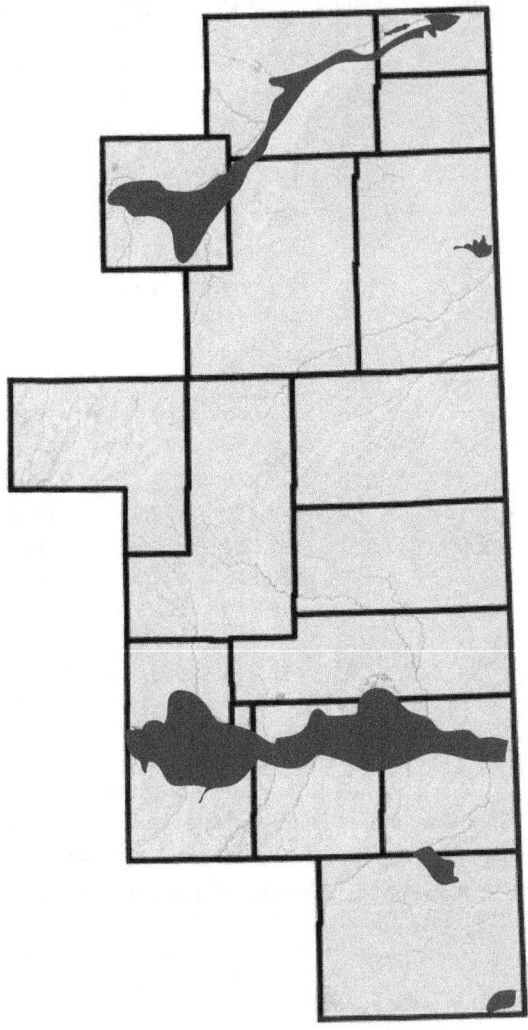

The map shows irrigated land in eastern Colorado in 1920. Irrigated farming was largely limited to land near the Arkansas and South Platte Rivers.

CHAPTER 2

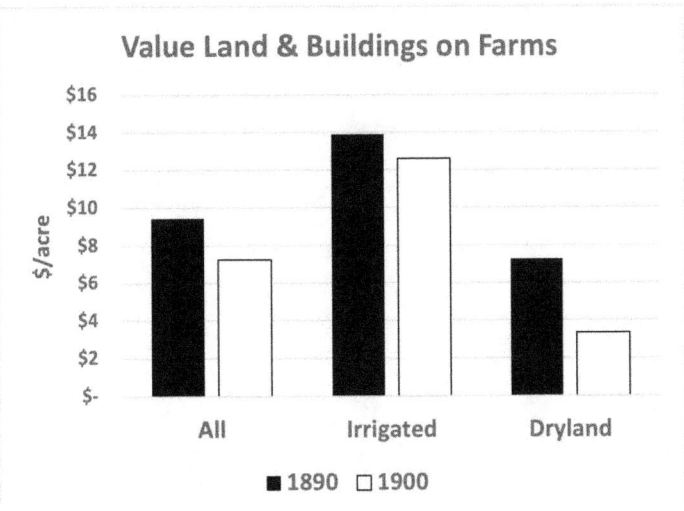

Sod house.

Farmland values fell over the 1890's. Dry weather early in the decade and abandonment of many farms were contributing factors. Values fell more in dryland counties than in irrigated areas.

The Mark Gill family's sod house in Morgan County. "Soddies" were constructed from bricks of sod cut from the prairie. They were smelly, leaked, and were plagued by insects and rodents, but provided shelter for homesteaders until better accommodations could be built.

Source: Census, based on county level data with irrigated county statistics covering entire county. The Denver Public Library, Western History Collection, Call number X-8493.

CHAPTER 3

The Golden Age of Agriculture: 1900 through Twenties

AMERICAN AGRICULTURISTS ENJOYED UNPRECEDENTED PROSPERITY IN THE EARLY twentieth century and eastern Colorado's farmers shared in the good fortune, thriving on both irrigated acreage and dryland. Prices for farm products rebounded. A combination of more effective equipment, improved techniques, and crop varieties better adapted to the regional climate led to more productive farms and ranches. Irrigation projects reduced the threat of limited rainfall, at least in the river valleys. The climate was more favorable; prolonged droughts were largely avoided until the 1930s. Industries processing farm produce, notably sugar beet refining and alfalfa dehydrating, became important contributors to the regional economy. The record numbers of migrants who settled on plains in the 1900s and the 1910s generally fared better than those who came earlier.

The Agricultural Environment

By the middle 1890s, crop and livestock prices had descended to levels that made it difficult for many farmers to survive. Gold discoveries in Alaska and South Africa late in the decade brought a reversal of post-Civil War deflation. Farmers' debt burdens lightened, and farm prices posted steady gains through the onset of World War I, bringing the healthiest agricultural economy in decades. By 1910 wholesale farm prices had risen 60 percent since the middle nineties and wheat sold for more than a dollar a bushel up from sixty cents in 1895.[256] Farm production costs also rose. But farmers as debtors and owners of land benefitted disproportionately from inflation, much as they had suffered more from earlier deflation. The average value of an acre of American farmland rose from under $20 in 1900 to almost $40 in 1910.[257] The early teens are often described as a "golden age" for American agriculture due to the favorable relationship between the value of the farmer's product and his cost of operation. This relationship was measured by the "parity ratio," and its value between 1910 and 1914 was to serve as a seldom-achieved benchmark for later farm support legislation.

Prospects would get even brighter. When the Turkish Navy blocked the Dardanelles in 1914, shipments of Russian wheat were halted, and the United States became a critical food supplier to the warring nations of western Europe. Farm prices accelerated in the face of growing demand by the belligerent powers, bringing unprecedented affluence to many plains farmers. The wholesale price index for agricultural products rose 82 percent between 1916 and 1919. Ian Frazier in his narrative of the Great Plains contended that "World War I changed the great plains more than any other event in recent history."[258, 259]

Plains famers could not have reaped the rewards from higher prices and improved farming techniques without favorable weather, most crucially adequate rainfall. Fortunately, drought was largely avoided. Las Animas, which reported average annual rainfall of less than ten inches in the 1890s, averaged fourteen inches annually over the next two decades. More importantly, prolonged dry spells were avoided. Farmers were better able to withstand brief dry periods through such techniques as soil packing, summer fallowing, or other moisture-retention strategies. Changes in plains agriculture were not limited to crop farming. Developments in cattle ranching, already well underway by 1900, resulted in a drastic transformation from the open range cattle kingdom.

Legislation designed to encourage western settlement had proved ill-suited for the western Great Plains. Lawmakers in Washington eventually awakened to some of its shortcomings and homestead laws were liberalized to better accommodate conditions in the arid west. The Enlarged Homestead Act of 1909 allowed claimants to patent 320 acres instead of 160. The Three-Year Homestead Act shortened residence requirement for perfecting a claim and allowed homesteaders to absent themselves for five months out of a year, making it easier to supplement farm income with off-farm jobs. The Stockgrowers Homestead Act of 1916 permitted the acquisition of 640 acres classified as grazing or forage crop land.

Farm prosperity was reflected in regional land values that had fallen during the 1890s when crop and livestock prices markets softened and drought limited crop yields and destroyed pastures. When conditions improved, they surged. The average price of an acre of land in Colorado's eastern plains tripled between 1900 and 1910 and rose by another two-thirds over the next ten years.[260] Average land values rose in all counties in the 1900-10 decade and in all but the Arkansas Valley counties of Bent, Otero and Prowers over the following decade. Land with water rights enjoyed a sizable premium. A 1908 promotional pamphlet for southeast Colorado quoted dryland at $5 to $30 per acre while irrigated land in the Arkansas Valley was priced at $80 to $150.[261] But dryland also enjoyed appreciation with the price of such property in Logan County reportedly rising from five to thirty dollars an acre between 1905 and 1910.[262]

CHAPTER 3

The Second Wave of Homesteaders

As the new century dawned, farming readily obtainable land on the western plains was once again viewed by many as a path to that era's version of the American Dream. Drought and low prices in the 1890s had forced countless dryland settlers to abandon their property. But by the early 1900s conditions improved, the difficulties of the previous decade were forgotten, and another round of feverish land accumulation was underway. The habits and skills brought by the settlers help fuel a rapidly growing rural economy and rising prosperity. As historian Bruce Garver pointed out in an article on Great Plains immigration, "the majority of pioneering settlers—whom many economists of the early twenty-first century would define as 'human capital'—arrived as ambitious, intelligent, and fully literate young adults, who were usually also married, in the best of health, and approaching the prime of life."[263]

Speculators, railroads, and state and local governments aggressively promoted eastern Colorado's farming potential, lauding available land in eastern Colorado as an opportunity to be exploited before the world learned of its promise. A 1910 pamphlet extolling Yuma County proclaimed, "The great agricultural possibilities of the unirrigated plains of eastern Colorado have not been understood or appreciated until within the last few years."[264] A land company affiliated with the Missouri Pacific Railroad promised moral as well as economic betterment in a land where "….there is also something in the sunshine that braces up the mental faculties and spurs the mind to higher and nobler deeds"[265] Another piece of hucksterism from the Amity Canal Company on the Arkansas claimed that on irrigated land "A man can make more money with less labor off forty acres than can be made off the best quarter section in the eastern states…."[266] A Washington County land company dismissed tales of the Great American Desert since improved farming techniques had overcome the need for plentiful rainfall. "There was a time when farmers thought that the rainfall determined the success of their crops, but thanks to our experimental stations, they have taught us that it is not the amount of water that falls, but the moisture that is retained in the soil."[267]

The Colorado state government joined the promoters when the Legislature authorized the State Board of Immigration in 1909, a successor to earlier agencies set up in the 1870s and 1880s but not reauthorized.[268] The mission of the Board as specified in its implementing legislation was "properly advertising the resource and attractions of the State of Colorado among the people of other States and nations, so that by immigration and investments the development of the State may be stimulated and its population increased."[269] In its 1916 Annual Report, the agency claimed that "It is impossible to state results of our work in dollars, but the evidence at hand would indicate at least $400,000 of new money has been brought into the State and we are safe in assuming that it might be twice this amount."[270]

There was plenty of land to sell. The Union Pacific still held substantial acreage and was eager to populate it with potential customers. Investors and speculators were able to buy claims called "relinquishments" from homesteaders who failed to prove up on their properties. These were often obtained from desperate sellers at low prices and could be resold at a handsome profit. Settlers could either claim government lands through the Homestead Act or other measures, or purchase plots that had been subdivided from large ranches. Speculative motives were not limited to large landowners. As noted earlier some small homesteaders hoped to resell their land for profit.

Promoters marketed their land at mass sales such as one in Burlington in June 1910. This event drew crowds from surrounding areas along with hundreds from farther away who were brought in by the Rock Island Railroad. The promoters provided entertainment for potential buyers including "trapeze performers [and] darkies' quaint songs in harmony with stringed instruments." But this event failed to live up to its promoters' hopes as both the volume of sales and prices received were reportedly disappointing.[271] Among the land promoters was Horace Davis, who came to Sterling as a station agent for the Union Pacific Railroad. He arranged with railroad officials to organize the Colorado Colony Company that conducted excursions for potential settlers to the South Platte Valley.[272]

The land promotion largely succeeded. Thousands came between 1900 and the and early teens, some in covered wagons driving their cattle and other livestock with their furniture and implements tied to the sides, while others came by train in "immigrant cars." The arrival of large numbers of homesteaders recalled the boom in the previous century. The *Lamar Register* reported in 1915 that "The new settlement on government land in the Lamar District has never been approached except during the famous boom of 1887. Thousands of newcomers have looked over these lands and filed on many hundred-thousands of acres and returned in a few months with their families and effects to make permanent settlement."[273] Census farm statistics reveal the magnitude of the flood of settlers. Both the number of farms and acreage farmed increased roughly fivefold between 1900 and 1920 with the fastest growth in the first decade. Much of the acreage in the river valleys had already been claimed, so the dryland counties that had lost farms during the 1890s saw a sharp rebound in the following decade, especially in the northeast. Phillips, Washington, and Yuma Counties all lost a third or more of their farms in the 1890s but registered large gains in the 1900s. Baca County's growth was delayed as it lacked a railroad until the middle 1920s, the only county in Colorado without one, making it less accessible to settlers and less influenced by the railway company's promotions. By the teens, when much of the better land in other counties had been settled, Baca County's farm numbers more than tripled.[274] Among the new settlers were Ike Osteen's parents who in 1911 rode to the railroad's end in Liberal, Kansas where they loaded farm and household equipment along with three children onto a wagon and, with their livestock, headed west. They spent the winter with a relative in Johnson, Kansas and proceeded to their homestead in Baca County sixteen miles south of today's Walsh.[275] Irrigated areas, especially the Arkansas Valley, saw steadier growth with the number of farms increasing in the 1890s, 1900s, and 1910s. The *Lamar Register* reported in mid-1916 that little government land was left for filing new claims.[276] By the 1920 the number of farms in the region reached an all-time high.[277]

Among the region's new farmers was the Adamson family from Russell Springs, Kansas. Thomas Adamson and his wife Annie arrived in Kiowa County in April 1910. He drove four horses pulling a covered wagon, Annie drove two horses pulling a spring wagon and their two children took turns riding a horse to herd the milk cows. The family settled on a 320-acre homestead, six miles north of Chivington in Kiowa County. They lived in a tent until September when they moved to a dugout with two cement sides. Fire for cooking and heat came from cow chips gathered by the children. The following spring Adamson broke sod with a four-horse team and a two-bottom plow and planted corn by hand. Their residence was later expanded to house their growing family; eventually there were eleven children. Adamson later acquired more land where he specialized in commercial Hereford cattle. He was an early practitioner of conservation methods. To limit soil erosion, he planted more grass as well as trees to prevent blowing. The Adamson farm thrived and was taken over by their son John and his wife in 1936.[278]

Marshall W. "Pop" Scott arrived with his wife and five children in Washington County in December 1914 on an immigrant train. The Scotts were one of five families who came together from south of Kansas City, all of whom homesteaded in the Akron area. The family brought with them a wagon, two horses, a walking plow, wood posts, a cow, and household effects. Within days Marshall filed for a 240-acre homestead, now available under the Enlarged Homestead Act. The family lived in Akron in a tent until the frame homestead house was ready to live in spring 1915. "Pop" dug a forty foot well, built a barn with a granary, dug a storage cellar, and built a chicken house. The Scotts raised barley, beans, cane, corn, wheat and turnips on 110 cultivated acres. The turnips were fed the to the farm's hogs.[279]

Finding the proper farming methods and crops was often a trial-and-error process. In 1908 Glen Durrell moved to Lincoln County from Earlville, Illinois in hopes that the climate in the new region would alleviate his respiratory problems. Along with his wife and four children, he arrived by train and settled with his family near Arriba where he had earlier claimed a quarter section under the Homestead Act. Upon reaching their homestead, a boxcar shared with another family homesteading nearby was shunted onto a sidetrack. It contained household goods, farm implements, and animals. Their land had been marked by public land surveys with mounds of earth at section corners and half mile markers, needed to delineate quarter sections were determined by siting from the section corners.

The Durrell family's first home was a tent where they lived through a summer and a fall. After fencing and planting, they built a dugout home for the winter. It was replaced the next summer by a frame house. Their first farming efforts were focused on supplying feed for livestock rather than crops for sale. The plot's square layout along section lines made it difficult to plow along contours or to accommodate stream crossings or excessive grades. Corn was planted the first two years on flat plowed land in rows as was practice back in Illinois, but the crop was poor. Corn eventually proved unreliable, so the land was shifted to sorghum and small grains which were cut with a grain binder or by hand and stacked to be fed in winter. A silo, ten feet in diameter and fifteen to twenty feet deep, was dug to store green corn or sorghum which supplied forage for milk cows. The Durrells also grew wheat which was harvested with a "header," a primitive combine pulled by five horses. The Durrell farm finally produced decent crops and achieved some degree of financial stability, but the absence of a nearby high school for the boys made it necessary to sell the farm. The family held a public sale of their horses, cattle, chickens, farm machinery and household goods and moved to a more populated area.[280]

Some immigrants settled on irrigated land, often purchasing it from previous owners. Claus Paulsen, a relatively prosperous Nebraska farmer, wished to relocate in the Arkansas Valley due to his wife's ill health. With a team and wagon, he examined several pieces of farmland before purchasing 320 acres of irrigated land eight miles north of Lamar using the proceeds from the sales of his Nebraska property. He brought his wife and seven children to the Arkansas Valley and another child would be born in Prowers County. Paulsen alternated crops of sugar beets and wheat, producing good yields from both. By 1910, having accumulated capital from his crops and perhaps having delegated some of the farm operation to his sons, he turned his attention to other ventures. In the early teens he represented the Payne Investment Company of Omaha, showing land in the area to would-be homesteaders. He wrote in a pamphlet prepared for prospective landowners that "any young man with a little ambition and perhaps a little money, can establish himself [in the Arkansas Valley] now, in five years be independent, and in ten years, wealthy." He also invested in a portable alfalfa meal grinding operation to take advantage of the Valley's rapidly expanding alfalfa crop. The grinder required a crew of eight and was pulled from farm to farm by a massive gasoline tractor as smaller and more efficient tractors were not yet available. The meal was processed on site, hauled to cars on a railroad siding, and shipped to Denver, Kansas City or other distribution points.[281]

Not all the new settlements were individual ventures. During the 1890s the American branch of the Salvation Army established colonies for the urban underprivileged, hoping to relocate them to rural areas where they could become farmers and independent landowners. One such colony was founded in Prowers County in 1898, called the Amity Colony or Fort Amity, in keeping with the Salvation Army's military posture. But the

Amity Colony's aspirations were continually thwarted. The land chosen was close to the ground-water table, so irrigation water tended to pool on fields resulting in alkaline deposits. But the Amity founders were determined to succeed and between thirty and thirty-five families arrived in April 1898 and were put to work constructing fences, irrigation ditches, and homes and planting crops. Each family was provided ten acres along with livestock, poultry, and tools. In 1901 forty to sixty orphans were brought to the colony and housed in an orphanage constructed on the site. The orphanage was to become self-sufficient through the sale of crops, dairy products, and poultry, which were all to be tended by the children, but this goal was not realized. The orphans were relocated, and the orphanage was converted to a sanitorium which proved no more profitable. The Army spent thousands of dollars attempting to solve the water-pooling problem, but these efforts failed, and the Colony incurred ongoing losses. The Amity Colony confronted floods, typhoid and scarlet fever outbreaks, and a bank robbery. Most of the colonists eventually left and the property was purchased by a Holly banker in 1909.[282]

The second wave of homesteaders transformed eastern Colorado's plains as much as any development in its history. What had been a sparsely populated zone in the Great American Desert became a prosperous agricultural region. Economic and demographic growth occurred at a record pace. Farm and ranch expansion brought industries processing farm products, and thriving communities providing necessary services to the growing population. But the region's prosperity would continue only so long as favorable weather and market conditions endured.

A Revolution in Agricultural Technology and Farming Techniques

The first quarter of the twentieth century saw changes in technology, crops and livestock, and techniques that brought dramatic improvements in farm productivity. The most important innovation was the tractor, probably one of the most significant advances in modern farming history. Prior to this machine, breaking the prairie sod required mechanical or animal assistance, and farm equipment was mostly pulled by horses or mules with the typical plains farmer requiring one horse for each fifty-three acres of farmland.[283] These animals were expensive and needed to be fed hay and grain that had to be purchased or grown on land which was then unavailable for cash crops. The first tractors, introduced in the late nineteenth century, were cumbersome and expensive steam driven behemoths weighing between ten and fifteen tons. Although they could be used on the open flat land of the Great Plains, they were practical only for sizable properties. The early gasoline powered machines were also large and costly. But World War I increased the demand for more and better tractors as horses were pressed into wartime service, fewer young men were available for farm labor, and higher grain prices raised the cost of feeding draft animals. Henry Ford introduced the Fordson which was lighter and cheaper, weighing two to six-thousand pounds and selling for under $1,000, making it practical for smaller operations. The introduction of rubber tires and the design of equipment for use with tractors made the machine vital for a growing number of farmers.

Other productivity-enhancing equipment included the one-way disc plow which set all the discs at the same angle and was ideal for plowing stubble and breaking hard-sunbaked soil. Combines could cut and thresh grain in a single operation, greatly reduced harvesting labor and cutting the number of man-hours needed to harvest an acre of wheat from an estimated 2.8 to 0.75.[284] The early combines were pulled by horses or tractors and had auxiliary power for cutting and threshing. But these were large and cumbersome. Smaller self-powered models were introduced in 1918. Logan County farmer Lorin Lindstrom recalled that in the late teens "our increasing acreage of wheat made it difficult to harvest with one small header. At about the same time a few small combines started appearing on the market. That same year International Harvester Company shipped in three twelve-foot pull-type combines. Earlier combines had drag sackers but ours came with a drag elevator that unloaded into a wagon. [The operator] scooped as many as 800 bushels per day when we could run well."[285] The level smoothing harrow, twenty-four feet wide was pulled by six horses or a tractor. With this machine a man could till thirty to sixty acres a day. In a dry climate, seeds needed to be separated to obtain enough moisture so the Midwestern practice of "broadcasting," or spreading seeds at random, was ineffective. The grain drill allowed planting seeds at specified intervals. Plains farmers invested heavily in the new equipment. The Census reported that the value of implements and machinery on farms in eastern Colorado counties at the turn of the century was less than a million dollars. By 1910 it had grown to $5 million and was almost $19 million in 1920.[286]

These innovations allowed the farmer to cultivate more land, and more extensive cultivation raised the productivity of his labor. The US Department of Agriculture estimated that the number of man-hours needed to produce 100 bushels of wheat fell from 152 in 1880 to 108 in 1900 and to 98 in 1910-14. For corn the corresponding figures were 180, 147 and 132.[287] Wheat production statistics for Colorado's plains counties suggest comparable gains. Most if not all the gains came from cultivating more land rather than producing more on existing acreage. Between 1900 and 1920, regional wheat output per acre increased only slightly while that for corn registered a decline. But corn production per farm more than doubled while that for wheat saw a greater than fourfold increase.[288]

Farming techniques also improved. By the turn of the century growers, especially those working dryland acreage, were developing greater knowledge of what worked and what didn't. Early settlers' experiences benefitted those who came later as the newly arrived farmers learned from their neighbors. These informal lessons were supplemented by government agricultural experiment stations that disseminated their findings to area farmers. The State of Colorado established the first dryland experiment station at Cheyenne Wells in 1893. The US government set up its first station at Akron in 1905 followed by several more.

The mix of crops and livestock was also changing. In 1910 H.M. Cottrell of the Agricultural Experiment Station at Colorado Agricultural College, now Colorado State University, summarized the strategies for success on the high plains. He first laid out the challenges plains farmers would face, describing dryland farming as "a continual fight against relentless unfavorable conditions."[289] Those arriving without funds were likely doomed to failure as a settler would need sufficient capital for buildings, teams and implements with money left over for seed, feed and living expenses. Diversification was an essential part of the successful business model. A farmer who relied on a grain crop such as corn or wheat was likely to go broke as three years out of five would see crops fail due to insufficient rainfall. The farmer's best hope, according to Cottrell, lay in a combination of dairy and poultry with crops principally for forage such as milo maize, a sorghum. Cottrell suggested at least 320 acres to support a family, eighty acres in crops, eighty in summer fallow, and 160 in grass to be supplemented by renting winter pasture. A well was vital but finding underground water was usually a challenge. Most of a farmer's cash flow could be expected to come from sale of eggs, cream, and male calves, perhaps supplemented with alfalfa raised for seed. Cottrell's views aligned with his "outside" job when he supplemented his income as the author of promotional material for the Rock Island Railroad. His rhetoric was definitely more in line with the Railroad's interest in encouraging settlement. While the extension bulletin warned of the obstacles dry land settlers would face, one of his railroad bulletins described eastern Colorado as "….one of the best countries for an energetic man with a good team and a few good cows to develop a good farm and an attractive home."[290]

As noted, the practices setters brought from the Midwest often failed on the Great Plains. Limited rainfall meant that successful crops required maximizing the amount of moisture captured and retained by the soil. The "Campbell System" of dryland farming, developed and promoted by early Dakota homesteader H. W. Campbell, would, its founder claimed, make family farming feasible on the Plains. It was widely disseminated by railroads and land developers. The principles of the system were deep plowing in the fall, subsurface packing, light seeding, thorough cultivation before and after seeding, and summer fallowing. Finally, the soil should be corrugated to limit the effects of wind which could increase evaporation as well as blow away the topsoil. Campbell's advice attracted some skeptics. As Vance Johnson noted in his history of dryland farming in eastern Colorado, Campbell's objectivity could be questioned as he had a financial interest in its adoption since it required machinery that his company manufactured.[291] Geoff Cunfer, who analyzed Great Plains agricultural land use from the late nineteenth century to the present day, contended that summer fallowing made a much greater contribution to soil conservation than deep plowing and packing.[292]

Dryland farmers increasingly adopted this practice which allowed one year's crop to benefit from moisture stored in the soil from earlier years.

Plains farmers learned to plant crop varieties appropriate to the region. Earlier settlers frequently brought seeds from their previous farms, but the yields were often meager as the plants did not develop the extensive root system needed to obtain enough moisture in an arid climate. Crops that matured early, before drought and hot winds became pervasive, fared better. These included wheat, sorghum, and milo maize. Turkey Red wheat, introduced by German-Russian settlers, could be a profitable cash crop on the high plains, although failures could still be expected in dry years. Sorghum thrived under arid conditions and could be stored to be used for animal feed. Drought-resistant varieties of corn with shorter stalks, limited foliage, and ears growing closer to the ground produced valuable forage and occasionally a marketable grain crop. Drought-resistant brome grass could be harvested as a hay crop or used for pasture.

Improvements were not limited to dryland cultivation. George Swink developed new varieties of melons and other vegetables. John Crowley, for whom the County was named, experimented with multiple varieties of fruit orchards. Sugar beet farming on a commercial scale began in the Arkansas and South Platte Valleys at the turn of the century. Alfalfa that had long been a raised for animal feed became an important cash crop in the early the twentieth century.

Crops

In 1900 the majority of cropland was devoted to some form of hay or forage to be consumed by livestock either on the farm or nearby. That year's Census reported that 108,000 acres were planted in alfalfa. Corn or wheat together were planted on 140,000 acres. Sugar beet acreage was not reported but was quite small. Twenty years later commercial crops were ascendant. Wheat and corn acreage totaled almost 1.4 million and more than 70,000 acres were devoted to sugar beets. Alfalfa was still planted on over 180,000 acres as it had become an important commercial crop.[293]

Farms got larger with a more liberal government land policy and greater awareness of the acreage needed for dryland farming. Farm size increased as smaller units either expanded or absorbed other properties. Although some ranches covered many thousand acres, most crop or mixed-use farms were small or medium sized. In 1924 less than 1 percent of the cropland in the sixteen counties was in farms of over five-thousand acres while another 6 percent was found in properties between one and five thousand acres.[294]

Sugar Beets

Sugar beets arguably had the greatest impact on the plains economy of any farm product in the early years of the twentieth century. Beets were introduced to the region around 1900 and soon became an important commercial crop and a vital revenue source for growers. According to Colorado assessors' data, sugar beets accounted for one-quarter of the 1923 value of crops in the seven counties in the South Platte and Arkansas Valleys and more than one-third in Morgan County.[295] Although the value of beets sold was exceeded by other crops and livestock, its influence in the South Platte and Arkansas Valleys was probably greater. Its economic importance extended beyond farming. Beet processing plants provided employment and income in the valley towns. Nor was the industry's influence on the region limited to the economy. The migrants brought in to work in the beet fields changed the social fabric of their communities.

The sugar beet plant's tuber has a high concentration of sucrose and can be processed to produce table sugar and food additives. In 1920 beets accounted for about one-sixth of US sugar consumption with Colorado the leading producer among the states. The rest came from cane with the majority imported from Cuba.[296] The soil and climatic conditions in the South Platte and Arkansas Valleys were ideal for growing beets, although the plant is sensitive to cold and had to be harvested by November. Beet growing and processing did not become profitable in the region until prices rose in the late 1890s when the Dingley Tariff of 1897, a comprehensive protectionist measure, doubled the import duty on sugar, and the outbreak of the Spanish American War interrupted Cuban supplies. The wholesale price for sugar rose by 20 percent between 1895 and 1900. Plans for the first processing plant in the region were developed in 1899.

Beet production was a partnership between the farmer and the processor. Growers contracted with the sugar companies to plant a specific acreage with seeds purchased from the companies. Payments to the farmers were made after delivery based on the weight and the sugar content of the beets. For example, in 1910 the going price was around $5 per ton with an additional 25 cents per ton for each one percent increase in the sugar content beyond a minimum.[297] Farmers brought their beets to dumps along the rail line where they then were loaded onto railroad cars and transported to the processing plants. By 1930 mechanical beet pilers replaced much of the hand labor required in unloading the beets and most beets were hauled to beet dumps by truck rather than by horse-drawn wagon, resulting in a three-fold increase in the quantity of beets per load.[298]

Sugar beet cultivation depended upon adequate water, a supply of laborers for fieldwork, and access to refining plants. About fifteen gallons of water were required to grow an average sized beet plant and normal precipitation in the region meant that the crop needed to be irrigated three times from July to September. The development of irrigation projects in the South Platte and Arkansas Valleys in the late 1800s and early 1900s was critical for the growth in beet farming. As cultivation expanded, additional projects were built, often with the urging and financial assistance of the sugar companies. During the first half of the twentieth century, beet farmers were the largest water users in the region.

The cost of transporting beets meant that the refining plants needed to be reasonably close to the growers, so extensive beet farming awaited the construction of factories. The earliest plants were in the Arkansas Valley. As noted earlier, the first sugar factory in the region was built by investors in the Colorado Canal and Twin Lakes Reservoir, who had spent $2 million on a reservoir near the headwaters of the Arkansas just east of the continental divide and the beginnings of an irrigation canal down river in what was then Otero County, but were short of customers for their water. In 1899 they developed plans for a processing facility in Otero County and a new town for workers to be called Sugar City.[299] The plant owned by National Beet Sugar, later the National Sugar Manufacturing Co., was completed and the company began recruiting workers. The town burgeoned, growing to two-thousand people in 1900 according to Dena Markoff with "a business district unsurpassed by those during gold rush times: two hotels, a newspaper, five general stores, two undertakers, five saloons, two houses of prostitution, a gambling casino, a billiard parlor and a race track."[300] The claim of two-thousand people should be viewed with some skepticism as the Census reported 639 residents in 1900, although the two-thousand figure may have included those living outside Sugar City's boundaries. The inventory of businesses might be correct as the clientele of the undertakers, houses of prostitution and other businesses was not limited to Sugar City residents.

Other factories followed. The Oxnard brothers, who had built beet plants in California and Nebraska, established the American Beet Sugar plant in Rocky Ford in 1900 with strong local support from George Swink, the pioneer Otero County farmer and community leader. The company that later became American Crystal Sugar built factories in Lamar in 1905 and Las Animas two years later. Holly Sugar constructed factories in the namesake Prowers County town in 1905 and in Swink the following year.[301]

The sugar factories' promise was fleeting for some Arkansas Valley communities. The combined production capacity of the Valley's plants soon exceeded farmers' available land, water, and willingness to grow beets. Competition among the sugar companies was intense. Two competing companies built parallel short-haul railroads to transport beets to their plants. The two firms hired armed men to tear up rival's tracks and shots were exchanged.[302] This phase of the battle ended when the two lines were taken over by the Santa Fe. Struggling sugar companies pressured growers to accept lower guarantees for their product. In 1908 the *La Junta Tribune* reported that "War between the sugar beet growers of the Arkansas Valley and the American Sugar Refining Company and the Holly Beet Sugar Company was declared by the farmers at a large and enthusiastic mass meeting held in Rocky Ford last Saturday, where the ultimatum of these two companies to not pay a $5 flat rate for sugar beets this year was read. The growers declared they could not possibly grow beets and make money for less than $5 per ton, and therefore would not grow any next season."[303] Investors in the sugar plants faced mounting losses and those in Lamar, Holly and Las Animas closed within a few years. Beet production in the Arkansas Valley grew only modestly after 1909 despite strong demand during the war years.

The first plants in northern Colorado were constructed by independent firms in Boulder, Larimer and Weld Counties with Colorado's mining magnates, facing declining profits since the repeal of the silver purchase act in 1893, providing much of the funding. In 1903 the Fort Morgan Times reported that the four plants in northern Colorado generated $2 million per year in payments to growers and $700,000 in wages to factory employees.[304] The prospect of a similar infusion of dollars into their towns was seized upon by community leaders in Logan and Morgan Counties.

While several firms competed in the Arkansas Valley, a single monopolist was soon to control the industry in the South Platte Valley. The dominant player in the US sugar market in the early years of the twentieth century was American Sugar Refining Company, in 1903 the sixth largest industrial enterprise in the country. It would eventually control 70 percent of the nation's beet sugar processing and enjoy a monopoly of cane sugar.[305] The company, popularly referred to as the "sugar trust," sought to protect its profits by crushing competition. According to William May in his University of Colorado PhD dissertation on Great Western Sugar, the trust would "first attempt to acquire a beet sugar company through a purchase offer; failing an acquisition, would attempt to bankrupt it through cut-throat underselling in its market."[306] This strategy succeeded in taking over northern Colorado's independent firms in Boulder, Larimer and Weld Counties, incorporating them in New Jersey as Great Western Sugar Company (GW), a subsidiary of the sugar trust. Chester Morey, who had been among the Greeley plant's developers and later became head of GW, was charged by the trust with "seeing to it that no beet sugar factories were built in which the American Sugar Refining Company did not have a controlling' interest."[307] Morey sought to vigorously enforce this edict on any new plants further down the South Platte Valley.

City fathers in Sterling, Fort Morgan and Brush eagerly sought sugar factories and investors soon saw the potential for plants there. Interest first surfaced in Sterling. In 1902 an industry executive from Chicago provided the following assessment of the town's potential: "There are thousands of acres of land contiguous to Sterling which are perfectly adapted to the raising of sugar beets, and every effort should be made by lower Platte Valley people to secure the establishment of a factory of large capacity for the manufacture of sugar from that crop."[308] Several prospective investors expressed interest in a Sterling factory. A *Logan County Advocate* headline proclaimed, "German Beet Sugar Manufacturer Was Pleased with Sterling."[309] But in December 1904, a factory site was purchased by an agent for Chester Morey.[310] Although the Sterling factory was initially owned by a supposedly independent entity labeled "The Sterling Sugar Company," it was acquired by GW the following January.

A contract was signed by the company with a committee of local beet growers committing the company to pay growers $4.75 per ton for the 1905 crop and $5 for the next two years.[311] The factory, completed in time for the 1905 harvest at a cost of the $1 million, could process six-hundred tons of beets with sufficient room to add equipment to double its capacity.[312] Sterling celebrated the completion of the plant with two-day of festivities including music, food, and speeches by local and state dignitaries.[313] The 1905 harvest was proclaimed successful by local growers. Logan County farmer W. L. Henderson received a $6,175 check for a crop of 1,300 tons from a hundred acres.[314]

The construction of long-delayed Bijou canal opened new acreage to irrigation and created an opportunity for a plant in Fort Morgan. The *Fort Morgan Times* editorialized, "Now that we have the Bijou ditch let us go after a sugar beet factory. We are in the swim and might as well have all there is going."[315] Independent investors vied with GW to build the facility.

Plans for an independent factory to open the following year were announced in 1903 at a site described as "admirably situated in regard to both transportation of beets and sugar. It lies directly between two railroads, the Union Pacific and Burlington, and although the building lot has not been given out, there is no point in the land watered by the Bijou Ditch company that does not lie within two and one-half miles of these roads."[316] Local sentiment favored an independent operation. According to the *Fort Morgan* Times independently owned factories in Fort Morgan and Brush would restrain the trust's bargaining position with growers as "the sugar trust's power in Colorado will be reduced to a minimum, as it will be impossible for that corporation to begin to compete on price. The reason for this is that with the enormous output of trust sugar, and the obligation to keep mills running, the trust will lose $1,000 to every $1 lost by the private concern. Should the corporation reduce the price of sugar in Colorado, it would be obliged to do so all over the country and the loss would amount to millions."[317] Investors in the proposed factory boasted, "there will be consternation in the sugar trust's camp when they find they are to be met by men who are fully as rich and determined as they are."[318] But GW persisted. A letter from American Sugar president and founder Henry O. Havemeyer to a Mr. E. F. Dyer who had secured contracts for plant sites in Brush and Fort Morgan stated, "It is our territory and…. We do not want any new people in what we regard as our territory."[319] The trust eventually prevailed, and GW presented plans to open a factory in Fort Morgan in 1906.

Before the company would proceed with construction, it needed contracts from regional farmers to grow enough beets to make it economical. Many farmers were initially reluctant to commit to a single crop but were persuaded by a Fort Morgan businessmen's campaign described in the *Fort Morgan Times*:

> They got hold of the landowners and repeated the argument of this paper in favor of beet planting with such zeal and earnestness as carried

conviction to the minds and pocketbooks of all listeners. If a landowner said he had so much on hand that he could not undertake to plant any more beets, straightaway a little syndicate would be formed to take the land and the landowner would sign for his acreage and go away rejoicing. In order to be sure of a sugar factory next year it was necessary to have contracts for 3,500 acres of beets signed September 1. The goal was almost reached. A little more rustling will mean victory.[320]

The goal was achieved, and construction got underway. William May wrote that to mark the opening of the Fort Morgan plant, "the Morgan County Fair Association had a huge celebration with bands, speakers, special trains, various amusements, a free lunch for all visitors and a half-day visit to the factory."[321] The plant's original capacity of six-hundred tons per day was later increased to 3,450. In October 1909 the *Fort Morgan Times* reported that "Since last week the farmers have been hauling great loads of beets to the factory dump and with the accumulated pile waiting to be rolled into the sluices all was in readiness for the run this morning. The beet train hauled twenty-two cars across the sugar switch this morning and reurned for a second load of like size."[322] The factory was a mainstay of the town's economy into the twenty-first century, and in 2016, operated by the grower-owned Western Sugar Cooperative, was the only sugar beet factory in Colorado.

Beet growing in the Brush began around 1900 and soon local leaders were soliciting possible investors in a Brush factory. A.J. Morey, a local sheep rancher and beet grower and the brother of GW's Chester Morey, recruited area growers to plant a crop sufficient to justify the plant and GW opened it 1906 with Morey as manager.[323] The factory had a capacity of six hundred tons per day[324] and, between 1916 and 1930, paid local farmers an averaged $1 million annually.[325] GW added another in plant Ovid in 1926.

The sugar trust maintained its grip on the South Platte Valley sugar economy through the teens. The federal government initiated an anti-trust suit against American Sugar in 1910 which was finally settled with a consent decree in 1921. American Sugar was allowed to retain its 31 percent interest in Great Western on the condition that it not increase its share nor exercise its votes, effectively ending the dominance of the east-coast firm in the Valley. During its years of control, the trust was able to provide the nascent Valley beet sugar industry with much needed capital as well as technical and management expertise. It also exercised its market power, often to the detriment of growers. In 1913 University of Colorado economist, Ward Darley, compared farmers' contracts in the South Platte Valley with those in the Rocky Ford area and concluded that the sugar trust was depressing receipts to its growers.[326] But the trust almost certainly contributed to the stability of the industry in its area in contrast to the more chaotic conditions in the Arkansas Valley. South Platte Valley beet farming enjoyed a dramatic expansion during American Sugar's suzerainty. In the early years of the industry, production in the Arkansas Valley exceeded that in the downstream counties in the South Platte Valley. By 1919 production in the three northern counties had grown to more than four-hundred thousand tons while that in the Arkansas Valley was just over three hundred thousand.[327] The now independent Great Western Sugar Company maintained its grip on South Platte Valley production until the company's collapse in the 1980s.

The sugar plants were sizable structures, and their construction and ongoing operation provided a significant boost to local economies. The plant in Lamar, the building of which reportedly required "1,000 Mexicans" who arrived in boxcars,[328] employed two-hundred workers.[329] Ava Betz described the Holly plant's short-lived impact on its town in her *History of Prowers County*:

> This was a boom time for Holly. Legions of employees trooped to work at the sugar factory each morning, donned aprons or head-to toe overalls, depending on their jobs, left the overalls at their lockers at noon and donned a freshly laundered set as they reported back to work after lunch. The factory meant jobs for townspeople, a market for farmers—the population growth and economic prosperity Holly's founding fathers were determined to obtain for their town.[330]

A *Logan County Advocate* editorial claimed that "the factory has been and is one of the great factors in the development of our resources."[331] In 1909 the Sterling factory had a workforce of 275 with a total annual payroll of $110,000.[332] Employment was mostly seasonal with production confined to the period between harvest and the first freeze. This meant that the plants only operated for a relatively brief period, usually around a hundred days, each fall.

The plants were stocked with equipment performing a multitude of tasks. The WPA Guide to 1930s Colorado described beet processing in the Great Western plant in Sterling.

> The beets are carried into factory through flumes filled with warm water which is agitated by a washer equipped rotating paddles. They fall upon hopper scales, are weighed, and then drop into a slicer which cuts them into long thin strips called "cossettes" but known as "chips" to the workers. These are carried along high-speed belts into a battery of cylindrical tanks where hot circulating water extracts the juices.
>
> What remains is diverted either to the wet-pulp silo where it is stored or is passed through heated drums where the pulp is dried. Part of the dried pulp is pressed into blocks known as "bull biscuits." The men handling the pulp, which has an unpleasant odor, as well as the truck transporting it, are called "high smellers."
>
> The juice is put through several chemical processes, repeatedly filtered, and run into evaporators, to emerge as "evaporator thick juice." Treated

with sulfur gas and carefully filtered, the clear sparkling liquor, known as "blow-up thick juice," passes into vacuum pans and is boiled until the sugar begins to crystalize. High speed centrifugal machines separate sugar crystals from the syrup. The wet sugar passes into granulators, where it is dried and screened; the dry sugar passes to the warehouse for packing in barrels, sacks and small packages. Workers engaged in the latter process say they are "making pups."

The two kinds of syrup produced "high green" and "high wash," are again filtered and returned to the vacuum tanks to be boiled and stirred for the recovery of some of the remaining sugar. After a third boiling the high green or mother liquor, called molasses, is sent to factories where the Steffen process is used to extract yet more sugar." [333]

Beet farming was labor intensive with a great deal of hand work involved in raising a crop. Blocking and thinning in the spring required hoeing and hand-pulling until plants were separated by eight to ten inches in rows approximately twenty inches apart. Topping or harvesting took place in the fall. The beets were plowed out and picked up by field hands who cut off green tops and "forked" the beets into open sided trucks that took them to railroad pickup stations or directly to factories. In 1985 the Wunsch brothers recalled their youthful work in the Morgan County beet fields. Older brother Henry remembered, "It was terribly hard work," while Bill commented, "even if it was 106 degrees you were thinning beets."[334]

Work was not limited to the man of the family as children and wives labored in the fields beside him. Typical contracts were with a father covering labor of the entire family.[335] Florence Riz recalled that among her relatives in Logan County, "Anyone that was old enough to lick a spoon was on hands and knees crawling along rows of tender plants, as life in the beet fields was difficult and every member of the family was expected to work."[336] The school that Ruth Browner attended on the Peetz highway north of Sterling closed for three weeks every fall so that the students could work in the beet fields.[337] Labor in the beet fields was unpleasant and intervals of several weeks usually lay between opportunities to work. As job opportunities and incomes improved, growers were unable to meet their needs for seasonal field employees locally. The necessary work force had to be found elsewhere. Sugar company representatives recruited the laborers, transported them to the area where they would be working, and distributed them among growers. A contract between laborer and the company guaranteed that the workers would be available for spring and fall work and specified levels of compensation.

Beginning in 1900, agents of the sugar companies recruited German Russians from Nebraska, Kansas, and other locations to be employed in Otero County. Similar efforts were undertaken by the South Platte Valley firms a few years later.[338] Trainloads of workers were brought from Nebraska after the Sterling plant opened. Most settled in the area but, when they achieved some financial success and acquired their own farms, many lost their appetite for stoop labor. After unsuccessful attempts to employ workers of Japanese ancestry, laborers of Mexican descent gradually assumed much of the field work. Mexican workers were introduced in the Sterling area in 1912 and in Brush ten years later.[339] (The experiences of German Russian and Mexican field workers are discussed in greater detail in chapter 4.)

Beet production grew rapidly during the teens as war cut off beet sugar production in Central Europe. Yields increased. The early growers in northern Colorado produced around a thousand pounds of sugar per acre; by 1910 virtually the same land would yield twenty-five hundred pounds and six thousand pounds by 1930.[340] Sugar prices surged in the war and post-war years, doubling between 1914 and 1919. GW paid Platte Valley growers $6.50 to $8.00 per ton in 1917 and $8.37 to $9.75 in 1918.[341] Payments to growers for the October 1917 deliveries to the Sterling plant amounted to $1.1 million.[342] Prices declined in the twenties, but production remained profitable in Otero County and the South Platte Valley.[343] In 1924 a Fort Morgan banker wrote, "The good sugar beet crop this year has put the agricultural interests of the county in better shape than they have been since the depression of 1920."[344]

The sugar beet industry pervaded the economy and life of Arkansas and Platte Valley farming communities. The naming of an Arkansas Valley town "Sugar City" and the designation of the Brush high school athletic teams as the "Beetdiggers" suggest the status of the industry in the region. "Beet Day" in October or November, when the growers received their largest checks, was an occasion for carnivals and street vendors in the beet towns. The small town of Wiley in Prowers County celebrated its annual "Sugar Beet Day" with a rodeo, races, and other entertainment.[345] The industry generated wealth for farmers; completion of the sugar factory in Fort Morgan reportedly caused the price of irrigated land in the area to increase from $40 to $250 per acre.[346]

Wheat

If sugar beets suffused the life of the irrigated farming communities, wheat played a similar role for drylanders. Communities outside the river valleys prospered or slumped with wheat prices and yields which varied widely with weather. Winter wheat, planted in the fall and harvested in mid-summer, was well suited to unirrigated high plains farmland. In 1921, almost 90 percent of the eastern plains wheat acreage was planted in winter wheat with the remainder spring wheat harvested in the fall. Only 5 percent was irrigated.[347] A successful winter wheat crop depended on moisture from either rain or snow in the fall, winter and early spring. As was the case with other crops, wheat cultivation had to be adapted to the peculiarities of the region. Perhaps the greatest contribution to early wheat-farming on the plains was by German Russians from the Steppes in southern Russia. The high plains climate was similar to that of the Steppes, a seven-hundred-mile-wide prairie stretching eastward from present day Ukraine through south-central Russia and into Kazakhstan, that was considered the breadbasket of Russia. Immigrants from the Steppes region knew how to grow crops on the arid plains and brought wheat varieties, such as Turkey Red, that thrived in the plains of the US and Canada.

Dryland wheat farming was a high-risk operation where crops could be expected to fail at least three years out of five. Small farmers were advised not to depend on it although it could supplement income from livestock and other crops. Because of the risk, plains farmers were cautious about planting wheat in the early years of the century. In 1899 112,000 acres were harvested in the plains counties, most of it in the South Platte and Arkansas Valley Counties, some of which was probably irrigated. But this changed when the price rose from around seventy cents a bushel at the turn of the century to neighborhood of one dollar by 1910. By 1909 the harvested acreage had grown to 214,000.[348] Dryland cultivation expanded with Kit Carson, Washington, and Yuma the leading wheat-producing counties.

The outbreak of hostilities in Europe in the teens radically transformed the fortunes of plains wheat growers as foreign demand for US grain surged. When America entered the war, the Federal Government issued patriotic appeals urging farmers to increase their output. This message was enthusiastically endorsed in eastern Colorado. The *Sterling Democrat* in a front-page editorial asserted, "Every acre of available land should be producing. Advantage should be taken of every daylight hour. It must not be a case of how much we can make. It must be a case of 'fight' with those who have gone over seas, but in our way, fight to win the war."[349] Government action was not limited to exhortation. The Food Control Act of 1917 guaranteed a price of $2.00 per bushel. The high price along with wet years in the mid-teens—reported rainfall in Lamar in 1915 was the greatest in at least 25 years[350]—encouraged more planting. Plains farmers plowed more grassland and sewed more grain. Wheat acreage harvested in the sixteen counties more than tripled between 1909 and 1917.[351]

The Great War brought unprecedented prosperity to dryland farmers. Timothy Egan wrote in his Dust Bowl narrative that "no group of people took a more dramatic leap in lifestyle or prosperity, in such a short time, than wheat farmers on the Great Plains. In less than ten years, they went from subsistence living to small-business class wealth, from working a few hard acres with horses and hand tools to being masters of wheat estates, directing harvests with wondrous new machines, at a profit margin in some cases that was ten times the cost of production."[352] Although many eastern Colorado wheat growers reaped sizable benefits, levels of prosperity for most fell somewhat short of the Croesus-like heights described by Egan. With a few exceptions in the late twenties, most wheat in eastern Colorado was still grown on relatively small farms with a diverse mix of crops and livestock.

High crop prices stimulated more investment in farm machinery and equipment. Cultivation was extended, often to marginal lands. The greatest increases in acreage during the teens and early twenties occurred in the northern plains counties of Logan, Phillips, Washington, and Yuma Counties.[353]

The boom times would not last. Peace allowed European farmers to return to their fields and world wheat surpluses accumulated. By the late teens, both price and US production had peaked. By 1922 the price had fallen by more than a dollar per bushel and US farmers had reduced their plantings by four million acres. But regional cultivation continued to increase. Because land was cheaper, farmers could still make money with dollar-a-bushel wheat if precipitation permitted; a decent yield and could even survive a dry year or two. The value of wheat produced in the region reached its peak in 1924 at almost $13 million despite the lower price.[354] The price remained low through the remainder of the decade before dropping further in the early thirties. By then growers in the northern counties had shifted much of their wheat land to other crops as wheat farming had become unprofitable.

Wheat cultivation in Baca County lagged that in the rest of the region, but it took a dramatic turn with the completion of a Santa Fe line from Santana, Kansas to Springfield in 1926, reducing shipping costs and making the County's wheat competitive. Although the price was depressed from its wartime level, low land prices still allowed a good return. The 1925 Census of Agriculture reported that farmland in Baca County was valued at $8.64 per acre compared with around $19 in Washington and Yuma Counties. Farmers could make a profit by cultivating more acres with the additional land that was often purchased with borrowed money. Among the first to take advantage of Baca County's prospects were large growers from nearby Kansas. According to the *Denver Post,* "Wheat farming began in Baca County in 1928, when Tom Hopkins, then the wheat king in southwestern Kansas, proved wheat could be raised in the area on summer-fallow soil and little moisture."[355] Wheat acreage in Baca County increased dramatically in the late twenties and early thirties, expanding from seventeen thousand acres in 1920 to 237,000 in 1931.[356]

Like the cattle boom forty years earlier, the Eastern-Colorado wheat bonanza saw its share of overexpansion and excessive borrowing. As was the case in the nineteenth century boom, prosperity was not sustainable. Much of the newly cultivated land produced a respectable return only in years with above-average precipitation. High debt and low wheat prices pressured farmers into planting more and more. In the 1930s the worldwide depression drove prices to even lower levels and the drought devastated yields.

Booming wheat production brought more economic activity to nearby towns. As cultivation surged in the northern dryland counties, Akron grew from 647 people to 1,401 between the 1910 and 1920 Censuses and Yuma posted an increase from 333 to

1,197. Springfield population exploded from less than 50 in 1900 to almost fourteen hundred thirty years later. Nearly every community in the wheat belt built a grain elevator along the railroad tracks to store the wheat until it could be transported to market. The early elevators were wooden with iron claddings built by local farmers and carpenters. By 1900 concrete was the preferred construction material as it reduced the danger of fire as well as losses from weevils. Several towns built flour mills in the 1890s. The Wray Milling Company, a partnership of a local entrepreneur and two Kansas investors, constructed a flour, feed, and grain mill in the Yuma County town in 1891. The mill was raised in three or four days by forty men including some local farmers. Three grades of flour were shipped as far as Denver in fifty-pound sacks and feedstuffs were sold in Yuma and Akron.[357] Lamar's flour mill was more substantial. Efforts to induce Denver entrepreneur J.K. Mullen to build a facility in the town began in 1890, but local businessmen were initially unwilling to meet Mullen's conditions regarding provision of land, water rights, and financing. Mullen's terms were eventually met in 1892 under pressure from banking interests and the Santa Fe Railroad. At the time, the Lamar Flour Mill with four-hundred-barrel capacity was the second largest in the state.[358] It continued to operate until the 1960s.

Corn and Other Dryland Crops

Although corn cultivation often disappointed early homesteaders, greater knowledge and varieties better adapted to arid conditions made it a more reliable crop after the turn of the century. Receipts from corn made a vital contribution to the plains farmers' success. On average, revenues from corn at least equaled those from wheat.[359] Most corn was grown without irrigation—in 1920 less than 5 percent of the corn acreage[360] in the region was irrigated—and was fed to cattle or hogs although sweet corn for human consumption was popular in the Arkansas Valley. Corn and wheat were sometimes grown in same fields with rows alternating between crops, especially in the northern dryland counties.

Corn prices also benefitted from wartime demand with the national price per bushel increasing from sixty cents in 1909 to seventy cents in 1914 and $1.63 in 1917 before declining slightly over the next two years. As was the case with wheat, the price surge was largely the result of foreign demand. The teens saw regional output more than double over the decade with Kit Carson, Lincoln, and Logan Counties the leading producers.[361] With the end of hostilities and resumption of near normal production overseas, the price fell to 55 cents a bushel in 1921 before recovering later, although falling well short of its wartime peak.[362] Regional farmers continued to plant more as new land was cultivated. Relative prices made corn a more attractive crop for some wheat farmers especially in the northern and central counties. In 1924 Kit Carson, Logan and Washington Counties each reported more than 100,000 acres of corn while Yuma County farmers planted over 200,000 acres.[363]

Other important dryland crops included broomcorn and sorghum. Broomcorn, used to make straw brooms, was introduced in Baca County in the late nineteenth century. The County became the leading producer in the state with significant cultivation also found in neighboring Prowers County. Harvesting broomcorn required extensive hand labor, much of it from seasonal migrant workers.[364] Substantial dryland acreage was devoted to sorghum, a term that included several grass-genus planted for grain or fodder. It was an ideal plant for marginal land, according to John Schlebecker, as it "resisted drought, defied grasshoppers and grew where nothing else would."[365] Because of its hardy character, sorghum cultivation was to become even more popular during the drought of the 1930s.

Alfalfa

Alfalfa, a perennial legume whose leaves have a high protein content, has been an important animal feed since at least Roman times. In the late nineteenth century, eastern Colorado farmers either fed it to their livestock as hay or pastured them on fields where the plant was grown. (Hay was also produced by drying grasses or other plants.) A single planting lasted for several years, and a good crop produced three or four cuttings per year. Alfalfa was often rotated with other crops, especially sugar beets, as it absorbs nitrogen from the atmosphere and converts it to ammonia that is metabolized by plants. This process, known as fixation, restores fertility to the soil depleted by other crops. Like sugar beets, alfalfa needs substantial moisture, so cultivation was largely limited to irrigated land although it was grown for seed on some dryland farms. Its importance in the South Platte and Arkansas Valleys was noted by the *Lamar Register* which, in the late teens, described alfalfa as "the agricultural king of the state."[366]

Although alfalfa was an important crop at the turn of the century, it was either consumed by on-farm stock or sold to buyers for resale. Demand picked up in the early 1900s with the development of a milling industry in the region. Alfalfa mills extracted the nutrients from the plants and formed them into meal or pellets that would still retain the food value of hay but could be shipped more cheaply. Alfalfa milling flourished in the Arkansas Valley after its introduction by my grandfather, F. M. Wilson. While working as a freight agent for the Missouri Pacific Railroad, he sensed a profitable opportunity after receiving inquiries from mixed-feed dealers about sources for alfalfa meal in Colorado. At that time the state had only a few mills along the Front Range. Milling operations depended upon both a relatively dry climate and the availability of irrigation. A dry climate was necessary because the early mills required sun-dried alfalfa; later advances allowed dehydration of the fresh-cut plants at the mill. Both the South Platte and Arkansas Valleys offered these prerequisites, but Wilson thought the Arkansas Valley a better location for the industry. According to a 1915 *Lamar Register* article, the lower reaches of the Arkansas Valley in Colorado boasted "the largest compact alfalfa acreage with the shortest haul to the eastern markets which must be looked forward to for the outlet for the finished product. And the climatic conditions were the most favored on account of the fall and winter months have the least precipitation allowing grinding and handling to proceed in these months."[367] Prowers County mills would also face less competition for hay from dairy farms and livestock feeders.

Wilson raised funds from well-to-do oil men in his Kansas hometown, and in 1908 built a mill in Hartman in Prowers County. The Hartman plant was soon followed by facilities in Wiley and Bristol, also in Prowers County. The early plants consisted of conveyors, a grinder, and a packer. Initially the dried alfalfa was ground into a medium or coarse meal. In 1918 a finer meal was produced for poultry feed. Alfalfa meal was packaged in hundred-pound bags and shipped to customers via rail. The principal buyers were large animal-feed firms in the mid-west such as Corno Mills and Ralston Purina, both located in St. Louis.[368] Alfalfa growers welcomed the mills which were more reliable and trustworthy purchasers than the itinerant hay buyers they had previously depended upon.

The Hartman plant was the beginning of Denver Alfalfa which, by 1920, operated eleven mills and eventually opened numerous others throughout the west and mid-west. The company moved its headquarters from Hartman to Lamar in 1918.[369] By the onset of World War II, the firm, renamed National Alfalfa, was the largest manufacturer of alfalfa products in the US. It had operations in eight states and exported it products to England, Scotland, Ireland, Holland, Denmark, Norway, and Cuba.[370]

Alfalfa cultivation spread in the early twentieth century with increased irrigation and mills. By 1917 Prowers County had twelve.[371] According to Robert Dunar's 1948 "History of Agriculture" in Colorado, alfalfa was "The most important crop in the Arkansas Valley."[372] Both growers and mills benefitted from improved technology. In the 1890s the plant was cut using horse drawn mowers and dried in the sun. Mechanical cutters and balers were introduced around the turn of the century. Further improvement came with powered harvesters that mowed hay, cut it into small portions, and fed it into trucks that hauled it to the dehydrating mills where it was dried in revolving drums heated with coal or gas and packed into pellets.[373] Land devoted to alfalfa in the sixteen regional counties grew from 115,000 acres in 1899 to 182,000 in 1919 and production increased from 242,000 tons to 396,000 tons. Output remained around that level through the early 1930s despite weaker prices.[374] In 1923 Colorado's county assessors valued the region's alfalfa crop at almost $8 million, slightly more than sugar beets although less than wheat or corn. Most years the leading producer was Prowers County while Logan, Morgan, and Bent Counties also grew sizable crops.[375] In 1939 Wilson could claim that that Prowers County was "still today hub of the great alfalfa production sections in eastern Colorado."[376]

Cantaloupe and Other Vegetable and Fruits

While the field crops—wheat, corn, sugar beets, alfalfa, and others—were typically grown on farms of at least 160 acres, vegetables could be raised profitably on more compact plots. Small vegetable farms with a variety of produce were common in the Arkansas Valley. In Otero County, the heartland of melon and onion farming, more than one-third of all cropland harvested consisted of farms of less than a hundred acres.[377] The County was noted for Rocky Ford cantaloupes that were first cultivated in the 1870s and eventually developed a strong national market. The introduction of standard crates and the railroads' ice cars expedited the shipment of the melons to midwestern and east-coast cities.[378] According to a Rocky Ford banker in the mid-twenties, 90 percent of the cantaloupe seed planted in the US was produced within a few miles of the town.[379] Onions and cucumbers were also popular, while other important cash crops included cabbage, tomatoes, peas, pumpkins, and celery. Bent, Crowley, and Otero Counties together grew almost one and one-half million dollars' worth of vegetables in 1929, more than 20 percent of the total value of the three counties' crops. In Otero County, the value of the vegetable crop was only slightly less than that of sugar beets and comfortably above any other crop.[380] Fruit orchards flourished for a time in Otero and Crowley Counties. According to the Crowley County Historical Society, the County once had 4,500 acres of fruit orchards. However, the damage to fruit orchards from early freezes caused most of this land to be converted to melons or field crops.[381]

A steady supply of vegetables and melons led to the development of a canning and processing industry in Otero and Crowley Counties. In 1890 Rocky Ford businessmen organized the Rocky Ford Canning Company that processed green beans, pumpkins, and pickles and, by 1899, employed a hundred women.[382] Local businessmen founded the Crowley Canning Company in 1913. The firm processed tomatoes and later cherries and employed thirty to fifty women and a smaller number of men for about six weeks a year. The company changed hands several times, and by the middle twenties employed seventy-two women and forty-five men.[383] Manzanola housed the Arkansas Valley's largest canning factory, the Manzanola Canning Company that was organized in 1900 and specialized in tomato products but also processed locally grown fruit. The firm acquired plants in Rocky Ford and La Junta and expanded its line to include apples, gooseberries, cherries, green beans, pumpkins, sweet potatoes, and pork and beans.[384] The Valley's fruit and vegetable processing plants prospered through the early teens and enjoyed a surge in demand during World War I but suffered from excess capacity in the post-war years.

Livestock

The passing of the open-range cattle ranches was not the death knell for the regional livestock industry. But the cattle and sheep businesses were transformed as vast ranches were broken up. More pastureland became available when land settled by homesteaders in the late eighties and early nineties was abandoned by the original settlers. The large ranches with absentee owners of the open range Cattle Kingdom were largely replaced by smaller ones with resident owners and operators.

One of the more successful ranchers of the era was A. B. "Bright" Ham. In 1887 he moved from Texas to Las Animas where his brother was an experienced trail boss. His first job was helping make bricks for Las Animas City Hall, but he was soon riding herd for large local rancher Judge R. H. Moore. Later he worked for a British-financed cattle company that encountered financial difficulties and was unable to meet its payroll. When Ham demanded his back wages, the company settled the debt by giving him twenty-six cows, four steers and one bull that he was able to pasture on the then widely available free-range land. In 1891 he leased a small property where he settled along with his wife and two sons and raised crops, cattle, and horses. In 1900 he acquired a quarter section with Fort Lyon water rights enabling him to raise alfalfa for a feed crop and for seed which he sold to help cover ranch expenses. With his sons' help, he raised horses and cattle with his "Tree top" brand which he registered in 1903. As free range disappeared Ham bought or leased more land. By keeping cows and heifers he was able to increase his herd and remained on the ranch for sixty years.[385]

Cattle ownership was not limited to ranchers. Many regional farms supplemented their crops with cattle, hogs, sheep, or poultry. Smaller farmers typically kept several head of cattle and businessmen in the plains communities often owned modest-sized herds. The industry grew much larger with the number of cattle in the early twentieth century far exceeding that of the open-range era. The Census reported 15,000 head in Bent County in 1880, near the peak of the early cattle boom. In 1930, the counties that made up the 1880 County reported 136,000 head. Nearly all counties saw sizable increases in populations, but the largest expansion occurred in dryland areas.[386]

Feeding became more important. The region's sizable grazing stock as well as abundant feed supplies made it an ideal location for fattening animals prior to slaughter. Cattle or sheep were purchased by feeders and fattened for a few months then sold to meat processors. In 1916 the *Sterling Democrat* reported that an estimated 3,500 cattle were turned out and fattened annually in local pens.[387] Cattle feeders developed a symbiotic relationship with the beet sugar industry. Beets required large quantities of nitrogen fertilizers, and manure, an excellent nitrogen source, was readily obtainable from feed lots or barnyard corrals. At the same time, the unused byproducts from sugar beet processing were an inexpensive feed for livestock. Sugar beet tops were retained by the farmer and fed to cattle or sheep. Beet pulp, a residue of the refining process, was sold in either wet or dry form to local farmers and commercial feeders. Beet molasses was mixed with alfalfa or grain and fed to lambs or cattle. W.C. Harris who arrived in Sterling in a covered wagon in 1875 built cattle feed lots in 1905 to take advantage of the beet pulp available from the recently opened factory. His company eventually operated numerous feed lots throughout the west and was recognized as one of the largest cattle feeders in the nation.[388] Great Western Sugar developed its own feed lots at Sterling, Brush, and Ovid where both cattle and sheep were fed pulp produced at local factories.[389]

With an expanding population on the plains as well as in the Front Range cities, demand for dairy products increased. A few dairy cows could furnish additional income for small farmers. Native grasses provided good feed supplemented with corn or sorghum fodder from the farm. In 1920 the region reported more than 120,000 dairy cattle valued at nearly $6.5 million.[390] Although many farms throughout the region had dairy cattle, the largest numbers were found in the northern counties close to Front Range markets. Local dairy products were processed for national markets. In 1914 the Helvetica Milk Condensing Company opened its plant in Lamar. The plant stimulated dairy farming throughout the Arkansas Valley. At the end of its first year, the plant was receiving milk from 1,850 cows owned by 225 farmers.[391] Other dairy processing firms soon followed. A Lamar banker reported in 1930 that the town also had "a large cheese factory, two ice cream factories and a butter factory."[392] Regional farmers sold more than $3 million in milk and other products in 1920, more than half from Elbert County and more than three hundred thousand from Prowers County.[393]

Sheep ranching also changed. During the open-range cattle era, sheep ranching on the eastern plains was limited to range land north of the Arkansas due to opposition from cattle growers. By the early twentieth century open range ranching diminished in importance as more of the animals were fed on irrigated farms or feed lots. The number of sheep and lambs in the region exceeded three-hundred thousand in 1920 with Bent, Morgan and Otero Counties all reporting large numbers of animals.[394]

Livestock ranchers and feeders shared in the wartime boom. When hostilities broke out in August 1914, US farmers received an average of $8 per hundred pounds for cattle and calves. Four years later the price had increased to $12 and prices for sheep saw a comparable increase.[395] The cattle and sheep markets peaked in the late teens along with those for other farm products and prices declined but remained above their 1910 levels through the twenties. By 1920 livestock on regional farms were valued by the Census at $34 million with cattle accounting for $28 million and sheep and hogs $3 million each.[396]

Farmers diversified with other livestock and poultry. They raised relatively few hogs before the teens, but by 1920 the region counted 160,000. Swine production was concentrated in areas where the animals could be pastured on alfalfa and fed corn. Kit Carson, Washington, and Yuma Counties, the leading corn producers, reported the largest numbers. Most farms had flocks of chickens and sometimes turkeys. With layers, Cottrell[397] estimated that a farmer could realize $2 per hen per year. Regional receipts from sales of eggs and chickens totaled slightly more than $1 million in 1920.[398]

CHAPTER 3

Plains Agriculture in 1920

By the 1920s dryland agriculture in eastern Colorado consisted of medium sized diversified farms and somewhat larger ranches. Irrigated farms in the river valleys were smaller with alfalfa, sugar beets and vegetables as the most important crops. Although the next several decades would bring significant changes to the industry, the patterns of land use would change little. According to Cunfer, they were "were well-established from Texas and New Mexico to Montana and the Dakotas." [399]

The late teens, in many ways, marked the apogee of high plains agriculture. The previous two decades had seen dramatic growth in farm production and profit. The number of farms in the region reached an all-time high. But the next twenty years would subject the industry to unprecedented stresses. It would be another quarter century before these levels of prosperity would be approached again.

Chapter 3 Exhibits

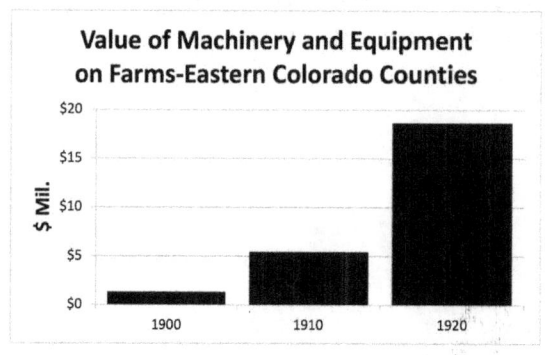

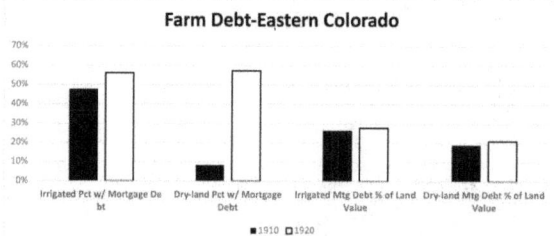

The early 20th century presented a more favorable environment for farming than the late 1880's and early 1890s. Prices rebounded through the early teens and accelerated after the outbreak of hostilities in Europe before declining in peacetime.

New technology and farmers' investments in machinery and equipment improved profitability.

Rising land values and healthy markets for agricultural products allowed farmers to borrow to finance improvements, additional land or new equipment. Although the share of farmers with debt rose during the teens, overall debt kept pace with the increase in the value of land.

Sources: Price indexes, BLS; Machinery and Equipment, Census; Rainfall, US Official Weather Observer & Bent County Soil Conservation District, Census of Agriculture

CHAPTER 3

Farms and Acreage in Eastern Colorado 1900-20

	Number of Farms			Acreage Farmed (000)		
	1900	1910	1920	1900	1910	1920
Baca	137	540	1,858	77.8	257.3	1,051.3
Bent	274	463	1,056	118.5	168.3	434.0
Cheyenne	57	791	674	116.2	216.2	490.4
Elbert	579	1,150	1,308	508.4	682.3	1,011.5
Kiowa	138	646	668	72.0	219.7	431.0
Kit Carson	305	1,767	1,461	88.3	566.6	729.8
Lincoln	138	1,334	1,385	163.1	428.1	1,208.0
Logan	413	1,359	1,874	182.5	409.5	857.4
Morgan	378	1,075	1,720	125.1	233.3	555.9
Otero *	814	1,498	2,229	244.6	254.2	597.6
Phillips	244	508	680	69.6	216.3	300.3
Prowers	478	991	1,469	217.3	250.3	669.3
Sedgwick	156	448	487	51.0	159.3	234.5
Washington	201	1,346	2,057	107.4	551.2	1,088.7
Yuma	291	1,829	2,179	93.6	658.3	1,203.8
Total	5,277	16,419	21,105	2,729.9	5,765.3	10,863.4
Dry Land	2,090	9,911	12,270	1,296.4	3,796.1	7,514.8
Irrigated	3,187	6,508	8,835	1,433.4	1,969.3	3,348.6

*1920 Otero total includes Crowley County

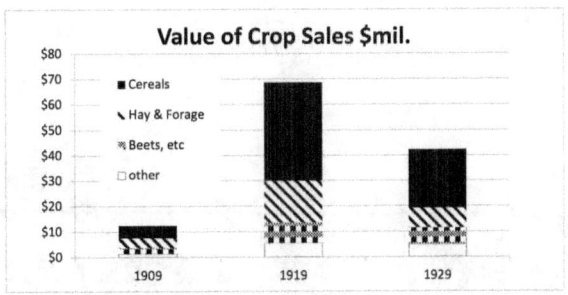

After drought drove away many settlers in the late eighties and nineties, a second wave of homesteaders came to eastern Colorado in the first two decades of the twentieth century. Both the number of farms and the acreage in farms and ranches increased roughly five-fold between 1900 and 1920. In the early 1900s the northeast and the central regions experienced a massive influx while most of the new settlement in Baca County occurred later.

Cereals, particularly corn and wheat, remained the most important cash crops. The value of all crops surged from just over $10 million in 1909 to almost $70 million in 1919. The gain was driven by both greater production and higher prices, even after the effects of inflation. Over the decade corn acreage more than doubled and the amount of land planted in wheat increased fivefold. Receipts from hay and forage, most of which were for alfalfa, increased with the introduction of dehydrating and milling in the early 1900s.

Source: Census. Arkansas Valley counties include Bent, Crowley, Otero and Prowers. Central dryland includes Cheyenne, Elbert, Kiowa, Kit Carson and Lincoln. Platte Valley includes Logan, Morgan and Sedgwick. NE dryland includes Phillips, Washington and Yuma; Census of Agriculture.

Livestock on Farms and Ranches

		1890	1900	1910	1920	1930
Cattle						
	Number (Thou.)	123.3	485.1	291.9	544.6	469.1
	Value ($ Ml.)			$ 7.9	$ 28.1	$ 22.3
Sheep						
	Number (Thou.)	252.1	680.9	433.4	306.9	345.4
	Value ($ Ml.)			$ 2.0	$ 3.0	$ 2.5
Swine						
	Number (Thou.)	19.1	32.6	75.2	159.8	257.9
	Value ($ Ml.)			$ 0.6	$ 3.0	$ 3.4

Cattle populations increased despite the disappearance of the big ranches. But the nature of the business changed. A farmer's cattle herd was often part of a diversified agricultural operation although many smaller ranchers remained. The dollar value of cattle far exceeded that of other livestock. Swine feeding also increased after the middle teens. The 1900 numbers for cattle and sheep are higher than those for other years because that year's estimates were based on June 1 populations while the others are for April 1. The later number contains more calves and lambs.

The sugar beet processing factory in Sugar City was and was the first in the eastern Colorado. Sugar factories were major employers in Arkansas and South Platte Valley towns.

Source: USDA, *Agricultural Statistics*, Census of Agriculture, Photo from The Denver Public Library, Western History Collection, call number z1818-

CHAPTER 4

The Non-Farm Economy, Population and Labor Force Through 1930

AGRICULTURE DOMINATED THE REGIONAL ECONOMY AT THE TURN OF THE TWENtieth century, but industry, commerce, and services were beginning to assume larger roles. Sugar beet plants, flour mills, and other firms processing farm products provided well-paying jobs in the rural communities while businesses supplying services and selling goods to the growing farm population flourished. Transformations in the work force were underway that affected both towns and farms including increased education levels and more foreign immigrants. The region's population grew rapidly, reaching all-time peaks in many counties, while undergoing changes in age, gender, and ethnic make-up.

Non-agricultural Industries

Between the Civil War and onset of the Great Depression, the United States was transformed from an agricultural economy to an industrial one. The national share of employed persons working in agriculture fell from 49 percent in 1870 to 21 percent in 1930. The economy was propelled by the rise of automobile, steel, and chemical manufacturing among other industries. Giant integrated businesses were able to exploit such technological advances as electricity, radio, and the internal combustion engine and to sell their products on national and world markets. But as the national economy moved into its industrial stage, Colorado's high plains, despite the emergence of some non-farm businesses, remained largely in a pre-industrial state with most of its jobs in agriculture, commerce, or services. In many respects it would remain so even to the present day.

Commerce sprang up quickly in the newly settled towns. David Dary's history of the Santa Fe Trail lists the commercial enterprises in the town of Las Animas shortly after railroad's arrival as including "two general stores, three restaurants, two hotels, several saloons, a number of frame houses, and even two lumber yards whose goods were largely freighted from the Rocky Mountains to the west."[400] Residents in early communities found jobs at businesses catering to farmers and ranchers. William Leroy opened a blacksmithing operation in La Junta in 1882 upon observing an absence of that service in town. He shoed horses and made plowshares needed for breaking prairie soil, capturing the bulk of business within in a fifty-mile radius.[401]

Occasional speculative ventures involving mining or oil and gas also made their appearances, although none seem to have come to fruition. According to Morris Taylor, 150 miners were brought to Carrisco Springs in western Baca County in 1887 in response to copper, lead and silver discoveries.[402] A thousand-foot mine was dug and thousands of tons of copper ore were extracted using the primitive methods of the late nineteenth century. The venture failed to generate the promised wealth due to the cost of hauling the ore to Omaha for refining.[403] In 1910 a claim was filed to mine copper from Two Buttes Mountain just north of the Baca-Prowers County border.[404] Oil wells were drilled in several counties, but none were commercially successful.

The eastern plains' comparative advantage in manufacturing lay in processing farm products. As described in the previous chapter, sugar beet plants, alfalfa dehydrating mills and flour mills were all leading employers in prairie towns and served as catalysts for growth in local economies. C.C. Huddleston of Lamar recalled that "The town began to take on a substantial nature in '92, the year the flour mill was built. And when we got a milk factory somewhere between 1906 and 1910, we thought the future was fixed."[405]

As the region grew in the teens and twenties the mix of businesses widened. Las Animas had been transformed from its early railroad days. Among the businesses listed in the 1928 Bent County Directory were three automobile dealers and five auto repair shops, four banks, one bakery, a building and loan, six grocery stores, two dry goods stores, two lumber yards, two newspapers and five hotels.[406] Smaller towns also boasted a wide collection of businesses. In 1924 a Holyoke banker listed the firms in his city of somewhat more than one thousand people.

> Holyoke has three banks, three grain elevators, one flour mill, two modern hotels, two large general merchandise stores, two lumber yards, two hardware stores, two furniture stores, two drug stores, five garages, one exclusive clothing store, one splendid theater, one modern hospital, two dental parlors, one creamery-cold storage and artificial ice plant, five grocery stores, three meat markets, four creamery and produce stations, three modern restaurants, one bakery, two jewelry stores, two millinery stores, one photo studio, one ten-cent store, three barber shops, two implement stores, two machine shops, one pump and windmill store, one plumbing shop, one shoe store, one suitorium, three wholesale oil stations,

two filling stations, two tire repair shops, one second-hand store, two rooming houses, one abstract company.[407]

As the lists of businesses in Las Animas and Holyoke suggest, most workers not engaged in farming or ranching were found in services, retail, or distribution with only a few employed in manufacturing.

The availability of electric power in the late nineteenth and early twentieth centuries served as the impetus for robust American growth as well as dramatic improvements in the average family's standard of living. Robert Gordon in *The Rise and Fall of American Growth* termed electric light power as one of the "two most important inventions of the late nineteenth century"[408] along with the internal combustion engine. Businessmen in plains communities soon realized the need for the new power source. Although some early firms depended upon coal or steam, electricity was becoming essential to successful business operation as well as indispensable for a modern lifestyle. A power plant could give a healthy boost to the local economy. In 1902 George W. Michiner claimed that "A good water and electric plant will double the value of every lot in Fort Morgan."[409] A 1913 editorial in the *Yuma Pioneer* lamented "Haigler, Nebraska, a town almost one-fourth the size of Yuma, is to have an electric plant in operation by September 15th, arrangement for the same having been completed last week. When, oh when, is Yuma going to wake up and become a real live town."[410]

Town leaders responded to these demands. A few local electric power companies were formed as early as the 1890s although these efforts were not always successful. La Junta's electric plant began furnishing power in 1892 but a boiler blew up in the plant the next year and further provision was delayed. The first home was not electrified until 1898.[411] Electricity was introduced in Rocky Ford in 1898 but was not available to all until 1912.[412] In Sterling, a franchise was granted for an electric light plant in 1902 but suspicions of residents about the new technology and a fire in 1905 prevented it from becoming fully operable.[413] Before long, most town residents could access electric power. A report prepared by the Colorado State Planning Commission observed that between 1905 and 1915 "the most extensive electric development in the history of the industry in Colorado occurred."[414] A group of local investors formed the Sterling Consolidated Electric Company's whose plant was built in 1908 or 1909. The company became part of Public Service Company of Colorado in 1924.[415] In 1905 A.E. Bent and Morton Strain formed the Lamar Light, Heat and Power Company that furnished electricity for the town along with steam heat for downtown offices and business. In 1920 the utility was supplanted by a new municipal plant.[416] Yuma, perhaps responding to local complaints such as that cited earlier, began the construction of a municipally owned power and light company in 1913.[417] Yet some regional towns waited until well into the 1920s for electricity. Springfield's power plant did not become operational until 1927.[418] Most rural areas lacked electric power until the necessary infrastructure was built under the auspices of the Rural Electrification Administration (REA) in the 1930s and later.

The most reliable picture of the makeup of the regional economy in this era comes from employment data in the 1930 Census that reported work force by industry for the first time. The Census estimates were based on county of residence rather than where the job was located but few 1930 plains workers commuted to another county. These data provide the first detailed picture of the makeup of the plains economy nearly fifty years after first sizable settlement by people of European ancestry.

Although the region's economy became more diverse, agriculture remained dominant. In 1930 farming and ranching still accounted for 55 percent of all employed persons[419] and the share of farm operators and workers in earlier years was certainly higher. As noted earlier, the US share of farm workers at the time was 21 percent. The counties in the river valleys with larger populations had more diversified economies while most of the dryland counties' laborers still worked on farms. Otero County reported the smallest proportion of the workforce in agriculture with all the rest employing at least half their workers that industry. La Junta and to a lesser extent Rocky Ford were important regional trade and service centers and nearly two-thirds of the County's workers were found in non-farm industries. In Elbert County with no towns over one-thousand persons and Washington County with only Akron with fourteen-hundred persons, at least three-quarters of employees worked on farms or ranches.

The thirty thousand agricultural workers in the region in 1930 included eighteen thousand farm owners or tenants along with 9,200 paid laborers and 2,900 unpaid family workers. These figures give a somewhat misleading picture of the work experience of rural residents as many farmers supplemented their income with seasonal or part-time jobs off the farm. Workers often moved between agricultural work and other jobs throughout their careers. Rufus Phillips, whose memories of roundups were described in chapter 1, came to Otero County in 1877 at age eighteen to learn the cattle business on his uncle's ranch near Rocky Ford. After several years as a cowpuncher, he was hired as manager of a newly established drug store in La Junta. Later he was appointed postmaster and then became owner-manager of a drug store in partnership with his brother. Upon selling the drug store, he and his brother purchased a herd of cattle and a newspaper that he operated for several years. Harsh winters in the middle eighties destroyed most of his herd ending his second stint as a cattleman. He then took a job in a bank in Las Animas and in 1888 organized a bank in La Junta.[420] Burt Ragan arrived in Kit Carson County in 1886 at age seventeen and was hired by the Republican Cattle Company as a cowboy with some additional duties hauling freight and foodstuffs. In 1899 he resigned when he was elected County Clerk and Recorder and later became assistant postmaster. He returned to ranching for eight years before joining a bank in Burlington as a part-owner. He sold his interest in the bank in 1929 and became a life insurance underwriter.[421] Gary Penley in his memoir of Prowers County farm life tells of his grandfather, George Blizzard, who homesteaded in 1914 but was unsuccessful and abandoned the farm after a couple of years. He moved to Lamar and worked odd jobs in town before once again attempting farming in 1935.[422]

The regional manufacturing sector was small as the high plains lacked easy access to raw materials or major markets that supported the mass production factories found in the East and Midwest. According to the Census, 36 percent of the nation's workers labored in manufacturing establishments while only 13 percent of those in the region were similarly employed. Almost two-fifths of the region's manufacturing employees, some twelve hundred persons, worked for firms which processed agricultural products with alfalfa mills and sugar beet plants accounting for the bulk of these jobs. (The development of these industries is discussed in the previous chapter.) Other agricultural processing businesses included flour mills, livestock slaughterhouses, meat packing plants, canned milk plants and bakeries.

The *1918 Colorado Yearbook* listed the most important firms in eastern Colorado's counties. All these businesses processed farm products, and all were found in the irrigated valleys:

Bent—1,000-ton American Beet Sugar factory

Crowley—2 beet sugar plants, 2 alfalfa meal mills and a canning factory

Logan—Great Western beet sugar plant

Morgan—2 beet sugar plants and 2 creameries

Otero—2 beet sugar plants, 2 alfalfa mills, 3 canning factories, a flour mill and a creamery

Prowers—a beet sugar plant, a milk condensing facility, 7 alfalfa mills and a flour mill[423]

Other manufacturing jobs were nearly with all small operations engaged in auto repair, metal fabricating, publishing and small-scale production and repair of farm implements. These firms employed 1,859 workers in 1930, many of which would not be classified as manufacturing employees under industrial classification system used today.[424]

Railroads were another important employer. Along with their critical roles in providing access to markets and bringing new settlers, they were an important source of income and jobs in several plains communities. As rail lines were being built in the nineteenth century, farmers supplemented their incomes with construction work during their off seasons. Residents assumed permanent well-paying jobs in maintenance and operations once the lines were completed. La Junta was considered a "railroad town" well into the twentieth century. Otero County reported more than 1,100 rail workers, 21 percent of all non-farm employees with nearly all in La Junta. The town was a division point for the Santa Fe and featured rail yards, repair facilities and a Fred Harvey hotel and restaurant. The reported rail workers also included La Junta residents who either began or ended their shifts when the train's crews switched in the town. Another thirteen hundred rail employees were found in the remaining counties with the largest numbers in Sterling and Limon that also served as rail centers in the early twentieth century.

As the plains population grew, more homes and stores and other commercial structures were needed. In 1930 more than two thousand residents reported employment in the building industry including those working on road construction. Most building jobs were in the larger counties although Baca Country, which was experiencing rapid growth in the late 1920s had 160 workers.

Purchases of household necessities and farm supplies from local merchants grew rapidly and rising affluence brought about increased demand for discretionary goods and services by both farm families and townspeople. The number and variety of stores in the region's towns grew through the late nineteenth and early twentieth century. In 1930 wholesale and retail trade accounted for almost four-thousand workers with the regional trading centers having the greatest numbers. The larger towns in Logan, Morgan, Otero and Prowers Counties sold to their own residents as well as to some from the surrounding more rural areas. Each of these counties reported more than five-hundred workers in trade establishments except Prowers County which had nearly that number. But even the smaller communities had several stores, often general stores that carried food, clothing, tobacco, feed, hardware, and numerous other wares. The son of the proprietor of Merino Mercantile in Logan County recalled the store in the teens and twenties:

> Dried fruits came in wooden boxes, were put in bags, and sold by the pound. One hundred-pound bags of sugar were hauled in an old trailer from the Sterling sugar factory to the Merino store where it was measured into paper bags to be sold. Flour came in 48-pound bags. A large coffee grinder stood in the middle of the store. All coffee came in bulk and was ground coarse or fine, according to the customer's specifications, and measured into paper bags. Gasoline pumps stood in front of the store.
>
> Practically all goods were sold on credit with 30 days to pay. Often terms were longer than that, and on occasion, a steer would be offered to settle up an account. Then [the merchant and his son] would shoot the steer in the evening, skin it out and let in hang from a rack till early morning when it was brought to the store, cut up and sold to customers. Some barter of good was made with eggs or garden produce.[425]

The surging popularity of the automobile led to new job opportunities. By 1918 more than twenty thousand automobiles were registered in the region, roughly one for every six and one-half persons. By 1928 the number had grown to forty-three thousand although the number of residents grew only modestly.[426] As motor vehicle ownership grew, garages and auto service businesses opened. The 1928 Bent County Directory listed three auto dealers and another twelve business that provided products or service to car owners.[427] The Census listed eighteen hundred jobs with automobiles dealers, repair shops, and service stations. Telephone or telegraph companies and those in other transportation and communication industries employed more than a thousand workers and some six hundred residents were government employees, mostly at the county or municipalities level.

Service businesses mushroomed to accommodate the needs of the increased population. Firms catering to local farms, households and businesses employed 11,436 persons in 1930. They worked in banking or real estate, entertainment such as the early movie theaters, laundries, domestic services, and many other areas. Most of the employers were small businesses typically set up by residents who saw an opportunity in a growing community. C.L. Denney arrived in Kiowa County in 1907 and homesteaded twenty-one miles southwest of Eads. In 1909 he sent for his family from Arkansas but soon realized that he wasn't making enough from farming to support his wife and four children. He moved to town and worked at casual jobs. He noted that the nearest undertaker was in Lyons, Kansas. He had some experience in burial preparation, so he took the state exam, was licensed, and established his business. The first hearse was a team and buckboard, and he made his own caskets. His business thrived as the county's sole provider of burial services.[428] More than eleven hundred residents worked at hotels or restaurants. Among these was Thomas Bell of Limon who expanded his barber and pool room in the early years of the new century to include a hotel and rooming house.[429]

The largest group of service workers were in the professional and semiprofessional services category with almost four thousand. Well over half were women, most of them schoolteachers, while many others worked as nurses or librarians. The mix of occupations is reflected in the 1928 Bent Directory that listed among its businesses three attorneys, three barbers, two chiropractors, two dentists, physicians, one undertaker, and one veterinarian.[430] Young doctor L. E. Likes arrived in southeast Colorado during the December 1913 blizzard, one the worst in history, and was recruited to accompany the Baca County sheriff via horse-drawn carriage to assist a farmer's wife with a difficult delivery. Upon their arrival at the farmhouse, the baby had arrived and was doing fine. Despite this harrowing experience, Likes was attracted to the area and decided to establish a practice in Lamar that continued for more than fifty years.[431]

Demographics and the Labor Force 1870-1930

In the 1870s most eastern Coloradans were ranchers or their employees and a few family members, along with a small number living in towns along the railroads. But by the mid-1880s completion of the railroads and the dwindling availability of land further east brought a surge of immigrants. Prospects for successful farming attracted tens of thousands of settlers through 1920. Growth was especially rapid in the first two decades of the twentieth century. Most of the counties reached their peak populations in the 1920s as did the region. As agricultural processing industries grew and the demand for commerce and services increased, an increasing share of residents lived in towns rather than on farms. Foreign-born migrants, especially those from Russia and Mexico, made an important contribution to the region's development and culture.

Population statistics are limited for 1880 and earlier years since most of region's counties were not yet established. The combined 1880 population in what were then Bent and Elbert Counties was almost thirty-five hundred, up from somewhat over a thousand ten years earlier.[432] The remainder of the region might have included an equal number. The arrival of settlers in the eighties brought the 1890 Census population in the then fifteen counties to almost thirty thousand, although it was probably somewhat higher a year or two earlier before the drought hit. By the end of the century the failures of many homesteads caused settlers to abandon their farms and population fell in most of the dryland counties. Irrigated land by contrast continued to attract immigrants. While the dryland counties lost thirty-six hundred people during the 1890s, population in the irrigated counties increased by twelve thousand four hundred. Baca and Kiowa Counties lost nearly half their populations. The losses were probably larger. According to some narratives, the peak population in the Baca County before the onset of drought reached six thousand although a more realistic figure is probably half that.[433] The 1890 Census indicated fewer than fifteen hundred residents. The number of people in Bent, Morgan and Otero Counties, all with substantial irrigated farmland, more than doubled. The Arkansas Valley towns of La Junta, Las Animas and Rocky Ford all posted strong growth.

As the agricultural outlook brightened in the new century the region enjoyed the fastest population growth in its history. The total number of residents increased more than four-fold between 1900 and 1920 reaching almost 164,000. Both irrigated and dryland counties saw burgeoning growth in the naughts with each group adding more than thirty thousand people. Cheyenne and Lincoln Counties saw more than fivefold expansions. Another sixty thousand persons were added in the teens fueled by the booming war-time farm economy.

The agricultural depression in the early 1920s brought population growth to a virtual halt. Fewer than six thousand people were added over the decade; only Baca and Sedgwick Counties posted gains greater than a thousand. The 1930 population reached 169,000, a number not to be achieved in any later census over the next eighty years. In 6 of the 16 counties, the 1920 Census population was never to be reached in a future Census. Six more reported their peak census populations in 1930.

An early Bent County rancher described the makeup of the inhabitants in the mid-1880s, just before the arrival of large numbers of homesteaders, as "… one-third women and children, one-sixth railroad employees, one-sixth businessmen and employees and one-third stockmen and employees."[434] This was probably a reasonably accurate description of the County's residents. In 1880 forty-three percent were males in their prime working ages of eighteen to forty-four, down from 60 percent in 1870. Only 20 percent were of school age, between five and seventeen, compared with 30 percent for the nation. There were almost two males for every female of all ages, down from almost three-to-one ten years earlier. Predominately male populations were typical of frontier communities. The cattle industry dominated the local economy, and most ranch hands were itinerant seasonal male workers without families. Ava Betz wrote that, according to local legend, "Until the influx of homesteaders in 1886, Mary Cain and Mrs. Marsena McMillin were the only white women between Las Animas and Kansas."[435] This may have been true in the early eighties, but it is likely that several white women worked as prostitutes during Granada's railroad boom some ten years earlier. As small-scale farming replaced open-range ranching, a growing number of homesteads were settled by men with wives and often children. But there were exceptions. Betz wrote of Nellie C. Bailey who homesteaded five miles south of Lamar in 1886 and whose history included a murder charge for the death of an English nobleman in Indian Territory.[436] By 1890 the male-female ratio in what had been Bent County fell below 1.5 and the surge of settler families in the early twentieth century brought it down to 1.1 by 1930.[437] The work force remained predominately male well into the twentieth century. In 1930 males held 87 percent of all jobs and 74 percent of non-farm jobs. Most employed women worked in retail trade, hotels or restaurants, domestic service or "professional and semi-professional services." Most in the last group were teachers.

Despite male dominance in numbers, or perhaps because of it, gender roles were less rigid than in more developed parts of the nation. Colorado enacted female suffrage in 1893 and women engaged in local politics and were quite active in social movements, particularly the push for prohibition. Wives played a vital role in the homesteader households, sharing the farm work and even taking on most of the it when the husband worked elsewhere. Females, married or single, made up the bulk of the teacher corps. When confronted with widowhood, a frequent situation in the late nineteenth and early twentieth centuries, women assumed substantial responsibilities. In 1888 my Great Aunt Stella and her well-off husband moved to Lamar, where her sister was a schoolteacher, in hopes of a cure for his tuberculosis. He invested his fortune in local property shortly before his unfortunate demise. Stella remained in Lamar, managing the property she inherited, teaching school, running her retail business, and taking an active part in community affairs.

Education and Literacy

Mechanization and advanced farming techniques, the need for skilled workers in agricultural processing plants, and the growing demand for professional and semi-professional services required greater skills from the work force. Plains settlers were able to meet these demands as they brought with them substantial "human capital" in the form of education and acquired work skills. According to the 1900 Census, plains residents' literacy and education levels compared favorably with those of other Americans. The average literacy rate for the region's adult males was significantly higher than for the nation in 1900 and, by 1930, that for all persons over ten exceeded the national rate. (The 1900 Census did not report literacy rates for females or those under twenty-one.) Although large numbers of former slaves and their families in the South depressed the nation's figure, the region's native whites had more years of education than in much of the nation. Regional literacy patterns refute the stereotype of the ignorant farmer. In 1930, plains residents living on farms reported higher literacy rates than either those living in small towns, i.e., rural nonfarm, or those living in communities with populations exceeding twenty-five hundred which the census classified as "urban areas."[438]

Claudia Goldin and Lawrence Katz, two Harvard economists, analyzed the role of education in the growth of the American economy, writing that by the beginning of the twentieth century "Americans had embraced the novel idea that the 'wealth of nations' would be embodied in its human capital stock."[439] They found that in the early 1900s, Iowa, with its small farms and rural towns, enrolled relatively high proportions of their young people in school. This practice contrasted with that in much of the South where skill demands were lower for workers in cotton or tobacco fields. They attributed this to the skills needed by small farmers and the ability of rural districts to organize and fund the schools.[440] Plains residents also valued education and were committed to ensuring that their children acquired the skills and knowledge needed earn an adequate income whether in farming or elsewhere. They heartily supported community investment in their children's schooling.

Free publicly funded common schools covering the first eight grades became the norm in most of the US in the last half of the nineteenth century. To encourage education, the state of Colorado designated two sections in each six-mile square township for schools. Settlers on Colorado's eastern plains started schools as soon as enough farm families had settled. Boggsville, in Bent County, established a private school in 1869. The first public school district in the County was organized in 1870 with its first-year rolls including students with such prominent family names as Bent, Carson and Prowers.[441] By 1875 the County boasted five schools with eight teachers and 329 pupils aged five through twenty-one.[442] The first school in Old Sterling opened in 1875 with twenty pupils age four to twenty. On Sundays, the building was used as a church.[443] Schools on the plains often struggled due to small student bodies, lack of supplies, and a shortage of qualified teachers. According to Ike Osteen's history of Baca County, teachers could be anyone able to read and write and pass a county exam. They were paid a few dollars a month plus room and board. Baca County teachers taught all eight grades in the small country schools as well as building a fire in the morning to warm the building and performing the necessary janitorial work.[444] In the 1930s, Mrs. J. M. Johnston, my Great Aunt May, recalled coming to Lamar in 1887 and teaching children age ten through seventeen. She noted the shortage of equipment although "skeletons for the study of human body were easy to get."[445]

By the turn of the century, the need had risen for greater skills and education. Families realized that common schools were no longer adequate for their children's needs in an increasingly sophisticated society. While schooling at the elementary level was almost universally available, high schools were academically oriented and mostly located in larger cities. Smaller communities responded by establishing public high schools that were in Claudia Goldin's words "places of practical and applied learning."[446] A 1915 La Junta newspaper article noted that:

> The view of the Secondary School changed very materially, in the decade between 1896 and 1906. Formerly the High School was regarded as an institution designed to accommodate only a few persons who wished to enter College and become Doctors, Lawyers or Preachers, hoping that they in turn might recruit other much needed into the ranks of these professions. This idea rapidly disappeared. In it's [sic] place the broader conception that each individual benefits society and enjoys fulfillment in his own life, largely in proportion to the extent in which he is educated.[447]

La Junta's Otero Union High school opened in 1906. High schools soon became common in eastern Colorado's rural communities. Julesburg citizens voted to form one in 1902; the first classes began the following year and a separate high school building was completed in 1910.[448] Holly, with about seven hundred residents at the time, reported its first high school graduation in 1907.[449] Goldin and Katz suggested that the growth of the road system and widespread auto ownership allowed smaller communities to enroll students from surrounding areas, thereby spreading the fixed expense of high schools over more pupils.[450] By 1918 the region reported forty one four-year high schools.[451] The share of six to seventeen year-olds that were enrolled grew from 81 percent to 89 percent between 1910 and 1930, largely due to more young people attending high schools.[452]

Early Towns

Although settlers formed a few villages on the plains in earlier years, the first incorporated towns did not appear until the 1870s. The 1880 Census listed seven towns in the region. Five were within the 1880 boundaries of Bent County while the other two, Hugo and Middle Kiowa, were in what was then Elbert County. West Las Animas, with 454 residents, was the largest town in the region. For a time, it was the endpoint of both the Santa Fe and Kansas Pacific railroads. Granada and Hugo, also railroad towns, each reported a population greater than one hundred.[453]

The first wave of homesteaders in the late 1880s led to the founding of more towns. Ralph Taylor described frenetic activity in Baca County where twelve towns were started between 1886 and 1888. An 1888 promotional advertisement for Boston in the southeast part of the County claimed six hundred residents. It was described as "the Utopian city of the plains" with five saloons, a bank, a drugstore, a hardware store, three livery barns, and the three-story Boston hotel, the "finest west of Wichita."[454] Two railroad companies with plans for lines in Baca County were incorporated, raising the prospect of more towns along the proposed routes. The railroad plans were soon abandoned followed by those for the towns. In 1887 the *Bent County Leader* reported "100 loads of lumber pull out of Lamar for new towns every 5 days."[455] Among the municipalities established in the 1880s were Fort Morgan, La Junta, Lamar and Sterling which would become the largest in the region by 1930.

As the population grew, new counties were created. Although large cattle ranchers opposed them as they wanted to pursue their business with minimal government interference, homesteaders felt the need for improved public services and facilities.[456] In 1889 Bent County was divided into six new counties while Baca County was split from Las Animas County. The northern and central counties in the region were formed from Weld, Arapahoe, and Elbert Counties, with Logan and Washington Counties created in 1887 and the rest in 1899. Of today's sixteen regional counties, only Crowley County, later carved from Otero, was not in existence in 1890.

The early towns often experienced vertiginous fluctuations between boom and bust. The surges accompanying the arrivals of railroads along with the collapse when the lines were extended west were described earlier. The arrival and later exodus of 1880s homesteaders had a similar effect. C. C. Huddleston recalled when he arrived in Lamar in 1887, "The town was less than a year old and quite a lively place. There were 16 saloons, 2 dance halls, 75 gay girls and about 180 tinhorn gamblers here." Huddleston opened a hardware store with business so brisk that he had difficulty keeping a stock of merchandise. But "The boom was over by '89 and everything fell flat. Owing to the scarcity of water, the ditches not being developed then, the farmers were short of water and there was nothing to support the boom."[457] Louise Merrill who settled with her parents in Granada in 1887 had similar memories. "Within a year after we came to Granada the boom dropped. Property values faded from sight, and most people moved away."[458]

As the population and economy expanded, economies of scale and agglomeration led to clustering of trade, government and service jobs, along with population in the larger communities. In 1890 only one town, La Junta, reported a population over one thousand people. By 1930 there were sixteen and their share of regional population grew from 5 percent to 26 percent. Most of the towns, particularly the larger ones, were found in irrigated areas where there were more rural residents to support local businesses. In 1900 the seven largest towns in the region were all in either the South Platte or Arkansas Valleys.[459]

Towns grew rapidly in the first two decades of the century, especially in the South Platte Valley. Between 1900 and 1920 Fort Morgan's population increased from 634 to 3,818 and Sterling's from 998 to 6,415. When farm prosperity waned in the 1920s, growth in many communities leveled off or reversed. An exception was Springfield which benefitted from the surge in dry land farming in Baca County as well as newly available rail service. In response to this growth the Springfield City Council optimistically voted in 1931 to accept a two-year contract to light its city streets, providing 36 lights and turning the town into "a brilliantly lighted whiteway."[460]

Often an entrepreneur served as a catalyst for the town's growth. Charles Maxwell came to Colorado as an orphan and trained as a barber. He was hired by flour milling magnate J. K. Mullen and in 1899 was appointed manager of the mill in Lamar. He soon became a leader in a myriad of local businesses and civic affairs. Maxwell's ventures included a furniture store, an implement company and an investment firm, and he built the town's leading hotel. When citizens voted down a levy for a new hospital, he financed it with his own funds. He served as mayor for twelve years.[461] George Henderson filled a similar role in Sterling. He opened a general store in 1887 and soon became Sterling's leading business and social leader. By the turn of the century, he was president of the First National Bank. Together with partners he built a new store advertised at its 1905 opening as "the largest store between Denver and Omaha." At the time of his death in 1928 he was thought to be the wealthiest man in northeastern Colorado.[462]

Foreign Immigrants

The late nineteenth and early twentieth century saw unprecedented numbers of migrants entering the United States. Immigration peaked in the first decade of the century when annual net influx averaged 1 percent of the nation's population. By comparison, immigration in the 1990s averaged only 0.3 percent of the population, the resulting political furor notwithstanding. Numbers of migrants remained high until legislation in the early 1920s limited southern and eastern European and Asian entry. Although the foreign-born share of the population in Colorado's eastern plains was less than that in many other parts of the country, those who came had a lasting impact on the work force and on rural communities. The two groups with the greatest influence were persons of German ancestry from the Russian Volga regions and those of Mexican ancestry. By 1930 more residents reported their births in either Russia or Mexico than in any other foreign nation.

Most of the immigrants from Russia spoke German and were known as German Russians or Volga-Germans. Nearly all descended from German Protestants who settled in southern Russia. They had moved there in the eighteenth century during the reign of Catherine the Great who sought to take advantage of their farming skills by offering privileges denied Russian peasants, particularly exemption from mandatory military service. By the late eighteenth century, many German settlements were found along the lower Volga where they largely maintained their language and culture. In the 1870s Czar Alexander II rescinded their military deferments and put rules in place that made land acquisition more difficult. A succession of poor harvests was followed by conscription for the Russo-Japanese war. These burdens encouraged many families to leave for the United States, often enticed by railroad agents who were actively recruiting new farmer-customers. They brought the farming techniques and plant varieties of their native region to the plains and many prospered, particularly in the cultivation of sugar beets and dryland wheat. Large-scale migration from Russia to the US lasted from the 1870s through the teens. Initially most settled in the upper Midwest in Kansas, Nebraska, or the Dakotas but many later moved to eastern Colorado. Some took jobs in railroad construction and remained in the state, many later becoming farmers on the plains. Others moved in search of better farming opportunities on Colorado dryland when late-nineteenth-century crop failures plagued the upper Midwest.[463]

Those who settled on the dryland applied the techniques and crop varieties from the Russian Steppes where soil and climate was not unlike that in their new homes. As they became successful, they encouraged friends and family from old country to join them, often providing financial assistance. Typical of the dryland German-Russian communities was "the settlement" in Kit Carson County near Burlington where the first recorded Russian immigrant arrived in 1887. In 1890 more than half the region's Russian-born residents lived in Kit Carson County. Most had migrated from the Odessa region in today's Ukraine.[464]

Among the Kit Carson County settlers was John Jacober who arrived in Burlington in 1892 with only one dollar. He filed a homestead claim and built a sod house. His wife whitewashed the walls every Saturday "so the house would always look fresh and clean."[465] Since he had no money, he found a job as a cattle herder. During the week he boarded in Burlington and walked fifteen miles home every Saturday night and back every Monday morning. The family struggled to afford food and clothing, especially during the drought. In 1896 he finally gave up, abandoning the homestead and moving to Brighton, a Denver suburb, where he got a job at the Globe Smelter plant, but he returned to Burlington ten years later. August Adolph, another settlement resident, left Russia with his wife and two children in 1888. He settled briefly in Scotland and South Dakota before arriving in Burlington in March 1890 where he homesteaded with other German families. August was a shoemaker by trade so, along with farming his homestead, he walked fifteen miles to Burlington to make and repair boots for twenty-five cents a day. His wife, Katherine, was one of the first midwives in the county. With August's help numerous family members followed him to the US and settled in Kit Carson County.[466]

CHAPTER 4

When labor shortages developed in the beet fields, the sugar companies recruited German Russians as described in the previous chapter. To attract the workers from the upper Midwest, the companies offered housing and the opportunity to eventually become tenant farmers. Great Western prepared a German-language booklet describing living and working conditions in the South Platte Valley and opportunities for new residents.[467] Trainloads of German-Russian families were transported from Nebraska.[468] They were viewed as willing to take on tasks that current residents were loath to perform. As the *Logan County Advocate* commented in 1904, "It has always been a source of trouble to secure adequate help in the fields during thinning and weed, few Americans caring to do this wearisome labor. The Russian apparently likes it, and as he in no way competes with the American laborer, his coming is a benefit rather than a detriment."[469] The workers rewarded their recruiters with hard work. Entire families including young children labored in the fields. Pay was not generous. A family in 1915 earned six dollars an acre for bunching and thinning, two dollars for a second hoeing and one dollar for a third hoeing.[470] During the harvest season many of the men worked in the sugar plants. The German Russians were thrifty as well as hard-working. The lived austerely and saved from their earnings.

Fred Ostwald of Fort Morgan recalled that his father came to America from Russian in 1906. He found a job at a tannery in Wisconsin and brought his wife and four children to the country. He held several jobs in the next few years including in the beet fields in Ohio. An uncle who worked summers in the beet fields in Weld County persuaded Ostwald to join him. He supported his family on an initial wage of $1 per day but was able to accumulate funds to buy a small farm and moved to Morgan County in 1918.[471] [472]

The German Russians typically had large families. Andrew Ament Sr.—the name would later be changed to Amen—and his wife Marie from Frank in the southern Volga region fled the revolution of 1905 and arrived at Ellis Island in 1906 with a family of seven. After a brief stay with friends in Nebraska, they moved to Sedgwick County where they began farming. Two years later Andrew was able to buy a farm twelve miles south-west of Sterling. His son John paid Katherine Koch's traveling expenses from Russia to become his bride in 1912. The couple homesteaded near Andrew Sr.'s farm and eventually had nine children. John drilled the first irrigation well in the area and grew sugar beets, beans, hay, corn, and small grains. He also cultivated dryland wheat and developed a herd of registered Herefords. Andrew Jr. married Anna Mary Weiderspan, a daughter of Russian immigrants, and moved in with his father along with two other families and several unmarried brothers. He and Anna eventually had thirteen children. Other brothers enjoyed similarly fecund marriages. Conrad sired nine children and Jake, eleven. The family farmed jointly for several years before the brothers acquired their own land. The family established the town of Amen along the Burlington railroad. The town's name was changed to Logan after the outbreak of

World War I, a reaction to anti-German feeling.[473] The Amen family has numerous descendants still living in the in area in the twenty-first century.

By 1930 the Russian-born population in the sixteen counties had grown to nearly three thousand from just over forty years earlier. Doubtless Russian revolutions in 1905 and 1917 and recruitment efforts by American railroads encouraged their exodus. In 1930 Logan County reported more than a thousand Russian-born residents and Morgan County more than nine hundred. They also settled in the Arkansas Valley. There were several sons of German Russian families on my late-fifties Lamar high school football team. In Sterling German Russian families lived in a carefully planned community of two or three room white wooden frame houses with picket fences referred to as "the Russian corner."[474] Their contributions to eastern Colorado were not all welcome. Mrs. Hans Christensen of Yuma County remembered, "A colony of Russians from South Dakota moved into the south end of the County in the late nineties. With them came the first weeds in the country, namely Russian Thistles."[475] This weed, when dry, is the source of tumbleweeds seen blowing through the plains in the late winter and spring. It depletes water from crops and can harbor crop viruses as well as being potentially toxic to livestock. It is believed to have been introduced by German Russian immigrants with the seed they brought from their native land.

As the German Russians became more affluent, they acquired their own farms and no longer needed to perform stoop labor for someone else. Their success meant a shortage of workers in the beet fields. In 1917 the *Sterling Democrat* commented that "There seems no possibility of securing Russian labor as in the past, and the company and growers are forced to turn to other quarters for the needed aid. The Russian has prospered so well during the ten years of sugar beet growing in the west that he has ceased to be a laborer and has become a planter."[476] The shortage worsened when young men joined the military as the nation mobilized for war while, at the same time, the demand for sugar increased.

The companies first attempted meet their labor demands by recruiting Japanese, but the new residents encountered racial animosity and many left. The companies then turned to workers of Mexican descent. Initially, most were seasonal laborers from southern Colorado or New Mexico who returned to their homes after the harvest. As demand grew the companies expanded their recruiting. GW canvassed Mexican families in the South Platte Valley for friends and relatives who might be prospective workers and prepared recruiting materials such as handbills, posters, and booklets. Texas provided a fruitful area for hiring. The company sent agents to Fort Worth and San Antonio every February and sponsored trains transporting the workers to the Colorado beet fields.[477] In 1909 an estimated 55 percent of the laborers in the sugar beet fields of northern Colorado were German Russians and 9 percent were Mexican. The remainder were almost evenly divided between Japanese and "miscellaneous white." By 1927 the Mexican share had grown to 59 percent while only 31 percent were German Russians.[478]

The sugar companies eventually found it more efficient to have a resident work force rather than having to recruit new workers each season so built permanent living quarters for the field workers and their families with rentals deducted from workers' wages.[479] William May outlined GW's objectives in setting up these settlements. "First, they were to demonstrate that Mexican laborers could build their own houses and then pay for the lot and the building material over a period of four years; secondly, the company could provide a limited number of houses for rent during the winter; and thirdly, the company could offer these houses for sale to deserving beet workers."[480] Many eastern Colorado communities had distinct sections of town with modest housing for Latino residents. These settlements or *colonias* were typically located across the tracks or highways or on the fringe of town. The companies, with the cooperation of local officials, often set up "company stores" to provide food, clothing, and other supplies. They often entrapped families in debt[481] and workers families sometimes faced higher prices than locals. In the South Platte Valley, GW established *colonias* in Brush, Ovid and Sedgwick.[482] The *colonia* in Lamar was referred to by local Anglos as "the Mexican Colony." The town's Hispanic residents had their own Catholic Church and a separate elementary school until after World War II. The Mexican migrants, unlike the Germans, were not encouraged to become tenant farmers or acquire their own farms.[483]

Despite harsh living and working conditions, some Mexican migrant were able to achieve that era's version of the "American Dream" for their families. One such was Marciano Aguayo who was born in Mexico in 1897. He ran away from home at sixteen and for a time worked as a stable boy for Pancho Villa. In 1921, after a succession of other jobs, he hopped a freight train ending up near Merino in Logan County where he got work in the beet fields. He was an excellent worker who put in long hours in the field. Great Western regularly evaluated and graded the field workers and he consistently received an A. A 1927 Certificate of Merit issued by the company showed that he thinned eighteen acres, hoed 18 1/2 acres, weeded forty acres and topped twenty acres. In 1929 he married Jovita Ortega, another beet-field worker, whom he met at a weekly dance held in Sedgwick for farm laborers. The family was able to purchase a small shack in Sedgwick where they raised their children. The Aguayo family's life was not easy. Jovita supplemented her husband's field earnings by taking in laundry, harvesting onions, picking potatoes, cleaning houses and other odd jobs. Marciano regularly struggled to pay his line of credit at the local store, a debt that was "never explained nor could be reviewed by debtor." In 1941 the family's lot improved when Marciano obtained a permanent job with Union Pacific Railroad that he held until he retired. The Aguayos were determined that their children would have a better life, and six of them completed college.[484] The Aguayos, although far from typical, were not alone. Several members of the Daniel Torres and Luis Delgado families of Logan

County, descendants of early immigrants who worked in the beet fields, attended or graduated from college.[485]

The Hispanic population grew rapidly. Only nineteen native Mexicans resided in the region in 1890. By 1910 this number had grown to nearly a thousand with most of them living in the Arkansas Valley in Bent, Otero, and Prowers Counties. The 1910 outbreak of the Mexican Revolution and wartime labor demand spurred further immigration. More than three thousand residents reported Mexican birth to the 1920 Census. The 1930 Census added the "Mexican" classification which included all persons born in Mexico or sons or daughters of Mexican-born parents not classified as Negro, Chinese or Indian. The number of "Mexican residents in the plains counties exceeded ten thousand.[486] They made up 8 percent of the region's total population and exceeded 15 percent of residents in Crowley, Cheyenne and Otero Counties. In the small Prowers County town of Granada, the Mexican population in 1933 was large enough to celebrate Mexican Independence Day featuring "two baseball games and other entertainment."[487] The Lamar *colonia* held a *Cinco de Mayo* celebration where both American and Mexican flags were displayed.[488]

The region's Hispanic population was an unfortunate exception to the pattern of progress in education. Mexican immigrants typically had less formal education than other arrivals and that provided their children usually fell well short of what offspring of Anglo families received. This failing often reflected the prejudices of local school officials and townspeople. Most Hispanics were employed as field workers in sugar beet and vegetable farming, occupations viewed as having little need for academically acquired skills. Goldin and Katz[489] noted similarly low school-enrollment rates for African Americans in the South where there seemed little need for school-acquired skills and knowledge among cotton and tobacco field laborers. Dennis Valdés, in his social history of sugar beet workers, observed that while both German Russian and Mexican families kept their children out of school to work in the fields, school officials discouraged this practice only among the former group.[490] Census data tend to confirm the lower educational attainment of immigrants from Mexico. In 1930 four counties, all in the Arkansas Valley with substantial irrigated farmland, reported more than 9 percent of their population as "Mexican," a significantly larger share than the rest of the region. Literacy was not reported for persons in the "Mexican" category, only for non-native-born-whites which included "Mexicans." In the four Arkansas Valley counties the rate for this group was 10 percent lower than for the same populations in the rest of the region.

By the 1920s increased migration from Mexico gave rise to resistance on both sides of the border. The Mexican government, concerned about population loss, set immigration and visa limitations and levied fees on Mexican nationals working in *El Norte*.[491] While the US enacted restrictions on immigration from nations outside northern Europe, there were no limits on immigration from Latin America, due in part to lobbying by the sugar companies. However, Mexicans entering the US had to pay an eight-dollar visa fee, submit to medical examinations and undergo bathing and delousing.[492] This led to considerable informal or extra-legal movement across the border.

High unemployment during the depression brought further domestic resistance to Mexican workers. During the thirties several hundred thousand US-residents of Mexican ancestry including American-born children were either deported or pressured to voluntary return to their native country.[493] In 1936 Colorado Governor Johnson responded to anti-Mexican sentiments by enacting martial law and stationing National Guard troops along state's southern border. A *Rocky Mountain News* front-page headline declared: "Troops Move Into Action at Dawn to Prevent Invasion by Indigent."[494] The Governor claimed that his action would prevent alien workers from depressing local wages and swelling state and local relief rolls.[495] Suspicious travelers were stopped and turned over to the authorities. The *Lamar Daily News* reported that "Two carloads of Mexicans were halted at Eads by Sheriff Lester Latham Tuesday morning and were brought to the state armory [in Lamar] about noon where they were turned over to the special detail of guardsmen."[496] The deployment, suspected by many to be a political stunt by the Governor to set the stage for a run for the Senate, was ended in eleven days, "after an apparent shortage of labor for the beet fields."[497]

The Aguayo family described earlier was exceptional. Unlike the German Russians, most Latinos remained manual laborers for decades. Some found employment outside the beet fields. Jose Reyes and Joe Alcala of Logan County were able to obtain jobs with the railroads.[498] Mexican workers were generally paid less than workers of other ethnicities and found it difficult to accumulate funds to acquire their own farms. Their aspirations were not encouraged by the rest of the population. The prevailing attitude of many Anglos was exemplified by Colorado University history professor Colin Goodykoontz who in 1948 wrote of the Mexican immigrants, "It is in the beet fields that they have made their chief contribution to the economic life of Colorado. …. The successful growing of sugar beets required intensive cultivation and, so far, a great deal of hand labor. Very few Anglo-Americans will stoop to this sort of work."[499] More than thirty years later in his 1982 University of Colorado doctoral thesis, William May wrote "the Mexican cultural heritage emphasize *mañana* attitude, characterized by a lack of concern or disregard for the future."[500] There was even some disdain for Mexican immigrants among Spanish surnamed natives. Sarah Deutsch in her examination of Anglo-Hispanic relationships in the Southwest noted divisions between the native "Spanish-American" population and Mexican migrants.[501] This distinction was more common among native Hispanics than Anglos who treated both groups poorly. Coloradans of Mexican descent would wait decades before obtaining respect as well as many of the rights and privileges enjoyed by other citizens.

The Plains Region in 1930

The first fifty years of non-indigenous settlement set patterns that, in many cases, prevailed into the twenty-first century. Nearly all agricultural land was settled. The larger towns were established along with government and primary and secondary educational institutions. Population levels reached their peaks in much of the region. The settlers had done well in their new home, but their optimism was soon to be tested by drought and depression.

CHAPTER 4

Chapter 4 Exhibits

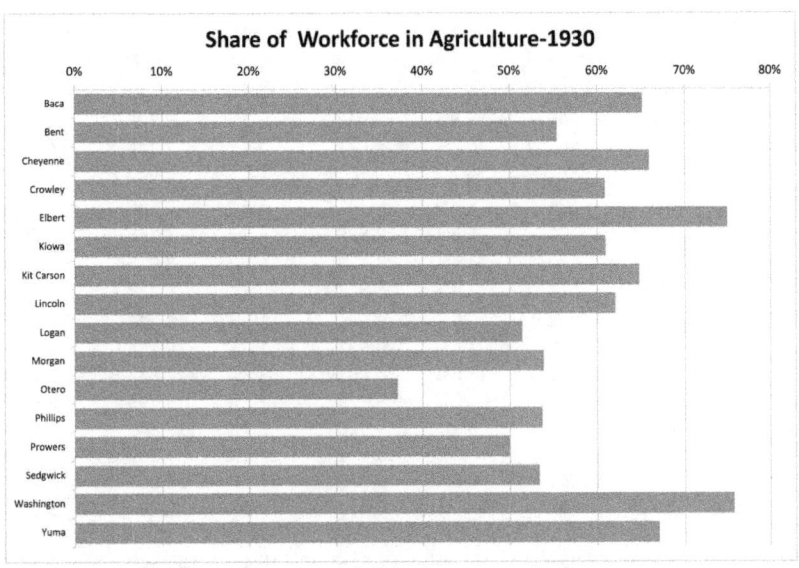

Share of Workforce in Agriculture-1930

Distribution of Nonagricultural Workers-1930

	Eastern Plains		US	
	Workers	Pct	Workers	Pct
Building	2,048	8%	2,561,535	7%
All food and	1,199	5%	876,904	2%
Non-food m	1,859	8%	13,440,631	34%
Railroads	2,426	10%	1,779,155	5%
Other Tansp	2,789	11%	2,659,450	7%
Trade	4,790	19%	6,113,780	16%
Professional	3,664	15%	2,976,811	8%
Other Servic	4,983	20%	6,184,427	16%
Other Indus	936	4%	2,761,254	7%

The 1930 Census provided the earliest data on the number of regional workers in different industries. Fifty-five percent were on farms or ranches compared with 21 percent in the US. Agriculture's share of the work force was lower in the more populated counties in the valleys but every county except Otero reported at least half its workers on farms or ranches.

Most workers outside agriculture were employed in trade and services. These included government workers, teachers and retail employees. Relatively few worked in manufacturing. While one in three nonfarm workers in the US were found in manufacturing firms, only one in eight regional workers were so employed.

Source: Census

Population By County 1890-1930

	1890	1900	Ann. Pct Ch	1910	Ann. Pct Ch	1920	Ann. Pct Ch
Baca	1,479	759	-6.5%	2,516	12.7%	8,721	13.2%
Bent	1,313	3,049	8.8%	5,043	5.2%	9,705	6.8%
Cheyenne	534	501	-0.6%	3,687	22.1%	3,746	0.2%
Crowley						6,383	
Elbert	1,856	3,101	5.3%	5,331	5.6%	5,980	1.2%
Kiowa	1,243	701	-5.6%	2,899	15.3%	3,755	2.6%
Kit Carson	2,472	1,580	-4.4%	7,483	16.8%	8,915	1.8%
Lincoln	689	926	3.0%	5,917	20.4%	8,273	3.4%
Logan	3,070	3,292	0.7%	9,549	11.2%	18,427	6.8%
Morgan	1,601	3,268	7.4%	9,577	11.4%	18,124	6.6%
Otero	4,192	11,522	10.6%	20,201	5.8%	22,823	1.2%
Phillips	2,642	1,583	-5.0%	3,179	7.2%	5,499	5.6%
Prowers	1,960	3,766	6.7%	9,520	9.7%	13,845	3.8%
Sedgwick	1,293	971	-2.8%	3,061	12.2%	4,207	3.2%
Washington	2,301	1,241	-6.0%	6,002	17.1%	11,208	6.4%
Yuma	2,596	1,792	-3.6%	8,499	16.8%	13,897	5.0%
Total	29,241	38,052	2.7%	102,464	10.4%	163,508	4.8%

* If Crowley County population included Otero growth 1910-20 is 3.8%.

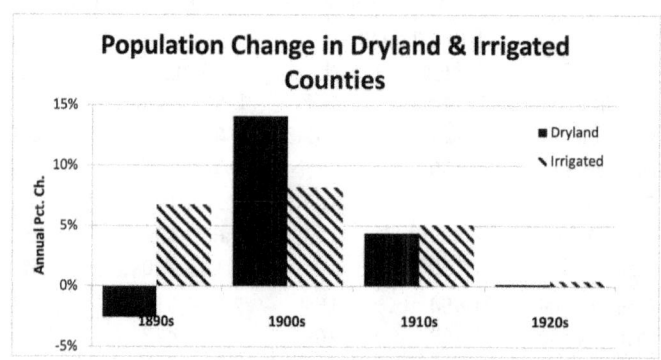

The counties with irrigation experienced solid growth in the 1890s, 1900s and teens while the dryland counties lost population in the nineties but rebounded over the next two decades. Populations stagnated through most of the region in the twenties.

Between 1890 and 1920 the region saw a five-fold expansion in population. The eastern plains population reached its all-time peak in the 1920s at around 170,000. Populations in twelve of the sixteen counties had also peaked by 1930. The surge of homesteaders in the early twentieth and farm prosperity during and after World War I were the major contributors to this growth.

Source: Census

CHAPTER 4

Eastern Plains Towns in 1880

Town	Population
Fort Lyon	64
Granada	121
Hugo	140
Las Animas	52
Middle Kiowa	74
Rocky Ford	47
West Las Animas	454

Towns with >1,000 Population in 1930

Town	County	1890	1900	1910	1920	1930
Akron	Washington	559	351	647	1,401	1,135
Brush	Morgan	112	381	997	2,103	2,312
Burlington	Kit Carson	146	183	368	991	1,280
Fort Morgan	Morgan	488	634	2,800	3,818	4,423
Holyoke	Phillips	649	451	659	1,205	1,226
Julesburg	Sedgwick	202	371	962	1,320	1,467
La Junta	Otero	1,439	2,513	4,154	4,964	7,193
Lamar	Prowers	566	987	2,977	2,512	4,233
Las Animas	Bent	611	1,192	2,008	2,252	2,517
Limon	Lincoln	N/A	N/A	534	1,047	1,100
Ordway	Crowley	N/A	138	705	1,186	1,139
Rocky Ford	Otero	468	2,018	3,230	3,746	3,426
Springfield	Baca	90	44	N/A	295	1,393
Sterling	Logan	540	998	3,044	6,415	7,195
Wray	Yuma	125	271	1,000	1,538	1,785
Yuma	Yuma	241	139	333	1,177	1,360
Share of population in towns > 1,000		5%	15%	18%	21%	26%

In 1880 most residents lived on farms or ranches rather than in towns. The table shows all incorporated towns at that time. All lay along railroads and West Las Animas, the largest town, had been the terminating point for two railroads, the Santa Fe and the Kansas Pacific.

In 1890 only one community, La Junta, reported a population greater than one thousand. By 1930 there were sixteen such towns in the region. The share of the population living in towns increased through the late nineteenth and early twentieth centuries due to a growing demand by farmers and ranchers for products and services that the towns offered. The largest towns were found in the South Platte or Arkansas Valleys where farms were smaller, and the rural population was more concentrated.

Source: Census

Foreign Born Population on Eastern Plains

Country of Origin	1890	1910	1930
Canada	382	650	439
Mexico	19	852	2,546 *
Great Britain	613	875	547
Ireland	385	333	133
Germany	1,052	1,793	1,373
Sweden	579	789	545
Russia	205	2,274	2,822
Other	646	2,164	2,022
Total Foreign Born	3,881	9,730	7,881

Foreign Born as Pct of Population**

Eastern Plains	13.3%	9.6%	5.8%
US	14.7%	16.3%	12.3%

The early homestead era brought large German-born populations, but by 1930 the largest non-native groups were from Mexico or Russia. The latter were mostly "German Russians" i.e. German speakers who had lived in Russia. Both groups were recruited by sugar beet companies. The region's share of foreign-born declined by 1930 as the nation enacted greater restrictions on immigration.

* 1930 number for Mexico based on share of those classified as "Mexican" that were foreign born.

** 1910 and 1930 for whites only including most Hispanics. The 1930 figure includes an estimate of those classified as "Mexican" that were foreign born.

Source: Census

CHAPTER 4

The early Mexican beet workers were seasonal laborers who returned to their homes in the winter. Later many became permanent residents and lived in *colonias* such as the one in Lamar pictured above.

Source: Photo courtesy of Big Timbers Museum, Lamar, Colorado

CHAPTER 5

Depression and Drought: the 1920s and 1930s

PLAINS FARMERS AND BUSINESSMEN ENJOYED UNPRECEDENTED PROSPERITY IN THE late teens, but the next twenty years were almost certainly the most challenging in the region's history. Wartime affluence quickly collapsed in a sharp but brief recession. Farm prices plummeted, recovering only modestly later in the decade. Most farmers were still in rather precarious condition when drought and world-wide depression delivered a further blow in the 1930s. Massive government intervention brought some relief, but farms and businesses suffered widespread failure and many residents left the region.

The Farm Depression of the 1920s

There were many reasons for optimism in 1919. The region had enjoyed two decades of solid growth. Cattle, wheat, and corn prices were near all-time highs and land values had soared to record levels. New industries, most based on adding value to farm products, were doing well. The end to the Great War and the homecoming of America's troops brought a sense of hope for the future, and the devastating Spanish Flu pandemic of 1918 seemed to be abating. In late December of that year, Dr. Leslie Parker, the Hugo town health officer, announced that the town's restrictions on public gatherings were declared off.[502]

But as world agricultural production recovered from the damage of war, demand for US grain and meat shrank and prices plummeted through the early 1920s. The "golden age" of American agriculture was over. In a belated attempt to curb post-war inflation, the Federal Reserve raised short-term interest rates to heights not to be reached again until the 1970s. Farm credit was severely restricted. A harsh recession and deflation followed, beginning in early 1920 and lasting through mid-1921.[503] Wholesale commodity prices that had more than doubled between 1916 and 1919 fell by two-thirds over the next two years.[504] Corn and wheat prices dropped to less than half of their wartime peaks.

111

When credit conditions were relaxed, the nonfarm economy embarked on a robust recovery and American business thrived in the "roaring twenties." But the decade was hardly roaring for farmers nor for the region still heavily dependent on agriculture. The combination of slackening foreign demand and domestic deflation was devastating for agrarian America. Grain prices saw a modest rebound and livestock prices a somewhat stronger recovery. But they remained well short of their wartime highs. Between 1919 and 1928 the Department of Agriculture's index of all farm commodity prices fell 29 percent and that of grain prices fell by 55 percent. Farmers costs also fell but by less than prices they got for their product.[505] Land values were devastated. National farmland prices dropped steadily through the decade. US farm bankruptcies increased almost eight-fold from 1920 to 1925.[506] Rural Americans left their land in droves. US farm population in 1920 was slightly over thirty million. During the ensuing decade those moving from farm to city or town exceeded those few relocating to farms by more than six million.[507]

Eastern Colorado farmers fought to survive in this difficult environment. Faced with lower prices, many attempted to increase revenues by purchasing more land or by plowing marginal acreage. Regional average wheat planting in the years 1922-24 grew by 383,000 acres or 56 percent over that in 1919-20 and farmers sowed 292,000 more acres of corn with most of the increase for both crops in the dryland counties.[508] Regional growers could expand their cultivation because ample reasonably priced land was still available while those in the rest of the nation generally had fewer opportunities for increasing their acreage.

Planting more may have helped farmers stave off financial ruin, at least temporarily. But it also increased their risk. In most cases, acquiring more land required more borrowing. For the sixteen counties, both the share of farms with mortgage debt and the amount of debt as a proportion of land value rose between 1920 and 1925.[509] Soon farmers could not continue their credit-fueled expansion as falling land prices limited their ability to borrow. The average value of an acre of eastern Colorado farmland fell by more than one-third between 1920 and 1925 and dropped another 11 percent by 1930.[510]

Beet growers and sugar companies faced wide gyrations in world prices. During the wartime boom, beet farmers prospered and pressured sugar companies for higher contract prices. But prices fell after the war as foreign demand flagged and a tariff reduction increased competitive pressure from foreign producers. By 1920 the market price of sugar had dropped more than 40 percent from its peak. The best that farmers could hope for was that companies could maintain their current offers.[511] But lower prices squeezed the companies' margins. In an open letter to South Platte Valley growers, GW management wrote, "This season's [1920] output of sugar is produced from beets paid for at the highest price in the history of the business with labor and other manufacturing costs at the highest point they have ever reached. We are now confronted with the prospect of having to sell our output of sugar at much lower prices than expected."[512] The contract price offered by the companies declined. Increasing acreage was usually not an option for farmers growing irrigated crops as planting was limited by the availability of water. Existing acreage could be farmed more intensively, and beet tonnage per acre rose by 14 percent between 1919 and 1924.[513]

Ranchers fared little better. A leading northern Colorado cattle feeder later wrote that during 1920s, "Virtually the entire cattle industry, including cow/calf producers, stocker/feeder operations and cattle feeders went broke and took many banks with them."[514] Between 1919 and 1922 the price of beef cattle fell from $9.00 per hundred pounds to $5.30 and the estimated value of sheep dropped from $11.63 per head to $4.79.[515] Ranchers responded by reducing their herds. The region's cattle and sheep populations both declined by more than one-quarter by 1925[516] leaving ranchers unable to take advantage when prices rose later in the decade. While prospects for cattle and sheep diminished, raising hogs became more attractive allowing farmers to use their increased corn output. The number of swine on eastern Colorado farms more than doubled between 1919 and 1924 with the largest increases in Kit Carson and Washington Counties, which also posted large increases in corn acreage.[517]

The outlook brightened somewhat toward the end of the decade as markets for most farm produce strengthened. The region's farmers could hope that the worst was behind them although sugar beet prices remained depressed. In 1925 an article in the *Akron News* noted optimism on the part of Washington County farmers who anticipated the "brightest prospects in eight years."[518] In 1926 a Rocky Ford banker reported that "the average farmer in much better shape than at any time since 1920."[519] By 1928 a banker in Hugo noted that "cattlemen and their bankers have an outlook materially altered from that prevailing since the depression of 1920." [520] While from Akron "a great deal of old indebtedness has been liquidated."[521]

For businessmen and nonfarm families, the 1920s marked the end of the agriculture-driven boom of the previous twenty years. Growth slowed in most of the region. County employment and income statistics are not available for the 1920s, but sluggish population growth suggests that the regional economy stagnated. After adding more than sixty-thousand people during the teens the region's population increased by less than six thousand in the twenties. Six counties saw a decline. Only Sedgwick and Baca Counties experienced growth on the scale of the previous decade. Weakness in the twenties made the region more vulnerable to the drought and depression that were to come.

The 1930s

It is difficult for twenty-first century Americans to appreciate the devastating impact of the Great Depression of the 1930s. According to Milton Friedman and Anna Schwartz's tome on US monetary history, the depression "may well have been the most severe in the whole of US history. Though sharper and more prolonged in the United

States than in most other countries, it was worldwide in scope and ranks as the most severe and widely diffused international contraction of modern times."[522] Virtually all industrial nations suffered deflation, high unemployment, declining real incomes, and often social unrest. It afflicted nearly the entire industrial world and persisted through most of the decade. Economic output collapsed. US real GDP fell 27 percent between 1929 and 1933. By contrast, the 2007-09 "Great Recession" saw a GDP drop only a bit over 3 percent. (Percentage declines are based on annual averages as only annual statistics were available for the 1930s.) More than eight million jobs were lost.[523] US real per capita personal income fell by more than one-quarter after 1929 and did not recover to its pre-Depression level until 1937.[524] Families hit with job and income losses lacked today's public safety net and were dependent upon family or private charity until government relief programs came into effect later in the decade. Some nine-thousand banks failed with depositors not protected as today by deposit insurance.

After suffering through the "farm depression" of the twenties, the outlook for agriculture darkened still further. Farmers and ranchers were particularly vulnerable to the combined effects of deflation and a severe drought that began in the early thirties. Crop and livestock prices collapsed. The index of prices received for agricultural commodities fell 55 percent between 1929 and 1932.[525] Foreign demand for US farm products plunged as other nations' incomes fell and their governments raised tariffs on farm produce in response to the high US levies in the Smoot-Hawley bill of 1929. The contribution of this infamous piece of legislation to the depression is often exaggerated, for example by Ben Stein's high school economics teacher in the movie *Ferris Beuller's Day Off*. But farmers and ranchers, who were the most exposed to world markets, bore the brunt of its damage. Wheat exports fell from 153 million bushels in 1929 to 41 million in 1932.[526] US gross income from farm production fell 55 percent between 1929 and 1932.[527]

The October 1929 stock market crash is often cited as marking the depression's onset in the US. But the crash appeared to have little effect in rural eastern Colorado. Baca County residents were particularly buoyant. The *Springfield Democrat-Herald* trumpeted 1930 as "the greatest year in the history of the town and county." The town's natural gas service was initiated, and electrical and water utilities were upgraded. Three new stores had opened, and plans were underway for a north-south railway through the town.[528] The outlook was nearly as ebullient in the northern plains. The *Julesburg Grit-Advocate* in October 1930 bragged that "Times are better here than in practically any other section of the nation"[529] Doris Monahan of Sterling remembered that "In Logan County, 1929 was the year the beets froze. The stock market crash was small potatoes comparatively."[530]

But the respite would not last. Eastern Colorado agriculture was already fragile, and farmers' burdens worsened as commodity prices sank and the real burden of farmers' debt increased. The price of wheat on the Chicago market, over $2 per bushel in the heady-post war days, fell as low as 50 cents and remained below one dollar for most of the decade. Many plains growers got even less. In 1931 Washington County farmers reportedly received between twenty-two and twenty-seven cents per bushel at local elevators.[531] Ted Sindt, who farmed west of Peetz, recalled a wheat price of eighteen cents.[532] The worst North American drought in three centuries spread over as much as 80 percent of the US. The greatest devastation was felt in the portion of the southern Great Plains, including parts of southeast Colorado, that became known as the Dust Bowl.

Hard times drove many plains residents to leave despite limited economic opportunities elsewhere in the depression-wracked nation. The region lost more than one-eighth of its population over the decade with only one of the sixteen counties adding any residents. Farmers saw much of their wealth destroyed as the average value of an acre of eastern Colorado farmland declined another 60 percent in the 1930s.[533] Economic suffering was not confined to agriculture. In-town businesses struggled, and banks failed. The number of nonfarm jobs fell 13 percent between 1930 and 1940.[534]

The Federal Government's Response to the Depression

The government's unprecedented intervention dominated the plains economy over the decade. The Federal role in the farm sector mushroomed with expenditures by the US Department of Agriculture increasing from less than $200 million in FY 1929 to $1.2 billion[535] in FY 1935 as both Hoover and Roosevelt administrations tried to revive the depressed farm sector. The Hoover administration cut taxes, expanded public works, and took measures to ease credit.

Franklin Roosevelt's New Deal, initiated when he assumed office in 1933 as the depression deepened, brought further expansion of the federal role in the economy and especially in agriculture. The overwhelming electoral support for change indicated a public demand for more aggressive action. But many New Dealers felt that merely seeking to return to the earlier status quo was insufficient, that the Depression exposed serious defects in American capitalism requiring a radical reconstruction. A nationally syndicated column written before the new president was inaugurated highlighted the contrasting views within the new administration: "Recovery, according to the language of the Brain Trust, is the progress of business toward the old days of prosperity under Calvin Coolidge, with the profit system remaining unchanged. Reconstruction, on the other hand, is the reform of the economic and social system by scaling down of profits, the scaling up of wages, and the creation of both government and consumer as virtual partners in industry."[536]

Nowhere was the perceived need for radical change more urgent than in rural America. With nearly one-fourth of US population living on farms,[537] New Deal planners viewed the condition of American agriculture as sufficiently threatening to warrant drastic measures. Secretary of Agriculture, Henry Wallace, characterized the early 1930s condition of the farm sector as one where "economic planning became not merely advisable but necessary."[538] The new administration embarked upon what Douglas Hurt described as a "form of state planning [that] imposed an unprecedented dependence upon the farmer."[539] The New Deal farm programs were a wrenching change from the status quo with emergency employment, government restriction on prices and production, expanded loan programs, currency depreciation and direct relief payments among its more significant programs. But these measures still fell short of some supporters' more utopian visions described by Paarlberg as "taking direct issue with existing institutions: the market mechanism, individual enterprise, the credit structure and the distributive system."[540] The tension between revolutionaries and pragmatists would manifest itself in the frequently schizophrenic quality of many New Deal farm programs.

President Roosevelt outlined his views of American agriculture's predicament in Julesburg from the rear platform of his campaign train. He saw three challenges: "The first is the immediate problem of taking care of the feeding of people during the summer. The second is the problem of taking care of people during the next winter until the next spring. The third problem relates to long-range planning, so we can beat this problem once and for all by the proper use of the land."[541] The administration dealt with the immediate problem of the farmer's inability to support his family and pay for feed and seed by directly distributing funds and generating paying jobs through emergency programs. The Federal Emergency Relief Administration (FERA), a continuation under a new title of a Hoover administration agency, distributed goods and emergency funds to needy farm families to be repaid with work, cash, or in kind.[542]

To deal with the second problem, a variety of programs expanded the government's role in farm credit to meet short-term operating needs. The Commodity Credit Corporation (CCC) enabled farmers to obtain non-recourse price support loans secured by their crops. The Emergency Farm Mortgage Act of 1933 increased the lending capacity of the Federal Land Banks to make loans against farmland and improvements. Emergency loans and livestock purchase programs were introduced in severe drought areas. The government also made short term feed and seed loans through Production Credit Associations.

The longer-term issues called for even greater changes, and FDR's planners replaced the ineffective direct purchase of agricultural commodities with measures designed to reduce farm production. The signature piece of New Deal farm legislation was the Agricultural Adjustment Act (AAA) enacted in 1933 in the frantic early days of the Roosevelt Administration. Although the AAA's overall goal of shrinking crop production was clear, the act itself was opaque and in places contradictory. Michael Hiltzik in his history of the New Deal described the AAA as

> "a typical product of the Hundred Days Congress. It was a hodgepodge passed in the heat of emergency, inadequately debated, taken mostly on

faith, and, in its delegation of authority to the executive branch, broad beyond measure. Its constitutionality was questionable but not deeply examined by the drafters or lawmakers.... It could be all things to all men, a quality that the New Deal of the Hundred Days regarded as a virtue, and it provoked suspicions about its true nature that Congress consciously repressed in the name of getting something, anything, done."[543]

The AAA attempted to control crop production by paying farmers to reduce their acreage, an approach consistent with other New Deal programs that aimed to suppress competition and maintain prices through government-enforced cartels. The supply of basic agricultural products was to be controlled through "allotments" developed by the Agricultural Adjustment Administration, that, like the law creating it, was also referred to as the AAA. Farmers were compensated for cutting their output to meet their allotments with funds raised from a levy on processors of farm commodities. This portion of the AAA was declared unconstitutional by the US Supreme Court in 1936 due to its funding scheme. It was quickly replaced by the Soil Conservation and Domestic Allotment Act of 1936 that was funded from direct Treasury appropriations and placed a greater emphasis on the soil conservation aspects of acreage reduction. Along with receiving payments for reduced plantings of targeted crops, farmers were compensated for a variety of soil conservation activities. Growers were paid for not planting soil-depleting crops and for cultivating grasses and other plants that helped limit wind erosion. The government advanced loans for purchase of seed and supported planting ground cover on land taken out of production.

The Agricultural Adjustment Act of 1938 incorporated most of the 1936 law as well as providing crop insurance and price support loans. The scope of the latter act was revealed in its title, "An Act to provide for the conservation of national soil resources and to provide an adequate and balanced flow of agricultural commodities in interstate and domestic commerce and for other purposes." The new law set the tone for farm policy for the next several decades. An analysis of the 1938 act by the Guarantee Trust Company described it as "the most ambitious experiment in farm relief ever tried by a democratic nation and one of the most important pieces of economic legislation in the history of the United States."[544] Other New Deal farm programs were more focused on aiding the farmer than on remaking the farm economy. These included research, education, loans, subsidies, and soil conservation activities by the Civilian Conservation Corps or CCC, not to be confused with the Commodity Credit Corporation also bearing the CCC acronym.

The Standard State Soil Conservation Districts Act of 1937 was designed to motivate states to pass legislation setting up districts that would provide conservation assistance and services to farmers and ranchers by encouraging and guiding more sustainable farming methods. It was hoped that the districts, either through assistance to famers or imposition of controls on their practices, would limit erosion. The Colorado Legislature authorized Soil Conservation Districts in the State in 1937 and eight districts were established in the eastern plains counties.[545]

County agents from the Agricultural Extension Service played a vital role in implementing New Deal policies in rural America. Douglas Sheflin's history of the Dust Bowl in southeast Colorado described how the federal government "relied on the Extension Service to identify rural problems and to strengthen the relationship between farmers and the federal government. The New Deal depended on local agents to ensure that residents were abiding by the new regulations and satisfying requirements to obtain newly created subsidies."[546] Financial support for county agents was increased. While viewed by many as providing welcome assistance in a time of dire need, they were criticized by others as yet another instance of federal government intrusion.

The government's aggressive intervention was not limited to agriculture. Other New Deal programs included the Works Progress Administration (WPA) that provided work for unemployed workers, usually in public infrastructure projects in cooperation with state and local governments. The National Recovery Administration (NRA), declared unconstitutional by the Supreme Court, was an attempt at government invention in the non-farm sectors of the economy analogous to that of the AAA in agriculture. The Rural Electrification Administration (REA) brought electricity to many previously unserved rural households. (Implementation of the various government programs in the region is described later in this chapter and in chapter 6.)

Drought and Depression on the Eastern Plains

The 1930s was a time of unprecedented suffering for eastern Colorado's people. Abandoned farms, impoverished families, failed businesses, and lost jobs haunted the region. In January 1936 Kit Carson County saw 48 percent of its population on relief, and more than half of Baca County residents were receiving public assistance.[547] Communities struggled to cope with an unprecedented level of distress. Doris Monahan recalled unemployed transients arriving in Sterling in boxcars in 1932; thirty-two of them slept in the Sterling jail. The men were given work in a wood yard that the town established to provide employment and income to unemployed residents. The Salvation Army gave them breakfasts in exchange for sawing wood.[548]

Along with low farm prices and the Great Depression, the region confronted a drought that reached historic proportions. It was most severe and prolonged in the southern counties. In the ninety-five years beginning in 1889, Lamar recorded twelve years when annual precipitation fell below ten inches; five of them were in the 1930s.[549] Record heat compounded the damage from lack of water. Virtually all weather-reporting stations in the sixteen counties registered above-average mean May-September temperatures through most of the decade. In 1934 average summer temperatures in Cheyenne Wells were more than six degrees above normal for the season. Las Animas reached a high of 114 degrees in July 1933, and in July of the following year, Lamar's temperature reached 111[550] and Sterling's a record 105 degrees.[551] The combination of heat and drought destroyed dryland wheat and corn crops and rendered pasture lands unable to support cattle. *The Lamar Daily News* reported in 1933 that Baca County wheat and corn crops had been "entirely burned out."[552]

The drought's damage was not confined to dryland farming and ranching. Reduced flows in the South Platte and Arkansas limited water for irrigation. Annual flow in the Arkansas fell to nearly half that of the previous twenty years. On July 21, 1934, the *Pueblo Chieftain* reported that the Arkansas had stopped flowing. Irrigators with junior water rights frequently received little or no water. Irrigators on the lower Arkansas saw water delivered from the Fort Lyon Canal drop from 248,000-acre feet in 1929 to 101,000 in 1934 and that from the Amity from 131,000 in 1924 to 32,000 in 1934.[553] Fort Lyon management attempted an equitable allocation that often meant denying farmers needed water. Some with dying crops reacted angrily breaking the locks on the gates that controlled flow to their fields, forcing the company to resort to lawsuits. Many farmers lacked funds to pay their assessment and the canal company barely avoided bankruptcy.[554] Board president M. M. Simpson lamented, "The old belt is up to the last hole."[555] Conflict between irrigators and the ditch companies became so heated in the summer of 1934 that the Colorado National Guard was called out to protect Rocky Ford Ditch users by shutting down upstream irrigators' illegal diversions.[556]

The lack of rainfall and below-normal flows in the rivers inspired political and business leaders to consider engineering projects that might in time alleviate the problem. These included diverting water from Colorado's western slope and building storage facilities to capture water in wet years. The first diversion project brought water to Twin Lakes Reservoir a few miles east of the Continental Divide. The reservoir was built shortly before the turn of the century to provide water for farmers in today's Crowley County as described in chapter 2. In response to the 1930s drought, a four-mile tunnel was dug just south of Independence Pass to collect water from the Roaring Fork River and its tributaries to be stored in the reservoir. The project was partially financed by the Reconstruction Finance Corporation and was completed in 1935.[557] Two larger projects were also initiated but not finished in time to provide relief during the thirties. The Colorado-Big Thompson project was designed to move water from the Colorado River under the Continental Divide to farmers and other users in northeastern Colorado. Planning and engineering studies were begun in 1934 and construction work was underway in 1938 but no water was delivered to South Platte Valley farmers until the 1950s.[558] Arkansas Valley boosters lobbied for Federal funds for construction of Caddoa Dam east of Las Animas. A *Lamar Daily News* editorial declared, "Caddoa Dam holds the key to the future prosperity of this Valley. It is not just an idle pipe dream of having the government spend a lot of money in this locality but is the determining factor as to whether or not farming is to be carried on in a region that has for many years been highly productive."[559] Construction of the dam, by the

Army Corps of Engineers began in 1938. War time demands forced construction to be halted in 1943 and completion was delayed until 1948.

Drought and dust were not the only natural hazards. Extraordinarily dry weather created ideal conditions for grasshoppers, and the insects responded with record hatches. In 1937 the *Springfield Democrat-Herald* declared "Colorado's Worst Hopper Plague."[560] Federal aid and resident volunteers were marshaled to confront the infestation. Etymologists and county agents recommended a multi-pronged attack including spraying, particularly important early in the season, fall plowing to bury the eggs, and raising turkeys to devour the hoppers.[561] In 1934 the state Agricultural Extension Service borrowed airplanes from the Army to spray.[562] In the summer of 1938, the Baca county agent warned of an impending hopper plague and urged farmers to spread poison and notify the agent of insects laying eggs.[563] The CCC camp at Hugo hauled five million pounds of grasshopper poison.[564] In a WPA grasshopper control project, ninety-two men spread poison on abandoned land.[565] J. D. Hughbanks, a Logan County farmer, reaped unexpected profited from his efforts to fight the grasshoppers. He bought a hundred turkeys to control the insects. Soon the demand for turkeys for holiday meals became a profitable business line. He later expanded his operation with a processing plant in Sterling for his and other farmers' birds.[566]

The jackrabbit population also exploded. Reasons for this proliferation are not clear although Douglas Hurt speculated that either the drought improved breeding conditions, or the hares migrated into the drought area in search of grass.[567] Residents confronted the animals with drives where the rabbits were forced toward a central point where they could be clubbed to death. In December 1934, a drive in Phillips County reportedly killed seven thousand animals.[568] The Baca County agent scheduled a drive in March 1935 urging residents to take part, "unless the dust is too terrific."[569] In 1939 CCC campers clubbed 805 rabbits to death near Hugo.[570]

The New Deal's depression programs furnished much of the funding for both relief projects and agricultural improvements as state and local governments' resources were limited in the depression economy. For the year ending July 1, 1935, payments on AAA contracts to farmers in eastern Colorado's sixteen counties totaled $4.3 million. Of this amount almost one third went to wheat farmers, 45 percent was paid to farmers enrolling in the corn-hog program and one-quarter to beet growers.[571] The Civilian Conservation Corps (CCC) employed young men on conservation and natural resource development projects, many of which benefitted farmers. John Martin, the Congressman representing Southeast Colorado, requested that Baca County be given the highest priority in locating a Civilian Conservation Corps (CCC) camp to aid in soil conservation projects. The Congressman wrote, "We estimate that the minimum acreage in this county alone which will need soil erosion work to be 500,000 acres. It is imperative that we have assistance thru CCC camps."[572] A camp near Springfield opened in July 1935.[573] Several CCC camps in eastern Colorado were assigned to the Soil

Conservation Service including those in Springfield, Cheyenne Wells, Hugo, Elbert and Sterling. Campers' work included range re-vegetation, tree planting and exterminating grasshoppers. In three years, the camp in Sterling constructed 145 earth dams, 143 miles of terraces, 1,683 miles of contour furrows, 7,861 acres of range re-vegetation, and planted 45,731 trees.[574]

The Works Progress Administration (WPA) provided jobs for the unemployed and upgraded local infrastructure. The WPA projects in eastern Colorado communities included constructing new school buildings and remodeling old ones.[575] In Vona, the town's water system was upgraded by replacing its aging water tank. A WPA project in Baca County employed some fifty-five women in what was described as a "repair sewing project."[576] The Rural Electrification Association (REA) brought electric power to farms and rural households. In 1939, one hundred miles of transmission lines were approved to serve Phillips and Sedgwick Counties.[577]

The burgeoning automobile age demanded more roads, and public works programs constructing new highways reached an unprecedented scale. Federal aid was supplemented by state government funds from an auto-users tax on motor fuel. A history of the Colorado Department of Transportation described the depression era as one that "proved a boon to road construction in Colorado."[578] In 1930 only seventy-nine miles of road in eastern Colorado were labeled "hard surface"; ten years later the region boasted more than nine-hundred miles of oiled or paved state highways.[579] Construction funds frequently provided work relief as well as new roads.

Eastern Plains Farming and Ranching in the 1930s

The plains farm economy weathered the early years of the depression reasonably well. The President of the Simla State Bank wrote, "Elbert County never really felt the current depression very badly until the latter part of 1931."[580] Farmers were able to partially offset the effects of lower prices through further expanding production. The value of crops in 1930 in the region was down only slightly from the previous year.[581] Rainfall was ample in most areas in 1930 and 1931.

But the good fortune was not to last. Plains crop farmers' incomes soon plunged as markets collapsed and drought cut yields. In 1931 the value of crops fell sharply with all counties except Baca, which enjoyed a record harvest, posting declines of at least half. The drought worsened in 1932, bringing a further decline in crop value of 43 percent, this time including all the counties.[582] Land prices plummeted. Joe Oswald recalled that in 1938 some of the best land in Kiowa County was only bringing two or three dollars per acre.[583] Farms were abandoned, especially later in the decade as operators were either forced out through foreclosure or gave up when faced with seemingly hopeless prospects. The number of farms in the sixteen counties fell by more than five thousand or roughly one-fourth between 1935 and 1940 with the largest declines in the southern counties where conditions were worse. In Baca County the number of farms was halved over the five years, and it fell by more than 30 percent in Kit Carson, Lincoln, and Prowers Counties.

Reports from regional bankers whose portfolios were heavily weighted toward agricultural loans reflected the desperate conditions. A La Junta banker wrote, "The year 1931 was possibly the poorest ever experienced by the Arkansas Valley." No improvement was forthcoming. A year later the president of a Limon bank reported, "the 1931 crop was poor and the 1932 crop was as near a complete failure as we have ever seen here." The bleak outlook continued into 1935 when, according to a Fort Morgan banker, "Crops on non-irrigated land were almost a complete failure and most dryland farmers did not raise enough feed to carry their livestock through the winter." From Wray came this cryptic comment: "summer drought, no wheat, no corn, cheap cattle, cheap hogs, very little feed crops." According to a Las Animas banker, "Arkansas River went dry and grazing pastures began to burn."[584]

Plains farmers and their families were forced to reduce their standards of living, often drastically. *The Sterling Farm Journal* reported more than five-thousand farm families in central and eastern Colorado in distress.[585] Rural communities reacted with anger and despair. In Sedgwick County a mob of five hundred farmers recovered $300 worth of farm machinery that had been repossessed from a County farmer by International Harvester,[586] and two hundred farmers gathered at the county courthouse to protest taxes.[587] A financially stressed Brush farmer killed his three family members and then hanged himself from his windmill.[588]

Eastern Colorado agriculture had long been at the mercy of weather and world markets. Now another uncontrollable was added: the vagaries of American politics. The expansion of federal farm programs cushioned some of the effects of weather and markets. But they also revealed the distance in mileage and perception between eastern Colorado and Washington although Washington's focus on the region sharpened when dust storms reached that city in 1934. The emphasis of the first AAA on limiting production failed to address the problems of the drought-plagued southern plains where production was already well below its earlier levels. Nonetheless, the government's acreage reduction programs were generally viewed as a good deal by farmers. If the land was producing nothing, taking it out of production cost little and farmers and ranchers received badly needed funds.

Wheat was the first regional crop affected by acreage reductions. Growers who signed up for the allotment program were required to reduce planting and were compensated with payments from the Treasury. For the first two years of the program, farmers who agreed to reduce their acreage by 15 percent received thirty cents per bushel and could keep the proceeds from selling their wheat. Most of the larger growers in the region enrolled but it was less beneficial to smaller operators, frequently the most distressed. Reduced cultivation left land barren and increased wind erosion and blowing dust.

Even a meager wheat crop helped hold the soil. This flaw was eventually corrected, and farmers were permitted to plant some corn or grain sorghum for roughage on land covered by the allocation contracts. After the AAA was ruled unconstitutional new legislation provided additional payment in drought areas for soil conservation. Logan County conservation measures included 770 miles of terraces, 1,724 miles of windbreaks, 115 miles of concrete ditches, 228 miles of underground irrigation pipe, over 100 miles of concrete ditch lining, and 760 watering facilities.[589]

Growers often discovered that the wheat they had planted in the fall was not worth harvesting the following summer. Acreage harvested as a share of that planted dropped sharply as both expected yield and price declined. Baca County growers harvested 85 percent of the acreage planted in 1929 through 1931 but only 32 percent in 1932 and 1933, while Phillips County saw the share harvested drop from 87 percent to 31 percent and Yuma County from 85 percent to 26 percent.[590] Wheat production continued to fall through the middle 1930s. Government programs explained only a part of the decline as output after 1933 fell by far more than mandated by the AAA and its successors or than in the rest of the nation. Regional growers raised more wheat toward the end of the decade as prices rose and precipitation increased, with the recovery more pronounced in the northern counties. In Yuma, Washington and Phillips Counties wheat production was beginning to pick up as early as 1937. Baca County, on the other hand, experienced only a modest increase by 1939.[591]

The corn program required reduction in both corn acreage and the number of hogs since a large portion of the corn crop was fed to swine. Farmers were, in effect, selling corn in the form of pork. The program got underway in the fall of 1933 by which time both corn and hog prices had fallen more than 50 percent from their 1929 levels.[592] Corn growers received payments of forty-five cents per bushel, based on average yield, for land taken out of production. Hog farmers were required to reduce their 1934 litters by one-fourth the number farrowed in the previous two years and received $5 per head. This program was one of the more controversial New Deal farm measures. It was plagued with administrative delays. The *Springfield Democrat-Herald* described the program as "the most difficult of any to administer and took the longest to get into operation."[593] Reducing litters gave rise to lurid stories about farmers killing baby pigs. Nonetheless most plains farmers signed up for the program. Corn acreage dropped by almost three-fourths in the southern and central dryland counties and by over half in the rest of the region, and swine population in the plains counties fell by two-thirds between 1933 and 1935.[594]

US sugar producers had long been protected by high tariffs that were raised further by the Smoot-Hawley Act. But prices still slumped, falling almost 30 percent between 1929 and 1933. The decline was felt by processors as well as by growers. GW reported a loss of almost half a million dollars in 1931 and more than a million in 1932.[595] Producers lobbied for further protection, but urban politicians and US trading partners balked. Sugar beets were not included as a basic commodity in the initial Agricultural Adjustment Act, and sugar's tariff protection was cut sharply in 1934. After further political pressure from growers and the sugar companies, the 1934 Jones-Costigan Sugar Act, sponsored by a Colorado senator, set up a marketing allotment. Quotas based on past production were set for regions of the country that were then allocated among sugar companies. The companies then determined how much to contract with their farmers. Growers signing up for the program would receive thirty cents per ton on their 1933 crop and $1.50 on their 1934 crop. Local politicians cited the act as a solution to most of the industry's ills. Eastern Colorado's congressman claimed assurance from a high government official that "The domestic sugar industry is today the best stabilized and protected industry in America."[596] According to the *Denver Post*, Logan County farmers received almost $1 million in beet payments in 1936.[597] The Act also included regulation of wages and working conditions for beet workers. It prohibited field labor by children under fourteen and limited work by those between fourteen and sixteen to eight hours daily with growers' offspring exempt.[598] The child labor provisions were unpopular with some producers who had become dependent on families working their fields. Production was largely maintained in the South Platte Valley where irrigation water was more plentiful, but in the Arkansas Valley irrigation companies discouraged planting of water-consuming beets.[599]

As prospects for corn and wheat deteriorated, dryland farmers planted more sorghum. It is a hardy plant and withstands drought well, thus providing some ground cover to limit wind erosion as well as a feed supplement for cattle. The crop was not covered by an allocation program, so it could be grown on land taken out of wheat or corn production. Dryland acreage in Baca, Kit Carson and Yuma Counties saw the sharp gains in sorghum cultivation. By 1939 regional acreage planted in sorghum had almost doubled from its level ten years earlier.[600]

Ranchers and feeders were also buffeted by drought and market conditions. Herd reductions in the late 1920s gave rise to higher prices in the early 1930s. The healthy market meant that neither ranchers nor the government wanted cattle included as a basic commodity in the AAA. But even as the market remained strong, cattle ranchers suffered from a shortage of credit when local banks failed or restricted their lending. Then the effects of depressed consumer incomes on beef consumption brought a collapse in the cattle market in 1933 with prices falling to less than half their 1929 levels. At the same time pastures deteriorated under drought conditions and ranchers became more dependent on supplemental feed. Reliance on the range for cattle sustenance throughout the Great Plains dropped from 80 percent in 1929 to 71 percent in 1935.[601] But feed crop yields had fallen, and many ranchers lacked funds to purchase additional fodder. In 1934 Prowers County's irrigated alfalfa crop was estimated at 40 percent of normal.[602] Some cattlemen cut Russian thistle to stave off starvation of their herds.[603] As distress mounted, regional ranchers became more receptive to federal assistance.

CHAPTER 5

The Jones-Connally Relief Bill (1934) authorized government cattle purchases in drought areas where pasture and feed were insufficient. The cattle were either destroyed or slaughtered to provide food for relief families. Bill Dodge recalled federal agents shooting cattle on a neighbor's ranch southwest of Granada.[604] The price for the cattle was determined by appointed local appraisers and was usually around $13 per head. This was far from a premium price as the Agricultural Marketing Service estimated the average cost per one-hundred pounds of cattle slaughtered in July 1934 at $4.55 and the average weight at 901 pounds.[605] Initial purchases under this program were confined to the northern plains but were extended to the southeast by mid-summer. Purchases began in Baca, Bent, and Prowers Counties in July 1934. The number of cattle purchased was limited by funding of the bill and amounted to only seven thousand Prowers County cattle in the summer of 1934.[606]

By fall conditions had worsened and southern plains ranchers urged increased purchases. Raymond McMillin, scion of an early ranching family whose homesteading experience was described in chapter 2, was president of the Bent-Prowers Cattle and Horse Growers Association. He pled with state program administrators, "There are approximately 168,000 head of livestock in this region and of this number 25,000 head should be moved immediately. Unless a greater quota can be obtained for this region many growers will be ruined financially through the loss of most or all of their herds."[607] An allotment was authorized for the purchase of an additional eight hundred head in October and three thousand more in December.[608] Although still short of the relief cattlemen desired, purchases did provide some needed cash and helped bring herd sizes somewhat closer to range capacity. Additional aid to ranchers came from the Farm Credit Administration's loans to cattlemen for transportation of their herds to new pastures and rangelands.[609]

Further assistance came from emergency financing for feed. The government also targeted the longer-term problems in the cattle industry by allocating funds for the restoration of pasture damaged by drought and overgrazing. Later legislation encouraged ranchers to limit the intensity of grazing by allowing pasture to lie fallow for part of the year and limiting the number of cattle on an acre of land. Cattlemen were paid thirty-five cents for each animal unit kept off grass in 1937. Federal programs also encouraged replanting grazing lands with grasses that were more drought and erosion resistant and subsidized digging wells.

Dust Bowl historian Paul Bonnifield, who was generally critical of the government's farm measures, characterized cattle purchases as the most successful program in providing relief and potential for recovery.[610] But the government programs were insufficient to sustain the industry. The number of cattle in the sixteen counties fell by one-third between 1934 and 1936.[611] The southern and central plains counties saw the largest drops. Baca County's beef cattle population fell 69 percent while Bent, Cheyenne, Crowley, Kiowa, and Prowers all saw the size of their herds fall by close to half. By contrast the northern counties of Logan, Phillips, Sedgwick, Washington, and Yuma experienced only modest reductions or even small increases.

Conditions for farmers and ranchers began to improve toward the end of the decade although falling well short of a return to earlier prosperity. Prices rose and the drought abated, more so in the northern counties. By 1936 and 1937, production restrictions in federal programs began to take effect, and regional crop revenues were showing signs of recovery. The total value of all crops sold in 1936 was more than twice that in 1932.[612] A Lamar bank president reported "….1936 had proved to be the best year the lower Arkansas Valley has had in six years." According to a Sterling banker, farmers in his area benefitted from heavy moisture early in the year although a drier summer and grasshoppers damaged crops. In 1938, a Rocky Ford banker claimed, "The Arkansas Valley enjoyed one of its best years as there was an ample supply of water to ensure the farmers under all of our ditches a sufficient amount to properly mature their crops." From Kit Carson: "crops and grass excellent." The Las Animas area enjoyed "the best beet harvest in terms of tonnage in 20 years." However, most bankers tempered their optimism as prices for both crops and livestock were still low. They reported shortages of irrigation water in the Arkansas Valley in 1939 except in Crowley County where farmers benefitted from the Twin Lakes diversion project.[613] By 1939-40 crop values in the irrigated counties had rebounded to more than 70 percent of their 1930-31 values while the dryland counties had reached just over 40 percent of their earlier peaks.[614]

Cattlemen's prospects also began to brighten. Prices edged upward in 1935, and increased rainfall toward the end of the decade improved grazing conditions. Ranchers and farmers restored their herds in much of the region. By 1940 beef cattle population was within 7 percent of its 1929 level. The cattle business, like the rest of agriculture, recovered more slowly in the southeast; in 1940 Baca County reported only ninety-three hundred head compared with more than twenty thousand in 1929 and Prowers County saw a drop of more than one-third.[615]

The Non-farm Economy

Eastern Colorado businesses struggled to survive in the face of a devastated agricultural sector and the worldwide depression. Although farmers and ranchers undoubtedly endured the greatest hardships, business owners and workers in the plains towns also suffered. The hard times endured in industry, trade, and services are borne out by employment figures in the 1930 and 1940 Censuses. The 25,000 odd workers outside agriculture in 1930, 44 percent of the total workforce, saw their numbers fall by more than 3,300 or 13 percent over the decade. Although the entire nation experienced the Great Depression, farming areas such as Colorado's plains saw larger job losses. Nationally the number of nonfarm workers fell by only 4.3 percent. (The 1940 figures exclude persons employed in public emergency work programs.) Decade-ending statistics almost certainly understate the job loss at the depths of the recession as US employment saw a resurgence toward the end of the decade, and it is likely that the region also experienced some rebound. Nearly all plains industries lost jobs during the decade and all counties except Bent and Washington saw a fall in nonfarm employment. Bent County benefitted from the expansion of the Veterans Administration neuropsychiatric facility at Fort Lyon and the construction of Caddoa Dam while Washington County posted a gain of only two jobs. The dryland counties in the southern part of the state fared the worst with Baca County losing two-fifths of its non-farm employees and Kiowa County more than one-third.

Census of Manufacturing estimates show that the number of manufacturing establishments in the region fell from 128 to 99 between 1929 and 1933. The industry's decline did significant harm as it removed many well-paying jobs from the economic base. The precise loss of manufacturing jobs over the decade can't be determined because of changes in the industrial classification system between the 1930 and 1940 Censuses. However, employment figures can be compared for the food and kindred products sector which accounted for nearly half the jobs in the sector including those at sugar beet plants, alfalfa mills, and other processors of farm products. Roughly one in eight food processing jobs had been lost over the decade with most in the early years when the economy was in near free fall. Sugar beet processors, with the largest numbers of workers, faced weak demand and reduced production by growers. All four firms operating in the Arkansas Valley flirted with bankruptcy[616] as the industry consolidated into larger more productive plants. As noted earlier, Great Western Sugar, dominant in the South Platte Valley, suffered major damage to its balance sheet.

With both passenger travel and shipments of goods plunging train traffic dropped sharply. La Junta, with its sizable Santa Fe presence, bore the brunt of downturn, losing over three hundred jobs. In 1926 eight trains from the east, six from the west, and five on the Denver line passed through town daily. By 1934 the numbers had been reduced to six, four, and three.[617] Santa Fe also closed its regional offices in La Junta and stopped the practice of passengers disembarking to eat at the city's Harvey House restaurant. However, operations continued at the railroad repair facilities. Other communities were also affected. In Limon the Rock Island reduced "its yard, shop and road forces to a minimum."[618] Santa Fe provided a brief stimulus to the region's economy in 1936 when the company undertook a 115-mile line from Boise City, Oklahoma through Springfield to Las Animas at a cost of $3.75 million providing temporary construction jobs for hundreds of men over the next two years.[619]

Merchants in the plains communities were forced to retrench or go out of business as loss of income and declining population made for a difficult sales environment. By 1933 automobile sales in Sterling had fallen to a third of their earlier peak.[620] Retail sales in the sixteen counties fell by 46 percent, after adjusting for inflation, between 1929 and 1933. Spending picked up later in the decade, but by 1939 sales were still 16 percent below their level ten years earlier.[621] Local tax bases shrunk as the economy contracted. Limon's city government reported slumping collections as well as difficulties collecting water bills and even dog taxes.[622] Total county tax collections for the region fell 32 percent between 1930 and 1934 and were still down 30 percent by 1939.[623]

The national economy had begun a slow recovery from the depression by the late 1930s, but the rebound in the eastern plains was even more modest. Receipts from Colorado's sales tax that the state began collecting in the spring of 1935 suggest that any improvement was, at best, meager. Receipts for the sixteen counties in 1939 and 1940 were down 2.2 percent over those in 1936 and 1937.[624]

Conditions were somewhat better in counties where the drought was less harsh. Otero County's irrigated farmers benefitted from more senior water rights than those further down the Valley and the town economies recovered more quickly. By 1936 accounts of the plains counties were becoming somewhat more positive. The *Denver Post* reported that in Rocky Ford, "farm produce is bringing a high price, and men are finding jobs" and that an upturn in business by the Santa Fe Railroad brought La Junta greater prosperity than "any year since 1929."[625] In Sterling, bankers noted the most deposits since 1929 and an improving real estate market.[626]

Banking

The collapse of the nation's banking sector in the early thirties was both a consequence and a cause of the severity of the depression. Many economic historians rate failures in the banking system as a most important contributor to turning an economic downturn into an unprecedented depression. Former Federal Reserve Chairman Ben Bernanke, a student of depression-era banking, described the condition of the US financial sector in the early 1930s. "The widespread banking panics of the 1930s caused many banks to shut their doors; facing the risk of runs by depositors. Even those who remained open were forced to constrain lending to keep their balance sheets as liquid as possible."[627] More than one-fifth of US commercial banks had suspended operations before the 1933 bank holiday.[628] Federal deposit insurance had not yet been established, and media coverage of a bank's problems spread the panic to other banks. Bank failures led to a vicious cycle of further restraints in lending, leading to more businesses failing, which in turn meant more bank failures. Agricultural banks were particularly vulnerable as falling land prices wiped out much of the value of their collateral. If the farmer couldn't service his loan, a frequent occurrence due to drought and falling commodity prices, the bank was unable to recoup the value of its asset through foreclosure. The resulting reduction in the bank's capital decreased its lending capacity and threatened the confidence of depositors.

Colorado's banking system was damaged by a struggling agricultural sector in the early twenties and faced even greater stresses in the thirties. In 1942 CU finance professor Fred Niehaus's *Development of Banking in Colorado* concluded that "Business depressions were responsible for many of the failures during 1921 and 1932. Likewise, deflation of farm values and unfavorable conditions in the agricultural regions of the State after 1920 produced a depressing effect on business and banking in many parts of the Commonwealth. Since farming had become one of the chief industries of the State by 1920, these poor agricultural conditions were especially depressing in Colorado."[629] Small-town banks were the especially vulnerable; most failures between 1919 and 1936 were in communities with populations less than one thousand.[630] One hundred twenty-eight banks were operating in the region in 1920; by 1930 only eighty-eight remained. Failures continued in the thirties with the first wave in late 1930 followed by another episode in the spring and early summer of 1931.[631] Among the closed banks were the Stockgrowers State Bank of Burlington that was shuttered due to "slow collections" and the Union Bank of Yuma, brought down by "heavy withdrawals."[632] More banks failed in late 1932 with further deterioration in early 1933, aggravated by rule changes requiring publication of the names of banks receiving loans from the Reconstruction Finance Corporation (RFC), a government entity lending to struggling banks. Not surprisingly, this led to runs on many of the banks so exposed. Only fifty-eight regional banks were still open at the end of 1933.[633] The experience of Lincoln County banks summarized below was typical of the region. Six national or state banks were chartered in first two decades of century; only two were still in business in the 1940s.

> **Lincoln County Banks in Early 20th Century**
> **Listed by Year of Founding**
>
> 1903—Lincoln County Bank re-chartered as First National Bank of Hugo in 1907-still operating in 1940s.
>
> 1907—Lincoln State Bank in Arriba, failed in 1928.
>
> 1908—Limon State Bank, reorganized as Limon National Bank in 1924, failed in 1931.
>
> 1909—Genoa State Bank, reorganized as First National Bank of Genoa in 1925, voluntary liquidation in 1931, attempted merger with Limon National Bank.
>
> 1917—Farmers and Merchants Bank of Limon, reorganized as First National Bank of Limon 1919, occupied vacated bldg. of Limon National Bank in 1931-still operating in 1940s.
>
> 1918—Farmers State Bank of Bovina, became inoperative in 1931.[634]

Bank failures made ordinary financial transactions difficult. Many communities considered currency substitutes. These typically took the form of "scrip" or locally generated paper that could be used to pay workers and would be accepted by local retailers. The State Bankers Association discussed plans for issuing scrip to banks outside Denver although these plans were never executed.[635] My father recalled that when merchants in Lamar met in March 1933 to consider introducing scrip in the community,[636] he, then a recent University of Chicago graduate, cited Gresham's Law in an attempt to convince the city fathers of the futility of issuing scrip. This maxim, formulated by Sir Thomas Gresham, a sixteenth century financial advisor to the King, is often expressed as "The bad money drives out the good." When two types of money are circulating the more valuable will be withdrawn and hoarded. In depression era Lamar, issuing scrip would only lead to hoarding legitimate currency. Presumably, my father's advice was taken as I could find no reports of scrip being issued in Lamar.

In 1933, faced with a collapse of the banking system, Colorado Governor Johnson declared a state bank holiday March 3, and President Roosevelt took similar action at the national level on March 6. All bank transactions except making change were suspended through March 10. One regional bank, the Farmers Bank of Fleming, failed to receive notification of the bank holiday and continued to operate, perhaps the only bank in the nation to remain open.[637] *The Sterling Journal Advocate* reported that some local banks were not accepting checks, causing extreme distress for a Sterling man whose request to his bank for "emergency" funds to get married was turned down.[638] The Emergency Banking Act of 1933, passed quickly after the President's bank holiday declaration, set requirements for banks' reopening including more stringent capital and liquidity requirements.

Regional bankers struggled to comply with the federal directives, and not all reopened after the bank holiday. Some were able to do so later, usually with some assistance from the Federal government. The Lamar National Bank reopened in August 1934, rescued by local businessmen and a $25,000 investment from the RFC. The First National Bank of Eads resumed operations in July 1934 with similar support. The First National Bank of Stratton in Kit Carson County, which survived a capital shortfall in 1924, was faced with another. The call to raise money from current stockholders was not met, but bank officers and directors came up with additional funds. In May 1934, the bank again confronted failure and had exhausted its options for raising more capital. According to directors' minutes "We thought it was better to liquidate the bank." Ultimately the bank was able to borrow money under the Reconstruction Finance Act and survived into the 1940s.[639] The reopened banks stressed their security in the uncertain environment. In their announcement of reopening, the directors of the Lamar National Bank assured depositors that "We shall be glad to handle your account, either large or small, giving you assurance of three-fold safety. First, the Federal government insurance of deposits up to $5,000. Second, a bank with ONE HUNDRED PERCENT CASH AND GOVERNMENT BONDS, and Third, the strength and assurance of the U.S. Government investing $35,000 with us."[640]

The banks that survived did so by imposing a regime of austerity and extreme caution. A Logan County resident recalled, "It was said that the healthiest of Sterling's banks stayed in business by cutting services to a bare minimum. For instance, no interest was allowed on savings accounts, salaries were reduced, and no loan was granted for an amount exceeding 10 percent of the value of collateral."[641] Bank's balance sheets shrank. Deposits in Fort Morgan, La Junta and Lamar all fell 60 percent or more between 1929 and the end of 1934.[642] By 1940 regional banks were showing signs of recovery although the volume of loans was still well below its pre-depression level. Many of the weaker banks were absorbed by other healthier institutions in their communities. Consolidation was also driven by the increased concentration of population and economic activity in the larger towns as well as the burden of an increased level of bank regulation on smaller institutions. The number of banks continued to decline; only forty-seven banks in the sixteen counties were still operating in 1940.[643]

Bank failures and lending caution on the part of the surviving institutions meant that traditional sources of credit diminished or disappeared. A Kit Carson banker commented in 1935: "The bank has plenty of money to loan but no good borrowers."[644] This was especially threatening for farmers who depended on local banks for such needs as loans at planting time that would be repaid after the harvest. Government programs filled some of the gap. The Farm Credit Administration (FCA) loaned funds for seed and feed and other operating expenses as well as writing mortgages. In August 1934

FCA made emergency feed and forage loans to farmers and ranchers in the drought area as well as seed and crop loans.[645] Federal Land Banks provided long-term mortgages to farmers and ranchers. The Agricultural Adjustment Administration made advance payments for basic crops when farmers signed up for allotments—in effect crop loans to cover early-growing-season expenses. Sugar beet growers were entitled to advance benefit payments of "more than a dollar per ton" [646] in 1934. The Farm Credit Act of 1933 authorized farmers to organize Production Credit Associations (PCAs) to deliver short- and intermediate-term loans to farmers and ranchers. PCAs also made loans to these borrowers for basic processing and marketing activities and to farm-related businesses.

Emigration

Population growth slowed in the twenties and the thirties brought unprecedented losses. As the agricultural sector collapsed and the towns' economies struggled many residents sought a better life elsewhere, even in depression-ravaged America. Many high-plains farmers abandoned their land and either left the region or moved to nearby towns. Grim economic prospects also raised the incentives for townspeople to move. The region's population fell by more than twenty-one thousand over the decade, a decline of 13 percent[647] while that of the nation grew more than 7 percent despite a declining birth rate and limits on migration. Fifteen of the sixteen eastern plains counties had fewer people in 1940 Census than in 1930 with only Bent County showing an increase. The arid central and southern plains saw the largest declines with Baca County losing more than 40 percent of its people. Cheyenne, Kiowa, Lincoln and Kit Carson Counties all lost more than one-fifth of their populations.

Population losses were greatest in the countryside as thousands of farms were abandoned. John Nolan attempted a hog-feeding operation on his Logan County farm, but three cents a pound for hogs and five cents a bushel for corn failed to cover his costs. He bought a gas station in Proctor.[648] Another Logan County farmer, Henry Nikel, moved to a dryland farm north of Padroni after his marriage in 1929, but was forced to abandon it in 1936 and took a job operating a water truck for the City of Sterling.[649] Fewer farms meant less demand for goods and services by farm families. Trade and service establishments in the smaller communities closed and population became more concentrated in larger trading centers. Most of the larger towns either added population or suffered relatively small losses as many who abandoned their farms or hamlets moved into nearby towns. Lamar's population grew 5 percent during the 1930s while the remainder of Prowers County lost 25 percent of its people. Similarly, Sterling grew 3 percent and the rest of Logan County declined by 14 percent. Springfield was an exception with a shrinking population, but by proportionally less than the rest of Baca County.[650]

Although birth rates dropped during the thirties the relatively young population meant that births still exceeded deaths for a positive "natural increase." But this gain was more than offset by people leaving. Over thirty-six thousand more people were estimated to have left the region than moved in.[651] Most of the migration was work related. The highest rates of out-migration were among young people who were entering the work force, those ten to nineteen years old in 1930. Men in this age group, and most workers were men, had less attachment to their jobs or farms and were more willing to risk pulling up stakes for better opportunities. Their wives and children followed them. School enrollments dropped sharply. Emigration left a much older population at the end of the decade. The proportion of those 55 and older in the region rose from 10 percent in 1930 to 15 percent in 1940.[652]

Out-migration was higher for the more rural counties and for those where the agricultural situation was the most precarious, particularly those in the Dust Bowl in the southeast. The highest rates of emigration occurred in Kiowa, Kit Carson, Lincoln and Baca Counties with the last of these by far the largest. As families left, school enrollments fell. The number of pupils in the sixteen counties dropped from more than 48,000 in 1932 to slightly less than 34,000 in 1940 with the largest losses in the central and southern counties.[653] Baca County enrollment fell by half and Cheyenne, Kit Carson, Lincoln and Prowers Counties all reported declines of close to 40 percent.

The Plains Region in 1940

By the end of the decade, residents were hopeful that the worst might be over. Prices for farm produce had begun to edge up. Precipitation was approaching normal levels. The national economy was emerging from the Great Depression, and early war mobilization brought additional spending and new jobs. But the scars of the drought and depression remained. The financial conditions of surviving farmers were often perilous, many businesses had closed, and local governments' resources were inadequate for meeting the needs of their still impoverished citizens. The population was, on average, markedly older than at the beginning of the decade and many workers still lacked jobs. The looming threat of world war brought further insecurity.

Chapter 5 Exhibits

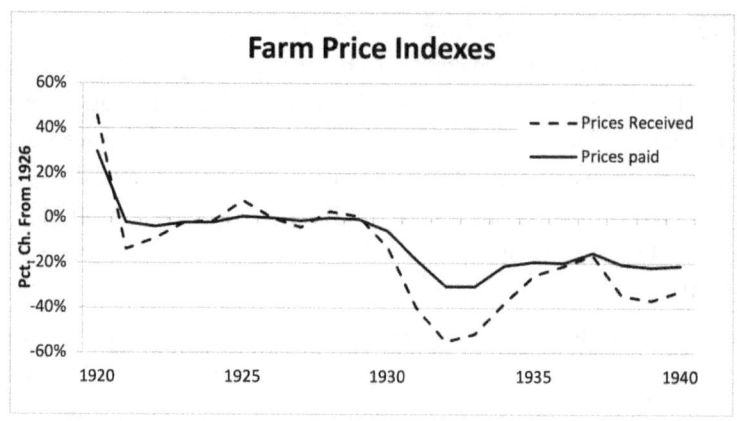

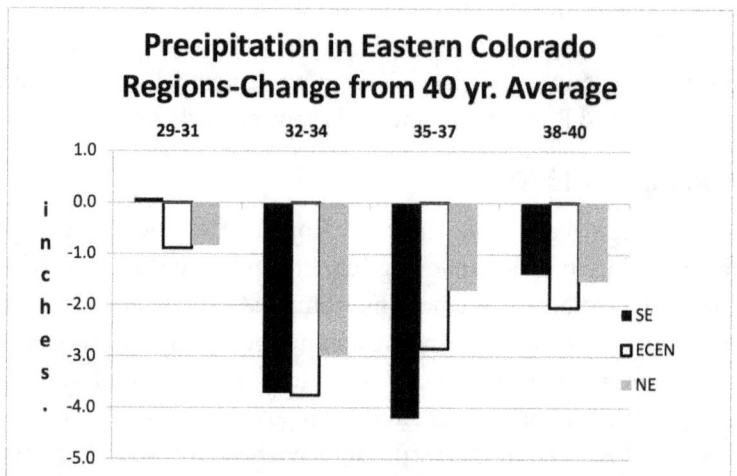

The overall index of prices received by farmers declined by more than that of prices paid. Record yields and diminished foreign demand reduced demand in the early and middle twenties, and the onset of the depression caused already depressed prices to drop even further.

Following the onset of the Depression, Colorado's plains economy was hit by severe drought that was worst in the southeast and central plains. Precipitation remained below its long-term average throughout the 1930s.

Source: USDA, Colorado Agricultural Yearbook 1941.The second chart includes counties outside plains region. SE includes Baca, Bent, Crowley, Custer, Fremont, Huerfano, Las Animas, Otero, Prowers and Pueblo Counties. E CEN includes Adams, Arapaho, Cheyenne, Denver, Douglas, Elbert, El Paso, Kiowa, Kit Carson, Lincoln Phillips, Washington and Yuma Counties. NE includes Boulder, Jefferson, Larimer, Logan, Morgan, Sedgwick and Weld Counties.

CHAPTER 5

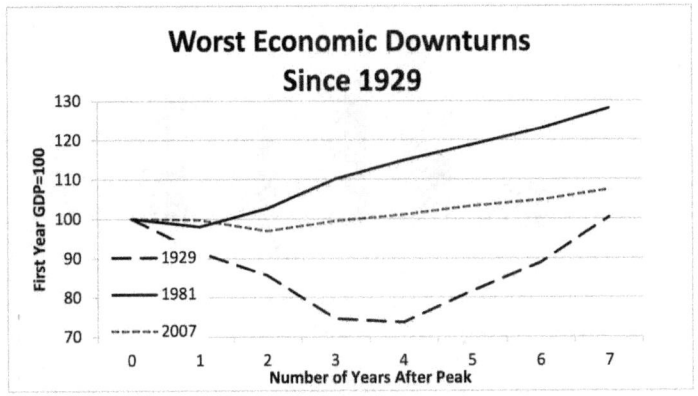

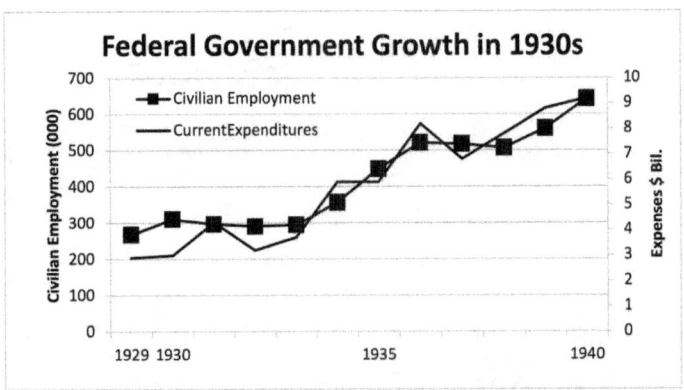

The Great Depression of the 1930s was the most severe in the nation's history. The top chart compares it to the two worst recent downturns, that in the early 1980s and the 2007-9 "Great Recession." In the thirties real GDP fell by more than one-quarter and did not return to its earlier peak for seven years.

The US government responded with unprecedented spending and intervention in the economy. Federal expenditures doubled and the number of Federal workers tripled by 1940.

Source: BEA

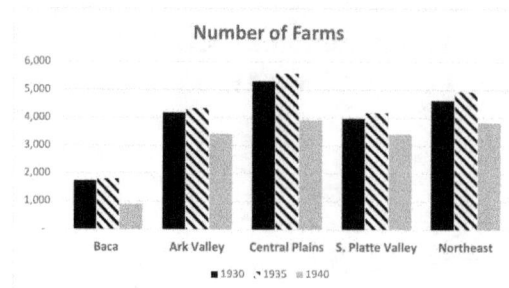

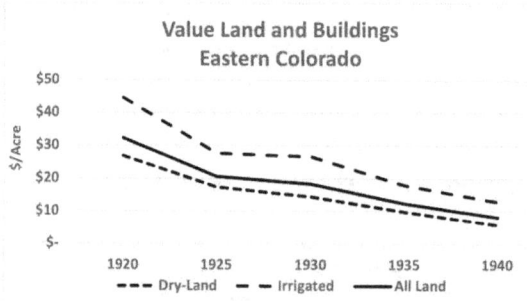

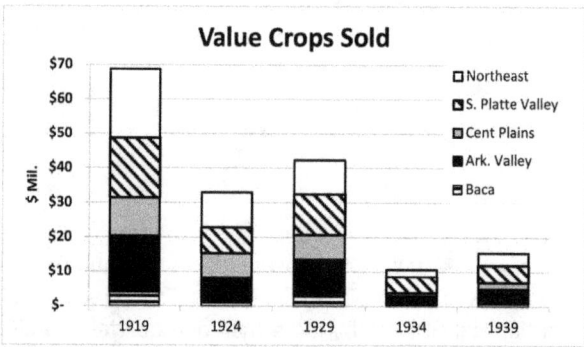

Most regional farmers continued to operate through the early thirties but by the latter part of the decade continuing drought and low prices drove many off their land. The decline in the number of farms was largest in the dryland counties, especially in Baca County and the Central Plains.

Land values peaked in the late teens and declined in the twenties as prices fell. The thirties saw further loss in value as conditions worsened. The dryland counties posted larger declines throughout the twenty years.

The value of crops sold by regional farmers fell in the early 1920s as post-war demand slackened. It recovered somewhat before plummeting again in the 1930s. The dryland farms in Baca County saw the greatest drop-off in the thirties.

Source: Census of Agriculture

CHAPTER 5

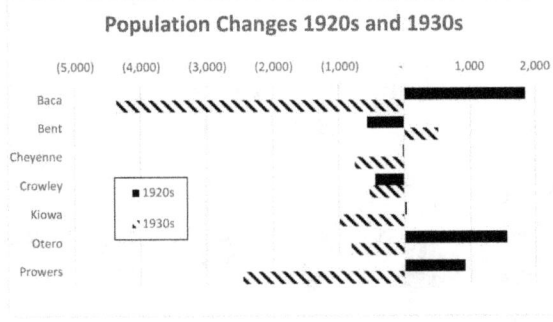

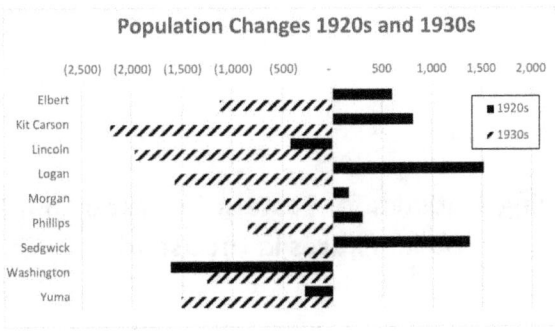

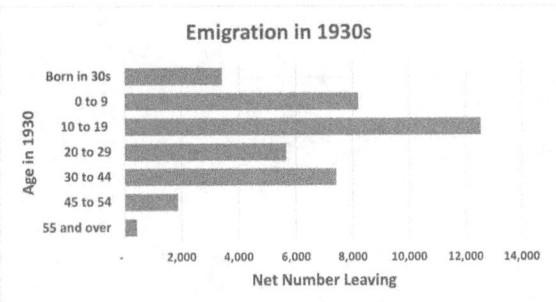

Population growth slowed in the twenties as the weak farm economy discouraged immigration. Worsening conditions in the thirties caused the region to lose more than twenty thousand people. All counties except Bent posted declines with the largest in the Dust Bowl counties of Baca and Prowers.

The greatest share of resident leaving the region were among young working-age people and their families. People in these age groups were less likely to have ties to the region such as jobs or homes they owned.

Source: Census. Migration estimates derived from Census population figures and national survival and fertility estimates for the decade. See Appendix for details.

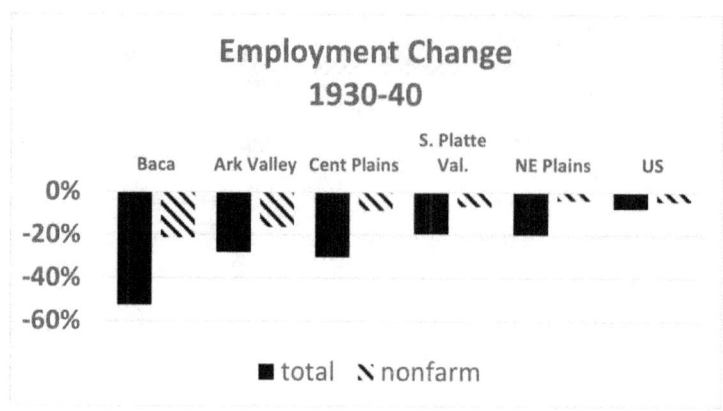

Banking Statistics for Eastern Colorado Counties
Dollar figures in thousands

	1929	1933	1940
Loans & Discounts	$ 16,669	$ 5,386	$ 10,170
Pct Ch.		-68%	89%
Deposits	$ 22,100	$ 9,506	$ 20,677
Pct Ch.		-57%	118%
Total Assets	$ 27,590	$ 14,210	$ 23,890
Pct Ch.		-48%	68%
Number of Banks	88	58	47

The devastation suffered by the region's farmers and ranchers as well as the worldwide depression wreaked havoc on the high-plains economy. Total employment in the region fell by one-quarter during the 1930s. Job losses were greater on farms and ranches, but most other industries also saw a decline in employment.

Bank failures were common in the late twenties and early thirties. After the bank holiday in 1933 many institutions did not reopen. Agricultural banks were especially vulnerable. Although conditions improved later in the decade, the number of banks continued to fall.

Source: Census; Colorado Banking Commission reported in *Colorado Yearbooks*

CHAPTER 6

The Dust Bowl

THE 1930S DROUGHT AND WIND EROSION THAT RAVAGED AMERICA'S SOUTHERN plains has been called one of the worst ecological disasters in world history[654] and has become a part of our nation's heritage and folklore. William E. Riebsame, a geography professor at the University of Colorado, characterized the dust bowl as "one of the enduring symbols of the American experience."[655] Its photographs of beleaguered farmers standing in front of their homes that were buried in dirt rank with apple stands and Hooverville shanty towns as icons of the Great Depression. The 1930s drought was the worst in the nation's history, affecting twenty-two states and almost three-fourths of US land area, with its most severe effects on the southern plains where rainfall remained at record lows for several years.

The national media coined the label "Dust Bowl" for the most affected parts of the plains, where throughout late winter and early spring, high winds carried dirt from fields that received insufficient precipitation to grow crop cover. Most of eastern Colorado experienced drought, wind erosion, and blowing dust during the thirties. But the climate was most destructive in the southeastern part of the state, especially in Baca along with southern Prowers and Bent Counties. These three counties along with twenty-three others in nearby portions of Kansas, the Oklahoma and Texas panhandles, and New Mexico suffered the worst soil erosion, were the focus of federal relief programs, and received the most publicity. These counties were the heart of the Dust Bowl.

Drought in Southeast Colorado

Drought and wind erosion on the plains were no surprise to long-time residents. Paul Bonnifield[656] and Douglas Hurt[657] in their writings on the Dust Bowl pointed out that blowing dirt had been noted by visitors to the region as early as the 1830s. Jacob Hasart, a Russian immigrant who settled near Akron in 1889, recalled that in 1904, "we had such a terrible dust storm that we lost almost everything, so we packed up and moved to Kansas."[658] Vance Johnson described drought and dust storms in Cheyenne County in 1912 and 1913.[659] The region may be uniquely vulnerable to wind erosion. Douglas Hurt pointed out that soil in the Dust Bowl differs from that elsewhere on the Great Plains. It is characterized by "flocculation" that causes tiny particles to cling together in clusters. With ample precipitation, channels separate the soil particles and facilitate the movement of moisture to the subsoil enhancing its productivity. But prolonged drought destroys flocculation, particularly when the soil is intensively cultivated. This causes the soil to break down into fine dust particles that are easily windblown.[660] Replacing prairie grass with commercial crops increases vulnerability to blowing. With adequate precipitation crops hold the soil in place, but when drought destroys the plants, it is exposed to the elements. Wheat was the principal dryland crop and, as Hurt pointed out, drought in the 1930s turned the wheat crop from an environmental asset into a liability. The dust storms came "not because southern Plains farmers grew too much wheat but because the drought prevented them from raising much wheat from 1932 to 1940."[661]

> During years of normal precipitation, the extensive root system of the wheat plant held the soil and offered excellent protection against wind erosion. In the droughty thirties, however, the inadequate moisture prevented a suitable growth of ground cover in the early spring "blow season." The drought then began a chain of events, the first of which was crop failure. Abandonment without a protective soil cover in turn allowed the nearly constant winds to begin erosion.[662]

If moisture was inadequate, fall plantings produced only meager ground cover for the late-winter and early-spring blowing season. Cash-strapped farmers were often unable to afford measures that might have helped hold the soil. In 1936 a plains farmer lamented to a *New York Times* reporter: "Seems like they are interested now in doing something about soil blowing. Trouble is, most farmers these last few years have had such poor crops, they don't have any money to do the things they'd like to do now."[663]

Dust Bowl narratives such as that in the documentary, *The Plow that Broke the Plains,* trace the origins of the dust bowl to a "great plow-up" in the late teens driven by the high war-time wheat price. But the surge in wheat planting in southeast Colorado lagged that in the rest of the southern plains by nearly a decade. Wheat farming in Baca County had been limited until a rail line through Springfield was completed in the late 1920s. Plantings accelerated in 1929, 1930, and 1931 with much of the new cultivation undertaken by large-scale wheat growers. Although suffering from depressed prices during the early years of the depression, southeast Colorado enjoyed more than adequate precipitation. In 1930 Springfield reported over twenty inches of rain and Lamar more than eighteen inches.[664] Farmers responded by planting more to compensate for the lower price. Early rains and a heavy late snow in 1931 produced a record crop. Baca

County farmers harvested nearly 3.6 million bushels, almost three times that in the previous year.[665] According to Ike Osteen, "wheat was everywhere. Elevators full, trains couldn't haul it all away, and every farm had great piles of wheat on the ground."[666]

Timothy Egan provides a vivid if somewhat hyperbolic description of the Baca County plow-up in his Dust Bowl narrative, The Worst Hard Time. "Baca County was the last big section of the southern plains to be torn up and planted. In ten years' time horse freighters had disappeared, cattle were run off the land, and the grass overturned."[667] Although the increase in wheat acreage was substantial, Egan exaggerates its extent and the impact on the cattle industry. According to the USDA, wheat acreage planted peaked at more than 355,000 acres in 1932, up from 120,000 in 1929, but the County has over 1.6 million acres of land. The 1930 Census reported almost 400,000 acres of cropland and nearly 700,000 acres of pastureland. If all the 235,000-acre increase in wheat planting from 1930 to 1932 had come from pasture, almost half a million acres of pastureland would have remained. Data on cattle populations exhibit no sign of reduced herds in the early thirties. Baca County tax assessors' records for 1933 show more than 32,000 range cattle not yet "run off the land," the largest number reported since the early twenties.[668] It is true that "in ten years' time" the cattle population saw a drastic decline, but it was caused by drought, depressed prices, and government programs that purchased excess cattle rather than by plowing up the County's pastureland.

By the late twenties, the wheat price had fallen substantially from its wartime high and would decline still further with the onset of the depression. In 1931 the Chicago price of No. 2 hard winter wheat was fifty-three cents per bushel, down from $1.30 only two years prior.[669] Farmers in the southern plains got even less, "somewhere around 25 cents per bushel" in the summer of 1932 according to the *Springfield Democrat-Herald*.[670] Growers struggled to increase their acreage enough to outpace the price decline. Many borrowed heavily to finance expansion, leaving them in precarious financial condition. Baca County Credit Association data showed that loans against the 1931-32 wheat crop totaled $904,000.[671] According to the local newspaper, growers would need another record crop of nearly four million bushels to clear their debt at the prevailing price.[672] Conditions remained reasonably favorable until the spring of 1932 when late freezes, dry weather, wind and hail cut prospective yields. Although a heavy rainfall in early June and warm weather promised some improvement, the *Springfield Democrat Herald* delivered a pessimistic assessment of wheat growers' prospects in the 1932 harvest. "Considering the fact that the price is no better than a year ago and that a large acreage has been hailed out, the chances of the farmer's clearing much of his indebtedness indeed looks slim."[673] The County's production that year was disappointing. Just over half the acreage planted in wheat was harvested and production was 1.5 million bushels, down almost 60 percent from the previous year, even though acreage planted had expanded by more than 40 percent.[674] While the crop was not a complete failure, it fell well short of what was needed to rescue the indebted farmers. In 1932 more than half a million acres of County agricultural land were listed as delinquent for taxes, up from fewer than a hundred thousand in 1929.[675]

Drought conditions worsened. Annual precipitation in central Baca County between 1932 and 1936 averaged six inches less than in the previous five years.[676] The fall and winter months, critical for the winter wheat crop, were even drier. A 1934 editorial in the *Lamar Daily News* lamented that precipitation in the last six months of the year had fallen from 12.3 inches in 1930 to 1.7 inches in 1931 and 3.1 inches in 1932. Although it rose to 7.3 inches in 1933, 3.8 inches of this fell in August before winter wheat had been planted.[677] In May 1935 the *Springfield Democrat-Herald* reported that "The County is starting on its fourth consecutive year of extreme drouth."[678] Residents reportedly "had taken recourse to superstitions, legends and ancient rituals of late to persuade the rain gods to smile upon them."[679] The Prairie City Sunday School near Pritchett asked the nation to join them in a prayer for rain.[680] A few showers fell on the county in the following weeks although not enough to end the drought. Buoyed by apparent success, the Sunday School repeated their plea the next year.[681] The infrequent rainstorms were often of little benefit to farmers. Rainstorms in Baca County were and still are often brief and intense. An old timer described one to me as like "a cow pissing on a flat rock." The rain from these storms quickly ran off the dry baked soil rather than being absorbed for the benefit of the crops.

The first large dust storms came in the winter of 1932. In May 1933, Baca County was hit with what the *Springfield Democrat-Herald* called "the worst storm in the memory of long-term residents." Bert Glasgow's barn was blown down as was Turk Rutheford's house. Floyd Patterson reported that his six-inch-high corn plants were completely covered with dust.[682] By 1934 the storms had become more severe and more frequent. The dusters were frightening, blackening the sky and depositing fine particles in homes. Letha Riggs, then a young girl living with her parents near Campo, recalled the family giving refuge in the basement of their home to worshipers who fled a nearby church when a dust storm hit, some fearing that they were witnessing the apocalypse.[683] The dust storms produced so much static electricity that drivers attached drag chains to their axels to prevent explosions in their gas tanks.[684]

Conditions may have reached their nadir in early 1935. A *Lamar Daily News* headline in February described a recent dust storm as the "WORST IN THIS AREA'S HISTORY."[685] The state Emergency Relief Act Director of Safety sent goggles and masks to the Baca County Relief Administrator.[686] A US Crop Service statistician reported that "Most of the range country is covered with two to three inches of fine silt. It is so dry that it is impossible to put in crops."[687] After an April duster in Baca County, a seven-year-old boy and a seventeen-year-old Walsh high school student died while being treated for dust pneumonia.[688] Red Cross emergency hospitals were set up in Springfield and Walsh.[689] Jeanne Clark, a child who had moved to Lamar from New York with her mother who sought relief from respiratory ailments, contracted dust pneumonia in the spring of 1935 and was put in the emergency ward in the town's hospital. Doctors did not know if she would survive until Easter.[690]

In April of that year, the *Springfield Democrat-Herald* described "a week of practically continuous dust storms."[691] Truck drivers coming into Springfield reported dust choked rabbits, squirrels, and other animals on the prairie. Schools and stores in the town were filled with dust. Children in Lamar's annual Easter egg hunt searched for eggs that according to a *New York Times* story were "hidden in the dust that lies deep on parks, lawns and streets."[692] CCC campers working west of Pritchett reported that "The air was so full of dust you could not see the ground you were standing on."[693] Ike Osteen, a teenager at the time, described being caught in the worst of the April storms. "Rabbits were running in front of the storm. The birds were darting and flying in all directions. We were just over the rises south of a hill. It came over the top of the hill and dropped down on us just like you would drop into a hand dug well. It was also just that dark. As it struck, we all stepped inside the Coulter house. It was so dark we could not see anyone standing shoulder to shoulder with us."[694]

Baca County agriculture was devastated. The dryness, heat, and wind virtually demolished the wheat crop. Planting, harvest, and yield all dropped sharply from record levels early in the decade. Wheat production in the County fell from 3.6 million bushels in 1931 to five thousand in 1935.[695] Damage was not limited to the wheat crop. More than one million bushels of corn were harvested in 1929; ten year later production had dropped to fewer than fifty thousand.[696] Between 1933 and 1936 the number of range cattle in the County fell from almost thirty-three thousand to fewer than ten thousand and the number of hogs from more than one-hundred-one thousand to under fourteen hundred. The average value of Baca County farmland dropped by 70 percent during the thirties. Many farmers abandoned their land. The number of farms fell by almost half over the decade.[697] But some persisted. In early 1935 as the drought and dust were at their worst, one Baca County farmer retained his optimism, certain that "If we can just get some moisture, we'll make it somehow."[698]

The economic damage extended beyond farmers and ranchers. Baca County lost more than 40 percent of its non-farm jobs over the decade.[699] Local government tax bases collapsed; Baca County's property tax valuation dropped by 20 percent between 1920 and 1936.[700] In 1929 Baca County collected over 98 percent of property taxes levied; by 1932 the share had fallen to less than 70 percent.[701] Fewer people and reduced incomes meant less business for local merchants. Baca County retailers reported that sales fell more than 60 percent between 1929 and 1933.[702] Dust was not just a burden for farmers. The Nu-Way Cleaners and the Ward Laundry in Springfield were frequently unable to delivery clean clothes during prolonged dust storms.[703] Although most larger plains towns experienced some population growth or, at worst, small declines, Springfield lost more than one-fifth of its population between 1930 and 1940 Censuses. Of the more than twenty communities established in the County in the teens and twenties, few survived the 1930s.[704] Robert T. McMillan, an economist with the Resettlement Administration, found that nearly half the dwelling units in the county had been abandoned by 1936.[705]

Rural folk leaving the dust bowl for California became a staple of Dust Bowl folklore, inspired in part by John Steinbeck's *The Grapes of Wrath*. But the Joad family in the novel was not from the arid plains but from more humid eastern Oklahoma as was the case with most of the "Okie" migrants to California. The famous passage describing a fearsome dust storm occurred during the Joad's journey west. James Gregory in his history of this renowned migration pointed out that "less than sixteen thousand people from the Dust Bowl proper ended up in California, barely 6 percent of the total from the Southwestern states. Journalists are to blame for this misunderstanding. Confusing drought with dust, and assuming that the dramatic dust storms must have had something to do with the large number of cars from Oklahoma and Texas seen crossing the California border in the mid-1930s, the press created the dramatic but misleading association between the Dust Bowl and the Southwestern migration."[706]

Although they may not have all moved to California, plenty of Dust Bowl residents left. More than five thousand of Baca County's 10,600 residents in 1930 had moved out to 1940.[707] Younger working age persons were the most likely to leave. More than half of those between five and nineteen in 1930 had moved elsewhere by 1940.[708] Ike Osteen, after graduating from Walsh high school, left his family farm in 1937 and found work on the railroad and in construction projects. He later joined the army where he fought in France before returning to Baca County after the war.[709] Baca County school enrollment dropped by more than half between 1932 and 1940.[710]

The plight of the Dust Bowl focused national attention, and the resulting publicity was often less than flattering. Media representatives flocked to Lamar or Springfield. Among the visitors were newsreel crews from Paramount News, Pathe News, and Hearst.[711] In 1937 *Colliers Weekly* published an article with the provocative title "Land Where Our Children Die." It devoted little space to children, dead or otherwise, but focused on the plains farmers and ranchers whose plight, according to the writer, was largely of their own doing. "As long as men and machines pulverize dry range land to plant wheat, the Dust Bowl will grow deeper and wider. As long as heedless greed (which will not be rewarded anyway) persists, we shall have more and bigger dust storms with all their miserable train—famine, violent death, private and public futility, insanity and lost generations." Farmers remained on their land only to feed at the public trough, and "They tell you quite candidly that they will stay here and eat their dust so long as they can farm the government, so long as the government gives them food and money."[712]

H. L. Mencken, perhaps the leading journalist and social commenter of the era, was even more derisive of struggling Dust Bowl farmers. In a 1936 article in *American Mercury* he wrote "They lack the hard diligence and pertinacity that are needed to wring a living from the earth, either where they languish or elsewhere. They are not conquerors of Nature but puerile parasites upon its bounty. …They are on their way back to the Stone Age."[713] Disdainful portrayals by outsiders were not limited to print. The influential 1936 documentary film *The Plow that Broke the Plains* generated passions on the parts of both Dust Bowl residents and outsiders.[714] It was financed by the Federal Government and directed by a consultant to the Resettlement Administration. Describing the film as "heavy handed" fails to convey its lack of context or subtlety. It portrayed relentless plowing of grasslands by long rows of large tractors pulling discs and raising billows of dust, accompanied by music that in a historic epic might provide background for pillaging Mongol hoards. Following its release, the film received praise from urban viewers for its artistic merit and its message. But it was harshly criticized by many plains residents as presenting a distorted and unfair view of their condition. The film and was withdrawn in 1939 under political pressure and not made available until 1961.

It is hardly surprisingly that these portrayals of their region were not well received by Baca County residents. The *Springfield Democrat Herald* complained that outsiders viewed their part of the nation as one where "the country is desert and the land is swept by wind and dust storms, making it literally a second Sahara."[715] A week later the paper claimed that "by the time the stories reached New York and Los Angeles it appears that most of us were dead or dying"[716] although admitting that "This County has been in the throes of about three weeks of the worst dust storms in the memory of old-timers."[717] Perhaps County residents achieved some satisfaction when an Associated Press reporter and a cameraman were trapped in their car by a dust storm although the photographer claimed to have taken "a picture I've been waiting twenty years to find."[718]

Government Response to the Dust Bowl

The brutally depressed Dust Bowl economy provided ample scope for New Deal relief programs and such assistance was generally welcome. The Federal Emergency Relief Administration (FERA) financed work for low-skilled residents. FERA distributed "Assistance either in cash or in kind sufficient to enable the family receiving the same to have adequate food, clothing, fuel and other necessities."[719] Government cattle purchases furnished food to destitute families as noted in the previous chapter. Along with direct relief, public funds created paying jobs for out-of-work residents. Unskilled workers were paid fifty cents per hour for thirty hours of work per week. The *Springfield Herald-Democrat* reported that in 1933 "hundreds of men" receiving relief funds were working cleaning and repairing streets and gutters.[720] The Civilian Works Administration (CWA) created temporary jobs for unskilled workers on public projects. The CWA hired more than thirteen-hundred men in Baca County in July 1933, who worked on highway projects for thirty hours a week with a minimum pay of fifty cents per hour. Farmers furnishing horses were compensated at fifteen cents per hour per head.[721] The CWA initiated its first major Colorado project in November 1933, with the Willow Creek Park in Lamar. In 1934 the CWA was succeeded by the Works Progress Administration (WPA) that invested heavily in the Dust Bowl. In 1935 projects in Baca, Prowers, and Kiowa Counties employed 149 men, 214 teams of horses and eight trucks with a monthly payroll of $44,367.[722] WPA projects included six bridges, the Hartman high school gym, curb and gutter at Wiley High School, Wiley street improvement, construction of a Wiley reservoir, a TB clinic in Lamar, a jail in Granada, grading and oiling streets in Holly, a school bus and manual training room in Walsh, a new Holly high school building, and Lamar High School's stadium.[723] Lamar's park was completed by the WPA. In 1938 the agency furnished 250 workers for the broomcorn harvest.[724] As late as 1940, some four hundred Baca County workers and almost five hundred in Prowers County were engaged in public emergency work programs.[725]

The government programs with the greatest impact on Colorado's Dust Bowl counties were those focused on agriculture. Several were described in the previous chapter. The early programs aimed at reducing overproduction were hardly a concern of farmers whose crops had largely blown away although the payments were welcomed. During the first six months of 1934, Baca County wheat growers received $190,000 in allotment payments and by July 1, 1936, had collected more than one million dollars.[726] In Prowers County all but 583 of the forty thousand acres allocated to wheat were approved for allotments.[727]

Later farm programs recognized the need to mitigate the damage from drought and erosion and included measures encouraging practices that reduced wind erosion. In 1933 the Soil Erosion Service of the Department of Interior established demonstration conservation projects in Colorado and other Dust Bowl states. In the spring of 1935, FERA initiated federal support for listing, a plowing technique that produced deeper furrows and reduced blowing. Those who wished to participate in the program required approval by a local committee and were paid forty cents per acre listed.[728] Congress appropriated $2 million for emergency listing of which $128,000 went to Baca County farmers to pay for applying the practice to four-hundred thousand acres of blowing land.[729] Other erosion-prevention or mitigation strategies included strip cropping or alternating soil holding crops such as wheat with contoured strips of densely growing feed crops such as sorghum.

Two Soil Conservation Districts were established in Baca County. One covered roughly the western half of the county and the other the southeast quarter. Together they included 1.25 million acres of the County's 1.6 million.[730] The districts, established through a vote of resident landowners, assessed erosion damage and developed programs for its reduction or prevention. They could restrict farming activities within their boundaries. Some of these restrictions, such as limiting plowing previously uncultivated grasslands, represented a drastic departure from existing practices.

CHAPTER 6

Some critics both inside and outside government viewed such measures as encouraging soil conservation and limiting production as merely palliative. They contended that preventing future Dust Bowls and providing a lasting solution to the desperate conditions of southern plains farmers called for a radical restructuring of existing farm and ranch practices. These utopians, including many academics and idealists for whom the Dust Bowl offered a laboratory to test their vision of a transformed American agriculture, considered most of the land on the arid plains unsuitable for crops and took an especially dim view of dryland wheat cultivation.

The seemingly irredeemable condition of much of the plains was summarized in the 1936 report entitled "The Future of the Great Plains" prepared by a committee appointed by the president.[731] The committee conducted hearings in communities throughout the plains including Lamar and Springfield. According to the report, agriculture on the plains was unsustainable in its current form. "There are perhaps 24,000 crop farms, covering a total of 15,000,000 acres, which should no longer be plowed. Of the range lands probably 95 percent have declined in forage value"[732] Conditions in southeast Colorado were particularly dire. "Forage in southeastern Colorado, the 'dust bowl' area, has lost 88 percent of its former value.... only about 8 percent can be classed as being in reasonably good condition."[733] Saving the Great Plains required a new strategy on the part of the government and a change in attitudes of plains farmers. "Therefore, rehabilitation of a great region in which it had been discovered that economic activities are not properly adjusted to basic and controlling physical conditions, is not merely a problem of encouraging better farming practices and desirable engineering works, and revision of such institutions as ownership and tenure. It is also one of revision of some of the less obvious, deep-seated attitudes of mind"[734]

A key player in the attempts at reconstructing Dust Bowl agriculture was Roy Kimmel, an Ivy League academician with roots in the Dust Bowl region and a cousin of my father, who was appointed by Secretary of Agriculture Wallace to coordinate the Department's anti-erosion programs in a hundred Counties in Colorado, Kansas, Oklahoma, New Mexico and Texas. In a 1940 academic journal article, Kimmel laid out his view of Dust Bowl agriculture's greatest underlying flaw, writing "wheat cannot be depended on as a major factor in the farmers' income…livestock and feed production must come more generally into the picture. A major shift in emphasis from wheat to livestock seemed called for."[735] Achieving this transformation would subject farmers and ranchers to disruptive changes. A Land Planning Committee of the National Resources Board appointed early in the Roosevelt administration estimated that 6.5 million acres in Great Plains farmland should be returned to grassland and sixteen thousand farmers needed to be relocated.[736]

Programs to achieve these aims were directed at farms judged "submarginal," in part a recognition that the AAA and its successors provided little help to farmers who did not own enough land to derive benefit from the crop allocation programs and could not obtain loans or credit from financial institutions. These "sub-marginal" operators were viewed by government planners as destined for failure without extensive change. As noted by Sheflin, the term "sub-marginal" was often misused, misunderstood, and ill-defined.[737]

New Deal planners believed that many sub-marginal farms could be salvaged through reorganization. They hoped to accomplish this by consolidating existing farm units into larger operations with diversified crops and livestock. Kimmel described the case of one Baca County farmer with 320 acres and a delinquent Federal Land Bank loan. Planners added twenty-one hundred acres to his land, ninety acres for cultivated crops and 930 of existing grassland with the remaining acreage restored to grass. An FSA loan of $2 thousand was used to purchase used equipment and cattle, pay delinquent taxes and cash lease, and meet operating expense. His cash income was to come from broomcorn and the sale of steers. He was to repay $200 in 1939 and $300 each spring for next six years. According to Kimmel, four hundred reorganizations of this type were done in first two years.[738] Not surprisingly, the reaction of residents to such plans was often less than enthusiastic. Bonnifield described heated conflicts between Kimmel and regional farmers.[739]

The operators of farms deemed unsalvageable were to be relocated to more promising sites. The administration issued an executive order in May 1935 creating the Resettlement Administration (RA) to remove "sub-marginal land" from cultivation and direct the farmers to more productive locations. The 1935 Yearbook of Agriculture described the RA's vision of the new settlements as "rural-industrial communities [that are] intended to provide home sites and tracts of land for stranded families, where products may be raised for home use. Likewise, it is intended to make part-time occupations, such as the production of handicraft goods, available for the earning of supplemental income. Eventually, it is hoped that a decentralization of industry may bring permanent employment to such communities."[740]

The RA purchased several hundred thousand acres in eastern Colorado and resettled families in newly formed communities near Grand Junction, Delta and Alamosa. The first such purchase involved one-hundred-fifty thousand acres of land in southern Otero County, an area west of Prowers County. Ninety percent of families were on relief and most agreed to the purchase of their land although some were unhappy about the government's offers. In 1937 the purchase of 377,000 acres in Baca County was approved. It was given the highest priority due to the severity of conditions there.[741]

The RA loaned the families money and provided houses and farms along with advice on farming in the new location. The resettled families were closely monitored by the RA. According to a recent article by Erin Cole on the RA's operations in Colorado, "Farmers accepted into the program had to agree to strict government management of their farms and households. Agricultural experts told them what to plant and how to treat the soil. Home economics experts instructed women in proper food storage. …. Family budgets were scrutinized and local resettlement offices had to countersign all checks residents wrote."[742]

Most relocation efforts did not go as smoothly as planners hoped. According to Clarence Wiley, the program was plagued by delays and red tape. "A farmer in a designated sub-marginal land purchase area could option his land to the government and wait possibly a year and a half before the Legal Division could pass on the abstract of title so he could obtain his pay. In the meantime, land values might be rising and farms once available already taken up. He was a big loser for his reluctant cooperation, and maladjustments were being incubated almost as fast as readjustments were consummated."[743] Bert and Mayme Stagner's Baca County farm failed in the early thirties. Mayme, by then expecting their fourth child, heard about the resettlement program and dreamed about an idyllic new location. But when the couple arrived in the San Luis Valley, reality fell far short of what she had envisioned. They moved into a dilapidated building on land that could not yet be farmed. Years passed before a new home was built and the land was cleared.[744] The Stagners were eventually able to buy their farm although they later sold it. Less fortunate were the Walkers who were resettled from a farm near Arriba in Lincoln County. They struggled to adapt to different soil conditions and their farm was repossessed and auctioned by the FSA which allowed them to keep two hundred dollars for a down-payment on a small home in town.[745] The number of farmers relocated was in fact quite small. Hurt noted that "most farmers within the project areas moved with their own funds and relocated in areas of their own choosing rather than accept federal land elsewhere."[746] As a result of farmer resistance and implementation difficulties the program was ultimately deemed a failure; the federal government sold most of the land it held for intended resettlement.[747] Much of the land purchased from submarginal farmers in Baca and Otero Counties later became part of the Comanche National Grassland.[748]

By the late thirties, the situation in the Dust Bowl was still judged to be dire. A soil conservation survey of the two Baca County districts completed in 1939 compiled an inventory of the area's soil conditions including extent of erosion, present land use, topography, and soil type as well as recommendations for future use. A report summarizing the survey findings was issued in 1944.[749] It found that 60 percent of the land in the two districts had suffered at least moderate erosion and 29 percent severe or very severe erosion. Only 225,000 acres or less than one-fifth of all cropland in the districts was found to be suitable for any type of crop. The report recommended that this land be limited to broomcorn or sorghum as the risk of wind erosion in dry years was too great to permit any wheat cultivation.

The government's agricultural programs furnished some relief to beleaguered agrarians and provided information that helped them improve farming techniques. But they fell far short of achieving the transformation envisioned by some New Dealers.

As the drought and depressed markets faded, pressures for reform also dissipated. Theodore Saloutos, in his analysis of federal farm policy on the Great Plains, concluded "the outbreak of the war, the need for increased food production to supply the United States and its allies, and the migration of people to the cities (and their replacement by new arrivals, who knew little about farming and soil conservation) tended to undo much, if not all, of what the New Dealers sought to accomplish."[750] A half-century after publication of "The Future of the Great Plains," Gilbert White, a University of Colorado geographer who served on the staff of the committee that drafted the report, expressed his views as to why its ambitious goals were not realized. He concluded that "the major directions in which it went astray were in overly modest assumptions about technological change and overly optimistic assumptions about the receptivity of society to radical alternations in traditional processes."[751] As Cunfer pointed out, neither the New Deal's interventions nor the disruptions of the Dust Bowl significantly changed the land use patterns in the southern plains. The proportions of land devoted to crops and to pasture were roughly the same in 1945 as in 1930.[752] In 1947 Baca County wheat farmers planted 360,000 acres, more than in any previous year.[753]

Causes of the Dust Bowl

The history of the Dust Bowl is still contentious more than three quarters of a century later. Interpretations are colored by current controversies about the environment and the role of government. Some narratives cast it as a morality play, a conflict between the private despoilers of the plains environment and government saviors with the latter ultimately triumphing, at least temporarily. Paul Bonnifield, a skeptic of the depression-era government farm policy, caricatured these views as claiming:

> "that there was no wind erosion until the buffalo grass was turned under by the plow; that selfish, greedy men sought quick wealth by raising wheat despite wise council given by scientists and government farm leaders. The spark that set off the great plow up, continued the theory, was the high price of wheat during World War I. In the mad race to achieve quick wealth, dust bowl farmers abandoned stock raising and other crops and turned to a single-crop agricultural system. To stop the advancing deserts the government had to apply heroic measures to right the wrongs to the soil and establish a permanent, stable agricultural economy in the stricken region." [754]

Recent portrayals such as Timothy Egan's *The Worst Hard Time* and the Ken Burns documentary *The Dust Bowl* are sympathetic to this narrative. While the morality-play scenario contains elements of truth, other explanations have also been advanced. They seem to fall into three categories.

The first might be simplified as "Blame mother nature." Extraordinary climatic conditions brought unparalleled damage and suffering. The drought of the 1930s was of unprecedented severity, and it was at its worst on the southern plains. Precipitation was at historic lows and temperatures in the summer months reached record highs. Soil conditions were particularly susceptible to wind erosion. A recent publication by Geoff Cunfer lends support to the case for drought and heat as the principal causes of the dust and wind erosion. He analyzed over 150 years of land use and weather data for Great Plains counties and examined their relationship to the frequency of dust storms. He concluded that "Drought and high temperatures explain the location of dust storms better than land use. .... dust storms, rather than being evidence of human ecological failure, are instead normal forms of ecological disturbance on the southern plains."[755] Yet it would be a mistake to characterize the Dust Bowl as a purely natural disaster. There is little question that the extent and the nature of cultivation in the 1920s and early 1930s made the region's farmland, especially its wheat land, more susceptible to extreme wind erosion.

A second narrative centers on darker forces in American society. Two historians of the Dust Bowl featured different villains in this drama. Donald Worster laid responsibility on the greed inherent in American capitalism, describing the plow-up as the work of "a generation of aggressive entrepreneurs, imbued with the values and world view of American agricultural capitalism."[756] The Dust Bowl was part and parcel of the ethos of interwar America. It was "made and delivered by socially destructive forces in modern American culture."[757] Greed drove Dust Bowl farmers to exploit nature's bounty, resulting in the ultimate destruction of both the land and the agrarian economy. But Baca County farmers were probably no greedier than their counterparts in Iowa or New Hampshire. And it is unlikely that Soviet-style collectives on the southern plains pushing to meet production quotas would have resulted in a better outcome. Worster's demonization of market forces should be tempered by the realization that the alleged wartime exploitation of the plains' soil was encouraged by government through both mandated high prices and propaganda, encouraging farmers to plant more.

For Paul Bonnifield, much of the blame falls on an inept and meddling federal government. He recognized that agricultural expansion and particularly mechanization contributed to increased soil erosion. But he minimized its significance, treating the Dust Bowl as just another episode of drought and blowing dirt which regional farmers would have adjusted to and overcome if only left alone. He contended that "the economy of the region was not worse than that of other areas of the nation and in many respects better."[758] The plight of the southern plains was exaggerated, in his view, by government propaganda and media distortion. However, by most measures the economy of the Dust Bowl area performed significantly worse than most of the nation. Certainly the results from government programs were at best mixed, and the view of many planners that the southern plains were largely the victim of a single crop economy was clearly an oversimplification. However, public assistance and support programs provided much needed funds to a desperate population. Although farmers undertook many anti-erosion measures on their own, federal assistance and guidance was welcomed by many, and it likely provided more benefit than damage.

A third narrative advanced by Harry McDean, based in part on late 1930s government sponsored sociological research, might be described, only a bit unfairly, as "the inevitable suffering of life's losers." McDean stressed the supposed unique cultural traits of Dust Bowl residents, describing their experiences as providing "instruction in the problem of marginality in modernizing societies: they show us how marginal people operate in a marginal economy. Here are people whose abilities do not square with the needs of modernizing societies.... They are therefore left to carve out for themselves a life in the margins."[759] According to McDean, farmers in the Dust Bowl counties had a more tenuous connection to their land than those in other parts of the nation. This was due to less dependence by farm owners on the output from their land. The southern plains region was more amenable to part-time farming since jobs were available in "part-time mining, lumbering, or oil work."[760] In addition, Dust Bowl farmers were prone to high-risk practices because they had not experienced previous failures.

These characterizations of Dust Bowl conditions do not seem applicable to southeast Colorado. There were few part-time employment opportunities of the sort described in Colorado's Dust Bowl counties, virtually no lumbering or mining, and very little oil work. Baca and Prowers County farmers, many having experienced homesteading failures in the 1880s and early 1890s or learned about them from elders, were hardly oblivious to climate risk. McDean, in keeping with much dust bowl mythology, casts nonresident farmers as leading villains in the tragedy. Such growers, often vilified as "suitcase farmers," were accused of buying their land at a low price, planting wheat and reaping great profits if the weather turned out favorable. If not, they abandoned the land to blow. Their demonization seems excessive. According to Leslie Hewes's in-depth study of the phenomenon, there is little evidence that absentee owners' stewardship of the land was any worse than that of resident owners.[761] He examined statistics on abandonment and wind erosion conditions by type of ownership in northeast Baca County. He found that, while absentee operators occasionally reckless practices certainly contributed to Dust Bowl conditions, their behavior was not very different than that of other classes of owners, and that conditions would still have been severe even without non-resident operators. Finally, the literacy and educational levels of Baca County residents exceeded national averages, hardly consistent with a "marginal" population. At the same time, many of the farms could fairly be characterized as marginal in that they were too small to be economically viable. In 1930 Baca County farms averaged 644 acres. While this figure seems large it includes many very large ranches. By 1940 many of the smaller farms had disappeared and the average size grew to 1180 acres.[762]

As is the case with most major social and economic events, the Dust Bowl can be attributed to a confluence of factors. The climate in the 1930s was uniquely harsh, and soil conditions in the southern plains were especially susceptible to wind erosion.

Erosion was undoubtedly worsened by the extent of cultivation initially stimulated by high wartime wheat prices and made possible by increased mechanization and later by the availability of cheap land in areas such as Baca County. The poor financial condition of many farmers after the 1920s agricultural depression made it difficult for famers to finance needed conservation measures. Low grain prices induced them to expand cultivation. Southeast Colorado wheat farmers had the misfortune to plow up more land just as the drought came on the horizon. While the results of government programs were mixed, they were probably beneficial on balance both to the farmers and for the condition of the land. There were certainly examples of speculative excesses, but it seems improbable that most southern plains farmers were more risk prone than their brethren elsewhere. But they had the misfortune of having their risky behavior coincide with climatic and economic disasters.

Legacy of the Dust Bowl

By the late thirties conditions had eased although southeast Colorado was still well short of a return to normal. After a heavy rain in 1935, the *Lamar Daily News* announced, somewhat prematurely as it turned out, "DROUTH BROKEN."[763] But precipitation eventually rebounded. In January 1939, the paper's headline proclaimed "Bumper Crop Promised by January Rain" describing a wet snow and rainstorm that brought 1.2 inches of moisture to Lamar.[764] The next month the area was buried under the heaviest snow in twenty years, leaving more than eighteen inches of snow and over an inch of precipitation.[765] The improved weather along with conservation measures helped ease wind erosion. Government programs and higher prices brought a measure of stability. Dust storms continued into 1938 and early 1939, but the worst seemed over. A syndicated article in the *Springfield Democrat-Herald* in October 1938 cheerily proclaimed, "The sun is beginning to shine through America's southwestern dust clouds."[766] In 1939 Baca County agent Claude Gausman reported that "Many rural families have just swept out the last dirt in their homes from the black period 1931-1938 and have produced enough from the farm in 1939-40 to pay off a portion of those unpardonable debts, thus many of them have just begin [sic] to live again rather than to exist."[767]

The Dust Bowl left southeast Colorado permanently changed. Many residents left the region; population would never again reach its earlier levels. Those remaining became more aware of vagaries of nature and its consequences. Farmers, scarred but perhaps wiser from the experience, became more prudent in their cultivation methods. Ranchers were less prone to overgrazing. Businessmen in the Dust Bowl communities were more cautious, maybe setting a little more aside for a rainy, or dusty, day. The people of southeast Colorado, though still fiercely independent, were more accepting of the role of the state as an emergency backstop for their farms, their banks, their businesses, or their families.

At the same time, they took pride in the resilience they demonstrated in the face of the catastrophic happenings of the thirties and were hopeful for a brighter future. But, as Douglas Hurt wrote, "The people who experienced the dust storms would never forget them..... The Dust Bowl years became an indelible mark on the minds of residents." [768] Perhaps the region never fully recovered. Colorado State University historian Douglas Sheflin concluded in *Legacies of Dust*, his exploration of the effects of the Dust Bowl in Baca and Prowers Counties, that "It is unclear whether the region will ever truly reach a point of stability. Drought and economic downturns continue to wreak havoc on locals."[769] Even eighty years later, as few who lived through it are alive, the Dust Bowl still haunts the region. A 2014 article in the *Denver Post* describing dry conditions in Baca County featured the headline "For Southeast Colorado a New Dust Bowl Is Blowing In."[770]

CHAPTER 6

Chapter 6 Exhibits

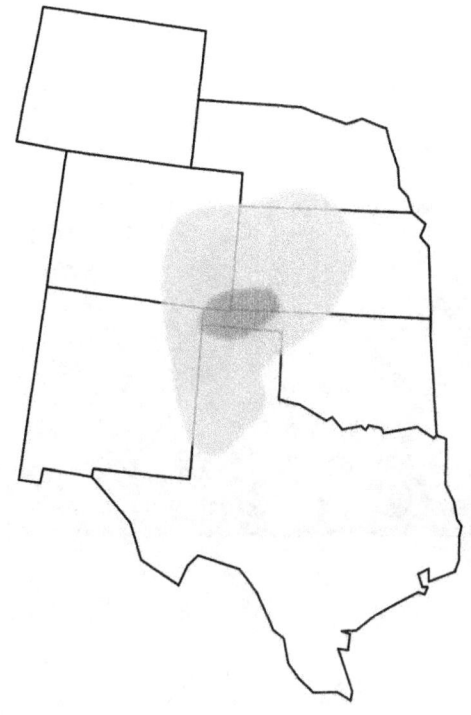

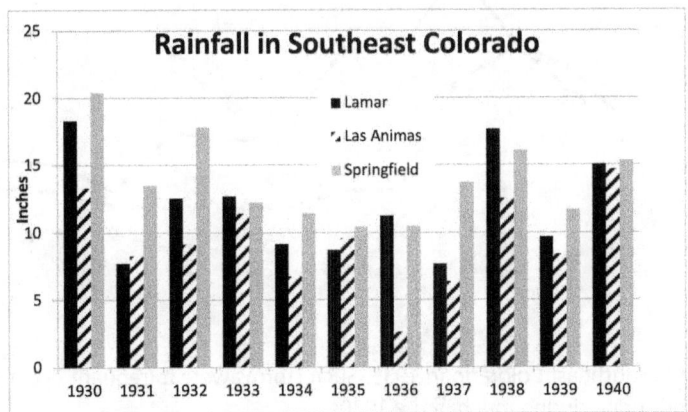

The area with the worst wind erosion in the 1930s, indicated by the darker shading on the map, included Baca County and parts of Prowers County as well as portions of four other states.

Southeast Colorado enjoyed wet years in the early 1930s but suffered a record drought in the middle years of the decade. The years 1933 through 1936 were the worst of the Dust Bowl.

Source: Lamar Centennial History, Bent County History.

Dust storm

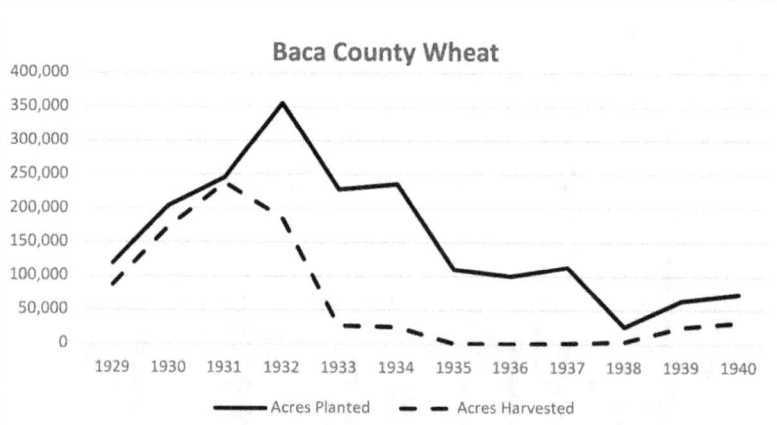

A dust storm in southeast Colorado in 1935. Such storms were a frequent occurrence in the late winter and spring during much of the 1930s.

The failure of its wheat crop was a major blow to the Baca County economy. After a record crop in 1931, plantings for the next year increased. But dry weather and hail rendered much of the crop not worth harvesting. The AAA resulted in further reductions in 1934 and by 1935 the County's wheat production had virtually disappeared. Continuing dry weather and government programs kept production low through the rest of the decade.

Source: Agriculture Reporting Service. Photo from The Denver Public Library, Western History Collection, call number X-17606

CHAPTER 6

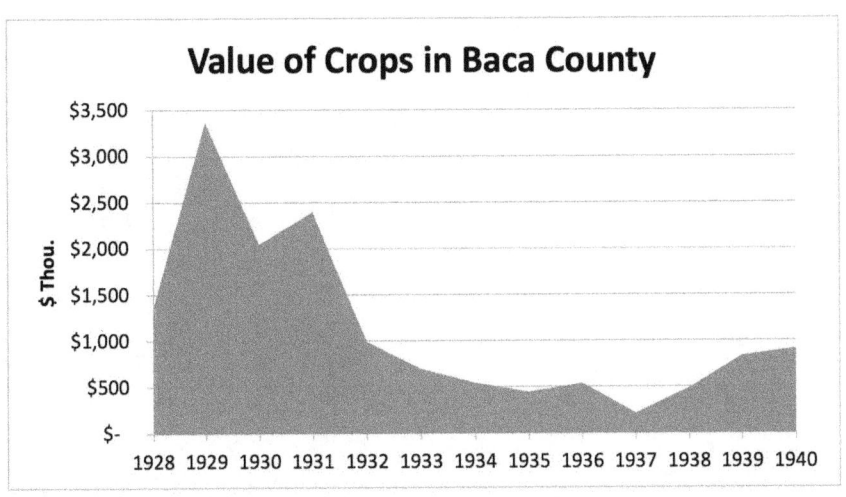

Baca County Indicators

	Year 1	Year 2		Year 1
Population	10,570	6,207	Number of Farms	1,805
1930 & 1940			1935 & 1940	
School Enrollment	3,380	1,686	Land Value/Acre	$ 15.23
1932 & 1940			1930 & 1940	
Total Employment	3,724	1,980	Value Crops ($000)	$ 3,367
1930 & 1940			1929 & 1937	
Nonfarm Employmer	1,297	994	Number of Range Cattle	32,581
1930 & 1940			1933 & 1938	

Baca County farmers enjoyed unprecedented prosperity in the late twenties and early thirties. Thereafter, their income from crops declined drastically as both prices and yields plummeted. The late thirties saw a very modest recovery.

These statistics show the severity of the County's agricultural, economic, and demographic deterioration during the 1930s. Different years have been selected for the various indicators because of data availability and to show the magnitude of the decline.

Sources: Agricultural Reporting Service, Census, Colorado Assessors and Colorado Dept. of Education in *Colorado Yearbooks*

CHAPTER 7

War and Postwar: The 1940s

THE NEW DECADE BROUGHT WELCOME PROSPERITY AFTER THE ANGUISH OF THIRties. A quarter century later Prowers County banker H.E. McKeever recalled, "From 1926 to 1940 things were really tough but with the advent of World War II and the breaking of the drought, things changed."[771] The region's economy rebounded vigorously from drought and depression. Rising farm prices, a recovering national economy, war-time mobilization, and a succession of years with above-average precipitation spurred robust growth in both farm and non-farm economies. Out-migration slowed, and all sixteen counties reported positive job growth in the 1940s with rate-of-gain for the region nearly matching that of the nation.

Wartime

World War II arguably brought the greatest economic disruption in American history, but many of the changes were welcome after the struggles of the Great Depression. The War's outbreak spurred a dramatic rebound in the economy, a large-scale mobilization of labor and industry, and severe restrictions on consumers and businesses. Mobilization efforts and the eventual entry of the US into the war produced similarly consequential developments for the plains region. Farmers' prospects improved as mobilization and foreign need for American farm output increased demand for their products. Prices for most agricultural commodities soared. At the same time, men entering the military and residents leaving the region for jobs in war industries depleted the supply of workers, particularly in agriculture.

Although not a center of war production, the region garnered some direct benefits from war-related activities. In April 1942 work began on an air base at La Junta to train forty-four hundred members of the British Royal Air Force. Contracts for the base called for around $5 million in expenditures and a peak construction employment of three thousand workers. Later, the size of the facility was approximately doubled to accommodate training American airmen. The military's footprint expanded further when a bombing range was developed south of La Junta to meet training needs.[772]

A more consequential development soon got underway some seventy miles down the Arkansas. In February 1942, shortly after the outbreak of war with Japan, President Roosevelt issued executive order 9066, mandating relocation all persons of Japanese ancestry residing in the Pacific military zone, which included the west coast states and Arizona. Those outside the zone were not relocated but were subject to some restrictions. Several Japanese American families who had settled in Sedgwick County in 1903-04 were permitted to continue working their farms but had to turn over their cameras, guns, and radios to authorities.[773]

The War Relocation Authority (WRA) sought sites that met the following criteria: 1) work opportunities for evacuees, e.g., labor shortages in critical sectors including agriculture; 2) adequate infrastructure such as road, power, and water; 3) absence of large Caucasian populations; and 4) absence of war industry plants or military installations minimizing the risk of sabotage.[774] The search centered on sparsely populated interior regions of the country including eastern Colorado. Residents' reactions to the possible presence of these unfortunates near their communities ranged from wariness to outright disapproval. The Denver Realty Board adopted a resolution opposing the transfer of any aliens to Colorado.[775] A March 1942 UP story headlined "NO JAP ALIEN CAMPS PLANNED IN COLORADO" quoted Colorado Governor Carr, saying that he had received federal assurances the allayed "all hysteria in Colorado regarding the influx of Japs from west coast defense areas."[776] Despite these assurances, the WRA announced in June plans for a relocation facility near Granada in Prowers County.[777] The WRA purchased some ten thousand acres of Arkansas bottom land formerly parts of the XY and the Koen ranches. By August one thousand men were at work preparing the camp at an estimated cost of $4.2 million on land described in a local paper as "A mile square plot of ground once trampled by buffalo as they fled from Indian hunters, and later grazed upon by the thousands of head of cattle that roamed the great XY ranch, [that] is being taken from the rattlesnakes, the prairie dogs, jackrabbits, and sagebrush."[778]

The camp provided a welcome boost to Granada's economy that had been in gradual decline since its salad days in the 1870s during its brief span as the terminus of the Santa Fe line. George Lurie's history of the Granada camp described the town's boom: "business at local stores increased one hundred-fold. Government advance teams descended upon the area in droves. So did enterprising businessmen and dozens of newspaper reporters. Granada's Main Street was teeming with automobiles and groups of strangers. The train station reopened; new enterprises were launched. Once again, Granada was bustling."[779] The town's population increased from 342 residents in 1940 to 551 ten years later by which time the camp had been closed for five years. The camp was officially entitled the Granada War Relocation Center. But the Granada post office was unable to handle all the mail for camp residents, so a new one was established named Camp Amache after John Prowers' Cheyenne wife.[780] This became the common designation for the camp through to the present day.

The first contingent of evacuees, made up of those with the skills to assist in construction, arrived in late August. More would soon come. The camp reached a maximum population of 7,567 which, if it had been an incorporated city, would probably have made it the largest in the region.[781] The facility consisted of more than two hundred buildings including barracks, houses, stores, a hospital and utilities. Residents built and operated schools for their children including a high school which fielded sports teams playing those from nearby towns. The *Lamar Daily News* regularly published an "Amache Notes" column similar to those for other small southeast Colorado communities. In 1943 it reported that four Amache High School students competed in the State Music Contest.[782] Camp residents published a bi-weekly newspaper whose staff included artists who had worked at Disney studios.[783] Many of the residents were skilled farmers. A Lamar banker reported that the Amache residents "operated their own farms and made an enviable record in production of farm product."[784] They cultivated fifty-five hundred acres of irrigated land and used the remainder for pasture. Crops included alfalfa, barley, sorghum, potatoes, spinach, and sugar beets. In 1944 the camp raised seven hundred head of cattle, thirty-six hundred chickens and nearly one thousand hogs.[785] A 1999 Department of Agriculture report stated that Amache "had one of the largest and most diversified agricultural enterprises of the ten relocation centers."[786]

Prowers County residents' attitudes towards Amache and its residents were colored by the awareness that many sons, brothers, and neighbors were engaged in combat against Japanese troops. These feelings were reflected in the headlines in adjacent front-page stories in a September 1942 edition of the *Lamar Daily News* reading, "1500 More Japs Coming to Granada This Week" and "Japs Smashed on New Guinea."[787] It used the same, today-politically-incorrect, term to refer to those trying to kill American men in the Pacific and fellow US residents who had the misfortune to be caught up in wartime hysteria and forcibly relocated into the paper's circulation area. Adam Schrager in his biography of Colorado Governor Ralph Carr claimed that "The town [Lamar] went out of its way make things difficult for evacuees."[788] This is probably an exaggeration. Several of my high school classmates remembered having camp residents to their homes for dinner and Bill Hosokawa in his history of the Japanese in Colorado wrote that the townspeople in Granada were friendly to camp residents.[789] But some Lamar stores had "No Japs Allowed" signs and the city council passed an ordinance forbidding the sales of alcohol to camp residents.[790]

Nonetheless, local businesses appreciated the boost to the economy. The city's Chamber of Commerce and Retail Merchants Association hosted a get acquainted dinner with Amache representatives where, according to the camp newsletter, the internees were issued "a cordial invitation to shop in their city and promised a hearty welcome." A Lamar store owner asked, "Their money is just as good as anybody else's isn't it?"[791] A 1943 editorial in the *Lamar Daily News* declared, "From a strictly selfish and material standpoint, it happens that to date the relocation center is the largest, and in fact, the only project this community has received out of the war effort. It has meant the expenditure of thousands of dollars in this region, which has meant much to local business in these days of high taxes and vanishing normal business."[792] An article in the *Democrat Herald* from nearby Springfield describing the harsh treatment of Americans in Japan at the war's outbreak declared, "The Japs have shown themselves to be a cruel race," but "it would not do any good to get revenge among those we interned."[793]

Amache, like most of the camps in the US, was classified as a "relocation center" where security measures were limited. Camp residents were granted leaves for seasonal work, usually in agriculture, and indefinite leaves for vocational or educational opportunities. Workers on leave were forbidden to move back to the west coast and were required to periodically report to the WRA. Many Amache residents found work outside the camp. Robert Harvey reported that by October 1942, more than one thousand had done so.[794] Rose Kikuchi, a young woman from the camp, lived in our home during the war and helped my mother take care of me and my two siblings. Rosie, as we kids called her, was a part of our family during the war years, and we maintained contact with her and her family long afterwards.

The internees' contribution to the local economy in this time of labor shortages was most welcome. In the fall of 1942, workers from Amache and from a camp in Wyoming assisted with the beet harvest. That fall the *Lamar Daily News* reported that nearly one thousand Amache evacuees were employed in farm labor including 235 commuting to farms in the immediate vicinity of the camp, 298 elsewhere in the Arkansas Valley, and 368 in the South Platte Valley.[795] Frank Torizawa's off-camp career was one of the more successful. While in the camp he started a fish market in an abandoned building in Granada, catering to fellow internees. A year later, the business was booming, and he moved his market to Denver where it thrived for decades in lower downtown as the Granada Fish Market.[796] Some 953 Amache residents served in the US military, many seeing combat duty in Europe.[797] They included Rose Kikuchi's brother who was killed in Italy.

The region hosted other smaller wartime facilities. In June 1943, a flight training facility in Fort Morgan began teaching at five training fields near the city. Some two hundred cadets were enrolled in a ninety-day course covering groundwork and flight training. The Fort Morgan based staff included three army officers, army ground school instructors, an army medical staff, seventy civilian flight instructors, fifty civilian maintenance men, and twenty-five mechanic helpers.[798] A dozen temporary POW camps were also established throughout the region to hold prisoners who performed seasonal farm labor.[799]

CHAPTER 7

Plains Agriculture in Wartime

By the late thirties, farm prices had risen from their depression lows. But inventories of surplus commodities soon grew well beyond expectations and prices began to weaken. International developments soon transformed markets. Germany's *blitzkrieg* attack on Poland in September 1939 signaled the outbreak of war in Europe and agricultural prices rebounded. Colorado director of agriculture, W. C. Sweinhart, lamented that hostilities started too late to benefit most farmers in current year but "If the war lasts the farmers should get good prices for everything they can raise by next fall."[800]

The war benefitted some commodities more than others. Massive worldwide surpluses kept the price for the grain below its government support level and planting remained under the control of the Commodity Credit Corporation through late 1941. The agency mandated a nationwide reduction of the 1942 wheat crop by two million acres.[801] Sugar beet farmers, on the other hand, quickly profited as the supply of sugar from the Philippines was cut off, and the demand from European allies increased. According to the Chairman of the state Agricultural Adjustment Act committee, 1942 beet growers "face the most favorable income outlook in more than 20 years."[802] Farmers were expected to receive $8.50 to $9.25 per ton compared to $6.75 over the previous three years and were initially allowed to freely increase production in response to higher prices although government later imposed price controls. Cattle prices surged within days after hostilities began in Europe. By early 1940 cattle fetched "the highest prices since 1930 and, with few exceptions, the highest profits since 1920."[803] The national average price of cattle rose from $6.54 per hundred pounds in 1938 to $10.70 in 1942.[804] Soon prices of all farm commodities were rising and continued to increase through the war years. The price of wheat rose from seventy cents per bushel in 1938 to $1.26 in 1942 and $1.60 in 1945.[805] Corn sold for forty-eight cents per bushel in 1938, ninety-one cents in 1942 and $1.94 in 1945.[806] As in World War I farmers were encouraged to view production as part of the war effort. In early 1942 the Prowers County Agent told local farmers that "The defense of the nation by its farmers is as important as the defense of the nation by its soldiers."[807]

Growers' opportunities to profit from higher prices were limited by lack of manpower and equipment. Most entered the war years with old or worn machinery because they lacked the money to purchase new gear. But even as their incomes improved, they were unable to replace their equipment as rationing of steel, rubber, and other materials severely limited production. Shortages of tractors and tires were the most pressing. Neighboring farms frequently pooled their equipment, and tasks requiring machinery were increasingly outsourced. Migrant combine operators and harvest workers who followed the wheat harvest from Texas to Canada each summer assumed a larger role.[808]

Wartime worker shortages were particularly problematic for labor intensive crops such as beets or vegetables. Federal and state governments provided some respite. As early as 1940, Baca County farmers faced a shortage of help for the broomcorn harvest and commissioners were asked to halt WPA projects so workers could be freed to pull corn.[809] The US Employment Service suggested that beet farmers in Colorado, Wyoming, and Montana hire women and children, perhaps unaware that whole families already worked in the fields.[810] Colorado Governor Vivian attempted to get local draft boards to halt induction of young men from farms, but his efforts were largely unsuccessful. Japanese Americans leaving the west coast were an early source of additional farm labor when the government encouraged them to move voluntarily. The Associated Press reported that as of April 2, 1942, before relocation began, some four hundred American citizens and 285 aliens had come into the Colorado. Many of these early arrivals worked on regional farms, many in Otero County.[811] But the military soon halted such voluntary relocation.[812] When the internment camps were established, farmers viewed camp residents as potential laborers. At a meeting of local farmers in early 1942 the Prowers County Agent discussed "plans for bringing Jap labor in this area."[813] In June 1942, the director of the Granada Relocation Center promised that "as many Japanese laborers would be furnished for farm work as could be spared at once" and that a thousand would be made available by October.[814]

The US Department of Agriculture brought more than three thousand mostly Latino farm workers from northern New Mexico.[815] Soon Mexican nationals became a vital source of seasonal labor under the *Bracero* program which began August 1942. The Spanish word "*bracero*" comes from the root *brazo* (arm) referring to the hand labor performed by the workers. The workers were "recruited, transported, placed and supervised by the FSA [Farm Security Agency] under terms of an agreement with the Mexican government."[816] The US government was employer of record and the contracts with laborers were relatively short, covering as few as forty-five days.[817] Under that agreement the workers were to be paid the prevailing wage, fed "Mexican-type food" when possible, provided reasonable and sanitary living conditions, and guaranteed employment three-fourths of the time they were in the US. The first contingent of 850 workers to be employed on Colorado farms, principally those growing sugar beets or onions, arrived by train in Denver in May 1943. Charles F. Brannan, regional director of the Farm Security Administration, said that the Mexican nationals would be the first of 3,315 workers to be brought under the program. One-hundred-thirty of the early arrivals were destined for the Lamar area and a hundred for Fowler. They were described in a *Rocky Mountain News* article as looking like "desperate characters out of a desperate pulp magazine, swarthy, multi-colored blankets up to their shining black eyes, straw sombreros down over their eyes."[818]

The *Bracero* program was conceived as a wartime measure, but growers remained dependent on Mexican workers after the war ended. The agreement between the Mexican and US governments expired at the end of 1947 although prospective employers could still enter Mexico and recruit workers on their own. Most of the recruiting for

Colorado was done by the sugar companies, with GW especially active. The Company claimed that a laborer could make as much money in six weeks in the Colorado beet fields as in three years on a Mexican farm.[819] However, lack of government oversight resulted in complaints about mistreatment of workers. In February 1946 the Mexican government excluded its nationals from eight states including Colorado on grounds of "discriminatory treatment and unsatisfactory earnings."[820] These issues were settled when a new agreement was arrived at in 1951 and *braceros* remained an important source of field workers into the 1960s.

Soldiers captured in the European theater provided yet more farm workers. In 1943 the Department of Agriculture and War Department developed a program to supply prisoners of war for agricultural labor. POWs working at Colorado farms included Italians from base camps in Douglas, Wyoming, and Scottsbluff, Nebraska and Germans from Camp Carson near Colorado Springs. Farmers contracted with army for POW labor and paid the local wage to the government with the prisoners receiving eighty cents per day. The workers were housed in work related camps located in several eastern Colorado communities ranging from Springfield to Yuma.[821] In 1943 some 125 German POWs from Camp Carson arrived to work the harvest in Sedgwick County. They worked on beet and potato harvests under agreement among GW Sugar, growers, and the government. The POWs were housed in two remodeled buildings in Ovid. The following year more German POWs along with Jamaicans and Indians from the Rosebud reservation were brought to work the harvest. The next spring two hundred POWs arrived in the spring to thin beets and another group came in fall for the beet, potato, and onion harvests.[822] The German and Italian prisoners/workers were well received and reportedly developed friendly relationships with townspeople and local farmers who often invited the prisoners to share meals in their homes. In June 1945 Camp Carson provided forty-nine hundred German POWs to work in beet fields in Logan County.[823]

Plains Agriculture in the 1940s

Wartime was good for US farmers and the postwar years were even better. According to Douglas Hurt, "Between the onset of World War II and the Korean War, the American farmer experienced the longest sustained period of prosperity in American history."[824] US agriculture benefitted from several favorable developments. The drought had abated, and new technology raised productivity. Government programs maintained prices at levels that were profitable for farmers. After wartime demand receded, the need to feed much of the war-ravaged world sustained the market for US farm produce. Between 1940 and 1951 national farm output rose by one quarter and net farm income tripled.[825]

The New Deal agricultural programs made American farmers dependent on the government for income support to the extent that more than one-third of US farmer's 1941 gross income came from direct government payments.[826] The federal role would only increase in wartime. The government encouraged production after the war's outbreak and guaranteed higher prices. The Emergency Price Control Act, enacted in January 1942 shortly after the US entered the war, prohibited farm prices from falling below 110 percent of parity and later legislation raised the guarantees still further. By 1943 farm prices had doubled from their 1939 level, far outpacing the rise in farmer's costs.[827] As farmers grew more crops and raised more livestock their total gross income more than doubled. When the war ended, farm price supports were extended. By 1951 both prices received by farmers and their gross income had risen another 50 percent.[828] Costs also increased as inflation accelerated but the rise in farm prices far exceeded both costs and overall inflation.[829]

The early 1940s not only brought a recovery in prices but also more precipitation. In the parched southeast both Lamar and Las Animas received less than ten inches of moisture in 1939. Two years later precipitation in both towns exceeded twenty inches, and it reached similar levels in two of the next three years. Bountiful rain and snow were not limited to the southeast; in 1941 annual rainfall in both Limon and Wray exceeded normal levels by more than ten inches.[830] Extreme dry spells were avoided through the remainder of the forties.

Plains farmers and ranchers' output surged in wartime. They harvested 3.1 million acres of cropland in 1945, up from 2.2 million in 1940.[831] Ranchers expanded their cattle herds from 434 thousand head to 666 thousand over the same interval.[832] Prosperity continued into the post-war period as total sales nearly doubled from their 1945 level.[833] Although prices softened in the late forties, the outbreak of the Korean War reignited demand. By 1951 prices for wheat, corn, and cattle had all risen to at least three times their pre-WWII levels.[834] Land values outpaced inflation throughout the period with the most rapid increases during the immediate post-war years. The average value of an acre of farm or ranch land in eastern Colorado rose from just under $8 in 1940 to almost $30 in 1950, more than doubling in real terms.[835] Vance Johnson reported that Cheyenne County land that could not be unloaded for $5 an acre in the thirties was fetching $40 in the late forties.[836]

Farmers also were able to profit from innovations in equipment, new plant and animal varieties, and advances in chemistry, although their application was often delayed until wartime shortages abated. Farm productivity accelerated. The rate of growth in farm GDP per worker in the decades after 1940 more than doubled from its pace the previous sixty years.[837] Yield per acre of major crops, which had changed little in the early decades of the twentieth century, began to increase. Nationwide corn yield per acre harvested had never exceeded thirty bushels prior to 1941; it achieved that level in nine of the next ten years. Similarly, winter wheat yield per acre seeded was greater than sixteen bushels in six of years in the 1940s after reaching that level only once previously.[838]

Farmers were able to take advantage of the higher prices with improved equipment along with new crop varieties, herbicides, and pesticides. The number of tractors on eastern Colorado farms more than doubled during the 1940s. By 1950 four-fifths of the region's farmers owned at least one tractor[839] and many acquired other machinery such as combines or corn pickers. By 1950 nearly one-half of all wheat growers in dryland counties owned a combine.[840] Chemical fertilizers raised yields while pesticides and herbicides limited losses from pests and weeds. Improved plant varieties were introduced. A 1941 article in the *Lamar Daily News* displayed the headline "HYBRID TAKES HAZARDS OUT OF CORN GROWING" describing how the introduction of Pioneer Hybrid overcame the "next to ruinous conditions" of raising corn in the high plains. The hybrid reportedly doubled previous yields.[841]

Changes were also underway in the cattle and sheep industries. Livestock feeding operations surged in the South Platte Valley but also flourished in the central plains and the Arkansas Valley. Increased feed grain yields led to several large feed lots being established in Kit Carson County.[842] In 1945 a Lamar banker reported one hundred thousand lambs and ewes fed in the area along with large numbers of cattle and hogs.[843] Thanks to the REA more farmers had electricity which allowed the use of electrical pumps for both surface and well irrigation. The number of regional farms with electricity increased by three thousand between 1945 and 1950.[844]

The greatest gains from labor saving innovations were achieved in the production of sugar beets, hastened by wartime shortages of workers. In the thirties GW management embraced the goal of eliminating stoop labor in the beet fields.[845] Harvesting was the first task to be mechanized. By the late forties, both Deere and International Harvester had developed mechanical beet harvesters[846] and by midcentury machines were harvesting nearly the entire crop.[847] Reducing the labor needed for thinning and topping proved more challenging. But in the late 1930s, the research staff at the Great Western Experiment Station, an arm of the sugar company, created a mechanical beet topper that accurately gauged the right height to cut the plant. The machine saved on labor costs as well as reducing loss from plants cut too high or too low by hand laborers.[848] Henry Herzog and Lawrence Wagner who grew beets near Iliff were the first in Logan County to own an electronic beet thinner operated by means of light beams across the rows of plants.[849] Although the new machinery did not eliminate the need for hand labor, it greatly reduced it. A test at the Colorado Agricultural Experiment Station showed that machine thinning decreased the necessary labor from 27.2 man-hours per acre to 2.5.[850] Chemicals and new seed varieties also enhanced productivity. According to Douglas Hurt, chemical weed killers cost sugar beet growers $5 per acre compared to $40 for weed-clearing hand labor.[851] Processed seed produced a more uniform crop that was suitable for mechanical blocking, thinning and cultivating. But financial constraints and resistance to change slowed adoption of these innovations. A document prepared for the Colorado Legislature in 1962 reported that by then virtually all beet harvesting in the state had been mechanized but that much of the pre-harvest work such as blocking and thinning was still performed by hand labor.[852]

Another Wheat Boom

The drought and depression years saw many plains residents suffer a vertiginous descent from prosperity to desperation, but none, arguably, were subjected to the distress visited upon wheat farmers. Plunging prices rendered virtually worthless whatever of their crop survived the drought, and government planners strove to eradicate their wheat-dependent farming models. But the outbreak of war and the return of rainfall short-circuited bureaucratic designs and brought back the good old days with a vengeance. Wheat prices surged through the war, and early post-war years and growers responded. Dryland was still relatively cheap in central and southeast Colorado, attracting the interest of large-scale and experienced growers along with some unknowledgeable speculators. But raising wheat in eastern Colorado without irrigation was still a risky and expensive business requiring "capital and experience and patience."[853] Turning a profit necessitated scale—successful operation often ran to thousands or even tens of thousands of acres—and a sizable investment in equipment. Some parts of the region still lacked grain elevators and railroad loading facilities. Despite wet years in the early forties, the climate remained predominately arid and unpredictable.

In addition to struggles with mother nature and the federal government, growers seeking to expand production often had to overcome local opposition. The legacy of the Dust Bowl made many residents and local officials resistant to farming prairie or grasslands that had been salvaged from blowing wheat fields or to the cultivation of virgin land. They had been inculcated with the New Deal philosophy of leaving "marginal" lands in grass. Soil Conservation Districts, set up with the goal of preventing cultivation of large swathes of new land, were viewed by many as saving the region from a replay of the thirties Dust Bowl. The districts instituted land-use ordinances that restricted planting.[854] Plowing grassland required a majority vote of resident landowners in the district, and local owners frequently opposed such undertakings, particularly if the cultivation was to be done by outsiders. But fear of drought and attitudes toward government programs to alleviate it were evolving. In 1946 the Springfield paper described a news story predicting dust storms in Baca County as "concocted by the soil conservationists who are seeking more money from the government to perpetuate themselves in a 'soft' job at the expense of taxpayers."[855] Changing economic incentives and lobbying by absentee owners brought loosening of some restrictions. The state law restricting voting on increasing cultivation to resident owners was changed in 1945.[856] Pressure was also brought to bear at the local level. Soil conservation districts in Baca County canceled their working agreements with the Soil Conservation Service.[857]

Large scale growers, many from neighboring Kansas, felt they had the expertise and capital to successfully grow dryland wheat in southeastern and central Colorado. In Baca County, Tom Hopkins from Haskell County, Kansas was reported to have harvested "130,000 bushels from his 5,000 acres there in five days in 1942 using twenty-six combines and fifty trucks."[858] George Gano from Hutchinson, Kansas acquired extensive holdings in eastern Colorado as well as constructing numerous grain elevators in the region. Among the largest landowners was Ray H. Garvey from Colby, Kansas. His operation was managed by John Kriss, whose ventures in eastern Colorado and western Kansas were described in H. Craig Miner's book *Harvesting the High Plains*.[859] Kriss grew up in Kansas wheat country some sixty miles east of the Colorado border. When his dryland-farmer stepfather abandoned his land and left for Arkansas in the early twenties, the young man remained and found work with area growers. By the late twenties, he was managing sizable farms for a local investor. Over the years he learned to grow dryland wheat successfully in the face of low prices and meager rainfall. This knowledge helped Kriss-managed operations survive with some profit through the thirties. He viewed the land as a valuable resource to be managed prudently. According to Miner, "Short-term profit maximization at the cost of long-term viability was never an option."[860] Kriss's practices included letting part of the land lie fallow each year, combining drilling and listing, and planting the wheat in rows to concentrate the moisture. He recognized the inherent riskiness of dryland wheat farming and was prepared for only two good crops every five years.

In 1933 Garvey, who held extensive acreage in Kansas, was impressed with Kriss's expertise and formed a partnership with him. Their operation in Kansas became immensely profitable by the 1940s as climate and market conditions improved. Hoping to build upon their earlier success, the partnership looked for opportunities in eastern Colorado. By late 1945 they had acquired nine thousand acres and eventually purchased tens of thousands of acres in Kiowa and Cheyenne Counties where land was still relatively inexpensive. They established headquarters in Sheridan Lake in Kiowa County and began to acquire the necessary equipment, soon owning twenty-seven tractors. The scale of their operation brought great efficiencies. Garvey claimed that seven tractors working night and day could drill a section of land in two days. The partnership maintained its long-term focus and continued to prosper over the next several decades, overcoming the hazards of drought and wind erosion. Garvey family members were farming some twenty-five thousand acres of land[861] in eastern Colorado in the mid-1960s and Kriss's family was still growing wheat as late as the 1990s.

Through the efforts of Kriss and others wheat acreage harvested in the sixteen counties grew from around five hundred thousand acres in the late thirties to over two million by 1947.[862] Many New Deal measures to limit dryland wheat cultivation were undone or weakened. According to Miner "lands that had been 'reclaimed' at federal expense were plowed again and produced high yields, often under the management of 'suitcase' farmers driving in from somewhere else."[863] Land classified as "unsuitable for cultivation" by the Soil Conservation Service in the thirties grew profitable wheat crops in the forties. In Baca County, which bore the brunt of the dust–bowl damage and government restrictions, the turnaround was dramatic. Fewer than one thousand acres were harvested in 1935 and 1936 and fewer than twenty-five thousand in 1939. In 1947 County growers harvested more than three-hundred-fifty thousand acres, nearly half-again that in the peak years of the early thirties and production more than doubled to nearly eight million bushels. (Baca County wheat acreage planted was only slightly greater than in 1932, but more than one-third of the earlier year's crop was not worth harvesting.)[864]

Nowhere was the surge in wheat growing more powerful than in the central plains counties where extensive uncultivated and relatively inexpensive land was still available. Only limited wheat planting took place in Kiowa and Cheyenne counties during the twenties and thirties. At their peaks in 1931 neither county harvested as much as twenty thousand acres. By the late forties Kiowa County's harvested wheat land had grown to two-hundred-five thousand acres and that in Cheyenne County to 185,000. Both Counties produced over three million bushels in their peak years compared to less than half a million in the 1930s.[865] A 1947 headline in the *Kiowa County Press* proclaimed, "Kiowa Co. Will Soon Harvest the Biggest Wheat Crop in History."[866] Absentee ownership, which had largely been limited to Baca County in the 1930s, mushroomed in the central plains counties in the forties. Cheyenne County tax rolls for 1946 showed 634 of 888 landowners were nonresidents,[867] and Census data showed substantial nonresident land ownership in Kiowa County.

Grain storage facilities were insufficient to handle the massive harvests and wheat piled up in the streets of small prairie towns awaiting shipment. In 1945 the *Lamar Daily News* reported that southeast Colorado storage bins were full, and grain was being stored on farms or in newly constructed bins. The flour mill in Lamar operated on a twenty-four-hour basis.[868] In the Prowers County town of Holly, wheat was stored in vacant buildings.[869] In July 1946 a half-million-bushel mound of wheat twenty-five feet deep covered a city block in the Kiowa county town of Brandon. Five years earlier no wheat had been shipped out of the County.[870] A Hugo banker reported that in 1948 "Wheat was piled on the ground."[871] In 1948 the wheat harvest around Haswell, a sleepy Kiowa County town of 150 or so residents, was estimated at more than half a million bushels. The Haswell elevator handled a million dollars' worth of wheat that summer.[872]

The post-war wheat boom brought a new level of prosperity. According to the *Kiowa County Press* "this year [1947] our farmers really hit the jackpot with remarkable production, good weather conditions during wheat harvest and handsome price—a combination that has made them wealthy."[873] The following year the same paper effused, "The gold rush to the mountains in the early days has nothing on the 1948 edition in Kiowa County."[874] The paper also noted, "One can easily see the result of good crop production in Kiowa County as reflected in the improvement of farm premises and general appearance of places where people live. A few years ago, most building were poorly kept and in bad repair."[875] Other dryland counties also prospered. Baca County reportedly had the highest per capita income of any county in the US in the late 1940s based on income tax statistics.[876] A breathless account in the *Rocky Mountain News* recounted that a "cattleman or farmer who doesn't carry a $1,000 bill in his pocket when he comes to Springfield is classified as penny-ante." The article claimed that local gambling games required a $5,000 buy-in and that farmers had deposited $3.5 million in the local bank.[877] There is little doubt that Baca County growers were doing very well. Income data from the 1950 Census show that 6.3 percent of the County's families and unrelated individuals reported incomes in 1949 that were greater than $10,000, equivalent to over $100,000 in the early twenty-first century. Growers in other dryland counties also prospered. Kiowa and Phillips Counties reported slightly higher proportions in the top income group than Baca, and in all three, the shares of high-income families were well above the comparable national figure.

The Nonfarm Economy in the Forties

Despite the disruptions from the war, the forties brought a welcome change from the previous decade for most American businesses and families. Wartime mobilization pulled the US economy out of the depression with the nation's employers adding nearly eight million jobs between 1940 and 1945. The war ended but prosperity continued. The feared post-war slump was avoided as pent-up demand and the application to civilian uses of innovative technologies developed during the depression and the war fueled a robust economy. The nation generated another eight million new jobs by 1950. Manufacturing, which comprised nearly one-third of all jobs at the time, accounted for half of the net increase in employment.[878] By almost any measure, the 1940s posted the strongest US growth of any past or future decade for which comprehensive data are available. US economic performance was marred only slightly by a high rate of inflation as consumer prices rose more than 70 percent over the ten years.[879]

Although lacking a manufacturing base comparable to the nation, Colorado's eastern plains economy also enjoyed a healthy expansion as the region reaped the benefits from excellent markets and favorable climate conditions for its still dominant farming and ranching sectors. Virtually all available statistics from the era suggest a vibrant economy. Sales tax collections in the sixteen eastern Colorado counties grew more than 150 percent over the ten years after adjusting for inflation while those for the state increased 95 percent in what was a prosperous decade for Colorado.[880] Similarly, Census data showed a nonfarm employment gain in the forties of more than nine thousand, a rate of increase roughly comparable to that of the nation and a dramatic improvement over the net job loss of more than three thousand in the 1930s.[881] As the region lacked many war related industries, most of the decade's job growth took place in the postwar years.

The southern and central dryland counties enjoyed the fastest growth in the forties as they benefitted most from the wheat boom and its spillover effects on local economies. The southeast and central plains saw gains in population, housing, and construction jobs. As a *Springfield Plainsman-Herald* proclaimed in late 1945, "We are going into 1946 with great hopes for the future…. the county has enjoyed five years of good crops and the farmers are prosperous which in turn makes the whole county prosperous. …. If the county could support 10,500 people in 1930 it could surely support 15,000 now."[882] As it turned out, the County's population approached eight thousand in 1950 but declined to less than half that by 2010.

Construction, manufacturing, and transportation complemented agriculture as driving forces for the region's growth. The three sectors together accounted of more than three thousand net new jobs over the decade. Manufacturing and transportation added around seven hundred jobs each while construction employment increased by almost nineteen hundred. Growth in these industries generated additional jobs elsewhere in the economy through the purchase by businesses and spending of earnings by their workers. Solid growth in these three industries along with strength in agriculture spurred a gain of more than six thousand jobs in trade, services, and local government.

Although the manufacturing sector enjoyed a healthy gain during the forties, it accounted for only 7 percent of all jobs. Its contribution to overall growth was much smaller than nationally where it comprised nearly one job in three. Well over one-third of the seven hundred new manufacturing jobs were found in the "food and kindred products" category which was dominated by processing of agricultural products. Most of the new jobs in this sector were found in the Arkansas Valley. Large manufacturers included three sugar beet plants: American Crystal in Rocky Ford, Holly Sugar in Swink, and National Sugar in Sugar City. Alfalfa milling was another major player with National Alfalfa operating ten dehydrating mills in the Arkansas Valley along with its headquarters in Lamar.[883] Approximately one-fifth of remaining new jobs were in various equipment and machinery production with the rest distributed among other durable and nondurable sectors.

A growing population and pent-up demand due to lack of new construction during depression and wartime led to surge of building in the late forties. The 1950 Census of Housing showed over six thousand homes had been built in the plains counties since 1944, more than in the previous fifteen years. In 1948 a La Junta banker reported surprising strength in the housing market. After the city's wartime expansion when population increased by a reported three thousand, many locals expected a falloff in the economy after closure of the air base, but no slowing occurred.[884] Baca County, with the fastest population growth of any county in the region, saw strong home building in the post war years as did Morgan, Otero and Prowers Counties.[885] The region also experienced a flurry of new retail and commercial building. All counties posted increases in construction employment except Bent County where the number of jobs declined late in the decade after the completion of the John Martin Dam where peak employment reached one thousand workers.[886]

Rail traffic rebounded during the war as gas rationing restricted automobile travel. The boom continued into the early post-war years, but it was beginning to fade by the end of the decade due to competition from autos, trucks, and airplanes. More than 350 railroad jobs were added, over half of these at Santa Fe's facility in La Junta. The Rock Island expanded its Limon work force to accommodate war-time traffic, recalling many workers laid off during the depression.[887]

Prosperity allowed the region's struggling banks to reach financial security and provide funds for local business and farmers. Total loans and discounts at plains banks grew from $99 million in 1943 to $284 million in 1950.[888] The First National Bank of Stratton's experience was typical of small-town institutions rebounding from the woes of the depression era. It was restructured in 1934 under provisions of the Reconstruction Finance Act. By 1944 it was free and clear from its RFC loan as a result of a record wheat crop. Deposits grew from $203,000 in 1940 to $2,233,000 by end of 1947.[889]

Growing sales meant more trade establishments and expansion of existing businesses. The decade saw more than twenty-five hundred new retail jobs including more than seven hundred in eating and drinking places. The *Lamar Centennial* book listed a radio shop, a jeweler, a gift shop and two women's clothing stores that opened their doors in the late 1940s.[890] A Piggly Wiggly grocery store opened in Limon.[891] Improved roads and widespread ownership of motor vehicles made it easier for rural residents to drive to town to shop. As a result, most of the new trade jobs were in the major trading centers in in Logan, Morgan, Otero, and Prowers Counties. The demand for services grew, driven by an increasing population and greater affluence. The medical and other professional services category, composed of lawyers, teachers including those in public schools, and medical professionals, added over eight hundred jobs. Public administration, including most government employees other than educators, saw a gain of nearly 250. Business and repair services made up of auto and machinery repair as well as such business services as janitorial firms added 541 employees.

Population and Labor Force

Despite the return of prosperity, more people left the region during the forties than moved in. Unlike the thirties their motivation was more pull than push. They moved to take advantage of attractive options elsewhere rather than to escape tough times at home. During the war young men joined the military and both men and women left to take well-paying jobs in the defense industries. Forrest Bellus who owned the Merino newspaper was forced to close the paper due to wartime rationing and took a job at the ordnance depot in Sidney, Nebraska.[892] Harold McKenney came to Logan County in 1940 to teach at the Harding School and married a local woman. But when war broke out, he moved to California to work in a defense plant.[893] Not all who left returned. After the war, now booming factories provided more attractive jobs than those available at home, and the GI bill allowed many young men to attend college. Despite the attractions of the nation's metropolitan areas, improving local economies in the 1940s slowed out-migration from that in the previous decade. Net outmigration in the forties totaled just almost nineteen thousand roughly half that of the previous decade.

Typically, younger people were most likely to move. Almost half of those leaving the region in the 1940s were between five and nineteen at the beginning of the decade. The aging of the population, so evident in the 1930s, slowed after 1940 but did not reverse. In 1930 the median age for the region was twenty-three years; it rose to 26.3 by 1940 and to 27.2 in 1950. However, the region's population was, by this measure, still almost three years younger than that of the US. The proportion of the population over sixty-five increased, rising from 4.5 percent in 1930 to 6.7 percent in 1940 and to 8.3 percent in 1950.[894]

The eastern plains, like the rest of the nation, experienced a "baby boom" in the post war period. Higher birth rates along with slowing out-migration helped the eastern plains counties post a modest three thousand population gain during the forties, a dramatic turnaround from the large loss in the 1930s. Still, population grew relatively slowly with annual gains of only 0.2 percent while the US saw a much faster growth of 1.4 percent per year. The southeast experienced the fastest growth in the forties, driven by wheat-boom-fueled prosperity. Baca and Prowers Counties added over three thousand new residents between them, more than accounting for region's entire increase. The central plains counties saw a slight increase while the South Platte Valley and the northeast plains reported small losses.

Perhaps the most dramatic demographic change during the decade was the sharp decline in the number of people living on farms. As more off-farm jobs became available, many farmers and their families left the land, some moving out of the region and others resettling in nearby towns. Those leaving farms more than accounted for all the out-migration, as towns and rural non-farm areas both saw net in-migration.[895] During the 1940s the Census count of farm residents fell by almost one-fifth while that in rural-nonfarm areas and in towns grew by 22 percent. But the farm population remained significant, comprising a much greater share of the total than the comparable national figure.

In 1940 drought and depression had left many residents either out of jobs or in undesirable ones, so enough workers were available to fill employers' needs even in the face of the exodus of younger people. Employers were able to hire those who moved from farms or were unemployed or underemployed at the beginning of the decade.

Only 40.6 percent of the regional population fourteen and over were employed in 1940 compared to 44.7 percent for the nation. (Both figures exclude those in depression-era emergency jobs such as those in CCC camps.) By the end of the decade the region's share of employed working-age residents had risen to just under 51 percent, close to that of the nation.[896]

Many of the new jobs were filled by women who entered the labor force in numbers far exceeding those in earlier decades. As the nation mobilized, men joining the military left jobs for women not previously employed in the formal economy. When farm families moved to towns, wives and daughters could find jobs with local businesses or governments. Female labor-force participation rose throughout the nation, but the increase was more pronounced in rural areas. In 1940 the share of regional working-age women who were employed was under 14 percent. By 1950 more than 22 percent held jobs. The growing number of women working accounted for more than two-fifths of the gain in regional employment during the forties.

How much did residents benefit from the strong economy? The 1950 Census reported household and family income estimates for the first time, and the Census data suggest that after a decade of solid growth plains residents' standards of living were at least comparable to those of most other Americans. The 1949 median income for regional families was $2,596.[897] Adjusted for inflation that figure is equivalent to nearly $26,000 in 2015 or less than half the level at the later date.[898] By this measure, the region appears to be poorer than the nation where median income was more than $400 higher. But regional living costs were lower than in large metropolitan area where costs of living were considerably higher. In 1950, 46 percent of the US population lived in what the Census designated "urbanized areas," defined as cities of 50,000 or more and surrounding "settled places" while none of eastern Colorado's population resided in a town with more than 8,000 people.

Comprehensive 1949 estimates of costs of living are not available, but the Census provided estimates of home values by county. Housing is the single largest cost for the most households and housing costs vary more by region than most other expenditures. As a result, comparative home prices provide a rough guide to differences in living costs. According to the 1950 Census of Housing, the median value of a single-family home, excluding those on farms, for most counties in eastern Colorado fell between four thousand dollars and the low five-thousands. Morgan County's figure of $6,329 was by far the highest in the region. The US median value of similar dwellings was $7,354, almost 40 percent higher than in most eastern plains counties and 15 percent higher than in the most expensive county.

Incomes in the region varied widely by county. Incomes of residents of the larger towns exceeded those in the rest of the region so the more rural counties usually had lower average incomes. The lowest family incomes were in Crowley and Elbert Counties with reported median incomes around $2,000 while the highest were in Kiowa and Logan Counties. The Arkansas Valley counties posted incomes below the regional average while those in the northeastern counties tended to be higher.

Eastern Colorado in 1950

At midcentury the eastern plains economy had overcome much of the damage from the depression and drought. Rural residents had enjoyed a prosperous decade and the towns were thriving. While the vagaries of weather, world markets, and federal farm policy still raised concerns, residents had ample cause for hopefulness. Looking back on the forties, an editorial in the *Lamar Daily News* effused that the region was "at the peak of an expansion period comparable to any in its 64-year history."[899] But the booming economy of the forties would stall in the early fifties.

CHAPTER 7

Chapter 7 Exhibits

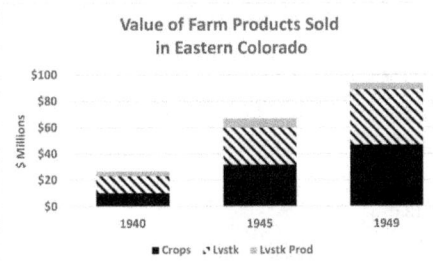
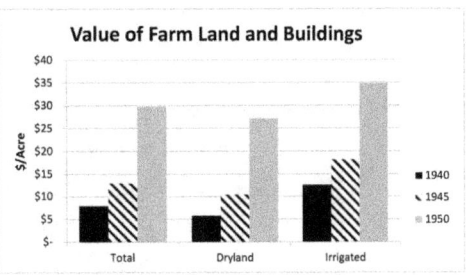

Camp Amache

American agriculture flourished during the forties and eastern Colorado farmers and ranchers shared the good fortune. The value of farm products sold more than tripled over the decade due to both higher prices and increased production. Grain sales surged in response to wartime and post-war demand giving rise to a boom surpassing that following WWI. Livestock sales also enjoyed a healthy increase and continued to account for the largest share of revenues.

Rising values of farmland provide evidence of this prosperity. The value of regional land and buildings rose from less than $10 per acre to nearly $30 over the decade.

Camp Amache near Granada. The site contained more than two hundred buildings. At its peak more than seven thousand Japanese American internees were housed there, more than of any town in the region at that time. Camp residents made a significant contribution to the lower Arkansas Valley economy during the war years.

Source: Census of Agriculture, The Denver Public Library, Western History Collection, call number x-6570

STRUGGLE ON THE HIGH PLAINS

Population Change 1940-50

	1940	1950	Pct. Ch.
Baca	6,207	7,964	28%
Bent	9,653	8,775	-9%
Cheyenne	2,964	3,453	16%
Crowley	5,398	5,222	-3%
Elbert	5,460	4,477	-18%
Kiowa	2,793	3,003	8%
Kit Carson	7,512	8,600	14%
Lincoln	5,882	5,909	0%
Logan	18,370	17,187	-6%
Morgan	17,214	18,074	5%
Otero	23,571	25,275	7%
Phillips	4,948	4,924	0%
Prowers	12,304	14,836	21%
Sedgwick	5,294	5,095	-4%
Washington	8,336	7,520	-10%
Yuma	12,102	10,827	-11%
Total	148,007	151,140	2%
Irrigated	91,804	94,464	3%
Dryland	56,204	56,677	1%
Baca	6,207	7,964	28%
Ark. Valley	50,926	54,108	6%
Central Plains	24,611	25,442	3%
Platte Valley	40,878	40,356	-1%
Northeast	25,386	23,271	-8%

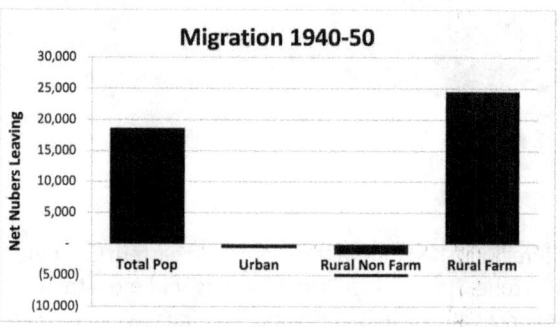

Regional population increased by three thousand or 2 percent during the 1940s. The gain was entirely due to the high birth rate as almost nineteen thousand people left the region on a net basis. War mobilization meant that many young men were called to military service and large numbers of both sexes left to work in the war industries. Out migration was dominated by those leaving farms as both urban and rural-non-farm areas experienced net in-migration. Prowers and Baca County populations both grew by more than 20 percent while the central plains counties of Cheyenne and Kit Carson posted gains of more than 10 percent.

Source: Census. See appendix for description of migration estimates.

CHAPTER 7

Employment Change 1940-50

	Total			Non-Agricultural		
	1940	1950	Pct. Ch.	1940	1950	Pct. Ch.
Baca	1,764	2,804	59%	778	1,415	82%
Bent	2,611	2,801	7%	1,677	1,801	7%
Cheyenne	939	1,336	42%	410	678	65%
Crowley	1,371	1,549	13%	582	782	34%
Elbert	1,877	1,633	-13%	518	565	9%
Kiowa	828	1,202	45%	354	709	100%
Kit Carson	2,221	3,504	58%	952	1,722	81%
Lincoln	1,913	2,189	14%	935	1,197	28%
Logan	5,541	6,544	18%	3,123	4,044	29%
Morgan	4,943	6,591	33%	2,662	3,889	46%
Otero	6,195	8,008	29%	4,359	6,267	44%
Phillips	1,623	1,762	9%	801	951	19%
Prowers	3,510	5,187	48%	2,152	3,457	61%
Sedgwick	1,721	1,838	7%	872	1,060	22%
Washington	2,741	2,823	3%	807	995	23%
Yuma	3,736	4,071	9%	1,452	2,126	46%
Total	43,534	53,842	24%	22,434	31,658	41%
Irrigated	25,892	32,518	26%	15,427	21,300	38%
Dryland	17,642	21,324	21%	7,007	10,358	48%
Baca	1,764	2,804	59%	778	1,415	82%
Ark. Valley	13,687	17,545	28%	8,770	12,307	40%
Central Plains	7,778	9,864	27%	3,169	4,871	54%
Platte Valley	12,205	14,973	23%	6,657	8,993	35%
Northeast	8,100	8,656	7%	3,060	4,072	33%
US (Thou.)	45,070	56,435	25%	36,621	49,527	35%

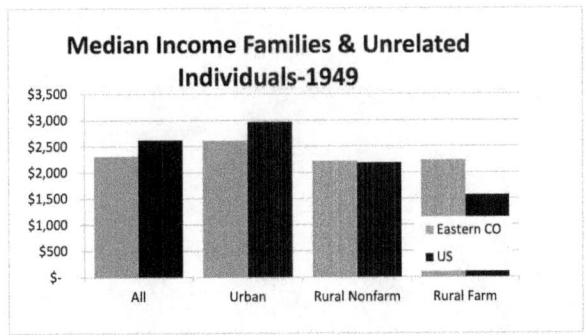

The plains economy in the forties was the strongest in a quarter century, benefitting from the wartime and post-war recovery as well as a buoyant agricultural sector. Employment gains were robust with more than ten thousand new jobs added, a rate of increase close to that of the nation. All counties except Elbert added jobs, and all added nonfarm jobs.

The Census first reported county household incomes for 1949. Regional median family incomes were some $400 below the national figure, a difference largely explained by the share of national urban dwellers in large metropolitan areas where living costs were higher. Regional farm residents' median household income was well above that of the nation and that for rural nonfarm income was also slightly higher.

Source: Census

CHAPTER 8

Post-War Exuberance Fades: 1950-1970

HIGH PLAINS' POST-WAR PROSPERITY ENDED IN THE EARLY FIFTIES. AGRICULTURAL markets weakened and drought returned to the southern and central plains. Though farming and ranching remained the dominant industries, their role in the region's economy continued to shrink as farms moved away from a model of smaller diversified units toward larger, more specialized, and commercial operations. The competitive advantages of the region's sugar beet industry were being eroded, most markedly in the Arkansas Valley. Irrigation spread as farmers took advantage of innovations and increased their use of underground water. The post-war surge in automobile ownership gave rise to an oil boom in northeastern Colorado. But the plains' rural settlement pattern and lack of manufacturing held its economy back in a time of increasing industrialization and concentration of population in large metropolitan areas. Growth over the twenty years fell well short of that of the surging US economy.

Return of the Dust Bowl

As the new decade opened the southern plains climate once again turned dry. Outsiders and plains residents alike viewed yet another drought with foreboding. A *New York Times* article in May 1950 filed from Springfield displayed the headline, "New Dust Bowl Threatened in 5 Arid Southwest States."[900] An AP story in April 1950 warned, "Drouth has it by the throat. Rain is 'a must' if a good soaking one doesn't come soon it looks bleak across the plains known as the nation's wheat belt."[901] But no relief came, and the dry years continued. Measured by the paucity of precipitation, the drought was comparable to that of the thirties. According to the Palmer Drought Severity Index, it lasted six years, reaching its nadir in 1954.[902] Annual precipitation in Springfield fell from eighteen inches in 1946 to ten in 1953 while Burlington's dropped from twenty-two to thirteen. In 1956 Cheyenne Wells, Eads, Kit Carson, La Junta and Springfield all reported less than ten inches of precipitation for the year.[903] John

Martin Reservoir on the lower Arkansas, viewed at its dedication in 1948 as a source of additional irrigation water, became virtually dry.[904]

The dust storms soon returned, extending as far as the northeastern plains. In the spring of 1950 the regional director of the Soil Conservation Service reported localized soil blowing on seventy-four thousand acres with mostly sandy soil south of Yuma.[905] An AP story described the March 25 and 26, 1950 duster in Sterling as the "worst since 1936."[906] But, as in the thirties, the storms were most damaging in the southeast. In January 1952 poor visibility from blowing dust caused a six-car crash on highway 287 between Lamar and Springfield.[907] The *Springfield Plainsman-Herald* described a February 1954 storm that combined blizzard conditions with blowing dust as "the worst dust storm since the depression days of the 1930s."[908] Colorado Governor Thornton, while flying back from Washington, observed a cloud of dust spreading across the plains from Omaha to the west and lamented, "I fear it is only a forerunner of what we are going to get."[909] In 1956 a Springfield teenager boating on Two Buttes Reservoir drowned in high wind and dust.[910]

The chance of relief through weather modification captivated farmers and businessmen. A *Lamar Daily News* editorial declared that a local Chamber of Commerce committee set up in 1954 to investigate rainmaking possibilities "may prove to be the most important committee of a number of committees that have been named by the Lamar Chamber of Commerce through the years."[911] That year Reuben W. Frost of Little Neck, New York, who claimed to have brought more rain in New York and Texas, established temporary headquarters in Lamar.[912] But the promises went largely unrealized, and the drought persisted.

Once again, the dust storms attracted the attention of the national media and government officials and, as in the thirties, the locals were less than thrilled with the attention. A Kansas newspaper reporter wrote derisively of Baca County's Dust-Bowl tourists: "Planeloads of dignitaries accompanied by newsmen, photographers and radio representatives are circling low over the area, then returning to air-conditioned offices to speak and write hysterically of the Gawdawfulness of the situation. Photographers are reviving the classic poses of 20 years ago, showing the desolate wind-swept plains, gaunt livestock and the weary sad-eyed farmers."[913] But downbeat reporting was not limited to outsiders. A July 1953 headline in the *Springfield Plainsman-Herald* on the Governor's trip to assess drought conditions declared "GOV. THORNTON INSPECTS BACA'S DESOLATE, PARCHED LAND."[914]

As in the thirties, wheat farmers suffered the greatest damage. Much of the crop was too poor to combine and haul to market. In five of the six years from 1951 through 1956, wheat was left in the field on more than a million planted acres or roughly one-third of plains counties' total. Most of the unharvested acreage was found in four southern counties: Baca, Cheyenne, Kiowa, and Prowers. The yield in these counties averaged more than twenty bushels per acre harvested in the best years of the forties. By 1954 it had fallen to between five and seven.[915] Baca County's 1954 crop was described as "destined for complete failure" by a National Farm Loan Association official. This official estimated that farmers who planted from four hundred to fourteen hundred acres would have a hundred to maybe a hundred and fifty acres worth cutting with an average yield from two to five bushels to the acre.[916] Production in the County fell from nearly eight million bushels in 1947 to just over two-hundred thousand in 1954. The central plains counties also saw declining yields. Cheyenne County produced nearly three million bushels in 1948 and Kiowa County 3.7 million. Seven years later output in the two counties had fallen to 168 thousand and 286 thousand, respectively. Growers in the northern dryland counties fared better as the drought was less severe and earlier production levels were largely maintained.[917] Pastureland also suffered from the lack of rain or snow. In 1950 the Crowley-Kiowa-Lincoln Counties Cattlemen's Association estimated that 90 percent of the range stock were either sold or moved out of the drought area.[918]

Federal and state governments were quick to respond to the crisis. By 1951 Baca and Prowers County farmers had received a total of more than half a million dollars to defray costs of conservation measures. In 1954 the Colorado Legislature passed a wind erosion law providing $1 million in aid,[919] and the Governor appointed a special long-range statewide erosion committee to "force compliance in soil conservation practices and land use by withholding state aid to those who refuse to follow procedures that benefit the entire community."[920] In 1954 and 1955 the US Department of Agriculture allocated funds for emergency tillage. A farmer could receive seventy-five cents an acre for listing, fifty cents for chiseling and $1.25 for contour strip cropping, all methods of plowing or planting that reduced wind erosion.[921] In 1954 growers applied these measures on some eight-hundred thousand acres of Baca County cropland or more that 90 percent of the County's cultivated acreage.[922]

The measure that proved most helpful to Colorado crop farmers was the 1956 legislation establishing a "Soil Bank" that enabled the federal government to pay farmers for removing crop land from production. The program had two elements. One involved a temporary set-aside where the farmer agreed to leave land idle. A second option required a long-term commitment to refrain from planting.[923] The Soil Bank was not universally popular. Selling the idea of paying farmers not to plant crops was at best challenging. The public also objected to the cost of the program that reached nearly a billion dollars a year. Rural economies suffered from what was described as "the negative impacts on rural businesses and institutions in communities where farmers placed whole farms in the Soil Bank."[924] If the farmer was cultivating fewer acres, he had less need for fertilizer or farm equipment. Outside investors taking advantage of this program provoked further cynicism. As Leslie Hewes wrote, "When in the late 1950s the government was again trying to bail out farmers and retire poor land from cultivation, loopholes in the regulations governing the conservation reserve of the Soil Banks permitted absentees to become landowners and nominal wheat farmers for the purpose of collecting government payments."[925]

Supporters of the program hoped that removing land from production would limit the crop surpluses the government was forced to purchase. Although it brought some reduction in output, planners' and politicians' more optimistic expectations were not realized. Farmers placed their least productive acreage in the Soil Bank, and surpluses continued to accumulate, eventually necessitating further government intervention. As noted by Paosour and Rucker in their critique of government farm policy, "The Soil Bank program provides another example of how government programs often create pressure for additional government action to cope with the undesirable consequences of the original program."[926] Supporters also hoped for a positive impact on soil erosion but, here too, the program may have had unintended negative consequences as Gary Penley observed in his memoir of his family's Prowers County farm:

> The program had a catch. For the landowners to qualify for Soil Bank money, the government somewhat naively required them to plow the designated farmland each year. They couldn't plant it, but they had to plow it. Of course, everyone would rather collect Soil Bank money than plant crops destined to fail, so they plowed their fields.
>
> The High Plains soil has the consistency of a very fine silt. In a severe drought, the dry soil would have remained more stable had it been left untouched, unplowed. The plowing program decreed by the government broke the soil down into the finest particles of silt. The wind could then lift it as much as a half mile high and carry it great distances, building volume as it moved across the land.[927]

For all its faults, the Soil Bank brought financial relief to drought-stricken wheat farmers, and they eagerly embraced it. Pressures from growers resulted in even more aid than envisioned in the original legislation. The program was intended to pay farmers only for land that was not planted. This meant that land with a winter wheat crop destroyed by drought and wind before harvest was not eligible for payment. After hearing complaints from beleaguered farmers, the Secretary of Agriculture agreed to make payments for land where the 1956 crops were lost. This change brought forth a surge in enrollments from eastern Colorado growers. Local agricultural offices were swamped; some eight hundred thousand acres in the region were expected to be enrolled.[928] Wheat acreage planted in eastern Colorado dropped by 40 percent or nearly one million acres between 1956 and 1957 as the Soil Bank program took effect.[929] In 1957 Baca County farmers received $2.6 million from the program.[930]

Relief finally came in the spring of 1957. A heavy snowstorm in March contributed to the most precipitation Springfield had received in that month since 1926, and April was also well above normal.⁹³¹ Both Lamar and Las Animas reported more than fifteen inches of precipitation in both '57 and '58. The water in John Martin Reservoir reached a record high.⁹³² I remember a boom in boat sales in Lamar and water skiing at area reservoirs in late fifties summers. In April 1957 the soil conservationist in Prowers County described the situation as "more promising than any time since the drought began."⁹³³ Wheat production rebounded; dryland growers in Baca County reported yields of ten to thirty-five bushels per acre in the 1957 harvest.⁹³⁴ A high school classmate who worked summers in the late 1950s at the Lamar grain elevator recalled trucks lined up for several blocks waiting to unload their wheat.⁹³⁵ Baca County output exceeded five and a half million bushels in 1958 while that in Cheyenne and Kiowa Counties reached four million.⁹³⁶ The entire region enjoyed bountiful harvests. A July 1957 headline in the Wray Gazette proclaimed, "This Region Is Harvesting a Bumper Wheat Crop."⁹³⁷ Despite some hail damage Yuma County wheat farmers were expected to average over thirty bushels per acre in 1958, and Kit Carson County's production reached an all-time high.⁹³⁸

Despite a drought at least as harsh as that of the 1930s, damage to the region's economy and ecology was much less severe. By 1959 the inflation-adjusted value of products sold by regional farmers had rebounded to 10 percent above its 1949 level.⁹³⁹ The dust storms were annoying and disruptive. I was in junior high and high school at the time and recall road visibility limited to the point where driving was virtually impossible, cancellation of outdoor school athletic events, and layers of fine dust piling up on the floor of our home. But according to those who experienced both episodes, the filthy fifties did not approach the severity of twenty years earlier. Wind erosion was much less damaging. A newsman visiting Baca County reported that "In spite of the extreme long dry period, wind erosion has been held to a minimum except in the Edler and Pritchett areas [in western Baca County] where sandy soil has made the problem more difficult."⁹⁴⁰ Both the agricultural and non-farm segments of the regional economy slowed but the business failures and economic destitution of the thirties were largely avoided. A reasonably healthy national economy and the absence of a collapse in farm prices limited the local damage.

Timothy Egan in *The Worst Hard Time* attributed the more favorable outcome to federal programs instituted in the thirties. Citing a 2004 academic journal article, Egan wrote, "What saved the land, this study found, was what Hugh Bennett had started: getting farmers to enter contracts with a soil conservation district and manage the land as a single ecological unit. By 1939, about twenty million acres in the heart of the Dust Bowl belonged to one of these units."⁹⁴¹ But this is only part of the story. The soil conservation districts indeed contributed to the better stewardship of the land, but as noted earlier, their power and influence had diminished by the late forties. Other factors also helped limit the damage. Growers were in better financial condition. The onset of the fifties drought followed a dozen or so years of almost unprecedented prosperity leaving farmers with greater resources and lower debt. As a result they were better equipped to take conservation measures with or without government assistance. The thirties drought was preceded by the twenties' agricultural depression, and, as noted earlier, even those farmers who were aware of the need for conservation measures, and many were, often could not afford to implement them.

Consolidation of acreage into larger farms increased incentives for conservation as well making it more affordable. The journal article referred to by Egan summarizes this argument: "The prevalence of small farms in the 1930s limited private solutions for controlling the downwind externalities associated with wind erosion."[942] The authors found that small farmers were less likely to let portions of their land lie fallow or employ other anti-erosion practices. A large operator such as John Kriss would be more motivated and more able to implement conservation measures as indeed Kriss did in Kansas in the 1930s and in eastern Colorado in the forties and fifties. The Census of Agricultural Census showed that more than one million acres of cropland in six eastern plains counties were reported as lying fallow in 1949.[943] The wider availability of irrigation, particularly the use of ground water in formerly dryland areas, was yet another advantage of the 1950s farmers. High plains farmers were better able to cope with the 1950s drought, as they would be in later dry spells in the seventies and in the early twenty-first century.

The Agricultural Environment in the 1950s and 1960s

American farmers enjoyed unparalleled prosperity during wartime and in the immediate post war years, but the good times did not last. Growers continued to produce crops in volumes that exceeded demand and markets softened over the next twenty years despite ongoing efforts by politicians to limit supply and maintain prices. By late 1940s government support programs had generated growing surpluses that only briefly disappeared during the Korean War. To deal with burgeoning stocks of grain in government backed storage, Federal programs were modified to make price supports more flexible and to further reduce potential supply as in the Soil Bank program discussed earlier. The government also attempted to increase demand for farm products with measures such as PL 480 or "Food for Peace," that subsidized the export of price-supported grain to third-world nations, and domestic food subsidies such as the food stamp and school lunch programs.

By 1960 the government had largely abandoned efforts to lower production through acreage control, and the Kennedy administration attempted to directly control production. Price supports were made contingent upon farmers voting to participate in production controls. But farmers frequently did not approve controls, and congress balked at allowing prices fall low enough to discourage production. Further legislation in 1964 authorized direct payments to farmers who participated in voluntary land retirement programs. All these programs contributed to the dramatic rise in the cost of farm programs during the period but were not terribly successful in limiting production or maintaining prices. Nor did they provide much help to small farmers. In Thomas Wessel's view, price supports were not "high enough to allow small farmers to stay in the industry and not low enough to induce large producers to voluntarily reduce the acreage they planted."[944] Prices, especially for crops, failed to keep pace with rising expenses. By the late sixties, corn and wheat prices had fallen to less than half their post-war peaks and surpluses reached record levels. The Department of Agriculture's index of prices received by farmers increased only 8 percent between 1950 and 1970 while that for prices paid rose 52 percent.[945] Total national farm proprietors' income over the twenty years was flat, a decline of almost one-third in real terms.[946] However, ranchers and feeders largely remained profitable as the price of cattle nearly doubled while feed costs declined.[947]

Impacts on Regional Farmers

The fifties and sixties were a difficult time for Eastern Colorado growers. They scaled back their operations in the early fifties as prices fell and drought returned. The acreage of cropland harvested declined almost one-fourth between 1949 and 1954 with the largest reductions in the southern and central dryland counties. Improved weather brought some recovery in the last half of the decade, but the sixties saw no further gains. The total value of crops sold reported in the 1969 Census of Agriculture Census was virtually unchanged from a decade earlier and acreage harvested was near the depressed 1954 level.[948] Since farmers' costs continued to rise, this reduced their incomes. Growers of the region's principal crops adjusted to changing conditions. Wheat farmers reduced plantings due to lower prices and increasing government restrictions. Corn growers shifted toward more irrigated land as use of ground water increased. Improved plant varieties and greater use of pesticides and herbicides greatly increased yields for both crops.

Like the nation, the region experienced a shift toward fewer but larger operators as the competitive environment for smaller farmers became more challenging. Farms had been growing larger for decades, but by the 1950s it was becoming clear that the small family farm was no longer economically viable. They were replaced by larger units more compatible with modern technology and market conditions. As depicted by John Opie, "Beginning in the 1950s the historic family farm in many cases became a private, heavily capitalized and mechanized operation. Today plains farmers resemble the nation's small businesses more than their pioneer forbears. [Successful farmers are] large scale, vertically integrated corporate operations."[949] As farms expanded, agricultural operations concentrated on commercial crops and livestock; growers became more specialized with a greater share of their cultivated land devoted to a single cash crop. Such a lack of diversification made them more vulnerable to fluctuations in world markets or local weather. Greater capital was needed to operate efficiently. In 1969 regional farmers reported the value of all machinery and equipment at $147 million, up from $31 million in 1945.[950] This amounted to an increase by a factor of roughly 3.5 in equipment per farm after adjusting for inflation.

Many smaller farms were abandoned or bought out by larger operators. Between 1945 and 1969 the number of farms fell by 4,000 while acreage increased by 600,000. Nearly all of increased acreage occurred in holdings greater than 1,000 acres.[951] Many rural residents, especially young people, left the land as nonfarm employment opportunities became increasingly attractive. Between 1940 and 1970 the number of people living on farms fell by three-fifths, a decline of more than forty thousand.[952]

Even as larger farms expanded, many of the region's marginal operations hung on. In 1949 almost one-sixth of commercial farms in eastern Colorado reported that the value of their farm products sold was less than $2,500.[953] Twenty years later that proportion was roughly the same even though the value of the dollar had shrunk by about one-third.[954] These small farmers typically had diversified output and frequently supplemented their income with off-farm jobs. In 1949 more than 12 percent of all commercial farms in the region reported operators working over a hundred days off the farm. By 1964 the share had risen to 23 percent.[955]

Midcentury saw the beginnings of decline in the region's sugar beet industry. Eastern Colorado was a leading producer in the early twentieth century, but by the 1960s its dominance was fading, especially in the Arkansas Valley. Strong wartime and postwar demand stimulated production by growers and plant expansion on the part of the sugar companies. But late 1940s legislation-based acreage allocations for farmers used a formula that disadvantaged Colorado beet growers. By the 1950s, regional sugar-beet plants' capacity exceeded farmers' production.

At the same time the sugar companies faced rising costs from operating below capacity and the obsolescence of factories that had been constructed early in the century. The newer plants could produce up to ten thousand tons per day, or as much as four times that of the older facilities and were able to achieve substantial economies of scale. Some of the older plants were expanded, but their decades-old structures limited options for increasing capacity or taking advantage of new technology.[956] American Crystal bought Holly Sugar's Swink plant in 1959 and closed it.[957] National Sugar shuttered its Sugar City plant in 1967 after many growers shifted to a new more efficient Great Western plant near Goodland, Kansas.[958] With the closing of the Sugar City plant, American Crystal's Rocky Ford plant was the industry's sole survivor in the Arkansas Valley. The loss of the beet plants was a blow to local economies. National Sugar at the time of its closing was the largest employer and the second largest taxpayer in Crowley County.[959] According the Chris Woodka, in his series in the *Pueblo Chieftain* on irrigation in the Arkansas Valley, Crowley County farmers were owed a quarter of a million dollars when the plant shut down.[960] Farmers' profits from growing beets diminished as they faced rising labor expenses and frequent shortages of irrigation water, but they continued planting to keep their allotments. When allotments were eliminated in 1967, farmers switched to more profitable crops.[961] By 1970 beet production in the four Arkansas Valley counties had fallen to less than 30 percent of its wartime peak.[962]

The sugar-beet industry in the South Platte Valley still thrived; production in the sixties exceeding that in the forties or fifties.[963] Cultivation expanded to new territory with greater use of ground water irrigation in Kit Carson and Phillips Counties. But growers in the northern and central areas were threatened when Great Western, with its monopoly of processing, encountered financial turbulence, making it difficult to fund the investments necessary to upgrade its out-of-date plants. In 1967 William M. "Billy" White, Jr., scion of a prominent southern Colorado banking family, gained control of GW, soon rechristened "Great Western United," through his ownership of Colorado Milling and Elevator (CM&E), a long-time Colorado flour milling company. He soon used the company's assets to diversify further, acquiring a Christmas tree grower and a developer of retirement and vacation communities to add to a pizza chain previously acquired by CM&E. White described his vision for the company as "part of the bigger question of how are the people of the world to be fed and how our companies are to be involved in feeding the people."[964] The views of beleaguered beet growers who depended on the company to purchase their output were less sanguine. In the late sixties, I attended a Great Western stockholder meeting where attendees included beet growers with long-time holdings of company stock. White was outlining his vision of the company and was asked by a farmer/stockholder about a recent financial transaction. White concluded his response with the comment, "I think we got a good deal."

The farmer replied, "I think we got a good screwin!"

The failure of many of White's new ventures along with the deteriorating conditions of GW's sugar operations led to pressures from stockholders and lenders. White resigned his position with GW, by then reorganized as Great Western United, in 1972. But the company's troubles and the attendant difficulties for Platte Valley growers were far from over.

Labor shortages were a growing problem for beet farmers as well as growers of onions, melons, tomatoes, potatoes, green beans and cucumbers in the Arkansas and South Platte Valleys and broomcorn in Baca County. In 1968 Morgan County pickle farmers complained that much of their crop went to waste in the fields for want of workers to pick the vegetables.[965] Mexican nationals brought in through the *Bracero* program had provided vital seasonal labor since the forties. In the early sixties, *Braceros* accounted for roughly one-third of the eighteen hundred Arkansas Valley seasonal workers used in May and June, about half the two thousand in September and three-fourths of the twenty-five hundred workers in May and June in the Sterling-Fort Morgan area.[966] But the federal government was under increasing pressure to end the program. Organized labor and worker-rights advocates complained about unfair competition as well as poor working conditions and mistreatment of field laborers and their families. Such complaints, although sometimes motivated by political or financial interests, had merit. In the late fifties, my summer job was delivering bakery goods to rural grocery stores. I was told by a store manager in Walsh, where underground irrigation had recently bought an increase in beet growing, that bread delivered on the day migrant crews were brought into town to shop should have no price tags. I don't think that was because he was giving them a discount. A report by the Colorado Legislative Council in 1962 found that some migrant housing "could not be considered adequate, even by minimum standards. [Some migrant camps] lacked minimum proper sanitary conditions proper sewage and garbage disposal and inadequately protected water supplies."[967] The federal government ended the *Bracero* program in 1964. Some local pundits attributed the difficulties of the sugar beet industry in the Arkansas Valley and the closure of the Sugar City plant to this action.[968]

Farmers and community leaders responded by improving conditions for the workers to attract domestic migrant workers in place of the *Braceros*. Growers in Prowers County upgraded workers' living quarters after pressure from the state health department and demands for better living conditions by new workers.[969] In Fort Morgan a community effort was launched to clean and improve conditions in the "Spanish Colony" near the city.[970] The La Junta school district explored options to improve the learning experience of Latino students.[971] But worker shortages persisted. Some growers contracted with undocumented migrants but were thwarted by stepped up enforcement of immigration laws. In 1966 the *Arkansas Valley Journal* wrote: "A critical farm labor shortage in the Arkansas Valley is swinging toward an acute stage and making a bad situation worse in a very drastic continuing roundup of Mexican 'Wetbacks' by the Border Patrol and Immigration officers."[972] The *Journal* reported that through August 1966, some 204 workers in the Arkansas Valley had been seized for deportation along with another twenty-four in northern Colorado. According to the farmers quoted in the *Journal*, the agents not only disrupted work of the crews but drove their vehicles through fields destroying crops. The demise of the *Bracero* program accelerated the trend toward automation. According to a recent *Economist* magazine article, "farmers swapped Mexicans for machines."[973]

Cattle ranchers and feeders, unlike their fellow agriculturists, enjoyed a prosperous decade and a half after overcoming the effects of the drought. Affluent Americans ate more beef, and cattle prices rose 23 percent during the fifties and another 21 percent during the sixties.[974] Important developments in biochemistry reduced costs and raised efficiency. Antibiotics such as Aureomycin combatted disease and increased gain when used as a feed supplement. Poisons controlled worms and insects while animal hormones accelerated weight gains.[975] Regional ranchers and feeders eagerly exploited the improved environment. The value of livestock and livestock products sold tripled during the sixties accounting for the entire increase in farm sales over the decade[976] with almost two-third of this increase taking place in the Platte Valley and Northeastern counties.

Much of the increase in cattle inventories was accounted for by expanded feeding operations. The Colorado Department of Agriculture reported nearly four hundred thousand cattle on feed in the eastern plains counties in 1970.[977] According to a US Department of Agriculture Report, the growing number and size of feedlots along the North and South Platte Valleys could be explained by the greater availability of feed.[978] The sugar beet industry provided livestock feed in the form of beet tops, pulp, and molasses, and more feed grain was produced as the use of underground water greatly increased corn yields. These developments encouraged more feeding by farmers as well as the development of large-scale commercial feed lots.[979] By the 1960s three large feedlots operated near Sterling: Seckler's Feed Lots, Lebsack Feed Yards, and E.E. Sonnenberg and Sons Feed Lot. Feeding also expanded in the Arkansas Valley with Otero and Prowers County reporting eighty-five thousand head on feed between them on January 1, 1970. According to the Powers County feeder Terry Turner, "The climate in the area is the best in the United State for finishing cattle."[980]

Although agriculture's importance in the region was declining, it was still critical to local economies. In 1969 the Bureau of Economic Analysis (BEA) began publishing estimates of earnings by industry. These data showed that over one-fourth of regional earnings were received by farmers or farm workers.[981] The comparable share for the state of Colorado was 3 percent. The dependence on agriculture varied widely by county, ranging for 60 percent in Kiowa County to less than 10 percent in Otero County. Three quarters of farm receipts came from the sale of livestock, 16 percent from sale of crops and the remaining 9 percent from government payments. Crop receipts and government payments were more important in the dryland counties. While government payments made up 16 percent of total receipts in the central plains, they accounted for only 3 percent in the South Platte Valley. Livestock sales were the greatest in the irrigated regions where most of the feedlots were located, especially in Morgan and Logan Counties.

Irrigation

Plains farmers who survived the thirties hoped to do better in the next drought through greater and more efficient use of irrigation. This would require new sources of water as well as investment in delivery systems. Until the late 1940s, most irrigation was based on gravity driven surface water flows, a practice known as flood irrigation, that was not too different from that employed in ancient Mesopotamia. The farmer diverted water from the small lateral ditches that carried it to his fields by damming the laterals and shoveling out a part of the ditch wall to channel water to the crops. When a portion of the field had been flooded, he repaired the ditch wall and repeated the process further down. Wartime technological developments allowed him to improve on this process. Concrete, plastic, or rubber lined the laterals. More efficient centrifugal pumps moved water through aluminum pipes to the fields, uphill if necessary. Most of the pumps were powered by gasoline that remained cheap until the 1973 oil boycott although REA electricity or natural gas were also used. As the water reached the field, the crop was then flooded using aluminum pipes at two-hundred-feet intervals.[982] The improvements required larger capital outlays by the farmers, often partially subsidized by the Department of Agriculture to encourage conservation of water. Use of pumps and aluminum pipes represented a sizable improvement although a great deal of hand labor was still needed, and substantial water was still lost to seepage and evaporation.[983]

Center-pivot irrigation, introduced in the early fifties, was yet more efficient. The system, invented by a farmer near Strasburg, Colorado, was patented in 1952 and was commercially available a year later. A center-pivot consisted of a central pump which fed several aluminum pipes with sprinklers along their lengths running out from it. The pipes were supported by trusses mounted on wheeled towers and moved around the pump at the pivot powered by water pressure. This created a circular irrigated area. Center-pivot systems used less water than earlier flood irrigation and could apply fertilizer, herbicides, and pesticides.[984] They could also repair the damage from commercial nitrogen fertilizers that would burn the soil during drought periods.[985] Larger operations often installed an even more efficient system that irrigated a field with a self-propelled system consisting of long pipes covering the widths of fields as they traversed them. But sprinkler systems were expensive. William Splinter's 1976 *Scientific American* article estimated the installation costs at $350 per acre.[986] John Opie placed the early fifties cost of a basic well and pumping system at $4,000.[987] But the threat of drought could justify the investment if the farmer could afford it.

Prowers County farmer Leabert Brazell realized the gains from sprinkler irrigation. He purchased an eight-hundred-acre farm northeast of Lamar in 1959 that had two miles of underground irrigation pipe and one mile of concrete ditch. But he still lost too much water due to the farm's sandy soil. He installed two self-propelled sprinklers, the shorter of these at one thousand feet irrigating one hundred acres with one inch of water every forty-eight hours while the thirteen-hundred-foot sprinkler watered 140 acres at the same depth every sixty-six hours. By the mid-sixties he was successfully raising wheat, milo, melons, and cucumbers.[988] John Gentz, a large landowner in Prowers and Kiowa Counties spent an estimated $42,000 to irrigate previously dry land. He laid two miles of plastic pipe four feet underground from a well to his dryland acreage with the water pressure delivered by a seventy-five-horsepower motor to power a fifteen-tower sprinkler.[989]

Wells made possible the irrigation of land not covered by the earlier systems of dams and ditches as well as supplementing the water from earlier sources. Nineteenth century settlers had relied on windmills to pump water for personal use or livestock.

But windmills could not deliver the volume needed to irrigate large fields, and much of the water in the aquifers was too far below the surface to be raised by wind power. Improved drilling and pumping technology overcame these barriers. Thousands of eastern Colorado wells were drilled near streams to draw water from alluvial aquifers. The ground water in these aquifers, also called tributary aquifers, is hydrologically part of a natural stream flow.

Vast amounts of water are also found in sedimentary aquifers deposited beneath the plains in earlier geologic eras. The largest in the American Midwest is the Ogallala Aquifer, a formation of water-saturated gravel beds extending through the central and southern plains. The Ogallala underlies 14,900 square miles of eastern Colorado farmland mostly in Baca, Kit Carson, Phillips, and Yuma Counties. It only recharges very slowly, so it is being "mined" as the water is depleted by irrigation. William Ashworth in his 2006 book on the Ogallala described the condition of Colorado's part of the aquifer:

> The state sits along the upstream fringe of the aquifer, and water has been draining out of it ever since this region of the High Plains was severed from the Rockies, roughly three million years ago. Irrigation has sped the outflow considerably. More than 10 percent of the state's historic portion of the Ogallala is now gone, half of it in the last twenty years. The water table, never healthy, has dropped an average of nine feet; in large parts of Yuma and Kit Carson Counties; along the state's eastern border, the decline is closer to fifty feet. Over the majority of Colorado's portion of the High Plains, the Ogallala's water today is less than fifty feet thick.[990]

Farmers increasingly relied on ground water from both alluvial aquifers and the Ogallala. Farmers in Phillips County reported experimenting with pump irrigation as early as 1940, and Kit Carson County saw extensive drilling after the dry years in the early fifties.[991] By 1959 one-third of irrigated farms in the sixteen counties used some ground water and one-fifth of them relied on it exclusively.[992] By 1972 the South Platte Basin contained an estimated thirty-two hundred wells pumping at least a hundred gallons per minute.[993] In 1969 irrigated crop land in the region had more than doubled from its 1940 total, an addition of more than four-hundred-fifty thousand acres. Over three-hundred thousand acres of this increase occurred in dryland counties where irrigation had been extremely limited. In 1940 fewer than a thousand acres were irrigated in either Baca or Kit Carson County and less than two thousand in Yuma County. By 1969 Baca County's irrigated farmland exceeded sixty thousand acres and that in Kit Carson and Yuma Counties was nearly ninety thousand in each. By the late sixties Baca County had some six hundred deep wells, 90 percent of them in the eastern part of the County near Walsh.[994]

Wells drawing on the Ogallala Aquifer greatly increased dryland yields of corn, milo, or wheat. Irrigated wheat helped compensate for a poor dryland harvest in Baca

County in 1962.⁹⁹⁵ New crops such as sugar beets, pinto beans and vegetables were now feasible on farmland that had formerly depended upon natural precipitation. Harvested acreage of irrigated corn in the dryland counties increased from two thousand in 1950 to more than a hundred thousand in 1969.⁹⁹⁶ Exploiting the aquifer allowed beet cultivation in dryland counties. GW planted test plots in Kit Carson County in the spring of 1956. Pleased with the results, the company met with local farmers urging them to apply for allotments, leased machinery to the farmers and helped them obtain the necessary transient workers.⁹⁹⁷ The first beets were planted in the Burlington area in April 1957 and at the end of May, thirty-two Mexican Nationals arrived by bus in time for thinning. In July the Rock Island Railroad announced plans for beet dumps along its line. Seventeen County farmers contracted for a crop but planting and thinning were delayed by heavy rains. Although the initial harvest was somewhat disappointing, the following year saw better results with yields increased by up to four tons per acre.⁹⁹⁸ By the late sixties the County produced more beets than any other in the region.⁹⁹⁹ Kit Carson County was not alone. A 1958 headline in the *Springfield Plainsman-Herald* proclaimed, "Irrigation Wells Boosts(*sic*) Economy."¹⁰⁰⁰ In 1962 residents of Walsh in eastern Baca County gazed at a huge pile of harvested beets 600 feet long, 125 feet wide, and 30 feet high.¹⁰⁰¹

Underground water use was mostly unregulated in its early years as the connection between alluvial aquifers and flowing streams was not well understood. But by the early sixties, it became apparent that surface irrigators and those drawing from wells in a river basin were competing for the same water. In 1965 the State Legislature enacted The Colorado Ground Water Management Act subjecting ground water to appropriation rules under the control of the State Engineer. The 1965 act affirmed that alluvial ground water was assumed to be tributary to a natural stream and subject to the priority system. A permit from State Engineer's office was required before drilling a well.¹⁰⁰² This restriction was not well received by owners of existing wells and the provisions of the act were not clear to many. An editorial in the *Arkansas Valley Journal* charged that the legislation "has stirred so much controversy and seems to be working so poorly than change is obviously needed."¹⁰⁰³ In 1967 the State Engineer tried to shut wells near the Arkansas River. This action was overruled by State Supreme Court thereby stripping the state of power to enforce provisions of the 1965 legislation. However, in its ruling the Court set standards that provided the basis for future regulation.¹⁰⁰⁴

The next major legislation was the 1969 Water Rights Determination and Administration Act that "set forth a method of incorporating wells outside areas set aside under the 1965 Act into the priority system."¹⁰⁰⁵ Alluvial waters, underground or surface, would be distributed by state engineers. A well permit would be necessary for the use of ground water, and all users would be governed by the rules of prior appropriation. This meant that if a user of a decreed right had insufficient water, the user could notify the Water Commissioner for the district requesting that upstream users with junior rights be restricted. The Commissioner could then limit junior upstream users, including those drawing from wells, to meet the shortfall.[1006] The act treated the use of sedimentary-aquifer water such as that in the Ogallala differently. It was classified under Colorado law as "designated groundwater." The prior appropriation system would apply in most cases but could be modified to permit full economic development of ground water resources.[1007] These measures provided some clarity but did not put an end to disputes over water use.

More irrigation water became available when two large projects, initiated in the thirties and described in chapter 5 but delayed by the war, were completed in the post war years. The completion of the John Martin Dam in time for the 1949 irrigating season fulfilled longtime dreams of Prowers and Bent County farmers. The dam provided 402,000-acre-feet of storage for irrigation purposes, allowing a more regulated flow to the lower Arkansas Valley[1008] It also enabled a settlement of a long-running dispute regarding the allocation of water between Colorado and Kansas and afforded flood protection. In 1965 the project proved its value when the Arkansas flooded causing substantial damage in Lamar and Holly. But losses would have been much worse in the absence of the dam.

The $160 million Colorado-Big Thompson diverted water from Colorado Basin on the western slope through the Adams Tunnel to several reservoirs in the South Platte Basin. It furnished electric power and water for municipal and agricultural use in the Northern Colorado Water Conservancy District that included portions of Morgan, Logan, Washington, and Sedgwick Counties. The tunnel was completed in 1944 and the first water was pumped through it in 1947.[1009] In 1953 it began delivering water to South Platte Valley farmers. Between 1957 and 1960 the project was estimated to have provided 40 percent of water used on seasonal crops as well as electric power for many rural cooperatives.[1010]

Oil Boom in the Denver-Julesburg Basin

In the early fifties, while most regional farmers suffered from low farm prices and meager precipitation, some fortunate landowners in northeast Colorado were enjoying renewed prosperity. Along with abundant grassland and fertile soil, Logan, Morgan and Washington Counties' natural resources included pools of oil beneath their land which became much more valuable after World War II. When gasoline rationing was lifted shortly after Japanese surrender, American motorists took to the streets and highways filling up their gas tanks and buying new cars that would guzzle still more fuel. The price of a barrel of oil rose 70 percent between 1946 and 1948[1011] spurring a search for more reserves. Among the promising sites was the Denver-Julesburg Basin, a geologic formation centered in northeastern Colorado and extending into southeast Wyoming and southwest Nebraska. Oil was first found in the Basin near Boulder in 1901, and sporadic exploration occurred in subsequent years. But few producing wells were found. In 1949 a major discovery in southwest Nebraska set off a flurry of activity in that state as well as elsewhere in the Basin with numerous new fields being developed in northeastern Colorado.[1012]

The initial stirrings of the boom were felt in Logan County. While exploration dated back to 1913, results had not been promising. A costly 1917 drilling operation near Padroni and another major effort in 1926 failed to produce enough oil to be profitable.[1013] Six wells were drilled near Sterling in 1949.[1014] The first success came the following April at the Segelke Well south and west of Peetz. Witnesses to the drilling test reported that "crude oil, of light green color and apparently high gravity, drenched the floor, drilling crew and machinery as joints of pipe were removed from the hole."[1015] The Segelke was the first of many producing wells discovered by the Plains Exploration Company of Sterling, one of the largest independents operating in the Basin that was controlled by Allan W. Biggerstaff of Sterling.[1016] Biggerstaff came to Sterling in 1917 to take a position at the local paper where he soon became editor. During his regular Sunday country drives, he asked his wife to take notes on the stakes in the ground with little ribbons indicating areas of interest to geologists. Based on this information and his growing knowledge of local geology, he acquired a sizable block of mineral leases in Logan County.[1017] When drilling began, he owned a portfolio of valuable rights and became a major figure in the regional oil industry. He was sometimes referred to in Logan County as "Mr. Oil."[1018]

The early discoveries gave rise to mounting optimism. The *Rocky Mountain News* proclaimed "Not only is the drilling easy because of the soft-sand structure of the subsoil but the wells are producing top, premium oil—38 to 40 gravity type."[1019] Demand for the Basin's oil increased with the completion in 1953 of a $2.5-million-dollar pipeline that could transport seventy thousand barrels of oil a day to a main line in Nebraska that connected to refineries in the Midwest.[1020] Exploration companies stepped up their activities. A compilation by the Colorado Department of Natural Resources showed eighty-three new fields discovered in Logan County in the 1950s.[1021]

Sterling, described by the *Rocky Mountain News* as the "hub of the entire boom," displayed the excesses and the strains that invariably accompany resource discovery and development. The *News* described the town as the "hottest, happiest, boomiest and most prosperous spot in the state."[1022] Residents either enjoyed or suffered from the growth surge, depending upon their financial interests in oil properties. Sterling's population, measured by the 1950 Census at 7,534, was reported to be "more than 10,000"[1023] in early 1952 and eleven thousand[1024] a year later. A survey in early 1955 by Sterling churches concluded that population in the area had grown to over twelve thousand.[1025] Plans were announced for a $2.5 million subdivision to house the burgeoning population.[1026] State sales tax receipts from Logan County grew by 37 percent between 1950 and 1953.[1027]

CHAPTER 8

Those fortunate enough to own mineral rights to land with productive wells suddenly became wealthy. Several Logan County farmers were said to receive as much as a million dollars a year.[1028] The new wealth was not limited to a few farmers. The police chief was reported to have supplemented his salary with revenue from six wells.[1029] Exploration and production spawned numerous supporting businesses. By early 1953 Sterling housed forty new service firms in addition to those directly involved in drilling and production.[1030] The 1960 Census showed a gain of 350 oil and gas industry jobs in Logan County over the previous decade. Spending by leaseholders and energy workers generated jobs in retail, hotels, restaurants and other services. The boom also brought headaches. Traffic increased, and crime rose. Demand for new homes surged along with housing costs and construction activity. The city issued a total of forty-nine residential building permits with a value of $290 thousand in 1948 and 1949. By 1954 and 1955 the building pace had grown to 274 permits with a value of $2.1 million.[1031] Burgeoning population put new pressures on local government. Salaries of government employees were increased substantially in the face of the inability to "get workers at the old prices because of oil field wages"[1032] in the words of a local official. School enrollments reached record levels necessitating the construction of new buildings. But the new wealth brought additional revenues. In 1952 voters approved a $375,000 bond issue for a new fifteen-room elementary school.[1033] The county commissioners took advantage of the expanded tax base to build new fairgrounds, buy an oiling plant, embark upon a county road improvement program, expand the local airport, and build a new Logan County Hospital.[1034]

Energy activity soon reached beyond Logan County. In February 1950 the *Sterling Advocate* reported "Scouts and 'lease hounds' for oil companies, who have been numerous in Sterling during the past months, today were reported intently watching the outcome of plans to test possible production at Adams-Lee No. 1 test, southwest of Brush."[1035] Within a few years forty-eight new oil fields[1036] and several important gas fields were found in Morgan County.[1037] Four refineries producing butane and propane were constructed within twenty-five miles of Fort Morgan.[1038] As oil and gas activity increased, Fort Morgan residents complained about high home prices.[1039]

Washington County, with sixty new oil fields shared in the prosperity. A representative of the Rocky Mountain Oil and Gas Association claimed that by the fall of 1950 some four million acres in the Denver-Julesburg Basin, including that in Front Range counties and in Nebraska and Wyoming, were under lease for exploration generating three million dollars annually in income.[1040] Oil activity made an important contribution to the economic health in the face of a weakening farm economy. Both Logan and Morgan Counties registered robust population gains in the fifties while the remaining plains counties saw declines.

The boom peaked in the middle 1950s and then, as booms inevitably do, it dissipated. In 1950 wells in Logan, Morgan and Washington Counties produced a combined total of just over one-hundred thousand barrels of oil; by 1955 output exceeded twenty-two million barrels. But production declined by the sixties. While drilling in the area was relatively easy and inexpensive, the pools of oil were small and short-lived. Despite conservation efforts and secondary recovery methods production in the basin fell. By 1970 output in the three major oil-producing counties had fallen to less than one third of its mid-fifties peak.[1041] But even with reduced output, oil and gas activity still accounted for more than one million dollars in earnings in both Logan and Morgan Counties.[1042]

Expectations for oil and gas production were also raised in the central plains and southeast. A *Lamar Daily News* editorial observed hopefully: "For half a century local and outside interests have been seeking to find the oil which most geologists have agreed is here."[1043] But exploration turned out to be less fruitful than further north. The early fifties saw some successful gas wells in in southeast Baca County.[1044] Bent and Elbert Counties reported exploration and limited production. The most activity outside the Denver-Julesburg basin was in Kiowa County. The County's first producing oil well, located southwest of Eads, was completed in winter of 1956.[1045] By 1968 the Brandon field boasted thirty-one producing wells and the *Arkansas Valley Journal* could report that oil and gas activity had "given the economy of Kiowa County a shot in the arm."[1046] But activity further south never approached that of the Denver-Julesburg Basin.

Other Key Industries

America's midcentury economy maintained its strong growth from the post war years. Inflation slowed in the fifties, and expansion was only briefly interrupted by three mild recessions. But the high plains lagged behind the rest of the nation. The US economy was dominated by large entities: big firms, strong labor unions, and an expanding government. Large corporations were controlling ever more of the economy. The strongest of these firms enjoyed high barriers to entry and were able to pass on the costs of generous worker compensation and heavy regulation. Most of the best new jobs were with large firms or federal agencies. America's people increasingly chose to live in cities or their suburban fringes limiting the customer base for businesses in rural areas. The mostly small businesses in the plains counties were at a disadvantage in that environment.

Although enjoying a temporary surge in the war and immediate postwar years, the economy in rural America failed to fully recover from the Great Depression. Nobel laureate economist Joseph Stiglitz[1047] theorized that the difficult transition from an agricultural economy to a manufacturing one was an important contributor to Great Depression. In his view, productivity gains along with drought and low prices greatly reduced the demand for farmers and farm workers. As a result, much of the workforce was unemployed or badly underemployed, and the economy stagnated from lack of demand. Eventually the wartime and post-war boom in manufacturing generated new jobs for the redundant laborers leading to a period of robust and sustained growth through the fifties and sixties. But the plains economy, lacking a manufacturing base, did not share in the nation's transition.

Buoyant agriculture concealed the region's underlying weakness during the war and post-war years, but it became apparent by the 1950s. While national growth was fueled by robust manufacturing, the regional economy was dragged down by a declining farm sector. Regional manufacturing and agriculture both outperformed their national counterparts as measured by job growth. But US manufacturing employment comprised 27 percent of all jobs in 1950 while it was only 4 percent of the regional total. Agricultural employment declined by at least half in both the nation and the region, but only accounted for 13 percent of national employment in 1950 compared to 41 percent in eastern Colorado.[1048] The plains' tiny manufacturing sector was unable to provide much impetus to the regional economy despite healthy growth, while weakness in agriculture depressed growth.

As agriculture languished and businesses struggled, the regional economy's fifties performance fell well short of that in the previous decade, and the sixties saw only modest improvement. Between 1950 and 1970, the region lost more than five thousand jobs and almost twenty thousand people. All but two counties registered declines in both employment and population. The exceptions were Logan and Morgan Counties, both benefitting from the oil and gas boom.[1049]

Homebuilding was no longer the spur to growth it had been in the immediate post-war years. By the early fifties most of the pent-up demand for new homes that accumulated during the war and depression had been satisfied. Stable or declining populations reduced the need for more homes and building slowed. During the last half of the 1940s nearly twelve hundred new homes were built in the region each year. This rate fell to around nine hundred annually in the first half of the 1950s and by another quarter over the next fifteen years.[1050] Building declined in all counties except Morgan and Logan where further population growth sustained the boom through the fifties. Total construction employment in the region fell by almost a quarter over the two decades.[1051]

Despite a shrinking economy and population, more people were employed providing health care, education, and repair services for both households and businesses as rising incomes and school enrollments increased demand for these services. Between 1950 and 1970 some forty-six hundred new jobs were added in the "Medical and other professional services" category with total employment more than doubling over the twenty years. Almost half of all workers in the category were employed at public or private elementary and secondary schools or colleges, and another third worked for health care organizations. Several communities added or expanded health care facilities. The Kit Carson County Hospital opened in Burlington in 1949, and Sterling's twenty-bed Logan County Hospital opened in 1954. Hugo also opened a hospital and nursing home in the fifties.

The region added almost twelve hundred retail trade jobs over these two decades. But this was less than half the number in the 1940s. Nearly all the new jobs were in the larger towns as shoppers demanded greater selections and often better prices. A study of the economy of the Arkansas River watershed by the University of Colorado School of Business in the mid-sixties found that the number of retail establishments declined markedly between 1948 and 1963 in largely rural Baca, Bent, Crowley, and Kiowa Counties while remaining roughly constant in Otero and Prowers Counties.[1052] Residents of Springfield, Eads, and Ordway reported losing trade to larger communities.[1053]

The healthiest economies were in the South Platte Valley which benefitted from the oil boom, growth in cattle feeding, and expansions of colleges and hospitals. The central dryland counties struggled in the fifties from the effects of the drought but rebounded to some extent in the sixties, as groundwater irrigation and feedlots expanded. The Arkansas Valley's economy was the weakest. The early fifties drought and the travails of the sugar beet industry took its toll on farm income with resulting weakness in the nonfarm economy. Reduced Santa Fe traffic through La Junta brought a reduction in railroad jobs in that city.

Some important employers were lost. Both the flour mill and National Alfalfa's headquarter ceased operations in Lamar. The Lamar Flour Mill, a fixture in the town since the late nineteenth century, closed in 1960.[1054] The relocation to Kansas City of National Alfalfa's headquarters, that had been housed in Prowers County since 1908, was a result of changes in the industry and the company's structure. As the firm's president explained: "In the beginning, the center of operations for the company was Eastern Colorado, but as mergers and expansion began to take place, the center of operations moved eastward, and therefore, while we regret to ask some of our staff to remove from Lamar, it is only good business to do so."[1055]

Farsighted community leaders realized the need for a more diversified economy. But the plains suffered from many competitive disadvantages. Labor costs were low, and the potential work force possessed adequate skills, but distances from major population centers rendered it uneconomical for production of bulky or heavy items other than agricultural products. Similarly, isolation made it unsuitable for service industries beyond those needed by the local populations. Most businesses serving national markets were unlikely to locate in eastern Colorado. As a Limon editorialist wrote, perhaps with excessive pessimism, "We are constantly being harassed by people who wish to know what the chances are of landing an industry in Limon. The chances, to put it bluntly—very thin." [1056]

CHAPTER 8

Community development strategies largely focused on two types of manufacturing firms: processors of farm products and relatively labor-intensive firms that could be attracted by the region's lower costs. The plains hosted a few firms in the latter category, most of them small. Regional metal and machinery manufacturing businesses including companies making auto trailers and mobile homes, which accounted for almost a quarter of all manufacturing workers. Nearly every plains town with at least a few hundred residents had several small machine shops. There were a few larger manufacturers. NIBCO of Colorado in La Junta, a maker of plumbing fixtures and supplies, employed more than a hundred workers in 1969. Clark-Feather Manufacturing, a long-time Fort Morgan firm, made more than forty different tools used throughout the nation. [1057]

The region was in a stronger position competing for agribusiness jobs. Food and kindred products producers, the category that included all the large regional manufacturers, accounted for about half the regional manufacturing workers in 1970. Four of the seven manufacturing facilities with more than a hundred workers in 1970 were sugar beet plants. [1058] Other farm-products processors included firms producing animal feed such as Mohrland Brothers in Brush or food processors such as Holbrook Turkey Growers in La Junta. Fruit and vegetable processors Western Canning in La Junta and Frozen Foods, Inc. in Rocky Ford employed more than a hundred workers each. The plains counties also hosted pet food manufacturers, creameries, flour mills and bakeries. Several firms produced supplies for farmers and ranchers including Colorado Plant Food in Otero County that made and distributed fertilizers and Nichols Tillage Tools, an Elbert County farm equipment manufacturer. [1059] In 1954 a subsidiary of National Alfalfa built a chemical plant in Lamar to produce chlorophyll from alfalfa. The product enjoyed a brief market boom in the fifties as it was believed to eliminate odors and was added to numerous products including gum, toothpaste, soap, and even cigarette filters. But soon researchers questioned its value and demand faded. [1060]

Lamar's economic development efforts, representative of those underway in most of the larger plains towns, experienced early failures followed by modest success. In 1959 community leaders formed the Greater Lamar Improvement Company (GLIC) with the goal of attracting manufacturing firms. [1061] Its first success was with Midway Homes, a Dallas based maker of luxury mobile homes, that located a facility in the city, taking advantage of local and federal government financing and favorable lease terms. But the business failed within two years and another mobile home manufacturer was equally unsuccessful. The property was then leased to WHO Manufacturing, a local firm making heavy duty feed grinding equipment that was looking for a larger plant site. [1062] In 1968 the firm employed thirty-two workers and had a payroll of $160,000. WHO's worldwide business improved in the late sixties, and it moved to larger quarters in 1968. Aspen Ski Wear, a Denver-based firm looking for a second facility in the state, leased part of the former WHO site. The portion of the facility not utilized by Aspen was leased to Cross Hydraulics, a producer of hydraulic cylinders for agricultural equipment. Lamar's economic development efforts would achieve their greatest success in the early eighties when the German bus company Neoplan opened a plant in the city.

Population and Incomes

Better economic opportunities elsewhere and the failure of many small and medium-sized farms encouraged many residents to leave the region. Between 1950 and 1970 more than fifty-five thousand people, or over one-third of 1950 population, are estimated to have moved from the eastern plains. This figure may appear surprisingly high. But in the absence of migration, population would have experienced healthy growth in both the fifties and sixties since the region's baby boom continued through the middle sixties. As a result, the number of people living in the sixteen counties fell by only 18,000 or 12 percent.[1063]

Young people were the most likely to leave as their job opportunities diminished. High school graduates left for college or the military or took jobs in metropolitan areas. An Arkansas Valley businessman lamented that his community was "nothing but a stud farm for Denver."[1064] More than three-quarters of net migration was accounted for by those under twenty-five in 1950.[1065] An attempt to track my Lamar High School class of 1957 showed that roughly 56 percent of those for whom information could be obtained pursued their adult careers outside the region, and some 85 percent of my classmates with college degrees, including those from two-year colleges, left.[1066] In 1999 Bob Ewegen, a columnist for *Denver Post,* described a survey he conducted of his Holyoke High School class of 1963. Of those surveyed, 93 percent expected to leave Phillips County upon graduation.[1067]

Once again, the largest population loss occurred among farm families as more rural residents chose to live elsewhere. In earlier times farmers were able to leave economically viable farms to many of their sons. Their daughters seldom received such an inheritance although their fathers often hoped they would marry other farmers' sons. By the fifties, the scale required for successful operations had eliminated this career option for many rural young people. Even among those who continued to farm, social amenities and better educational opportunities for their children often persuaded them to move to town. Over the twenty years some forty-four thousand rural farm residents either moved to one of the nearby towns or left the region, and the number living on farms fell by more than half.[1068]

Like others in post-war America, plains residents increasingly relocated to cities or suburbs. By 1970, 58 percent of the nation's people were dwelling in what the Census calls "urbanized areas," made up of a city with a population of at least fifty thousand and its surrounding settled areas, compared to 46 percent twenty years earlier. Population gains in these conurbations, none of which were found in eastern Colorado, accounted for nearly all national growth between 1950 and 1970. Plains residents who remained in the region were also more likely to live in larger communities, albeit more diminutive ones. By 1960 more eastern Colorado residents lived in towns larger than twenty-five hundred than lived on farms. By 1970 Sterling had grown to more than ten thousand people and populations in La Junta, Lamar and Fort Morgan all exceeded seven thousand.[1069]

Economic activity also shifted toward the larger towns. Some businesses were attracted to the region but, because of better public services and such amenities as superior schools and a wider selection of homes, they were more likely to locate in La Junta or Sterling rather than in Manzanola or Merino. The smaller towns struggled to survive. Main streets displayed abandoned and shuttered buildings and schools were closed. By the sixties many smaller plains communities evoked images from *The Last Picture Show,* the Larry McMurtry novel and 1971 movie about a dying Texas town. Grocery stores, restaurants, law offices, and other local businesses closed, and, as in McMurtry's fictional town, movie houses succumbed to struggling local economies and competition from rivals in larger communities. The Rialto Theatre in Haxtun, operated for years by the Muchie family who served as ushers, janitors, cashiers, and projectionists when necessary, screened its last movie around 1970.[1070] Three quarters of Colorado's eastern plains towns with fewer than a thousand people lost population between 1950 and 1970 as did half of those between a thousand and twenty-five hundred.[1071]

A robust economy meant unprecedented prosperity for American families in the fifties and sixties with median family income, after adjusting for inflation, doubling between 1949 and 1969. Despite sluggish growth, regional families also enjoyed an improving standard of living although their income gains fell short of those in the rest of the nation. Regional families' real median income grew by 80 percent in twenty years. But the 1969 family income of $7,154 was almost $2,500 lower than the comparable national figure, compared to a $500 gap twenty years earlier. The South Platte Valley registered the highest income, nearly $1,200 or 18 percent higher than that in the Arkansas Valley.

The region's lagging income growth can be explained by a combination of a lethargic economy, the absence of large metropolitan areas where incomes were higher, and a greater proportion of elderly, many with limited assets or earnings. In 1970, 14 percent of the region's residents were sixty-five or over compared with 10 percent of the nation's population.

Gains in regional incomes were, at least in part, a result of a better educated and therefore more productive work force. In 1950 roughly one-third of residents over twenty-five were high school graduates. By 1970 this share had risen to more than half. The proportion with college degrees rose from 4.6 percent to 7.5 percent over the same period. However, the nation's more urbanized population had higher levels of education than the plains' rural and small-town residents.[1072]

The Eastern Plains Economy in 1970

The post-war euphoria had long since worn off. The plains economy was still heavily dependent on a declining agricultural sector and failed to benefit from booming manufacturing or the movement to the suburbs that drove national prosperity in the fifties and sixties. The shrinking numbers of farmers and ranchers meant they made a smaller contribution to the economy. Oil and gas brought wealth to many residents of the Denver-Julesburg Basin, but production had declined by 1970. Lack of job opportunities encouraged many younger people, particularly those with more education or marketable skills, to leave the region. As young adults moved out, the falling share of working age population presented a burden on local economies and a challenge to future growth. The early seventies would bring renewed prosperity for farmers and ranchers. But it would be relatively short-lived and its impact on the overall economy would be less than in earlier agricultural booms.

Chapter 8 Exhibits

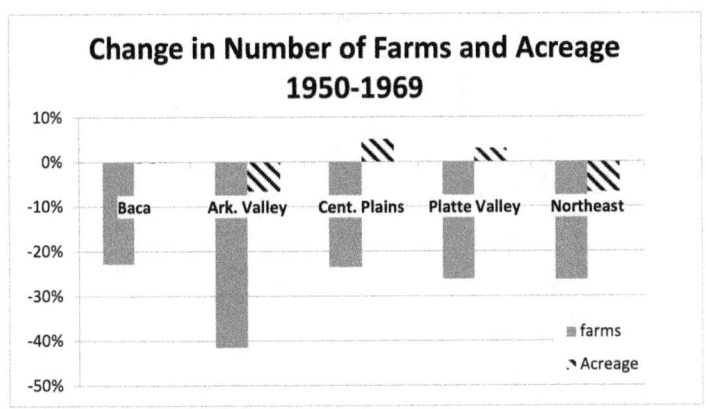

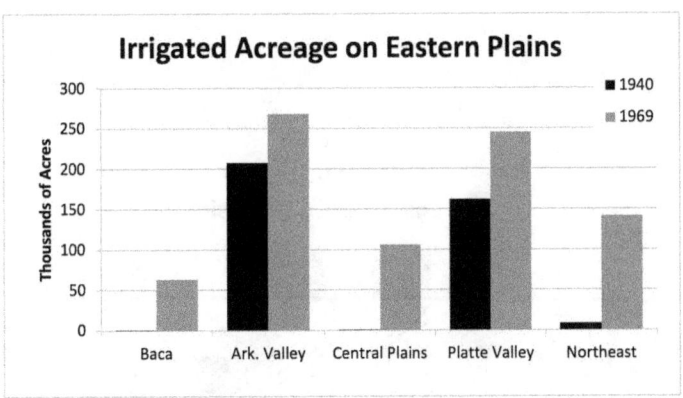

Scale became essential in American agriculture, and the post-war era saw the virtual disappearance of the small family farm as an economically viable entity. Many small operators remained but they became increasingly dependent on off-farm income. The total number of farms in the region declined nearly 30 percent between 1950 and 1969.

Droughts in the thirties and fifties made irrigation more attractive, and new technology made it more affordable. The most dramatic increase occurred in areas that had earlier lacked access to surface water. Dryland farmers were now able to pump sufficient water to irrigate crops and pastures. Wells drawing on the Ogallala Aquifer accounted for most of the increase in Baca County, the northeast and the central plains.

Source: USDA, Census of Agriculture

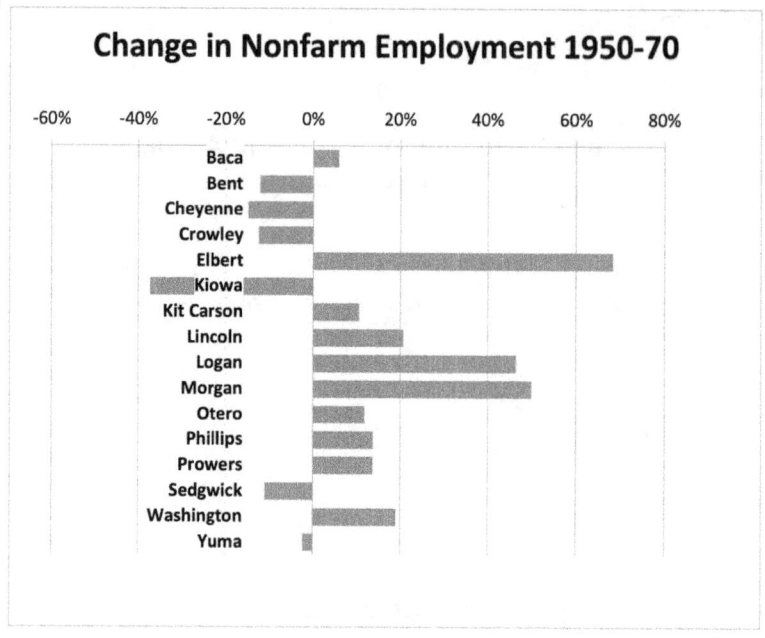

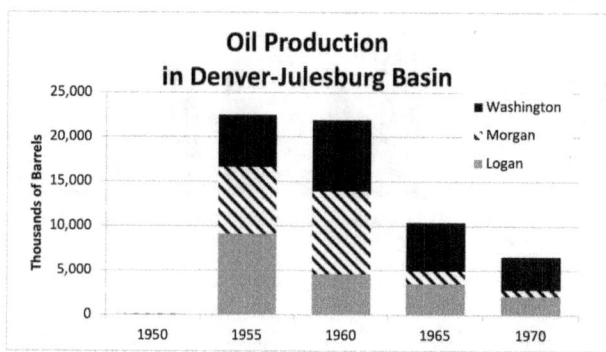

Nonfarm employment for the region increased by almost 5,400 or 17 percent over the twenty years, well short of the US gain of almost 55 percent. Logan and Morgan Counties posted large gains stimulated by the 1950s oil boom and a healthy agricultural sector. Elbert County's strength was due to its proximity to Metro Denver.

Oil production in the eastern-plains portion of the Denver-Julesburg Basin peaked at over twenty-two million barrels in 1955 but declined through the sixties. While drilling was relatively easy and inexpensive, the pools of oil were small and short-lived, and the boom did not last into the sixties.

Source: Census. Colorado Oil and Gas Conservation Commission

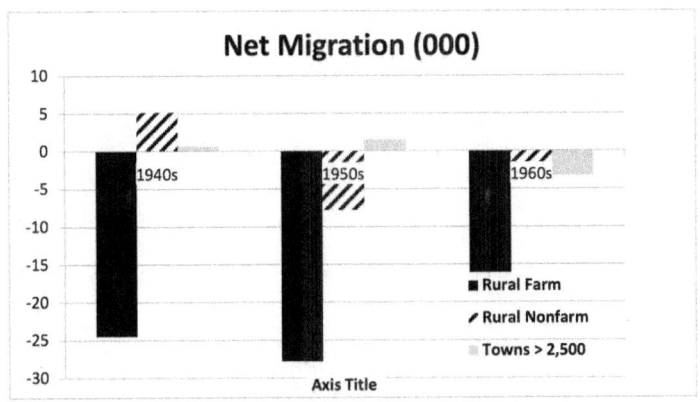

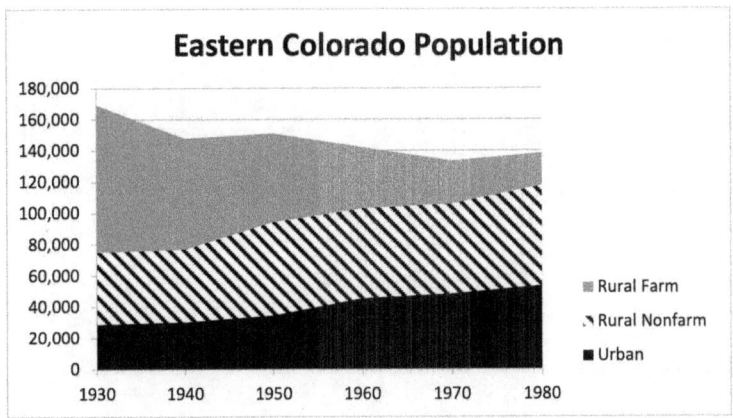

Net out-migration totaled over 34,000 during the fifties and almost 22,000 during the sixties. Only high post-war birth rates prevented a large population loss. Working-aged people and their families were most likely to leave. The overwhelming majority net migration was accounted for by those leaving farms. The classification, towns>2,5000, was based on population at the beginning of the decade.

The most striking demographic development in the middle years of the twentieth century was the dramatic reduction in the farm population. Over the fifty years covered by the chart regional farm population fell by nearly 75,000 while the number of persons living in towns or in rural-non-farm areas increased in every decade. The urban population consists of those living in towns with more than 2,500 residents. Rural nonfarm residents are those living neither on farms or in the larger towns.

Source: Census. See appendix for description of migration estimates.

CHAPTER 9

Boom and Bust Once More: The 1970s and 1980s

THE GOOD TIMES RETURNED IN THE EARLY SEVENTIES AND PLAINS OLD TIMERS must have had a sense of *déjà vu*. The regional economy seemed to boom every third decade. The 1880s saw burgeoning investment in cattle ranching and later an influx of homesteaders. The wartime surge in demand for farm products and a rush of new settlers fueled the economy in the 1910s. World War II and the post war commodities boom brought renewed prosperity in the forties. The seventies perpetuated this pattern as an export-led demand for farm commodities drove agricultural incomes and farmland prices to unprecedented heights. Like earlier periods of exuberance, the seventies prosperity ended unhappily. The farm economy was in desperate straits by the end of the decade, and the region continued to struggle through most of the eighties.

Agricultural Prosperity in the Early 1970s

American farmers enjoyed exceptional good fortune in the early seventies. A Federal Land Bank official speaking in Lamar called 1972, "the greatest year in the history of American agriculture."[1073] As in the earlier booms in the teens and the forties, robust foreign demand for American produce provided much of the impetus. World population surged and incomes in most nations were rising. The dollar weakened as President Nixon removed its peg to gold and allowed it to float against other currencies, making American farm products cheaper for foreigners.[1074] US wheat exports more than doubled between 1968 and 1973, jumping from just over one-third of domestic production to more than 70 percent with sales to Soviet bloc nations accounting for much of the growth. Previous agricultural exports to the nation's cold war adversaries had been minimal. This changed in the summer of 1972 when the US sold the Soviet Union some 440 million bushels of wheat, equivalent of 30 percent of annual American production and more than 80 percent of domestic consumption.[1075] While some blamed the deal for subsequent food price increases, it only added fuel to what was already underway.

The Russian wheat deal was followed by sharp rises in the price of most agricultural commodities. The government responded to high food prices by authorizing planting on previously idled land, some forty million acres nationwide for the 1974 crop, raising the specter of another dust bowl in eastern Colorado.[1076]

Inflation, caused in part by the unwise macroeconomic policies of the Johnson and Nixon administrations, took off in the late sixties and continued through the seventies with annual CPI increases reaching double-digit rates. The 1973 OPEC oil boycott put further pressure on domestic prices. But inflationary periods are generally good for farmers and ranchers, at least for a while, and the early seventies were no exception. Between 1970 and 1974 the price of a bushel of wheat on the Kansas City exchange rose from $1.56 to $4.20 while that for corn increased from $1.45 to $3.08.[1077] Livestock prices reached record heights. At Omaha auctions, choice steers sold for less $30 per hundred pounds in 1970; by 1973 they brought over $90.[1078] In some rural communities the turnaround was even more dramatic. The *Limon Leader* reported that the wheat price at the local elevator reached $5.50 a bushel in February 1974 after bringing as little as ninety-nine cents in the fall of 1968.[1079]

Farmers' costs also accelerated; prices for machinery, farm labor, feed, seed, and especially for fuel all rose. In 1973 Arab oil producers instituted a boycott of sales to the US and other nations supporting Israel, along with a cut in total production. The price of oil soared, raising the operating cost of trucks, tractors, combines, and gasoline powered irrigation pumps. Regional farmers' outlays for petroleum products nearly doubled from pre-boycotts years.[1080] Potential fuel shortages threatened growers' ability to take advantage of the record prices. Custom cutters that had worked the eastern plains in past years indicated that they might not come without a guarantee of sufficient fuel.[1081] Although a government allocation program was supposed to ensure adequate gasoline and diesel for agriculture, allocations left many farmers short, and they were forced to pay exorbitant prices. In late 1973 Gerald Quattlebaum who farmed three thousand acres in Prowers County paid thirty-nine cents a gallon for five hundred gallons of diesel fuel. Prior to the boycott a gallon cost eighteen cents.[1082] Total production expenses incurred by farmers in the sixteen eastern plains counties increased almost 50 percent between 1970 and 1974.[1083]

But prices outpaced costs and farm incomes soared. In August 1973 the parity ratio, based on the relationship between farmers' costs and prices in 1910-14, exceeded 100 percent for the first time in decades.[1084] Between 1970 and 1974 regional farmers' cash receipts from marketing crops and livestock rose by $515 million while production expenses increased only $247 million.[1085] Plains agriculturists enjoyed a brief period of almost unprecedented prosperity as realized net earnings almost doubled even after adjusting for accelerating inflation.[1086] Land values soared. The Census of Agriculture reported that the per-acre value of farm and ranch land and buildings in the sixteen eastern Colorado counties nearly doubled between 1969 and 1974.[1087]

CHAPTER 9

But a consumer backlash erupted when higher farm prices showed up at the supermarket. The cost of beef attracted the greatest media attention. A *Time* magazine cover featured a cartoon of an angry housewife confronting a rancher. The magazine described the rapidly developing movement urging wives to refrain from purchasing expensive beef as the "most successful boycott by women since *Lysistrata*" as "thousands of women took to the streets in protest."[1088] Not surprisingly, plains residents were not sympathetic to urban housewives' complaints. This was especially true in southeast Colorado where, as the national beef boycott got underway, an early April blizzard caused an estimated $20 million in losses to area ranchers.[1089]

While news media buzzed with stories of enraged shoppers, ranchers in Baca and Prowers Counties were struggling through deep snow trying to save as much of their herds as possible. A Cleveland city councilman called for the boycott to "bring the meat industry to its knees." A group of southeast Colorado ranchers sent the councilman a telegram urging him to see their side of the story and offering to pay for him to come and work alongside farmers and ranchers. The councilman, however, was too busy with "personal involvement in coordinating the boycott" to consider the offer.[1090] *Newsweek* published an angry retort to American homemakers from my high school classmate Sandy Reifschneider, a Prowers County farmer's wife. Ms. Reifschneider characterized the typical boycotting housewife as being too "involved with just yourself" and "so self-centered." She wrote "Tell me, why should my husband work long hard hours—and I mean hard hours—for people who don't give a damn?"[1091] In Fort Morgan local farmers, ranchers, and feed growers defied the boycott with a mass purchase of almost $5,000 worth of packaged meat from local grocery stores.[1092] Defiance was not limited to farm and ranch families. An editorial in the *Bent County Democrat* observed, "A check with local supermarkets did not indicate any boycott support by local citizens and we are pleased that they are supporting our cattlemen."[1093] A discussion at a family dinner between my wife and sister-in-law about participation in the boycott brought an icy comment from my mother that the Kendalls were still involved in the cattle business. We were hardly big-time ranchers but ran a hundred head or so on some pastureland near our home, descendants from my brother's and my high school vocational ag projects.

The federal government attempted to slow accelerating inflation, but its efforts failed to slake consumer anger and raised the ire of producers. Wage and price controls were instituted in August 1971, but farm prices were exempt, allowing retailers to pass on increases to consumers. As beef prices shot up, the government relaxed restrictions on imports, an action not welcomed by ranchers or feeders. The president of the Colorado Cattlemen's Association claimed that the rancher was getting the same price as in 1952 while overall prices and wages have risen more than 50 percent and called the measure "damaging" and "political."[1094] Inflation slowed somewhat, aiding the President's reelection bid. Finally in April 1973, responding to voter unhappiness, President Nixon imposed controls on beef, lamb, and pork that did not directly restrain farm prices, but restricted retailers and wholesalers from selling at a price above the maximum in the previous thirty days. The latest action was no more welcome than earlier efforts. Consumer and labor groups thought prices should have been rolled back while ranchers and feeders complained they were being taken advantage of in a rare good year. Beef prices remained frozen through mid-September. Sporadic and largely ineffective attempts to restrain prices continued through the Ford and Carter administrations.

The government's floundering efforts brought chaos to all parts of the beef industry. Controls of beef prices without any restraint on costs of feed or cattle on the hoof created severe pressures on packers and feeders. Housewives hoarded meat, packers cut their purchases, and when more animals came on the market after controls were ended, prices slumped. In December 1974, the Colorado Cattlemen's Association met to consider "Today's cattle crisis created by the grim reality of high grain prices and depressed cattle prices that threaten to bankrupt cattlemen."[1095] An editorial in the *Arkansas Valley Journal* described the government's actions as "tragic for everyone concerned" and that "disrupted the beef pipeline for years to come."[1096]

High crop prices encouraged eastern Colorado farmers to make greater use of underground water. Between 1970 and 1974, regional corn output rose by almost fifteen million bushels or 55 percent with much of the increase due to the addition of 141,000 irrigated acres.[1097] Most of the newly cultivated acreage was in Kit Carson, Phillips and Yuma Counties where growers were able to tap the Ogallala Aquifer. But concerns were already being raised about sustainability. An analysis of the Kit Carson County water table found that in eastern parts of the County water levels declined two feet per year between 1964 and 1971.[1098]

The End of the Boom

The good times were not going to last. A *Washington Post* reporter visiting southeast Colorado in 1973 described farmers' trepidations: "But what the farmers here see ahead are rising costs, sliding prices and perhaps a return to the more marginal existence of the not-very-distant past."[1099] These forebodings were soon realized. The increase in farm prices slowed while costs continued to rise. The parity ratio that had peaked at over one hundred in the summer of 1973 dropped to seventy-eight a year later.[1100] As the end of the decade approached, American farmers' prospects appeared bleak, and the next few years brought no respite. Fuel and energy prices that had doubled between 1970 and 1978 doubled again by 1981 as the Iran-Iraq war put further pressure on world supplies.[1101] Foreign demand for US grain weakened due to the now more expensive dollar and the 1980 US embargo on wheat sales to Russia. By 1983 prices paid by farmers had more than doubled since 1974 while prices received were up only 10 percent.[1102] The Federal Reserve sharply restricted the money supply in an attempt to tame inflation that had once again reached double digits. Short-term interest rates approached 20 percent and rates on loans rose accordingly, increasing the burden on farmers who had earlier borrowed heavily against soaring land values. Vernon Franke, a dryland farmer from Akron, complained that his 1981 interest payments rose to $114,000, saddling him with a $70,000 loss for the year.[1103] The level of indebtedness of US farmers quadrupled between 1970 and 1983,[1104] and interest charges payable on farm real estate debt outstanding increased from $1.8 billion to $11 billion.[1105]

Eastern Colorado farmers attempted to compensate for the cost squeeze by expanding production further. Between 1974 and 1978 regional wheat growers harvested an additional 156,000 acres and corn farmers another 145,000.[1106] This required additional land and equipment, and, as in the 1920s, much of cost was paid for by borrowing against now more valuable land. Unsurprisingly, growers elsewhere reacted similarly putting further downward pressure on prices. US wheat stocks at the beginning of 1974 totaled 340 million bushels, but by the beginning of 1978 they had grown to 1.2 billion.[1107] The Limon elevator where wheat had reached $5.50 a bushel in early 1974 reported a price of only $2.17 three years later.[1108] Revenues from crop sales slumped. Between 1974 and 1978 regional farmers' receipts from crop sales dropped 40 percent despite the increased output. Larry Hall, a Baca County wheat grower, called his 1977 harvest the best in decades but with the low wheat price he was "losing money on every bushel." Hall estimated his break-even price at around three dollars per bushel but was getting less than two.[1109]

Ranchers fared somewhat better as cattle prices remained historically high although well short of their 1973 peaks and lower grain prices benefitted feeders. Regional livestock receipts posted a gain of more than $200 million between 1974 and 1978 which approximately balanced the decline from crops. Although total current-dollar receipts from crop and livestock sales were essentially unchanged, higher costs were cutting into margins. By 1978 the total net farm earnings estimate for the region showed a small loss.[1110]

Just as all parts of the region enjoyed the prosperity of the early seventies, the suffering in the latter years was widely shared with twelve of the sixteen counties reporting a decline of at least 80 percent in net farm earnings from their earlier peaks.[1111] Many farmers found themselves in desperate situations. Dean Nichols who farmed north of Walsh lamented, "There were a few good years there in 1973 and 1974 that allowed of people to get current on their debts, and some may have allowed themselves to get overextended on machinery and land prices went sky high…. I'm not in debt yet, but in another year, we'll be in that position again. I've gotten behind by $40,000 the last two years."[1112]

Farmers' travails continued through the early eighties. Commodity prices rebounded from their lows in 1978 but failed to keep pace with rising costs. A study by Chase Econometrics estimated that the 1982 average cost of producing a bushel of wheat in the US exceeded $6 while the price was below $4.[1113] Farmers and ranchers fared no better with other crops nor with livestock. In 1985 an Otis banker commented, "What we've experienced over the last three or four years is that no particular agricultural commodity has been profitable."[1114] By 1983 realized net earnings in the region, although now positive, had fallen to an eighth of their early seventies peak if adjusted for inflation.[1115] The president of the Federal Land Bank Association of Pueblo assessed the plight of regional farmers: "Right now survival is about all farmers can expect."[1116] Over the next few years cost increases slowed but so did prices.[1117] By the end of the eighties, prices had stabilized, cost inflation had slowed, and government payments to farmers had become more generous. Regional farm incomes increased somewhat but, when adjusted for inflation, were still well below those achieved in the halcyon days of the early seventies.[1118]

The acceleration in land values eventually reversed. In the long run, the price of land, like that of any earning asset, is the discounted value of its projected earnings. In the early 1970s, exports and farm prices soared, and earnings achieved record highs. Interest rates, which determine the rate at which future earnings were discounted, failed to keep pace with inflation so the gains in the value of farmland rose much faster than overall prices. By the 1980s interest rates were much higher, and earnings remained well below levels in the early 1970s. By 1987 the average value of an acre of land in eastern Colorado was lower than it had been nine years earlier despite a 75 percent increase in overall prices.[1119] Falling land values reduced farmers' abilities to borrow and increased pressures from lenders as collateral values fell.

As in the past the Federal government responded to farmers' distress by making agricultural support programs more generous. The 1977 Farm Bill raised subsidy levels for both wheat and corn but required farmers to agree to reduce production.[1120] Subsidies were raised further the following year. The greatest relief to the region came from the 1985 Conservation Reserve Program (CRP) that paid growers to permanently withdraw their land from production. The program was established by the Food Security Act of 1985 as a voluntary long-term cropland retirement program. It was designed to preserve highly erodible and environmentally sensitive land as well as remove surplus commodities from production and provide income security to farmers. Participants in the program received per-acre rental payments plus half the cost of establishing land cover (usually grass or trees) over a ten- to fifteen-year contract. Farmers wishing to enroll their land applied at their local Consolidated Farm Service Agency offices, with enrollments limited by available funds. In the 1990 fiscal year more than 1.3 million acres in eastern Colorado were enrolled. Rental payments averaged roughly $40 per acre and totaled $54 million that year. Most of the CRP land had been planted in wheat with the southeastern and central plains counties the largest participants. Baca County reported the greatest acreage at 254 thousand followed by Kiowa County with

181 thousand and Cheyenne and Prowers Counties, both with 148 thousand.[1121] The CRP provided a lifeline to dryland farmers and saved many rural banks from failure.

The Return of Farm Populism

As in earlier agricultural depressions, rural distress spawned political unrest, and militant farmers organized to protest their plight. For a few months, national attention focused on the American Agriculture Movement (AAM) that had its birth in the small southern Baca County town of Campo following summer-1977 discussions over coffee in a local café. The discussants, described by political scientists John Dinse and William Browne in their article on the AAM as "locally respected large-scale farmers and farm-related businessmen,"[1122] emerged as leaders of an organization committed to changing the existing political system and its perceived unfair treatment of American farmers. AAM founders viewed the US agricultural economy as plagued by low prices, prohibitive costs, and unresponsive politicians. They felt that government farm policy catered to large operators and were particularly troubled by the 1977 farm bill which they considered grossly inadequate in the face of difficulties facing US agriculture. Although its leaders portrayed the movement as a populist uprising by society's underdogs, the organizers were hardly struggling dirt farmers. Laurence "Bud" Bitner, one of AAM's founders, farmed nearly fifteen hundred acres, flew his own small plane, was a member of the state highway commission, and co-owned a farm supply store.[1123]

AAM's leadership envisioned the solution to US farmers' unhappy state as government support of agricultural prices at "parity" or the relationship between farmers' prices and costs that existed in agriculture's "golden age" between 1910 and 1914. Such a development, in their view, would not only benefit farmers but would relieve the malaise afflicting wider segments of the nation. According to the AAM, the health of the national economy was closely tied to the prosperity of the small farmer. As Alvin Jenkins, one of the Baca County founders of the movement, explained to an audience in Lincoln County's Arriba High School gymnasium, the parity-base years were "the most prosperous time we'd ever had in America and what was causing it was agriculture—which is the backbone of America—that was being highly successful due to the fact that it was on an even keel with all the rest of the economy. They called that 'parity.'"[1124] The movement demanded 100 percent of parity for all domestically consumed agricultural products and for all exports. In August 1977 achieving parity would have required a 64 percent increase, on average, of all prices for farm products. The price of wheat would need to increase 40 percent, that of corn 48 percent and beef cattle 77 percent.[1125] Most experts were skeptical of the AAM proposal. US Department of Agriculture economists predicted dire results.[1126]

The movement quickly gathered momentum in southeast Colorado. By mid-September Baca County farmers had assembled a mile-long caravan of tractors along highway 160 near Walsh sporting signs promising a strike if demands were not met.[1127] Support spread beyond the farm community. Merchants in Lamar and Walsh displayed signs backing the strike, and it was endorsed by the Springfield Chamber of Commerce.[1128] The American Agriculture National Strike Office raised more than $6,000 from Baca County residents and businesses at a benefit auction at the County Fairgrounds.[1129] The Movement soon established national headquarters in Springfield and by December 1977 claimed eleven hundred chapters in forty states.[1130]

AAM's leaders waged a grass roots campaign based on rallies and protests throughout rural America designed to climax with a demonstration in Washington that would put pressure on lawmakers. The rallies opened with a meeting with local farmers where the Movement's grievances were presented. Organizers and a few farmers laid out the dire condition of US agriculture and AAM's vision for alleviating it. Attendees were then encouraged to participate in a discussion followed by a rousing diatribe from an outside speaker, usually one of the founders or someone with a similarly apocalyptic view of the farmers' prospects. Farmers then formed a "tractorcade" of tractors and farm trucks parading through the local business district, usually at peak shopping hours. Pamphlets outlining the AAM's philosophy and strategy were distributed throughout the meeting and during the tractorcade. The first such rally was held in Campo in early September followed a week later by a larger assembly in nearby Springfield. AAM rallies were held in many eastern Colorado communities including Sterling, Fort Morgan, and Holyoke.[1131] By the end of the month a nationally televised Pueblo rally attracted some two thousand participants including US Agriculture Secretary Bob Bergland.

The rallies continued in eastern Colorado and elsewhere through the fall and winter of 1977. The *Limon Leader* described that town's tractorcade as "perhaps the largest parade ever seen in Limon." Cattleman Charlie Dodge opened the Limon meeting declaring: "Go ahead and smile. Just because you're mad, you're starving to death, and your kids aren't going to have any place to farm…. go ahead and smile—enjoy it! That's just what these political boys seem to think we ought to do about it. Just enjoy it! Well, we're not going to do that!"[1132]

Publicity was critical, and the Movement received coverage far beyond local and farm-based media. According to the *Springfield Plainsman Herald*, the coverage included the *New York Times*, AP and UPI, ABC's Good Morning *America*, NBC's *Today Show* and the CBS *Morning Show*.[1133] Both *Time* and *Newsweek* carried stories.[1134] Even readers of *Penthouse* magazine could take a break from viewing pictures of naked women to read about the AAM.[1135] But the stories often expressed skepticism about the movement's prospects. *Newsweek* quoted a scoffing farmer: "Some of these guys that are striking haven't watched the economics of their own farming. They bought high-priced land. Now they want the government to bail them out."[1136] The regional media remained largely defiant. A *Lamar Daily News* editorial responded to the *Wall Street Journal's* disparagement of the farmers' pleas with, "The *Journal* thinks 'The

Year of the Farmer' with his 'goats, tractors and trucks' would wreck the economy. Well we'll see."[1137]

The farmers strike that would reinforce movement demands was called for December 14. AAM leadership vowed to withhold all production of farm products until the demand for 100 percent of parity was met. Gene Shroder, one of strike leaders, told *Farm Journal*, "The strike will be continued as long as necessary."[1138] This bravado proved rather short-lived. At a rally in Pueblo on the strike date, movement farmers picketed local businesses although few instances of the picket lines being honored by local resident or workers were reported.[1139] By January the movement had backed off their earlier ultimatum as famers' fervor weakened under pressures from landlords and bankers. Leaders put forth a revised goal calling for a 50 percent reduction in output, but even they did not anticipate widespread participation, although it was hoped that the threat would bring about the desired legislative action.[1140]

The critical Washington rally on January 18 drew three thousand participants and a long tractorcade. As described in by the *Denver Post*, the farmers "paraded on tractors and in pickup trucks on Constitution Avenue in freezing rain and ankle-deep slush during Friday morning's rush-hour traffic. [Several] tractors broke down or ran out of gas."[1141] Movement members released a herd of goats on the floor of the House of Representatives and forced Agriculture Secretary Bergland to flee through a window.[1142] Movement leaders and farmers met with legislators and administration officials. The Senate passed a bill incorporating many of AAM's demands, but the Carter administration lobbied the House to oppose the measure, and it stalled in the lower chamber.

It was hoped that a new threat of a withholding production would prod recalcitrant legislators into action. In March 1978 the movement leaders urged Colorado wheat farmers to engage in a "plow down" destroying their crops. An AAM spokesman claimed that seventy-three farms, forty-one ranches and four dairies in Elbert, El Paso, and Lincoln Counties had committed by either plowing under their crops or otherwise restricting output.[1143] More than one hundred Baca County farmers reportedly plowed under portions of their wheat crop.[1144] But overall participation in the plow down was limited. Acreage and output of both wheat and sorghum rose in eastern Colorado.

The farm bill that was finally passed in May brought only a modest increase in price support levels which movement leaders viewed as a sellout. But by then the AAM's moment had passed. It soon faded as a political force eventually evolving into an increasingly paranoid populism that blamed the legislative failures on corporations, banking interests, and internationalists. A second Washington tractorcade in January 1979 was largely ignored. The media fueled the AAM's rise to national prominence and, as other causes gained attention, its visibility receded along with whatever political power it once exercised. As depicted by Douglas Hurt, "In the end, the public grew tired of the AAM's radical activities and pronouncements. When the AAM no longer made the news, the Movement essentially died."[1145]

Although national interest in the movement cooled, its founders remained committed. Increasing pressure by lenders on debt-saddled farmers rekindled the fervor of remnants of the movement at a five-year reunion in Campo in 1982. A spokesman vowed to "fight farm foreclosures till Hell freezes over."[1146] About a hundred Baca County farmers donned red armbands and gathered to help Kinan Burk of Springfield stop a forced liquidation sale of his farm equipment and household goods.[1147] In early 1983 an AAM inspired crowd of more than 250 farmers from several states gathered at the Springfield courthouse confronting sheriff's deputies in riot gear who were attempting to repel them with tear gas and mace. The crowd's aim was to prevent a public-trustee sale of Jerry Wright's 320-acre wheat and milo farm near Campo. Several participants were arrested and charged with assault and obstructing peace officers. The effort to save Jerry Wright's farm was ultimately unsuccessful as he soon abandoned it and left the state in 1985, owing more than $500,000 to various banks.[1148] But AAM members persisted, vowing to "appear at future land sales to try and block them."[1149] A few weeks after the foreclosure protests *Denver Post* story described AAM-sponsored classes instructing members in the production of explosives with home-made black powder. AAM spokesman Alvin Jenkins denied any destructive intent but, he said, "once you learn to use explosives you can use it for whatever you want."[1150]

But the AAM was fading even in its home county. Some of the founders became entrepreneurs in the gasohol industry, building and operating plants converting grain into alcohol which was then mixed with gasoline for use in internal combustion engines. Derral Shroder, who had been active the AAM, claimed that gasohol demand would double the price of grain, bringing farmers closer to the desired 100 percent of parity.[1151] Alvin Jenkins, apparently eschewing his interest in explosives, became vice-president of Baca Food and Fuel Cooperative that opened a plant in Campo employing fifteen workers.[1152] Bud Bitner became president of Colorado Gasohol with a twenty-two-employee plant near Walsh.[1153] But the AAM's days of national notoriety had passed.

Challenges for Plains Bankers

Farmers' financial distress soon spread to the area's banks. Soaring prices for crops and livestock in the early 1970s encouraged farmers to expand production through acquisition of additional land and the purchase of more equipment. They usually financed these expansions by borrowing against their now more valuable land and bankers were more than willing to extend the necessary credit. It seemed a mutually beneficial transaction. Borrowers were able to take advantage of a favorable market situation, and the interest they were paying reduced taxes on their soaring incomes. Bankers saw these as profitable loans with minimal risk. In the early seventies, farmers' cash flows were easily enough to service the loans and the value of farmland provided more than adequate collateral. By 1977 local banks' farm and agriculture-related loans in Prowers, Baca, and Kiowa Counties exceeded $2 billion.[1154] An eastern Colorado banker remarked to me, as his bank's condition deteriorated in the early eighties, that a decade ago, "We couldn't make a bad loan."

Farm loans remained profitable for banks only so long as farmer's incomes held up and collateral retained its value. But crop prices began to fall and costs to rise threatening both banks and their borrowers. A plains banker assessing the situation observed that "Some of these farmers bought when they shouldn't have been buying. They purchased all sorts of new equipment and land when wheat was $5, and then when it dropped to $2, they found they couldn't pay for it."[1155] Of course the bankers were eager to facilitate this imprudence. By the end of the decade, farmers' incomes had fallen, and they struggled to service their loans. Rural bankers faced unhappy choices. They did not want to lend more to heavily indebted farmers, but foreclosures and forced sales increased pressure on the region's economy, further threatening the health of the banks. They also forced banks to recognize their losses and reduced their capital. As an Eads banker complained in 1977, "Ya can't keep loaning to a losing cause, but for these rural banks, if the farmer goes under, we do too."[1156] More than a few plains farmers were close to going under. A USDA survey of rural banks in April 1977 found that many grain growers would be unable to obtain operating credit for the 1977 growing season.[1157] One-third of farmers' loans from the surveyed banks reported difficulties. Land prices remained relatively high through the early eighties although they were soon destined to fall. This permitted many agricultural bankers to deal with their problem loans through a strategy of "extend and pretend." Rather than recognizing losses on loans that could not be serviced, they relaxed payment terms and frequently loaned more so the farmers could continue operating.

Well-intended actions by the federal government to ease farmers access to credit may have worsened things for both farmers and banks. The Farm Credit System (FCS), established in the 1910s and greatly expanded under the New Deal, included twelve Federal Land Banks along with hundreds of local cooperatives, intermediate credit bank, and production credit associations all involved in providing agricultural credit. These entities were owned by farmers but were implicitly guaranteed by the federal government. The Farmers Home Administration (FmHA), a federal agency designed to extend credit to farmers deemed "credit worthy" but unable to obtain funds elsewhere, was another source of funds for struggling farmers. If they could not get loans from a bank or had exhausted their credit they could, for a time, borrow from FCS or FmHA. In many cases the borrowers already had substantial debt to commercial banks. Federal agricultural credit programs eased borrowing terms for farmers often leading the banks to exercise less scrutiny of their borrowers figuring, or hoping, that the additional credit would allow the farms to survive and their loans to be repaid. They also reduced incentives for the borrowers to confront their financial problems.

Between the early seventies and the early eighties, the volume of loans by both the FCS and the FmHA increased more than five-fold and their share of farm lending rose from one-third to nearly one-half. As wheat farmer Vernon Franke remarked, "They didn't push farmers into loans, but they lent them all they could."[1158]

A day of reckoning finally arrived. Farmers' balance sheets worsened, and the banks began to approach their lending limits. Eventually the value of their collateral deteriorated. The Kansas City Federal Reserve surveying its district reported that in the first quarter of 1984 interest rates continued to rise, loan repayment rates were falling, and values for all categories of farm real estate declined.[1159] A Walsh banker observed "We can't continue the way we're going."[1160] Regulators, charged with protecting depositors and government guarantees, put more pressure on the banks. By the mid-eighties they were forced to recognize their imperiled loans by writing them down, thereby depleting their capital and putting many in a precarious position. In late 1984 Denver based Colorado National Bank, one of the state's largest and a heavy agricultural lender either directly or through correspondent relationships with rural banks, was forced to add $5 million to its loan loss reserve. The *Denver Post* reported that the bank's problem loans were "centered in the agricultural industry and a few small rural banks which are experiencing financial difficulty."[1161] Some banks failed. In December 1984 Colorado's State Bank Commissioner closed the Holyoke Farmers State Bank when stockholders were unable to meet a requirement for additional capital. The bank had received a capital infusion the previous summer but deteriorating loans required yet more.[1162] In February 1985 the ninety-seven-year-old First National Bank of Eads was declared insolvent and sold to a Denver bank holding company.[1163] In April the FDIC closed the First National Bank of Springfield after it experienced "substantial deterioration in the quality of its loan portfolio over the past two years" according to the agency's statement.[1164] In October 1987 the First National Bank of Brush was declared insolvent and closed. The "bank's loan losses impaired and finally exhausted the bank's capital."[1165]

Bankers who were able to continue operating became more cautious, aggravating the squeeze on the farmers. In the eighties I served on the board of directors of a Lamar bank where my family had a substantial interest. The board faced tough decisions under pressure from regulators to choose between the financial survival of farmers, often long-time customers and friends, and the viability of the bank. A leading Colorado Ag banker told the Colorado Bankers Association that highly leveraged farmers "will probably have to retrench—sell off their assets."[1166] Farmers lost some or all their land and equipment. Lots overflowing with repossessed combines, tractors, and other farm machinery could be seen along plains highways.

Farmers pressured the government for more assistance. In April 1986 a group of farmers parked their tractors outside the Federal Land Bank in Yuma refusing to leave until local officials agreed to discuss restructuring loans and making changes in the bank's lending and management policies.[1167] A year later a tractor convoy picketed the Farm Credit System's national headquarters in suburban Denver. An estimated one hundred farmers and ranchers demanded more opportunity to restructure loans, lower interest rates, a moratorium on foreclosures and more control by local farmers.[1168] Quasi-governmental agencies' loan terms were made more generous in response to the political pressure and the worsening agricultural picture. Limits on loans as a share of assets were increased, credit-worthiness requirements were relaxed, and their interest rates remained below market during a time of rising rates. A portion of the 1978 Emergency Agricultural Act, inspired in part by pressure from the AAM, further liberalized emergency lending by the FmHA. In November 1988 FmHA allowed farmers delinquent on their loans an opportunity to restructure them including writing loans down to the current value of collateral.[1169] But despite politicians' sensitivity to rural voters, the federal credit providers' generosity could not be sustained. The number of Colorado farm properties owned by the federal government through repossession or abandonment grew from seven at the beginning of 1981 to sixty-three four years later.[1170] By 1988, 652 of the of the state's FmHA borrowers were delinquent and the agency held title to another 169 obtained through conveyance or foreclosure. The FCS reported large losses and approached congress with a request for a six-billion-dollar bailout.[1171] The ability of struggling farmers to tap the federal Treasury was finally curtailed. As an official at the Springfield FmHA office commented, "borrowing is not substitute for profit."[1172] As the eighties drew to its end, neither farmers nor bankers could claim financial health.

Surface Irrigation Threatened

Irrigators faced not only an inadequate stream flow and a declining water table but the possibility that some of their current sources of supply might be lost or diminished. The early seventies saw the first large-scale efforts to purchase agricultural water rights for municipal or industrial use. The growing urban areas along Colorado's Front Range needed ever more water, and the bulk of water rights in the State were owned by agricultural interests. Colorado law permitted the transfer of water from agricultural use dating back to an 1891 Colorado Supreme Court decision.[1173] Such transfers had been quite common but most involved expansion of urban settlement onto farmland. As the state's metropolitan areas added ever more people, municipalities looked to purchase large blocks of water rights from more distant areas. These transfers, it was argued, resulted in a net gain as the return from water in municipal or industrial use typically exceeded that in agriculture. As an analysis from the University of Colorado Law School asserted, "From a purely economic perspective such transfers make good sense. The dollar value of water used in agriculture is generally much lower than the value of the water in urban uses. Moreover, the cost of developing new supplies of water increases to a point that transfers of agricultural water were likely to be less expensive in many cases."[1174] However, James Sherow contended that the damage to rural economies was not fully considered. He wrote, "Some economists have argued that irrigation farmers prohibit healthy urban growth in the semiarid and arid West by controlling a disproportionate amount of water. But these scholars have not yet dealt with devastating social and environmental consequences occurring in such areas as the Arkansas River Valley."[1175]

In 1970 and 1971 the city of Pueblo completed two relatively small purchases from ditch companies in Bent County resulting in the loss of eighteen hundred acres of irrigated land.[1176] In 1972 rumors surfaced of an offer to purchase Amity Ditch water rights by the Pueblo West metropolitan district, threatening a loss of as much as fifty-thousand acres of irrigated Prowers County farmland[1177] and raising the specter of substantial economic damage to the region. The *Lamar Daily News* editorialized, "Do you want a land of fertile farms, owned and operated by independent citizens and service institutions in the hand of individual businessmen or do you want to be herded into Front Range urban nursing homes or housing developments, depending on the size of check you get from the government?"[1178]

The Amity sale did not go through, but two sizable transfers further upriver threatened the economies of Otero and Crowley Counties. The Colorado Canal Company had long provided irrigation water to Crowley County farmers. The Company possessed relatively junior rights, and its operation was plagued by substantial losses due to seepage and evaporation. An investors' group purchased the bulk of the Company's water rights which were then marketed to Front Range municipalities. A large sale to Colorado Springs was consummated in 1985 at a total price of $35 million.[1179] More sales of Colorado Canal Company water were to come, often by individual farmers at higher prices than in the earlier transaction. The Rocky Ford Ditch Company, with relatively senior water rights described earlier, had irrigated Otero County farmland for nearly a century. American Chrystal Sugar owned a controlling interest in the Company, and when its Rocky Ford plant was shut down in 1976, a Denver-based limited partnership purchased the plant, land, and 46,800 acre-feet of water rights. The rights were then sold to the city of Aurora for $22 million.[1180]

The motivation of financially strapped farmers is understandable. A *Denver Post* article covering the Rocky Ford Ditch transfer noted that Valley corn farmers felt that at current prices the water offered are a much better deal.[1181] Hal Holder, a Rocky Ford farmer, commented that "Farmers don't like to sell their water. They hate like hell to do it. But since they can't make a living and make payments through farming it's their only way out."[1182] Losses of irrigated farmland threatened the economies of the Arkansas Valley. Morgan Smith, the Colorado Agricultural Commissioner, in a July 1981 "Ag in Focus" column wrote that due to water-rights sales, Crowley and Otero Counties are "facing debilitating economic decline."[1183]

Economic effects from water transfers through the eighties are difficult to detect, although tax assessors' data show that property values dropped in Crowley County.[1184] As the municipalities did not need all the water at the time of sale, a portion was leased back to the farmers so that irrigation only diminished gradually.[1185] According to the Census irrigated acreage in Crowley and Otero Counties fell by roughly 6,000 acres or less than 7 percent between 1969 and 1987. University of Colorado economist Charles Howe and two co-authors conducted an economic study of historical and potential impacts of water transfers in the Arkansas Valley.[1186] They concluded that through the late 1980s, transfers of water rights shifted irrigation from low value to higher value crops. As a result, the net economic impact was minor. They found no reduction in vegetable or specialty crops or any effect on the expansion of feed lots in the region, the two areas with the greatest impact on the overall economy. However the authors also forecast that proposed future transfers, potentially affecting nearly 60 percent of the irrigated acreage, would be damaging. It would be more than offset by gains to urban municipalities. But the authors conclude that in such transfers, "the incidence of the costs is always on the area of origin, while the benefits accrue to the area of new use."[1187] With growth continuing along the Front Range, the threat to Valley farmers and communities would only increase.

The Nonfarm Economy

Farm prosperity in the early seventies fueled a resurgence in the rest of the economy and, for a few years, plains businesses and townspeople enjoyed a return of the good times. Steady growth continued even in the face of the reasonably severe national recession that began in late 1973. In 1973 and 1974, per-capita personal income in the sixteen counties edged above that of the nation, an occurrence that was to prove temporary and not to be repeated. These atypically high incomes were largely accounted for by healthy farm incomes, but businesses in the towns also thrived. Real nonfarm earnings increased at a 5.9 percent annual rate through the first three years of the decade,[1188] and retail sales over the same period grew at 7 percent a year after adjusting for inflation.[1189] The Census showed healthy job gains in the seventies, following a decline in the sixties, with most of the increase in the early years of the decade.[1190]

The nation bounced back from the recession and posted solid growth through the rest of the decade, although marred by high inflation. But the plains economy languished. The squeeze on farmers' incomes meant reduced purchases from in-town merchants with sellers of farm equipment and supplies feeling the greatest distress. A Walsh implement dealer lamented "We'd like to see equipment move but there's just no money to buy things after the farmers pay back their operating expenses from crop revenue."[1191] Dealers reported that only repair business enabled them to meet their expenses. The damage was not confined to those dealing directly with farmers. Both total sales and income in the region slackened through the remainder of the 1970s. Job growth slowed, and net out-migration increased.

The continuing slump in the farm economy and the deep national recession of the early eighties brought further grief. Local economies suffered from the closures of vital businesses. In the middle 1980s, Morgan County lost three major employers.[1192] According to the *Denver Post,* Sterling was suffering from "one of its deepest depressions both in oil and agriculture."[1193] In 1989 the Rocky Ford school superintendent recalled that since his arrival six years earlier, "A car dealer, hospital, lumber yard, movie theater, J.C. Penney's and a sporting goods store have all gone out of business."[1194] In a rare positive development, Public Service Company of Colorado announced plans for two coal powered electrical plants in the region. The first of these was to be built in Brush[1195] with a second promised in Las Animas.[1196] But demand growth fell short of expectations and plans for the Las Animas plant were later dropped. An improving farm economy brought some relief by the end the decade. But the reduction in the number of farmers and the increase in absentee ownership limited the benefits to local economies. As a *Denver Post* columnist observed, businesses in the rural towns "are not going to bounce back just because the large farm operators, often absentee owners, are able to get better prices or contemplate rising land values."[1197]

Economic data reinforce the narrative of a struggling eighties economy. Nonfarm employment was essentially flat after 1981, and retail sales[1198] adjusted for inflation declined. The region had added almost twelve thousand non-farm jobs from 1970 through 1981 but posted a small decline through the remainder of the decade.[1199] Shuttering of all but one sugar plant took its toll on the South Platte Valley economy where the meat packing industry was also encountering difficulties. Between 1984 and 1986 Morgan County lost 852 jobs or 10 percent of its workforce on nonfarm payrolls. Over the same two years Logan County posted a decline of 479 jobs or 6 percent while Sedgwick County's job number fell by 178 or 19 percent.[1200] In 1985 Morgan County food stamp applications rose 30 percent,[1201] and rumors of retail closings circulated in Fort Morgan.[1202] The mayor of the Morgan County town of Wiggins raised the prospect of her town, that had seen no growth in the past two years, becoming "a desolate main street."[1203] Archbishop Stafford, the Catholic prelate of northern Colorado, urged a gathering of farmers north of Ovid to keep their faith during the crisis.[1204]

The Arkansas Valley's sole beet processing plant closed in the 1970s, and the eighties brought no respite as more jobs were lost in durable manufacturing and railroads. Lamar's Neoplan bus manufacturing plant boosted Prowers County employment although the firm's layoffs in the late eighties brought a slowdown. The real nonfarm earnings for the sixteen counties grew by nearly one-third by 1981 but dropped 5 percent over the next nine years.[1205] Only Elbert County experienced consistent growth through the twenty years of the seventies and eighties.

CHAPTER 9

Interstate Highways and Railroads

Since its earliest settlements, the economic viability of plains communities depended upon access to transportation. Bent's Fort, the first significant commercial entity in the region, was located on the Santa Fe Trail, the principal route from St. Louis and Kansas City to the southwest. In the late nineteenth century, railroads dictated development patterns. With the coming of the automobile, highways became the principal links among settlements, benefitting communities along such major routes as US-50 through the Arkansas Valley. Manufacturers profited from access to supplies and markets while service industries benefitted from business of travelers.

The next transformation of the plains' transportation network was launched when President Eisenhower signed the Federal Aid Highway Act of 1956 authorizing a national system of Interstate Highways. Construction of the new limited-access motorways altered traffic patterns to the benefit of those communities lying on the thoroughfares. A town fortunate enough to be on an Interstate route possessed a significant advantage. Retail activity, especially gas stations, restaurants, and motels, gained from the increased traffic. Manufacturers and distributors enjoyed quicker and less expensive means of shipping goods to markets. As Douglas Hurt wrote, "Access to markets by residents, manufacturers and suppliers became essential. The towns bypassed by an interstate highway, like those bypassed by a railroad during the nineteenth century, struggled economically."[1206] Nowhere was the increasing importance of the Interstates more evident than along Interstate 70 running through Burlington and Limon to Denver. Even before I-70 was finished in 1976 it had become the most convenient motor route to Denver and the Rockies. Colorado Department of Highways traffic data show that the number of daily vehicles crossing the Kansas line on I-70 or the US highways along the route that was to become I-70 steadily increased from 2,450 in 1964 to 3,500 in 1974 and 4,350 in 1980.[1207] Interstate 80-S, later to be renamed I-76, completed in 1968 and extending from Denver through Sterling into Nebraska exhibited a similar increase in traffic.

Towns bypassed by the interstates could still ship or receive goods on the older US highways or by rail. But shipment by truck was becoming more important and truck traffic gravitated to the interstates. Communities not on their routes saw a reduction in traffic and attendant economic activity. No local economies suffered more than towns along US Highway 50, bordering the Arkansas River through Prowers, Bent and Otero Counties. Through the forties and the fifties Valley businesses profited from the heavy east-west traffic along the highway. In the early sixties US50 was used by an estimated 7.5 percent of the tourists entering the state.[1208] But change was coming. A 1966 editorial in the *Lamar Daily News* warned "that we have our work cut out for us to maintain our share of travel into the state."[1209] The warning proved prescient. As traffic along I-70 surged the daily number of vehicles using US-50 at the Kansas state line remained stagnant, rising from 1,250 in 1948 to 1,450 in 1966 before declining to 1,350 in 1974 and then increasing slightly to 1,500 in 1980. Most other non-Interstate highways also reported flat or declining travel.[1210]

Concerns about the effects on local economies were borne out. Sales and employment statistics suggest that the economies along I-70 and I-76 (80-S) performed much better than those along US-50. Between 1971 and 1989 retail sales adjusted for inflation declined in both Bent and Otero Counties and posted a meager 10 percent gain in Prowers County. At the same time, Lincoln and Kit Carson Counties along I-70 posted increases of 72 percent and 50 percent respectively.[1211] Both Otero and Bent Counties saw declines in total employment while Prowers County posted an increase due to strong gains from its new bus plant. Lincoln and Kit Carson Counties showed solid employment gains as did Morgan and Logan Counties along I-76.[1212]

The arrival of an interstate was not always greeted enthusiastically by local merchants as the thoroughfares typically bypassed the towns' business districts. In Limon, Dale Cooley from the local Chamber of Commerce assured townspeople that the "By-pass [routing I-70 north of the community] Won't Stop Limon's Growth."[1213] Construction work provided a short-term stimulus; the Colorado Highway Department Resident Engineer for the central plains estimated that highway work resulted in some four hundred construction workers in his district.[1214] But sales dropped off for some in-town firms after the by-pass was completed. Businesses in Limon along the old US-40 though the middle of town, especially motels and gas stations, reported declining sales in the months following the opening.[1215]

But Limon soon reaped the benefits from the new highway. Rip Griffin, a developer of travel centers along interstates in Texas, purchased land at the intersection of US-24 and I-70 northwest of the town for a planned travel center catering to truckers and tourists. The facility was projected to cost between one and three million dollars exclusive of land acquisition and would employ fifty to seventy-five workers.[1216] The developer estimated it would generate fourteen million dollars annually from fuel sales, motels, restaurants and miscellaneous services.[1217] When completed in January 1979, the complex included eight gas pumps, a convenience store, a 165-seat restaurant, and a lounge and locker room for truckers. More gas stations, motels, fast food restaurants, and other services for travelers soon followed.[1218] The complex provided a significant boost to the Limon economy. Between 1969 and 1989, Lincoln County reported an 11 percent growth in employment by auto dealers and gas stations.[1219] While this increase seems unimpressive it occurred at a time when gas stations were changing to self-service and cutting their work forces. Lincoln County posted the largest increase in retail sales of any county in the region between 1971 and 1989.[1220]

Railroads were still important, and rail service cutbacks, in part a reaction to competition from the interstates, raised concerns in central plains communities. An editorial in the *Eastern Colorado Plainsman* regarding the Union Pacific's proposed closure of the Hugo depot was headlined, "Union Pacific Requests Spell Disaster for Eastern Colorado."[1221] The depot was closed in 1973, and business was transferred to Limon where the Union Pacific continued freight service, maintaining a yard and equipment storage but its economic impact on the region was greatly diminished.[1222]

The Rock Island, the principal line through the central plains, grappled with financial problems throughout the seventies. The line's bankruptcy filing in March 1975 threatened rail service,[1223] but the firm struggled on in receivership. In 1977 the president of the company assured the public that the Rock Island was heading toward survival and eventual prosperity. He heralded plans for rebuilding track and buying rolling stock. But the economic environment for railroads remained hostile, and the firm ceased all rail operations in early 1980, resulting in the loss of a hundred jobs and two million dollars in payroll in Limon. Passenger service had ceased; an excursion train to Colorado Springs was attempted but it soon shut down.[1224] The collapse of the Rock Island was a harbinger of railroads' future on the eastern plains. Service was unprofitable and traffic would be reduced further in the coming years. Central plains residents held out hope that Amtrak would designate a passenger route between Kansas City and Denver passing through Kit Carson and Lincoln Counties.[1225] Amtrak officials chose the Santa Fe line along the Arkansas instead, a decision greeted with enthusiasm by Valley communities and disappointment by those on the central plains.[1226]

Manufacturing in the Seventies and Eighties

In the late twentieth, many US manufacturers facing competitive pressures sought to relocate production facilities to lower cost locations, often in rural America. Jason Henderson, writing for the Kansas City Federal Reserve Bank, noted that rural America "accounted for 20 percent of all U.S. manufacturing jobs by the mid-1990s, up from 16 percent prior to the 1970s."[1227] Eastern Colorado was among the newly desirable sites. The plains communities' economic development efforts undertaken in the sixties increased awareness of the region's advantages and often offered incentives to firms considering relocating or opening new plants. Real estate was relatively inexpensive. Indeed, many communities had existing structures which could be rehabilitated such as abandoned sugar beet plants. But the availability of relatively inexpensive and productive workers was even more important. Farmers and their family members usually had good mechanical skills and work habits. They were available much of the year and, as the farm economy worsened, were eager to supplement their incomes. The lower cost of living meant that the local work force could be supplemented with migrants who could meet living costs on pay from unskilled jobs.

Processors of products from the region's farmers were still responsible for most of the region's manufacturing. Food and kindred products accounted for 36 percent of manufacturing jobs in 1990. These included employment at sugar beet plants, long mainstays in several eastern Colorado communities, but now encountering challenges. The industry provided livelihoods to workers and farmers and tax support for school districts and local governments. But low sugar prices and rising transportation costs in the early seventies cut into processors' margins. Plants built in the early twentieth century were no longer efficient, irrigation water was increasingly expensive, and beet sugar faced increasing competition.

The Arkansas Valley had already seen several plant closures and acreage had fallen by more than half by 1970.[1228] Rocky Ford's American Crystal factory, the lone facility still operating in the Valley, faced declining profits. The company leased its plant to Colo-Kan, Inc., a cooperative of Arkansas Valley growers, with the option to extend the lease or purchase it after five years.[1229] Depressed sugar prices at the time the lease was signed meant the new owners faced the possibility that many beet growers would shift to other more profitable crops. But the outlook soon brightened. Sugar prices recovered due to a failure in the world cane crop. By early 1974 the price approached $20 per hundred pounds, up from $13 the previous September, with projections of the future price as high as $30.[1230] In early 1974 Harry Bates, president of Colo-Kan told a meeting of growers, bankers and implement dealers that he had "never felt more optimistic about the sugar beet industry since he started growing beets in 1939."[1231] But prosperity proved ephemeral. Health concerns on the part of US consumers caused sugar consumption to decline and beet sugar faced increasing competition from imports and cheaper high-fructose corn sugar. Sluggish prices and potential shortages of labor and water discouraged farmers from planting enough to make the Rocky Ford plant viable. In November 1977 American Crystal president Jack Tanner reviewed the history of the industry in the Arkansas Valley for a meeting with growers, noting the number of plants in the Valley that had already closed. He pointed out that prices the previous summer were the lowest ever in relation to growers' costs.[1232] The Rocky Ford plant's survival was in doubt. In 1977 a letter from Colo-Kan president Bates informed the coop's growers/stockholders that "your Coop is facing a real possibility of closing the Rocky Ford Sugar Factory, because of an apparent lack of interest in growing sugar beets."[1233] The cooperative refrained from exercising its purchase option on the plant, and it closed permanently in 1979, signaling the end for sugar beet farming and processing in the Arkansas Valley.[1234]

Beet growers and processors in the South Platte Valley also faced increasing pressures. In 1979 the Colorado Agriculture Commissioner speculated that the industry "may be extinct within three or four years."[1235] At the beginning of the seventies Great Western Sugar, which had dominated the Valley's industry since the beginning of the century, was laboring under depressed profits and the heavy debt load accumulated through the exuberance of Billy White, the firm's recently resigned head. A group of growers attempted to organize a cooperative to purchase Great Western Sugar Company, owner and operator of the Valley's sugar beet plants, that was owned by Great Western

CHAPTER 9

United (GWU), the conglomerate built by White in the sixties. (See discussion in chapter 8.) In 1972 after protracted negotiations, GWU management agreed to the sale, and the company's board of directors concurred. The president of the buyers' cooperative expressed confidence in the grower-owned company's future.[1236] But the sugar market's recovery described earlier led to a sharp gain in earnings, and GWU stockholders refused to approve the sale.[1237] A new buyer appeared in late 1974 when the Texas-based Hunt brothers began buying stock in GWU. They eventually acquired a controlling interest in the firm, and the sugar factories continued to operate through the reminder of the seventies.[1238]

GWU had become a part of the Hunt brothers' holdings, a complicated assortment of properties in oil and gas, real estate, and coal leases along with more exotic assets such as art, coins, and racehorses. In late 1979 the Hunts began to invest heavily in silver, pushing the price up from $11 to $50 an ounce.[1239] To help finance this undertaking that many viewed as an attempt to corner the market, the Hunts took GWU private. By then the corporation was renamed Hunt International Resources Corporation (HIRCO), and its assets were used as collateral to acquire more silver.[1240] But the Hunt's scheme foundered as the silver price collapsed in early 1980, falling to $6 by May.[1241] Meanwhile high sugar prices kept HIRCO afloat for a time despite the brothers' neglect of the company's management problems.[1242] But the sugar price fell in 1981 just as oil and gas prices slumped, jeopardizing another important part of the Hunts' empire. Despite their difficulties the Hunts' net worth was still in the billions although, as Bunker Hunt famously remarked at the time, "a billion dollars isn't what it used to be."[1243] But the bulk of the Hunts' assets were insulated by what *Fortune* described as "a remarkably intricate network of meticulously built fire walls—private corporations and trusts that insulate the Hunt wealth from creditors, the tax collector, the public eye, and even different wings of the Hunt family itself."[1244] HIRCO was not going to be bailed out by the Hunts, and its sugar operation was in peril.

In September 1984 HIRCO was unable to make interest payments due holders of Great Western debentures,[1245] and a month later the company was reported struggling to reach an agreement on a loan package for the next fiscal year.[1246] After lengthy delays the firm reported $92 million in losses in the previous three fiscal years and announced plans to sell its assets at auction in early 1985. An effort the to sell the sugar factories to a growers' coop failed when the Hunts demanded a price twice what the growers were willing to pay.[1247] In February 1985 the firm failed to issue some $7 million in checks to growers in Colorado and four other states and stated that it did know when the checks would be sent.[1248] Then sugar plant employees' payroll checks bounced[1249] and widespread layoffs were announced.[1250] The company soon shut down its factories including those in Ovid, Sterling, and Fort Morgan[1251] and declared bankruptcy on March 7.[1252]

The plants in Wyoming, Nebraska, and Montana were soon sold but not those in Colorado or Kansas.[1253] The Mountain State Beet Growers Cooperative attempted to negotiate a purchase of the Colorado and Kansas plants. In the spring of 1985, as bargaining dragged on and planting time approached, growers were reluctant to commit to a crop without certainty of being paid. The *Fort Morgan Times* urged the cooperative to come to terms with HIRCO's creditors so "growers will be able to get their seed in the ground before they decide to drop plans for planting beets this year."[1254] An agreement was finally reached in April. In order for the sugar plants to operate, the cooperative required farmers in the South Platte Valley and elsewhere in northeast Colorado and northwest Kansas to commit to plant a hundred thousand acres.[1255] It was now up to the growers, in the words of a *Fort Morgan Times* editorial, to "determine the future of the sugar industry in the state."[1256] But the depressed sugar price and uncertainties about the plants' reopening had already caused many growers to turn to other crops, and the necessary acreage commitment was not reached.[1257] The sale agreement was no longer operative and, for the first time in over eighty years, no sugar beets were planted in eastern Colorado.[1258]

South Platte Valley communities faced the prospect of the permanent loss of a critical industry. The Morgan County Economic Development Association estimated that the local sugar beet plant's closure would cause a loss of $23 million per year from beet payments, payroll, utilities, and local purchases.[1259] But in early 1986, the Fort Morgan plant was acquired by Western Sugar Company of Denver and reopened, leaving it the lone facility on the eastern plains.[1260] Western Sugar announced plans to add $1.4 million dollars of new equipment, and the fall of 1986 once again saw a beet harvest. Morgan County beet farmers enjoyed a successful growing season and received $9.1 million in the first checks.[1261] But role of sugar in the regional economy was much diminished. Acreage harvested by eastern plains growers had fallen below fifteen thousand, less than a fifth of its peak in the sixties, virtually all of it in Logan and Morgan Counties.[1262]

GW had long been vital to the industry in the South Platte Valley, but the company's troubles were not the only contributor to the industry's decline. Finding field workers was still challenging, and owners of water rights began to realize that massive quantities consumed in raising the crop could be put to more profitable uses. By the end of the century most of the nation's sugar beet production had moved to northern states including Minnesota, North Dakota, Michigan, Montana and Wyoming. Western Sugar Company was purchased by a consortium of beet growers in 2002. The new company which operated the Fort Morgan factory along with four others was renamed Western Sugar Cooperative.[1263] The Fort Morgan plant remains the sole beet processing plant in eastern Colorado.

While the region's sugar beet industry fought to survive another agribusiness offered greater promise. Meat packing was undergoing a transformation. Whole beef carcasses were no longer shipped from slaughtering plants. Instead, steaks, loins, and other cuts were prepared at the plants saving the cost of shipping waste portions of animals. Companies were relocating their plants to where the animals were fed, closing plants, in larger cities such as Chicago, Omaha, or Denver.[1264] Expensive unionized labor was replaced with less skilled and cheaper workers. Most of the jobs in the packing plants were unpleasant and poorly paid. Rather than relying on residents, the packers recruited unskilled workers from outside, often migrants. As Donald Hurt observed, "Meatpacking jobs did not require a skill, education, or command of English. Overall, the meatpacking towns primarily attracted unskilled Latino workers who accepted the dangerous jobs that local residents rejected."[1265]

The South Platte Valley's extensive production of feed grains, access to rail and highway transportation, and weather conditions favorable to weight gains attracted a growing number of feed lots that provided a ready supply of finished animals for slaughter. In the middle eighties some two million stocker and feeder cattle were shipped into Colorado, many of them to the northeastern portion of the state. On January 1, 1986, Morgan County reported 106,000 cattle on feed, Logan County had ninety-seven thousand and Yuma County fifty-five thousand.[1266]

The first large-scale packing plants opened in the middle sixties, but they were often poorly capitalized and vulnerable to market fluctuations and labor problems. The Sterling Beef plant, in its namesake city, began operations in 1966. By the early seventies the work force had grown to more than three hundred and the daily slaughter to fifteen hundred head.[1267] The plant's annual payroll reached $3 million, and it spent $132 million each year purchasing livestock, much of it from local feeders.[1268] By 1980 the *Directory of Colorado Manufacturing* reported that the firm employed between 500 and 999 employees.

Meat packing debuted in Fort Morgan with the locally financed Fort Morgan Dressed Beef's plant in June 1966. Within a year the operation was in the process of liquidation by the Small Business Administration, and the plant closed in November 1967. American Beef Packers, an Iowa firm, bought the plant in a bankruptcy auction in April 1968.[1269] The new owner's operation encountered financial difficulties through the early seventies compounded by issues with the Fort Morgan City government concerning waste disposal. In 1975 the firm filed for reorganization under Chapter 11 of the bankruptcy code. The Fort Morgan plant closed and remained shut for eleven months.[1270] A consortium of local feeders reopened it as Morgan Colorado Beef.[1271] A hog and sheep slaughtering plant that opened in Brush in 1966 also encountered difficulties and experienced closures and changes in ownership.[1272] The industry's hopes of avoiding labor troubles were not fully realized. Strikes and threats of strikes plagued operations in Brush, Fort Morgan, and Sterling. Labor troubles would continue over the next several decades.

In 1980 the Fort Morgan and Sterling packing plants merged to form Sterling-Morgan Colorado Beef later changed to Sterling Beef Company (SBC).[1273] But SBC experienced financial instability due to fluctuating beef prices and ongoing labor problems and announced several sizable layoffs. In the mid-eighties reports surfaced about difficulties with creditors and possible sale of the company.[1274] In January 1985, responding to what were described as "severely depressed economic conditions," SBC management announced a temporary closing of portions of both Fort Morgan and Sterling plants. Total layoffs amounted to seven hundred workers.[1275] The packing plants' trouble along with the loss of sugar beet factories rippled through the South Platte Valley economy already suffering from years of depressed farm incomes.

The outlook brightened in 1987 when SBC's plants in Fort Morgan and Sterling were purchased by Excel Corporation, a subsidiary of agribusiness giant Cargill.[1276] Excel was able to restore some stability to the South Platte Valley meat packing industry. The closed plants finally reopened and 550 of the workers were rehired, 350 at Fort Morgan, and 200 at Sterling.[1277] By the end of the decade the regional economy had stabilized. In 1990 both the Sterling and Fort Morgan operations reported employment of more than a thousand workers.[1278]

The Arkansas Valley also offered potential packing plant sites. The area already boasted several large feed lots, and the demand for fed animals from a local packing plant would bring further growth.[1279] A Valley feed lot manager told the Lamar Rotary Club, "I believe it's time for the people of the area to realize they have one business, one industry of benefit to all and that is cattle feeding and related industries."[1280] Local business leaders agreed and sought to attract the industry to their area. In 1970 a group of boosters from several Valley towns set in motion a plan to accomplish this goal.[1281]

Hopes were raised in 1979 when Iowa Beef Processors (IBP) purchased an option on two thousand acres east of the Lamar as a possible site for a $50 million, 2,400 employee slaughtering facility.[1282] The company was also considering Garden City, Kansas some hundred miles east, but the local paper reported that, according to a BP executive, "right now Lamar is our chosen site."[1283] Despite these assurances, Garden City was ultimately chosen for what became one of the largest meat processing operations in the nation.[1284] IBP's decision was reportedly influenced by incentives offered by Garden City and water supply issues in Lamar as well as hints of local opposition.[1285] Failure to land the IBP plant caused a reexamination of Lamar's growth prospects affecting many aspects of the town's life. The *Lamar Daily News* reported that reductions in projected school enrollments after IBP spurned Lamar led the school board to consider revising the classification of the town's high school sports teams to avoid competing with schools from much larger communities.[1286]

Lamar's disappointment over the IBP failure was forgotten when community leaders joined a combined state and local effort to attract an assembly plant proposed by the

German bus manufacturer Neoplan. The company sought a facility in the rural United States to take advantage of labor costs and quality as well as proximity to American markets. Among the advantages Lamar offered was an affordable workforce with skills needed for metal fabrication operations as demonstrated by the previous success of fabrication firms such as Cross Hydraulics and WHO Manufacturing. The recruiting efforts were successful, and the plant began production in May 1982. The *New York Times* described Lamar's optimism with an article headlined, "Colorado Town Looks to Better Days, With a German Bus Factory." The opening of the plant was celebrated with cheerleaders and band from the local high school along with speeches by state dignitaries and German executives.[1287]

Within three years the plant was producing as many as four buses a day. It employed 650 workers drawn from a sixty-mile radius. Neoplan's operation attracted complementary firms to a nearby industrial park developed by Suetrak, a Dallas-based manufacturer. Suetrak and other firms in the industrial park made components for Neoplan as well as other customers. Products included air conditioning systems, compressors, pulleys and clutches, fiberglass products, prototype designs, electrical systems, and metal work.[1288] The local economy became heavily dependent upon the firm and its suppliers. In the 1987 Neoplan accounted for at least 16 percent of the County's payroll and its satellite firms undoubtedly added additional jobs.[1289] The economy prospered as County employment grew from forty-five hundred in 1981 to fifty-one hundred six years later.[1290] But the community soon became aware of the risks of its reliance on a single firm when the company laid off more than half the plant's work force in January 1988[1291] and another 180 in March.[1292] As a result, the Prowers County economy registered losses in both nonfarm employment and real nonagricultural earnings late in the decade.[1293]

Although manufacturing still comprised a relatively small share of economic activity, it made an important contribution to overall growth in the seventies and eighties. The sector posted a gain of over a thousand jobs between 1970 and 1990, 785 of which were with firms making electrical machinery, nonelectrical machinery, and transportation equipment.[1294] In addition to the Prowers County bus plant and its suppliers, regional firms included Wisdom Manufacturing in Merino a maker of carnival rides; Mohrland Manufacturing in Brush that made farm machinery; Colt Production in Sterling producing semi-grain trailers, and Oliver Manufacturing of La Junta, a manufacturer of gravity separators.[1295]

Population and Labor Force

As in the previous several decades, the region did not generate enough new jobs for all the young people entering the work force. Even during the early seventies when the local economies were expanding, net out-migration continued although at a moderate pace. As job markets weakened over the next decade and a half more and more people moved out. Net out-migration averaged just over five hundred per year between 1970 and 1980 while the region added one thousand nonfarm wage and salary jobs annually.[1296] As local economies slowed and job opportunities diminished, more people left. In the 1980s employment was essentially flat over the decade and more than two thousand people moved from the region each year.[1297] Young people were the most likely to relocate. As her community faced plant closures and farm sales in the mid-eighties, Brenda Endsley a high school senior, told the *Fort Morgan Times* "I feel most of us will have to move, to Denver or even out of state, to find anything worthwhile."[1298] The Applied Population Laboratory at the University of Wisconsin estimated that during the seventies more than seven thousand young people, those between ages fifteen and thirty at the beginning of the decade, left the region. In the eighties the number increased to nearly eleven thousand.[1299] These figures amounted roughly one-fourth the population in those age groups at the beginning of the seventies and one-third at the beginning of the eighties.

Despite outmigration the region's employers were able to fill many of their jobs with women who had not previously been part of the work force. The regional female labor force participation rate for the sixteen counties increased by 17 percentage points between 1970 and 1990. Women were entering the job market throughout the nation, but the region's female participation rate grew much faster, mostly due to women moving from rural areas to towns where employment opportunities were better. Male participation fell slightly over the same period, also paralleling the national trend.[1300]

The excess of births over deaths kept population from declining in the seventies, and the number of people in the sixteen counties increased over the decade for the first time since the forties. Growth was strongest in the early 1970s when the economy was booming, but it continued through the early eighties. Some eight thousand people were added between 1970 and 1983. Thereafter, most counties lost population, and by 1990 the number of people living in the region was virtually unchanged from twenty years earlier. All but two counties either lost population or saw only small gains over the twenty years. The exceptions were Crowley County where a new prison opened in the late eighties, adding nearly a thousand involuntary residents, and Elbert County where a growing number of new residents commuted to Metro Denver. In 1970 seventy percent of workers in the County reported that they worked outside its boundaries. Population more than doubled, increasing from under four thousand in 1970 to more than ninety-seven hundred by 1990. The town of Elizabeth grew from 493 people to 818.[1301]

The seventies and eighties saw the region's Hispanic population begin to grow after several decades of stability as migration across the nation's southern border increased. Between 1970 and 1990 the number of Latinos grew by almost thirty-two hundred, an increase of 19 percent. Over half of this gain occurred in Morgan County, largely a result of demand for migrant workers in the meat packing industry.[1302]

CHAPTER 9

The Plains Economy in 1990

Although markets for farm products were beginning to improve, changes in the structure of American agriculture led to a diminished role as a driver of the regional economy. Manufacturing offered an alternative source of growth, but the seventies and eighties showed both its promise and its vulnerability to outside forces. Food processing and assembly plants provided boosts to local economies, but the manufacturers that located in the plains communities were either independent companies or facilities owned by major corporations. They were vulnerable to market conditions as well as changes in company goals and strategies. While recovery in agriculture in the nineties promised improvement over the previous fifteen years, a return to the exuberance of the early seventies seemed unlikely.

Chapter 9 Exhibits

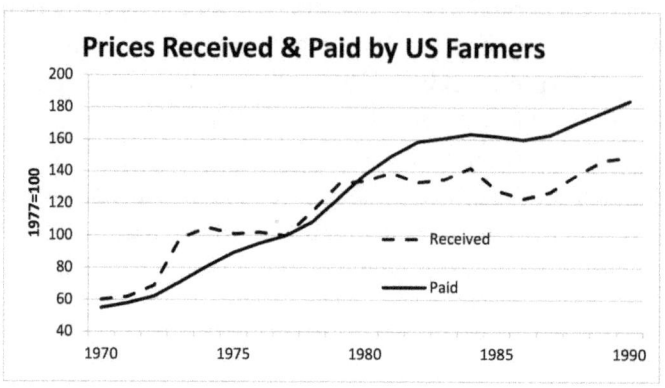

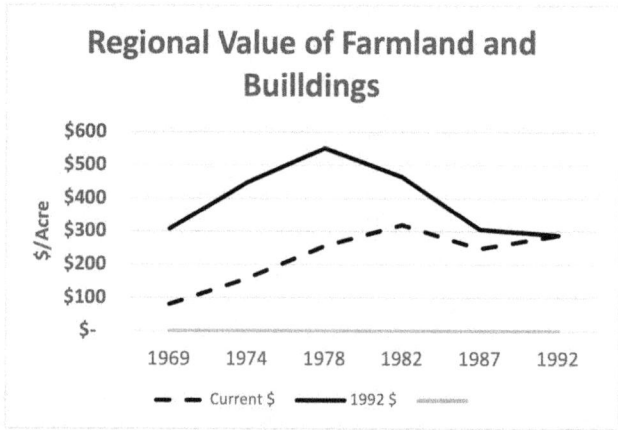

Price increases outpaced the rise in costs in the early 1970s, giving rise to several prosperous years for US farmers. But prices stabilized later in the decade while costs continued upward. Costs continued to outpace prices throughout the eighties.

The real value of farmland peaked as income declined and the Federal Reserve raised interest rates. By the late eighties real land value reached a twenty-year low, creating problems for both farmers and lenders.

Source: USDA, Census of Agriculture

CHAPTER 9

Tractor motorcade.

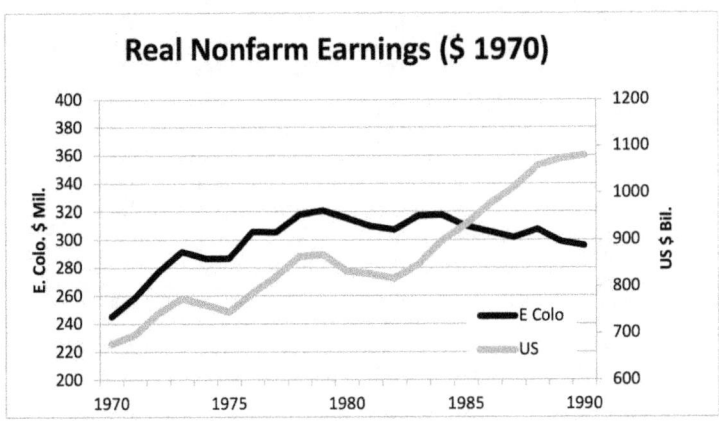

"Tractorcade" in support of American Agricultural Movement. The parade down Lamar's Main Street in December 1977 was described as "festive" despite the twenty-six-degree temperature. The event concluded with a meeting and speakers at the county fairgrounds. Similar rallies were held in many plains communities.

The region's nonfarm economy performed relatively well through the 1970's. Its rate of growth through 1983 exceeded that of the nation which was buffeted by two major recessions. Thereafter the nation rebounded vigorously while real regional earnings declined.

Source: Courtesy of Big Timbers Museum, Lamar, Colorado. BEA

STRUGGLE ON THE HIGH PLAINS

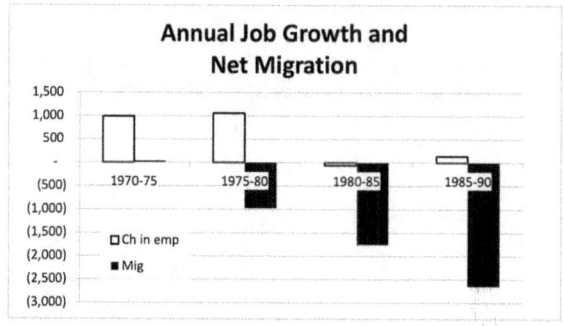

Population

	1970	1975	1980	1985	1990
Baca	5,653	5,625	5,407	4,873	4,516
Bent	6,488	6,337	5,944	5,699	5,023
Cheyenne	2,396	2,224	2,164	2,294	2,396
Crowley	3,085	3,307	2,983	2,997	3,927
Elbert	3,912	4,919	6,904	8,560	9,754
Kiowa	2,022	2,051	1,948	1,847	1,678
Kit Carson	7,579	7,661	7,582	7,547	7,128
Lincoln	4,861	4,982	4,632	4,588	4,514
Logan	18,881	19,243	19,797	19,063	17,508
Morgan	20,268	21,729	22,498	22,431	21,933
Otero	23,398	23,934	22,559	21,760	20,110
Phillips	4,085	4,235	4,533	4,421	4,185
Prowers	13,274	13,684	13,075	14,374	13,329
Sedgwick	3,406	3,374	3,256	2,991	2,674
Washington	5,520	5,135	5,287	5,396	4,768
Yuma	8,501	8,750	9,697	9,853	8,925
Total	133,329	137,190	138,266	138,694	132,368
Dryland	44,529	45,582	48,154	49,379	47,864
Irrigated	88,800	91,608	90,112	89,315	84,504
Baca	5,653	5,625	5,407	4,873	4,516
Ark Valley	46,245	47,262	44,561	44,830	42,389
Central Plains	20,770	21,837	23,230	24,836	25,470
Platte Valley	42,555	44,346	45,551	44,485	42,115
NE Plains	18,106	18,120	19,517	19,670	17,878

Source: Colorado State Demogaphy Office

Net migration was negative throughout the seventies and eighties as job growth was insufficient to meet the employment needs of young people entering the work force. As the economy slowed the pace of out-migration accelerated.

Buoyed by a healthy farm economy early in the decade, the seventies saw the first population gain since the 1940s. But as the economy slowed population declined in most counties. Only the increase in commuters from Elbert County and the opening of a state prison in Crowley County prevented a larger decline. Population losses were largest in the southern part of the region including Baca County and the Arkansas Valley.

Source: BEA and SDO

CHAPTER 10

Coping with the New Economy: 1990-2015

THE US ECONOMY ENJOYED HEALTHY GROWTH IN THE 1990S FUELED BY TECHNOLogy and information services. But the new century brought a marked slowdown punctuated by two recessions, the latter the worst since the 1930s, followed by a historically anemic recovery. The concentration of population and economic activity in urbanized areas continued. Between 1990 and 2015 the US urban population grew 44 percent while the number of non-urban residents fell by 8 percent. The fastest growth was in post-industrial cities that became magnets for what Richard Florida termed the "creative class" of knowledge-based workers. Many of the new jobs supported the lifestyle of these workers and their families. The lack of "creative class" workers was yet another headwind faced by the region's economy.

The regional economy experienced neither the exuberance of the nineties nor severe downturn in new century but, like that nation, suffered a sluggish recovery from the "Great Recession." The nineties saw solid growth in agriculture and a manufacturing rebound in the South Platte and Arkansas Valleys. The next decade turned out less benign. Farmers and ranchers endured a drought and then a devastating blizzard. Two major manufacturers closed their plants in the Arkansas Valley placing a further burden on struggling local economies. The outlook brightened when commodity prices soared in the early teens, bringing brief prosperity for the region's farmers, but agriculture was again under pressure by 2015. As the importance of agriculture shrank, the plains evinced greater vulnerability to changes in other parts of the economy. Elbert County continued to prosper as a bedroom community and the South Platte Valley profited from a healthy farm economy and strong agribusiness. But the Arkansas Valley languished after the turn of the century.

Agriculture 1990-2011

Regional farmers experienced both prosperity and privation during the 1990s and the early 2000s but overall, the years were an improvement over the eighties. Lengthy periods of depressed commodity prices were avoided. The region experienced both drought and harsh winters, but neither caused prolonged damage.

The nineties began on a positive note as real farm earnings in the plains region reached their highest levels since the middle seventies. But the good fortune was largely limited to the livestock industry. Surging crop production throughout the world along with the Gulf War and the collapse of the Soviet Union weakened export demand, and plains growers faced depressed prices for corn and wheat. In early 1991, Alan Foutz, who farmed twenty-eight hundred acres near Akron, estimated his producing wheat cost him $2.60 to $2.70 per bushel while the best price he could get was around $2.30.[1303] At the same time cattlemen were enjoying near record profits. Low prices in the late eighties caused ranchers to reduce their herds and even forced some out of business. This meant fewer animals coming on the market and a rebound in prices. When combined with low feed costs, this produced what the *Denver Post* described as a "nearly unprecedented period of profitability"[1304] for ranchers and feeders. Cash receipts from cattle sales reached an all-time high. But the cycle soon turned. By the middle of the decade, vast numbers of cattle were hitting the markets driving prices down. At the same time feed prices were increasing. In 1996, according to Marvin Eisenach, Morgan County extension agent, losses on cattle sometimes reached $100 per head.[1305] By 1997 regional real realized net farm income had fallen to one-third its level four years earlier.

As Congress considered a new seven-year farm in 1996, dryland wheat growers were most concerned about the fate of the Conservation Reserve Program (CRP) that was scheduled to expire. Their worries were relieved when the program was renewed with no major changes. By 2008 nearly 1.7 million acres in plains counties were enrolled in the program.[1306] In Baca, Kiowa, and Prowers County almost 30 percent of the crop land was covered, and farmers in the region received nearly $1.3 billion between 1995 and 2019, an average of $40,000 annually for each recipient.[1307] Farmers could obtain additional funds from their CRP land by sequestering carbon dioxide by not tilling and allowing grasses and roots to grow and accumulate $CO2$. The credits averaged one ton of CO_2 per acre at a 2008 price of $6.45/ton.[1308]

Good times returned in the late nineties. Near record quantities of wheat were harvested in 1998 and 1999. Cattle prices rebounded and incomes returned to their highs earlier in the decade and remained reasonably strong though much of the early 2000s. By 2008 farmers were able to profit from surging crop prices with wheat selling from more than $6 per bushel and corn above $4.[1309] The value of farmland increased at the fastest rate since the early 1970s; by 2007 it was up a third from twenty years earlier.[1310]

Arkansas Valley melon growers suffered a major blow in 2011 when a Listeria outbreak resulting in thirty-three deaths and 125 people falling ill was traced to cantaloupes grown at the Jensen Brothers farm near Holly. The Jensens were eventually charged by the FDA with adulteration of food and pled guilty to a misdemeanor but avoided prison. [1311] Although the Jensen property was some ninety miles down the Arkansas from Rocky Ford, their melons were marketed as "Rocky Ford Cantaloupes" as were most grown in the Valley. The fallout from the Listeria panic "caused the Lower Arkansas Valley melon growers to struggle as sales plummeted when the Jensen Farm's voluntary recall was issued."[1312]

Destructive Weather

The eastern plains were spared a repeat of past meteorological disasters such as the 1930s' Dust Bowl or even the drought of the early 1950s. This was not entirely due to a more benign climate. Advances in farming and increased irrigation made agriculture less vulnerable to drought. But the region was still afflicted with several climatological events that brought distress to its farmers. Wheat growers in Logan, Sedgwick, and Washington Counties were hit with drought, a late freeze and hail in 1992. The worst drought in fifteen years struck northeast Colorado in 1994. The flow in the South Platte dropped to the point where farmers with rights junior to 1871 could not draw water.[1313]

An even more severe drought, called the harshest in Colorado history, developed in 2001. A US Geological Survey task force study characterized 2002 as the driest in 117 years of records based on stream flow in Colorado's eight river basins.[1314] The Governor declared a state of agricultural emergency for half the State's counties and called a special session of the legislature in 2002. The worst conditions in Colorado were in the San Juan Basin in the southwestern part of the state but the eastern plains faced near-record dry conditions. A group of churchgoers in Lamar handed out flyers urging residents to "Pray that God would pour out a blessing of rain on Prowers County."[1315] As the 2002 growing season approached, farmers anticipated poor crops and ranchers were culling their herds. The dryland wheat crop was especially hard hit. Farmers in Kiowa County had relied on the subsurface moisture from earlier wet years, but by 2001 the subsurface moisture was gone. Kiowa County's wheat harvest totaled 9.4 million bushels in 1998. By 2001 it had dropped to 2.7 million and it fell further to less than half a million bushels in 2002.[1316] Burl Scherler, a wheat grower near Sheridan Lake, assessed the precarious situation commenting, "You've got to hit home runs on the good years so you can make it on the bad years."[1317] Baca County farmer Terry Swanson did not harvest any of the two thousand acres of wheat he planted while Jan Kockhis's farm near Limon yielded only six thousand bushels compared with sixty thousand in an average year.[1318] In Baca County 110,000 acres of cropland were destroyed or failed in 2002 because of drought.[1319] Regional wheat production which had exceeded eighty million bushels in good years fell to only sixteen million bushels in 2002.[1320]

The damage was not limited to dryland. Farmers in the Arkansas Valley faced shortages of water for irrigation as moisture conditions reached a twenty-year low. John Martin Reservoir storage at the beginning of 2002 was 63 percent of normal but fell to 30 percent by June. Both Fort Lyon and Amity Canals reported well below average storage in their reservoirs.[1321] Well irrigators were warned that their usage could be curtailed. Dick Evans, President of the Arkansas Groundwater Users Association warned, "Farmers need to consider that sufficient water may not be available to support historic cropping levels."[1322] At least half of the farmland in Otero County was left idle.[1323] Gary Shane, a Rocky Ford cantaloupe farmer refrained from cultivating 30 percent of his acreage due to lack of irrigation water.[1324] Bent County alfalfa growers reported getting two cuttings instead of the normal three or four. Much of the corn crop was unsuitable for feed and was cut up for silage.[1325]

The 2002 drought also reduced the flow in the South Platte. Owners of surface rights whose seniority dated back to the nineteenth century, claimed that alluvial-well irrigators up-river were drawing upon its flow. Most of these wells had been drilled in the thirties, forties or fifties before any regulation of underground water use. In normal years the South Platte's flow was adequate for both ditches and well irrigators. But in the 2002 drought year, surface irrigators facing shortages sued demanding that well irrigation be curtailed. The Colorado Supreme Court ruled in favor of the surface irrigators and gave the State Engineer authority to restrict well owners' usage.[1326] In March 2003, the state official formally notified owners of affected wells that their pumping would be limited.[1327] Fifteen hundred wells along the river were shut down and many others faced pumping restrictions.[1328] Some farmers defied the order to turn off their pumps. Surface irrigators hired private investigators to find those evading the order and the State Engineer responded by filing complaints with potential fines.[1329]

Most of the affected wells were in Weld, Boulder, and Morgan Counties while the senior surface irrigators were located further downstream. Both sides attempted to reach compromises. Well-water users were allowed to file augmentation plans with the State Engineer to continue to pump from their wells for three years if they arranged to replace the water they used.[1330] Farmers' groups attempted to arrange exchanges with municipal users or other farmers, but negotiation often failed due to lack of assurance that the water would be replaced.[1331] Well irrigators faced threats to their future livelihoods. The Kobobel family's 1,750-acre operation near Wiggins in Morgan County irrigated corn and wheat with six high volume wells. Glen Kobobel, one of the second-generation brothers operating the farm, lamented, "We think it's inevitable that we're going to be shut down."[1332] Morgan County farmer Bill McCracken estimated that shutting down his wells wiped out much of the value of his land. According to McCracken, "I had a farm worth probably close to a million dollars. Now it's worth practically nothing."[1333] In 2007 the owner of an auction company handling land sales in the South Platte Valley reported half his auctions were related to well restrictions.[1334]

CHAPTER 10

Irrigated acreage declined, falling by nearly 30 percent in Morgan County between 2002 and 2007.[1335] Effects from well shut-downs and limitations extended beyond farmers. A Colorado State University study estimated that the wells, which by one estimate were taking 170,000-acre feet of water per year,[1336] contributed $131 million annually to farming communities along the river.[1337]

Ranchers also suffered. Lack of precipitation left pastures with meager grass, so cattle had to be fed. But with the shortage of water, little hay was grown, and it could only be purchased at near-record prices. The government provided some relief by allowing grazing[1338] and growing hay[1339] on CRP land. Ranchers were forced to sell off much of their herds and some went out of business. The Calhan Auction Market in Elbert County sold twice as many animals as usual with many of the sales to buyers from Midwestern states. Winter Livestock in La Junta, which usually traded five hundred head a week, sold eight thousand one week in June.[1340] Bill Gray, owner of a twenty-thousand-acre ranch north of Ordway, had sold almost half his herd by early 2003 and was keeping the remainder alive with hay purchased from Kansas. He planned to sell the rest if rains didn't come by April.[1341] By 2003 Baca County's cattle population had declined by thirteen thousand from two years earlier.[1342]

A big blizzard in March 2003 brought relief and hopes that the drought was over. Mountain snowpack returned to near normal levels. Prices for farm products surged, but the aftereffects of the drought kept many regional farmers and ranchers from taking advantage of them. Poor soil moisture limited planting despite wheat prices at a seven-year high. Beef prices rose sharply, but ranchers were unable to profit as they had sold off much of their herds.

The region was also plagued with several harsh winter storms. The worst began on December 29, 2006, when snow started falling on the southeastern plains. It soon turned into a blizzard with heavy snowfall, fifty-mile-per-hour winds and drifts as high as fifteen feet. Recovery was impeded by at least two more major blizzards over the next several days. Tens of thousands of cattle both on the range and in feedlots were threatened with eventual losses estimated at ten- to fifteen-thousand head.[1343] The Federal Emergency Management Agency (FEMA) declared an emergency in Baca, Bent, Prowers, and Otero Counties making them eligible for federal assistance. Colorado National Guard helicopters and cargo planes dropped hay bales for stranded cattle.[1344] When the storms finally receded, ranchers faced the expense of disposing of the dead animals. The continued cold and lack of feed left pregnant cows weak, threatening further losses in the upcoming calving season. Many calves were stillborn while others were under-weight and would soon die. Feed bills soared as the price of hay climbed from $150 a ton to as much as $210.[1345]

Another Farm Boom

In the early teens, fortuitous developments brought about what Jason Henderson of the Kansas City Federal Reserve described as "another golden era"[1346] comparable to those in the two post-world-war periods and the early seventies. World crop supplies fell due to unfavorable weather in the US corn belt along with droughts in the southern US, parts of eastern Europe, and Russia. At the same time, ethanol demand jumped, requiring more corn, and Chinese imports of corn and soybeans escalated. Crop prices surged over the next few years with wheat approaching $8 per bushel and a bushel of corn reaching nearly $7.[1347] The cattle cycle also entered a favorable phase. Many livestock producers had culled their herds in the late 2000s after experiencing losses and, as the economy began to recover, prices soared. The average price received for cattle and calves increased more than 60 percent between 2009 and 2012.[1348]

The Federal Reserve, attempting to revive the sluggish economy after the Great Recession, drove interest rates to all-time lows, thereby capitalizing rising farm incomes into record-high land values. Increases in non-irrigated cropland values in the Tenth Federal Reserve District, which includes Colorado, averaged over 20 percent per year in 2010, 2011 and 2012.[1349] The 2012 average value of an acre of land in the region was nearly twice what is had been ten years earlier.[1350] Escalating land prices raised concerns about a possible "bubble" as the value-to-rent ratio, an indicator corresponding to the price-earnings ratios for equities, rose well above its previous highs in the early 1970s.[1351] Realized net farm income in the sixteen eastern Colorado counties reached a thirty-eight-year high in 2012 and, although declining in the following year, remained at a historically elevated level.[1352]

But, as in past booms, prosperity was fleeting. High crop prices brought forth increased supply as well as squeezing cattle growers and feeders' margins. By 2015 three years of robust US production along with flat consumption increased grain stocks putting downward pressure on prices. Export demand for US wheat also softened due to weakness in the currencies of other major world grain suppliers, notably Argentina and Russia.[1353] Crop prices peaked in late 2012, and by 2016; the price of wheat was down more than 40 percent and that of corn by over half. Regional growers' receipts from crop sales were off more than 40 percent.[1354] By 2015 cattle prices were also declining, and ranchers and feedlot operators were reporting losses. Regional farm incomes slumped. Realized net farm income fell almost three quarters between 2012 and 2016.[1355] Farm credit conditions deteriorated, and land values were flat in 2014 and declined in 2015 and 2016.[1356]

Agriculture Consolidation Continued

As farming became more capital intensive and technologically sophisticated, earning a decent living became more difficult for small and medium-sized operators.

CHAPTER 10

Farm consolidation that had been underway since at least mid-century continued. As reported by the Federal Reserve Bank of Kansas City in 2017, "Both the crop and livestock sectors are changing from an industry dominated by smaller, family-based, relatively independent firms to an industry dominated by larger businesses more tightly aligned across the value chain."[1357] Economies of scale accruing to larger units increased. Farm Business Farm Management data showed that in 2015 Illinois crop farms reported machinery investment of $640 per acre for one-thousand-acre farms, $590 per acre for two-thousand-acre farms, and $540 per acre for three-thousand-acre farms.[1358] Larger farmers had greater bargaining power in both purchasing and selling along with greater access to capital that facilitated acquisition of more land and incorporation of the latest technology.

Farmers on Colorado's eastern plains followed the national trend. If large farms are considered those with sales greater than $250,000 in 1978, and $500,000 in 2017, roughly comparable after adjusting for inflation, the number of regional operations in the largest category grew by 60 percent in thirty-nine years. In 2017 those with $500,000 or more in sales made up 10 percent of farms but accounted for 88 percent of sales. The 26 percent of farms harvesting one thousand acres or more of crops accounted for 79 percent of the acreage harvested. Measured by either sales or acreage, eastern Colorado agriculture was more concentrated in large farms than the nation.[1359]

At the same time, the number of very small farms increased. Those with sales under $5,000 in 1978 and $10,000 in 2017 more than tripled. Undersized operations did not become profitable. As the economic situation of the marginal farmer deteriorated, he became more dependent on off-farm work. Instead of moving to town the farmer took a job there but kept his rural residence. At the same time urban dwellers along the Front Range with well-paying jobs or comfortable retirement or investment incomes purchased hobby farms. According to the 1978 Census of Agriculture 28 percent of regional farmers reported a primary occupation other than farming and 19 percent worked two hundred or more days off the farm. By 2017 percentages had risen to 53 percent and 24 percent respectively. The greater dependency on off farm work was seen in all sixteen counties.[1360] Elbert County, where proximity to Metro Denver afforded the opportunity for those with ample assets or well-paying urban jobs to embrace the rural life, saw the largest gain in the number of small farms.

As large farms prospered and small farms became part-time operations, mid-sized commercial farms faced increasing cost and competitive pressures. In 1984 Tim Shultz, Colorado's Agricultural Commissioner, noted, "The trend today is toward a 'two-pole' agriculture: more corporate-type farms and more small 'hobby' farms. Caught in the middle are medium-size 'family farm' operations, declining in numbers because of economic and political forces largely outside of farmer control or even influence."[1361] Between 1978 and 2017 the number of mid-sized farms, those in neither the smallest nor largest sales categories, fell by 48 percent. These farms enjoyed neither the economies of scale of the large operations nor the support from off-farm income that sustained the smaller ones. As Crowley County farmer Chris Tomky lamented, "It's just so hard to make a living on a small acreage now. Fifty years ago, a family could survive on 80 acres or 150 acres. Now, there's no way."[1362]

Hog Farms

Few developments in the nineties generated more controversy in plains communities than the advent of large-scale corporate hog farms. They brought new money into often struggling rural communities along with jobs for locals and a ready market for grain farmers along with some less desirable side effects. The prospects of an industrial-scale hog farm generated both enthusiasm and revulsion. According to the *Burlington Record*, residents viewed the location of a large-scale hog operation in their town as either a "promising future" or a "bane of existence."[1363]

Industrial-scale hog farming in the US began in the 1970s following similar trends in chicken production. The modern farms had separate units for farrowing (birthing), nursery, and finishing. Improved techniques, medicines, and feeds allowed handling far more animals at a single site where thousands could be processed. Large hog farms were estimated to operate at a cost advantage of $3 to $5 per hundred pounds over that of traditional small farms.[1364] They could quickly adapt new technology and take advantage of market information. They enjoyed greater access to inputs and capital and, with high volumes and consistent quality, were in a better bargaining position with buyers.[1365] Industrial-scale hog farms first flourished in the Midwestern corn belt and later in North Carolina. But objections to pollution and "unfair" competition with family farms gave rise to lawsuits and statutory restrictions, and producers were attracted to less populated areas such as Colorado's eastern plains. By 1994 hog farms with thousands of animals were located near Holyoke, Julesburg, Lamar, and Yuma.[1366] Yuma County with four large operations by 1995 was the epicenter of the industry in the state. The number of animals sold by County farms of all sizes grew from thirty thousand in 1987 to more than four hundred thousand ten years later and almost nine hundred thousand by 2003.[1367]

The hog farms provided welcome boosts to plains economies. Midwest Farms' proposed twenty thousand sow-multiplier operation near Burlington was estimated to cost $80 million and promised two hundred jobs, a $5.6 million payroll, and more than $9 million in grain purchases from local farmers.[1368] This was a significant stimulus to Kit Carson County which at that time reported roughly twenty-five hundred employees and a covered payroll of $42 million.[1369] Bell farms paid about $300,00 annually in property tax in Bent County.[1370] The Yuma city manager, noting the increase in local sales tax collections after the hog farms began operation, commented, "We're experiencing and little bit of a boom here," and noted the town's plans for a recreation center with the new revenue.[1371]

But attitudes of locals remained mixed. Waste from the animals was collected in lagoons that produced unpleasant odors. Concerns were not limited to the smell. Water supplies could be threatened. Hog effluent is rich in nitrogen and phosphorous and can be an excellent fertilizer. However, when not applied properly, it can percolate through the soil and collect in the water table. Large hog farms were also heavy users of scarce local water. Midwest's plans for its Burlington operation were threatened when the State Engineer denied the firm's application to drill twenty-five wells to tap the Ogallala Aquifer. The wells were eventually approved after Midwest altered its application and the company was able to proceed with its plans. [1372]

Many rural residents felt an attachment to traditional agriculture and opposed corporate farming. A spokesperson for the Rocky Mountain Farmers Union commented, "We're very opposed to corporate agriculture in general, and corporate hog farming in particular. I personally would rather drive through eastern Colorado and see a thousand small hog farms than one giant operation." [1373] Opposition was not limited to agricultural groups. Residents of farm communities viewed changes in the traditional agricultural structure, whatever the economic advantages they might bring, as threats to their way of life. A consultant to the Center for Rural Affairs, a group that studied rural communities, reported, "Any time you go to the people and ask them what they want, in every instance they say they don't want corporate farming. It says people understand better than a lot of policy makers what kind of impacts corporate farming has on the community, independent producers, and the quality of life in the area." [1374]

Disputes pitting defenders of aesthetics, traditional values, and the environment against the boosters of local economies raged through the nineties. Both sides pushed for changes in state laws. The conflict intensified in 1998 when Colorado voters faced opposing amendments to the state's Constitution. Industry-sponsored Amendment 13 limited the ability of local governments to place constraints on factory hog farms by requiring that all livestock operations be regulated in a comparable manner, thereby guaranteeing opposition to changes from cattle and chicken operations. Opponents backed Amendment 14 that mandated state regulation of large hog farms. The state's responsibilities would include regulation of the disposal of wastewater and manure and limiting odor. The Amendment also allowed local government to impose even more stringent regulations. State voters expressed their disapproval of hog farms when Amendment 14 passed by a large margin while the industry sponsored measure was soundly defeated.

As Amendment 14 was being implemented, operators and many community leaders expressed concern about the regulations, particularly the controls of air pollution. [1375] Under the powers granted by the Amendment, the Colorado Air Quality Control Commission adopted rules that required covering waste lagoons to control odors. [1376] Covering lagoons was expensive. Seaboard Farms near Holyoke claimed that a single lagoon cover would cost $100,000[1377] and would, in the industry's view, prevent the farms from using other techniques to limit undesirable odors.[1378]

Tighter regulation raised fears of damage to local economies. A Prowers County commissioner voiced worries about the ability of the farms to continue operating in the County. He noted that four hundred to five hundred people worked in the industry in southeast Colorado and felt that "The hog farms have stabilized Main Street in Lamar."[1379] Phillips County native and *Denver Post* columnist Bob Ewegen wrote of his concerns about threats to D&D Corporation's facility near Holyoke. He noted that many farmers were able to survive through day jobs with D&D and characterized the air pollution standards as so strict that they "could not be met by most businesses in Denver."[1380] The new rules appear to have constrained large-scale hog farms but hardly eliminated them. The Census of Agriculture reported that the number of hog farms with inventories greater than one thousand fell from thirty-one in 1997, the year before the referendums, to seventeen in 2017. The counties with the greatest number of large operations saw declines. In Logan County the number of farms with at least one thousand hogs fell from seven to six and in Yuma County from six to three.[1381]

Further Threats to Irrigation

Water transfers from agricultural to municipal use continued. Demands by Colorado's Front Range municipalities accelerated as the counties stretching from the Wyoming border through Pueblo added more than eight-hundred thousand people during the nineties and over a million in the next fifteen years.[1382] Resistance from environmental interests to further depletion of mountain streams, exemplified by the Environmental Protection Agency's rejection of the Denver Water Board's proposed Two Forks Dam, and Western Slope opposition to further diversion projects left eastern plains irrigation water the least costly and most politically feasible source for meeting future municipal needs.

Most of the water transfers were from the Arkansas Basin. By the early nineties, 85 percent of Crowley County's irrigation water had been sold, the bulk of it for use by Colorado Springs or Aurora.[1383] By the end of the century, 755 of the 800 shares in the Rocky Ford Ditch had either been sold or were committed to be sold.[1384] The municipalities were sometimes able to ameliorate the damage caused by their acquisition of water. In 2011 the Arkansas Valley endured a severe drought while Aurora enjoyed a temporary surplus of water due to snow in Colorado's northern mountains and heavy rains on Front Range. Aurora aided the Valley farmers by providing water, on a temporary basis, to Otero County ditch companies.

Crowley and Otero County saw the largest losses, but buyers extended their quests down-river to Bent and Prowers Counties where the rights were usually more junior. The largest water owner in these counties was the Fort Lyon Canal that irrigated farms extending from Otero County to near the Kansas line, and whose development a century earlier was described in chapter 2. In 1992 Colorado Water Supply, a sister company of Colorado Interstate Gas, extended an offer to the Canal's owners of $2,228 per share with the proceeds reduced by brokers fees, revegetation costs and other expenses.[1385] The planned purchase could have amounted to $110 million but was ultimately cancelled when the buyer failed to get commitments from enough owners.[1386]

Threats to the Fort Lyon were not over. Some ten years later a Nevada investment company, High Plains A&M, began purchasing land with rights to the Canal's water. The firm reportedly offered $1,750 per acre to several farmers in Bent, Prowers and Otero Counties. The first sale by a Bent County farmer closed in June 2002 for nearly $1.3 million.[1387] According to the *Denver Post* the price for an acre of land with Fort Lyon rights had been bid up to $4,000 and by mid-2003 and High Plains had acquired a reported twenty-five thousand acres controlling a hundred thousand acre feet, more than a quarter of the Fort Lyon's annual flow.[1388] The Canal Company went to court attempting to stop High Plains' actions.[1389] The case eventually reached the state Supreme Court which rejected the attempt to change the water rights from agricultural to other unspecified use on the grounds that it was not legal to buy up water rights for speculative purposes in Colorado, and the Fort Lyon's water was restored.[1390]

Critics of the transfers continued to warn of the potential harm to agriculture and to the local economies. By the 1990s, these apprehensions were being realized. Between 1987 and 2017 irrigated acreage in Crowley County dropped from twenty-one thousand to five thousand and that in Otero County fell from fifty-six thousand to forty-nine thousand.[1391] As he viewed the water transfers *Denver Post* environment columnist Mark Obmascik wrote, "The high plains of Colorado are clearly in deep trouble."[1392] Bob Rawlings, publisher of the *Pueblo Chieftain*, lamented, "How sad it is that these water sales dry up fine farmland just to permit Aurora to grow even bigger."[1393] John Stencel, president of the Rocky Mountain Farmers Union, expresses the concerns of many when he noted, "I fear the whole high plains area drying up."[1394] Damage went beyond the loss of water for irrigation. The Director of the State Soil Conservation Board expressed fears that the loss of irrigation was "creating a miniature dust bowl in the Arkansas Valley."[1395] More upstream use increased the salinity of the Arkansas, worsening an already troublesome problem.

Agreements with metropolitan purchasers often called for rehabilitating the no-longer-irrigated land by reseeding it to return the acreage to grassland. But reseeding was often a lengthy undertaking. Years of irrigation had increased the salinity of the soil, making it a hostile environment for grass. Reseeding efforts in Crowley County took five to seven years to produce an acceptable stand.[1396] Prospects for dryland crops on the reclaimed land were meager. According to Otero County Soil Conservation agronomist John Knapp, "we can expect dramatically lower production value of the land…. At worst it becomes useless."[1397]

The loss of irrigated farmland placed a heavy financial burden on local governments dependent on property tax revenues. When irrigation rights were lost, the land was reclassified as grassland on the tax rolls. The Otero County assessor estimated that an acre served by a ditch was assessed at $1,750 to $2,000, a figure that would drop to around $300 after the water rights were sold.[1398] Although both Crowley and Otero added jobs in the nineties, the loss of irrigated farming was an important contributor to the declining economies in the two counties after the turn of the century.

Growers drawing on the Ogallala Aquifer were not immediately affected by drought, transfers, or well restrictions but faced growing threats to their long-term water use. By the late nineties the State Engineer estimated that 20 percent of the aquifer had been drained in the past quarter century.[1399] The Colorado Groundwater Commission imposed a virtual moratorium on new wells in northeastern Colorado. In the Southern High Plains Basin underlying Baca County, drilling new wells was still allowed although measurements of underground water at five locations in the County showed the water level had dropped an average of forty-five feet.[1400] The promised bonanza from the Aquifer had receded. Yuma County irrigated acreage fell by sixty-four thousand between 1992 and 2017 and that in Kit Carson County dropped by twenty-one thousand.[1401] In 2015 *Bloomberg Business Week* reported that Yuma County farmer Marvin Pletcher was able to pump only half the volume of water that he did ten years earlier. He was forced to switch crops from corn to wheat, sorghum, sunflowers, and pinto beans, which used less water but were not as profitable. Pletcher lamented, "I have four wells in operation. In 10 years, I'll be lucky if I have one."[1402]

The Non-farm Economy

In the nineties the US economy posted its strongest growth in three decades, profiting from the end of the Cold War, low inflation, and the incorporation of productivity-enhancing information technology. Although the plains region lacked high-tech industry, it benefitted from the strength of the national economy as well as the region's cost advantages, as prices for labor and real estate accelerated in metropolitan areas. This created a favorable climate for vehicle and machinery manufacturing with Lamar's Neoplan bus plant a prime example. Food processors also thrived, especially meat packing. That industry added more US jobs than any other four-digit NAICS manufacturing categories between 1990 and 2000.[1403]

As a result, plains businesses enjoyed a prosperous decade. Regional real non-agricultural earnings grew almost 3 percent per year.[1404] The sixteen counties added more than 11,000 wage and salary jobs with every county experiencing an increase.[1405] The new century was less kind. While a strong national economy aided the region in the 1990s, sluggish US growth exposed the plains communities to stiff headwinds that contributed to stagnation in the 2000s and the early teens. The region lost 1,500 jobs through 2015.[1406]

CHAPTER 10

Apart from Elbert County, the region was spared the housing bust that plagued the nation since the rural plains had not experienced an earlier housing boom. As a result, eastern Colorado's downturn in the Great Recession was less severe than in much of the nation. Regional nonfarm GDP actually increased between 2007 and 2009 at a rate close to the previous six years while that of the US fell. But the region's recovery from the recession was weaker.[1407] Post-recession experiences varied within the region. The Arkansas Valley's GDP growth was barely positive while the rate of increase in the South Platte Valley was well above that of the nation.[1408] Morgan County again saw the most new jobs among the rural counties, an additional eight hundred between 2009 and 2015.[1409]

The region's burdens in the new century were not limited to national recessions and a stressed farm sector. As international flows of capital increased, intense foreign competition and a strong dollar eroded plains communities' advantages in manufacturing. Plants reduced their scale of operations or closed. With jobs demanding ever higher skills, the lower education level of the population acted as a further impediment to growth.[1410] While more than fifteen-hundred manufacturing jobs were added during the nineties, nearly two-thirds of them were lost over the next fifteen years.[1411] Meat packing in the South Platte Valley was a loan bright spot.

Regionwide data obscure differences among local economies. The northern part of the region was relatively healthy while southern counties fell behind. The South Platte Valley and the northeast plains enjoyed solid growth, led by Morgan County which added more than nine hundred wage and salary jobs between 2001 and 2015 and Yuma County with over three hundred. The Arkansas Valley and Baca County registered the slowest nonfarm income growth in the region between 1990 and 2015. Bent, Otero and Prowers Counties all saw sizable job losses.[1412] The Arkansas Valley economy is discussed in greater detail in the next section.

Elbert County's economy was by far the most buoyant. New workers in trade, professional and business services and local government were needed to serve the County's rapidly growing population. Employment nearly tripled with more than twenty-four hundred jobs added between 1990 and 2015. The central plains also enjoyed healthy growth with Lincoln and Kit Carson County each adding several hundred jobs aided by opening of prisons in Limon and Burlington in the nineties[1413] and traffic along Interstate 70. In 2016 Burlington boasted more than five hundred motel rooms catering to tourist traffic.[1414]

The performance of the smaller counties reliant on agriculture varied. Yuma County thrived, driven by record corn crops, several commercial hog farms and some oil and gas activity. The County's rate of employment growth between 1990 and 2015 lagged only that in Elbert County. Baca and Washington Counties, heavily dependent upon dryland wheat and cattle, experienced a sluggish economy while Phillips County benefited from a hog farm in Holyoke and posted a job gain over the twenty-five years.[1415] Kiowa County and Cheyenne, also dependent on dry land farming, saw little or no growth. According to a 1998 *Denver Post* article, "More than half the businesses in Eads stand empty."[1416]

Energy activity provided a boost in some counties. Oil and gas activity picked up as prices began to rise. Production increased in Cheyenne and Lincoln Counties and the energy industry was still a major player in Washington, Logan, and Morgan Counties although at levels well below those in the boom times of the fifties. Between 1990 and 2015 the nine regional counties that reported employment in the natural resources and mining sector added more than two thousand jobs with Morgan and Yuma Counties adding almost seven hundred each.[1417] The introduction of fracking led to increased activity in the Niobrara Shale Basin that included parts of northeast Colorado. The executive director of the Morgan County Economic Development Corp. noted that drilling in the County benefitted many businesses in Fort Morgan. "Your hotels are full, your gas stations are full, and your restaurants."[1418] But oil and gas activity was not universally welcomed by locals. Oil producers clashed with landowners over legal and financial recourse for damage done from drillers taking advantage of mineral rights on farm property.[1419]

The most striking energy developments were in renewables, especially wind. Subsidies and regulatory mandates helped make electricity generated by wind power competitive. A federal government production-based tax credit took effect in 1992 and the state of Colorado enacted Renewable Portfolio Standards (RPS) that required electric utilities to produce a specified share of their power from renewable sources.[1420] These incentives led to the siting of several large windfarms on the plains, taking advantage of the region's brisk winds and the availability of vast unpopulated stretches where the turbines could be sited. The first large one, a partnership of General Electric and Xcel Energy, was built south of Lamar. Completed in 2003 with a 162-megawatt capacity, it was, at the time, the fifth largest in the nation. It brought hundreds of temporary construction jobs to the County and generated $700,000 annually in property tax revenue.[1421] By 2012 there were eight commercial scale windfarms in eastern Colorado, two each in Prowers, Lincoln, Logan and Phillips Counties.[1422] While windfarms produced few local jobs once construction was completed, they provided a healthy increase in the local property tax base and lease payments that were welcomed by landowners. The windfarm near Peetz in Logan County reportedly paid landowners more than $5,000 per year for each turbine.[1423] The largest wind project, begun in the middle teens, was Xcel Energy's $1 billion six hundred-megawatt Rush Creek project in Cheyenne, Elbert, Kit Carson and Lincoln Counties. It included three hundred turbines and a ninety-mile transmission line to the Front Range and was completed in 2018.[1424]

The region's ample corn crop gave rise yet another alternative energy industry. As noted in chapter 9, several smaller biofuel plants were built in the 1980s. By the 2000s state and federal subsidies and mandates for biofuels led to several regional plants including the 42 million-gallon-a-year Sterling Ethanol.[1425] In 2007 two plants were built near Yuma. One, priced at $61 million, was estimated to generate 180 construction jobs and a permanent work force of forty earning an average wage of $40,000.[1426] But ethanol's future might be less promising than that of wind energy as doubts arose about its contribution to either America's energy independence or to greenhouse-gas reduction.

Prisons: A New Economic Driver for Rural Communities

In the nineties, rural communities discovered a promising new target for their economic development efforts: public and private penal institutions. Since crime seemed unlikely to go away, the long-term prospects for such institutions appeared brighter than some of the more ephemeral industries the plains region had attracted in the past. In Colorado, as in the nation, the eighties and nineties saw a sharp increase in incarcerated populations. Driven by the "war on drugs," harsher sentencing laws, and political responses to fears of rising crime, more and more people wound up behind bars. Colorado's adult prison population increased from 3,114 in 1982 to 13,666 in 1998 with another six thousand inmates projected by 2005.[1427] Growth in the prison population led to overcrowding of existing institutions and demand for new facilities. The combination of "nimbyism" (not in my back yard) in metropolitan areas and the desire for new employers in the hinterlands led to many of Colorado's new penal institutions being placed in eastern plains communities. Between the late 1980s and the early 2000s, seven state correctional facilities including private operations and youth institutions opened in plains counties.

The prospect of a new prison was attractive to community leaders striving to sustain their economies in the face of the shrinking impact of agriculture and declining manufacturing. Geographer Deborah Che wrote, "Rural communities, where traditional productive economic sectors such as agriculture, manufacturing and resource extraction have declined, view correctional institutions and jobs as a route to economic growth, population stabilization and a middle-class life style for residents without college degrees."[1428] A new prison seemed to promise a steady source of reasonably well-paid employment and, with private facilities, a welcome addition to the tax base. Expenditures by the institutions' employees and by families from urban areas visiting their incarcerated relatives would boost sales of merchants, restaurants, and motels. Prisons were environmentally clean and seemingly invulnerable to economic cycles.

Despite these benefits, the prospect of a prison in the community was not received with universal approval. Residents expressed concerns about safety and some businesses feared that prisons' pay scales would make it difficult to find workers.[1429] In 1997 Dominion Leasing, an Oklahoma firm, proposed a thousand bed private medium security facility in the small Morgan County town of Wiggins. The project promised 240 jobs and more than $200,000 annually in additional taxes.[1430] But some residents were not pleased. A woman complained, "I just think a correctional facility is totally wrong for a small town."[1431] The issue was put to a vote and passed by the narrow margin of twelve votes out of 296 cast.[1432] But continuing protests including a demonstration by unhappy farmers on their tractors convinced the firm to abandon its plan.[1433] Simla also rejected a correctional facility[1434] and a Lamar campaign to attract a private prison that would have employed three hundred workers was dropped.[1435]

But other towns welcomed a large new employer. The first state prison built on the plains was the state owned Arkansas Valley Correctional Facility near Ordway in Crowley County that opened in 1987 with a capacity of one thousand inmates.[1436] It was soon followed in 1989 by the High Plains Youth Facility in Brush, a private institution for troubled youth. By 1993 it employed 150 with a payroll of $1.5 million.[1437] The Bent County Correctional Facility, also private, opened in 1993 with 335 inmates and 84 workers. In 1997 it was taken over by Corrections Corporation of America (CCA), later rebranded CORECIVIC, the nation's largest private prison company, which planned a $9.5 million expansion that would increase the population to 700 and staff to 160.[1438] The Kit Carson Correctional Center in Burlington, also operated by CCA, opened in 1998. By 2000, publicly funded facilities were built in Limon, Sterling, and Akron and a private one in Olney Springs in Crowley County. Yet another new custodial facility was created when the Fort Lyon Veterans Hospital was converted into a state facility for chronically ill and infirm inmates. It was later converted to a transitional facility for homeless persons.

The prisons delivered the promised population and jobs. The *Denver Post* reported in 2001 that "The Limon prison brought 950 residents who can't leave and 350 jobs."[1439] As noted earlier, Crowley County was one of the few eastern plains counties that did not lose population during the 1980s, even if the direct economic contribution of incarcerated individuals to the local economy was limited. But the impetus to the local economy was sometimes outweighed by other less favorable developments. Despite the new prison opening in 1991, Lincoln County only added two net new jobs between 1990 and 1995. In Logan County, where the twenty-four hundred bed Sterling Correction Facility opened in 1998, the number of jobs declined between 1995 and 2000.[1440] The prison jobs did not necessarily go to locals. Construction contracts often went to outside firms, and most of the better jobs in state operated facilities were filled by nonresidents through competitive examinations.[1441] Many of the workers at plains community's prison commuted from outlying areas. Almost 30 percent of the employees at the Burlington facility lived in Goodland, Kansas where better and more affordable housing was available.[1442] Many staff positions at the Limon prison were filled by retired military personnel who commuted from Colorado Springs. Although the seventy-mile drive might have seemed a burden, one commuter claimed that it could be completed within an hour "if you know the sheriff."[1443]

CHAPTER 10

The growth in demand for prison beds eventually slowed. Politicians were beginning to consider the costs, both fiscal and social, of rising rates of incarceration. Between 2009 and 2015 population in Colorado's public and private prisons fell from 18,327 to 16,522. It stabilized over the next several years.[1444] Most of the burden from smaller inmate populations fell on private facilities as the decline coincided with the construction of new government facilities or the expansion of existing ones. When Sterling's state penal institution opened in 1998, it left nineteen hundred empty beds in the four private institutions.[1445] In 2001 the private prison in Crowley County reported 300 empty beds while the Bent County facility had 500 and Burlington 350.[1446] In late 2001 CCA reported 575 empty beds in Colorado.[1447] Falling occupancy put severe pressures on the private operators as much of their cost was fixed while revenues varied with the number of beds filled. Eric Schlosser in a recent *Atlantic* article described the private prisons' dilemma:

> The economics of the private-prison industry are in many respects similar to those of the lodging industry. An inmate at a private prison is like a guest at a hotel—a guest whose bill is being paid and whose checkout date is set by someone else. A hotel has a strong economic incentive to book every available room and encourage every guest to stay as long as possible. A private prison has exactly the same incentive. The labor costs constitute the bulk of operating costs for both kinds of accommodation. The higher the occupancy rate, the higher the profit margin. The private-prison industry usually charges its customers a daily rate for each inmate; the success or failure of a private prison is determined by the number of "man-days" it can generate.[1448]

The private prison industry's troubles were not only financial. Criticism of private prisons grew through the 1990s and early 2000s, although many of the facilities' shortcomings were also found in government institutions in Colorado and elsewhere. Unlike the hotel industry, private prisons had little incentive to accommodate their "guests" who could not "check out" if displeased nor choose the location for their confinement based on on-line reviews. Private operators were accused of lacking motivation to reduce recidivism as it was as a source of potential repeat business. The prisons' management frequently focused on minimizing operating costs often resulting in the hiring of untrained and poorly paid staff. According to critics, this could lead to mistreatment of inmates. A 1999 story in the Denver weekly *Westword* cited "allegations of sexual misconduct and smuggling of contraband by staff, as well as inmate gripes about inadequate medical care, canteen ripoffs, unsanitary kitchen conditions and other issues,"[1449] at the Kit Carson Correctional Center. In 2004 inmates rioted at the private Crowley County Correctional Facility, chasing staff from the building, lighting fires, and causing millions of dollars in damages. The Colorado Department of Corrections released a critical report citing inadequate training and emergency procedures, and a lawsuit was filed against the prison operator by a public-interest law firm.[1450]

As populations in private facilities fell, communities faced the possibility of a major blow to their economies. By the middle teens, the Kit Carson Correctional Center was coming under severe cost pressures. In 2016 inmate population had fallen to 402 in a facility with a capacity of 1,450. The Center was viewed as vital for the local economy and the state legislature approved an additional $3 million to keep it open. The prison's operator considered the additional funds insufficient and announced plans to close in July. Burlington confronted the loss of both jobs and tax base. The prison employed 142 staff at the time of closing, many of whom lived in the community. It accounted for 9.8 percent of the Kit Carson County's assessed valuation, paid over one million dollars in property tax, and was the largest customer for city owned utilities. Most prison employees left the town when their jobs disappeared. By early 2017 Burlington's population had dropped from forty-two hundred to thirty-six hundred with some four hundred of that decline accounted for by the loss of inmates.[1451] To long-time Burlington resident Daniel Gonzales, "It was like half the town left."[1452]

The Arkansas Valley Economy Slumped in the 2000s

Between 2000 and 2015, the Arkansas Valley, along with adjacent Baca and Kiowa Counties, suffered the weakest growth in the region following a solid gain in the 1990s. Over a thousand jobs were lost between 2001 and 2005 and another two thousand over the next ten years, a total of nearly one-sixth of all wage and salary employment.[1453] Population declined by more than five thousand.[1454] Between 2000 and 2015 Otero County lost 15 percent of its wage and salary jobs and Prowers County 25 percent.[1455] Real median incomes declined almost everywhere after 2000 but they fell by a shocking 20 percent in Otero County between 1999 and 2013-17. Poverty rates in the Arkansas Valley counties were well above those in the nation as a whole.[1456]

Valley communities were beginning to exhibit many of the woes afflicting the "Rust Belt" in the American Midwest with declining incomes, falling population, and social pathologies such as spreading drug addiction. A 2016 *Denver Post* headline declaimed, "Strapped towns in southeast Colorado struggle to fight heroin's spread."[1457] According to the article the heroin, most of which was thought to be distributed from Pueblo, led to sharp increases in the incidence of overdoses between 2002 and 2014. Valley counties showed high rates of disability among older working-age adults, often an indicator of social and economic distress.[1458] A 2017 survey by the Economic Innovation Group using Census data and based on new business formation and job growth ranked the Arkansas Valley towns of Granada, Las Animas, Sugar City and Rocky Ford as "distressed."[1459]

The Valley suffered a major blow when Lamar's Neoplan bus plant closed. As the new century opened, Prowers County's manufacturing sector was thriving. Demand for buses was robust and almost five hundred well-paying manufacturing jobs had been added over the previous decade.¹⁴⁶⁰ At the 1982 dedication of the company's Lamar plant, the founder had proclaimed, "We are here forever."¹⁴⁶¹ But increased pressure from both domestic and foreign competitors threatened the firm's survival. The plant had originally been part of a German corporation, but the US division was spun off, and the new entity did not have the resources to compete with several larger manufacturers under the more difficult conditions in the new century.¹⁴⁶² Management reduced the workforce in the early 2000s, citing increasing competition along with less demand from local governments as federal transportation funding was cut. The company's executive offices relocated from Lamar to Denver. Finally, in November 2005 management announced that its Lamar plant was closing. According to a company spokesman, "Despite everyone's best efforts, we could not continue to operate against larger, stronger competitors."¹⁴⁶³ The loss to employees and the community from Neoplan's closing was estimated by the company at $10 million.¹⁴⁶⁴ Prowers County was left with some $200,000 in unpaid taxes.¹⁴⁶⁵

The closure was a shock to the community and especially to employees who had been attracted to what appeared to be stable and well-paying jobs. A laid-off employee recalled, "When I started working there in 1995, we were pushing four busses a day out the door. I thought I was going to retire from there."¹⁴⁶⁶ Community leaders voiced determination to find another employer to occupy the former Neoplan facility, and the many small satellite manufacturers in Lamar issued optimistic statements about their ability to maintain their business.¹⁴⁶⁷ But these efforts faced significant obstacles. As the Lamar City Administrator pointed out, "We want businesses to come here, but we have no control if they choose to or not. In the six-county area the population is under 70,000 and that is a disadvantage to companies considering bringing businesses here because of the work force."¹⁴⁶⁸

Neoplan's closure reflected developments in its industry, but also revealed that the plant's ties to the regional economy were weak and transitory. Lamar was close to neither inputs nor markets. The company employed local workers and had developed a supply chain of small manufacturers near its Lamar plant. But buses could be built anywhere. Workers with the necessary skills could be found in elsewhere in the US or abroad and new supply chains could be developed as they were in Lamar.

The bus plant's situation contrasted with that of another large regional manufacturer, Cargill's meat packing plant in Fort Morgan was anchored to its northeast Colorado location by the supply of fed cattle that in turn depended on regional ranches and growers of feed grains. As discussed in the chapter 9, the Arkansas Valley was also potentially attractive to meat packers, but once the industry settled in the South Platte Valley and the large IPB plant was established in Garden City, Kansas, there was little demand for another sizable facility in the region. The Cargill plant was largely responsible for Morgan County adding almost three hundred manufacturing jobs between 2001 and 2015 while Prowers County lost more than six hundred.¹⁴⁶⁹ The failure of

Arkansas Valley to secure the IBP plant in the 1970s may have destined it to a sluggish economy in the 2000s, although the loss of irrigation through water transfers might have limited Arkansas Valley cattle feeding in any case.

A day after the Neoplan announcement, Bay Valley Foods revealed plans to shut down its La Junta pickle and relish plant with an annual payroll of $3 million and 153 employees. The plant, under several owners, had been a major employer in La Junta for sixty-five years and was an important buyer of the county's cucumber crop. The company attributed the closure to declining market share, rising costs, and competition from overseas producers. According to the company, the cost of local farmers' cucumbers was well above that of those shipped from elsewhere, and La Junta labor costs averaging $12 per hour greatly exceeded the one dollar or less paid in foreign plants.[1470] By 2007 Otero County's manufacturing employment had fallen by 126 and total private jobs by more than five hundred since 2001.[1471]

The closing of the Fort Lyon Veterans Hospital delivered yet another blow. The hospital, located a few miles east of Las Animas, had been an important Bent County employer for decades. The facility housed six hundred neuropsychiatric patients in the early nineties.[1472] When it was shut down in 2001 only ninety-nine patients remained, and the staff had seen a comparable reduction. The facility was converted to a state operated prison for elderly and ailing inmates. The staff size at the new Fort Lyon was roughly the same as when the hospital closed, but the employees were generally paid less than the professionals at the veterans' hospital. The Fort Lyon payroll was reduced further when the prison was converted to a facility providing transitional housing to homeless persons.

The closures were not the sole contributor to the Valley's struggling economy. Manufacturing dominated the Prowers County economy but was less important elsewhere in southeast Colorado. Although timing of the Bay Valley Food closing coincided with that of Neoplan, its longer-term impact on the Otero County economy was small. Only sixteen manufacturing jobs were lost between 2001 and 2005 as most of Bay Valley's loss was eventually offset by increased employment at other firms.[1473] But other industries also struggled. The loss of irrigated farmland meant less business in the trading centers that depended on farmers' spending. The effect was greatest in Otero and Crowley Counties but was also felt elsewhere. The lack of access to the interstate highway was a continuing disadvantage. The Arkansas Valley counties lost more than six hundred retail trade jobs between 2001 and 2015. Otero County employment in transportation and warehousing fell by one-fifth as railroad operations in La Junta were scaled back.[1474]

Population and Labor Force

Between 1990 and 2015 the plains region saw population gains which appear quite healthy with more than twenty-six thousand people added over the quarter century.

This picture is somewhat misleading as three groups—prison inmates, commuters and Hispanics—more than accounted for all the growth. The adult inmate population in the sixteen counties grew by seven thousand, all of whom were included in population counts of the counties where the prisons were located. Commuters to Metro Denver were largely responsible for Elbert County's fifteen thousand new people over the twenty-five years. Finally, the Latino population rose by eighteen thousand. These categories are not mutually exclusive as some Latinos were included in the prison population or the commuters. Nonetheless, without gains in these three groups the regions' population would have shown a significant decline. The non-Hispanic, non-inmate population outside Elbert County fell by an estimated ten thousand or 9 percent over the twenty-five years.[1475] By 2002 total population in the region exceeded 162,000 approaching its peak reached during the 1920s. In the following years, all sixteen counties' growth slowed and, by 2015, and the region's population had declined more than two thousand from its peak, more than five thousand if Elbert County's gain is excluded. The population decline was greatest in the Arkansas Valley. While growing number of prison inmates stabilized populations in Bent and Crowley Counties, Prowers and Otero Counties each lost more than a thousand residents.[1476]

The two largest towns in the region, Sterling and Fort Morgan, saw healthy growth, between them adding about six thousand people from 1990 to 2015. All the larger towns in the struggling Arkansas Valley lost population. In a contrast with most of the twentieth century, the latest quarter century did not see a large rural exodus. Rural areas outside towns and towns with fewer than one thousand people each posted small gains.[1477] The growth in small farms with operators dependent on outside income accounts much of this gain.

Explosive growth in Metro Denver meant more people moving into its bedroom communities such as those in western Elbert County. The County's population growth in the 1990s was the third fastest of any county in the nation. (The fastest occurred in neighboring Douglas County.) By 2015 the County had over twenty-five thousand residents, with nearly all the growth in the Census County Subdivision of Elizabeth, which made up roughly the western half of the county.[1478] While local governments and business leaders elsewhere in the region strove to attract additional jobs and people, many Elbert County residents resisted the disruption in their communities from the influx of people and to intrusions on what they consider a rural way of life. As one of them complained in 2004, "We moved out here for a lifestyle, and we don't want Aurora moving in next door."[1479] Disputes over this issue often became heated. In a confrontation over growth in the town of Elizabeth, a seventy-three-year-old member of the town planning commission called the town manager a "bastard" and advocated his castration.[1480]

With a large share of the population made up of commuters and their families, Elbert County residents had distinctly different economic and demographic characteristics than those in the rest of the region, more closely resembling dwellers in urbanized areas than the rural and small-town residents on the plains and in the river valleys. In 1969 the County's median family income was only slightly above the regional average. By the mid-teens it grown to nearly twice that in the other counties. There were relatively more rich families; 30 percent reported incomes above $150,000 compared only 5 percent for the other plains counties, and its population was concentrated in the prime working age group; 57 percent of its residents were between twenty-nine and forty-nine, some six percentage points higher than in the remainder of the region. Education levels were higher. The share of residents with a bachelor's degree was nearly twice that in the other counties.[1481]

After decades of more people leaving the region than moving in, net positive migration over the twenty-five years nearly reached fifteen thousand, of which thirteen thousand was in Elbert County. Migration to Logan, Morgan and Cheyenne Counties exceed one thousand, some of which was accounted for by prison inmates. Almost thirty-five hundred people left Prowers County on a net basis and over twenty-five hundred moved from Otero County.[1482] As the economy worsened and more young people left, rural communities offering little in the way of opportunity and birth rates declined. Migration estimates from the University of Wisconsin show net emigration between 2000 and 2010 concentrated among the region's residents in their twenties.[1483] Jodi Schreilber, a high school senior in Cheyenne Wells, expressed the views of many young plains dwellers when she told a *Denver Post* reporter, "I'd like living in a smaller town, but there is nothing to do around here, like jobs in my field. It's not that I want to move out. It's more that I have to move out."[1484]

The "graying" of the plains population continued. Aging accelerated after the turn of the century. Births declined as the population aged and many couples decided to postpone childbearing in a weak economy. Deaths in 2015 exceeded births in seven counties.[1485] The plains population was an older one. Its 2015 median age of over forty-one, up from just over thirty in 1970, was nearly three years greater than the figure for the US, and the share of those over-sixty-five was 2.6 percentage points higher.[1486] The aging trend was greatest in counties without large towns where younger people were most likely to leave. Baca, Kiowa and Sedgwick Counties all reported 2015 median ages exceeding forty-eight years.[1487] The work force was also aging. In Baca County an estimated 34 percent of primary jobs were held by workers fifty-five or over.[1488]

Declining numbers of working age adults had some damaging consequences. Providing for the young and the old took a larger share of income leaving less for public and private investment that could raise productivity and wealth. The needs of those outside the work force could be furnished through government, financed at least in part by local taxpayers, or privately as parents cared for children or family members assisted aging relatives. Of course, neither every young or old persons were wholly dependent on others nor were all working age residents contributing to local output.

Employment and unpaid farm work were common among both young and old and many contributed services in their homes.

The ratio of those too young or too old to work compared to those of working age, termed the "dependency ratio" by economists, is an indicator of the burden of providing necessary services to those who cannot contribute their labor. A higher dependency ratio suggests that the burden of supporting young and the old is greater. In 2015 the region's dependency ratio was 0.73 compared to 0.61 for the US. (The population in state prisons was excluded from regional dependency ratio calculations as inmates neither contribute to the support of local dependent populations nor rely upon support of working-age residents.) This meant that on the eastern plains there were fewer than 1.4 working age residents to provide for each person too young or old to work. The dependency ratio was highest in the more rural counties with Baca, Phillips, and Kiowa Counties all .84 or greater. Elbert County had by far the lowest at .55.[1489] The region's higher dependency ratio was almost entirely accounted for by a larger proportion of the population over sixty-five.

As a result of its relatively large share of older residents and its higher incidence of poverty, the proportion of income from transfer payments was large and growing. These included public and private pensions, Medicare and Medicaid, income maintenance payments, and unemployment insurance. In 1970 transfers accounted for 10 percent of regional personal income. By 2015 this proportion had nearly doubled and was two-and-one-half percentage points higher than the comparable national figure. The counties reporting the greatest dependence on transfers were those with a large poverty population. Baca, Crowley and Otero Counties all reported transfer payments over 30 percent of personal income.[1490]

Plains residents in 2015 were better educated than their counterparts twenty-five years earlier although their average years of schooling still fell short of that in the nation. The share of adults twenty-five and over who had graduated from high school rose from 74 percent to 89 percent. Those who had attended college increased from 39 percent to 55 percent and the proportion with at least bachelors' degrees grew from 13 percent to 20 percent with Elbert County's markedly higher. The make-up of the labor force changed. The share of women working continued to rise. Farm employment became less important.[1491]

Regional Incomes

Most people in the world's advanced economies saw income growth slow markedly in the 1970s following a quarter century of solid gains. Economists attributed this development to such factors as globalization, technological change and policy measures that favored the wealthy. Plains families' median income adjusted for inflation, which had grown by 2.8 percent annually between 1949 and 1969 slowed to a rate of only 0.5 percent over the next forty-six years.[1492] The 2013-17 median family income for the region almost $61,000 in 2017 dollars, more than $10,000 below that of the nation and $25,000 lower than in Metro Denver.[1493]

While incomes were lower for rural plains counties, so was the cost of living, as noted earlier. Unadjusted income comparisons overstate differences in standards of living as a dollar of earnings will go further in a lower cost community. A now-available comprehensive measure of relative living costs in Colorado's counties allows us to adjust for these differences. Colorado's State Demography Office (SDO) has compiled cost-of-living indices for each of the State's counties based on data collected for allocating state funds to school districts.[1494] Living-cost estimates were calculated for a three-person household with an annual income of about $50,000. The latest available estimates were based on 2013 costs, but, while prices had changed since 2013, relative costs were roughly the same. The indices for Colorado counties ranged from 82.4 for Kiowa County to 172.7 for Pitkin County with one hundred the statewide average. This means that living costs were more than twice as high for a middle-class family in Aspen, if such a family should exist, as for one in Eads. Costs for the rural counties were all well below those along the Front Range or the mountain resort areas; eleven of the fifteen lowest cost counties in Colorado were on the eastern plains. Elbert County had the highest costs among the plains counties at 97.2.

Adjusting county income estimates for differences in the costs of living gives a more accurate measure of the relative economic well-being in the different counties. All figures were benchmarked to the US 2017 Consumer Price Index (CPIU) allowing comparisons of plains counties incomes with national figures.[1495] Even after accounting for price differences, plains counties incomes remained relatively low. The adjusted regional median family income of just over $65,000 in 2017 dollars was more than $5,000 below the US median family income and $18,000 lower than that in Metro Denver.

Differences between counties narrowed, but they remained sizable. On average, Arkansas Valley residents were the poorest in the plains region. Bent and Otero Counties registered the lowest cost-adjusted incomes among the sixteen counites, a figure more than 25 percent below that of the nation. Incomes in Crowley and Prowers were somewhat higher, but still in the lower half of the region's counties.[1496] Elbert County residents were markedly more affluent. Incomes in the South Platte Valley and the northeast plains were greater than in the southeast.[1497]

The region's relatively low incomes are largely a result of lower skills and a lack of well-paying jobs. Incomes ultimately depend upon the productivity of workers, or the efficiency with which labor and capital are utilized to produce goods and services. It is the key source of wealth, economic growth, and competitiveness. Geographic income differences are closely related to variations in productivity. Workers' productivity depends upon both the skills of workers and the availability of jobs in industries able to take advantage of these skills. To the extent that education is a proxy for worker skills, the plains are at a disadvantage relative to urban areas. But that is not the whole story. Prosperous urban areas have a larger share of employment in high-productivity and well-paying industries such as professional services, information, and management while jobs in rural areas are concentrated in retail and lower paying service industries. In 2017 only 9 percent of the regions workforce were employed in the six highest paying industries as measured by national wages and salaries per full-time employee. In Metropolitan Denver, including Boulder, 22 percent of the workforce were so employed. Some of the difference can be explained by the plains' large share of employment in agriculture. But, if these jobs are excluded, the region's share in high-paying industries was only half that in the metro area. Even within the relatively well-paid manufacturing sector, two-thirds of the region's jobs were in the food and kindred products sector where average US earnings were 70 percent of those in all manufacturing.[1498] Workers' skills and the industry mix are not independent. High productivity industries are attracted to areas with greater workforce skills and more skilled workers are likely to move to these locations.

The Surging Latino Population

The nation's Hispanic population increased dramatically in the late twentieth and early twenty-first centuries. The share of US residents in this group had already been rising, increasing from less than 5 percent in 1970 to 9 percent in 1990, and growth accelerated in the nineties. Strong demand for workers in such industries as agriculture, tourism, domestic service, labor-intensive manufacturing, and construction attracted migrants from Mexico and Central America. The 1986 enactment of the Immigration Reform and Control Act, which granted amnesty to over two million undocumented persons, made residence north of the border more attractive as did a healthy US economy in the late eighties and nineties. At the same time, Mexico saw increasing gang violence and an economy that suffered from the government's default in 1982 and the Peso Crisis in 1994, rendering that nation less appealing. Central American nations experienced similar conditions. Although demand for immigrant labor slackened as the US entered the Great Recession relatively high fertility rates among Latinas meant that their US population continued to increase from twenty-two million to fifty-seven million between 1990 and 2015 and doubling to 18 percent as a proportion of the national total.[1499]

Most Hispanic plains residents are migrants from Mexico or their descendants although the ancestors of some lived for generations in what was northern Mexico prior to its annexation by the US after the Mexican war in the 1840s. As described in chapter 4, the first large movement of Latinos to the plains occurred in the first three decades of the twentieth century when most were recruited for field work in the sugar beet industry. The 1930 Census showed a little over ten thousand persons in the region classified as "Mexican" which included persons born in Mexico or their children. It is probable that the number of Hispanics based on the current Census definition would have been somewhat higher.

The Latino population was relatively stable between 1930 and 1970, by which time there were more than sixteen thousand living in the region. Conservative assumptions about birth and death rates suggest there was little net immigration over the previous forty years although many seasonal workers labored in the fields in the Arkansas and South Platte Valleys, and as noted in chapter 4, significant numbers of residents of Mexican descent left the US in the 1930s under government pressure.

The seventies and eighties saw large gains in the region's Latino population as migration across the nation's southern border increased. By 1990 it had risen to twenty thousand and reached almost thirty-two thousand a decade later. Another six thousand were added over the next fifteen years.[1500] By the middle teens they were 24 percent of the non-inmate population in the region compared to 15 percent a quarter century earlier, contributing more than 70 percent of the population increase over the previous twenty-five years and more than accounting for the entire gain outside Elbert County.[1501]

Most plains Latinos can trace their residence in the region either to those who came in the early twentieth century or who arrived after about 1980. Descendants of the early migrants differ from those who came more recently. These differences are obscured in the statistics cited in this section as Census data do not distinguish between the two groups. The long-time residents more closely resemble the rest of the population. They are older on average. Since they have had more time to acquire property and better jobs, they likely have attained a higher socio-economic status including greater incomes and education levels. Most are found in the Arkansas or South Platte Valleys. Some of the more recent arrivals settled in smaller plains communities such as Yuma, Holyoke, or Burlington. Many live in Fort Morgan.

In 2015 Latinos made up a third or more of the population in Bent, Morgan, Otero and Prowers Counties. Morgan County had the largest number of any county in the region with over ten thousand compared to 2,665 in 1980, largely a result of the growth in job opportunities for migrant workers at packing plants. By contrast, Otero County with fewer new low-skilled jobs reported a relatively stable Latino population of between seven and eight thousand over the thirty-five-year period.[1502] Counties with growing cattle and hog feeding operations that previously had only a few Latinos also saw rapid increases that offset some or all of the decline in the number of non-Hispanic residents. Yuma County added more than two thousand between 1990 and 2015 and Kit Carson County nearly one thousand. Phillips County's Hispanic population increased by eight hundred.[1503] They made up an estimated 30 percent of Holyoke's Seaboard Food work force[1504] and approximately half the students in the local school system.[1505]

Immigration was often a thorny issue for residents in these communities. While they supported controls on the border, they depended upon the labor of many undocumented immigrants. The head of human resources at Smithfield's hog processing operation in Yuma expressed frustration at her inability to hire more residents as many potential workers lacked documentation. She lamented, "There's some great people [in Yuma County] we would like to keep. I don't know the right answer."[1506] The region's Hispanic population was increasingly found in larger towns rather than in rural areas. By 2010, 46 percent of La Junta residents were Hispanic as were 43 percent in Fort Morgan and 40 percent in Lamar. Some smaller towns also had large shares of Latino residents, including Granada where it exceeded 70 percent.[1507]

In the middle teens 82 percent of the Latino population reported their ancestry as "Mexican." The ancestry of the rest was widely distributed among Puerto Rican, Cuban, Central American, South American and "other." An estimated 31 percent of all adults were foreign-born, with 25 percent reporting that they were not US citizens, both having increased over the previous twenty-five years. At the same time, many were long-time residents of Colorado. The share of regional Latinos who reported being born in the State at 56 percent, was only slightly lower than the 58 percent of Colorado natives in the rest of the regional population. (The estimates in this paragraph include the inmate population.)[1508]

Hispanics were relatively young with a median age of twenty-nine compared to forty-six for the remainder of the population. They made up one-third of all residents under eighteen and around half in Morgan, Otero and Prowers Counties. As many were recent immigrants and their families, the share sixty-five or over was relatively small, with most in counties with large long-time Latino populations.[1509] They had less education on average than the rest of the population with 35 percent of those twenty-five and over having less than a high school education compared with only 8 percent for the remaining population.[1510] Seven percent held bachelor's degrees with females reporting a somewhat higher share. They were, on average, poorer with a median family income of $41,000 compared to more than $66,000 for non-Latinos, and 19 percent reported incomes below the poverty level compared with 14 percent for the remainder of the population.[1511]

In the early and middle twentieth century most of the employed Hispanics were farm workers. This was changing by the seventies as they acquired more education and skills, and farm work became more automated. In 1990 fewer than 8 percent of employed Hispanics in the five counties with a sufficiently large population to be reported in the Census listed their occupation as "farm worker." Some who remained in agriculture became farm managers or owners. Perfecto Hijar from Sugar City began as a farm laborer and eventually became a successful farmer and cattleman.[1512] In the middle teens 18 percent of employed Latinos in the region worked in management occupations and 27 percent in service occupations and 15 percent in sales.[1513] Many were small business owners such as Johnny Abitia of Lamar who owned a liquor store and a Mexican café. Hope Arriola whose mother came to Logan County to work in the beet fields in 1944 became an independent businesswoman in 1970 when she bought Sterling's Acapulco Restaurant.[1514] Others served as government officials including Rocky Ford police chief Chris Lucero who held the position for twenty-five years in beginning in the 1970s.[1515]

In contrast to the early twentieth century, many families were able to achieve better jobs, incomes, and education. Fort Morgan native Roger (Rogelio) Segura's father had no formal education, and his grandfather had fled Mexico during unrest in the late 1920s. His father worked in a dairy while his mother raised seven children and worked in potato harvest. The family struggled, but Roger completed his bachelor's degree. He worked more than twenty-five years for County Department of Human Services and served as president of the district board of education. His wife Anna, the daughter of migrant field workers, was employed at a local bank for eleven years before taking a job with a government agency.[1516] Twenty-two percent of the region's Latinos worked in construction, maintenance, or natural resources. This category includes farm workers, but most were employed elsewhere. Production workers made up another 19 percent of workers including more than twelve hundred in Morgan County, most of whom worked in meat processing.[1517]

Rapid increases in Latino populations caused some disruptions in plains communities. Small school districts struggled to accommodate students lacking English language proficiency. Older Anglo residents were sometimes uncomfortable dealing with service workers who spoke mostly Spanish. But young people soon adjust to the new residents. Jesse Ruiz, Jr., who arrive in Holyoke some fifty years ago at age three, noted the merging of the Latino and Anglo populations. Latina girls have been selected as homecoming queens at the local high school.[1518] The Hispanic influx revitalized towns facing a shrinking population and a shortage of workers. Between 1990 and 2010 Lamar lost 1,857 non-Hispanic residents but roughly half this loss was offset by an increase in the number of Latinos, while Holyoke lost 339 Anglos and gained 739 Latinos.[1519]

The High Plains in the Twenty-First Century

After a relatively prosperous 1990s the early years of the new century were challenging for much of the region. Local businesses, governments, and households were forced to cope with many difficult issues confronting rural America. The plight of the US hinterlands was summarized in a *Wall Street Journal* headline proclaiming, "Rural America is the New 'Inner City'—Small Counties Fare Worst by Key Measures of Socioeconomic Well-being."[1520] The persistent issues of lack of good jobs, poor public services and a declining population were compounded by falling farm incomes in the middle teens. Colorado's eastern plains counties coped with these difficulties with varying success. The status and prospects of the region in the late 2010s will be examined in chapter 12.

CHAPTER 10

Chapter 10 Exhibits

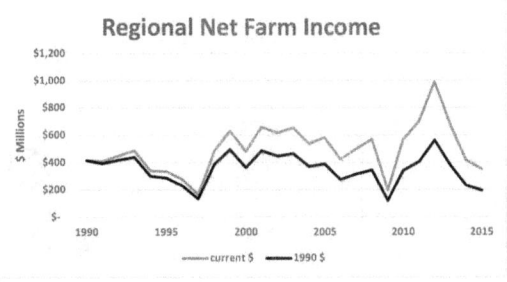

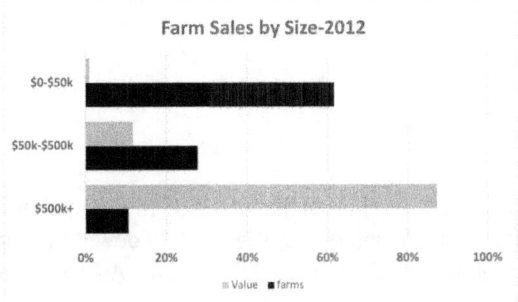

Real regional farm incomes reflected changes in prices, fluctuating through the 1990s and early 2000s, reaching a peak in 2012 and falling in subsequent years.

A relatively small number of large producers accounted for most farm production and sales. Although some of the large farms were held by corporations, most were still family owned and operated. Many of the region's farms were too small for to be economically viable without outside income.

Regional employment patterns mirror the nonfarm economy. Eastern Colorado posted relatively healthy growth through the 90's. It slowed thereafter although it was not greatly affected by the 2007-2009 Great Recession.

Source: Prices, USDA; Incomes and employment, BEA; Size, Census of Agriculture

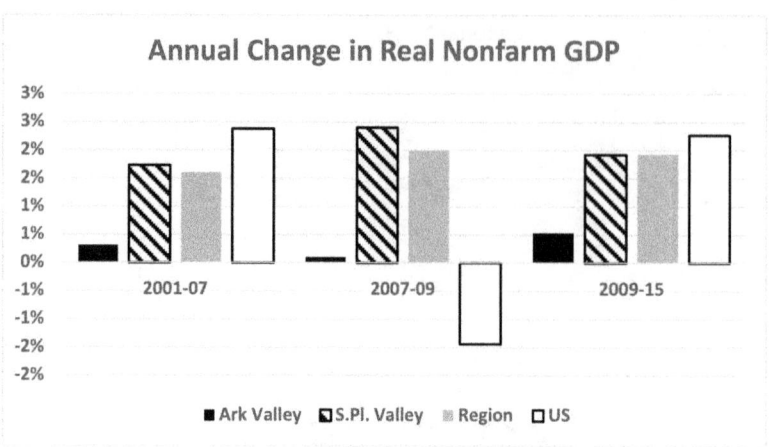

Regional nonfarm GDP growth fell short of that of the US throughout the twenty-first century, although it outperformed the nation during the 2007-09 downturn. The South Platte Valley posted solid gains throughout the 2001-15 period while the Arkansas Valley saw little growth.

Source: BEA.

CHAPTER 10

With its sparse population and windy conditions, the plains made an ideal location for wind farms. Xcel Energy's-Colorado's Rush Creek project in Cheyenne, Elbert, Kit Carson and Lincoln counties, that began operating in 2018, includes two wind farms, three hundred Vesta wind turbines, and approximately eighty-three miles of transmission line to connect and carry wind power output to homes and businesses across the state. It produces enough electricity to power about 325,000 homes.

Source: Xcel Energy.

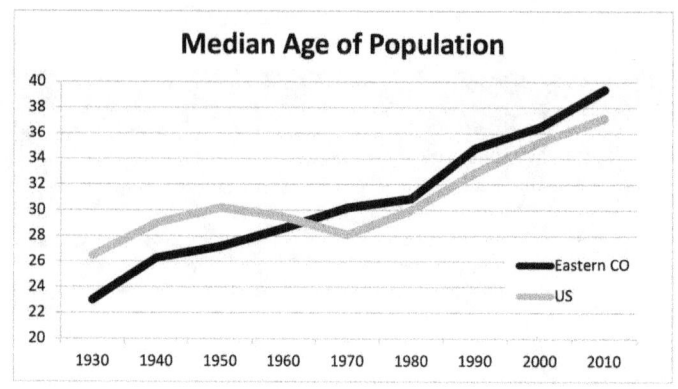

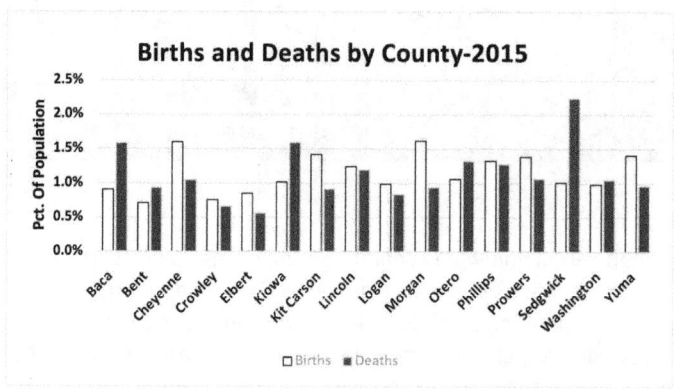

The region's median age has risen steadily and increased by more than sixteen years since 1930 as younger residents have left. The nation has followed a similar pattern except in the "baby boom" decades of the fifties and sixties. Populations in both the US and the plains region have become older since 1970.

Deaths exceeded births in several dryland counties while the reverse was true in most counties in the Arkansas and South Platte Valleys. Bent and Otero Counties with declining economies and older populations were exceptions.

Source: Census and SDO

CHAPTER 10

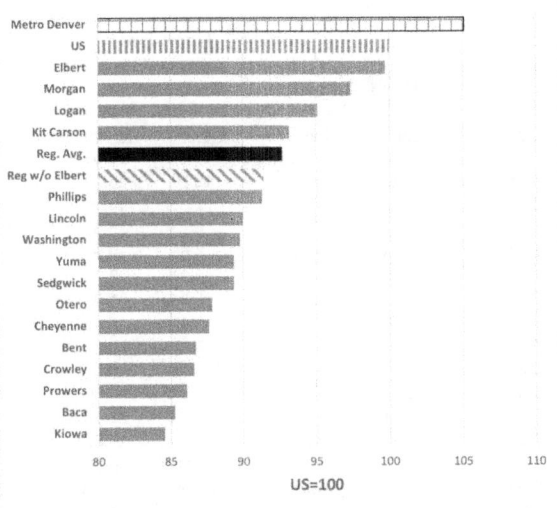

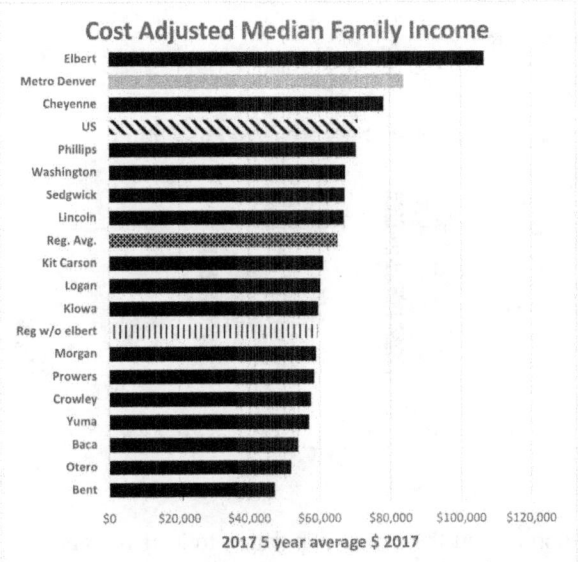

Living costs varied among counties but all were lower than Metropolitan Denver or the US average. The lower chart shows median family incomes adjusted to account for these differences among county incomes. Despite the adjustment the wealthier counites retained their status and inflation adjusted family incomes in the nation and in Metro Denver and were still higher than those in most of the region.

Source: Income from ACS,.Cost data from SDO.

Latino and Non-Latino Poulation in Eastern Plains-2015

	Share Latino	Median Age Latino	Median Age Non-Latino	Proportion of Population 65 & over Latino	Proportion of Population 65 & over Non-Latino	Proportion of Population Under 18 Latino	Proportion of Population Under 18 Non-Latino
Baca	10.5%	31.7	49.1	12.8%	26.6%	33.0%	19.5%
Bent	35.2%	32.3	51.0	13.8%	26.1%	23.9%	18.6%
Cheyenne	14.9%	25.8	38.8	1.9%	14.7%	42.0%	29.3%
Crowley	28.9%	31.6	57.0	6.5%	30.5%	32.3%	23.7%
Elbert	6.5%	30.6	46.2	4.6%	14.9%	32.3%	21.6%
Kiowa	4.4%	17.2	43.0	0.0%	22.3%	55.0%	26.4%
Kit Carson	19.1%	30.1	44.9	5.8%	21.0%	38.3%	20.4%
Lincoln	22.9%	31.1	48.6	2.4%	25.6%	17.2%	25.7%
Logan	14.8%	24.6	42.2	7.3%	20.4%	30.4%	23.0%
Morgan	35.8%	26.0	44.8	5.6%	20.5%	36.4%	20.8%
Otero	41.5%	32.3	46.7	12.9%	23.8%	30.4%	18.8%
Phillips	20.1%	25.6	45.3	0.8%	21.6%	41.2%	20.8%
Prowers	37.2%	26.5	45.3	8.2%	21.8%	36.3%	19.1%
Sedgwick	11.2%	41.8	48.2	16.0%	26.1%	22.4%	21.9%
Washington	9.6%	28.6	45.2	0.9%	21.2%	34.8%	21.5%
Yuma	22.6%	25.2	43.7	5.2%	21.2%	40.5%	22.9%
Total	24.0%	28.5	45.6	7.8%	20.6%	33.6%	21.5%

Inmate populations excluded

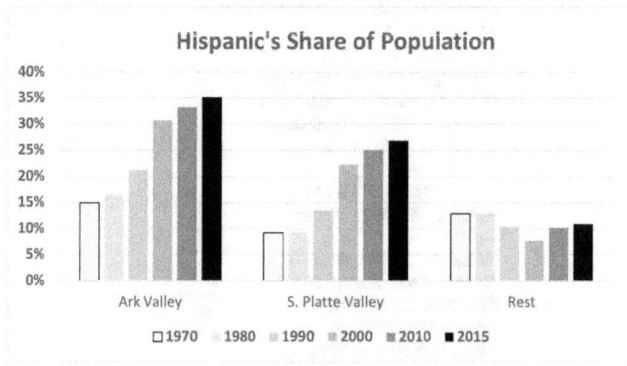

Large-scale migration caused the Latino population to increase rapidly in the 90's and the 2000s. By 2015 they made up nearly one-fourth of the region's population with much larger shares in the Arkansas Valley and Morgan County. Latinos were younger on average. Their median age was seventeen years less than that of other residents and they comprised more than one-third of those under eighteen.

The Arkansas and South Platte Valleys accounted for most of the growth although the northeast and central plains also attracted Latino migration in response to demand for workers at feed lots and hog farms.

Source: Shares in table estimated from ACS 2013-17. Chart from SDO. Chart includes inmate populations.

CHAPTER 11

The Prairie Towns

MOST EARLY SETTLERS RESIDED ON FARMS, BUT THE IMPORTANCE OF EASTERN Colorado's towns grew through increased trade and service activity as rural populations increased. The first settlements other than military or trading forts or native villages sprouted at railroad junctions or at their temporary end points. Julesburg in 1867 was the first of these, located at the transcontinental railroad's brief incursion into Colorado. A few others followed in the 1870s. The two waves of homesteaders in the late nineteenth and early twentieth centuries led to the founding of yet more towns. Over the next century a handful grew into small cities with populations nearing or even exceeding ten thousand. Others became small towns, some remained tiny villages, and many disappeared altogether.

This chapter examines the history of several of the more important towns in the region. The narrative relies heavily on population data as the availability of other indicators on a consistent basis is limited. Healthy economies attracted migrants, and town populations usually grew fastest during prosperous periods. Conversely, weakness drove outmigration and declining populations. Population statistics give a consistent measure of plains towns' longer-term trajectories as well as cyclical growth and decline.

Evolution of the Plains Towns

As the regional economy developed the role of its towns changed. The early settlements were established along railways. In 1880 the three largest towns listed in the Census were West Las Animas, later to become Las Animas, and Granada, both on the Santa Fe line, along with Hugo on what was then the Kansas Pacific. Many of the railroad towns enjoyed brief booms followed by a waning as the track was extended on westward and they lost much of their economic rationale. La Junta proved an exception. With only a brief interruption in the late 1870s, it thrived as a location for crew changes and rolling-stock repair for the Santa Fe through the middle of the twentieth century.

From its incorporation in 1881, it boasted the largest population of any city in every decennial census until it was surpassed by Sterling, then also a railroad town, in 1920.

Important government offices such as county courthouses or federal land offices also spurred early growth. Community boosters competed fiercely for these plums. In 1889 Prowers County, Granada and Lamar newspapers hurled invectives during an election to determine the county seat.[1521] In 1891 a Wray saloon keeper bribed residents with pigs' feet and whiskey to obtain their votes in an election that would move the county seat from Yuma to his town.[1522] Federal relief agencies in Lamar and Springfield during the Dust-Bowl era were a welcome source of jobs and income. In the thirties and forties Las Animas benefited from its proximity to a major federal construction project at Caddoa Dam, later John Martin Dam, and a veteran's hospital at nearby Fort Lyon. Wartime facilities boosted local economies in the forties. State prisons brought steady well-paying jobs to several plains communities in the 1990s.

The growth of farming both on dryland and in the river valleys in the late nineteenth and early twentieth centuries led to large numbers of new business in the prairie towns. Their main streets featured stores where farmers and ranchers could purchase necessary supplies and equipment and their families could buy food, clothing and other consumer goods. Other early commercial establishments included business and financial services such as local banks, law firms, and machinery repair shops as well as personal services such as doctors or barber shops. Farmers and ranchers marketed their produce in nearby towns where it was either processed locally by flour mills, sugar beet plants, or alfalfa dehydrating mills, or shipped to more distant markets. Finally, local governments provided judicial and protective services along with schools for farm and town children.

The first towns of any size were in the irrigated farming areas of the South Platte and Arkansas Valleys. Community businessmen and outside investors spurred the development of major reservoir and ditch projects that opened more land to irrigation, leading to more farms and the demand to support more local businesses. The early twentieth century saw rapid growth in the region's towns. In 1900 the only three cities with more than one thousand people were La Junta, Rocky Ford, and Las Animas, all in the Arkansas Valley. Ten years later they were joined by Lamar, also on the Arkansas, along with Fort Morgan and Sterling in the South Platte Valley. By 1920 there were sixteen such municipalities in the region including five with more than twenty-five hundred people. Between 1890 and 1920 the four largest towns added sixteen thousand people and the next eight largest another eleven thousand.[1523] But most of the growth occurred on farms and smaller settlements where population grew by more than one-hundred thousand.

The post war agricultural decline along with the Great Depression and Dust Bowl in the thirties caused struggling farmers to abandon their land. Many left the region, but others moved to nearby towns. Although jobs were scarce, the communities offered government funds and services for their families. Local governments grappled with declining tax bases and an increased demand for public services for destitute townspeople and farmers. Infusions of state and federal government funds helped. Local economies languished, but conditions were not a lot better elsewhere and most communities didn't experience mass departures. Many young people chose to remain in their hometowns where family and friends provided some assistance. Between 1920 and 1940, the dozen largest towns in the region added eighty-five hundred people while the rest of the region was losing more than twenty-two thousand.[1524] The 1930 Census reported Sterling, La Junta, Fort Morgan and Lamar as the four largest towns in the region, a distinction they maintained into the second decade of the twenty-fist century.

The war and postwar decades were a time of solid growth for the region's larger municipalities. Wartime mobilization pulled the nation out of the depression and strong demand for farm products provided an extra boost to regional growth. Between 1940 and 1970, the dozen largest towns added fifteen thousand people; Fort Morgan, Lamar and Sterling each grew by at least twenty-seven hundred.[1525] At the same time, greater agricultural efficiencies and the lure of jobs in metropolitan areas caused rural residents to leave. But the smaller populations on the farms and in the smaller towns could no longer support the growing number of workers in the larger communities. They had to find new sources of demand for their products and services. In some cases they expanded the processing of farm products. While the number of farms fell, their output did not. Light manufacturing such as machinery and equipment was another option.

In the late twentieth and early twenty-first centuries agriculture's continuing decline forced further changes in local economies. Trading centers that had benefitted from the gains of their rural hinterlands saw agriculture became less important. During the first five years of the 1970s, farm earnings accounted for 28 percent of the region's personal income. Forty years later, this share had shrunk to 11 percent.[1526] The farm demand for products and services from the towns diminished. Thomas Johnson of the Kansas City Federal Reserve, examining America's rural economy in the twenty-first century, observed that farms were becoming more reliant on rural towns while the towns dependence on agriculture lessened.[1527] Farmers and ranchers still needed local suppliers of equipment and inputs such as fertilizer or seed as well as marketers of their produce, even as local economies were diversifying their bases away from agriculture.

Some plains communities received a boost from national or international businesses siting facilities in rural areas. These firms faced cost pressures that made less expensive areas such as the high plains more attractive. Johnson observed that in some respects rural communities were becoming attractive for operations that were larger than those that had located in rural communities in the past. He explained, "The imperative of scale is leading to larger and larger firms and more complex agglomerations of businesses. In urban areas small to medium firms can cluster to capture the benefits of agglomeration economies—savings due to proximity to a diverse labor force, specialized producer services, and high-quality public services. In rural areas, economies of scale are more likely to be achieved internally to firms."[1528] In other words, a large firm locating a part of its operation in a rural area could still enjoy many of the efficiencies of size that it experienced in urban areas and could also take advantage of lower labor and land costs. The most important regional examples of such facilities were Neoplan's bus plant in Lamar and Cargill's meat packing plant in Fort Morgan.

At the same time, regional trading centers were losing some of their business to metropolitan areas. Economies of scale and easier access often provided cheaper and more convenient shopping and better financial services in Denver or Pueblo rather than Fort Morgan or La Junta. Hospitals in the smaller towns could not afford the equipment necessary for the latest medical services and often had trouble attracting and keeping professional staff. The growth of internet sales in the 2000s was yet another threat to small-town business.

By the late twentieth century the economic spillover from manufacturing or agricultural activity was declining. The amount of local spending and jobs generated by a dollar of farm sales or factory output was less than in an earlier day. This relationship, represented in economic models by multipliers, became smaller. Increased labor productivity and greater capital intensity had reduced the linkage between production and employment.[1529] As farms became larger and more capital intensive, the need for farm labor declined along with local wages. Absentee ownership meant more of the earnings flowed outside the region. Something similar was happening with retail and service industries. When Walmart supplanted local retailers, the number of employees was reduced, and the stores' profits went to shareholders throughout the world although local consumers benefitted from lower prices and a wider selection. The effects of these changes were not uniform. Some communities thrived while others stagnated or declined.

The Larger Towns

Ease of travel and consolidation of businesses have concentrated activity in larger towns, four of which, Fort Morgan, La Junta, Lamar, and Sterling, accounted for a growing share of the region's population and economic activity. In 1890 slightly more than one-tenth of the region's population resided in these four towns. By 1930 their share had risen to almost 14 percent, and it reached nearly 19 percent by midcentury. In 2015 they held more than 30 percent of eastern plains residents outside Elbert County.[1530] These four cities, whose development is described in the following pages, played an ever-larger role in the economic history of the region.

CHAPTER 11

Fort Morgan

Since the town's founding, Fort Morgan's economy has depended on bountiful irrigated farming in the South Platte Valley and processing of local agricultural products. Its sugar beet factory provided jobs and income from the early twentieth century, while meat packing got its start in the 1960s. The town also benefitted from relatively easy access to Metro Denver, approximately eighty miles via Interstate highway, along with good road and rail links. Its population increased every decade since 1890, growing to over eleven thousand in 2015, making it the second largest municipality in the region.

The first permanent residents near today's Fort Morgan were stationed at an army fort established to protect emigrants along the Overland Trail and settlers in the South Platte Valley. The fort with sod walls three feet thick was completed in July 1865 and was renamed Fort Morgan in June 1866.[1531] It was abandoned in 1868 as a peace treaty with the Cheyenne and Arapaho reduced the threat to settlers, and military operations became more centralized with the development of railroads across the plains.[1532]

Abner Baker, whose role in developing Colorado's early irrigation canals was described in chapter 2, is generally recognized as the founder of Fort Morgan. Baker and fellow investors saw the potential for irrigation in the South Platte Valley and undertook the construction of the Fort Morgan Canal that opened approximately twenty-five thousand acres to irrigation when completed in 1884. The town of Fort Morgan was platted just south of the ruins of the old Fort in the same year. Baker acquired considerable land in and around the new town and recruited family, including his father, brothers and others to settle there. The Bakers came from the Union Colony, a utopian Christian community in nearby Weld County that was inspired by east coast newspaper magnate Horace Greeley. They brought with them the values of that community and prided themselves on their good moral character, especially the avoidance of demon rum. The town was founded as a dry community and remained so until 1965.[1533] In 1939 city voters rejected alcohol sales by a five to one margin.[1534] Baker required that sale of liquor be forbidden upon the forfeiture of the property as part of any contract for land sold.[1535] Early Fort Morgan was connected to the adjacent village of Deuel by a wagon bridge across the South Platte River built in 1875. Deuel residents, unlike those in Fort Morgan, could purchase liquor. Despite this possible advantage, Deuel was fated to soon wither away and be absorbed by its neighbor.

The town profited from proximity to two major rail lines, the Union Pacific completed in 1881 on the north side of the South Platte River and the Burlington line on the south side finished a year later. The UP station was in Deuel, but Abner Baker realized the importance of rail access for his community and persuaded Burlington officials to bring a station to Fort Morgan on a flat car from Nebraska. To secure the station and ensure regularly scheduled train stops, Baker deeded substantial portions of his land in the new town to a company owned by railroad executives.[1536] He was also able to persuade the UP to increase its service to its station in Deuel which was soon renamed North Fort Morgan. [1537]

The town's formation set off a flurry of building. One of first businesses was the Killebrew and Burk brickyard, soon joined by Hallack and Howard Lumber. In 1884 H. Clatworthy's hardware store housed the first post office and soon the Bank of Fort Morgan. By 1886 Main Street had "a restaurant, a bank, a hotel, a drug store, a confectionary store, a livery, a barber shop and a number of hardware and dry goods stores."[1538] By 1889 three hotels had been constructed.[1539]

The optimism of Fort Morgan's founders and early investors in new businesses rested upon the promise of irrigated farming under the Fort Morgan Canal. (The development of irrigation around Fort Morgan is discussed in chapter 2.) Yet growth fell short of expectations. Irrigation was unfamiliar to farmers who had come from areas with ample rainfall. Some were taken in by claims about the "rainbelt" and did not see the need for additional water. As a result, they often preferred making their claims on dryland further east[1540] where drought and low farm prices soon forced many to abandon their farms.

Among the casualties of the depressed economy of the 1890s was Baker's dream of the Bijou Ditch that he and other local interests had envisioned as means to greatly expand irrigated acreage and thereby reinvigorate growth in Fort Morgan. Baker had invested a large share of his fortune in the Bijou but died before it was finally completed in 1900 after new investors were found. The new canal opened an additional forty- to fifty-thousand acres to irrigation[1541] and provided the impetus for a fresh surge of economic activity. The *Denver Times* effused, "The Bijou Ditch, which was once proved a failure in Morgan County, was opened yesterday…This event will double the population of Fort Morgan in a year and will make Morgan County one of the richest counties in the state."[1542] The local paper was similarly enthusiastic in claiming the town would grow to ten thousand people,[1543] a goal not realized until nearly a century later.

The developers of the Bijou, hoping to profit from their investment, opened a real estate office, offering plots to settlers attracted by the area's new promise. The *Denver Times* reported that "management is having no trouble convincing people that Fort Morgan is a good place in which to locate while property can be had at ground floor prices." In 1901 alone some thirty-five new buildings were constructed.[1544] A municipal water works for fire protection as well as commercial and residential use was completed in 1904.[1545] By 1905 town had twenty-seven business houses, two banks, two hotels, two restaurants, two lumber yards, two grain elevators, a steam laundry, a planeing mill and a canning factory. Some two hundred homes had been built over the prior three years.[1546]

Fort Morgan's city fathers embraced further development. The expansion of irrigated land made the town a prime location for a sugar beet factory and, as described in chapter

3, city fathers were ultimately successful in attracting the necessary investment and commitments from growers for a plant to open in 1906. Fort Morgan had become an important agricultural trade and processing center with an economy based on ranching, sugar beet farming, livestock feeding and processing of agricultural products from the fertile surrounding countryside. Between 1900 and 1910 the town's population grew from 639 to twenty-eight hundred and by 1920 it exceeded thirty-eight hundred.

Over the next twenty years growth slowed. The collapse in farm prices in the late teens and early twenties had already diminished the community's economic base in agriculture and the onset of the 1930s depression brought further difficulties. Between 1929 and 1936 Fort Morgan's assessed valuation fell 22 percent, and deposits in local banks declined by 23 percent.[1547] The outlook brightened by the late thirties and improved further with war-time mobilization. During the forties bank deposits more than tripled, and population continued to increase. It grew at a rate of a little over 1 percent per year between 1920 and 1950, a markedly more moderate pace than the 9 percent annual growth over the previous twenty years.

Fort Morgan shared in the fifties' oil and gas boom described in chapter 9. The town added more than two thousand people over the decade with population reaching nearly seventy-five hundred. Although many residents profited from the boom and the towns economy flourished, some viewed it with mixed emotions. Homes became more expensive, local businesses confronted difficulties hiring workers, and schools were overcrowded. Oil workers' enthusiasm for Fort Morgan may have been restrained as it was still dry, and they had to drive ten miles to Brush for an evening of legal drinking.

Meat packing got its start in the middle sixties as described in chapter 8. The local economy flourished, and the town added fourteen hundred residents by 1980. But the meat-packing industry suffered reverses in the early eighties culminating in sizable layoffs. These layoffs were soon followed by closure of Great Western's sugar beet plants throughout the South Platte Valley when the company declared bankruptcy as recounted in chapter 9. At the time the Fort Morgan sugar factory employed sixty full-time workers and another 250 to 300 during harvest season.[1548] The town's misfortune was compounded by the generally depressed condition of South Platte Valley agriculture. A January 2, 1986, story in the *Fort Morgan Times* summarized the previous year as characterized by "Poor economic conditions—in some cases miserable economic conditions."[1549] The slump dealt a blow to local government finances. The Fort Morgan School District anticipated losing almost $100,000 in property tax revenues due to the beet plant closure and faced the possibility of increasing the mill levy to pay off bonds.[1550] Pessimism about their futures spread among young people. A local news article described Fort Morgan High School students' plans for their future observing "most of them indicated those plans included leaving Fort Morgan."[1551] The town's population declined by more than five hundred between 1983 and 1986.[1552]

By early 1986 the worst seemed over. The sugar factory was purchased by Denver-based Western Sugar Co. in March and County farmers enjoyed a successful growing season. SBC's Fort Morgan slaughter plant reopened in June after a seventeen-month long shutdown[1553] and was later purchased by a subsidiary of meat industry giant Cargill.[1554] Despite its difficulties Fort Morgan had by far the healthiest economy of any municipality in the region during the seventies and eighties. The city added 1,162 employees over twenty years, benefitting from the late eighties improvement in the South Platte Valley economy and the expansion of the meat packing industry. More than two hundred nondurable manufacturing jobs were added along with 380 in wholesale and retail trade and almost fifteen hundred new residents.[1555]

Cargill expanded its operation through the 1990s and 2000s eventually employing more than two thousand workers and becoming the dominant business in the city. The company's reliance on foreign workers changed the demographic makeup of the town. The 1980 Census reported 947 Latinos in the town or 11 percent of total population. By the middle-teens their numbers had grown to 5,276 or 47 percent of all residents.[1556] The Cargill plant also recruited other immigrant groups creating a culturally diverse work force that led to friction between management and workers. Some two hundred Cargill employees walked off their jobs in 2015 after a dispute over Muslim workers' prayer breaks.[1557]

The town prospered in the late twentieth and early twenty-first centuries. In 2003 the closure of Greeley's sugar beet plant left the Fort Morgan operation the sole producer in Colorado. While sugar beet production had declined from its heyday—according to the Census of Agriculture, Weld County acreage in 2012 was down one-third from its level thirty years earlier—the Fort Morgan plant benefitted from access to beets grown in the northern Front Range and formerly processed in Greeley. Leprino Foods' cheese plant was a steady source of employment. Between 1990 and 2015, total employment in the town increased by more than a thousand, a 20 percent gain that does not include workers at Fort Morgan plants who lived outside the city, and population increased from 9,068 to 11,157.[1558]

La Junta

The Santa Fe railroad and flourishing irrigated agriculture in the Arkansas Valley served as the basis for La Junta's economy, helping it enjoy healthy growth well into the second half of the twentieth century when competitive pressures on American railroads forced Santa Fe to reduce its footprint. The town also confronted the loss of highway traffic to the Interstate system, and the decline of irrigated farming as water rights in Otero and Crowley Counties were transferred to metropolitan areas. The city struggled to maintain manufacturing jobs, compounding its difficulties. Both population and employment declined through the late twentieth and early twenty-first centuries.

CHAPTER 11

From its earliest days, La Junta was a railroad town as described in chapter 2. In 1875 two lines pushed into the site of today's municipality. The Kansas Pacific arrived in December followed by the Santa Fe a few days later. The two sets of tracks lay fifty feet apart on the south side of the Arkansas. Messrs. Rice and Smith, who owned land bordering the rail lines, opened a store and soon filed a plat for the town of La Junta, Spanish for "the junction." A collection of tents appeared along with commission houses offering warehouses for goods to be shipped to the southwest, buying or selling produce from the area on commission, selling goods to residents and transients, and outfitting wagons for the New Mexico trade. One of first buildings was a saloon soon followed by a fire station, several mercantile stores, a dance hall, and a post office. The *Rocky Mountain News* reported, "The new town [La Junta] is twenty miles west of Las Animas and is likely to absorb the business of the latter place very soon—indeed Otero, Seller[sic] & Co. have already moved their extensive warehouses to the new town."[1559] Soon a livery stable, a restaurant and a hotel opened for business. The booming economy attracted new residents including some young girls brought to La Junta from the east for "good jobs" although many wound up working as dance hall girls or prostitutes.[1560]

The town had fifty inhabitants in 1876 and soon grew to a reported three hundred.[1561] But with the completion of the Rio Grande line from Pueblo to El Moro near Trinidad, shipping goods via wagon from La Junta to New Mexico was no longer competitive, and many of the new town's businesses disappeared. The Kansas Pacific removed its tracks in 1878, economic activity came to a standstill, and population reportedly fell to only four persons.[1562] But recovery was at hand in 1878 when the Santa Fe began construction on the extension of its line to Trinidad and on to the city of Santa Fe. La Junta was designated as the railroad's Colorado Division Point. Eventually, the town became headquarters of the Railroad's northern division which extended from Denver to Newton, Kansas to Albuquerque. The Railroad built a stone roundhouse and thirty-two small homes for employees. A larger wood depot was constructed in 1880 replacing one that had been hauled in five years earlier. By 1881 Santa Fe had added an office for the division superintendent, a small hotel and a Harvey House restaurant to feed passengers. James C. Denney, who arrived in town in 1877 as the Santa Fe's station agent, became the first mayor when town was incorporated in April 1881. Denny was also La Junta's first attorney and editor of the *Tribune* newspaper. Articles of incorporation claimed a population of 256 males and 33 females.[1563] The town retained its wild-west character. A visitor described it as "a very small town, boasting several saloons," and another observed that "the main street was lined with saloons and dance halls."[1564] La Junta became the county seat of the newly formed Otero County in 1889.

The town grew rapidly in 1890s and 1900s. Population increased from 1,439 in 1890 to 2,513 in 1900 and 4,124 by 1910.[1565] Electricity became available in 1892, a telephone exchange was established in 1894 and sewer lines were laid in 1898. A movie theater opened in 1908 and the city built a new water plant the same year.[1566] The railroad was still an important driver of growth. In 1884 the $20,000 Santa Fe hospital was built for care of employees of the northern division.[1567] In 1907 the Railroad reportedly employed a thousand men with a total monthly payroll of $85,000. Sixteen passenger trains ran through daily in 1914.[1568]

Rail and agriculture remained the dominant industries in the teens and twenties. Irrigated farming and cattle ranching in Otero County reached new heights. In the 1920s the Santa Fe shops employed an average of 1,334 workers with yard annual payroll of $2.4 million.[1569] But the economy was beginning to diversify. A report prepared for the local Chamber of Commerce by the University of Colorado's Business Research Division characterized La Junta in the 1920s as experiencing "a shift from a city entirely dependent on the farm trade toward an industrialized community."[1570] New firms included a refrigerating and icing plant, a packing plant, a manufacturer of brick and clay products, a creamery, three grain elevators and a like number of milling companies.[1571] National retailers Montgomery Ward, J.C. Penny, Three Rules, Duckwalls, National Tire, Snodgrass, Piggly Wiggly and Skaggs Safeway all opened outlets in the town.[1572] By 1930 the number of residents exceeded seven thousand.[1573] According to a Santa Fe agent the population gain in the twenties was fueled by "a decided increase in the migration of Mexican Nationals into the area for track, extra gang and farm labor."[1574] The 1930 census reported thirty-nine hundred "Mexicans" in Otero County, a category that included those born in Mexico or their children, by far the most of any county in the region.

The depression era slump in farm incomes and rail traffic brought La Junta's growth to a halt. Santa Fe's national operating revenues fell from $267 million in 1929 to $133 million 1932.[1575] By 1937 employment in the town's railroad shops had declined by 250 from its 1929 level.[1576] Traffic did not recover until 1940-41 when war mobilization got underway. La Junta's population was essentially unchanged during the 1930s with a reported net loss of 153 persons over the decade.[1577]

Wartime mobilization promised economic revival as construction of the air training field north of the city brought in a reported workforce of more than three thousand.[1578] Prosperity continued in the post-war years as new businesses were formed including a rendering plant and a concrete products company. Scarf Brother's pickle plant, built in the 1930s, expanded as did a potato chip company and a packing company. Winter Livestock, a large cattle auctioneer, flourished in the post-war years. Otero Junior College, an important contributor to the town's economy and culture over the next three-quarters of a century, was established in the early forties. The city added nearly a thousand people during the forties and fifties; its 1960 population exceeded eight thousand.[1579]

The railroad remained the most important employer past the middle of the century when La Junta housed a roundhouse and the largest Santa Fe shop system outside

Topeka, Kansas.[1580] But the economics of American railroading were changing. The growth of airlines and the interstate highway system made alternative forms of travel and shipping more attractive. Fewer passengers and the greater use of dining cars threatened the Harvey House restaurant business. A wartime revival proved temporary, and it was closed in 1948. The station building was torn down in 1953 to make room for a combination freight and passenger office.[1581] Fifty railroad mail service workers no longer laid over in La Junta for twelve hours as mail trains were replaced by planes and trucks. In 1987 the Railroad's Colorado Division was eliminated and its headquarters building in town was abandoned.[1582] The railroad reportedly employed a thousand workers in La Junta in 1949. Their numbers fell to seven hundred by 1954 and 484 by 1963.[1583]

The local economy languished. The 1970 Census reported fewer La Junta residents employed than in 1950. The seventies and eighties saw some improvement. Despite a failed effort to obtain a packing plant and the loss of railroad jobs, the city added more than two hundred net new jobs between 1970 and 1990.[1584] Among the large employers listed in a 1980 Chamber of Commerce Report were: Nibco of Colorado a major supplier of copper pipe fittings with twenty-seven salaried and 290 hourly employees; Eagle Upsetters, a firm with twenty-four full time jobs that prepared pipe to be delivered to well-drilling suppliers; Prior Manufacturing, a clothing manufacturer with seventy-two employees in a sewing plant; and a Western Food Products plant, a long-time La Junta employer with three hundred year-round workers and another 150 during harvest season. In addition, sixty-nine air force personnel were stationed at an installation at the city's airport and staff positions at Otero Junior College totaled eighty.[1585] Population growth after 1969 was modest. The number of La Junta residents reached its peak in 1983 at 8,365 or only slightly more than in 1960.[1586]

The next quarter-century was a time of decline and stagnation. Railroad activity fell further, and the loss of irrigated farmland eroded the purchasing power in La Junta's trade area. The pickle plant that, under various ownerships, had been an important local employer for sixty-five years closed in 2005. Employment in La Junta fell by more than three hundred between 1990 and the middle teens.[1587] The city's population declined to seven thousand in 2010 some thirteen hundred below its peak, and by 2015 it had fallen further to just over sixty-eight hundred, fewer than in 1930.[1588]

La Junta had some success in the teens offsetting the earlier loss of manufacturing jobs. The city's largest industrial employer, Lewis Nut & Bolt Company, a railroad supplier, added one hundred workers. Other firms locating in La Junta included Sprout Tiny Homes; Whole Hemp Company, a producer of non-marijuana hemp products; and Miller International which located a brewery in the space abandoned by the pickle factory.[1589] Despite such hopeful developments, the La Junta economy was still far from robust. The community's prospects were hindered by an older and less affluent population; its median age in the middle teens was the highest of any of the four large plains towns.[1590] The most recent population and economic data suggest an economically stressed community.

Lamar

Since its founding in the 1880s, Lamar has experienced a succession of booms and busts. A flour mill, a sugar beet plant, a major alfalfa milling company headquarters, and a bus manufacturer all brought jobs and income to the community. But all eventually folded or relocated. The town prospered during the farm booms following the two wars and in the early 1970s. But it suffered from the declines that followed as well as from the effects of the Dust Bowl in the thirties. Since the turn of the century, the loss of manufacturing jobs has meant a continuing decline in jobs and population.

Most plains towns were established at critical sites such as railroad termini, river crossings, or military forts. Lamar was an exception to this pattern in that its location was entirely the result of speculation and land promotion. Prior to the town's founding in 1886, Lamar's future site was an empty space between two large ranches. With established communities of Granada to the east and Las Animas to the west, there was little reason to believe that this bit of prairie had any economic potential other than as farmland. But it was the height of the first homestead boom and settlers were surging into what was then eastern Bent County. Promoter I. R. Holmes, a former Santa Fe land man, spearheaded a campaign to turn the site into a settlement that would generate profit for him and his partners. With support from the railroad, they filed claims on the land that was to become Lamar.[1591] They arranged the clandestine relocation of a Santa Fe station to the proposed site and lobbied for locating a land office there. The latter effort, ultimately successful, was aided by naming the town for Secretary of Interior L. Q. C. Lamar. More than $25,000 in transactions were recorded on the land office's opening day.[1592] On the morning of May 24, 1886, still celebrated in the town as "Lamar Day," an excursion train from Garden City, Kansas stopped at the recently relocated station. Banners proclaimed, "I. R. Holmes, Excursion, Garden City to Lamar, future 'Mascot City of the Plains', First Sale Town Lots Today." Passengers disembarked and the auction began. By the end of the day $42,000 worth of lots had been sold.[1593]

The new town grew quickly; streets were laid out, and business and homes sprouted on what had been open prairie only a few months earlier. Within a week, a handful of saloons, restaurants, and real estate offices were open for business. A hundred residences were built within two months, and a special election to organize the new town was held in November.[1594] In 1889 Lamar became the county seat of Prowers County, one of six new counties created from the former Bent County.[1595] The 1890 Census reported 566 residents. The town's early population was a peripatetic lot. Cowboys, land speculators, and other frontier denizens came and went. The noted frontier lawman and jack-of-all-trades, Bat Masterson, made his home in Lamar for six months in 1887 before leaving for California for the winter.[1596]

CHAPTER 11

Despite the travails of southeast Colorado dryland homesteaders, irrigated farmers helped support a population of almost one thousand in 1900. The early history of Lamar, like that of many plains towns, was marked by frenetic entrepreneurial activity. New business seemed to be starting up almost daily. The most significant of these for the town's future was the Lamar flour mill completed in 1892 after a difficult campaign to raise the necessary funds from local citizens. It was soon joined by plants processing sugar beets and alfalfa. A 1909 article in the *Lamar Register* extolled the prospects of these two industries, contending that

> "The American Beet Sugar Company has during the past year finished the enlargement and extension which have a combined capacity of over one thousand tons per day….One of the greatest industries in the country and one which has done more for the enhancement of land values and which will do a great deal more in the future in that line is the four alfalfa meal mills in the county, all of which have been constructed in the last four years."[1597]

Alfalfa milling would thrive through the next half century as Denver Alfalfa, later retitled National Alfalfa and slated to become one of the leaders in the industry, moved its headquarters to Lamar from nearby Hartman. But the sugar beet factory soon failed.

Many enterprising businessmen contributed to the town's early growth, among them Morton Strain who arrived in the late 1880s. He soon involved himself in several local businesses including a transfer and ice business, a coal business and an alfalfa seed brokerage. With local partners, he built a hotel billed as "the best hotel in the state outside the large cities." He was a partner in the town's first electric light plant and its first telephone system. In 1900 he sold his seed and coal business and opened a bank. Morton Strain capped his career by serving two terms as Lamar's mayor.[1598] Other important local businessmen included A. E. Bent, from the family of the founders of the eponymous fort, who played a key role in developing the town's early electric utility and later served as Colorado's State Auditor and State Treasurer. Charles Maxwell, whose role in Lamar's development was described in chapter 4, was another important community leader until his death in the late thirties.[1599]

By 1910 the town's population approached three thousand, almost tripling over the previous ten years. The *Lamar Register* reported continuing prosperity describing a "usual steady growth and constant spreading out of the business district." The article noted two large business blocks and "A number of new fine residences."[1600] In 1914 the Helvetica Milk Condensing Company built a plant producing canned milked to be sold under the Pet Milk label. At the end of its first year the plant was reportedly received milk from 1,850 cows and produced twenty-three thousand pounds per day.[1601] In 1920 the board of aldermen negotiated a purchase of the assets of the private firm then furnishing electricity and created Lamar Light and Power, a municipal utility.[1602] As the farm economy struggled and the influx of new homesteaders can to an end, growth slowed but by 1930 more than four thousand people resided there.[1603]

Lamar lay on the northern edge of the Dust Bowl and was afflicted by drought, extreme heat, high winds, and blowing dust during the thirties. The Dust Bowl along with the national recession took its toll on the local economy, although it benefitted from an influx of federal bureaucrats arriving to provide relief and assistance to struggling farmers and townspeople. Between 1929 and 1940, the town's assessed valuation declined by 16 percent and deposits in the community's banks fell by 23 percent.[1604] A rare positive development was the founding of Lamar Junior College, later Lamar Community College, in 1937. The town's population grew by some two hundred people during the decade, although most of the new residents were farm families abandoning their land and moving into town.

Lamar posted solid growth in the forties adding some twenty-four hundred people benefitting from the buoyant war and post war economies as well as the farming boom that lasted through most of the decade. The economy received a boost from the construction of the Amache relocation center at nearby Granada. Growth slowed in the fifties and sixties with fewer than one thousand new residents added over the two decades. In 1960 the town lost two major employers when the flour mill closed, and National Alfalfa relocated its headquarters to Kansas City.

Santa Fe's main line and as well as east-west and north-south US highways traversing the town brought customers for many local businesses. Motels, gas stations and restaurants depended upon travelers for an important part of their sales, and access to truck and rail routes made Lamar attractive to manufacturers. The larger number of travelers passing through the community also made it a prime location for the brothels that Lamar hosted for several decades before they were finally closed under federal pressure in 1962.[1605] By the seventies Lamar's transportation advantages were eroding. The interstate highway system bypassed the Arkansas Valley causing growth in traffic along US-50 to stagnate as described in chapter 9. Rail passenger traffic continued to decline, and falling revenues raised questions about the viability of Amtrak's passenger service that had replaced Santa Fe's although it had not been terminated by the middle teens.

The seventies and eighties saw Lamar diversify from its dependence on agriculture toward light manufacturing. By the mid-seventies the city could claim a skiwear producer and a maker of hydraulic cylinders, each with more than a hundred employees, as well as several smaller companies.[1606] After an ardent effort to attract a large meat packing plant failed, local businessmen and state development officials succeeded in persuading the German bus firm Neoplan to locate an assembly plant on the northern edge of town as noted in chapter 9, the Bus plant attracted several firms supplying components and related products. Increased manufacturing activity brought a surge of growth, and the town added more than one thousand persons between 1980 and

1985 with total population expanding to more than 8,800.[1607] It would remain near that level until the end of the century. The town gained 822 jobs between 1970 and 1990.[1608] But Lamar's dependence upon the German bus firm made it vulnerable to the company's fortunes.

Prosperity continued into the nineties. Farming and ranching still generated jobs. Local feed lots with a capacity of 100,000 head employed 250 workers. Although east-west highway traffic along US-50 slowed, truck shipping along north-south US287/385 continued at a healthy pace. Lamar boasted motels with more than 450 rooms, the largest of these employing nearly a hundred workers.[1609] The town reached its all-time population peak of 8,854 in 2000.[1610] But concerns about Neoplan's future in the community surfaced as the firm, now independent of its German parent, was plagued with quality and financial problems. As described in chapter 10, the company began to reduce employment in the late 1990s.[1611] Finally, in November 2005, management announced closure of the Lamar factory resulting in elimination of jobs for a workforce that had already been reduced to three hundred.[1612]

Lamar endured trying times in the new century. As Neoplan was winding down, the city government undertook what turned out to be an unfortunate investment in a coal-fired electrical generating plant that never produced any power. Threatened water transfers and a severe drought in the early 2000s added to the community's concerns. By 2015 manufacturing employment had dropped to half its 1990 level,[1613] and Lamar's population had fallen by almost fifteen hundred from its peak.[1614] One of the town's elementary schools was closed due to declining enrollment. But, by most measures, Lamar fared better than other towns in the Arkansas Valley.

Sterling

Sterling has been the largest municipality in the region for most of the last hundred years.[1615] The city exhibited an ability to adapt to changing conditions as the fortunes of important local industries rose and fell. Sterling, like La Junta, owed much of its early development to railroads, but has been more successful than its Arkansas Valley counterpart in continuing to grow after rail traffic diminished. The city was a major regional trading center and hosted sizable sugar beet refining and meat packing plants through most of the twentieth century. When changes in markets forced closure of these facilities, Sterling was able to diversify its economy and resume healthy growth driven by health care, education, travel, and a large state prison.

The first settlers in what became known as "old Sterling" arrived in the early 1870s. By 1875 the village consisted of twelve houses each on a quarter-section of land and a school that opened in the fall of that year.[1616] In 1881 the Union Pacific completed a line from Julesburg to La Salle, creating a more direct connection between Denver and the main UP line through Wyoming. Landowner M.C. King offered the railroad company eighty acres of land along lines right of way provided railroad located its shops there.

New yards built on this site and a sizable livestock shipping business got underway.[1617] This became the new location for Sterling three miles south of the earlier settlement.[1618]

The town soon grew up around the railroad yards. Among the early buildings were a hotel, a laundry house, a lunchroom, tenement housing, an icehouse, coal chutes, and blacksmith shops.[1619] Sterling incorporated in 1884 and later became the county seat of the newly created Logan County. UP facilities included a depot, a coal house, a long platform, a section house and a water tank. A five-stall roundhouse and an iron turntable for turning steam locomotives were soon added.[1620] In 1899 UP built a railroad-owned hotel[1621] and completed a new depot in 1903.[1622] The railroad's monthly local payroll in April 1900 was $4,000.[1623] Sterling acquired a second rail line in 1887 when the Burlington route from Holdrege, Nebraska to Cheyenne, Wyoming traversed the city. The Census reported a population of 540 in 1890 with an increase to 908 ten years later despite drought and depressed farm prices in the nineties.

As was the case in other South Platte and Arkansas Valley towns in the early 1900s, Sterling's city fathers saw a sugar factory as a key to future prosperity. As described in chapter 3, the completion of the plant in 1905 and the construction of the North Sterling Reservoir some five years later provided a significant boost to the town's economy. Other agriculture-related industries soon sprang up. W. C. Harris, who arrived in Sterling in a covered wagon in 1875, got his start in the cattle business collecting and selling the carcasses of stock that died in the hard winters of the 1890s. He established feed yards in Sterling in 1906, using the beet pulp from the newly opened sugar beet factory. Mr. Harris, with partners, operated grain elevators and feed lots in Colorado and other western and midwestern states.[1624] Other Sterling manufacturers included an alfalfa mill [1625] and a canning factory.[1626]

The town was beginning to transcend its rural roots. Teams of horses had become a hazard on Main Street so, in 1905, town officials prohibited tying horse teams on that thoroughfare. The problem of cows wandering the streets was dealt with by impounding the loose critters.[1627] In 1907 board sidewalks were replaced with cement ones, streets were graded, and hitching racks on Main Street were removed. Sterling's water works were expanded, a sewer system was installed, and building codes were established.[1628] The city embraced the automobile age. In 1908 a garage capable of accommodating twenty vehicles was built. The garage owners soon established a Ford agency and a Studebaker agency quickly followed.[1629] In 1915 the City Council passed an ordinance restricting driving to the right side of the road.[1630]

The lure of irrigated farmland drew large numbers of settlers, and the first two decades of the twentieth century saw the fastest growth in Sterling's history. The town's population increased from less than one thousand at the beginning of the century to almost sixty-five hundred twenty years later.[1631] Like Fort Morgan, Sterling remained a "dry" city in the pre-prohibition era. A city ordinance adopted in 1906 made it "illegal to store liquor of any character in any building."[1632] Despite the stresses of hard times, residents voted to remain dry when national prohibition was repealed in 1933.[1633]

Growth slowed in the twenties as farmers and ranchers confronted depressed postwar markets. Two of the town's three banks were among the many rural financial institutions forced to close in the 1920s, but two new ones soon formed.[1634] By the late twenties, conditions were improving. The town's retail potential led to the opening of a Montgomery Ward branch and a J.C. Penney store in 1928.[1635] Auto dealers offered a full line of vehicles including Willys Knight, Overland, Whippet, Hudson, Essex, Chrysler, and Chevrolet.[1636] But the depression brought the fledgling recovery to a halt. Farm prices fell further, and drought and blowing dust worsened although conditions were less severe than in southeastern Colorado. The town's business slumped. New automobile sales fell by two-thirds and the value of building permits declined by 60 percent from the previous decade.[1637] Yet, in the face of the declining national economy and a depressed farm sector, Sterling added almost a thousand new residents between 1920 and 1940.[1638]

Northeastern Junior College was founded in 1941 with fifty-five students and soon established a pilot training program and Navy officer procurement classes. Its contribution to the community was to grow over the years with enrollment expanding to ninety-one full-time students by 1948.[1639] In the mid-fifties a report from one of the state's leading banks described Northeastern JC as "Colorado's fastest growing institution of higher learning."[1640] By 1987 full time equivalent enrollment had grown to 1,658, and the college served four thousand students in community education programs.[1641] With the outbreak of war, several hundred Japanese Americans resettled in Sterling. They were not forcibly relocated as those at Camp Amache but chose to move from the west coast states to avoid internment.[1642] The Logan County Fairgrounds housed 140 Italian prisoners of war.[1643] Despite the flurry of war and post-war activity Sterling only added slightly more than one hundred people during the 1940s.

In the fifties Sterling's economy was dominated by the oil boom described in chapter 8. At its peak more than three hundred wells in Logan County pumped over twenty-two million barrels annually, with much of production and exploration managed from Sterling. In 1955, 44 companies were engaged in drilling or oil field services in the county.[1644] Increased tax receipts allowed the expansion of the county fairgrounds, construction of a new modern hospital and upgrading the airport.[1645] A new 12,500 square foot Red Owl grocery store opened in 1960.[1646] The Census reported Sterling's employment grew by 965 during the decade. These figures were based on the residence of the worker rather than the location of the job so the number of jobs in the community was probably larger. Among the new jobs were 158 in the mining sector, nearly all of which were in oil and gas exploration and production. Professional and related services grew by 339 workers, many of them supporting services for exploration and drilling activity. The town's building boom was responsible for another 137 in construction. The

Census reported that population grew from 7,534 to 10,751 over the decade although some local sources estimated larger numbers of people at the height of the oil boom.[1647]

As the competitive position of American railroads faltered in the 1950s, their contribution to the Sterling economy declined. The loss of mail contracts in 1955 forced UP to discontinue two daily passenger trains through the town.[1648] Three years later the Burlington eliminated its car repair shops.[1649] The jointly operated Union Pacific-Burlington freight depot was closed in 1968, and its operations were moved to the passenger depot.[1650] The UP abandoned its passenger depot in 1985 and presented the building to the City of Sterling which moved it to a new location and reopened it as a visitor center.[1651] The UP also discontinued service on the Julesburg to LaSalle line in the eighties ending any connection with the city.[1652] Sterling's endangered rail business received a reprieve in the 1980s with an expansion of coal train traffic from Wyoming's Powder River Basin to power plants in southern Colorado, Nebraska, and Texas. Burlington Northern, formed by a merger of the Burlington with three other lines, shipped the coal from Cheyenne through Sterling and La Salle, thereby avoiding running coal trains through cities in Colorado's heavily populated northern Front Range. By 1985 coal traffic accounted for two hundred employees in Sterling.[1653]

The decline in railroad activity along with the lack of new oil and gas exploration caused growth to slacken in the sixties and Sterling's population registered a small decline over the decade. But farm prosperity limited the damage. Great Western's Sterling sugar factory provided a steady source of local employment and revenue for area farmers despite the company's ongoing management problems. The number of feedlots in the region suggested potential for a packing plant and Sterling Colorado Beef opened one in 1966. The sixties saw the construction of a new shopping center and the opening of a new bank. Two new elementary schools were built.[1654] The local economy also received a boost from the 1970 completion of Interstate 80-S, later renamed I-76.

After a few prosperous years in the early seventies, the farm economy suffered a sharp correction. Both the town's major agri-business employers struggled. Sterling Colorado Beef experienced financial instability due to fluctuating beef prices and ongoing labor disputes leading to layoffs and a temporary shutdown in 1987 before the plant was acquired by Cargill subsidiary Excel.[1655] Great Western Sugar suffered from weak sugar prices and its parent corporation's financial problems and the Sterling plant ceased operations in 1985.[1656] More jobs were lost with the closing of Evans Rail Car Service, with thirty workers, and the shuttering of three local alfalfa mills.[1657] But the health care sector was a steady source of jobs and income. The Logan County Hospital expanded further in the seventies employing almost three hundred full and part-time workers with a $1.6 million annual payroll.[1658] By the 1980s the town's overall employment growth had slowed sharply from its pace in the fifties.[1659] The 1990 Census reported 274 fewer residents than twenty years earlier.

Sterling's difficulties continued into the early nineties By 1992 population had declined by nearly fifteen hundred over the previous decade.[1660] But a rebound was at hand as the local economy diversified from its agriculture and railroading roots. A 1995 *Rocky Mountain News* headline proclaimed, "A Sterling Resurgence for Once Ailing Town." According to the *News*, the community now faced a housing shortage instead of the vacant dwellings of a few years earlier. Wal-Mart replaced its store with a twenty-four-hour supercenter. The Sterling regional medical center planned a $5 million expansion. Northeastern Junior College enjoyed a surge in enrollment. Meatpacker Excel-Cargill and computer support company Sykes both increased their payrolls and plans were underway for the state's newest prison with 2,532 inmates and nine hundred employees.[1661] The prison opened in 1998, but earlier optimism about the meatpacking plant turned out to be misplaced. Cargill cut its Sterling work force in half in 1995[1662] and announced plans to close the plant in November 1997 putting 335 people with a total payroll of $7.5 million out of work.[1663] But Sterling was able to prosper despite this loss. The new prison, the college and medical center, along with the city's services and transportation jobs, helped to strengthen the local economy in the new century. Between 1990 and the middle teens employment increased by over fifteen hundred or more than one-third.[1664] The town's 2015 population exceeded 14,000 a gain of nearly four thousand over the previous twenty-five years.[1665]

Other Economically Important Towns

Other somewhat smaller towns also played important roles in the region's development. The fortunes and influence of these communities varied since the first influx of settlers. Las Animas and Rocky Ford enjoyed vibrant economies in the late nineteenth and early twentieth centuries but have struggled more recently as the fortunes of the Arkansas Valley waned. Brush and Yuma, on the other hand, experienced solid growth over the latest quarter century, benefitting from healthy agriculture and related businesses in the northeast Colorado. Jobs from a state prison and a large traveler service complex on I-70 sustained Limon's economy through the middle 1990s although it has since lost some population. Burlington took advantage of similar factors, but its prison's closure in 2016 was at least a temporary interruption of its growth. Springfield's population peaked during the post war wheat boom and has subsequently fallen by one-third. A brief history of these towns follows.

Brush

Cattle and sugar beets were the driving forces in Brush's economy throughout most of its history although it also benefitted from the fifties oil boom and proximity to Fort Morgan's food processing factories. Settlement began in 1882 with completion of the Burlington line from McCook to Denver. The Lincoln Land Company, associated with the Railroad, acquired substantial land in and around the town. Some of it became the location of the railroad's station and yards and rest was sold to settlers.

The town was incorporated two years later, taking the name of prominent northeast Colorado cattleman Jared Brush who may never have set foot in the community.[1666] With completion of the railroad, Brush became an important shipping point for cattle in northeast Colorado. A reported twelve hundred carloads of cattle were shipped from the town in 1884.[1667]

Development of irrigation in the area was well underway before the town's incorporation beginning with the Weldon Valley Canal completed in 1880. Later, northeast Colorado irrigation pioneer, Abner Baker, spearheaded the construction of the Fort Morgan and Beaver Canals.[1668] The availability of irrigation attracted homesteaders in the 1880s and 1990s. Dryland homesteading also surged in the area south and east of Brush although many left as the drought took hold.[1669] The growing rural population led to a demand for retail and other services in the town. William Knearl, who served two terms as mayor, operated a general merchandise store in Brush beginning in 1888.[1670] By 1900 Brush's population had grown to 881.[1671]

The 1906 opening of Great Western's plant marked the beginnings of the sugar beet production that would prove pivotal in the Brush economy for the next half century. It spurred rapid growth in the teens when population more than doubled, reaching 2,103 in 1920.[1672] Between 1916 and 1930 sugar payments to farmers averaged $1 million annually, and the plant's payroll averaged $150,000. As the mix of beet-field workers shifted from German Russian to Mexican, the Company built a "colony" with 8 adobe houses.[1673] By 1915 Brush boasted three banks: First National Bank, Stockmen's Bank, and Farmer's State Bank.[1674]

Growth slowed and population grew by only another three hundred between 1920 and 1950. Cattle and sheep feeding assumed greater importance taking advantage of the abundance of feed crops in the area. The Brush Auction and Livestock exchange was established in 1937.[1675] Boxer & Weisbart built a large feed lot with supporting storage elevators and feed grinding machinery which fed twenty to thirty thousand head at a time through the 1940s and early 1950s.[1676] Brush was the largest origination point between Denver and Omaha for Burlington Railroad livestock shipments.[1677] A prisoner of war camp housed Italian, German, and Austrian prisoners who worked in the fields during the beet harvest.[1678] The completion of US highway 34 meant Brush was located along an important route to the Front Range and the Colorado mountains.[1679]

The 1950s oil boom spurred growth and new construction. Brush's population surged with much of the increase accounted for by transient energy workers. Buildings erected between 1954 and 1960 included five churches, nineteen stores and office buildings, two grain elevators, three storage buildings, and 177 homes.[1680] Even the closure of the sugar-beet plant in 1955 had little effect on the town's buoyant economy. Brush added some twelve hundred people during the 1950s.[1681]

The Census reported an additional four hundred people during the 1960s and 1970s. A hog and sheep slaughtering plant opened in 1966 and expanded in the early seventies although it was closed in the eighties.[1682] The Chamber of Commerce reported that the Brush Livestock Commission Company handled between ninety and 160 thousand head annually and three large cattle finishing feeding pens had a combined capacity of a hundred thousand head.[1683] The completion of I-76 increased traffic and boosted activity at local restaurants, motels and gas stations. The town claimed thirteen motor freight carriers operating with Brush as a home base.[1684]

The economy encountered difficulties in late eighties as local farmers struggled to survive. Unemployment hit 14 percent after the closing of the pork processing plant, and the First National Bank failed in 1987.[1685] But conditions soon began to improve. The High Plains Youth Facility, a private institution for troubled young people, opened in 1989 with 150 employees and a payroll of $3.4 million. Colorado Power Partners built a $28 million cogeneration steam power plant and a greenhouse which together provided 150 jobs and a $1.5 million payroll.[1686] Between 1990 and the middle teens, an additional 185 manufacturing workers reported residing in the town, many commuting to the Cargill meat packing plant or the Leprino Foods cheese plant, both in nearby Fort Morgan.[1687] In 1994 the *Denver Post* described a housing shortage, especially for affordable housing for the low-wage workers on farms or in the Fort Morgan packing plant.[1688] City officials were reportedly planning to move forty-five housing units from Lamar to be refurbished for living quarters for workers and their families.[1689] By 2015 the population had grown to 5,415, a gain of more twelve hundred or almost 30 percent over the previous twenty-five years, and the median family income was the second highest of any of the towns described in this chapter.[1690]

Burlington

Burlington has long served as a major trading center for the central plains' farm economy. The opening of I-70 and the introduction of irrigated farming added to its economic base. The town got its start in September 1887 when the Rock Island Railroad laid out its line running from Kansas to Denver. The owners of the railroad purchased a tract of school land along the proposed line that became the town of Burlington. Businesses in the town's early days included several real estate firms, a livery stable, feed stores, banking, and hardware and grocery stores, but there were no saloons or dance halls as the open range era had passed.[1691] The 1890 Census reported 146 residents.

The arrival of homesteaders in the early twentieth century caused population to grow from 183 in 1900 to 991 twenty years later. The community struggled through the farm crisis of the twenties and the drought and national recession in the thirties. The Stock Growers Bank failed[1692] and population was unchanged over the decade. The onset of war brought prosperity to area farmers as well as local businesses. A half-million-bushel grain elevator was built along with the Kit Carson Memorial Hospital.[1693] The war and postwar years saw another thousand people added during the 1940s.

Growth slowed in the fifties, but the introduction of ground-water irrigation in eastern Kit Carson County in the 1960s and 1970s led to a resurgence. The completion of I-70 in the seventies provided a stable base of expenditures by tourists and business travelers from the Midwest to Colorado's mountains and Front Range eventually leading to the construction of more than five hundred motel rooms and a Love's Travel Stop.[1694] Between 1960 and 1980 the town's population increased by more than a thousand.[1695]

Burlington gained two major employers in the nineties. Midwest Farms, Inc. constructed a twenty-thousand-sow-hog farrowing operation south of the town in 1995 with as many as two hundred workers. In 1998 Corrections Corporation of America opened its Kit Carson Correctional Facility as described in chapter 10.[1696] It operated for eighteen years until declining occupancy forced its closure in 2016. At that time, it held only 402 inmates in a facility with a capacity of fourteen hundred.[1697] Shuttering the prison meant a loss of 142 jobs and a shortfall in the city's revenue base. When the prison closed, Burlington's population exceeded four thousand, but it dropped sharply thereafter from the loss of inmates as well as staff and families.[1698]

Las Animas

The town is one of the oldest in the region and was by far the largest on the eastern plains in 1880 with more than five hundred residents in two towns that were to become Las Animas. The first settlement was Las Animas City founded in 1869 on the south side of the Arkansas across from Fort Lyon, then a military installation. A toll bridge was built across the river from the Fort to the new town. Las Animas City boasted saloons and dance halls along with general stores and was patronized by settlers, cowboys and soldiers from the Fort. It soon reported 150 people and thirty buildings.[1699] But four years later the Kansas Pacific Railroad, then constructing a spur from Kit Carson to the Arkansas Valley, balked at bridging both the Arkansas and the Purgatoire that flowed into the Arkansas west of the town. When the citizens of Las Animas City voted down a bond issue that would have helped fund the Purgatoire bridge, the railroad formed a land company that, through what were described as "fraudulent means,"[1700] acquired land west of the Purgatoire and founded the town of West Las Animas. The railroad bypassed Las Animas City, crossing the Arkansas a few miles to the west at the site of the new city named West Las Animas. The first train arrived in October 1873.

By the end of 1873 the new town boasted around fifty permanent structures including dance halls, saloons, and three hotels. The first school opened in November 1873 and by mid-March 1874 the town had three hundred residents. John W. Prowers and his brother-in-law built a two-story adobe commission house south of the railroad tracks to handle shipments to New Mexico. A second rail line, the Santa Fe, reached the town in 1875. The first bank in the Arkansas Valley, The Bent County Bank, was organized that year.[1701] The town, now at the end of two lines, became a leading shipper of meat to the east and Midwest and important site for shipping products arriving by rail to the southwest. Demand for livestock stock from local ranchers increased. Bent County's livestock population was estimated at seventy-two hundred pure American cattle, twenty-nine thousand pure Texas cattle, 37,500 mixed and half-breed cattle, and 35,500 sheep.[1702]

When the two rail lines were extended on to La Junta, wagon traffic to the southwest moved to the new rail terminus. West Las Animas changed its name to Las Animas and incorporated in 1882.[1703] Although the importance of rail traffic diminished, the new town prospered with the arrival of settlers in the Arkansas Valley, aided by the construction of several large irrigation projects. By 1910 the town's population exceeded two thousand. American Beet Sugar built a factory in the town in 1907 that processed beets grown on six thousand acres in Bent County. But beet production dwindled, and the factory closed in 1921.[1704]

Unlike nearly all other plains communities Las Animas experienced relatively healthy growth during the 1930s when population grew by 28 percent. Two government projects were largely responsible for its good fortune. Fort Lyon, whose mission was changed several times, was a consistent source of steady and well-paying jobs. The Army abandoned the Fort in 1889, and the property was reclaimed in 1906 by the US Navy, which turned it into a tuberculosis sanitarium that was later acquired by the Veterans Bureau. When the number of TB patients declined, the sanitarium was converted to a neuro-psychiatric hospital in 1929. The facility was expanded with several large brick buildings built before and during WWII.[1705] In the fifties and early sixties the number of the hospital's employees, many of them highly paid professionals, varied between 470 and 535.[1706] Las Animas also benefitted from construction of the John Martin dam some ten miles east of town. Between 1938 and 1949, more than a thousand workers were employed on the project.[1707] The town's population exceeded 3,200 at mid-century, virtually unchanged from 1940, and remained stable over the next decade.

The 1950s marked the apex of the city's population and economic activity. Over the next fifty-odd years the town lost nearly one-third its residents. Water transfers reduced irrigated farming in Bent County. Hope for an economic stimulus were raised when Las Animas was chosen as the site for a large electrical generating plant but, in 1982, the State's major energy utility canceled its plans.[1708] The payroll at Fort Lyon decreased as it evolved from a veterans' hospital to a state prison for elderly and medically needy inmates and then to a transitional facility for homeless persons, resulting in a progressively smaller and less-well-paid staff. The town gradually lost trade and service business to nearby Lamar or La Junta. These losses were somewhat offset by the opening in 1993 of the private twelve hundred-bed Bent County Correctional Facility on the outskirts of the city. In 2015 Las Animas had only twenty-two hundred residents, and the lowest median family income of any regional town its size or larger.[1709] (Inmates at the prison which lies outside the town were not included in the population count.)

Limon

Limon's history has been tied to its proximity to important transportation routes as reflected in its appellation as the "Hub City of the Plains."[1710] The town traces its beginnings to an 1888 Rock Island Railroad camp for construction workers. The site was a division point between tracks running to Colorado Springs and those to Denver as well as the intersection of the proposed Rock Island line and that of the Union Pacific. The collection of tents for workers was soon supplemented by a small roundhouse, a coal chute, a section house, and an eating house for workers and train passengers.[1711] The two railroads remained important Limon employers through the middle of the twentieth century, with a peak work force of as many as three hundred.[1712] In addition to railroad activity, the town, which was not incorporated until 1909, served as a trading center for open range ranchers on the central plains. It featured a hotel and saloon and a general merchandise store.[1713] Settlement by homesteaders in the early days of the twentieth century led to more new businesses including a bank and a lumber company.[1714] The population of 75 in 1900 grew to 534 by 1910.[1715] The teens brought a water system, an electric utility and expanded automobile traffic[1716] along with another five hundred residents.[1717]

The local economy worsened in the twenties and thirties. In 1924 a fire destroyed several businesses in Limon's downtown.[1718] The 1930s depression and drought brought abandonment of local farms, a cutback in employment and the failure of the Limon National Bank.[1719] Population remained around a thousand through the early 1940s before a war and post-war boom raised it to 1,470 at mid-century.[1720] Rail's presence in Limon was beginning to decline. By the middle fifties the Rock Island had drastically cut back its employment in the town.[1721] The Rocky Mountain Rocket, one of the line's premier streamliners that made daily stops in Limon to separate its passenger cars with one group destined for Denver the other for Colorado Springs, was discontinued in 1966.[1722] The Rock Islands footprint on the town disappeared when it went into bankruptcy in 1980. However, the Union Pacific continued to run trains through Limon and house a small maintenance crew there.

Dryland agriculture in Lincoln County remained stable in the latter part of the twentieth century but did not generate enough demand to support a town of over twelve hundred people, Limon's population in 1970. But the community was able to obtain two new economic drivers. The Interstate Highway System designated the route that became I-70 just north of the town. When completed in 1974, the interstate bypassed Limon's business district and connected with US 40, 287 and 24 north and west of the town. The Rip Griffin Truck Service Center at the highway interchange opened in 1979. The Center and other traveler-based businesses that would locate nearby became a major contributor to the local economy as related in chapter 9. Another economic boost occurred in 1991 when the State of Colorado completed the Limon Correctional Facility south of the town. These two employment centers enabled Limon to avoid the decline that afflicted most other dryland farming communities and to survive a devastating tornado in 1990 that destroyed much of the downtown business district. Population exceeded two thousand at the beginning of the century before declining slightly after 2008-9 Great Recession.[1723] (The population figure does not include the more than nine hundred inmates at the correctional facility located outside the city limits.) The median family income in the middle teens was the highest of any town described in this chapter.[1724]

Rocky Ford

The Rocky Ford economy flourished during Otero County's irrigated-farming heyday, but the waning of the Arkansas Valley sugar beet industry and the loss of irrigation water rights led to stagnation and decline in the late twentieth and early twenty-first centuries. The town traces its beginnings to 1875 when the Santa Fe laid out its route from Las Animas to Pueblo. George Swink, who had founded an earlier town of Rocky Ford two miles north of today's location, and two others filed homestead claims on land along the proposed rail route at the right distance from La Junta for a siding. Soon the line was completed, and a depot erected. Swink built a twenty-by-forty-foot adobe store near the tracks.[1725] A flurry of canal building was soon underway including expansion of the Rocky Ford Ditch. As noted earlier this canal, begun by Swink in the early 1870s, held some of the most senior water rights in the Arkansas Valley, a boon to irrigators given the often-erratic flow of the river.[1726]

Newly available land under the irrigation canals attracted settlers. To accommodate the new residents' families an adobe schoolhouse opened with twenty pupils in 1877.[1727] Ten years later an auction of lots in the town attracted hundreds of buyers who came by train from as far away as St. Louis.[1728] Cattle and sheep grazing expanded around Rocky Ford in the 1890s. But it was most noted for its cantaloupe and cucumbers. The town established a reputation for producing "Rocky Ford" cantaloupes and fine seed for melons with buyers from all over the world.[1729] Its high school athletic teams still reflect this legacy in their "Meloneer" nickname. Businesses in the 1890s included a canning factory, a flour mill, a brick yard, and two new hotels. At the end of the century its population of 2,018, was second in size only to La Junta among communities on the eastern plains.[1730]

In 1900 Rocky Ford staked its claim in the burgeoning sugar beet industry when American Beet Sugar built a factory and bought seven thousand acres of land and a controlling interest in the Rocky Ford Ditch.[1731] The plant, whose parent was re-christened American Crystal Sugar Company in 1934, remained a mainstay of the Rocky Ford economy through the 1970s. The town continued to grow with the booming farm economy in the early twentieth century; population reached 3,746 in 1920. But depressed farm prices and the national recession took their toll and population declined over the next two decades.

Prospects brightened in the forties as Otero County agriculture prospered and growth continued with population peaking at 4,859 in 1960. By the seventies the Rocky Ford plant was the sole sugar beet factory in the Arkansas Valley, but it was becoming increasingly less profitable and was closed in 1979 as described in chapter 9.[1732] The jobs lost when the plant closed were never replaced as nearby La Junta offered superior conditions for manufacturing operations and more attractive options for shopping. The town lost jobs between 1970 and 1990 and registered a population decline of almost seven hundred. Census data showed a 23 percent drop in Rocky Ford's median family income over that period after adjusting for inflation. The loss of Otero County irrigation through water transfers in the 1990s and 2000s further eroded the community's economic base.

In the mid-eighties, the state economic development agency prepared an assessment of Rocky Ford's potential.[1733] The report seems discouraging but perhaps prophetic. Among its findings: "Does not have a very attractive downtown," "Labor attitudes are good, and wage levels are low enough for most cash flows but probably too low to support one-income families," and "Recreational opportunities are borderline and cultural opportunities are poor."[1734] The report set two growth targets for the year 2000. The more ambitious called for an end-of-century population of 5,820 while the more modest one was 5,070, both significant increases from the slightly more than forty-five hundred residents at the time. The targets were not achieved; by 2000 population had fallen to less than forty-three hundred. Over the next fifteen years the town lost another nine hundred people. Recent data show a relatively poor population with the median family income in the middle teens the second lowest of any of the nine towns covered in this chapter. Nearly 60 percent of Rocky Ford's residents were Latinos, predominately youngsters or older working-age adults.[1735]

Springfield

In its early decades Springfield's economy waxed and waned with the local agricultural economy, followed by a gradual decline after the middle of the twentieth century. The town came into existence in the spring of 1887 at the peak of the first wave of homesteaders and became the county seat of newly formed Baca County in 1889. It briefly flourished, boasting four grocery stores, two clothing stores, three livery stables, two banks, and five or six saloons by the summer of 1888.[1736] Thomas Harper in his University of Denver thesis on Baca County history estimated the peak population at around three hundred.[1737] But a succession of dry years drove out many of the homesteaders and the town languished. A new boom began in the teens fueled by war-time demand for farm products. The growing rural population was a boon to local merchants. A typical weekend saw "thirty cars, a dozen wagons, and two schooner wagons on the streets of Springfield as rural residents came to town to do their business."[1738] Population grew from 150 in 1914 to 295 in 1920.[1739]

Growth accelerated with the completion of a railroad from western Kansas in 1926 providing a less costly means of shipping Baca County grain and livestock to markets. Relatively cheap land led to a massive expansion of dryland wheat cultivation in the late twenties. Natural gas service was instituted in 1930, and the population that year reached 1,393.[1740] In 1931 the city signed a contract for streetlights.[1741] But the Dust Bowl soon brought the boom to an end as Baca County's agriculture was devasted by drought and wind erosion. As noted in chapter 6, national media flocked to the town to breathlessly report on the ruin wrought by the climatic disaster. By the middle of the decade, the arrival of federal funds from New Deal relief programs limited the damage to the Springfield economy,[1742] and construction of Santa Fe's rail line from Las Animas to Boise City, Oklahoma provided a further boost. But the effects of the drought and depression persisted. The 1940 Census reported that population had declined by 22 percent over the decade, by far the largest loss of any of the larger towns in the region during the thirties.

Wartime demand for grain brought a revival, and growth accelerated in the postwar period with high wheat prices and adequate rainfall. Springfield prospered from the newly acquired fortunes of Baca County wheat growers. By 1950 the population had nearly doubled to more than two thousand.[1743] But another drought in the early fifties once again extinguished the community's prosperity. Over the next six decades Springfield was forced to rely on a shrinking number of dryland farmers and retirement spending by an aging population. By 2015 the number of residents had fallen by a third to 1,383.[1744] The main street of Springfield was described in a recent *Denver Post* article as lined with "mostly empty storefronts."[1745]

Yuma

While other plains communities have attempted to shift their economic foundations to manufacturing or services, Yuma has thrived while retaining its agricultural base. In the middle-1880s the site of today's town consisted of only a Chicago, Burlington & Quincy railway station and a water tank. As homesteaders settled in the area W.A. Sheedy saw a business opportunity and established a mercantile store that thrived on sales to farmers coming to town to shop on weekends.[1746] According to a history of the region published a century later, "During the week, the town was deserted, the main street was grown into grass and weeds with a single wagon track down the center. When Saturday came, the farm wagons from surrounding territory began to arrive."[1747] A petition was filed for incorporation in 1887. When the town incorporated it had 105 residents.[1748] But area homesteaders soon faced the perils of dryland farming. Good harvests in 1891 and '92 were followed by drought-caused failures over the next two years. By the middle 1990s farmers were abandoning Yuma County in droves. By 1900 population that had reached 241 ten years earlier shrank to only 134.[1749]

Growth returned in the early 1900s and teens as western Yuma County experienced another flood of settlers. Fueled by wartime demand for farm products, the town's population surged. The number of residents reached 333 in 1910 and exploded to almost twelve hundred by 1920. School buildings proved inadequate for rapidly growing enrollments. Additional streets were laid out and hundreds of new houses were built. The town's water and electricity capacities were expanded.[1750]

Depression and drought brought challenging times. Two of the three Yuma banks failed, and the school board cut teachers' salaries by a quarter and eliminated the principal's job.[1751] But farm families abandoning their property and moving to town brought an additional 250 residents by 1940. Yet another three hundred were added in the forties to bring the total population to nearly two thousand in 1950.[1752] A history of west Yuma County compiled in the 1980s reported that by the early fifties the town had its own light and power plant, a twenty-bed hospital, two grade schools, a high school, a Lutheran parochial school, a public library, a bank, four grocery stores, six clothing stores, five restaurants, two drug stores, two furniture stores, one theatre, two hotels, and eight auto show rooms.[1753]

The 1960s saw the introduction of irrigated farming on former dryland as improved technology enabled the exploitation of the Ogallala Aquifer as described in chapter 8. Irrigated acreage grew rapidly by the late 1980s. Sugar beets were introduced, and the proliferation of feed lots and large-scale hog farms in northeast Colorado led to increased grain cultivation. Yuma County corn production, less than a million bushels a year in the early sixties, grew to thirty-two million bushels in 1981 and over forty million by the 2000s.[1754] Four large hog farms opened in the 1990s. The town benefitted from farm prosperity and continued to grow; its population exceeded twenty-eight hundred in 1980 and grew to over thirty-five hundred by 2015.[1755]

Although it lacked major manufacturing firms—only fifty-six of its 1,876 workers were employed in that industry in the middle teens—and was not located on an interstate highway, Yuma continued to prosper through the early twenty-first century. The community remained a farm trading center and benefitted from the health of northeast Colorado agriculture. Its median family income in the middle teens was a healthy $47,368, and only 9.1 percent of families reported incomes less than the federal poverty level.[1756]

The Smaller Towns

For a few summers in the late fifties, I delivered bakery products to small town restaurants and grocery stores in southeast Colorado. Although this was a reasonably prosperous time for the region, I could not help but notice how the survival of these businesses was threatened as they lost more and more of their customers to the larger trading centers. The varied fortunes of different sized plains communities were described in 1955 by Karl Frederick Kraenzel[1757] who characterized Great Plains settlements as divided between the *sutland* and the *yonland*. The former included the more densely settled areas along major transportation routes, while the outlying stretches were part of the *yonland*. Kraenzel's *sutland* appellation was derived from the term "sutler" for suppliers to army posts on the frontier. It would include the larger towns in the South Platte and Arkansas Valleys and the I-70 corridor and most of the cities described earlier in this chapter. The smaller towns described in this section would be relegated to the *yonland*.

By the 1950s the plains' shrinking population along with advancing technology led to greater concentration of population and economic activity in the *sutland*. As transportation improved, firms in the larger trading centers were able to exploit economies of scale and offer a wider scope of goods and services along with better prices, while those in the outlying areas became increasingly uncompetitive. Farmers and ranchers moved to the larger communities to take advantage of such amenities as better health care and education for their children while they continued to run their operations. Residents of smaller communities moved to larger ones for similar reasons. The *yonland* communities faded. As their customer bases shrank main-street retail outlets were abandoned, and banks, hospitals, and legal offices were absorbed by those in the larger towns. This in turn brought a further downward spiral. Governments were unable to raise enough revenue to maintain services. The lack of amenities made it difficult to retain young residents or to attract new ones. The remaining aging populations put further burdens on local service providers, and even many older residents moved to be nearer to their children or for better access to medical care.

Many of what might be termed the "larger small towns," those that at some point exceeding one thousand persons, reached their peak populations in the fifties or early sixties. Julesburg achieved its maximum size of nearly two thousand around mid-century, but population declined by more than a third by 2015. Other towns, including many of those in the Arkansas Valley or the central plains followed similar paths. Eads, Cheyenne Wells, and Holly reached populations greater than a thousand in 1950, but all saw significant losses by 2015. Some communities benefitted from positive economic development, but these were exceptions. Wray benefitted from the booming farm economy in the northeastern plains and continued to grow, reaching 2,345 persons in 2015 while Akron's population remained relatively stable at around seventeen hundred. A new prison allowed Ordway's population to remain above one thousand. Towns near Front Range cities also continued to grow, exemplified by Elizabeth whose population increased from 253 in 1950 to 1399 in 2015.[1758]

The even smaller communities with maximum populations of a few hundred or less had, in many cases, vanished by the twenty-first century. Most of the towns were founded during one of the two homestead booms in the late 1880s and the early twentieth century. At their inception, they had grand ambitions with many boasting hotels and impressive public buildings. Although most lost population over the longer-term, their fortunes waxed and waned with weather cycles, agricultural markets, and changes in railroads or highways. Towns dependent on a single business shriveled. Ovid and Sugar City, where sugar beet plants closed, each lost more than half their residents.[1759] In 2001 a *Denver Post* writer commenting on the closure of the sole grocery store in the Kiowa County hamlet of Haswell wrote, "A century after the Census Bureau stopped drawing an American Frontier line, the places where almost nobody lives haven't changed that much."[1760] While towns such as Haswell give a sense of permanence with many of the same buildings that existed as long as a century ago, the Post writer's comment is misleading. If residents of a century or even a half century ago could return, they would certainly dispute the view that the town hasn't "changed much." Long-time Haswell residents recalled population of "about three hundred" in the 1920s, and local businesses that included "two grocery stores, a hardware store, a bakery, post office, bank, hotel, butcher shop, café, garage, harness shop, drug store, lumber yard, two blacksmith shops."[1761] My father-in-law, after completing college under the GI bill, got his first teaching job at Haswell high school in the early fifties. The school was tiny—its high school graduating class consisted of six students—but it featured school colors, sports teams, and many other activities chronicled in the school's annual. Today the schools are closed and young people from Haswell and the surrounding farming areas are educated in larger towns. As the *Post* noted the combination general store/gas station/post office that served local needs in the fifties is gone. The town's population of 163 in 1950 had fallen to sixty-eight by 2015.[1762]

While most of the smaller towns faced a seemingly inevitable decline, a few were able to exploit a unique advantage. One fortunate community was Sedgwick, with a population of approximately 150, located less than ten miles from the Nebraska border. According to the *Colorado Springs Gazette*, the town's financial situation had become so dire by the early twenty-first century that community leaders discussed shutting down the local government through disincorporation. But Colorado's legalization of medical marijuana offered possible salvation. In 2012 Sedgwick passed an ordinance allowing a dispensary to open and permitted recreational sales when the state legalized them two years later. Sedgwick's location on I-76 made it easily accessible to Nebraskans crossing the border to purchase medicinal cannabis products or to partake of a few recreational tokes. Nebraska law-enforcement officials claimed that a not-insignificant portion of the purchases was transported across the border for resale. While the town is hardly booming—the latest population estimate shows only a slight change[1763]—its imminent collapse has been staved off. Townspeople are more optimistic about their community's future. The local government's financial outlook has brightened. According to the town clerk, the general fund has grown, and the municipal government invested

CHAPTER 11

in some new equipment. The proprietors of the local pot shop have plans to expand their grow operation.[1764]

The futures of many plains towns are in doubt. They have confronted the perils of a declining agricultural sector and an increasingly urbanized economy. Some achieved at least limited success. The larger towns and those within commuting distance of the Front Range metro areas will survive and, in many cases, grow. But those unable to secure new rationales for their economies face the prospect of becoming merely holding places for their aging populations.

Chapter 11 Exhibits

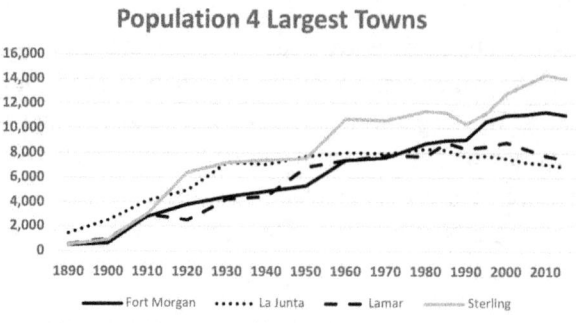

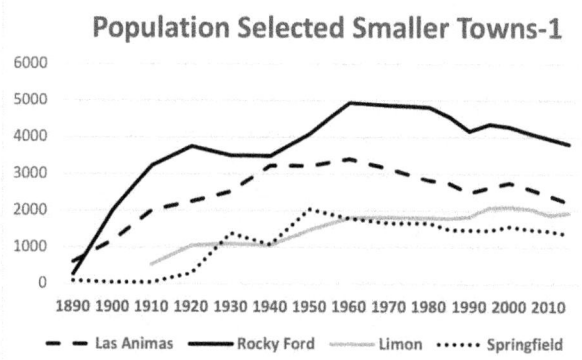

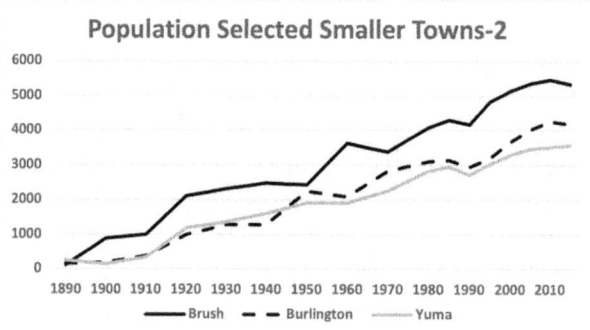

Most of the region's towns posted rapid population increases through 1920 fueled by the two waves of homesteaders. Growth slowed in the late 1920s and 1930s before resuming in the war and postwar eras. La Junta and Lamar experienced declining populations in the early twenty-first century as the Arkansas Valley economy struggled while Fort Morgan and Sterling continued to expand. Smaller communities showed a similar divergence when Yuma and Brush grew steadily while Springfield, Las Animas and Rocky Ford lost population after 1960.

Source: Census and SDO

CHAPTER 11

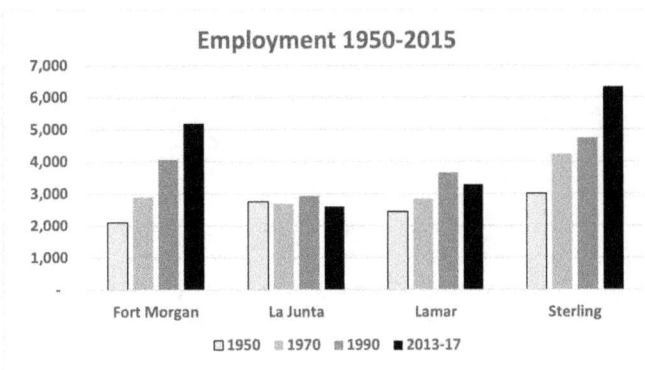

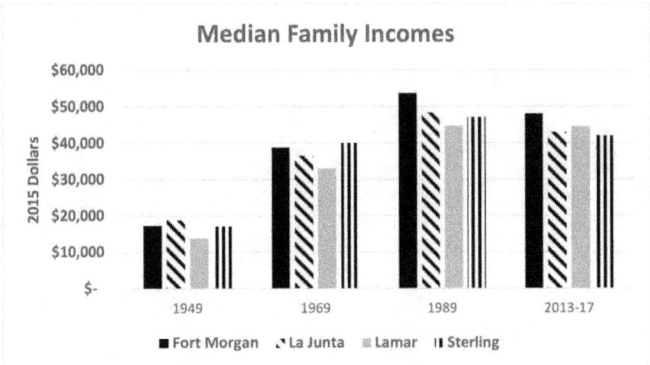

Employment grew steadily in the Fort Morgan and Sterling. Lamar's employment grew through 2000 and then declined with the loss of its largest employer. La Junta's employment has changed little since 1950.

Median family incomes were generally lower for towns in the Arkansas Valley. The highest incomes were in the smaller towns in the central and northeast plains.

Source: Census and ACS, Employment based on estimates by place of residence.

CHAPTER 12

The Eastern Plains Today

As Colorado's eastern plains approach a century and a half of significant non-indigenous settlement, its local economies confront many of the challenges facing the rest of rural America along with some others that are unique to the region. Consolidation and changes in farm organization reduced agriculture's economic contribution to local economies. Technology and foreign competition eliminated most manufacturing other than small scale operations and processors of farm products. Local retail and service jobs are shifting to urban areas. Aging populations limit labor availability and increase the cost of delivering government services. An influx of mostly Latino migrants has disrupted living patterns of residents in many communities even as it slowed the population decline. Water rights transfers to urban areas and depletion of aquifers threaten irrigated farming. Rapid growth along Colorado's Front Range reduced the political leverage of plains communities. Some local economies dealt with these trials with greater success than others. This chapter is an attempt to assess the current condition and prospects for the eastern plains economy.

The first part of this chapter relies heavily on information from the Colorado State Demography Office (SDO). As an agency of the Colorado Department of Local Affairs, Division of Local Government, SDO is a trusted source of comprehensive local demographic and economic information. Its staff has long experience dealing with Colorado's geographically diverse economies. The information SDO compiles incorporates input from local officials, businesses, citizens, and data from federal, state, and private sources. I have worked with SDO for many years in a variety of roles and feel very confident using their information.

The Structure of Plains Economies

What are the key industries in eastern Colorado in the late teens? Which contribute the most to economic growth? SDO has developed a data base that helps answer such questions. It is described as "economic base analysis" and is available for all Colorado counties on an annual basis.[1765] The data were prepared using a wide selection of economic and demographic statistics and were reviewed by local officials, planners, and industry representatives. They provide a consistent picture of the structure of Colorado's local economies.

The estimates in SDO's data base are premised on an "export base" model that assumes the driving force in a local economy is the net inflow of funds. In other words the health of the local economy is largely determined by the purchases by outside entities of locally generated goods and services and the expenditures of funds from elsewhere by residents and businesses. The dollars flowing into an economy determine its export base. When the export base increases the local economy grows; it will decline when the base is reduced. Examples of effects of changes in the export base include the burgeoning employment and population growth in Logan County during the fifties oil boom. Prowers County's slumping economy that resulted from the closure of Lamar's Neoplan bus plant in the 2000s showed a similar effect from a reduction in basic activity. In both instances the change in local employment, income and population exceeded that directly due to the change in either the oil industry or the bus plant.

SDO measures the export base of a county's economy by "basic" jobs or those generated by outside spending. Basic employment can be viewed as the "driver" of economic activity as spending by basic workers results in further employment in other industries through their local expenditures. Thus, workers in a factory whose output is sold outside its region are considered basic employees as are those providing health services through Medicare, as these are paid for by federal government funds. SDO also estimates jobs at local firms resulting from sales to business in the basic category These are call "indirect basic" jobs.

Farmers along with employees in the oil and gas industry and most manufacturing workers are obvious inclusions in the basic category as nearly all their product is purchased by outsiders. Basic jobs also include those with retailers or restaurants that sell to tourists and other visitors as well providers of services, such as legal advice or transportation, to nonresident persons or businesses. Federal and state government jobs are considered basic as they are financed by outside funds. The basic category also includes those jobs resulting from residents spending outside funds such as the earnings of commuters, government transfer payments, pensions, and income from outside investments. The following pages describe the current structure of the plains' economy as measured by SDO's economic base estimates.

Agriculture

The eastern plains economy is still heavily dependent on farming and ranching. Agriculture, along with a very small forestry and fisheries industry, was responsible for 20 percent of the regional GDP in the years 2015-17.[1766] This probably understates the industry's contribution as substantial portions of the next largest sector; finance, real estate, rentals, and leasing with 17 percent of the total, were rents and leases of farmland. Agriculture's share of GDP was approximately twice that of government and three times as large as manufacturing. SDO estimated a regional total of more than ten thousand basic jobs as farm or ranch operators or laborers including those at feed lots or hog farms. These positions, described as "agricultural production," made up 19 percent of all basic jobs in the region.

But agricultural production only includes what takes place on the farm. Other businesses such as processors of farm output or suppliers to farms and ranches are directly dependent upon agriculture, and SDO includes them in agriculture's basic employment. In 2017 there were almost nine thousand such jobs in the region. They included some thirty-three hundred workers in "processing," nearly all of them in manufacturing industries such as meat packing or sugar beet refining. "Agricultural inputs" employed thirty-six hundred workers in the manufacture or sales of farm services and products such as equipment or fertilizer. An additional eighteen hundred held jobs in "other processing and trade" such as transportation or marketing of farm products. In 2017 the agricultural sector included 35 percent of all basic jobs in the region, a total of nearly nineteen thousand.

Agriculture and related industries were vital contributors to the local economies throughout the region. In six counties, more than 50 percent of all basic workers were found in one of the agricultural sectors. In all but one of the counties a majority of these were on farms or ranches. The exception arose in Morgan County where nearly two-thirds of workers so classified were employed by processing firms, among them Cargill's meatpacking plant with almost two thousand workers, cheese producer Leprino with a work force of 420 and Western Sugar with almost two hundred.[1767] Agriculture's proportion of basic employment was greater than 20 percent in all counties except Elbert. By contrast, Metro Denver's share was only 5 percent.

Although still a vital part of local economies, agriculture's importance had diminished by the twenty-first century. Farm earnings as a share of total regional earnings in 2017 were less than half that in 1969. Even the farming-dependent counties experienced a sizable decline. Baca's farm earnings share fell from 50 percent to 17 percent and Washington's decreased from 52 percent to 21 percent.[1768] Some of this decline can be explained by poor farm earnings in 2017, but most was due to agriculture's shrinking role in local economies.

The Non-Farm Economy

Despite agriculture's importance, most regional workers made their livings in other pursuits. In 2017 only around one in seven[1769] were found on a farm or ranch although, as noted earlier, many non-farm workers were found in industries closely related to agriculture.

Although industries such as manufacturing or oil and gas production are typically cited as critical to local economies, the largest number of basic nonagricultural jobs were those labeled "household basic" by SDO. These workers were paid with outside dollars but did not directly produce a good or service for export. Their impact on the economy is similar to that of workers in the more traditional basic industries. Expenditures by a hospital worker supported by Medicare payments or one whose job is a result of spending pension funds by a retiree affect the local economy in the same way as those of a worker in a manufacturing plant. These employees accounted for 33 percent of all basic jobs in the region or eighteen thousand jobs, some eight thousand more than on farms or ranches and only slightly fewer than in the expanded agricultural category.[1770]

Retiree spending was responsible the largest number of such jobs in most counties. Retirees' impact on local economies comes from their expenditures of social security payments, other retirement income and disability benefits along with government expenditures on Medicare health services for the elderly. Most of the retiree jobs were in the trade and service industries, especially health care. Retiree jobs were 17 percent of all basic jobs and were a greater share of the total in the southeast. Their share of basic jobs in Metropolitan Denver, with its younger population, was only 13 percent.[1771]

Residents' expenditures of earnings from work outside their home counties were responsible for additional local jobs that were also included in household basic employment. The estimate of "commuter" jobs was based, not on the number of commuters, but on those jobs resulting from commuters' spending. They totaled over thirty-nine hundred in the region, nearly all of them in counties close to the Front Range population centers. Elbert County accounted for more than thirty-three hundred or 41 percent of all that County's basic jobs. An estimated 88 percent of employed residents worked outside the County, mostly in Denver and its suburbs.[1772] The importance of commuter expenditures in local economies within commuting distance of the Front Range should grow in the coming decades as more Front Range workers settle in Elbert, Morgan, Lincoln, Crowley, and Otero Counties.

Spending outside funds by younger residents also generated local jobs, among them an estimated twenty-four hundred jobs caused by expenditures of federal or state government payments to residents under sixty-five such as welfare benefits, unemployment payments and Medicaid. Another twenty-four hundred were attributed to younger residents spending their investments earnings.

The next largest group of nonagricultural basic jobs were "regional center" jobs, those providing a service to nonresident households or businesses. (Jobs due to tourist spending are in a separate category.) Regional center jobs accounted for nine thousand or 17 percent of all basic jobs in the region. These jobs resulted from treating nonresident patients at local hospitals, serving students enrolled in local colleges, or local construction firms working on projects for out-of-county entities. Nearly two-thirds of regional center jobs were in health care, many treating residents of the less populated counties lacking medical services. Logan, Morgan, and Otero Counties all with major regional trading centers, medical centers and local colleges each had more than a thousand regional center jobs as did Elbert County where most were in construction.

Government activities have been important contributors to local economies since the 1880s when towns vied for designation as county seats or sites for federal land offices. In 2015-17 government accounted for 11 percent of GDP, the largest share in the non-farm economy outside finance and leasing.[1773] Nearly five thousand government jobs were considered basic, making up 9 percent of the regional total. Most were with the federal or state government, civilian or military, or were paid for by federal or state dollars. Prisons were responsible for large numbers of basic government jobs in Bent, Crowley, Lincoln and Logan Counties. Most local government jobs were non-basic.[1774]

Jobs catering to tourists and other travelers made important contributions to several counties' economies. While the region boasted relatively few tourist sites, many travelers on I-70 or other plains highways were customers of regional motels, restaurants or gas stations. In 2017 there were eighteen hundred basic travel and tourism jobs in the region. Kit Carson and Lincoln Counties received a large economic boost from heavy highway traffic. In addition to I-70, US highways 24, 40 and 287 extend through Limon while 24, 40 and 385 traverse Burlington. Tourism contributed 8 percent of basic employment in Lincoln County and 6 percent in Kit Carson County.

Manufacturing has traditionally been viewed as an important driver of local economies and was often the prime target of economic development efforts. Its reputation is not unjustified, although often exaggerated. The industry accounted for 7 percent of the region's 2015-17 GDP,[1775] a figure that includes output of firms processing farm products. SDO allocates these processing jobs to agriculture. The rest of manufacturing had almost a thousand basic jobs or about 2 percent of the total. Otero and Prowers Counties housed significant manufacturing activity although both have lost important local employers since 2000. Almost one thousand basic jobs were found in mining, which included oil and gas production, sand and gravel quarries and supporting activities. Most these were in Logan and Morgan Counties. Although mining was responsible for only 2 percent of the region's basic jobs, it accounted for 5 percent of GDP[1776] as a small number of employees produced a highly valued output.

The fifty-four thousand basic jobs in the region were estimated to have generated an additional twenty thousand jobs. These include seven thousand indirect basic jobs. The remaining thirteen thousand are considered "local resident service" jobs, filled by workers supplying goods and services to residents. Among these are K-12 school staff, most workers at retail stores, most local government employees, and other providers of other services to residents.

The impact of changes in basic industries on the local economy will vary depending upon the extent to which workers in these industries spend their funds in the local economy and how dependent basic industries are upon local suppliers. This relationship is referred to as an "employment multiplier" defined as the change in total employment resulting from one additional job in the basic industries. As existing data do not allow calculating this incremental change, SDO estimates the employer multiplier as the ratio of total employment to direct basic employment.[1777] The employment multiplier for the eastern plains region in 2017 was 1.36. This means that each additional basic job increases total employment by 1.36 workers including the basic job and an additional 0.36 jobs elsewhere in the economy.

Employment multipliers are low for sparsely populated counties with fewer opportunities for local spending and for Elbert County where most residents' shopping and recreation take place in Metropolitan Denver. They are higher in the counties with major trading centers such as those with the larger towns in the Arkansas and South Platte Valleys. The multiplier of 1.36 for the region is well below the 2.05 estimate for Metro Denver. The difference shows how dependent the hinterlands are on the metro area for goods and services. Greater isolation from Front Range municipalities usually increases the share of local spending. Long distances limit local firms' access to markets and supplies and make big-city amenities harder to reach. A shopping trip to Denver or driving to a Bronco game and returning that evening is convenient for Fort Morgan residents but challenging for people living in Lamar. But isolation also enables local suppliers and retailers to capture a larger share of outlays by resident families and businesses. Prowers County's 2017 multiplier of 1.54 is among the highest in the region.

Although historical estimates are not available, regional multipliers for the plains counties have almost certainly become smaller over time. Labor saving technology and structural changes, greater dependence on distant supply chains and the shift to more shopping in urban areas or online are among the factors contributing to this trend. The declining impact of agriculture was discussed in chapter 10. Most other basic industries have probably experienced a similar effect and this trend is expected to continue.

What do the economic base data tell us about the structure of the regional economy in the late teens? First, agriculture is still important, but its role has diminished, a trend likely to continue. Second, the region's basic manufacturing is largely limited to agricultural processing. Third, many of the most important economic drivers are not locally based industries but expenditures by residents of funds from elsewhere. These include commuters' earnings, public and private retirement expenditures, residents' outside investments, and government transfers as well as government funding of medical services to residents. Finally, the impact of local basic industries on the region's economy, measured to by the employment multiplier, is relatively small and likely becoming smaller.

CHAPTER 12

Future Population Trends

In 2017 nearly 160,000 people lived in the sixteen plains counties. Almost half resided in the three largest counties: Elbert, Logan and Morgan, each with between twenty thousand and thirty thousand people. Latinos made up a quarter of residents, most of them in the Arkansas or South Platte Valleys. Nearly eight thousand prison inmates were also included, although most had permanent residences elsewhere. Total population was little changed from 2000, and much of the region saw more people leaving than moving in.

Recent growth trends are expected to persist. SDO prepares projections of future population for all Colorado counties based on employment forecasts and future demographic developments. SDO's 2019 projections show the region adding twenty-one thousand residents between 2017 and 2030 and another twelve thousand by 2040 with the three largest counties expected to account for nearly all the increase. Population declines are anticipated in the Arkansas Valley as well as in many of the dryland counties.[1778]

SDO projects a further loss of more than five hundred people in Baca County by 2040. County Commissioner Glen Ausmus is more optimistic. He contends that the current population of roughly one-third that in the late 1920s is "about what the land will support."[1779] In the Arkansas Valley, Prowers and Otero Counties are expected to lose population while Crowley County should add residents, as it will house an increasing number of commuters to Pueblo who move to escape rising home prices. It seems likely that some of these commuters will also settle in western Otero County.[1780] In the Central Plains, both Kiowa and Cheyenne Counties are projected to lose population while Lincoln and Kit Carson Counties grow over the next quarter century. Lincoln County will add more than seventeen hundred people as rising home prices in the Front Range cause more settlement further east along I-70.[1781] Kit Carson County is expected to add more than six hundred residents by 2040 although depletion of the Ogallala Aquifer poses some threat to future expansion. With more than a million new people in the Denver-Boulder area, Elbert County is forecast to add nearly twenty thousand to its current population of almost twenty-six thousand. In contrast to the many plains counties struggling with declining population, Elbert County's most pressing issues will involve coping with growth. In the South Platte Valley, SDO expects eighty-eight hundred new residents in Morgan County with commuters to the Front Range accounting for much of the increase. Logan County, with its diversified economy is forecast to add more than forty-five hundred people. Crop and livestock industries in the northeast are expected to remain healthy which will allow Phillips, Sedgwick and Washington Counties to retain most of their populations and Yuma County to grow by 8 percent.[1782]

Those moving out will be mostly working-age persons and their families leaving for jobs or education in urban areas and birth rates are expected to remain low. As a result, the population will, on average, continue to age, especially through the 2020s. By 2030 the share sixty-five and older will increase by three percentage points from the middle teens. Aging will slow after 2030 as the older working wage population will have been reduced by earlier outmigration. In other words, the numbers of older people will grow slowly or even decline because many residents will have left the region before they grow old.[1783]

Challenges Facing Plains Economies

In the coming decades, as over the past century and a half, eastern Colorado's rural economies will be buffeted by outside forces, many of which will be threaten their ability to prosper, or even survive. They must adapt to the new realities or face inevitable decline. As Drabenstott and Henderson of the Kansas City Fed recently wrote. "The swift currents of global markets mean that rural areas can no longer rely on old economic engines to fuel future growth."[1784] Changes in the nation's industrial structure and particularly in the farm sector have transformed the environment that eastern plains local economies must navigate. Much of past growth was driven by the provision of services to farmers and ranchers along with labor-intensive manufacturing attracted by lower costs and firms processing local farm products. But the economic impact of the agricultural sector has diminished, overseas competition has reduced the advantage of low labor costs, and opportunities for further expansion of agricultural processing are limited. In most plains communities, resident spending of public dollars may insure survival but often little more. Efforts to reverse or even stem the economic decline in plains economies have seen only limited success.

Some of the challenges facing plains communities were outlined in a recent report prepared for the Colorado Division of Economic Development and Foreign Trade by the Business Research Division of the University of Colorado Leeds School of Business. The document entitled "Rural Colorado Economic Resiliency"[1785] evaluated the robustness or lack thereof in Colorado's rural counties. As the title implies the report focused on resiliency which it defined as "the ability of an economy to withstand and recover from an exogenous shock."[1786] The plains region has endured many such shocks over the years from weather, markets, and transformations in the world economy, and more are certain in the future. The report asserted that "As Colorado communities around the state continue to confront different economic challenges, certain communities seem to demonstrate a resiliency that others do not."[1787] The report examined forty-seven rural counties in Colorado of which fifteen are on the eastern plains. (Elbert County, considered urban, was not included.) The report suggests that many eastern plains counties may lack the resiliency necessary to thrive in twenty-first century. Recent performance indicates such concern is warranted. Nine of the fifteen plains counties ranked in the lowest quartile of Colorado's rural counties based on population growth between 1990 and 2014, and eight fell in the bottom quartile of job growth over the same period.[1788] This section discusses some of the barriers that plains economies face.

Issues Confronting Agriculture

Perhaps the greatest threat to plains agriculture comes from dwindling water supplies. As discussed in earlier chapters, both surface and well irrigation have declined due to water transfers, climate change, and depletion of the aquifer. The effects of transfers are most noticeable in the Arkansas Valley. The 2017 *Census of Agriculture* reported that irrigated cropland in the four Valley counties had fallen by one-third over the previous thirty years. Losses will continue, even if no more transfers occur, since some municipalities purchasing the water often did not have an immediate need and leased it back to the farmers. Losses from transfers are aggravated by climate change that threatens to reduce snowpack and the resulting flows in the rivers. As the Ogallala Aquifer is mined, farmers' ability to irrigate in dryland counties on eastern edge of the region is being limited. Pumping from the Aquifer has caused the water level to drop by between fifty and a hundred feet since 1950 in some parts of Yuma and Kit Carson Counties.[1789]

The Colorado Water Plan,[1790] a document prepared with input from state agencies and other interests, anticipates that by 2050 irrigated acreage will decline between 8 percent and 17 percent in the Arkansas Basin, by 20 percent in the Republican Basin, and by 22 percent to 32 percent in the South Platte Basin. Growers are adjusting by making better use of reduced supplies through techniques such as drip-irrigation and the introduction of crops that need less water. But such improvements can be expensive and beyond the capabilities of many smaller operators, and their impact is limited. As a Yuma County commissioner noted, "Technology has been helping, but at some point that won't be enough."[1791]

The expected loss of irrigated acreage will be felt beyond agriculture, as is already evident in the Arkansas Valley. The northeast has so far avoided this fate, but its good fortune may not continue. As the SDO notes in its 2015 Region 1 Planning and Management Report (Region 1 includes counties in the South Platte Valley and Northeast Plains): "Over the next five to ten years, irrigated cropland in the Eastern South Platte Basin will be reduced by 150,000 acres. This reduction of cropland will have a serious direct and indirect economic impact on Northeastern Colorado. The economic impact of this loss of revenue could include fewer employees in both agricultural production and in the manufacturing plants that are dependent on agricultural production."[1792]

Along with a shortage of water, plains agriculture faces an impending shortage of farmers as today's operators are getting older, and fewer young people are coming up to take their places. This issue is faced throughout the rural economy but may be most severe in farming. In 2017 the average age of those listing themselves as "principal producers" on all eastern-plains farms was over fifty-five and exceeded sixty in Baca, Bent, Crowley, Kiowa, and Prowers Counties.[1793] Young would-be farmers need substantial capital to be competitive in today's environment, and few have the necessary resources to do so. Urban amenities have made agricultural life less attractive to many farmers' sons or daughters, and the latest squeeze on incomes has led many operators to encourage their children to pursue different careers. The opportunity to cash in on municipal demand for water rights has allowed many older operators to keep their farms and live off the proceeds from the sales but leaving little for their heirs. As forty-year Bent County farmer Kim Siefkas lamented, "What I see happening is the older people hanging on the farms a little longer, and pretty soon there aren't going to be any young people to buy them."[1794]

Transportation and Communication

Since its early settlement, the region has long been disadvantaged by its distance from major population centers, leading to higher transportation costs, lack of access to important suppliers and markets, and difficulty keeping pace with the latest developments in technology and business practice. As a result, the location of most economic activity was heavily influenced by availability of transportation. Nearly all the plains towns were founded next to rail lines. Later, location on a major highway was an important asset. But as a growing share of highway traffic has moved to the interstate system and rail service has been reduced, many towns have become less accessible. The plains counties have no commercial service airports.[1795]

But are traditional means of transportation still as important in the information-based economy of the twenty-first century? To some observers, the IT revolution seemed to hold the promise of obviating many of the handicaps of rural isolation. Location, it was hoped, would become less important with the development of the internet, and more high-productivity economic activity would migrate to lower-cost areas. The idea of "lone eagles," highly skilled workers who preferred a rural lifestyle and used computers and other technology to serve distant markets was popularized by, among others, Phil Burgess of the Denver based Center for the New West.[1796] The vision of high-six-figure-income professionals resettling in plains communities and revitalizing local economies captivated planners and economic development gurus.

But the anticipated internet-based prosperity did not occur. To the contrary, the development pattern of the American economy over the past three or so decades produced a growing regional inequality. Some communities did spectacularly well—Silicon Valley along with such Colorado cities as Boulder and Fort Collins thrived—while others lost population and jobs as high productivity firms clustered in a few prime locations. It turned out that clustering was not just a matter of transport costs and connectivity. Firms in the favored sites benefited from their ability to interact with suppliers, competitors, and customers that the internet could not fully replicate. Employers could tap a larger potential work force with the skills needed in the new economy. Economists refer to these advantages as economies of agglomeration. Drabenstott and Henderson concluded that "Research increasingly shows that locations with more agglomeration appear to be growing faster in the 21st century economy."[1797] If anything, the prospects for rural communities have deteriorated in the internet age. The population in rural lone-eagle aviaries turned out to be rather sparse. As even Burgess later concluded, "Lone eagles have always been concentrated in urban areas."[1798] Technology may someday eliminate the disadvantages of geographical isolation, but that day still seems well in the future.

But if the internet is no panacea, neither can it be ignored. Although not overcoming all rural locational disadvantages, fast and accessible on-line connections can greatly enhance a community's economic prospects in much the same manner as location on a main rail line in the late nineteenth century or proximity to the interstate highway system a hundred years later. In the 2010s the quality of service in many plains communities falls well short of what is needed in the modern economy. The result, as a recent *Wall Street Journal* article noted, is that "residents sacrifice not only their online pastimes but also their chances at a better living."[1799]

Both state and federal governments have provided funds and promise more to improve rural internet service. Despite government efforts to achieve universal high-speed service, many rural internet users still struggle with inadequate connections. The available data suggest that service for plains households, businesses and schools is at best uneven. Broadband maps of Colorado show large expanses on the plains with slow or no service while the urban Front Range enjoys premium access.[1800] This disparity, according to a recent *Denver Post* article, creates "a digital dichotomy that feeds the 'have-have not' narrative that in many ways marks the relationship between urban and rural Colorado."[1801]

Labor Availability and Quality

A shortage of skilled workers discourages opening new businesses as well as expanding or even continuing existing ones. It may seem counterintuitive that finding workers is often difficult in struggling rural communities with limited job opportunities. But emigration is concentrated among younger and more skilled working-age residents, leaving the very young, the old and the less productive. Employers face shortages of workers with the needed skills. The tight labor market in 2017 forced the manager of a Yuma County farm supply firm to employ drivers in their seventies and eighties.[1802] Jobs with educational requirements are especially difficult to fill. While an increasing number of young people graduated from college over the past several decades the education gap with urban areas widened. In middle teens 20 percent of plains residents over twenty-five had bachelors' degrees but the share in Metro Denver exceeded 40 percent.[1803]

Since few new homes have been built, particularly in the price range that most workers could afford, the condition of the housing stock makes attracting and keeping workers difficult. The CU-BRD Report noted that "The first major issue that prevents business growth is a lack of affordable housing for employees."[1804] The Report characterized much of the available housing stock in the Southeast Colorado Business Retention, Expansion & Attraction program (SEBREA) area, the Arkansas Valley counties along with Kiowa and Baca, as "uninhabitable and run down due to asbestos concerns and a lack of maintenance."[1805] Housing shortages were reported as an obstacle to business growth in Rocky Ford,[1806] Lamar,[1807] Brush[1808] and Limon[1809] and a reason for nearly one-third of the workers at Burlington's now closed private prison residing in Goodland, Kansas.[1810] Southeast Colorado Enterprise Development reports that constraints on borrowing limit the supply of new homes, resulting in a "dilapidated housing stock."[1811]

Struggling local education systems affect both the quality of labor forces and the attractiveness of communities to new residents. Depressed property values in many rural communities make funding education more difficult despite equalization efforts through the state's school finance acts.[1812] School districts with a growing migrant population lack resources for educating diverse student populations with language and cultural issues. Plains school districts, like other employers, frequently encounter difficulties attracting teachers.

In 2005 a state legislative committee report on economic development issues stated that in rural Colorado, "one of the main concerns tied to recruiting and retaining workforce professionals is the ability of an employer to offer affordable health insurance. Regarding health care professionals, the committee heard that there is an acute shortage of nurse practitioners in rural Colorado, it is difficult to recruit physicians to work in rural communities."[1813] In 2017 the *Denver Post* reported that thirteen counties in rural Colorado had no hospital and two, including Crowley County, had no doctor.[1814] Plains residents and businesses not only face a lower quality of care but also higher costs. A study conducted by the Network for Regional Healthcare Improvement surveyed spending levels of private health insurers and found those on the eastern plains the highest in the state.[1815] Small town hospitals face financial pressures as the region's older and poorer populations mean a high proportion of patients covered by Medicare or Medicaid, both with reimbursement rates that often fall short of covering costs. Along with its burden on employers and workers, the lack of a local hospital or a shortage of doctors can dissuade retirees who otherwise might be attracted by lower living costs and a less stressful rural lifestyle.

Rural communities not only face a shortage of potential employees but encounter difficulties replacing owner/operators of their current small businesses who are facing retirement, a frequent occurrence with the region's aging population. SDO's 2017 Region 5 (Central Plains) Planning and Management Report describes the plight of many small-town retailers in the central plains region:

> As small "Mom and Pop" stores that have provided basic service for years come up for sale there are few interested buyers. While such a business may still have cash flow under the original owner, that owner probably has limited debt. Added debt for the new buyer plus the impact of an ever-declining market means the continued existence of the small hardware stores and grocery stores in towns with a population under one thousand becomes doubtful.[1816]

Some barriers to attracting and maintaining a productive labor force are not measurable. The CU-BRD Report termed these "Quality of Life" issues that bring" a sense of passion for one's community, factors that cause people to stay and continue to work, even when they could leave to find different opportunities."[1817] Many would-be residents of rural towns are discouraged by the absence of such urban amenities as entertainment options, quality restaurants, exciting night life and varied shopping experiences. When my father, contemplating retirement, sought buyers to take over his Lamar firm, prospective purchasers with experience in the baking business were deterred by lack of amenities, a grievance often expressed by family members. One prospect's wife complained of having no place to shop. Plains communities have tried to sell the region's desirable qualities. The Region 6 (Southeast Colorado) Colorado Planning and Management Region Report cites efforts to attract millennials and by featuring "the attractiveness of wide-open, non-congested living conditions."[1818]

Financing Local Businesses

The closure of small-town banks, a trend that accelerated after new regulations following the Great Recession, has limited local businesses' ability to obtain loans. The number of rural counties in the US without a locally owned community bank has doubled since 1994.[1819] In 2014 Crowley and Kiowa Counties each had only one bank branch and borrowers in three other regional counties were limited to two.[1820] The *Wall Street Journal* reported in 2017 that "Even as lending revives around cities, it is drying up in small communities. In-person banking, crucial to many small businesses, is disappearing as banks consolidate and close rural branches."[1821] My experience as a rural bank director in the eighties is consistent with this finding. Our bank was too small to handle most credit needs of the German bus manufacturer Neoplan, the dominant employer in Lamar, but was an important source of financing for smaller local businesses. Local lending is especially vital for the fledgling business that provide much of the impetus for local growth. A study by Conroy, Low and Weiler, economists at University of Wisconsin, the US Department of Agriculture, and Colorado State University found that small business loans were critical for startups in rural communities. The study concluded, "county-level lending has a positive relationship with future employers' establishment births, generally, and that this result is strongest in rural (nonmetro) counties."[1822]

Social and Cultural Issues

Eastern plains residents have become increasingly alienated from their fellow Coloradans on the urban Front Range while the attitude of urbanites toward their rural brethren is often one of indifference. In 2017 more than 4.5 million people resided in the counties stretching along the eastern edge of the Rockies from the Wyoming border to Pueblo. Fewer than 135,000 people dwelled in the plains counties outside Elbert County.[1823] The people and businesses in the Front Range corridor wield economic and political power that is often feared and resented by those in outlying areas. As a recent *Denver Post* article declared, rural and urban Colorado are separated by "a chasm that reveals itself across a range of issues and clouds a collaborative vision of the state's future."[1824]

Colorado's urban-rural divide is not a new development, but it has been exacerbated by the surge immigrants to the Front Range who have few relationships with outlying areas with the possible exception of mountain resorts. Rural dependency on the Front Range metropolitan areas has grown while urban linkages with outlying counties weakened. An increasing share of spending by rural households and businesses flows to the Front Range as shown in the county economic multipliers discussed earlier in this chapter. Plains households do more shopping in Denver, Colorado Springs, or on-line and many main street stores in plains communities are being shuttered. Even the money spent at home more often goes to Walmart and other big box stores rather than local merchants. Retail is not the only sector affected. Consolidation and modern communications have made rural communities more dependent on metropolitan areas for financial, legal, and medical services. At the same time Front Range businesses rely less on products or services from outlying areas. Processing agricultural products from rural Colorado has become less important in the Denver economy. The state's sugar beet firms' Denver headquarters in that industry's heyday and the city's stockyards and packing plants, important businesses through much of the twentieth century, are no more. While Denver supermarkets still advertise Rocky Ford cantaloupes, more and more items on their shelves come from distant locations throughout the nation or the world.

Social linkages have also been transformed. Plains residents' ties to the metropolitan areas have remained and even strengthened while those of urbanites to the hinterlands have diminished. Brush residents make frequent trips to Denver while the typical Denverite's interaction with the Morgan County town is limited to a fleeting view from I-76. The share of Front Range residents who, like me, grew up in rural Colorado is shrinking. While many older plains residents have children or grandchildren in Metro

Denver, Fort Collins, or Colorado Springs, a growing number of new Front Range residents lack any family roots on the plains. As small-town newspapers have either gone out of business or drastically cut coverage, plains residents have grown to depend on Front Range media or the internet. Recreation and entertainment have become more concentrated in the large cities. Eastern plains sports fans are increasingly likely to follow the Denver Broncos more closely than the local high school football team.

As voting power shifted to the Front Range, rural Colorado experienced a sense of abandonment by state and federal governments. Ken Salazar, a prominent Colorado politician who grew up in the rural San Luis Valley, commented, "the leadership of our country, and indeed our state, has not been sensitive to the challenges of rural America."[1825] Plains and Front Range citizens' views often diverge on such issues as oil and gas regulation, water use, and gun control. The overwhelming voting power of the urban areas typically carries the day, and rural residents feel rejected and ignored. State leaders are not insensitive to rural Colorado's problems, and they are frequently cited in debates at the Capitol. But, despite efforts at reconciliation, the divide between eastern plains and Front Range seems likely to widen. This sense of alienation surfaced in 2013 when eleven rural counties, nine of them on the plains, called for a vote on the question of secession from the state of Colorado. Actual secession was extremely unlikely as it had not happened in the US in peacetime in over two hundred years. Nevertheless, the poll asking citizens whether their county commissioners should pursue steps to secede provided an opportunity for venting frustrations. As a secession advocate declared, "We just want to be left alone to live our lives without heavy-handed restrictions from the state Capitol."[1826] In the election, six of the nine plains counties voting on the issue delivered a majority-supporting secession.

The High Plains: Looking Back

Almost two centuries since Stephen Long's expeditionaries rendered their bleak assessment of the Great Plains' prospects, eastern Colorado's isolation and aridity still present formidable challenges to farmers, ranchers, business owners, and community leaders. The regional economy's trials have been further compounded by the vicissitudes of world markets and the vagaries of state and national politics. Episodes of prosperity have often been fleeting and followed by dispiriting reversals. Yet the region's economic performance since Long's excursion has not borne out those early forebodings.

Josiah Gregg, an explorer and trader on the southern plains in the 1830s, was not optimistic about the prospects for the prairies north of the Red River that today marks the border between Texas and Oklahoma. He wrote in his journal that "Unless with the progressive influence of time, some favorable mutation in nature's operations to revive the plains and upland prairies, the occasional fertile valleys are too isolated and remote to become the abodes of civilized man."[1827] Fortunately, advancing technology and the perseverance of plains residents were able bring about a "favorable mutation" even without any improvement in "nature's operations." Settlers adapted to local conditions. Farmers learned to exploit the seasonal moisture. Reservoirs and canals were built, and bountiful irrigated farming developed in the South Platte and Arkansas Valleys. Although the experience of dryland homesteaders in the late nineteenth century seemed to vindicate earlier apprehensions, farming without surface irrigation became more productive when mechanization allowed operators to cultivate more acreage. Manufacturing soon sprang up. Flour mills, sugar beet plants, and other agricultural processing operations were established in plains communities.

Twice responding to the outbreak of world war, the region's farmers helped feed the American military and much of the world, while at the same time bringing prosperity to their region, if only briefly. The economy rebounded after the devastating drought of the thirties as well as from several milder instances of destructive weather. As agriculture's boost to local economies diminished, they diversified. In the second half of the twentieth century labor-intensive manufacturing firms were drawn to the region although the local tenure of some was depressingly brief. Bountiful pastureland, plentiful feed grains, favorable costs, and the development of technology to tap underground aquifers gave rise to a ranching, grain cultivation, cattle feeding and meat processing industry in the South Platte Valley. Commuters and retirees helped sustain many local economies.

Colorado's eastern plains, like the rest of rural America, face daunting challenges. The decline of industrial areas in the Midwest has focused national attention on regional disparities in economic opportunity. But government efforts to revive rural economies have at best achieved limited success. As Nobel Prize economist Paul Krugman recently opined, "There are powerful forces behind the relative and in some cases absolute decline of rural America—and the truth is that nobody knows how to reverse those forces."[1828]

But history suggests that the region will endure. Although still vulnerable to weather and market cycles, the plains economy continues to support many healthy communities. While the more utopian visions of the region's future have not been borne out, neither have the harshest prognoses. Residents learned to cope with the plains' challenges. The history of the region's settlement as Walter Prescott Webb wrote, "is the history of adjustments and modifications, of giving up old things that would no longer function for new things that would, of giving up an old way of life for a new way in order that there might be a way."[1829] The story of Colorado's eastern plains since the first settlement by Europeans has been one of struggle and too often of failure but also of survival and, at times, prosperity as residents have managed the necessary "adjustments and modifications." There is no reason to believe that this pattern will not persist.

CHAPTER 12

Chapter 12 Exhibits

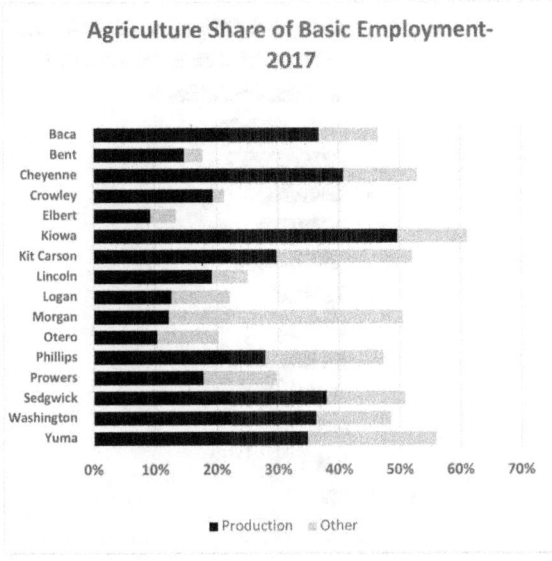

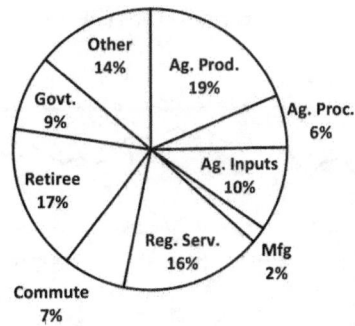

The degree of dependence on agriculture, which also includes agribusinesses such as meat packing, varies widely among the counties. It is greatest in the dryland counties as well as Morgan County with its extensive agricultural processing industry.

The economic base of the eastern plains is still heavily weighted toward agriculture which makes up more than 35 percent of all basic employment. Retiree spending contributes another 17 percent as does regional service. The latter category includes providers of services to businesses or individuals outside the region. Most commuter spending jobs are found in Elbert County. Manufacturing, excluding agricultural processing, makes up a small share everywhere.

Source: SDO

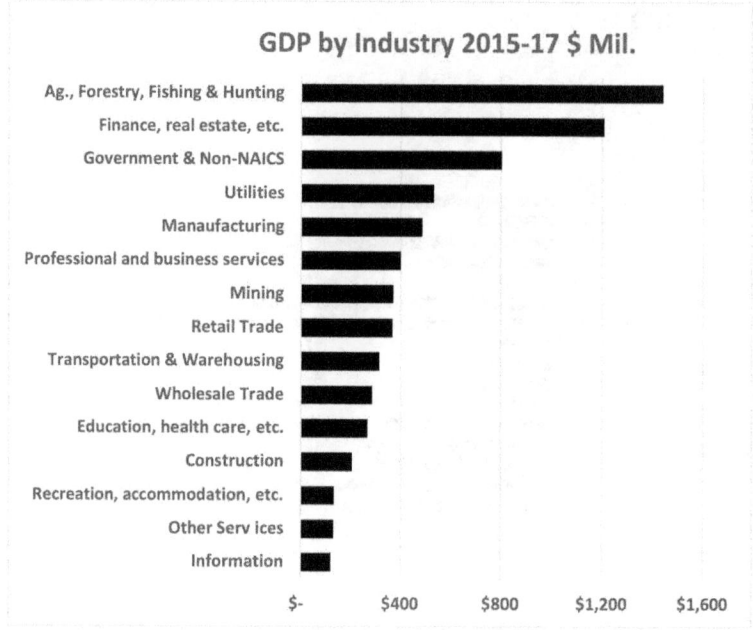

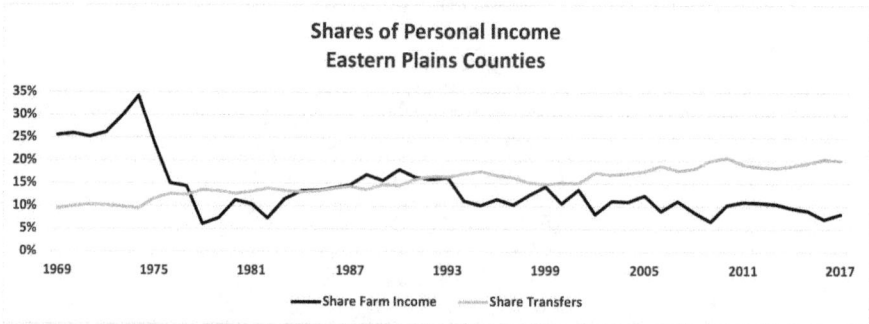

Agriculture accounted for 20 percent of the regional GDP total followed by finance and rents, government, and manufacturing. Rents on farm properties account for a sizable share of finance and rents GDP. Manufacturing includes agricultural processing.

Farm income has diminished in importance while transfer payments, that include such items as social security, Medicare, Medicaid, and income maintenance payments, have risen.

Source: BEA. GDP data were missing for some of smaller industries in a few counties. These numbers were estimated from other years' values or from 2014 value added data estimated by implant in CU-BRD report.

CHAPTER 12

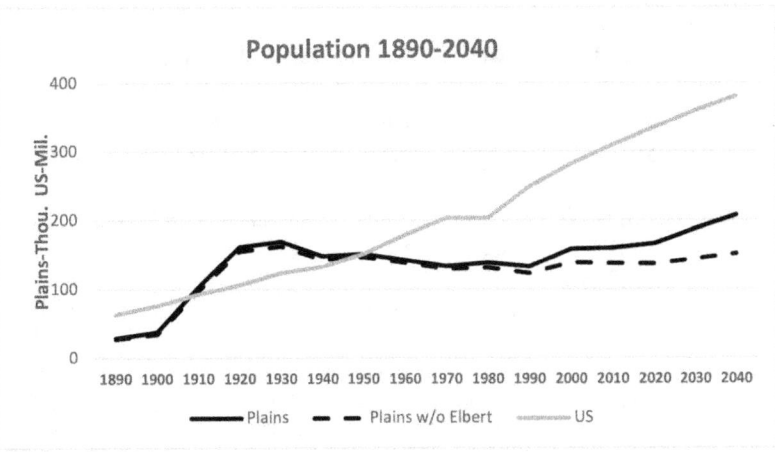

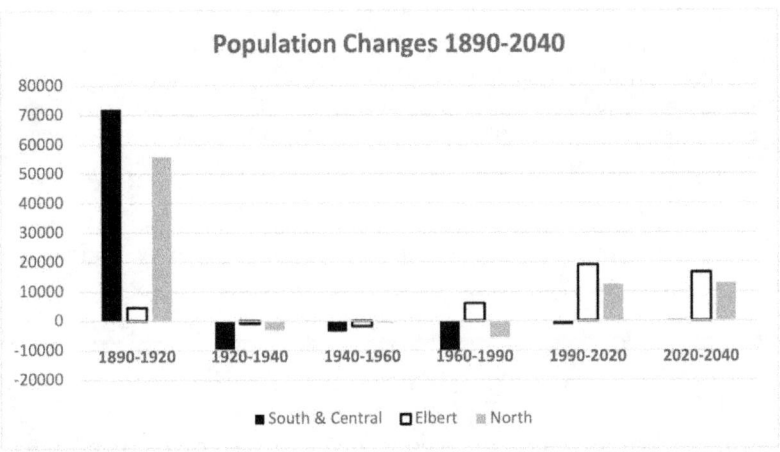

The region's fastest population growth occurred during the homestead era that ended by 1920. It slowed during the 1920s, fell markedly in the 1930s, and gradually declined through the late twentieth century. The region's population exclusive of Elbert County peaked in the 1920s and has since declined by 18 percent.

After robust growth in the late nineteenth and early twentieth centuries most of the region lost population through the next seventy years. Elbert County began to grow after 1970 and the northern counties after 1990. Future population increases are expected be largely limited to the South Platte Valley and Elbert County.

Source: County population, Census through 1960, SDO (2019) 1970-2040. US population from Census, 2015 projections. South and Central includes Baca, Arkansas Valley, Central Plains except Elbert. North includes Northeast plains and South Platte Valley.

Population Projections by County

	1990	2017	Ann Pct Ch	2030	Ann Pct Ch	2040	
Baca	5,407	3,542	-1.6%	3,258	-0.6%	3,025	-0.7%
Bent	5,944	5,835	-0.1%	5,752	-0.1%	5,631	-0.2%
Cheyenne	2,164	1,858	-0.6%	1,858	0.0%	1,749	-0.6%
Crowley	2,983	5,777	2.7%	6,256	0.6%	6,618	0.6%
Elbert	6,904	25,701	5.4%	38,117	3.1%	44,901	1.7%
Kiowa	1,948	1,364	-1.4%	1,296	-0.4%	1,205	-0.7%
Kit Carson	7,582	7,162	-0.2%	7,641	0.5%	8,264	0.8%
Lincoln	4,632	5,520	0.7%	6,559	1.3%	7,247	1.0%
Logan	19,797	21,889	0.4%	24,847	1.0%	26,543	0.7%
Morgan	22,498	28,144	0.9%	32,620	1.1%	36,930	1.2%
Otero	22,559	18,362	-0.8%	17,756	-0.3%	16,687	-0.6%
Phillips	4,533	4,292	-0.2%	4,262	-0.1%	4,187	-0.2%
Prowers	13,075	12,021	-0.3%	11,912	-0.1%	11,660	-0.2%
Sedgwick	3,256	2,319	-1.3%	2,284	-0.1%	2,194	-0.4%
Washington	5,287	4,762	-0.4%	5,007	0.4%	4,788	-0.4%
Yuma	9,697	10,037	0.1%	10,643	0.5%	10,870	0.2%
Total	138,266	158,585	0.5%	180,066	1.0%	192,498	0.7%
Total w/o Elbert	131,362	132,884	0.0%	141,949	0.5%	147,597	0.4%

Population projections show growth between 2017 and 2040 concentrated in 3 counties: Elbert, Logan and Morgan. Crowley and Lincoln Counties will experience some settlement by commuters to the Front Range. Counties in the Arkansas Valley and much of the dryland will see flat or declining populations.

Source: SDO 2019

Appendix

Description of Data Sources

Statistics covering employment, population, income, other socio-economic indicators, and various agricultural indicators are frequently cited. Different sources are cited from different years depending upon availability and quality. Below is a list of sources with brief descriptions of the series. For more detailed information consult the source agencies' web sites.

Employment

Census & American Community Survey (ACS)—A measure of workers by place of residence, i.e., the number of persons rather than jobs. It covers all employed residents and is based on samples. ACS estimates are based on a smaller sample of households so most of numbers in book were five-year averages as the samples for many counties are quite small. Decennial census data are available from 1930, ACS annually from 2002. These data are available at sub-county levels for more recent years.

QCEW—A measure of jobs by place of work. Estimates include all wage and salary employees covered by unemployment insurance. They exclude railroads and some service and nonprofits workers. Available after 1970.

SDO—A measure of jobs by place of work. Includes all wage and salary workers and an estimate of self-employed that excludes workers earning marginal income that is not from primary job. Available from 2000.

BEA—A measure of jobs by place of work. Includes all wage and salary positions and all self-employed including those not in SDO estimate. BEA includes as self-employed some workers for whom the position is not their primary job, and their earnings are quite small. Examples include those doing casual consulting work. BEA also estimates wage and salary employment. Available from 1969

County Business Patterns—A measure of jobs by place of work. Based on social security payroll taxes. Available for selected years from 1940s.

BLS—County estimates by place of residence based on allocations of the agency's household survey to the county level. Includes all employed residents. Available from 1970. BLS produces estimates of jobs by place of work based on data from employers, but these estimates are not available at the county level.

Population

Census—A count of residents based on responses from all households that can be identified. Census does extensive follow-up so nearly all residents are counted. Available every ten years from 1870 for eastern Colorado counties. Data are available for all counties in existence in Census year. Census also reports on various characteristics of population such as age, ethnic group, occupation or income, some of which is based on a sample of respondents. Census also prepares estimates for inter-census years.

ACS—Similar to Census but based on sample. Available annually from 2002. (See further discussion of ACS above.)

SDO—Estimate based on decennial Census with inter-census years estimated from SDO's data on births, deaths, school enrollments and housing stock. Benchmarked to decennial Census estimates.

BEA—Estimates of total population for inter-census years. Based on Census estimates.

Income

Census & ACS—Median incomes of resident households and families and count of households and families by income class. Available from 1949 in decennial census and annually from ACS from 2002.

BEA—Total income by all persons and earnings by industry with some industry data from smaller counties suppressed. Available from 1969.

Miscellaneous Social and Economic Indicators

Census and ACS—estimates of such variables as education, ethnic group, or household and family composition.

Colorado Yearbooks—A collection of state and local statistics from various sources compiled by Colorado Planning Commission for years 1918-1973.

Agricultural Statistics

Census—Agricultural statistics were collected as part of decennial census through 1920. For 1925 and following years they were reported by Department of Agriculture roughly every five years with occasional variation. Census reports include such data as size of farms, value of land and buildings, livestock inventories and characteristics of farm operators.

Other Department of Agriculture Data—The National Agricultural Statistical Service (NASS) produces a variety of annual, quarterly and monthly agricultural data. Some statistics are collected by Department, and some are from other sources. The are available in the annual *Agricultural Statistics* publications or from the NASS website. Endnotes on sources either cite Agricultural Statistics for data obtained from publication or USDA for those for Department's website.

Colorado Property Tax Statistics. Statistics of crop production and livestock inventory are based on data collected by County Assessors. They were published in *Colorado Yearbooks* through the early 1960s.

Migration Estimates

Estimates for the years 1930 through 1970 were calculated by applying ten-year survival and birth rates to the 1930 population and comparing the results to the actual 1940 population. In other words, the 1930s net migration estimates compared an estimate of who would have been around in 1940 if no one left with those on hand at the end of the decade. The initial "no-migration" 1940 population was then reduced by an estimate of the number of children who would have been born to women after they emigrated. Estimates for later decades were prepared in a similar manner. Mortality estimates were those for entire US population and were derived from Social Security Administration, *Life Tables for United No. 120,* 2005. Birth rates were those for white women and were derived from US HEW, Public Health Service, Department of *Fertility Tables for Birth Cohorts by Color, United States 1917-73*, DHEW Publication No. (HRA) 76-1152 (1976). SDO prepared annual migration estimates for all counties for all years from 1970. The migration estimates for the urban, non-farm rural and farm populations in chapters 7 & 8 were adjusted for the change in classification from rural-nonfarm to urban of Brush in 1960 and Burlington in 1970 when their populations exceeded twenty-five hundred. They were based on classification at the beginning of the decade.

Endnotes

Abbreviations—Newspapers
AVJ-Arkansas Valley Journal
BCD-Bent County Democrat
BR-Burlington Record
DBJ-Denver Business Journal
DP-Denver Post
DT-Denver Times
ECP-Eastern Colorado Plainsman
FMT-Fort Morgan Times
LCA- Logan County Advocate
LDN-Lamar Daily News
LJDD-La Junta Daily Democrat
LJTD-La Junta Tribune Democrat
LL-Limon Leader
NYT-New York Times
SA-Sterling Advocate
SJA-Sterling Journal Advocate
SDH-Springfield Democrat-Herald
SPH-Springfield Plainsman-Herald
SD-Sterling Democrat
SFJ-Sterling Farm Journal
SJA-Sterling Journal Advocate
SPH-Springfield Plainsman Herald
RMN-Rocky Mountain News
WG-Wray Gazette

Abbreviations—Data Sources

BEA-US Department of Commerce, Bureau of Economic Analysis

BLS-US Department of Labor, Bureau of Labor Statistics

SDO-Colorado Department of Local Affairs, State Demography Office

QCEW-US Department of Labor, Bureau of Labor Statistics, Quarterly Census of Employment and Earnings

USDA-US Department of Agriculture

Overview

1. Stenzel, Richard and Cech, Tom, *Water: Colorado's Real Gold* (Richard Stenzel, 2013), p.11
2. Lecture at University of Denver, Oct. 24, 2017
3. Quoted in Allen, John L., "The Garden-Desert Continuum: Competing Views of the Great Plains in the Nineteenth Century", Great Plains Quarterly, Fall 1985, p. 212
4. Rosenberg, Norman J., "Climate of the Great Plains Region of the United States", Great Plains Quarterly, Winter 1987, p.23
5. Wolfskill, George, "Walter Prescott Webb and the Great Plains: Then and Now", *Reviews in American History*, Vol. 12, No. 2 (Jun.,1984), pp. 296-307
6. Webb, Walter Prescott, *The Great Plains*, Grosset & Dunlap (New York, 1931). p.vi
7. Quoted in Allen, John L., *op. cit.*, p. 211
8. Powell, John Wesley, *Report on the Lands of the Arid Region of The United States: With a More Detailed Account of the Lands of Utah,* Edited by Wallace Stegner, Belknap Press of Harvard University Press (Cambridge, MA 1962).
9. Popper, Deborah Epstein and Frank J., "The Great Plains: From Dust to Dust", *Planning Magazine*, December 1987
10. *DP*, Apr. 2, 2015
11. Allen, *op. cit.*
12. Frazier, Ian *The Great Plains,* Picador Press (New York 1989, p.2
13. Schnell, J. Christopher, "William Gilpin and the Destruction of the Desert Myth", *Colorado Magazine*, spring 1969 p. 134
14. Nelson Chas. J., "Agricultural Possibilities of Eastern Colorado, Wonderful Opportunities for the Homeseeker or Investor, Lands in Yuma and Washington Counties, Colorado" circa 1910
15. Colorado Division of Commerce and Development, "Regional Profiles" for Planning and Management Regions 1, 5 and 6, 1975
16. Bent County was created in 1870 when Colorado was still a territory. It included much of the southeastern portion of the Territory. Estimate for original Bent County for 1870 includes Bent County and one-half the population of Greenwood County. Estimates for 1890 and following years include Bent, Cheyenne, Crowley (beginning in 1920), Kiowa, Otero and Prowers Counties.
17. 2015 estimate from SDO.

Chapter 1

18 Fowler, Loretta, *The Columbia Guide to American Indians of the Great Plains* Columbia University Press (New York, 2003) pp. 8-9
19 Webb, *op. cit.*, p.44
20 Bowman, Charles W., *History of Bent County*
21 Webb., *op. cit.*, p.121
22 Webb *op. cit.*, p. 88
23 Lavender, David, "Bent's Fort: Outpost of Manifest Destiny", in *Essays and Monographs in Colorado History*, No. 6, 1987, Colorado Historical Society, pp. 12-13
24 Hafen, Leroy, editor, "The W.M. Boggs Manuscript About Bent's Fort, Kit Carson, and the Far West and Life Among the Indians," *The Colorado Magazine*, Mar. 1930, p.49-50
25 Lavender, David, *Bent's Fort* University of Nebraska Press (Lincoln, 1954) pp.154-8
26 Hafen, *op. cit.*, p. 49
27 Farnham, Thomas J., 1843 *Travels in the Great Western Prairies, the Anahuac and Rocky Mountains, and in the Oregon Territory*, Reprinted by Da Capo Press, NY 1973, reported in Butler op. cit. p.116
28 Hafen, *op. cit.*, p.67
29 Butler, William B., *The Fur Trade in Colorado*, Western Reflections Publishing Company, Lake City Colorado, 2012, p.51
30 Lavender, *Bent's Fort, op. cit.* p.155
31 Cronon, William J.; Miles, George and Gitlin, Jay, "Becoming West" in *Under an Open Sky: Rethinking America's West* W.W. Norton & Company (New York 1992) p. 14
32 The Book Committee, *Bent County History* (Las Animas 1987), p. 10 & 20
33 Ellis, Richard N, "Bent, Carson and the Indians, 1965", Colorado Magazine, Winter 1969, pp 56-66
34 Garst, Shannon, *William Bent and His Adobe Empire*, Julian Messner, Inc., New York 1957
35 Knowlton, Christopher, *Cattle Kingdom, The Hidden History of the Cowboy West*, Houghton Mifflin Harcourt (New York, 2017), p.30
36 *AVJ*, June 13, 1974
37 Civil Works Administration (CWA), Interviews Conducted During 1933 and 1934, Stephen H. Hart Library and Research Center, History Colorado, Denver
38 CWA interview with Charles D. Farr, *op. cit.*, Kit Carson County
39 CWA interview with J. L. Tanner, *op. cit.*, Prowers County
40 Wells, Bud, Editor, *Logan County: Better by 100 Years: A Centennial History of Logan County Colorado 1887-1987*, Curtis Media Corporation, 1987, p. T16
41 Peake, Ora Brooks, *The Colorado Range Cattle Industry*, The Arthur H. Clark Company (Glendale, CA 1937).
42 Taylor, Ralph C., *Colorado South of the Border*, Sage Books (Denver 1963), pp.203-209

43 Accounts of the legal status of the National Cattle Trail and Trail City differ. See Betz, Ava *A Prowers County History,* The Prowers County Historical Society (Lamar, 1986), p.96 for a more in-depth discussion of this issue.
44 Peake, op. cit. p. 27
45 Knowlton, *op. cit.,* pp. 102-03
46 Wishart, David J., *The Last Days of the Rainbelt,* University of Nebraska Press (Lincoln 2013), p.41
47 Wells, Bud, Editor, *op. cit.*
48 CWA interview with J. L. Tanner, *op. cit.,* Prowers County
49 Phillips, Rufus "Early Cowboy Life in the Arkansas Valley", The Colorado Magazine, Sep. 1930, pp.165-179
50 *AVJ,* June 13, 1974
51 *AVJ,* June 4, 1970
52 Kendall, Charles, "A History of the Lamar Economy", draft for Lamar Centennial Publication (unpublished, 1986), p.2
53 Scott, P. G., "John W. Prowers, Bent County Pioneer", The Colorado Magazine Sep 1930
54 Scott, *op. cit.* p. 186
55 Merrill, George B., "Early History of Lamar, Colorado", *The Colorado Magazine,* July 1929 p. 120
56 Reported in *AVJ,* May 7, 1984
57 RMN, May 31, 1874
58 RMN Apr. 16, 1874
59 *LDN,* Jun. 7, 1966
60 *LAL,* Feb. 8, 1877
61 Sections on J.W. Prowers relied heavily on "A Pioneer Colorado Cattle King: John Wesley Prowers"-Seminar paper by Arthur R. Cook, Student at University of Colorado 1953-4; and West, Elliot, *The Contested Plains: Indians, Goldseekers, and the Rush to Colorado,* University Press of Kansas (Lawrence 1998) and Peake, op. cit.
62 Frink, Maurice; Jackson, W. Turentine; Spring, Agnes Wright; *When Grass Was King, Contributions to the Western Range Cattle Industry Study,* University of Colorado Press, Boulder 1956 p. 361
63 The section on Iliff relied on Peake and West, *op. cit.,* Bureau of Land Management, *The New Empire of the Rockies: A History of Northeast Colorado,* BLM Cultural Resources Series (Colorado: No. 16) and Wells, Dale, *The Logan County Ledger* (Logan County Historical Society, 1976), p.p. 11-12
64 Conklin, Emma Burke, *A Brief History of Logan County, Colorado* (Denver 1928) p.191
65 Steinel, Alvin T., *History of Agriculture in Colorado: 1858-1926,* State Board of Agriculture 1926, p. 135
66 *Cincinnati Enquirer,* Feb. 23, 1878
67 *LL,* Sep. 13, 1973
68 *Bent County History,* book committee, p. 280

Endnotes

69 Holly Chieftain, February 19, 1904 in CWA Interviews, *op. cit.* Prowers County
70 USDA, *1930 Annual Yearbook of Agriculture,* p.824
71 Webb *op. cit.* pp. 234-35
72 Brisbin, Gen. James S., U.S.A., *The Beef Bonanza or How to Get Rich on the Plains: Being a Description of Cattle-growing, Sheep-farming, Horse-raising, and Dairying in the West*, J.B. Libbincott & Co. (Philadelphia 1881), p. 55
73 Steinel, *op. cit.,* p. 137
74 Knowlton, *op. cit.,* pp. 70-73
75 Based on FRB New York Cost of Living Index through 2013 and CPIU thereafter
76 Steinel, *op. cit.,* p.137
77 Baxter, A.H. notes in Bent and Prowers County Cattle and Horse Growers Brand Book, Western History Collection, Denver Public Library
78 Frink, *op. cit.* p.8
79 Motherhead, Harmon, "Protection to Promotion in the Range Cattle Industry", in *A Taste of the West: Essays in Honor of Robert G. Athearn,* Pruett Publishing Company (Boulder 1983), p.78
80 Steinel, *op. cit.,* p. 139
81 Jordan, Terry G., *North American Cattle-Ranching Frontiers*, University of New Mexico Press (Albuquerque, 1993).
82 Webb, *op. cit.,* p. 239
83 Osteen, Ike, *A Place Called Baca,* Fifth edition, The Baca Weekly (Springfield, CO, 1997), p. 30
84 Baxter, *op. cit.*
85 Interview with Isaac D. Messenger, CWA Interviews, *op. cit.*, Kit Carson County
86 Schweninger, *op. cit.*, p 175
87 Wishart, *op. cit.*, p.43
88 Wishart, *op. cit.*, p.39
89 Knowlton, *op. cit.*, p.181
90 See McFerrin, Randy and Wills, Douglas, "Searching for the Big Die-Off: An Event Study of 19th Century Cattle Markets", *Essays in Business and Economic History,* Vol. XXXI 2013 an article which questions the extent of overgrazing.
91 NYT January 7, 1986
92 CWA Interviews, from Holly Chieftain, *op. cit.,* Prowers County
93 CWA Interviews, from Holly Chieftain, *op. cit.,* Prowers County
94 Stegner, Wallace, *Beyond the Hundredth Meridian,* Penguin Books (New York, 1992) p. 295
95 Bent County Soil Conservation District, from *History of Bent County*
96 Interview with C.M. Webster in CWA Interviews, *op. cit.,* Yuma County
97 Gressley, Gene M. *Bankers and Cattlemen*, Alfred A. Knopf (New York 1966).
98 Census 1880
99 Steinel, *op. cit.,* p. 147
100 Census 1880, v3-20, pp. 48-54
101 Steinel, *op. cit.,* pp. 148-49

102 Wells, Dale, *op. cit.*, p. 43
103 AVJ, Jul. 1, 1954
104 *Bent County History,* book committee, *op. cit.*, p. 282
105 Bureau of Land Management, *The New Empire of the Rockies: A History of Northeast Colorado,*
BLM Cultural Resources Series (Colorado: No. 16).
106 Webb. op. cit. p. 226
107 Phillips, *op. cit.*
108 Scott, *op. cit.*
109 Robert William Fogel, *Railroads and American Economic Growth: Essays in Econometric History* (Baltimore: Johns Hopkins Press, 1964
110 Webb, *op. cit.*, p. 274
111 Greever, William S. "A Comparison of Railroad Land-Grant Policies", Agricultural History, Apr. 1951, p.84
112 For example, see trinityhistory.org
113 Greever, *op. cit.*, p. 85
114 Athearn, Robert G., *The Coloradans,* University of New Mexico Press (Albuquerque 1976), p. 78
115 English, Don, *The Early History of Fort Morgan, Colorado,* Fort Morgan Heritage Association, 1975, p. 18-19
116 Mercer, Lloyd J., "Land Grants to American Railroads: Social Cost or Social Benefit?", *The Business History Review* (Summer, 1969), pp. 134-151
117 Mock, S.D., "The Financing of Early Colorado Railroads", *Colorado Magazine,* November 1941 p. 208
118 Poor, *Manual of the Railroads of the United States, 1873-74,* p. lii, cited by Webb p. 278
119 White, Richard, *Railroaded: The Transcontinentals and the Making of Modern America,* W.W. Norton & Company, Inc., New York, 2011, pp. 192-93
120 White, *op. cit.*, p. 373
121 The Kansas Pacific was known as the Eastern Division of the Union Pacific until 1863 although it was an independent entity. It became part of the Union Pacific in 1880. Such changes of ownership and confusing titles were typical for late nineteenth century western railroads.
122 Bryant, Keith L. Jr., *History of the Atchison Topeka and Santa Fe Railway,* University of Nebraska Press (Lincoln 1974), p.37
123 Taylor, *op. cit.*, p. 332
124 Taylor, *op. cit.*, p. 337
125 Hauk, Cornelius W., "La Junta, The Santa Fe's Colorado Connection", in *Santa Fe and the Intermountain West,* Colorado Rail Annual No. 23, Colorado Railroad Historical Museum
126 Due to bankruptcies, acquisitions and organizational changes the names of the railroad companies changed frequently and often. Sometimes the name in which a rail line was registered in Colorado did not correspond to the national firm that

controlled it. Here an attempt was made to use the name of the controlling company in the late nineteenth century.
127 Greever, *op. cit.*, p. 90
128 Byers and Parker, "Choice Farming, Grazing, Coal and Timber Land in Colorado along the Kansas Pacific and Denver Pacific Railways" (Denver 1873) p. 2
129 Union Pacific Land Company, "Eastern Colorado and Denver Outskirts in the Big Development Race", circa 1906
130 Byers and Parker, *op. cit.*, p. 15
131 Jones, James R. and Collman, Russ, *Sterling Colorado: Crossroads on the Prairie*, Sundance Books (Denver 2000), p. 35
132 BLM, *Northeast Colorado, op. cit.*, p. 4
133 Garver, Bruce, "Immigration to the Great Plains, 1865-1914: War, Politics, Technology, and Economic Development", Great Plains Quarterly, Summer 2011, p.192
134 W.E. Webb, "Air Towns and Their Inhabitants", Harper's Magazine 1875 quoted in Hudson, John C. "Towns of the Western Railroads", Great Plains Quarterly, Winter 1982, p.42
135 Klein, Murray, *Union Pacific: Birth of a Railroad 1862-1893*, Doubleday & Company, Inc. (Garden City, NY, 1987), p.101
136 Quoted in Monahan, Doris, *Julesburg and Fort Sedgwick: Wicked City—Scandalous Fort* (Sterling, CO 2009), p.170
137 Klein, *op. cit.*
138 Monahan, *op. cit.*, p.175
139 *Las Animas Leader*, Jul. 20, 1873
140 *LDN*, June 14, 1973
141 Dary, David *The Santa Fe Trail*, Alfred A. Knopf (New York, 2000), p.289
142 *Las Animas Leader*, Dec. 26, 1873
143 Cited by C. Kendall, *op. cit.*, p.3
144 Athearn, *High County Empire, op. cit.*, p.159
145 Taylor, *op. cit.*, p. 254
146 Fell, James E, Jr., *Limon Colorado: Hub City of the High Plains, 1888-1952*, Limon Heritage Society, 1997, p. 8
147 DP, Jun. 10, 2001
148 Taylor, *op. cit.*, pp. 330-337, and Hockmeyer, M. F., "Don Miguel Antonio Otero 1829-1882", Otero County Genealogy and History
149 White, *op. cit.*, p. 488

Chapter 2
150 Census
151 *NY Tribune*, Feb. 18, 1854, cited by Smith, Henry Nash, *Virgin Land*, Vintage Books (New York 1950), p.234
152 Harris, Katherine, *Long Vistas: Women and Families in Colorado Homesteads*, University of Colorado Press, Niwot 1993. p.49

153 Betz, *op. cit.*, p.104
154 J. T. Kearns based on *Wray Republican*, Jul. 12, 1889, CWA Interviews, *op. cit.*, Yuma County
155 Centennial Farms documentation at Colorado History Museum.
156 *Smith, Henry Nash, Virgin Land, Vintage Books (New York 1950)*, p.147
157 Wishart, *op. cit.*, p. 19
158 Wishart, *op. cit.*
159 Interview with Henry Wells, CWA Interviews, *op. cit.*, Yuma County
160 Smith, *op. cit.*, pp.209-212
161 Emmons, David M., *Garden in the Grasslands: Boomer Literature of the Central Great Plains,* University of Nebraska Press (Lincoln, 1971), p.158
162 Emmons, *op. cit.*, p. 159
163 "Boards of Immigration" in Wishart, David J., editor *The Encyclopedia of the Great Plains,* University of Nebraska Press (Lincoln 2004).
164 Elbert County in 1880 also included today's Kit Carson County and those parts of Lincoln and Cheyenne Counties not in Bent County
165 Census
166 Steinel, *op. cit.*, p. 255
167 *Bent County Leader,* June 15, 1889
168 Interview with Wallace Hoze Wilcox, CWA, *op. cit.*, Kit Carson County
169 Harris, *op. cit.*, p.59
170 Interview with Wallace Hoze Wilcox, CWA, *op. cit.*, Kit Carson County
171 Schweninger, Lee, editor, *The First We Can Remember: Colorado Pioneer Women Tell Their Stories,* University of Nebraska Press (Lincoln 2011), p.154
172 Harris, *op. cit.*, p. 50
173 Schweninger, *op. cit.*, p. 125
174 Johnston, M.D., "Eastern Colorado Fifty-seven Years Ago", Colorado Magazine, May 1944, pp.116-118
175 bauderhistory.com, "TheBirthoftheGermanSettlement.pdf"
176 Harris, *op. cit.*, p.65
177 Many early Colorado migrants came for relief from respiratory diseases.
178 *Lamar Register,* Sep. 23, 1893
179 Betz, *op. cit.* pp.108-120
180 Wells, Dale, *op. cit.*, p.38
181 Cather, Willa, *O Pioneers!,* Kindle Edition, Loc .156
182 Fort Sedgwick Historical Society, *The History of Sedgwick County, Colorado* (1982) p. 142
183 *History of Sedgwick County, op. cit.*, p. 142
184 FMT, May 31, 1968
185 Schafer, Thomas C., "Specialization and Diversification in the Agricultural System of Southwestern Kansas, 1887-1980", in Char Miller, editor, *Fluid Arguments: Five Centuries of Western Water Conflict,* University of Arizona Press (2001), p. 207

Endnotes

186 Dunbar, Robert G., "Agricultural Adjustments in Eastern Colorado in the Eighteen-Nineties", *Agricultural History,* Jan. 1944, p. 43
187 Interview with Timothy Burns, CWA Interviews, *op. cit.,* Yuma County
188 Bent County Soil Conservation District, from History of Bent County, *op. cit.*
189 McHendrie, A. W., "Boyhood Recollections of Springfield, Colorado", *Colorado Magazine,* 1944 pp 93-100
190 1890 Census Vol.5 pp 102-135
191 *RMN,* Jan. 2, 1891
192 *RMN,* Jan. 8, 1891.
193 Dunbar, Agricultural Adjustments, *op. cit.,* p. 46
194 Wishart, *op. cit.* p xvi
195 Some sources date the dry years to the early 1890's. The notes from the Census cited here suggest that, at least in eastern Colorado, the drought began somewhat earlier.
196 Average of weekly quotations for No. 2 or better from reports of Chicago Board of Trade, Source: Agricultural Statistics 1936 Table 37
197 Letter from Lelia Walters, CWA Interviews, *op. cit.,* Kit Carson County
198 Census
199 McMath, Robert C. Jr., *American Populism,* Hill and Wang (New York 1993), p.126
200 Jordan op. cit. p. 267-9
201 *History of Sedgwick County, op. cit.,* p. 142
202 Limerick, Patricia Nelson, *The Legacy of Conquest: The Unbroken Past of the American West,* W.W. Norton & Company-Kindle Edition (New York 1987), loc. no.2078
203 *LDN,* Sep. 21, 1982
204 Powell, *op. cit.,* p.20
205 Aiken, J. David, "Development of the Appropriation Doctrine: Adapting Water Allocation Policies to Semiarid Environs", *Great Plains Quarterly,* Winter 1988
206 Powell, *op. cit.,* p.16
207 See Emmons, David M., *Garden in the Grasslands: Boomer Literature of the Central Great Plains,* University of Nebraska Press (Lincoln, 1971), pp. 175-82
208 McHendrie, A. W., "The Early History of Irrigation in Colorado and the Doctrine of Appropriation" in The Colorado Water Conservation Board, *A Hundred Years of Irrigation in Colorado* (1952) p.17
209 Hobbs, Gregory J., Jr., "Colorado Water Law: An Historical Overview", *University of Denver Water Law Review,* Fall 1997, p.8
210 McHendrie, A. W., Irrigation, *op. cit.* p.15
211 Stenzel, and Cech, *op. cit.,* pp. 51-3
212 Wells, Dale, *op. cit.,* p. 17
213 Stenzel and Cech, *op. cit.,* p.130
214 Van Hook, Joseph O., "Development of Irrigation in the Arkansas Valley", *Colorado Magazine,* Jan. 1933, p. 8
215 Census

216 Sherow, James Earl, *Watering the Valley, Development along the High Plains Arkansas River, 1870-1950.* University of Kansas Press (Lawrence, Kansas 1990) p.18
217 Harris, *op. cit.*, p.44
218 Pisani, Pisani, Donald J., *To Reclaim a Divided West: Water, Law and Public Policy, 1848-1902*, University of New Mexico Press (Albuquerque 1992), p. 105
219 Fortier, Samuel, "The Greatest Need of Arid America", in *Official proceedings of the Fifteenth National Irrigation Congress* [Sacramento 1907] quoted in Pisani *op. cit.* p. 105
220 Sherow, Utopia, *op. cit., p. 167*
221 Census 1890, vol. 5 p. 120
222 Census 1890, vol. 5, p. 126
223 Stenzel and Cech, *op. cit.* p.147
224 Hamman, A. J., "Theodore C. Henry—Champion Irrigation Project Promoter", in The Colorado Water Conservation Board, *A Hundred Years of Irrigation in Colorado* (1952), p.82
225 Woodka, Chris "Taming the Land" Series of articles about development of Arkansas Valley published in Pueblo Chieftain (2008-09), March 8, 2009
226 Stenzel and Cech, *op. cit.* p.155
227 Stenzel and Cech, *op. cit.* p.150
228 LDN, Jan. 23, 1965
229 Sherow, James E., "Utopia, Reality, and Irrigation: The Plight of the Fort Lyon Canal Company in the Arkansas River Valley", *Western Historical Quarterly*, May 1989, p.170
230 The information on the Fort Lyon Canal is from Sherow, *Valley, op. cit.*, pp.17-19 and Utopia, *op. cit.*, and from article by Arthur C. Gordon, a long-time attorney for the Canal in the *LDN*, Jan. 23, 1965
231 Chapman Publishing Company, *Portrait and Biographical Record of the State of Colorado,* , Chicago 1899 pp. 286-7
232 English, History, *op. cit.*, p. 17
233 English, History, *op. cit.*, p. 17
234 FMT Dec. 19, 1907
235 FMT, May 23, 1967
236 FMT, Feb 21, 1896
237 *Denver Times,* Dec. 31, 1891
238 Sherow, *op. cit.*, p. 17
239 *History of Sedgwick County, op. cit.*, p. 138
240 Markoff, Dana, "A Bittersweet Saga: The Arkansas Valley Sugar Industry, 1900-1979", *Colorado Magazine*, Summer/Fall 1979
241 May, *op. cit.*, pp. 288-9
242 May, William J. Jr., *The Great Western Sugarlands: History of the Great Western Sugar Company,* Thesis (Ph. D.), University of Colorado at Boulder, 1982, pp. 285-86
243 Wells ed., Logan County, *op. cit.*, p. 50
244 Jones and Collman, *op. cit.*, p.57

Endnotes

245 SD, Mar. 14, 1912
246 Census
247 These data cover all counties in the state and include, for the irrigated counties, all farms including those without irrigation. Thus, they include effects from factors other than irrigation.
248 Sherow, *Utopia, op. cit.,* p.170
249 Sherow, *Watering, op. cit.* pp.28-29
250 Woodka, *op. cit.,* March 22, 2009
251 "Rocky Ford" in CWA Interviews, *op. cit.,* Otero County,
252 Stenzel and Cech, *op. cit.* p.130
253 Woodka, *op. cit.,* Mar. 22, 2009
254 Source: 1900 Census
255 Woodka, *op. cit.,* March 8, 2009

Chapter 3

256 *Agricultural Statistics,* Wheat price is Chicago Range No. 1 Northern Spring and No. 2 Red Winter
257 Census
258 Frazier *op. cit.,* p.195
259 Source: 1890-1950, BLS, *Handbook of Labor Statistics,1950 edition*
260 Census
261 Passenger Department, Missouri Pacific Iron Mountain, *Eastern Colorado, Its Opportunities and Resource-A New Region Opened to Agriculture by the Development of Dry Farming and Irrigation-Reliable Facts for Homeseekers* (1908), p.7
262 Wells, Dale, *op. cit.,* p. 77
263 Garver, Bruce, "Immigration to the Great Plains, 1865-1914: War, Politics, Technology, and Economic Development", *Great Plains Quarterly,* Summer 2011, p.186
264 Nelson, Charles J., *Agricultural Possibilities for the Homesteader or Investor, Lands in Yuma and Washing Counties, Colorado.* (1910), p.1
265 Missouri Pacific, *Eastern Colorado* op. cit. p.5
266 Mohl, Fred, General Traveling Agent, Amity Canal Co. *About Farming by Irrigation Under the Amity* (Circa 1900), p.3
267 Clarey Land Company, *Golden Prairie Lands, Washington County Colorado,* Akron 1909 p.2
268 Blodgett, op. cit.
269 1909 Session Laws of Colorado
270 Annual Report of the Colorado State Board of Immigration-1916, p.7
271 *History of Kit Carson County, op, cit.,* p. 22
272 Interview with Horace B. Davis in CWA Interviews, *op. cit.,* Logan County
273 *Lamar Register,* December 29, 1915. The Lamar District included Baca, Bent, Cheyenne, Kiowa, Las Animas, Lincoln and Prowers Counties.
274 Census of Agriculture

275 Osteen, *op. cit.,* p. 59
276 *Lamar Register,* Jul. 12, 1916
277 Census of Agriculture
278 *Kiowa County* Bicentennial Committee, *Kiowa County,* Johnson Publishing Company (Boulder 1976), *op. cit.* p.65-6
279 Centennial Farms Documentation, Colorado History Museum
280 Durrell, Glen R., "Homesteading in Colorado", *Colorado Magazine* Spring 1974, pp 93-114
281 The section on Paulson was based on Betz, *op. cit.,* pp. 339-341
282 Stenzel and Cech, *op. cit.,* pp. 133-138, and Betz, *op. cit.,* pp. 127-143
283 Cunfer, Geoff, *On the Great Plains: Agriculture and Environment,* Texas A&M University Press (College Station 2005), p. 114
284 Miner, H. Craig, *Harvesting the High Plains: John Kriss and the Business of Wheat Farming, 1920-55,* University Press of Kansas (Lawrence 1998), p.21
285 Wells ed., Logan County, *op. cit.,* p. 68
286 Census
287 *Progress of Farm Mechanization,* Miscellaneous Publication No. 630, October 1947, and Economic Research Service, *Labor Used to Produce Field Crops,* Statistical Bulletin No. 364, May 1964
288 Census
289 Cottrell, H.M., *Dry Land Farming in Eastern Colorado,* Bulletin 145, Experiment Station (Fort Collins, 1910), p.4
290 Cottrel, H.M., *Dry Farming in Eastern Colorado,* Passenger Traffic Department, Rock Island Lines, Chicago 1910, p.23 V
291 Johnson, Vance, *Heaven's Tableland: The Dust Bowl Story,* Farrar, Straus and Company (New York 1947), pp. 82-3
292 Cunfer, *op. cit.,* pp. 100-101
293 Census
294 Census
295 Colorado Yearbook, *op. cit.*
296 *Agricultural Statistics 1942,* Tables 183 & 187
297 May, *op. cit,* p.77
298 May, *op. cit.,* p. 189
299 Markoff, Dena S., "The Sugar Industry in the Arkansas River Valley: National Beet Sugar Company", *The Colorado Magazine,* Winter 1978, p. 78
300 Markoff, Dena S., *op. cit.,* pp. 82-83
301 Markoff, Dena S., "A Bittersweet Saga", op. cit., pp. 165-68
302 Markoff, "A Bittersweet Saga", *op. cit.* p. 168
303 La Junta Tribune, Feb. 15, 1908
304 *FMT,* Oct. 16, 1903
305 Hamilton, Candy, *Footprints in Sugar: A History of the Great Western Sugar Company,* Bates Publishers (Ontario, Oregon 2009), p. 61
306 May, *op. cit.,* p. 45

307 May, *op. cit.*, pp. 67-8
308 DT, Dec 23, 1902
309 LCA, Sep. 22, 1904
310 LCA, Dec. 15, 1904
311 LCA, Dec. 22, 1904
312 LCA, Mar. 9, 1905
313 LCA, Oct. 26, 1905
314 LCA, Dec. 21, 1905
315 FMT, Apr. 6, 1900
316 FMT, Feb. 13, 1903
317 FMT, Feb. 13, 1903
318 FMT Feb. 13, 2003
319 Darley, Ward, *Sugar: The Tariff, The Trust and The Truth* (Denver, The Author, 1913), p.17
320 FMT, Sep. 1, 1905
321 May, *op. cit.*, based on *Greeley Tribune*, Feb. 26, 1907
322 FMT Oct. 7, 1909 reproduced in FMT Oct. 3, 2014
323 "Observations about Longmont, Colorado", http://longmontian.blogspot.com/2010/01/brush-colorado-sugar-factory.html
324 Mills, James E., *A History of Brush, Colorado*, M.A. Thesis, University of Colorado, 1964, p. 31
325 Mills, *op. cit.* p.51
326 Darley, *op. cit.*, p.16-17
327 *Census of Agriculture*
328 Kessler, H.H.., *Lamar Colorado Its First Hundred Years: 1886-1986*, pp.25-26
329 Lamar Centennial, Inc., *op. cit.*, p. 25
330 Betz, *op. cit.*, p. 308
331 LCA, Jul. 4, 1907
332 Wells, Dale, *op. cit., p. 53*
333 *The WPA Guide to 1930s Colorado,* University Press of Kansas (Lawrence 1987), pp.201-02
334 *FMT,* May 10, 1985
335 This paragraph is based on May, *op. cit.*, pp. 355-361
336 Wells ed., *Logan County, op. cit.,* p. T19
337 Wells ed., *Logan County, op. cit.,* p. 264
338 Kloberdanz, Timothy J., People Without A Country: The Russian Germans of Logan County. Colorado, in D. Wells, *op. cit.,* p. 232
339 May, *op. cit.*, p.287 and p. 290
340 May, *op. cit.*, pp. 159-60
341 May, *op. cit.*, p.77
342 SD, Nov. 8, 1917
343 *Agricultural Statistics 1936,* Table 120
344 *Rocky Mountain Banker,* January 1924

345 Betz, *op. cit.*, p.378
346 May, *op. cit.*, p. 292
347 Based on Assessors' data, *Colorado Yearbook 1922*
348 Census
349 SD, July 12, 1917.
350 Lamar Centennial, *op. cit.*, p.115
351 Census
352 Egan, *op. cit.*, p. 42
353 Hewes, Leslie, "Early Suitcase Farming in the Central Great Plains", *Agricultural History*, Jan. 1977, p. 24
354 Source: Colorado Assessors Data, *Colorado Yearbook 1925*
355 DP Aug. 27, 1942
356 Source: 1920 Colorado Yearbook, 1931 Colorado Agricultural Statistics, cited in Harper, *op. cit.*, Appendix Table 6. Different sources provide alternate estimates but all show dramatic increase in acreage.
357 Pickle, J.W., "History of WrayMill", manuscript in Denver Public Library, Western History Collection (1907).
358 Kendall, C, *op. cit.*, pp.5-6
359 Source: *Colorado Yearbook*
360 Source: Assessors data from *Colorado Yearbook 1921*, p.47
361 Census
362 No. 3 Yellow, Average of Daily Prices, Chicago Board of Trade, *Agricultural Statistics 1936*, Table 37
363 All acreage and production figures are from the Census.
364 Osteen, *op. cit.*, p. 82
365 Schlebecker, John T. *Raising Cattle on the Plains 1900-1961,* University of Nebraska Press (Lincoln 1963) p. 163
366 Lamar Register, January 3, 1917
367 Lamar Register, January 20, 1915
368 Christie, *op. cit.*
369 Much of the information on the alfalfa milling industry comes from Robert Christie, "The Denver Alfalfa Milling & Products Company, 1908-1946" (Lamar 1965), "Floyd M. Wilson and the Alfalfa Milling Industry", *Colorado Magazine* 1944 pp. 100-101 and National Alfalfa Dehydrating and Milling Co., a report prepared by the company and found at the Big Timbers Museum in Lamar.
370 *Pueblo Chieftain,* Dec. 10, 1944
371 Lamar Register, January 3, 1917
372 Dunar, Robert G., "History of Agriculture" in *Colorado and Its People: A Narrative and Topical History of the Centennial State,* Hafen, LeRoy R. editor, Lewis Historical Publishing Co., Inc. (New York, 1948) p. 144
373 Christy, Robert "The Denver Alfalfa Milling & Products Company 1908-1946" Unpublished Manuscript (1965), p.36
374 Census

Endnotes

375 Census of Agriculture
376 LDN Jul. 24, 1939
377 Census of Agriculture, 1925
378 Sheflin, Douglas, *Legacies of Dust: Land Use and Labor on the Colorado Plains*, University of Nebraska Press (Lincoln, 2019), p. 35
379 *Mountain States Banker*, Jan. 1926
380 Census 1930
381 Woodka, *op. cit.*, Mar. 22, 2009
382 Scamehorn, Lee, *Colorado's Small Town Industrial Revolution: The Arkansas Valley and the Western Slope*, Dog Ear Publishing (Indianapolis 2012), pp.47-48
383 Scamehorn, *Small Town, op. cit.*, pp. 29-32
384 Scamehorn, *Small Town, op. cit.*, p.50
385 *Bent County History*, book committee, p.499
386 Census
387 SD, Nov. 12, 1916
388 Wells, Dale, *op. cit.*, pp. 56 and 102
389 May, *op. cit.*, pp. 150-154
390 Census
391 *Lamar Register*, Mar. 3, 1915
392 *Rocky Mountain Banker*, Jun. 1930
393 Census
394 Census of Agriculture
395 US Department of Agriculture, Average price received per cwt
396 Census
397 Cottrell, op. cit., p.10
398 Census of Agriculture
399 Cunfer, *op. cit.*, p. 5

Chapter 4

400 Dary, David *The Santa Fe Trail*, Alfred A. Knopf (New York, 2000) p.289
401 Interview with William Leroy in CWA Interviews, op. cit., Otero County
402 Taylor, "Town Boom", op. cit.
403 *LDN*, Jul. 2&3, 1965
404 *LDN*, Mar. 13, 1965
405 Interview with C.C. Huddleston in Prowers County, CWA Interviews, *op. cit.*
406 Bent County History, book committee, *op. cit.*, pp. 81-83
407 *Rocky Mountain Banker*, June 1924
408 Gordon, Robert A., *The Rise and Fall of American Growth*, Princeton University Press (Princeton, 1916) p.555
409 *FMT*, August 11, 1902
410 *Yuma Pioneer*, July 4, 1913
411 Keck, Frances Bollacker, *Conquistadors to the 21st Century: A History of Otero and Crowley Counties Colorado*, Otero Press (La Junta 1995) , *op. cit.*, p. 180

412 Keck, *op. cit.,* p. 203
413 Wells, Dale, *op. cit.,* p. 58
414 Colorado State Planning Commission, *Development of Electric Power Industry in Colorado: 1916-1936* (Denver, 1938), p.5
415 Hershberger, Forrest, *Images of America, Sterling,* Arcadia Publishing (Charleston, SC, 2011), p.27
416 *Lamar Colorado 1986, op. cit., pp. 27 & 43*
417 *West Yuma County History, op. cit.* p.15
418 Colorado State Planning Commission, *op. cit.*
419 Census
420 CWA Interview with Rufus Phillips, op. cit., Otero County
421 CWA Interview with Burt Ragan, *op. cit.,* Kit Carson County
422 Penley, Gary, *Rivers of Wind: A Western Boyhood Remembered,* Filter Press (Palmer Lake, Colorado 1998).
423 *Colorado Yearbook 1918*
424 Neither auto repair nor publishing are classified as manufacturing industries in the current North American Industrial Classification System (NAICS) currently in use.
425 Wells, ed., *Logan County, op. cit.,* p.T12
426 Source: *Colorado Yearbook 1918*. Population estimate based on interpolation between 1910 and 1920 figures. The 1928 figure includes only automobiles owned by individuals.
427 *Bent County History*, book committee, *op. cit.*, pp.81-83
428 Kiowa County Bicentennial Committee, *op. cit.,* p. 263
429 Fell, *op. cit.,* p. 10
430 *Bent County History*, book committee, *op. cit.*, pp.81-83
431 Betz, *op. cit.,* pp. 264-5
432 Census; 1870 based estimates of Bent and Greenwood Counties
433 Taylor, *op. cit.*, pp.253-258. Today's Baca County was part of Las Animas County prior to 1889. Taylor cites a 6,000 peak population while Harper, Thomas Alan, *The Development of a High Plains Community: A History of Baca County*, Colorado, M.A. Thesis, University of Denver, 1967, estimates peak population at 3,000.
434 Newspaper article by Marsena McMillin 1892 reported in *Lamar Colorado Its First Hundred Years: 1886-1986,* Lamar Centennial, Inc. p.7
435 Betz, *op. cit.,* p.74
436 Betz, *op. cit.,* p.219
437 The 1870 and 1880 figures are not strictly comparable as Bent County boundaries had changed.
438 Census
439 Goldin, Claudia and Katz, Lawrence F., *The Race between Education and Technology,* Harvard University Press (Cambridge, MA 2008), p.11
440 Goldin, *op. cit.,* pp.205-8
441 The Book Committee, *op. cit.* p. 222
442 *Bent County History,* book committee, *op. cit.,* p. 10

Endnotes

443 Wells ed., *Logan County, op. cit.*, p. 72
444 Osteen, *op. cit.*, pp. 60-61
445 Interview with Mrs. J. M. Johnston, CWA interviews, *op. cit.*, Prowers County
446 Goldin, Claudia, "A Brief History of Education in the United States", NBER Historical Paper 199, National Bureau of Economic Research (Cambridge, MA 1999) p.11
447 *Industrial Edition of La Junta Tribune*, 1915, cited in *AVJ*, Jul. 2, 1970
448 *History of Sedgwick County, op. cit.*, p. c97-98
449 Betz, *op. cit.* p.294
450 Goldin and Katz, *op. cit.* p.166
451 Colorado Department of Education from *1918 Colorado Yearbook*
452 Census
453 Bent County was divided into 5 counties in 1889.
454 Taylor, Morris W., "The Town Boom in Las Animas and Baca Counties", *Colorado Magazine*, Spring/Summer 1978, p.114
455 *Bent County Leader*, Apr. 30, 1887
456 Interview with Helen Slater in CWA Interviews, *op. cit.* Yuma County
457 Interview with C.C. Huddleston in CWA Interviews, *op. cit.*, Prowers County
458 Schweninger, *op. cit.*, p.188
459 Census
460 *SDH*, Nov. 26, 1931
461 Betz, *op. cit.* pp.235-6
462 Wells, Dale, *op. cit.*, p.30
463 Rock, Kenneth W., "Uesere Leute: The Germans from Russia in Colorado", *Colorado Magazine*, Spring 1977, pp.156-183
464 Bauderhistory.com, "The Birth of the German Settlement at Burlington Colorado."
465 Interview with John Jacober, CWA Interviews, *op. cit.*, Kit Carson County
466 Interview with August Adolph, CWA Interviews, *op. cit.*, Kit Carson County
467 May *op. cit.*, p.386
468 May *op. cit.*, p.388
469 LCA, Oct. 13, 1904
470 Kloberdanz, *op. cit.*, p. 235
471 *FMT*, Aug. 4, 1967
472 *Logan Country History, op. cit.*, p. 458
473 Wells ed., *Logan Country, op. cit.*, pp.233-6
474 Wells ed., *Logan County, op. cit.*, p.T19
475 Interview with Mrs. Hans Christensen, CWA Interviews, *op. cit.*, Yuma County
476 SD, Nov. 8, 1917
477 May, *op. cit.*, pp. 406-7
478 Taylor, Paul, *Changes in Nationality among Hand Labor in Sugar Beet Fields of Northern Colorado 1909-1927* cited in *Colorado Heritage*, March/April 2015, pp.30-31
479 Valdes, *op. cit.*, p.114
480 May, *op. cit.*, p.413
481 Valdes, *op. cit.*, p.115

482 May, *op. cit.*, p.413
483 Valdés, Dennis Nodín, "Settlers, Sojourners, and Proletarians: Social Formation in The Great Plains Sugar Beet Industry, 1890-1940" Great Plains Quarterly (1990), pp.113-14
484 Aguayo story is based on family papers at Western History of Denver Public Library and *History of Sedgwick County*, p. f1
485 Wells, *Logan County, op. cit.*, p. 222
486 Census.
487 LDN Sep. 9, 1933
488 LDN May 6, 1938
489 Goldin and Katz, *op. cit.*
490 Valdés, Dennis Nodín, "Settlers, Sojourners, and Proletarians: Social Formation in the Great Plains Sugar Beet Industry, 1890-1940", *Great Plains Quarterly* (1990), pp. 114-115
491 Hamilton, op. cit., p.273
492 Norris, Jim, *North for the Harvest*, Minnesota Historical Society Press (St. Paul 2009), p.27
493 Sheflin, *op. cit.*, p. 190
494 *RMN,* Apr. 20, 1936
495 *RMN, Apr. 19, 1936*
496 LDN Apr. 21, 1936
497 UPI Apr. 29, 1936 in LDN Apr. 30, 1936
498 Wells, *Logan County, op. cit.*, p. 217
499 Goodykoontz, Colin B. *"The People of Colorado" in Hafen, Editor, Colorado and Its People: A Narrative and Topical History of the Centennial State*, Lewis Historical Publishing Company, Inc. (New York 1948), vol.2, p.99
500 May, op. cit., p.403
501 Deutsch, Sarah, *No Refuge: Culture, Class and Gender on an Anglo-Hispanic Frontier in the American Southwest, 1880-1940,* Oxford University Press (New York, 1987).

Chapter 5

502 *The Range Ledger,* Dec. 28, 1918
503 Based on National Bureau of Economic Research cycle dates. For discussion of Fed policy during this period see Friedman and Schwartz pp. 221-35
504 Bureau of Labor Statistics Wholesale Price Index for All Commodities
505 *Statistics of Agriculture 1936,* Tables 450 and 451
506 *ibid.*, Table 456
507 *ibid*. Table 445
508 Colorado County Assessors from *Colorado Yearbooks*
509 Census
510 Census
511 BLM N.E. Colorado, op. cit. Chapter XI and SD Nov. 11, 1920
512 Published in SD, December 16, 1920

Endnotes

513 Census
514 Matsushima, John and Farr, W.D., *A Journey Back: A History of Cattle Feeding in Colorado and the United States*, Cattlemen's Communications (Colorado Springs 1995), p.44
515 Source: cattle NASS, Sheep, Bureau of Agricultural Economics, *Agricultural Statistics 1936*, Table 333
516 Colorado Assessors data in *Colorado Yearbooks,* change from 1919 to 1925.
517 Swine population and corn acreage both based on Colorado assessors data in *Colorado Yearbooks.*
518 *Akron News*, Mar. 5,1925
519 *Rocky Mountain Banker,* Jan. 1926
520 *Rocky Mountain Banker,* Jan 1928
521 *Rocky Mountain Banker,* Jan.1928
522 Friedman, Milton and Schwartz, Anna Jacobson, *A Monetary History of the United States 1867-1960,* Princeton University Press (Princeton 1963), p. 299
523 BEA, full and part-time employment.
524 BEA personal Income deflated by personal consumption deflator.
525 *Agricultural Statistics 1936*, Tables 450 and 452
526 *Agricultural Statistics 1936*, Table 1
527 *Agricultural Statistics 1936*, Table 442
528 Harper, *op. cit.,* p.79
529 Leonard, Steven J., *Trials and Triumphs: A Colorado Portrait of the Great Depression, With FSA Photographs,* University Press of Colorado (Niwot 1993), p.20
530 Wells ed., *Logan County,* Wells ed., op. cit., p.92
531 *Akron News Reporter,* Jul. 16, 1931
532 Wells ed., *Logan County,* op. cit., p.478
533 Department of Agriculture
534 Census
535 Paosour, E.C. Jr., and Rucker, Randal R., *Plowshares and Pork Barrels: The Political Economy of Agriculture,* Independent Institute (Oakland CA 2005), p.92
536 Pearson, Drew and Allen, Robert, *The Washington Merry Go Round,* in LDN, Jan. 5, 1934
537 Census 1930, farm population was 24.8 percent of US total
538 US Department of Agriculture, *Yearbook of Agriculture, 1934,* US Government Printing Office (Washington, 1933).
539 Hurt, R. Douglas, *American Agriculture: A Brief History,* Iowa State University Press (Ames 1994), p.293
540 Paarlberg, Don, *American Farm Policy: A Case Study of Centralized Decision Making,* John Wiley & Sons, Inc. (New York 1964) pp.19-20
541 Ellis, Edward Robb, *A Nation in Torment: The Great American Depression, 1292-1939,* Kodansha America, Inc. (New York 1995) p.466
542 Saloutos, Theodore, *The American Farmer and the New Deal,* Iowa State University Press (Ames, 1982), p.19

543 Hiltzik, Michael A., *The New Deal, A Modern History,* Free Press (New York, 2011), p. 104
544 NYT, Mar. 28, 1938
545 Source: Colorado Yearbook
546 Sheflin, *op. cit.,* p. 47
547 Colorado Preservation Inc., *Drought, Depression and Dust: The New Deal in Eastern Colorado: Phase I* (2005) p.30-31. This includes direct relief (cash, commodities) and initial Federal Emergency Relief Administration (FERA) programs.
548 Wells, editor, *Logan County, op. cit.* p.92
549 U.S. Weather Observer in *Lamar Colorado* 1986, *op. cit.,* p. 115
550 Climatological Data, US Department of Agriculture, Weather Bureau
551 SFJ, Aug. 3, 1934
552 LDN, Sep. 11, 1933
553 Sheflin, *op. cit.,* p.144
554 Based on Sherow, *Watering, op. cit.,* pp.38-39 and Sherow, *Utopia, op. cit.,* pp. 175-176
555 Sherow, *Utopia, op. cit.,* p. 176
556 Stenzel and Cech, *op. cit.,* p. 247
557 Taylor, *op. cit.,* p.30
558 BLM NE Colo
559 LDN Jan. 18, 1934
560 SDH Jul. 8, 1937
561 SDH, Aug. 6, 1936
562 Wickens, James F., *Colorado and the Great Depression,* Garland Publishers (New York 1979), p.232
563 SDH, July 7, 1938
564 Colorado Preservation, Inc., Drought, Depression and Dust; the New Deal in Eastern Colorado-Survey Report (2005), p.13
565 SDH Jul. 1, 1937
566 Wells ed., *Logan County, op. cit.,* p. 358
567 Hurt, *Dust Bowl,* op. cit., p.50
568 *Those Were the Days, op. cit.*
569 SDH, March 21, 1935
570 Audretsch, Robert W., *The Civilian Conservation Corps in Colorado 1933-1942,* Dog Ear Publishing (Indianapolis 2008), Vol. II, p. 206
571 Colorado State College Extension Service, Reported in SDH, September 26, 1935
572 SDH, May 2, 1935
573 Audretsch, *op. cit.,*Vol. II, p. 208
574 Colorado Preservation, Inc., *op. cit.* p.13
575 Leonard, *op. cit.,* p.98
576 SDH, November 7, 1935
577 Phillips County Historical Society, Book Committee, *Those Were the Days, 18889-1989 Centennial History Phillips County Colorado (Holyoke, 1988).*

Endnotes

578 Colorado Department of Transportation, *100 Years of Colorado Transportation History (2010)*
579 Source: US Bureau of Public Roads and State Highway Department from *Colorado Yearbook*
580 *Rocky Mountain Banker*, January 1932
581 Source for value of crops: Colorado Assessors reports in *Colorado Yearbook*
582 Source: Colorado Assessors Reports from *Colorado Yearbook*
583 Kiowa County Bicentennial Committee, *op. cit.*, p.262
584 Source: Bankers' reports from the *Mountain States Banker*, January and February issues.
585 SFJ, Sept. 1, 1932
586 UPI reported in *LDN*, Feb. 3, 1933
587 Wickens, *op. cit.*, p.221
588 UPI reported in *LDN*, Sep. 18, 1934.
589 Wells ed., *Logan County, op. cit.*, p. 128
590 US Department of Agriculture, Bureau of Agricultural Economics
591 US Department of Agriculture, Bureau of Agricultural Economics
592 US Agricultural Statistics. Hog price based on average farm value and corn price from Chicago Board of Trade.
593 SDH Mar. 21, 9135
594 Colorado Assessors Data from *Colorado Yearbooks*
595 Leonard, *op. cit.* p. 93
596 *LDN*, Oct. 4, 1934
597 *DP*, Dec. 31, 1936
598 May, *op. cit.* p.375
599 Sherow, *Utopia, op. cit.*, p.175
600 *Census of Agriculture*
601 Schlebecker, John T. *Cattle Raising on the Plains 1900-61* University of Nebraska Press (Lincoln 1963), p.150
602 LDN, Aug. 24, 1934
603 Keck, *op. cit.*, p.376
604 DP Feb. 9, 2003
605 *Agricultural Statistics, 1940,* Table 477
606 LDN, August 24, 1934
607 LDN, Oct. 20, 1934
608 LDN, Oct. 29, 1934 and Dec. 3, 1934
609 SDH, Aug. 9, 1934
610 Bonnifield, Paul, *The Dust Bowl; Men, Dirt and Depression,* University of New Mexico Press (Albuquerque 1979), p.126
611 *Colorado Agricultural Statistics* based on assessment data
612 Colorado Assessors data reported in *Colorado Yearbook*
613 Bankers' reports are from the *Mountain States Banker*'s January and February issues.
614 Colorado Assessors data from *Colorado Yearbooks,* based on assessors data

615 USDA
616 Markoff, Dena S., Bittersweet, *op. cit.*, pp.161-78
617 Hauk, Cornelius, "La Junta, The Santa Fe's Colorado Connection" in *Santa Fe in the Intermountain West, Colorado Railroad Annual No. 23*, Colorado Railroad Historical Museum
618 Fell, *Limon Colorado, op. cit.*, p.38
619 SDH March 26, 1936
620 Wells, *Register, op. cit.*, p.128
621 Based on Census Reports, data in *Colorado Year Books*, adjustment for price changes based on US Consumer Price Index
622 Fell, *Limon Colorado, op. cit.*, pp. 38-40
623 Source: *Colorado Year Books*
624 Colorado Department of Revenue in *Colorado Yearbooks*
625 *DP*, Dec. 31, 1936
626 Wells, Dale, *op. cit.*, p. 129
627 Bernanke, Ben S., "The Financial Accelerator and the Credit Channel, The Credit Channel of Monetary Policy in the Twenty-first Century Conference, Atlanta, Georgia". Federal Reserve Bank of Atlanta, June 15, 2007
628 Friedman and Schwartz, *op. cit.*, p.299
629 Niehaus, Fred R., *Development of Banking in Colorado*, Mountain States Publishing Company (Denver 1942) , p.46
630 Niehaus, *op. cit.*, p. 46
631 Bank statistics from *Colorado Yearbook*, various years
632 *Mountain States Banker*, Nov. 1931
633 Bank Statistics from *Colorado Yearbooks*
634 East Central Council of Local Governments, *Our Heritage, A Collection of tales of East Central Colorado, Vol. I* (1983), p.57
635 *SJA*, Mar. 7, 1933
636 *LDN*, Mar. 8, 1933
637 Wels, Dale, *op. cit.*, p.88
638 *SJA*, Mar. 7, 1933
639 *History of Kit Carson County, op. cit.*, p. 811
640 LDN Aug. 27, 1934
641 Wells, editor, *Logan County, op. cit.*, p.92
642 Bank Statistics from *Colorado Yearbooks*
643 Bank Statistics from *Colorado Yearbooks*
644 *Mountain States Banker*, January 1935
645 LDN, Aug. 28, 1934
646 SFJ, Jul. 5, 1934
647 All population figures in this section are from Census unless otherwise noted.
648 Wells ed., *Logan County, op. cit.*, p. 432
649 Wells ed., *Logan County, op. cit.*, p. 431
650 Census

Endnotes

651 Calculation based on 1930 and 1940 populations and estimates of fertility and mortality. See Appendix for details.
652 Census
653 Colorado Department of Education, from *Colorado Yearbooks*

Chapter 6

654 Borgstrom, George, *World Food Resources*, Intext Educational Publishers (New York 1973) P. 203, cited by Worster, p.4
655 Riebsame, William E., "The Dust Bowl: Historical Image, Psychological Anchor, and Ecological Taboo", *Great Plains Quarterly*, Spring 1986, p.128
656 Bonnifield, *op. cit.*, p.7
657 Hurt, *Dust Bowl*, op. cit., p.7
658 Interview with Jacob Hasart, CWA interviews, *op. cit.*, Kit Carson County
659 Johnson, *Heaven's Tableland*, *op. cit.*, p.104-05
660 Hurt, *The Dust Bowl*, *op. cit.*, p.18
661 Hurt, R. Douglas, *American Agriculture: A Brief History*, Iowa State University Press (Ames 1994), p.100
662 Hurt, *The Dust Bowl*, *op. cit.*, p. 30
663 NYT, Jul. 26, 1936
664 Lamar Centennial History, Bent County History
665 USDA, NASS
666 Osteen, *op. cit.*, p.120
667 Hurt, *The Dust Bowl*, *op. cit.*, p.80
668 Colorado Assessors' data in *Colorado Yearbooks*
669 *Agricultural Statistics, 1940*, Table 1
670 *SDH*, July 7, 1932
671 *Ibid.*
672 Ibid.
673 *SDH*, Jun 30, 1932 and Jun 9, 1932
674 Source: USDA
675 Source: CWA Project No. F-6, Bureau of Agricultural Economics and Colorado Agricultural Experiment Station, reported in *Colorado Yearbook, 1933-34*
676 US Forest Service Land Utilization Project reported at station 8 miles south of Springfield in *SDH*, Jan 3, 1964
677 LDN Jan. 18, 1934
678 SDH, May 2, 1935
679 LDN Jun. 16, 1934
680 SDH May 2, 1935
681 SDH Apr. 2, 1936
682 SDH May 25, 1933
683 Riggs, Letha Wilcox, "Recollections of Baca County in the Early 1930s", Oral History in Western History/Genealogy Department, Denver Public Library
684 LDN Mar. 18, 1935

685　LDN Feb. 22, 1935
686　RMN, Mar. 24, 1935
687　RMN, Mar. 24, 1935
688　*LDN*, Apr. 26, 1935
689　Harper, *op. cit.* p.108
690　Egan, *op. cit.*, p. 174
691　SDH, Apr. 11, 1935
692　NYT, Ap. 22, 1935
693　Audretsch, *op. cit.*, Vol. II, p. 208
694　Osteen, *op. cit.*, p. 123-124
695　USDA
696　Census
697　Colorado Assessors Data from *Colorado Yearbooks*
698　SDH Mar. 28, 1935
699　Census
700　Hurt, *Dust Bowl, op. cit.*, p.96
701　*Colorado Year Book*s
702　Source: compiled from Census data, reported in *Colorado Year Books*
703　SDH, Apr. 1, 1935
704　Colorado Preservation, Inc., *Historic Baca County*
705　Sheflin, *op. cit.*, p. 76
706　Gregory, James N., *American Exodus, The Dust Bowl Migration and Okie Culture in California*, Oxford University Press (New York, 1989), p.11
707　This is a net migration figure. See Appendix for description of migration estimates.
708　*Ibid.*
709　Egan, *op. cit.*, p. 132
710　Colorado Department of Education from *Colorado Yearbooks*
711　SDH, May 2, 1935
712　Davenport, Walter, "Land Where Our Children Die", *Colliers Weekly*, Sept. 18, 1937
713　H.L. Mencken, "The Dole for Bogus Farmers", *American Mercury,* December 1936
714　A disc or disc harrow is an implement pulled by a tractor and used for tilling soil. It consists of many parallel concave metal disks attached to a frame.
715　SDH, Mar. 21, 1935
716　SDH, Mar. 28, 1935
717　SDH, Mar. 28, 1935
718　SDH, Apr. 18, 1935
719　General order concerning relief in drought areas from Harry L. Hopkins, National Administrator, Federal Emergency Relief Administration, in *Springfield Herald Democrat*, March 22, 1934
720　SDH, March 30, 1933
721　*SDH* July 7, 1933.
722　LDN Dec. 16, 1935
723　LDN, various dates 1934-38.

Endnotes

724 SDH Aug. 25, 1938
725 Census 1940
726 Hurt, *Dust Bowl, op. cit.* p.93 and SDH, October 1, 1936
727 LDN Nov. 28, 1933
728 SDH, March 26, 1936
729 Hurt, *Dust Bowl, op. cit.* p.72
730 Source: Colorado Yearbook
731 US Government Printing Office, "The Future of the Great Plains: Report of the Great Plains Committee", Washington, D.C., December 1936
732 Future of the Great Plains, *op. cit.* p.5
733 Future of the Great Plains, *op. cit.* p.50, quote from US Department of Agriculture, *The Western Range*, Senate Document No. 199, Govt. Printing Office, Washington 1936 p. 88
734 Future of the Great Plains, *op. cit.* p.63
735 Kimmel, Roy I., "Unit Reorganization Program for the Southern Great Plains", *Journal of Farm Economics* (1940, Vol.22, Number 1), p. 265
736 Hurt, R. Douglas, "Federal Land Reclamation in the Dust Bowl", Great Plains Quarterly, Spring 1986, p.93
737 Sheflin, *op. cit.,* p. 81
738 Kimmel, *op. cit.*
739 Bonnifield, *op. cit.,* pp.129,171-3
740 US Department of Agriculture, *Yearbook of Agriculture 1935,* US Government Printing Office (Washington, 1934).
741 Hurt, "Reclamation", *op. cit.* pp.100-101
742 Cole, B. Erin, "A Second Change: The Resettlement in Administration in Dust Bowl-Era Colorado", *Colorado Heritage*, September/October 2013, p.21
743 Wiley, Clarence A., "Settlement and Unsettlement in the Resettlement Administration Program", *Law and Contemporary Problems-1937,* p.472
744 Cannon, Brian Q., *Remaking the Agrarian Dream: New Deal Rural Resettlement in the Mountain West,* University of New Mexico Press (Albuquerque, 1996), pp. 25-6
745 Cannon, *op. cit.,* p.140
746 Hurt, "Reclamation", *op. cit.,* p.103
747 Wickens, *op. cit.*p.256
748 Sheflin, *op. cit., pp. 121-22*
749 Underwood, John J., *Physical Land Conditions in the Western and Southeastern Baca County Soil Conservation Districts, Colorado,* US Department of Agriculture, Soil Conservation Service (Washington, DC, 1944).
750 Saloutos, *op. cit.,* p. 207
751 White, Gilbert F., "The Future of the Great Plains Re-visited", *Great Plains Quarterly,* Spring 1986, p.93
752 Cunfer, *op. cit.,* p. 6
753 Source: Colorado Assessors data from *Colorado Year Books* and *Colorado Agricultural Statistics*

754 Bonnifield, *Dustbowl, op. cit.*, p.3
755 Cunfer, *op. cit.*, p.156
756 Worster, Donald, "The Dirty Thirties: A Study in Agricultural Capitalism" in Americans View Their Dust Bowl Experience, edited by Wunder, John R., Kaye, Frances W., and Cartensen, Vernon, University Press of Colorado (Niwot, 1999), p.358
757 Worster, *Dirty Thirties, op. cit.*, p.361
758 Bonnifield, *Dust Bowl*, op. cit., p.201
759 McDean, Harry C., "Dust Bowl Historiography" in *Americans View Their Dust Bowl Experience*, edited by Wunder, Kaye and Cartensen, University Press of Colorado (Niwot, 1999), p.381
760 McDean, *op. cit.*, p.367
761 Hewes, Leslie, *The Suitcase Farming Frontier: A Study in the Historical Geography of the Central Great Plains,* University of Nebraska Press (Lincoln, 1973).
762 Census of Agriculture
763 *LDN*, May 18, 1935.
764 Jan. 9, 1939
765 LDN Feb. 27, 1939
766 *SDH* Oct. 20, 1938
767 Sheflin, *op. cit.*, p. 167
768 Hurt, R. Douglas, *The Big Empty: The Great Plains in the Twentieth Century,* The University of Arizona Press (Tucson 2011), p.96
769 Sheflin, *op. cit.*, p. 323
770 DP, Apr. 6, 2014

Chapter 7

771 *LDN*, Jun. 14, 1973
772 *Colorado Yearbook 1943-1944*, p. 512 and *LDN*, May 28, 1942
773 *History of Sedgwick County*, op. cit., p. C79-80
774 Harvey, Robert, *Amache: The Story of Japanese Internment in Colorado during World War II,* Taylor Trade Publishing, Lanham MD,2003, p.58
775 *LJDD*, February 27, 1942
776 *LDN*, March 25, 1942
777 LDN, June 3, 1942
778 LDN, Sep. 19, 1942
779 Lurie, George, *A Legacy of Shame: The Story of Colorado's Camp Amache*, G. L:Uire (c1985), p.40
780 Hurt, R. Douglas, *The Great Plains During World War II*, University of Nebraska Press (Lincoln 2008), p.295
781 Lurie, *op. cit.,* p.67, La Junta and Sterling both reported 1940 Census populations of over 7,000 but fewer than the peak numbers at the camp.
782 LDN, Apr. 21, 1943
783 LDN, Sep. 7, 1945

Endnotes

784 *Mountain States Banker*, January 1945
785 Harvey, *op. cit.*, p. 124
786 Hosokawa, Bill, *Colorado's Japanese Americans; From 1886 to the Present*, University Press of Colorado, Boulder 2005, p. 103
787 *LDN*, September 1, 1943
788 Schrager, Adam, *The Principled Politician: the Ralph Carr Story*, Fulcrum Pub., Golden, CO 2008, p. 287
789 Hosokawa, *op. cit.*, p. 103
790 Schrager, *op. cit.* p. 287
791 Schrager, *op. cit.* p. 287
792 *LDN*, January 16, 1943
793 SPH Sep. 3, 1942
794 Harvey, *op. cit.* p.79
795 *LDN*, October 8, 1942
796 Lurie, *op. cit.*, p.125
797 Holsinger, Paul M., "Amache", *Colorado Magazine,* Winter 1964, p.58
798 DP, May 22, 1942
799 Hamilton, *op. cit.*, p.358-ii
800 LDN Oct. 26, 1939
801 Hurt, *World War II, op. cit.*, p.158
802 LDN, Feb. 19, 1942
803 Hurt, *World War II, op. cit.*, p.174
804 *Agricultural Statistics 1952*, Average Price Received by Farmers
805 *Agricultural Statistics 1952*, No. 2 Hard Winter. Kansas City
806 *Agricultural Statistics 1952*, No. 2 yellow, Chicago
807 LDN, Feb. 19, 1942
808 Johnson, *Heaven's Tableland, op. cit.*, p.275
809 LDN Aug. 17, 1940
810 Hurt, *World War II, op. cit.*, p.193
811 *LJDD*, March 26, 1942
812 FMT, Apr. 2, 1942
813 LDN, Feb. 19, 1942
814 LDN, Sep. 16, 1942
815 LDN, May 6, 1942
816 *DP*, May 7, 1943
817 Cohen, Deborah, *Braceros: Migrant Citizens and Transnational Subjects in the Postwar United States and Mexico*, University of North Carolina Press, 2011, p.23
818 *RMN*, May 13, 1943
819 May, *op. cit.*, p. 423
820 LDN Feb. 2, 1946
821 Worrall, Janet E. "Prisoners on the Home Front", *Colorado Heritage*, Issue 1, 1990 and Paschal, Allen W., "The Enemy in Colorado: German Prisoners of War, 1943-46", *Colorado Magazine*, Summer/Fall 1979

822 *History of Sedgwick County, op. cit.,* pp. C149-51
823 Jones and Collman, *op. cit.,* p.187
824 Hurt, R. Douglas, *Problems of Plenty: The American Farmer in the Twentieth Century,* Ivan R. Dee (Chicago 2002), p.120
825 Farm output is index of gross farm production minus production from power of horses and mules. Source: Bureau of Agricultural Economics, *Agricultural Statistics 1952,* Table 681. Farm income is net income from farm sources of persons living of farms. Source: Bureau of Agricultural Economics, *Agricultural Statistics 1952,* Table 702.
826 Hurt, *Problems, op. cit.,* p.94
827 US Department of Agriculture, Bureau of Agriculture Economics, Index of Prices Received by Farmers for All Farm Products, *1952 Agricultural Statistics,* Table 694
828 *1952 Agricultural Statistics,* Table 633
829 USDA and BLS
830 US Weather Bureau, reported in *Lamar Centennial, Bent County History* book committee, p. 322 (from Bent County Soil Conservation District), and *Colorado Yearbook 1941-42,* p.60
831 *Census of Agriculture 1945*
832 Colorado assessors' data, reported in *Colorado Yearbooks,* includes all cattle
833 Census of Agriculture
834 *Agricultural Statistics 1962,* Wheat price-average per bushel year beginning in July at Kansas City; corn-average price per bushel year beginning in October at Chicago; Cattle-average price per 100 lbs. received by farmers.
835 *Census of Agriculture*
836 Johnson, *Tableland, op. cit.,* pp.276-77
837 Gardner, Bruce L., *American Agriculture in the Twentieth Century,* Harvard University Press (Cambridge, MA 2002), p. 5
838 *1952 Agricultural Statistics,* Tables 2 and 38
839 *Census of Agriculture*
840 *Census of Agriculture*
841 LDN, May 15, 1941
842 *History of Kit Carson County, op. cit.,* p.32
843 *Rocky Mountain Banker,* January 1945
844 *Census of Agriculture*
845 May, *op. cit.,* p. 193
846 Hurt, R. Douglas, *Agricultural Technology in the Twentieth Century,* Sunflower University Press, Manhattan, KS 1991, p. 82
847 Hurt, *Technology, op. cit.,* p.78
848 May, *op. cit.,* p. 190-91
849 Wells ed., *Logan County, op. cit.,* p.348
850 May, *op. cit.,* p. 195
851 Hurt, *Problems, op. cit.,* p.116

Endnotes

852 Colorado Legislative Council, *Report to the General Assembly: Migratory Labor in Colorado,* Research Publication No. 72, December 1962, p.15
853 Miner, *op. cit.*, p. 141
854 Hewes, *op. cit.*, p.131
855 SPH Sep. 26, 1946
856 Johnson, *Heavens Tableland, op. cit.*, p.282
857 Johnson, *Heavens Tableland, op. cit.*, p.278
858 Miner, *op. cit.*, p. 161
859 Miner, *op. cit.*
860 Miner, *op. cit.*, p. 96
861 LL, September 23, 1965
862 USDA
863 Miner, *op. cit.*, p.142
864 Source: USDA
865 Source: USDA
866 KCP, Jun. 20, 1947
867 Miner, *op. cit.*, p.283
868 *DP*, January 1945
869 *LDN*, July 24, 1942
870 *DP*, July 7, 1946
871 *Mountain States Banker*, January 1949
872 Hewes, *op. cit.*, p.106
873 KCP, Aug. 15, 1947
874 KCP, July 16, 1948
875 KCP, Jun. 4, 1948
876 RMN, Oct. 18, 1946
877 RMN Oct. 18, 1946
878 BLS
879 Based on CPIU
880 Source: Colorado Department of Revenue, in *Colorado Yearbooks*
881 The comparison with the nation is based on Census data rather than the Bureau of Labor Statistics numbers citied in the beginning paragraph in this section. Comparable BLS data were not available for Colorado counties.
882 SPH, Dec. 27, 1945
883 University of Colorado Business Research Division, *Directory of Colorado Manufacturers*, 1948
884 *Mountain States Banker*, Jan. 1948
885 Based on 1950 Census reports of homes built after 1945
886 *LDN*, Jan 13, 1943
887 Fell, *op. cit.*, p. 46
888 Colorado Banking Commission from *Colorado Yearbooks*
889 History of *Kit Carson County, op. cit*, p. 811
890 *Lamar Colorado 1986, op. cit.*, pp.102-3

891   Fell, *op. cit.*, p. 54
892   Wells ed., *Logan County, op. cit.*, p.249
893   Wells ed., *Logan County, op. cit.*, p.335
894   See endnote 21 above
895   Net migration was estimated from beginning and ending populations by age and sex and national estimates of mortality and birth rates as described in Chapter 6.
896   Census
897   All income estimates in this section are based on data from the *Census of Population and Housing*. Regional estimates were computed based on sums of county estimates of income in each income range and interpolation within the ranges.
898   Adjusted by national CPIU.
899   *LDN*, Jan. 3, 1949
900   *NYT*, May 30, 1950

Chapter 8

901   *SA*, Apr. 8, 1950
902   Ashworth, William, *Ogallala Blue: Water and Life on the High Plains*, W.W. Norton & Company, New York 2006, p.268
903   Historical rainfall data in various local newspapers
904   *LDN*, Jan. 15, 1957
905   *SA*, Feb. 18, 1950
906   *SA*, Apr. 10, 1950
907   Hurt, *Dust Bowl, op. cit.*, p.142
908   *SPH*, Feb. 25, 1954.
909   *SPH*, Feb. 25, 1954
910   *SPH*, Apr. 12, 1956
911   *LDN* Oct. 7, 1954
912   *SPH* Jul. 22, 1954
913   *Hutchison News Herald*, Jul. 4, 1953 reported in *SPH*, Jul. 9, 1953
914   *SPH*, Jul. 2, 1954.
915   USDA
916   *SPH*, Jun. 24, 1954
917   USDA
918   *LDN* Jul. 26, 1950
919   Hurt, *Dust Bowl, op. cit.*, p.144-45
920   *SPH* Apr. 22, 1954
921   Opie, John, *Ogallala: Water for a Dry Land*, University of Nebraska Press (Lincoln 1993), p.109
922   *SPH*, April 22, 1954.
923   Diebert, Edward J., "Soil Bank" in *Great Plains Encyclopedia*
924   Paosour and Rucker, *op. cit.*, p.118
925   Hewes, *op. cit.*, p.4
926   Paosour and Rucker, *op. cit.*, p.119

Endnotes

927 Penley, *op. cit.*, p. 124
928 *NYT*, Jul. 22, 1956
929 USDA
930 SPH, Jun. 6, 1957
931 SPH, April 4, 1957 and May 2, 1957
932 *LDN*, Jul. 26, 1957
933 *NYT*, Apr. 7, 1957
934 SPH, Jul. 11, 1957
935 Interview with Larry Webster, August 21, 2014
936 USDA
937 *The Wray Gazette*, Jul. 18, 1957
938 *BR*, Jul. 17, 1958
939 Census of Agriculture
940 *Hutchison News Herald*, July 4, 1953 reported in SPH, Jul. 9, 1953
941 Egan, *op. cit.*, p.311
942 Hansen, Zeynep, K., and Libecap, Gary D., "Small Farms, Externalities, and the Dust Bowl of the 1930s", *Journal of Political Economy*, June 2004
943 *1949 Census of Agriculture*. The six counties are Baca, Cheyenne, Kiowa, Kit Carson, Prowers and Washington.
944 Wessel, Thomas R., "Agricultural Policy Since 1945" in *The Rural West Since World War II*, R. Douglas Hurt, Editor, University Press of Kansas, 1998, p.86
945 USDA
946 BEA, Personal Income Accounts
947 USDA, Measured in dollars per hundred pounds
948 *Census of Agriculture*
949 Opie, *op. cit.*, p.110-111
950 *Census of Agriculture*
951 *Census of Agriculture*
952 1940 and 1970
953 *1954 Census of Agriculture*
954 *1974 Census of Agriculture*, change in dollar value based on CPIU.
955 *Census of Agriculture*
956 Hamilton, *op. cit.*, p.402
957 Keck, *op. cit.*, pp.209-10
958 *Cervi's Rocky Mountain Journal*, May 3, 1967
959 *AVJ*, Dec. 1, 1966
960 *Pueblo Chieftain*, Mar. 29, 2009
961 See Markoff, Dena S., Bittersweet, *op. cit.*, pp. 161-178
962 USDA
963 USDA
964 *Cervi's Rocky Mountain Journal*, Mar. 1, 1967
965 *FMT*, Aug. 19, 1968
966 Colorado Legislative Council, *op. cit.*, pp.18-19 and p.134

967 Colorado Legislative Council, *op. cit.,* p. xxxv
968 Editorial in *LL*, Dec. 5, 1968
969 *LDN*, May 5, 1964
970 *FMT*, Mar. 1, 1968
971 *LJTD*, Mar. 17, 1967
972 *AVJ*, Aug. 25, 1966
973 *The Economist,* Feb. 4, 2017
974 USDA, Survey of national price received, $/cwt.
975 Schlebecker, *op. cit.,* p. 229
976 Census of Agriculture
977 Colorado Agricultural Statistics, 1970
978 US Department of Agriculture, Economic Research Service, Farm Production Economics Division, In cooperation with Colorado Agricultural Experiment Station, "Changes in the Cattle-feeding Industry Along the North and South Platte Rivers, 1953-1959" (Washington, 1963).
979 Hurt, *Agricultural Technology, op. cit.,* p.73
980 *AVJ,* Oct. 15, 1970
981 BEA, Regional Employment and Earnings, Earnings by Industry
982 Opie, *op. cit.,* p. 140
983 Opie, *op. cit.,* p. 140
984 Splinter, William E., "Center-Pivot Irrigation", *Scientific American,* June 1976
985 Hurt, *Agricultural Technology, op. cit.,* p.72
986 Splinter, *op. cit.,* p.90
987 Opie, *op. cit.,* p. 136
988 *LDN*, Jun. 24, 1966
989 *AVJ*, Jan. 23, 1969
990 Ashworth, *op. cit.,* p.25
991 *Rocky Mountain Banker,* January 1941
992 *1959 Census of Agriculture*
993 Stenzel, *op. cit.,* p. 411
994 *AVJ, Jan. 4, 1968*
995 *SPH,* Jun. 7, 1962
996 *Colorado Agricultural Statistics*
997 *BR,* Jan. 3, 1957
998 *BR.,* Jun. 13,1957, July 18, 1957, Dec. 5, 1957 and Nov. 27, 1958
999 USDA
1000 SPH Jun. 5, 1958
1001 *SPH, Nov. 22, 1962*
1002 Jones and Stenzel, *op. cit.,* p. 89
1003 *AVJ,* Jan. 12, 1967
1004 Templer, Otis W., "The Legal Context for Groundwater Use" in *Groundwater Exploitation in the High Plains,* Edited by David E. Kromm & Stephen E. White, University of Kansas Press (1992), pp75-76

1005 Jones and Cech, *op. cit.*, p.68
1006 Jones and Cech, *op. cit.*, pp. 101-102
1007 Jones and Cech, *op. cit.*, p. 160
1008 *LDN*, Apr. 1, 1949
1009 Tyler, Daniel, *The Last Water Hole in the West: The Colorado-Big Thompson Project and the Northern Colorado Water Conservancy District,* University Press of Colorado (Niwot, CO, 1992), pp. 136 & 158
1010 U.S. Department of the Interior, *The Story of the Colorado-Big Thompson Project,* , US Government Printing Office, Washington, 1962
1011 InflationData.com
1012 Scamehorn, Lee, *High Altitude Energy: A History of Fossil Fuels in Colorado,* University of Colorado Press (Boulder 2002), p.117
1013 Wells, Dale, *op. cit.,* pp. 89 and 117
1014 *SA*, Jan. 2, 1949
1015 *SA*, Apr. 1, 1950
1016 Scamehorn, Energy, *op. cit.,* p. 117
1017 Wells ed., *Logan County, op. cit.,* p 138
1018 Wells, Dale, *op. cit.,* p.163
1019 *RMN*, Feb. 3, 1952
1020 *DP*, Feb. 15, 1953
1021 Colorado Department of Natural Resources, Colorado Geological Survey, *Oil and Gas Fields of Colorado: Statistical Data* (Denver 1976).
1022 *RMN*, Feb. 3, 1952
1023 *RMN*, Feb. 3, 1952
1024 *DP*, Feb. 15, 1953
1025 *SA*, Jan. 2, 1949. As the 1960 Census listed Sterling's population at 10,751 the reports cited here might include some hyperbole.
1026 *DP*, Sep. 28, 1955
1027 Colorado Department of Revenue
1028 *RMN*, Feb. 3, 1952
1029 *RMN*, Feb. 3, 1952
1030 *DP*, Feb. 15, 1953
1031 Sterling Industrial Promotion Fund, *Industrial Report for Sterling, Colorado and Area 1959,* p. 40
1032 *RMN*, Feb. 3, 1952
1033 *DP*, Feb. 15, 1953
1034 Wells, Dale, *op. cit.,* p.165
1035 *SA*, Feb. 10, 1950
1036 Colorado Department of Natural Resources, *op. cit.*
1037 Scamehorn, Energy, *op. cit.,* p. 136
1038 The Fort Morgan Chamber of Commerce, *An Economic and Industrial Survey of Fort Morgan, Colorado,* Prepared for The Fort Morgan Industrial Foundation, Reviewed by The Bureau of Business Research, University of Colorado, Circa 1958, p.I-2

1039 DP, Feb. 27, 1955
1040 SA, Oct. 25, 1950
1041 Colorado Oil and Gas Conservation Commission
1042 BEA Personal Income Estimates
1043 LDN, Aug. 12, 1966
1044 SPH, January 21, 1953
1045 *Kiowa County* Bicentennial Committee, op. cit., pp.46-47
1046 AVJ, Sep. 5, 1968
1047 Stiglitz, Joseph E., *The Great Divide: Unequal Societies and What We Can Do About Them*, W.W. Norton (New York, 2015).
1048 Census
1049 Census
1050 Estimate based on *Census of Housing* statistics on year homes built.
1051 Census
1052 Lymberopoulos, P. John, Working Paper #6: "Retail Sales: Levels and Patterns", in University of Colorado School of Business, Arkansas Valley Study, Trade and Services Sector of the Arkansas Valley Economy in Colorado, 1965, Appendix Tables 1.1-1.10
1053 Kline, John B., Working Paper #10, "Summary of Field Study Investigations, Phase I." in University of Colorado School of Business, Arkansas Valley Study, Trade and Services Sector of the Arkansas Valley Economy in Colorado, 1965, pp. 8, 13 & 14
1054 LDN, Feb. 18, 1966
1055 LDN, Jan. 27, 1960
1056 LL, Apr. 20, 1967
1057 FMT, Sep. 12, 1968
1058 Census
1059 *Directory of* Colorado *Manufacturers*, op. cit., 1968-69.
1060 C. Kendall, op. cit., p. 6
1061 *Lamar Colorado 1986*, op. cit., pp. 125-26
1062 AVJ, Jun. 20, 1968
1063 Net migration was estimated by projecting 1960 and 1970 population using national mortality and fertility rates for each age group in the regional population. This was the same methodology used to prepared estimates in earlier chapters.
1064 Gilmore, John S. and Ryan, John J., "The Manufacturing Sector of the Arkansas Valley Economy", prepared for The Colorado Division of Commerce & Development, Denver Research Institute, June 1965. p. N2
1065 Estimate based on Census population by age and national natality and mortality rates.
1066 Estimates based on 50th reunion biographies, a 2014 listing of class addresses and the writer's personal knowledge. Reliable information was obtained for 71 of 79 students listed in 1957 Annual of which 41 migrated. Eighteen of 21 college graduates moved away. Those who moved from Lamar to another location in the region were treated as non-migrants.
1067 DP, Apr. 5, 1999

Endnotes

1068 Estimate based on differences between estimated population in absence of migration and actual population. Because of rural births exceeded deaths the numbers moving off the farms exceeded the change in population.
1069 All population figures in this section are from *the Census of Population*.
1070 *Those Were the Days, op. cit., p.157*
1071 SDO
1072 Education data from Census

Chapter 9

1073 *LDN*, Oct. 16, 1973
1074 Duncan, Marvin and Bickel, Blaine, "U.S. Agricultural Exports-A Boon to Farmers", *Federal Reserve Bank of Kansas Monthly Review*, July-August 1976
1075 Luttrell, Clifton B., "The Russian Wheat Deal-Hindsight vs. Foresight", *Federal Reserve Bank of St. Louis Review*, October 1973, pp. 2-8
1076 ECP, Feb. 14, 1974
1077 Source: US Department of Agriculture, NASS, Annual average, Wheat, No. 1 Hard Winter, Ordinary Protein-Kansas City, corn no. 2 yellow Kansas City
1078 USDA, Average price per 100 pounds at Omaha
1079 *LL*, Jan. 27, 1977
1080 BEA, County Farm Income
1081 *AVJ*, Jun. 21, 1973
1082 *LDN*, Dec. 5, 1973
1083 BEA, State and Local Personal Income Accounts.
1084 *AVJ*, Sep. 13, 1973
1085 BEA, State and Local Personal Income Accounts.
1086 BEA, State and Local Personal Income Accounts. Realized net farm earnings includes other small items on both income expenditure side in addition to receipts and expenditures attributable to crop and livestock production
1087 Census of Agriculture
1088 *Time*, "Changing Farm Policy to Cut Food Prices," Apr. 19, 1973
1089 *LDN*, Apr. 23, 1973
1090 *LDN*, Apr. 2, 1973
1091 *Newsweek*, Apr. 30, 1973
1092 *DP*, Apr. 4, 1973
1093 Reported in *LDN*, Apr. 11, 1973
1094 *LDN*, Mar. 13, 1972
1095 *AVJ*, Nov. 21, 1974
1096 *AVJ*, Sep. 6, 1973
1097 USDA, Based on 1974 yields for 16 eastern Colorado counties
1098 *BR*, May 18, 1973
1099 *LDN*, Dec. 5, 1973
1100 *AVJ*, Sep. 12, 1974

1101 Based on index for farmers' fuel and energy costs, *1982 Agricultural Statistics*, Table 603
1102 *1982 Agricultural Statistics,* Tables 601 and 603; *1992 Agricultural Statistics,* Tables 563 and 566
1103 *AVJ,* Apr. 1, 1982
1104 Combined real estate debt and non-real estate debt excluding CCC loans, *1982 Agricultural Statistics,* Tables 625 and 633 and *1992 Agricultural Statistics,* Tables 586 and 587
1105 *1982 Agricultural Statistics,* Table 631 and *1992 Agricultural Statistics,* Table 551
1106 USDA
1107 *1982 Agricultural Statistics,* Table 5
1108 *LL,* Jan. 27, 1977
1109 AP story in SJA, Jul. 8, 1977
1110 BEA State and Local Personal Income Accounts
1111 US Department of Commerce, Bureau of Economic Analysis, State and Local Personal Income Accounts
1112 *LDN,* Nov. 30, 1977
1113 *AVJ,* Jun. 10, 1982
1114 *DP,* Dec. 29, 1985
1115 BEA State and Local Personal Income Accounts
1116 *AVJ,* Apr. 15, 1982
1117 *1992 Agricultural Statistics,* Table 631 and 565
1118 Based on net farm income adjusted by CPIU
1119 Based on *Census of Agriculture* average value of land and buildings and US CPIU.
1120 *NYT,* Aug. 3, 1977
1121 Source: USDA, Economic Research Service
1122 Dinse, John and Browne, William P. "The Emergence of the American Agriculture Movement, 1977-79" in *Great Plains Quarterly",* Fall 1985, p. 222
1123 NYT, Dec. 15, 1977
1124 LL, March 30, 1978
1125 *SPH,* Sep. 29, 1977 based on August 15 prices.
1126 UPI story, reported in *LDN,* Mar. 3, 1978
1127 *LDN,* Sep. 15, 1977
1128 *LDN,* Sep. 19, 1977
1129 *SPH,* Nov. 3, 1977
1130 Hurt, *The Big Empty,* op. cit., p.232
1131 *SPH,* Oct. 16, 1977 and Dec. 15, 1977
1132 *LL,* Feb. 2, 1978
1133 *SPH,* Sep. 22, 1977 and Sep. 29, 1977
1134 *Newsweek,* "The Tractor Rebellion", Dec. 19, 1977 and *Time,* "Furious Farmers", Dec. 19, 1977
1135 Dinse and Browne, op. cit., p. 233
1136 *Newsweek,* Dec 19, 1977

1137 *LDN*, Apr. 13, 1977
1138 *Farm Journal*, "The Farm Strike", Jan. 1978, p.36
1139 DP, Dec. 14, 1977
1140 DP, Jan. 26, 1978
1141 *DP*, Jan. 21, 1978
1142 Bovard, James "The Farm Credit Quagmire", Cato Policy Analysis No. 122, July 27, 1989
1143 *LL*, Mar. 30, 1978
1144 SPH, *Mar. 23, 1978*
1145 Hurt, *The Big Empty, op. cit.*, p.233
1146 *LDN*, Dec. 12, 1982
1147 *LDN*, Dec. 12, 1982
1148 *DP*, Mar. 31, 1985
1149 *DP*, Jan. 3, 1983
1150 *DP*, Feb. 13, 1983
1151 *AVJ*, Feb. 5, 1981
1152 *LDN*, Apr. 24, 1981
1153 *LDN*, Sep. 9, 1981
1154 *LDN*, Nov. 2, 1977
1155 *LDN*, Nov. 2, 1977
1156 *LDN*, Nov. 2, 1977
1157 LDN May 18, 1977
1158 *DP*, May 25, 1987
1159 *DP*, May 27, 1984
1160 *LDN*, Nov. 2, 1977
1161 *DP*, Dec. 11, 1984
1162 *DP*, Dec. 8, 1984
1163 *DP*, Feb. 15, 1985
1164 *DP*, Apr. 19, 1985
1165 *DP*, Oct. 9, 1987
1166 *DP*, Apr. 11, 1984
1167 *DP*, Apr. 11, 1986
1168 *DP*, Apr. 3, 1987
1169 *DP*, Jul. 26, 1988
1170 *DP*, Feb. 10, 1985
1171 The previous 2 paragraphs on federal farm credit are based on Nyberg, Bartel, "Hard Times Clobber Farm Credit agencies" and Tatge, Mark, "System Failure", both in *DP*, May 25, 1987 and Harl, Neil E., "History and Unique Features of the Farm Credit System", *Choices*, 1st quarter, 2005 and Bovard, *op. cit.*
1172 *LDN*, Nov. 2, 1977
1173 Rice, Teresa A., MacDonnell and Lawrence J., "Agricultural to Urban Water Transfers in Colorado: An Assessment of the Issues and Options", Colorado Water Resources

Research Institute University of Colorado Boulder. Natural Resources Law Center (1993).
1174 Rice and MacDonnell, *op. cit.*, p.1
1175 Sherow, Utopia, *op. cit.*, p. 183
1176 *Pueblo Chieftain*, Jan. 13, 1985
1177 LDN, Feb. 7, 1973
1178 LDN, Mar. 28, 1972
1179 AVJ, Mar. 28, 1985
1180 DP, Apr. 7, 1983
1181 DP, Aug. 4, 1985
1182 DP, Oct. 29, 1986
1183 AVJ, Jun. 10, 1982
1184 AVJ, Nov. 1, 1984
1185 Taylor, R. G. and Young, Robert A., "Rural-to-Urban Water Transfers: Measuring Direct Foregone Benefits of irrigation Water under Uncertain Water Supplies", *Journal of Agricultural and Resource Economics* 20(2).
1186 Howe, Charles W., Lazo, Jeffrey K. and Weber, Kenneth R., "The Economic Impacts of Agriculture-to-Urban Water Transfers on the Area of Origin: A Case Study of the Arkansas River Valley in Colorado", *American Journal of Agricultural Economics*, Vol. 72, No. 5, Proceedings Issue, pp. 1200-1204 (Dec., 1990).
1187 Howe, *op. cit.*, p. 1203
1188 BEA State and Local Personal Income Accounts
1189 Colorado Department of Revenue, Estimates calculated by averaging fiscal year figures.
1190 Decade gains from Census. Regional employment reported in County Business Patterns shows a gain of 4,501 between 1970 and 1974 and of 881 over the next four years.
1191 LDN, Dec. 9, 1977
1192 DP, Apr. 3, 1986
1193 DP, Mar. 29, 1988
1194 DP, May 20, 1989
1195 DP, Jun. 11, 1975
1196 LDN, Dec. 21, 1979
1197 DP, Mar. 1, 1988
1198 BEA and Colorado Department of Revenue, fiscal year data deflated by USCPIU
1199 BEA
1200 Based on BEA non-agricultural wage and salary employment
1201 FMT, Nov. 20, 1985
1202 FMT, Feb. 6, 1985
1203 FMT, Nov. 20, 1985
1204 FMT, Sep. 15, 1986
1205 BEA, deflated by USCPIU
1206 Hurt, *The Big Empty, op. cit.*, p. 213

1207 State of Colorado Department of Highways, *Colorado Traffic Volume Study 1966, 1974, 1980*
1208 *RMN*, Dec. 7, 1962
1209 *LDN, Aug. 12, 1966*
1210 *Colorado Traffic Volume Study, op. cit., 1966 and 1974*
1211 Colorado Department of Revenue. Statistics are for fiscal years deflated by US CPIU.
1212 BEA, nonagricultural wage and salary employment.
1213 Headline in *LL*, Jan. 10, 1974
1214 *LL* Mar. 7, 1974
1215 *LL* Feb. 6, 1975
1216 *LL* May 5, 1977 and Jun. 6,1978
1217 *LL* Aug. 24, 1978
1218 Miller, Lyle, *Limon, Colorado: A Place to Call Home 1953-2016,* Western Reflections Publishing Company (2016) pp. 136 & 149
1219 Census
1220 Colorado Department of Revenue, based on fiscal year data.
1221 *ECP,* Sep. 28, 1972
1222 Miller, *Limon, op. cit.,* p.101
1223 *LL* Mar. 20, 1975
1224 Miller, Lyle, *op. cit.,* p. 98
1225 *ECP,* May 31, 1974
1226 *LL* Oct. 31, 1974
1227 *Henderson, Jason,* "Rebuilding Rural Manufacturing", Federal Reserve Bank of Kansas City, *The Main Street Economist*: Issue 2, 2012, p.1
1228 USDA
1229 *AVJ,* Mar. 8, 1973
1230 *AVJ,* Feb. 26, 1974
1231 *AVJ,* Feb. 28, 1974
1232 *LDN,* Nov. 30, 1977
1233 *SPH,* Dec. 29, 1977
1234 Markoff, Bittersweet, *op. cit.,* pp. 161 & 176
1235 *FMT,* May 10, 1985
1236 *SJA,* Jan. 29. 1972; Mar. 16, 1972; Oct. 16, 1972; November 20, 1972; *BR,* Feb. 3, 1972; Mar. 30, 1972
1237 Hamilton, *op. cit.,* p. 406
1238 Worthy, Ford S., "The Battered House of Hunt", *Fortune,* April 1, 1985
1239 Worthy, *op. cit.*
1240 Hamilton, *op. cit.,* pp. 410-19
1241 Worthy, *op. cit.*
1242 Worthy, *op. cit.*
1243 Worthy, *op. cit.*
1244 Worthy, *op. cit.*
1245 *DP,* Sep. 29, 1984

1246 *DP*, Oct. 19, 1984
1247 *DP*, Dec. 22, 1984
1248 *DP*, Feb. 22, 1985
1249 *DP*, Feb. 27, 1985
1250 *FMT*, Feb. 4, 1985
1251 *DP*, Mar. 2, 1985
1252 *DP*, Mar. 8, 1985
1253 *DP*, Mar. 29, 1985
1254 *FMT*, Mar. 29, 1985
1255 *FMT*, Apr. 8, 1985
1256 *FMT*, Apr. 13, 1985
1257 *DP*, May. 7, 1986
1258 USDA
1259 *FMT*, May 11, 1985
1260 Hamilton, *op. cit.*, pp. 406-425
1261 FMT Jan. 2, 1987
1262 USDA
1263 FMT Jul. 16, 2012
1264 Drabenstott, Mark, Henry, Mark, and Mitchell, Kristin, "Where Have All the Packing Plants Gone? The New Meat Geography in Rural America", *Federal Reserve Bank of Kansas City, Economic Review*, 3rd quarter 1999
1265 Hurt, *The Big Empty, op. cit.*, p.206
1266 Colorado Agricultural Statistics
1267 Wells, Dale, *op. cit.*, p. 173
1268 SJA, Apr. 30, 1972
1269 FMT Feb. 1, 1985
1270 FMT Feb. 1, 1985
1271 RMN Nov. 19, 1975
1272 *RMN*, Apr. 26, 1966, Jan. 15, 1973 and Aug. 6, 1984
1273 RMN Feb. 21, 1980
1274 *SJA*, Mar. 1 and Mar. 5, 1985
1275 FMT Jan. 17, 1985
1276 DP Apr. 8, 1987
1277 *RMN*, Jun. 17, 1986
1278 *Directory of Colorado Manufacturers, op. cit.*, 1990
1279 *DP*, Feb. 11, 1970
1280 *LDN*, Mar. 12, 1973
1281 *AVJ, Feb. 5, 1970*
1282 *LDN*, Mar. 5, 1979
1283 *LDN*, Apr. 26, 1979
1284 *LDN*, Sep. 4, 1979
1285 *RMN*, Sep. 5, 1979 and Oct.22, 1979
1286 *LDN*, Jul. 11, 1979

1287 NYT May 5, 1981
1288 *Lamar Colorado 1986, op. cit.,* p.127
1289 Based on employment and wages figures in ES202 Report from Colorado Department of Labor and Employment. Estimate assumed 650 employees paid average manufacturing wage for county.
1290 BEA Wage & Salary Employment
1291 *DP,* Jan. 15, 1988
1292 *DP,* Mar. 15, 1988
1293 BEA County Personal Income
1294 Census
1295 *Directory of Colorado Manufacturers, op. cit.*
1296 BEA
1297 Migration estimates fromSDO, jobs estimates from Bureau of Economic Analysis
1298 *FMT,* Mar. 1, 1985
1299 Winkler, Richelle, Johnson, Kenneth M., Cheng, Cheng, Beaudoin, Jim, Voss, Paul R. and Curtis, Katherine J., *Age-Specific Net Migration Estimates for US Counties, 1950-2010.* Applied Population Laboratory, University of Wisconsin- Madison, 2013. These estimate differ slightly from those of the State Demographer cited elsewhere.
1300 Census
1301 SDO
1302 Census: Hispanic definitions differed somewhat between the Census years.
1303 DP Feb. 17, 1991

Chapter 10

1304 DP Dec 12, 1990
1305 FMT Dec. 31, 1996
1306 DP May 18, 2008
1307 https://farm.ewg.org/region.php
1308 DP May 18, 2008
1309 Based on average price received by farmers. Source: NASS
1310 Census of Agriculture
1311 Associated Press, Sep. 27, 2013
1312 LJTD, Oct. 24, 2011
1313 DP Jul. 28, 1994
1314 DP Nov. 24, 2004
1315 LDN Aug. 9, 2002
1316 USDA
1317 DP May 27, 2001
1318 DP Oct 29, 2002
1319 DP Jun. 20, 2003
1320 USDA
1321 LDN Jan 10, 2002 and Jun. 20, 2002
1322 LDN Jan. 24, 2002

1323 LDN Sep. 27, 202
1324 DP May 19, 2002
1325 LDN Sep 27, 2002
1326 SJA Jun. 23, 2005
1327 DP Mar. 14, 2003
1328 DP Nov. 23, 2006
1329 DP Nov. 24, 2006
1330 FMT May 1, 2003
1331 DP Jun. 4, 2006
1332 SJA Jun 23, 2005
1333 DP Nov 23, 2006
1334 DP April 15, 2007
1335 Census of Agriculture
1336 DP Nov. 23, 2006
1337 DP Jan. 14, 2003
1338 SPH May 30, 2002
1339 SPR Jul. 22, 2002
1340 LDN Jul. 23, 2002
1341 DP Feb. 9, 2003
1342 DP Jun. 20, 2003
1343 LDN Jan. 5, 2007
1344 LDN Jan. 4, 2007
1345 LDN Jan. 5, 2007
1346 Henderson Jason, "Is This Farm Boom Different?", *The Main Street Economist: Federal Reserve Bank of Kansas City*, Issue 5, 2011, p.1
1347 Average price received per bushel. Source: USDA
1348 Average price received per cwt. Source: USDA
1349 Federal Reserve Bank of Kansas City
1350 Census of Agriculture
1351 Henderson Jason, *op. cit.*, p.3
1352 BEA, Regional Personal Income Series
1353 Cowley, Cortney, "Supply and Demand Fundamentals Weighing on Ag Economy,", Federal Reserve Bank of Kansas City, Jan. 13, 2016
1354 Prices from USDA, wheat KC no. 1 hard winter, corn KC no. 2 yellow, receipts for BEA county personal income
1355 BEA county personal income
1356 Federal Reserve Bank of Kansas City
1357 Langemeier, Michael and Boehlje, Michael, "Drivers of Consolidation and Structural Change in Production Agriculture," *Federal Reserve Bank Kansas City Economic Review*, Special Issue 2017, p. 22
1358 Langemeier and Boehlje, *op. cit.*, p.7
1359 Census of Agriculture
1360 Census of Agriculture

Endnotes

1361 *AVJ*, Nov. 15, 1984
1362 DP Sep. 24, 2017
1363 BR, Dec. 22, 1994
1364 Rhodes, *op. cit.*, p.110
1365 Rhodes, V. James, "The Industrialization of Hog Production", *Review of Agricultural Economics,* May 1955, p. 111
1366 DP, Jul. 31, 1994
1367 Census of Agriculture
1368 BR Nov. 17, 1994
1369 QCEW
1370 DP Mar. 8, 1998
1371 Dexheimer, Eric, "Corporate Swine", *Westword,* Feb. 15, 1995
1372 BR, Feb. 9, 1995
1373 Dexheimer, *op. cit.*
1374 NYT, Sep. 22, 1997
1375 Legislative Council of the State of Colorado, "Analysis of the 1998 Statewide Ballot", Research Publication 438 (1998), pp. 6-10
1376 DP Feb 2, 1999
1377 DP Feb 14, 2006
1378 DP Oct 18, 1998
1379 DP Mar. 29, 1999
1380 DP Apr. 5, 1999
1381 Census of Agriculture
1382 SDO
1383 DP Jul. 20, 1992
1384 DP Apr. 24, 2000
1385 AVJ Jan.6, 1992
1386 DP Feb. 27, 1992
1387 LDN Jun. 12, 2002
1388 DP Jul 28, 2003
1389 DP July 28, 2003
1390 Colorado Politics, Aug. 29,2018
1391 Census of Agriculture
1392 DP Mar. 7, 1992
1393 DP Dec. 16, 2001
1394 DP July 11, 2004
1395 *DP,* Sep. 6, 1985
1396 AVJ Mar 5, 1992
1397 *Pueblo Chieftain*, Jan. 14, 1985
1398 DP Dec. 16, 1999
1399 DP Sep. 27, 2000
1400 DP Oct. 4, 1998
1401 Census of Agriculture

1402 Bjerga, Alan "The Great Plains' Looming Water Crisis: Depletion of a Giant Aquifer Threatens Vital U.S. Farmland", *Bloomberg Business Week,* July 2, 2015
1403 Wilkerson, Chad R. and Williams, Megan D., "The Transformation of Manufacturing Across Federal Reserve Districts: Success for the Great Plains", *Federal Reserve Bank of Kansas City Economic Review,* Second Quarter 2012, p. 115
1404 BEA deflated by US CPIU
1405 BEA
1406 BEA
1407 BEA
1408 BEA
1409 BEA
1410 Henderson Jason, "Rebuilding Rural Manufacturing", *The Main Street Economist: Federal Reserve Bank of Kansas City,* Issue 52, 2012
1411 QCEW. Only data from those counties reporting manufacturing employment in all three years included.
1412 BEA
1413 BEA
1414 University of Colorado, Leeds School of Business, *2017 Colorado Business Economic Outlook* (Boulder, 2016), p. 120
1415 Based on BEA wage and Salary Employment
1416 DP Mar. 4, 1998
1417 QCEW
1418 FMT Sep. 15, 2014
1419 DP Apr. 16, 1993
1420 Brown, Jason P., "The Cycles of Wind Power Development", *The Main Street Economist: Federal Reserve Bank of Kansas City,* Issue 3, 2013
1421 DP Nov. 20, 2002 and Jun. 16, 2005
1422 Open Energy Information
1423 SJA Apr. 25, 2005
1424 DP Feb. 3, 2017
1425 DP Jul. 19, 2005
1426 DP Mar. 5, 2007
1427 Colorado Legislative Council, *An Overview of the Colorado Adult Criminal Justice System,* Research Publication No. 452, 1998, p. 115
1428 Che, Deborah, "Constructing a Prison in the Forest: Conflicts over Nature, Paradise and Identity", *Annals of the Association of American Geographers",* Dec 2002, p. 809
1429 LDN Jan. 15, 2004
1430 FMT Feb. 10, 1997
1431 FMT Feb. 5, 1997
1432 FMT Feb. 5, 1997
1433 DP Mar. 14, 1997
1434 DP Jul. 10, 1997
1435 LDN Aug. 10, 2004

Endnotes

1436 Colorado Department of Corrections
1437 DP Apr. 11, 1993
1438 DP Feb 24, 1997
1439 DP Jun. 10, 2001
1440 Based on QCEW reports
1441 Yanarella, Ernest J. and Blankenship, Susan, "Big House on the Rural Landscape: Prison Recruitment as a Policy Tool for Economic Development", *Journal of Appalachian Studies,* Fall 2006, p. 125
1442 Hudler, *op. cit.*
1443 Based on interviews with Colorado State Demography Office staff.
1444 Colorado Department of Corrections
1445 Colorado Department of Corrections
1446 DP Jan. 22, 2001
1447 DP Dec. 17, 2001
1448 Schlosser, Eric, "The Prison-Industrial Complex", *Atlantic Monthly*, Dec. 1998
1449 *Westword*, Sep. 30, 1999
1450 *Westword*, Dec. 21, 2011
1451 Hudler, *op. cit.*
1452 DP Feb. 26, 2017
1453 BEA
1454 SDO
1455 BEA
1456 ACS, 2013-17
1457 DP Aug. 16, 2016
1458 ACS 2013-17
1459 DP Sep. 25, 2017
1460 QCEW Prowers County figures
1461 LDN Oct 4, 1982
1462 LDN Nov 23, 2005
1463 DP Nov. 16, 2005
1464 LDN Nov. 23, 2005
1465 LDN Sep. 29, 2006
1466 LDN Dec. 16, 2005
1467 LDN Nov. 16, 2005
1468 LDN Dec 15, 2005
1469 BEA
1470 LJTD Nov. 21, 2005
1471 QCEW
1472 DP Jul. 1, 2002
1473 QCEW
1474 BEA
1475 Based on SDO population estimates and Department of Corrections inmate counts adjusted for estimates of Latinos in Elbert County and in state prisons.

1476 SDO
1477 SDO
1478 Census and SDO
1479 DP, Oct. 22, 2006
1480 DP Oct. 27, 1995
1481 Census and ACS 5 year average 2017
1482 SDO
1483 Winkler *et. al.,* University of Wisconsin, *op. cit.*
1484 DP Nov. 22, 1992
1485 SDO and ACS, 5-year estimate 2013-17adjusted for Colorado prison population
1486 ACS, 5-year estimate 2013-17 adjusted for Colorado prison population
1487 Calculation based on SDO estimates adjusted for prison population.
1488 US Bureau of Census, "OnTheMap", 2015
1489 Based on Census
1490 BEA
1491 ACS 2013-17 estimate and 1990 Census
1492 Census and 2017 ACS 5-year average, adjusted for inflation with US CPIU
1493 ACS 2013-17 average
1494 SDO, "Cost of Living Differentials Across the State" (2015).
1495 Adjustment factor for national income and Metro Income based on BEA "Regional Price Parities by State and Metro Area".
1496 ACS 2013-17 average
1497 ACS 2013-17 average
1498 Based on BEA estimates of US wages and salaries per full-time employee and SDO estimates of jobs by NAICS category.
1499 Census
1500 SDO
1501 ACS 2013-17 estimate adjusted for inmate population
1502 SDO and ACS 2013-17 estimate adjusted for inmate population
1503 Source: ACS 2013-17 and 1980 Census
1504 DP, Nov. 12,2017
1505 DP, Nov. 12,2017
1506 DP Jun. 30, 2019
1507 2010 Census
1508 ACS 2013-17 estimate
1509 ACS 2013-17 estimates adjusted for inmate population which was excluded
1510 ACS 2013-17
1511 ACS 2013-17
1512 Keck, *op. cit.,* p. 342
1513 ACS 2013-17
1514 D. Wells, *op. cit.,* p. 221
1515 Keck, *op. cit.,* p. 341
1516 FMT Jan. 16, 2015

Endnotes

1517 ACS 2013-17
1518 DP, Nov. 12, 2017
1519 1990 and 2010 Census
1520 WSJ, May 27, 2017

Chapter 11

1521 Betz, *op. cit.*, pp.227-8
1522 DP Jan. 25, 2017
1523 Census. Compares population in towns in each size class in 1890 with those in same size classes in 1920.
1524 Census Compares population in towns in each size class in 1920 with those in same size classes in 1940.
1525 Census Compares population in towns in each size class in 1940 with those in same size classes in 1970.
1526 BEA County Personal Income
1527 Johnson, Thomas G., "The Rural Economy in a New Century" in *Beyond Agriculture: New Policies for Rural America,* Center for the Study of Rural America, Federal Reserve Bank of Kansas City 2000
1528 Johnson, Rural Economy, *op. cit.* p.17
1529 Johnson, Rural Economy, *op. cit.*
1530 SDO: Elbert County is excluded from the 2010 figure because its population is predominately those living on the fringe of Metro Denver while in the earlier years the County's share of population was small and mostly rural like the rest of the region.
1531 Patten, Jennifer, *In View of the Mountains: A History of Fort Morgan, Colorado* (2011), p. 211
1532 Patten, op. cit., p.256
1533 FMT, Mar. 14, 2018
1534 FMT Nov. 8, 2014
1535 English, History *op. cit.*, p. 22
1536 English, Don, History, 1975 p. 18-19
1537 English, Don, "Fort Morgan" in Colorado Magazine, September 1946; and *FMT,* May 23, 1967
1538 Patten, op. cit., p.329
1539 Patten, op. cit., p.334
1540 English, in Colorado Magazine, *op. cit.* p. 13-14
1541 *Denver Times,* Dec. 31, 1891
1542 *Denver Times,* Oct. 31, 1899
1543 FMT, Oct. 13, 1899
1544 *Denver Times,* Dec. 31, 1891
1545 FMT Mar 5, 1904
1546 English, in Colorado Magazine, *op. cit.*, p.34
1547 Colorado Yearbooks

1548 United Banks of Colorado, Economic Development Department, *Fort Morgan, Colorado: An Economic Overview* 1978
1549 FMT Jan 2, 1986
1550 FMT May 11, 1985
1551 FMT Mar. 1, 1985
1552 SDO
1553 FMT Jun. 11, 1986
1554 DP Mar. 8, 1987
1555 Census
1556 2013-17 ACS
1557 DP Dec 30, 2015
1558 Census and ACS
1559 RMN, Dec. 22, 1875
1560 Keck, *op. cit.*, p.162
1561 Keck, *op. cit.*, p.163
1562 Keck, *op. cit.*, p.164
1563 Hauk, op. cit., p. 272
1564 Hauk, op. cit., p. 273
1565 Census
1566 Keck, *op. cit.*, p.180
1567 Keck, *op. cit.*, p.169
1568 Keck, *op. cit.*, p.171
1569 Bureau of Business and Government Research (1930), *op. cit.*, p.14
1570 Business Research Division, University of Colorado, "La Junta Business Survey", Prepared for La Junta Chamber of Commerce-1948, p.85
1571 Bureau of Business and Government Research (1930), *op. cit.*, pp. 15-17
1572 Bureau of Business and Government Research (1930), *op. cit.*, p. 22
1573 Census
1574 Business Research Division (1948), *op. cit.* pp. 14-15
1575 Hauk, op. cit., p. 285
1576 Business Research Division (1948), *op. cit.* p. 16
1577 Census
1578 LDN May 28, 1942
1579 Census
1580 Keck, *op. cit.*, p.171
1581 Hauk, op. cit., p. 275
1582 Keck, *op. cit.*, p.171
1583 Hauk, op. cit., p. 286
1584 Census
1585 La Junta Chamber of Commerce, 1980
1586 SDO
1587 Census and ACS, compares 1990 Census estimate with 2013-17 ACS estimate
1588 Information from Cindy DeGroen of SDO, Dec. 19, 2008

Endnotes

1589 Stevens, Ryan, "Manufacturing Spurs Economic Growth in La Junta" in *Colorado Business Review*, Number 4, 2015, University of Colorado, Leeds School of Business, pp. 8-9
1590 ACS 2013-17
1591 C. Kendall, *op. cit.*
1592 LDN May 26, 1950
1593 This paragraph draws heavily upon Betz, *op. cit.*, pp.190-193
1594 Betz, *op. cit.*, pp.197-199
1595 These Counties were Otero, Bent, Prowers, Kiowa, Cheyenne and Lincoln. Crowley County was formed later from part of Otero.
1596 Betz, *op. cit.*, p. 217
1597 *Lamar Register*, Dec 29, 1909
1598 Betz, *op. cit.*, p.199
1599 Betz, *op. cit.*, p. 234
1600 *Lamar Register*, Jan. 4, 1910
1601 *Lamar Register*, Mar. 3, 1915
1602 *Lamar Colorado 1986*, *op. cit.*, p. 44
1603 Source: Census. The Census shows Lamar's population declining 16 percent during 1910's and increasing 69 percent during 1920's. This is inconsistent with Prowers County figures showing gains of 46 percent during 1910's and only 6 percent during 1920's. It is likely that much of the towns growth between 1910 and 1930 occurred in the 1910's and the Census results reflect boundary changes or some other quirk.
1604 *Colorado Yearbooks*
1605 *RMN*, Apr. 7, 1962
1606 United Banks of Colorado: *Lamar, Colorado: An Economic Overview* 1975
1607 SDO
1608 Census
1609 Lamar Chamber of Commerce, *op. cit.*
1610 SDO
1611 LDN, Jan. 10, 2002
1612 LDN, Nov. 16, 2002
1613 Census and ACS
1614 SDO
1615 Based on Census and SDO estimates. The 1950 Census showed La Junta's population some 2 percent greater than Sterling's.
1616 Wells, Dale, *The Logan County Ledger*, Logan County Historical Society (1976), p. 18
1617 Wells ed., Logan County, *op. cit.*, p. 28
1618 Dale Wells, *op. cit.*, p. 25
1619 Jones and Collman, *op. cit.*, p.17
1620 Jones and Collman, *op. cit.*, p.17
1621 Jones and Collman, *op. cit.*, p.35
1622 Jones and Collman, *op. cit.*, p.43
1623 Jones and Collman, *op. cit.*, p.43

1624 Dale Wells, *op. cit.*, p. 56-7
1625 LCA, Dec. 21, 1905
1626 SD Feb. 1, 1912
1627 Dale Wells, *op. cit.*, p. 67
1628 Dale Wells, *op. cit.*, p. 69
1629 Dale Wells, *op. cit.*, p. 55
1630 Dale Wells, *op. cit.*, p. 84
1631 Census
1632 LCA, May 24, 1906
1633 Dale Wells, *op. cit.*, p. 116
1634 Dale Wells, *op. cit.*, p. 105
1635 Dale Wells, *op. cit.*, p. 105
1636 Dale Wells, *op. cit.*, p. 108
1637 Dale Wells, *op. cit.*, p. 128
1638 Census
1639 Wells ed., *Logan County, op. cit.,* p. 110
1640 United Banks of Colorado, Inc., Economic Development Department Sterling, Colorado: An Economic Overview, circa 1972
1641 Wells ed., Logan County, *op. cit.,* p. 110
1642 Jones and Collman, *op. cit.*, p.182
1643 Dale Wells, *op. cit.*, p. 146
1644 Jones and Collman, *op. cit.*, p.220
1645 Dale Wells, *op. cit.*, p. 164; Jones and Collman, *op. cit.*; RMN, Apr. 11, 1951
1646 RMN Jul. 10, 1960
1647 See Chapter 8
1648 Jones and Collman, *op. cit.*, p.220
1649 Jones and Collman, *op. cit.*, p.223
1650 Jones and Collman, *op. cit.*, p.302
1651 Jones and Collman, *op. cit.*, p.323
1652 Jones and Collman, *op. cit.*, p.329
1653 Jones and Collman, *op. cit.*, p.325
1654 Dale Wells, *op. cit.*, p. 175
1655 SJA, Jun. 22, 1987
1656 SJA, Apr. 22, 1985
1657 RMN Apr 26, 1986
1658 Dale Wells, *op. cit.*, p. 177
1659 Census
1660 SDO
1661 RMN, Sep. 11, 1995
1662 Jones and Collman, *op. cit.*, p.335
1663 Jones and Collman, *op. cit.*, p.337
1664 Census and ACS, compares 1990 Census estimate with 2013-17 ACS estimate
1665 SDO

Endnotes

1666 Mills, *op. cit.*, p.9
1667 Mills, *op. cit.* p.11
1668 Mills, *op. cit.* p.16
1669 Mills, *op. cit.* pp. 37-38
1670 Mills, *op. cit.* p.21
1671 Census
1672 Census
1673 Mills, *op. cit.* p.71
1674 Mills, *op. cit.* p.43
1675 Mills, *op. cit.* p.87
1676 Mills, *op. cit.* p.84
1677 Bureau of Business Research, University of Colo. *Brush Industrial Survey*, 1954, p.18
1678 Mills, *op. cit.* p.90
1679 Mills, *op. cit.* p.88
1680 Mills, *op. cit.* p.104-05
1681 Census
1682 RMN Apr. 26, 1966 and Jan. 15, 1973
1683 Brush Chamber of Commerce & Public Service Company of Colorado, *Brush, Colorado*, circa 1967, p.i
1684 Brush Chamber of Commerce, *op. cit.* p.25
1685 DP Apr. 11, 1993
1686 DP Apr. 11, 1993
1687 ACS, job figures based on place of residence
1688 DP Oct. 20, 1994
1689 DP Apr. 11, 1993
1690 SDO and ACS 2013-17
1691 *History of Kit Carson County op. cit.*, pp. 162-3
1692 *History of Kit Carson County, op. cit.*, p.170
1693 *History of Kit Carson County, op. cit.*, p.173
1694 DP Feb. 26, 2017
1695 Census
1696 See Chapter 10
1697 DP Feb. 26, 2017
1698 SDO
1699 *Bent County History*, book committee, *op. cit.*, pp.46-47
1700 *Bent County History*, book committee, *op. cit.*, pp. 9-10
1701 *Bent County History*, book committee, *op. cit.*, p. 80
1702 *Bent County History*, book committee, *op. cit.*, p. 10
1703 *Bent County History*, book committee, *op. cit.*, pp.47-54
1704 *Bent County History*, book committee, *op. cit.*, p. 78
1705 *Bent County History*, book committee, *op. cit.*, pp. 22-23

1706 Gilmore, John S. and Ryan, John J., "The Government Sector of the Arkansas Valley Economy", prepared for The Colorado Division of Commerce & Development, Denver Research Institute, June 1965, p. C.2
1707 *Bent County History*, book committee, *op. cit.*, pp. 201-202
1708 BCD, Apr. 22, 1982
1709 SDO & ACS 2013-17 estimate
1710 For example, Fell, *op. cit.*
1711 Fell, *op. cit.*, p. 7
1712 Limon Heritage and Railroad Museum
1713 Fell, *op. cit.*, p. 9
1714 Fell, *op. cit.*, p. 14
1715 Census
1716 Fell, *op. cit.*, pp. 21, 22 & 26
1717 Census
1718 Fell, *op. cit.*, p. 35
1719 Fell, *op. cit.*, p. 38
1720 Census
1721 Fell, *op. cit.*, p. 53
1722 Miller, Lyle, *op. cit.*, p.93
1723 SDO
1724 ACS 2013-17
1725 Keck, *op. cit.*, p. 197
1726 Sherow, Watering, *op. cit.*, pp. 13-14
1727 Keck, *op. cit.*, p. 198
1728 Keck, *op. cit.*, p. 201
1729 Keck, *op. cit.*, p. 203
1730 Source: 1900 Census
1731 Keck, *op. cit.*, p. 204
1732 See Chapter 9
1733 Russell, Randy, *Rocky Ford, Colorado: Targeted Industry Study* prepared for Southeast Colorado Office of Business Development, 1987
1734 Russell, *op. cit.* p. 12
1735 ACS
1736 Harper, *op. cit.*, p. 14
1737 Harper, *op. cit.*, p. 15
1738 Harper, *op. cit.*, p. 59
1739 Harper, *op. cit.*, p. 59 and Census
1740 Census
1741 Harper, *op. cit.*, p. 84
1742 Harper, *op. cit.*, p. 117
1743 Census
1744 SDO
1745 DP Jul. 30, 2017

Endnotes

1746 Yuma Colorado Centennial Book Committee, *West Yuma County Colorado: A History of West Yuma County 1886-1986*, Taylor Publishing Company (1985), pp. 14-15
1747 Yuma Colorado Centennial Book Committee, *op. cit.*, p. 15
1748 Yuma Colorado Centennial Book Committee, *op. cit.*, p. 14
1749 Census
1750 Yuma Colorado Centennial Book Committee, *op. cit.*, p. 15
1751 Yuma Colorado Centennial Book Committee, *op. cit.*, p. 16
1752 Census
1753 Yuma Colorado Centennial Book Committee, *op. cit.*, p. 16
1754 USDA
1755 SDO
1756 ACS 2013-17
1757 Kraenzel, Carl Frederick, *The Great Plains in Transition*, University of Oklahoma Press (Norman 1955), pp.194-211
1758 Census prior to 1980 and SDO thereafter.
1759 Census and SDO
1760 DP June 10, 2001
1761 Kiowa County Bicentennial Committee, *op. cit.*, p. 397
1762 Census and SDO
1763 SDO
1764 *Colorado Springs Gazette*, May 1, 2017

Chapter 12

1765 See SDO, "Program Description of Location Economic Information and Forecasting Assistance", Technical Documentation, Revised August 2011
1766 BEA
1767 Email from Chris Akers of SDO, Sep. 5, 2017
1768 BEA Regional Personal Income
1769 SDO Total employment less agricultural production
1770 SDO
1771 SDO
1772 Census "OnTheMap" 2015
1773 BEA
1774 SDO
1775 BEA.
1776 BEA
1777 Basic employment is divided into "direct basic" and "indirect basic". The former includes workers in organizations directly supported by outside dollars while the latter category are workers at suppliers to these organizations. The discussion in this chapter will focus on direct basic employment and when the term "basic employment" is used it will mean direct basic employment unless specified otherwise.
1778 SDO 2019 projections

1779 DP Jul. 30, 2017
1780 SDO projections Dec. 2018 and email from Chris Akers of SDO, Jan. 9, 2018
1781 Email from Chris Akers of SDO, Jan. 9, 2018
1782 Population growth figures in this paragraph based on SDO 2019 projections
1783 SDO 2019 projections
1784 Drabenstott, Mark and Henderson, Jason, "A New Rural Economy: A New Role for Public Policy", Federal Reserve Bank of Kansas City, *The Main Street Economist*: Issue 4, 2006
1785 Business Research Division, Leeds School of Business, University of Colorado, Boulder, *Rural Colorado Economic Resiliency: Study of Factors Impacting Rural Economic Growth 1990-2014,* Final Draft Report, August 18, 2016
1786 *Rural Colorado Resiliency, op. cit.*, p.5
1787 *Rural Colorado Resiliency, op. cit.*, p.47
1788 *Rural Colorado Resiliency, op. cit.*, pp. 14 & 32
1789 DP, Oct. 8, 2017
1790 Colorado Water Plan, Colorado.gov\cowaterplan, p.6-32
1791 DP Jun. 30, 2019
1792 SDO, "'2015 Colorado Planning & Management Region Report", Region 1
1793 Census of Agriculture 2017
1794 DP Sep. 24, 2017
1795 *Rural Colorado Resiliency, op. cit.,* p.39
1796 Pendergast, Alan, "Winging It", *Westword,* Apr. 11,1996
1797 Drabenstott, and Henderson (2006), *op. cit.*
1798 Young, Jeffrey S., "Not so lonely eagles", *Forbes,* May 19, 1997
1799 WSJ, Jun. 16, 2017
1800 MapBroadbandNow.org, Mar. 2020
1801 DP Sep. 10, 2017
1802 WSJ, Jun. 2, 2017
1803 Census for 1970 and 1990, ACS for 2013-17
1804 *Rural Colorado Resiliency, op. cit.*, p.47
1805 *Rural Colorado Resiliency, op. cit.*, p.52
1806 DP Oct 18, 1998
1807 DP Apr. 26, 1996
1808 DP Nov. 20, 1994
1809 McCue, Roy, "Lincoln County—A Rural County in the Crosshairs of Transportation and Energy Expansion", *Colorado Business Review,* Nov. 2016
1810 Hudler, Rol, "The Economic Impact of Prison Closing in Burlington", *Colorado Business Review,* Nov. 2016
1811 SDO, 2017 Colorado Planning & Management Report, Region 6
1812 DP Dec 24, 2017, The section of the Colorado constitution is referred to as the "Gallagher Amendment." As described in the DP article, "The convoluted rules of Colorado state finance mandate additional relief for Front Range homeowners whose property values are soaring but take another bite out of the budgets of rural

governments, schools and fire districts that are already struggling to provide basic public services."

1813 Interim Committee on Rural Economic Development, Issues Report to the Colorado General Assembly, Colorado Legislative Council Research Publication No. 544 December 2005, p.12
1814 DP, Dec. 10, 2017
1815 Reported in DP, Feb. 21, 2018
1816 SDO, "2017 Colorado Planning & Management Region Report", Region 5
1817 *Rural Colorado Resiliency, op. cit.*, p.51
1818 SDO, "2017 Colorado Planning & Management Report, Region 6"
1819 WSJ Dec. 26, 2017
1820 Source: *Rural Economic Resiliency, op. cit.*
1821 WSJ Dec. 26, 2017
1822 Conroy, Teressa; Low, Sarah A.; and Weiler, Stephan; "Fueling Job Engines: Impacts of Small Business Loans on Establishment Births in Metropolitan and Nonmetro Counties", *Contemporary Economic Policy,* July 2017, p. 589
1823 SDO. Front Range includes, Denver and Boulder PMSAs; Fort Collins, Greeley, Colorado Springs and Pueblo MSAs; and Elbert County.
1824 DP, Jul. 23, 2017
1825 DP, Dec. 24, 2017
1826 DP, Nov. 6, 2013
1827 Gregg, Josiah, *Commerce of the Prairies,* Narrative Press, Santa Barbara, CA 2001
1828 NYT Mar. 18, 2019
1829 Webb, W.P., *op. cit.,* pp. 507-8

Bibliography

Books

Ashworth, William, *Ogallala Blue: Water and Life on the High Plains*, W.W. Norton & Company (New York 2006).

Athearn, Robert G., *High Country Empire*, University of Nebraska Press (Lincoln, Nebraska 1965).

----. *The Coloradans*. University of New Mexico Press (Albuquerque 1976).

Audretsch, Robert W., *The Civilian Conservation Corps in Colorado 1933-1942*, Dog Ear Publishing (Indianapolis 2008).

Betz, Ava A., *Prowers County History*, The Prowers County Historical Society (Lamar 1986).

Bonnifield, Paul, *The Dust Bowl; Men, Dirt and Depression*, University of New Mexico Press (Albuquerque 1979).

Bowman, Charles W. *Bent County History*, from *The Historical Encyclopedia of Colorado* Volume 1

The Book Committee, *Bent County History* (Las Animas 1987).

Brisbin, Gen. James S., U.S.A. *The Beef Bonanza or How to Get Rich on the Plains: Being a Description of Cattle-growing, Sheep-farming, Horse-raising, and Dairying in the West*, J.B. Libbincott & Co. (Philadelphia 1881).

Bureau of Land Management, *Land of Contrast: A History of Southeast Colorado*, BLM Cultural Resources Series (Colorado: No. 17).

Bureau of Land Management, *The New Empire of the Rockies: A History of Northeast Colorado*, BLM Cultural Resources Series (Colorado: No. 16).

Butler, William B. *The Fur Trade in Colorado*, Western Reflections Publishing Company (Lake City, Colorado 2012).

Bryant, Keith L. Jr., *History of the Atchison Topeka and Santa Fe Railway*, University of Nebraska Press (Lincoln 1974).

Cannon, Brian Q., *Remaking the Agrarian Dream: New Deal Rural Resettlement in the Mountain West*, University of New Mexico Press (Albuquerque 1996).

Chapman Publishing Company, *Portrait and Biographical Record of the State of Colorado* (Chicago 1899).

Civil Works Administration, *Interviews Collected During 1933-34 for State Historical of Colorado,* History Colorado Library

Cohen, Deborah, *Braceros: Migrant Citizens and Transnational Subjects in the Postwar United States and Mexico* (University of North Carolina Press 2011).

Colorado Department of Transportation, *100 Years of Colorado Transportation History (2010).*

Colorado Preservation, Inc., *Drought, Depression and Dust; the New Deal in Eastern Colorado-Survey Report* (2005).

----. *Historic Baca County* (Denver 2010).

Conklin, Emma Burke, *A Brief History of Logan County, Colorado* (Denver 1928).

Crisler, Carney Clark, *The Mexican Bracero Program with Special Reference to Colorado,* MA Thesis (University of Denver 1968).

Cunfer, Geoff, *On the Great Plains: Agriculture and Environment,* Texas A&M University Press (College Station 2005).

Darley, Ward, *Sugar: The Tariff, The Trust and The Truth* (Denver, The Author, 1913).

Dary, David, *The Santa Fe Trail,* Alfred A. Knopf (New York 2000).

Deutsch, Sarah, *No Refuge: Culture, Class and Gender on an Anglo-Hispanic Frontier in the American Southwest, 1880-1940,* Oxford University Press (New York 1987).

East Central Council of Local Governments, *Our Heritage, A Collection of tales of East Central Colorado, Vol. I* (1983).

Egan, Timothy, *The Worst Hard Time* Houghton Mifflin (New York 2006).

Ellis, Edward Robb, *A Nation in Torment: The Great American Depression, 1292-1939,* Kodansha America, Inc. (New York 1995).

Emmons, David M., *Garden in the Grasslands: Boomer Literature of the Central Great Plains,* University of Nebraska Press (Lincoln 1971).

English, Don, *The Early History of Fort Morgan, Colorado,* Fort Morgan Heritage Association (1975).

Farnham, Thomas J., 1843 *Travels in the Great Western Prairies, the Anahuac and Rocky Mountains, and in the Oregon Territory (*Reprinted by Da Capo Press, NY 1973).

Fell, James E, Jr., *Limon Colorado: Hub City of the High Plains, 1888-1952* (Limon Heritage Society 1997).

Frazier, Ian, *The Great Plains,* Picador Press (New York 1989).

Fort Sedgwick Historical Society, *The History of Sedgwick County, Colorado* (1982).

Fowler, Loretta, *The Columbia Guide to American Indians of the Great Plains* Columbia University Press (New York 2003).

Friedman, Milton and Schwartz, Anna Jacobson, *A Monetary History of the United States 1867-1960,* Princeton University Press (Princeton 1963).

Gardner, Bruce L., *American Agriculture in the Twentieth Century,* Harvard University Press (Cambridge, MA 2002).

Bibliography

Galbraith, John Kenneth, *The New Industrial State*, Third Edition, Revised, Houghton Miflin Company (Boston 1978).

Garst, Shannon, *William Bent and His Adobe Empire*, Julian Messner, Inc. (New York 1957).

Gregory, James N., *American Exodus, The Dust Bowl Migration and Okie Culture in California*, Oxford University Press (New York, 1989).

Griffiths, Mel, *Colorado, A Geography*, Westview Press, Inc. (Boulder 1983).

Goldin, Claudia and Katz, Lawrence F., *The Race between Education and Technology*, Harvard University Press (Cambridge, MA 2008).

Gressley, Gene M. *Bankers and Cattlemen*, Alfred A. Knopf (New York 1966).

Halas, Eugene T., *The Banking Structure in Colorado*, University of Denver (1969).

Hamilton, Candy, *Footprints in Sugar: A History of the Great Western Sugar Company*, Bates Publishers (Ontario, Oregon 2009).

Harper, Thomas Alan, *The Development of a High Plains Community: A History of Baca County Colorado*, MA Thesis, University of Denver (1967).

Harvey, Robert, *Amache: The Story of Japanese Internment in Colorado during World War II*, Taylor Trade Publishing (Lanham MD,2003).

Harris, Katherine, *Long Vistas: Women and Families in Colorado Homesteads*, University of Colorado Press (Niwot 1993).

Hiltzik, Michael A., *The New Deal, A Modern History*, Free Press (New York, 2011).

Hurt, R. Douglas, *American Agriculture: A Brief History*, Iowa State University Press (Ames 1994).

----. *The Big Empty: The Great Plains in the Twentieth Century*, The University of Arizona Press (Tucson 2011).

----. *The Dust Bowl, An Agricultural and Social History*, Nelson Hall (Chicago 1981).

----. *The Great Plains During World War II*, University of Nebraska Press (Lincoln 2008).

----. *Problems of Plenty: The American Farmer in the Twentieth Century*, Ivan R. Dee (Chicago 2002).

----. *Agricultural Technology in the Twentieth Century*, Sunflower University Press (Manhattan, KS 1991).

Hewes, Leslie, *The Suitcase Farming Frontier: A Study in the Historical Geography of the Central Great Plains*, University of Nebraska Press (Lincoln 1973).

Hosokawa, Bill, *Colorado's Japanese Americans; From 1886 to the Present*, University Press of Colorado (Boulder 2005).

Hudson, John C., *Plains Country Towns*, University of Minnesota Press (Minneapolis 1985).

Johnson, Vance, *Heaven's Tableland: The Dust Bowl Story*, Farrar, Straus and Company (New York 1947).

Jones, James R. and Collman, Russ, *Sterling Colorado: Crossroads on the Prairie*, Sundance Books (Denver 2000).

Jones, P. Andrew and Cech, Thomas, *Colorado Water Law for Non-Lawyers,* University Press of Colorado (Boulder 2009).

Jordan, Terry G., *North American Cattle-Ranching Frontiers,* University of New Mexico Press (Albuquerque, 1993).

Keck, Frances Bollacker, *Conquistadors to the 21st Century: A History of Otero and Crowley Counties Colorado,* Otero Press (La Junta 1995).

Kessler, H.H., Lamar Centennial Inc., *Lamar Colorado Its First Hundred Years: 1886-1986,* Kes-Print (Shawnee Mission, KS, 1986).

Kiowa County Bicentennial Committee, *Kiowa County,* Johnson Publishing Company (Boulder 1976).

Kit Carson County History Book Committee, *History of Kit Carson County, Colorado,* Curtis Median Corporation (1988).

Kit Carson County Cattlemen's Association, *Kit Carson County and Its Cattlemen* (1963).

Klein, Murray, *Union Pacific: Birth of a Railroad 1862-1893,* Doubleday & Company, Inc. (Garden City, NY, 1987).

Knowlton, Christopher, *Cattle Kingdom, The Hidden History of the Cowboy West,* Houghton Mifflin Harcourt (New York, 2017).

Kraenzel, Carl Frederick, *The Great Plains in Transition,* University of Oklahoma Press (Norman 1955).

Lavender, David, *Bent's Fort,* University of Nebraska Press (Lincoln, 1954).

Leonard, Steven J., *Trials and Triumphs: A Colorado Portrait of the Great Depression, With FSA Photographs,* University Press of Colorado (Niwot 1993).

Limerick, Patricia Nelson, *The Legacy of Conquest: The Unbroken Past of the American West,* W.W. Norton & Company-Kindle Edition (New York 1987).

Lurie, George, *A Legacy of Shame: The Story of Colorado's Camp Amache,* G. Lurie (c1985).

Matsushima, John, and Farr, W.D., *A Journey Back: A History of Cattle Feeding in Colorado and the United States,* Cattlemen's Communications (Colorado Springs 1995).

May, William J. Jr., *The Great Western Sugarlands: History of the Great Western Sugar Company,* Thesis (Ph. D.), University of Colorado at Boulder (1982).

McMath, Robert C. Jr., *American Populism,* Hill, and Wang (New York 1993).

Miller, Lyle, *Limon, Colorado: A Place to Call Home 1953-2016,* Western Reflections Publishing Company (2016).

Mills, James E., *A History of Brush, Colorado,* M.A. Thesis, University of Colorado (1964).

Miner, H. Craig, *Harvesting the High Plains: John Kriss and the business of wheat farming, 1920-55,* University Press of Kansas (Lawrence 1998).

Monahan, Doris, *Julesburg and Fort Sedgwick: Wicked City—Scandalous Fort* (Sterling, CO 2009).

Moretti, Enrico, *The New Geography of Jobs,* First Mariner Books (ebook-2013).

Bibliography

Niehaus, Fred R., *Development of Banking in Colorado,* Mountain States Publishing Company (Denver 1942).

Norris, Jim, *North for the Harvest,* Minnesota Historical Society Press (St. Paul 2009).

Opie, John, *Ogallala: Water for a Dry Land,* University of Nebraska Press (Lincoln 1993).

Osteen, Ike, *A Place Called Baca,* Fifth edition, The Baca Weekly (Springfield, CO, 1997).

Paarlberg, Don, *American Farm Policy: A Case Study of Centralized Decision Making,* John Wiley & Sons, Inc. (New York 1964).

Paosour, E.C. Jr., and Rucker, Randal R., *Plowshares and Pork Barrels: The Political Economy of Agriculture,* Independent Institute (Oakland, CA 2005).

Patten, Jennifer, *In View of the Mountains: A History of Fort Morgan, Colorado* (2011).

Peake, Ora Brooks, *The Colorado Range Cattle Industry,* The Arthur H. Clark Company (Glendale, CA 1937).

Penley, Gary, *Rivers of Wind: A Western Boyhood Remembered,* Filter Press (Palmer Lake, Colorado 1998).

Phillips County Historical Society, Book Committee, *Those Were the Days, 1889-1989 Centennial History Phillips County Colorado* (Holyoke, 1988).

Pisani, Donald J., *To Reclaim a Divided West: Water, Law and Public Policy, 1848-1902,* University of New Mexico Press (Albuquerque 1992).

Powell, John Wesley, *Report on the Lands of the Arid Region of The United States: With a More Detailed Account of the Lands of Utah,* Edited by Wallace Stegner, Belknap Press of Harvard University Press (Cambridge, MA 1962).

Robertson, Donald B., *Encyclopedia of Western Railroad History,* Taylor Publishing Company (Dallas 1991).

Saloutos, Theodore, *The American Farmer and the New Deal,* Iowa State University Press (Ames 1982).

Scamehorn, Lee, *High Altitude Energy: A History of Fossil Fuels in Colorado,* University of Colorado Press (Boulder 2002).

----. *Colorado's Small Town Industrial Revolution: The Arkansas Valley and the Western Slope,* Dog Ear Publishing (Indianapolis 2012).

Sheflin, Douglas, *Legacies of Dust: Land Use and Labor on the Colorado Plains,* University of Nebraska Press (Lincoln 2019).

Schrager, Adam, *The Principled Politician: the Ralph Carr Story,* Fulcrum Pub. (Golden, CO 2008).

Schlebecker, John T. *Raising Cattle on the Plains 1900-1961,* University of Nebraska Press (Lincoln 1963).

Schweninger, Lee, editor, *The First We Can Remember: Colorado Pioneer Women Tell Their Stories,* University of Nebraska Press (Lincoln 2011).

Sherow, James Earl, Watering the Valley, Development along the High Plains Arkansas River, 1870-1950. University of Kansas Press (Lawrence, Kansas 1990).

Shoven, John L., *First Majority-Last Minority: The Transformation of Rural Life in America*, Northern Illinois University Press (De Kalb, 1976).

Smith, Henry Nash, *Virgin Land*, Vintage Books (New York 1950).

Stegner, Wallace, *Beyond the Hundredth Meridian*, Penguin Books (New York 1992).

Steinel, Alvin T. *History of Agriculture in Colorado*, State Board of Agriculture (1926).

Stenzel, Richard and Cech, Tom, *Water: Colorado's Real Gold* (Richard Stenzel 2013).

Stiglitz, Joseph E., *The Great Divide: Unequal Societies and What We Can Do About Them*, W.W. Norton (New York, 2015).

Taylor, Ralph C., *Colorado South of the Border*, Sage Books (Denver 1963).

Tyler, Daniel, *The Last Water Hole in the West: The Colorado-Big Thompson Project and the Northern Colorado Water Conservancy District*, University Press of Colorado (Niwot, CO 1992).

Underwood, John J., *Physical Land Conditions in the Western and Southeastern Baca County Soil Conservation Districts, Colorado*, US Department of Agriculture, Soil Conservation Service (Washington, DC 1944).

Webb, Walter Prescott, *The Great Plains*, Grosset & Dunlap (New York, 1931).

Wells, Bud, Editor, *Logan County: Better by 100 Years: A Centennial History of Logan County Colorado 1887-1987*, Curtis Media Corporation (1987).

Wells, Dale, *The Logan County Ledger*, Logan County Historical Society (1976).

West, Elliot, *The Contested Plains: Indians, Goldseekers, and the Rush to Colorado*, University Press of Kansas (Lawrence 1998).

White, Richard *Railroaded: The Transcontinentals and the Making of Modern America*, W.W. Norton & Company (New York 2011).

Wickens, James F., *Colorado and the Great Depression*, Garland Publishers (New York 1979).

Wishart, David J., *The Last Days of the Rainbelt*, University of Nebraska Press (Lincoln 2013).

----, editor, *The Encyclopedia of the Great Plains*, University of Nebraska Press (Lincoln 2004).

Worster, Donald, *Dust Bowl, The Southern Plains in the 1930s*, Oxford University Press (New York 1982).

----. *Rivers of Empire*, Pantheon Books (New York 1985).

Wood, Richard E., *Survival of Rural America: Small Victories and Bitter Harvests*, University Press of Kansas (Lawrence 2008).

Woodka, Chris "Taming the Land" Series of articles about development of Arkansas Valley published in Pueblo Chieftain (2008-09).

Writers' Program of the Works Progress Administration, *The WPA Guide to 1930s Colorado*, University Press of Kansas (Lawrence 1987).

Yuma Colorado Centennial Book Committee, *West Yuma County Colorado: A History of West Yuma County 1886-1986*, Taylor Publishing Company (1985).

Articles and Pamphlets

Aiken, J. David, "Development of the Appropriation Doctrine: Adapting Water Allocation Policies to Semiarid Environs", Great Plains Quarterly, Winter 1988

Allen, John L., "The Garden-Desert Continuum: Competing Views of the Great Plains in the Nineteenth Century", *Great Plains Quarterly*, Fall 1985, pp 207-220

Bartlett, E.T. and. Trock, W.L, "The Conservation Reserve Program: An Economic Perspective" in *Rangelands*, Aug. 1987 pp. 147-48

bauderhistory.com, "TheBirthoftheGermanSettlement.pdf"

Baxter, A.H. notes in Bent and Prowers County Cattle and Horse Growers Brand Book, Western History Collection, Denver Public Library

Bernanke, Ben S. "The Financial Accelerator and the Credit Channel, The Credit Channel of Monetary Policy in the Twenty-first Century Conference, Atlanta, Georgia". Federal Reserve Bank of Atlanta, June 15, 2007

Blodgett, Ralph E." The Colorado Territorial Board of Immigration" in *Colorado Magazine,* Summer 1969

Bovard, James "The Farm Credit Quagmire", Cato Policy Analysis No. 122, July 27, 1989

Brown, Jason P. "The Cycles of Wind Power Development", *The Main Street Economist: Federal Reserve Bank of Kansas City,* Issue 3, 2013

Byers and Parker," Choice Farming, Grazing, Coal and Timber Land in Colorado along the Kansas Pacific and Denver Pacific Railways" (Denver 1873).

Che, Deborah, "Constructing a Prison in the Forest: Conflicts over Nature, Paradise and Identity", *Annals of the Association of American Geographers" (Dec 2002).*

Christy, Robert "The Denver Alfalfa Milling & Products Company 1908-1946" Unpublished Manuscript (1965).

Clarey Land Company, *Golden Prairie Lands, Washington County Colorado* (Akron 1909).

Clemens, Michael A., Lewis, Ethan G. and Postel, Hannah M., "Immigration Restrictions as Active Labor Market Policy," *American Economic Review (*June 2018).

Cole, B. Erin, "A Second Change: The Resettlement Administration in Dust Bowl-Era Colorado", *Colorado Heritage* (September/October 2013).

Colorado Magazine, "Floyd M. Wilson and the Alfalfa Milling Industry" (1944).

----. "Fort Morgan", Sep. 1946

Conroy, Teressa; Low Sarah A.; and Weiler, Stephan; "Fueling Job Engines: Impacts of Small Business Loans on Establishment Births in Metropolitan and Nonmetro Counties," *Contemporary Economic Policy,* July 2017, pp. 578-595

Cook, Arthur R., "A Pioneer Colorado Cattle King: John Wesley Prowers," Seminar paper at University of Colorado 1953-4

Cottrell, H.M., *Dry Land Farming in Eastern Colorado,* Bulletin 145, Experiment Station (Fort Collins, 1910).

----. *Dry Farming in Eastern Colorado*, Passenger Traffic Department, Rock Island Lines (Chicago 1910).

Cronon, William J.; Miles, George and Gitlin, Jay, "Becoming West" in *Under an Open Sky: Rethinking America's West* W.W. Norton & Company (New York 1992).

Davenport, Walter, "Land Where Our Children Die", *Colliers Weekly*, Sept. 18, 1937

Diebert, Edward J., "Soil Bank" in *Great Plains Encyclopedia*

Dinse, John and Browne, William P. "The Emergence of the American Agriculture Movement, 1977-79" in *Great Plains Quarterly"*, Fall 1985, pp. 221-235

Doty, Michael C., and McFarland E.M, "Rocketing the Rockies" in *Colorado Rail Annual, No. 17* (Colorado Railroad Museum, 1987), pp. 9-124.

Drabenstott, Mark and Henderson, Jason, "A New Rural Economy: A New Role for Public Policy", Federal Reserve Bank of Kansas City, *The Main Street Economist*: Issue 4, 2006

----. Henry, Mark; and Mitchell, Kristin, "Where Have All the Packing Plants Gone? The New Meat Geography in Rural America", *Federal Reserve Bank of Kansas City, Economic Review*, 3rd quarter (1999)

Dunbar, Robert G., "History of Agriculture" in *Colorado and Its People: A narrative and Topical History of the Centennial State*, Hafen, LeRoy R. editor, Lewis Historical Publishing Co., Inc. (New York 1948).

----. "Agricultural Adjustments in Eastern Colorado in the Eighteen-Nineties", *Agricultural History*, Jan. 1944, pp. 41-52

Duncan, Marvin and Bickel, Blaine, "U.S. Agricultural Exports-A Boon to Farmers", *Federal Reserve Bank of Kansas Monthly Review*, July-August 197

Durrell, Glen R., "Homesteading in Colorado", *Colorado Magazine* Spring 1974, pp 93-114

English, Don, "Fort Morgan" in Colorado Magazine, September 1946

Everett, Derek R., "Colorado and World War I" in *Colorado Heritage,* Winter 2018/19, pp. 4-13

Falcon, Priscilla, "Soldiers of the Field: Mexican Labor in Northern Colorado", in *Colorado Heritage, March/April 2015,* pp .30-31

Ellis, Richard N, "Bent, Carson and the Indians, 1965", Colorado Magazine, Winter 1969, pp. 56-66

Farm Journal, January 1978 "The Farm Strike", pp.35-6

Frink, Maurice; Jackson, W. Turentine; Spring, and Agnes Wright; "When Grass Was King", *in Contributions to the Western Range Cattle Industry Study,* University of Colorado Press,(Boulder 1956

Fort Morgan Heritage Foundation, "From the Steppes to the Prairies: A Brief History of the German People from Russia in Fort Morgan, Colorado" (Fort Morgan 1984).

Garver, Bruce, "Immigration to the Great Plains, 1865-1914: War, Politics, Technology, and Economic Development", *Great Plains Quarterly*, Summer 2011

Bibliography

Gilmore, John S. and Ryan, John J., "The Government Sector of the Arkansas Valley Economy", prepared for The Colorado Division of Commerce & Development, Denver Research Institute, June 1965

----. "The Manufacturing Sector of the Arkansas Valley Economy", prepared for The Colorado Division of Commerce & Development, Denver Research Institute, June 1965

Greever, William S. "A Comparison of Railroad Land-Grant Policies", *Agricultural History*, Apr. 1951, pp. 83-90

Goldin, Claudia, "A Brief History of Education in the United States", NBER Historical Paper 199, National Bureau of Economic Research (Cambridge, MA 1999).

Goodykoontz, Colin B. "The People of Colorado" in Hafen, Editor, Colorado and Its People: A Narrative and Topical History of the Centennial State, Lewis Historical Publishing Company, Inc. (New York 1948), vol. 2, pp. 77-120

Gordon, Dan "Where the Money Flows", Denver Post September 9, 2012

Hafen, Leroy, editor, "The W.M. Boggs Manuscript About Bent's Fort, Kit Carson, and the Far West and Life Among the Indians," *The Colorado Magazine*, Mar. 1930, pp. 45-69

Hamman, A. J., "Theodore C. Henry—Champion Irrigation Project Promoter", in The Colorado Water Conservation Board, *A Hundred Years of Irrigation in Colorado* (1952).

Hansen, Zeynep K., and Libecap, Gary D., "Small Farms, Externalities, and the Dust Bowl of the 1930s", *Journal of Political Economy*, June 2004

Harl, Neil E., "History and Unique Features of the Farm Credit System", *Choices,* 1st quarter, 2005

Harshbarger, C. Edward and Duncan, Marvin, "Parity-Is It the Answer?", Federal Reserve Bank of Kansas City, *Economic Review*, June 1978, pp. 3-14

Hauk, Cornelius W., "La Junta, The Santa Fe's Colorado Connection", in *Santa Fe and the Intermountain West*, Colorado Rail Annual No. 23, Colorado Railroad Historical Museum

Henderson, Jason, "Rebuilding Rural Manufacturing", Federal Reserve Bank of Kansas City, *The Main Street Economist*: Issue 2, 2012

Hewes, Leslie, "Early Suitcase Farming in the Central Great Plains", *Agricultural History*, Jan. 1977, pp. 23-37

Hobbs, Gregory J., Jr., "Colorado Water Law: An Historical Overview", *University of Denver Water Law Review*, Fall 1997

Hockmeyer, M. F., "Don Miguel Antonio Otero 1829-1882", Otero County Genealogy and History

Holsinger, Paul M., "Amache", *Colorado Magazine*, Winter 1964

Howe, Charles W., Lazo, Jeffrey K. and Weber, Kenneth R., "The Economic Impacts of Agriculture-to-Urban Water Transfers on the Area of Origin: A Case Study of the Arkansas River Valley in Colorado", *American Journal of Agricultural Economics*, Vol. 72, No. 5, Proceedings Issue, pp. 1200-1204 (Dec. 1990).

Hudler, Ron, "The Economic Impact of Prison Closing in Burlington", *Colorado Business Review*, Nov. 2016

Hudson, John C. "Towns of the Western Railroads", *Great Plains Quarterly*, Winter 1982

Hurt, R. Douglas, "Federal Land Reclamation in the Dust Bowl", *Great Plains Quarterly*, Spring 1986, pp. 94-106

Johnson, Thomas G., "The Rural Economy in a New Century" in *Beyond Agriculture: New Policies for Rural America*, Center for the Study of Rural America, Federal Reserve Bank of Kansas City (2000).

Johnston, M.D., "Eastern Colorado Fifty-seven Years Ago", *Colorado Magazine*, May 1944, pp116-118

Kandel, William and Parrado, Emilio A., "Restructuring of the US Meat Processing Industry and New Hispanic Migrant Destinations", *Population and Development Review*, Sep. 2005, pp. 447-471

Kepfield, Sam S.," Great Plains Legal Culture and Irrigation Development: The Minitare (Mutual) Irrigation Ditch Company, 1887-1896", *Environmental History Review* (Winter, 1995), pp. 49-66

Kendall, Charles, "A History of the Lamar Economy", draft for Lamar Centennial Publication (unpublished 1986).

Kirby, Russell S., "Nineteenth-century Patterns of Railroad Development on the Great Plains", *Great Plains Quarterly, Summer 1983), pp. 157-170*

Kimmel, Roy I., "Unit Reorganization Program for the Southern Great Plains", *Journal of Farm Economics* (1940, Vol22, Number 1).

Kline, John B., Working Paper #10, "Summary of Field Study Investigations, Phase I." in University of Colorado School of Business, Arkansas Valley Study, Trade and Services Sector of the Arkansas Valley Economy in Colorado (1965).

Kloberdanz, Timothy J., "People Without a Country: The Russian Germans of Logan County Colorado" in Wells, Dale, *The Logan County Ledger,* Logan County Historical Society (1976), pp. 225-47

Langemeier, Michael and Boehlje, Michael," Drivers of Consolidation and Structural Change in Production Agriculture", *Federal Reserve Bank Kansas City Economic Review*, Special Issue 2017, pp. 5-24

Las Animas Leader, "Railroads" (West Las Animas, Dec. 26, 1873).

Lavender, David, "Bents Fort: Outpost of Manifest Destiny", in *Essays and Monographs in Colorado History*, No. 6, 1987, Colorado Historical Society

Limerick, Patricia Nelson "Making the Most of Words" in *Under an Open Sky: Rethinking America's West* W. W. Norton & Company (New York 1992).

Longmontian blog, "Observations about Longmont, Colorado",

http://longmontian.blogspot.com/2010/01/

Luebke, Frederick C., "Back to the Future of the Great Plains", *Montana: The Magazine of Western History* (Autumn, 1990), pp. 60-65

Luttrell, Clifton B., "The Russian Wheat Deal-Hindsight vs. Foresight", *Federal Reserve Bank of St. Louis Review*, October 1973, pp. 2-8

Bibliography

Lymberopoulos, P. John, Working Paper #6: "Retail Sales: Levels and Patterns", in University of Colorado School of Business, Arkansas Valley Study, Trade and Services Sector of the Arkansas Valley Economy in Colorado, 1965

Markoff, Dena S., "A Bittersweet Saga: The Arkansas Valley Beet Sugar Industry, 1900-1979", *The Colorado Magazine*, Summer/Fall 1979, pp. 161-178

----. "The Sugar Industry in the Arkansas River Valley: National Beet Sugar Company", *The Colorado Magazine,* Winter 1978, pp.69-92

McDean, Harry C., "Dust Bowl Historiography" in *Americans View Their Dust Bowl Experience*, edited by Wunder, Kaye and Cartensen, University Press of Colorado (Niwot, 1999)

McFerrin, Randy and Wills, Douglas, "Searching for the Big Die-Off: An Event Study of 19th Century Cattle Markets", *Essays in Business and Economic History,* Vol. XXXI 2013

McGerr, Michael E. "Is There a Twentieth-Century West?" in *Under an Open Sky: Rethinking America's West* W.W. Norton & Company (New York 1992).

McHendrie, A. W., "Boyhood Recollections of Springfield, Colorado", *Colorado Magazine*, 1944 pp 93-100

----. "The Early History of Irrigation in Colorado and the Doctrine of Appropriation" in The Colorado Water Conservation Board, *A Hundred Years of Irrigation in Colorado* (1952).

Mencken, H.L., "The Dole for Bogus Farmers", *American Mercury 39,* December 1936

Mercer, Lloyd J., "Land Grants to American Railroads: Social Cost or Social Benefit?", *The Business History Review* (Summer, 1969), pp. 134-151

Merrill, George B., "Early History of Lamar, Colorado", *The Colorado Magazine,* July 1929 pp.117-126

Mintz, Sidney "Sweetness and Power" Fort Collins History Connection Archive (1985).

Mock, S.D., "The Financing of Early Colorado Railroads", *Colorado Magazine*, November 1941 pp. 201-9

Mohl, Fred, General Traveling Agent, Amity Canal Co. *About Farming by Irrigation Under the Amity* (Circa 1900).

Motherhead, Harmon, "Protection to Promotion in the Range Cattle Industry", in *A Taste of the West: Essays in Honor of Robert G. Athearn,* Pruett Publishing Company (Boulder 1983).

Musick, J.T., and Stewart, B.A., "Irrigation Technologies" in *Groundwater Exploitation in the High Plains,* Edited by David E. Kromm & Stephen E. White, University of Kansas Press (1992).

Nelson Chas. J., "Agricultural Possibilities of Eastern Colorado, Wonderful Opportunities for the Homeseeker or Investor, Lands in Yuma and Washington Counties, Colorado" circa 1910

Newsweek," The Tractor Rebellion", Dec. 19, 1977

Passenger Department, Missouri Pacific Iron Mountain, *Eastern Colorado, Its Opportunities and Resource-A New Region Opened to Agriculture by the Development of Dry Farming and Irrigation-Reliable Facts for Homeseekers* (1908).

Riebsame, William E., "The Dust Bowl: Historical Image, Psychological Anchor, and Ecological Taboo", *Great Plains Quarterly*, Spring 1986

Paschal, Allen W., "The Enemy in Colorado: German Prisoners of War, 1943-46", *Colorado Magazine*, Summer/Fall 1979

Pendergast, Alan, "Winging It", *Westword*, Apr. 11,1996

Phillips, Rufus "Early Cowboy Life in the Arkansas Valley", *The Colorado Magazine*, Sep. 1930, pp.165-179

Pickle, J.W., "History of Wray Mill", manuscript in Denver Public Library, Western History Collection (1907).

Popper Deborah Epstein and Frank J. "The Great Plains: From Dust to Dust", *Planning Magazine* -December 1987

Probst, Nell Brown, "The New Americans" in D. Wells, *op. cit.*, pp. 194-224

Rice, Teresa A., and MacDonnell, Lawrence J.," Agricultural to Urban Water Transfers in Colorado: An Assessment of the Issues and Options", Colorado Water Resources Research Institute, University of Colorado Boulder. Natural Resources Law Center (1993).

Riggs, Letha Wilcox, "Recollections of Baca County in the Early 1930s", Oral History in Western History/Genealogy Department, Denver Public Library

Rock, Kenneth W., "*Uesere Leute*: The Germans from Russia in Colorado", *Colorado Magazine*, Spring 1977

Rosenberg, Norman J., "Climate of the Great Plains Region of the United States", *Great Plains Quarterly*, Winter 1987

Schafer, Thomas C., "Specialization and Diversification in the Agricultural System of Southwestern Kansas, 1887-1980", in Char Miller, editor, *Fluid Arguments: Five Centuries of Western Water Conflict*, University of Arizona Press (2001).

Schlosser, Eric, "The Prison-Industrial Complex", *Atlantic Monthly*, Dec. 1998

Schnell, J. Christopher, "William Gilpin and the Destruction of the Desert Myth", *Colorado Magazine*, spring 1969 pp. 131-144

Scott, P. G., "John W. Prowers, Bent County Pioneer", *The Colorado Magazine*, Sep. 1930, pp. 183-187

Sherow, James E., "Utopia, Reality, and Irrigation: The Plight of the Fort Lyon Canal Company in the Arkansas River Valley", *Western Historical Quarterly*, May 1989, pp. 162-184

Smith, Garry "Sugar Beet Production in the Arkansas Valley of Colorado" www.SugarJournal.com (2009).

Southeast Colorado Enterprise Development, Inc., *Southeast Colorado: Emerald of the Plains: 2000 Overview and Annual Report* (Lamar 2000).

Splinter, William E., "Center-Pivot Irrigation", *Scientific American*, June 1976

Stevens, Ryan, "Manufacturing Spurs Economic Growth in La Junta" in *Colorado Business Review*, Number 4, 2015, University of Colorado, Leeds School of Business

Bibliography

Taylor, Morris W., "The Town Boom in Las Animas and Baca Counties", *Colorado Magazine*, Spring/Summer 1978

Taylor, R. G. and Young, Robert A., "Rural-to-Urban Water Transfers: Measuring Direct Foregone Benefits of irrigation Water under Uncertain Water Supplies", *Journal of Agricultural and Resource Economics* (1995), pp. 247-262

Templer, Otis W., "The Legal Context for Groundwater Use" in *Groundwater Exploitation in the High Plains,* Edited by David E. Kromm & Stephen E. White, University of Kansas Press (1992).

Time, "Furious Farmers", Dec. 19, 1977

Time, "Changing Farm Policy to Cut Food Prices", Apr. 9, 1973

Union Pacific Land Company, "Eastern Colorado and Denver Outskirts in the Big Development Race", circa 1906

Valdés, Dennis Nodín, "Settlers, Sojourners, and Proletarians: Social Formation in the Great Plains Sugar Beet Industry, 1890-1940", *Great Plains Quarterly* (1990).

Van Hook, Joseph O., "Development of Irrigation in the Arkansas Valley", *Colorado Magazine,* Jan. 1933, pp. 3-11

Wessel, Thomas R., "Agricultural Policy Since 1945" in *The Rural West Since World War II,* R. Douglas Hurt, Editor, University Press of Kansas, 1998

White, Gilbert F., "The Future of the Great Plains Re-visited", *Great Plains Quarterly,* Spring 1986

Wiley, Clarence A., "Settlement and Unsettlement in the Resettlement Administration Program", *Law and Contemporary Problems-1937*

Wilkerson, Chad R. and Williams, Megan D., "The Transformation of Manufacturing Across Federal Reserve Districts: Success for the Great Plains", *Federal Reserve Bank of Kansas City Economic Review,* Second Quarter 2012

Wolfskill, George, "Walter Prescott Webb and the Great Plains: Then and Now", *Reviews in American History*, Vol. 12, No. 2 (Jun. 1984), pp. 296-307

Worrall, Janet E. "Prisoners on the Home Front", *Colorado Heritage,* Issue 1, 1990

Worster, Donald, "The Dirty Thirties: A Study in Agricultural Capitalism" in *Americans View Their Dust Bowl Experience,* edited by Wunder, John R., Kaye, Frances W., and Cartensen, Vernon, University Press of Colorado (Niwot, 1999).

Worthy, Ford S., "The Battered House of Hunt", *Fortune,* April 1, 1985

Yanarella, Ernest J. and Blankenship, Susan, "Big House on the Rural Landscape: Prison Recruitment as a Policy Tool for Economic Development", *Journal of Appalachian Studies,* Fall 2006

Young, Jeffrey S., "Not so lonely eagles", *Forbes,* May 19, 1997

Newspapers and Periodicals

Akron News and News-Reporter

Arkansas Valley Journal

Bent County Democrat

Burlington Record

Cervi's Rocky Mountain Journal

Denver Post

Denver Times

Eastern Colorado Plainsman,

Fort Morgan Times

Fortune

Kiowa County Press

Limon Leader

Lamar Daily News-also Tristate Daily News

Lamar Register

Las Animas Leader-also Bent County Leader

La Junta Tribune Democrat

Logan County Advocate

Mountain States Banker

Newsweek

New York Times

Pueblo Chieftain

Rocky Mountain News

Springfield Democrat-Herald

Springfield Plainsman-Herald

Sterling Advocate-also Sterling Journal Advocate

Sterling Democrat

Sterling Farm Journal

Time Magazine

The Wray Gazette

Yuma Pioneer

Government Reports and Data Sources

Brush Chamber of Commerce & Public Service Company of Colorado, *Brush, Colorado*, circa 1967

Bureau of Business and Government Research, University Extension Division, University of Colorado, "Industrial Survey of La Junta Colorado", prepared for La Junta Chamber of Commerce -1930

Bureau of Business Research, University of Colorado, *Brush Industrial Survey,* 1954

Bibliography

Business Research Division, Graduate School of Business Administration, University of Colorado, Boulder, *Colorado Regional Profiles, Regions 1,5, and 6,* prepared for Colorado Department of Local Affairs (1975)

Business Research Division, Leeds School of Business, University of Colorado, Boulder, *Rural Colorado Economic Resiliency: Study of Factors Impacting Rural Economic Growth 1990-2014,* Final Draft Report, August 18, 2016

Business Research Division, University of Colorado, "La Junta Business Survey", Prepared for La Junta Chamber of Commerce-1948

Colorado Department of Agriculture, *Colorado Agricultural Statistics,* 1948-1970

Colorado Department of Highways, *Colorado Traffic Volume Study 1966, 1974, 1980*

Colorado Planning Commission, Colorado Yearbook, 1918-1973

Colorado State Board of Immigration, *Annual Report -1916*

Colorado Department of Natural Resources, Colorado Geological Survey, *Oil and Gas Fields of Colorado: Statistical Data* (Denver 1976).

Colorado Department of Labor and Employment, Labor Market Information, *Quarterly Census of Employment and Wages* (Denver, various years).

Colorado Department of Natural Resources, Colorado Geological Survey, *Oil and Gas Fields of Colorado: Statistical Data* (Denver 1976).

Colorado Department of Revenue, *Annual Report* (Denver, various years).

Colorado Division of Commerce and Development, "Regional Profiles" for Planning and Management Regions 1, 5 and 6, 1975

Colorado Legislative Council, *Report to the General Assembly: Migratory Labor in Colorado,* Research Publication No. 72, December 1962

Colorado State Demography Office, "Program Description of Location Economic Information and Forecasting Assistance", Technical Documentation, Revised August 2011

Colorado State Planning Commission, *Development of Electric Power Industry in Colorado: 1916-1936,* 1938

Colorado Water Conservation Board, *Colorado's Water Plan,* 2017

Division of Economic Development, Regional Service Institute, Southern Colorado State College, "A Feasibility Evaluation of La Junta as a Location for a Beef Slaughtering and Packing Plant" prepared for The Southern Colorado Economic District, Inc. Pueblo 1969

Division, Economic Research Service, U.S. Department of Agriculture, Statistical Bulletin No. 925

Fort Morgan Chamber of Commerce, *An Economic and Industrial Survey of Fort Morgan, Colorado,* Prepared for The Fort Morgan Industrial Foundation, Reviewed by The Bureau of Business Research, University of Colorado, Circa 1958

Interim Committee on Rural Economic Development, Issues Report to the Colorado General Assembly, Colorado Legislative Council Research Publication No. 544 December 2005

Lamar Chamber of Commerce, *Lamar Colorado Lifestyles,* Circa 1984

Osborn, C. Tim, Llacuna, Felix, and Linsenbigler, Michael, *The Conservation Reserve Program, Enrollment Statistics for Signup Periods 1-12 and Fiscal Years 1986-93*. Natural Resources and Environment

Russell, Randy, *Rocky Ford, Colorado: Targeted Industry Study* prepared for Southeast Colorado Office of Business Development, 1987

Scales, Kathy E., *Fort Morgan, Community Profile*, prepared for Colorado Division of Commerce and Development 1972

Sterling Industrial Promotion Fund, *Industrial Report for Sterling, Colorado and Area 1959*

Sterling Area Promotion Corporation, *Sterling, Colorado*, circa 1963

United Banks of Colorado: *Lamar, Colorado: An Economic Overview*—1975

United Banks of Colorado, Economic Development Department, *Fort Morgan, Colorado: An Economic Overview* 1978

United Banks of Colorado, Inc. Economic Development Department, *Fort Morgan, Colorado: An Economic Overview 1981*

United Banks of Colorado, Inc. Economic Development Department, *Sterling, Colorado: An Economic Overview*, circa 1972

United Banks of Colorado, Economic Development Department, *Sterling Colorado: An Economic Overview 1982*

United Banks of Colorado, Economic Development Department, *Las Animas, Colorado: An Economic Overview 1978*

United Banks of Colorado, Economic Development Department, *Lamar Colorado: An Economic Overview 1982*

University of Colorado Business Research Division, *Directory of Colorado Manufacturers*, 1948 ff.

US Department of Agriculture, *Progress of Farm Mechanization*, Miscellaneous Publication No. 630, October 1947

US Department of Agriculture, Economic Research Service, *Labor Used to Produce Field Crops*, Statistical Bulletin No. 364, May 1964

US Department of Agriculture, Economic Research Service, Farm Production Economics Division, In cooperation with Colorado Agricultural Experiment Station, "Changes in the Cattle-feeding Industry Along the North and South Platte Rivers, 1953-1959" (Washington 1963).

US Department of Agriculture, *Agricultural Statistics*, US Government Printing Office (Washington, various years).

US Department of Commerce, Bureau of Census, *Census of Population and Housing* US Government Printing Office (Washington, various years).

US Department of Commerce, Bureau of Census and US Department of Agriculture, *Census of Agriculture*, US Government Printing Office (Washington, various years).

US Department of Commerce, Bureau of Census, *County Business Patterns*, US Government Printing Office (Washington, various years).

Bibliography

U.S. Department of Commerce, Office of Business Economics, *Growth Patterns in Employment by County; 1940-1950 and 1950-1960, Volume 7 Rocky Mountain*, U.S. Government Printing Office (Washington 1965).

U.S. Department of the Interior, *The Story of the Colorado-Big Thompson Project*, US Government Printing Office (Washington, 1962).

US General Land Office, *Report of the Commissioner of the General Land Office: 1887-1905*, Washington

US Government Printing Office, "The Future of the Great Plains: Report of the Great Plains Committee", Washington, D.C., December 1936

Winkler, Richelle, Johnson, Kenneth M., Cheng, Cheng, Beaudoin, Jim, Voss, Paul R. and Curtis, Katherine J., *Age-Specific Net Migration Estimates for US Counties, 1950-2010*. Applied Population Laboratory, University of Wisconsin- Madison, 2013. Web. < http://www.netmigration.wisc.edu/>.

Index

A

Abitia, Johnny, 265
Acapulco Restaurant, 266
Adamson, Thomas, 59
Adolph, August, 98
Agricultural Adjustment Act (AAA),
116–117
    Agricultural Adjustment Act of 1938,
117
    controls on farm output, 117
    declared unconstitutional, 117
    Soil Conservation and Domestic Allotment Act of 1936, 117
    sugar beet exclusion, 124
Agricultural Adjustment
Administration (AAA), 117
Agricultural Extension Service, 13, 118,
120, 240
agriculture 1990–2015, 240–250
    blizzard in 2006, 243
    boom in early teens, 244
    drought 2001–02, 241
    farm consolidation, 244–246
    farm sales by size 2012, chart, 267
    hog farms, 246–248
        constitutional amendment restricting, 247
        controls, 247–248
        growth in early 1990s, 246
        local opposition to, 247
    Listeria outbreak in 2011, 241
    net farm income 199–2015, chart, 267
    renewal of CRP, 240
    water issues, 242, 248–250
agriculture in 1920s and 1930s; *see also*
Dust Bowl, 121–126
    Baca County wheat acreage 1929–
1940, chart, 156
    county agents, role of, 118
    drought, 122
    farm depression of 1920s, 111–113
        cattle ranchers, 113
        falling prices after World War I, 111
        increased planting and debt, 112
        pressures on sugar companies and
beet growers, 112
    farm populism, 122
    government programs, 115–118
    grasshoppers and jack rabbits, 120
    gross farm sales 1919–1939, chart, 136
    improving conditions late in decade,
126
    limits on credit, 131–132
    number of farms by subregion 1930–
1940, chart, 136
    precipitation by subregion 1929–1940,
chart, 134
    prices paid and received by farmers
1920–1940, chart, 134
    rural poverty increases, 122

value of crops in Baca County 1928–1940, chart, 157
value of crop sales 1919–1939, chart, 136
value of farm land and buildings 1930–1940, chart, 136
agriculture in 1940s, 163–171; *see also* World War II
  electric pumps for irrigation, 167
  government support programs, 165
  innovations, 166–167
  labor and equipment shortages, 163–164
  land values, 166
  livestock feeding, 167
  precipitation, 166
  prices, 166
  productivity, 166
  sugar beets, labor saving innovations, 167–168
  value of farm products sold in eastern Colorado 1940–1949, chart, 177
  value of farm land and buildings 1940–1950, chart, 177
  wheat boom, 168–171
agriculture in 1950s and 60s, 182–195
  change in number of farms and acreage 1950–1969, chart, 205
  contribution to regional economy, 191
  consolidation, 188
  declining sugar beet industry, 188–189
  government programs, 186
  increased cattle feeding, 191
  irrigated acreage 1940 and 1969, chart, 205
  irrigation, 191–195
  labor shortages, 189–190
  prices, 186–187
  soil bank, 183–184, 186
  strong cattle market, 190

agriculture in 1970s and 80s, 209–218
  beef boycott, 211
  boom in early 70s, 209–215
  Conservation Reserve Program (CRP), 214
  export demand, 209, 212
  falling land prices in 80s, 214
  farm populism, 215–218
  government programs, 214
  higher fuel costs, 210
  higher interest rates in early 1980s, 212
  increased debt in late 70s, 213
  irrigation, 221–223
  price controls, 211–212
  prices received and paid by farmers, 1970–1990 chart, 236
  Russian wheat deal, 210
  "tractorcade", picture, 237
  underground water use, 212
  value farm land and buildings 1969–1992, chart, 236
agriculture in early 1900s, 55–81; *see also* homesteaders, various crops
  a Golden Age, 55
  agricultural experiment stations, 62
  alfalfa, 76–77
  broomcorn, 76
  cattle, 78–80
  change in wholesales prices for farm products 1890–1929, chart, 82
  combines and tractors, 62
  corn, 75
  crop sales 1909–1929, chart, 83
  dairy, 80
  farm debt—eastern Colorado 1910 and 1920, chart, 82
  farms and acreage in eastern Colorado 1900–1920, table, 83
  hogs and poultry, 80
  increased precipitation, 56

innovations, 61–64
irrigation, 65
livestock on farms and ranches, 1890–1930, table, 84
melons and vegetables, 78
productivity, 62
rising prices, 55
settlers, 57–61
sheep ranching and feeding, 80
sugar beets, 64–72
value machinery and equipment on farms, 1900–1920, 82
value of crop sales, chart, 83
wheat, 72–75
WWI impact, 56, 73
agriculture in mid 2010s, 308–309, 315–316
agriculture processing industries, 309
agriculture's share of direct basic employment by county 2017, chart, 323
share of local economies, 309
water issues, 315
agriculture pre-1900, 27–50; see also homesteaders
choice of crops, 35
combined 1880 Bent & Elbert Counties, selected economic statistics, 1880 and 1890, table, 50
drought in late 80s, 35–36
George Swink's fruit and vegetable cultivation, 64
irrigation development, 38–47
irrigated farming number of farms and acreage, table 51
irrigated farmland, map, 52
number of farms by county, 1890 and 1900, chart, 50
obstacles to high plains farming, 27
rain follows the plow, the rainbelt, 30
settlers, 28–38
shortcomings of midwestern corn varieties, 35
value land and buildings on farms, 1890 and 1900, chart, 53
Aguayo, Marciano, 101, 103
Akron, 63, 74, 88, 254, 279
Alcala, Joe, 103
alfalfa, xiii, 38, 44, 46–48, 63, 76–78, 81, 91, 127, 172, 200, 242, 274, 284, 288, 290
conditions for successful mills, 76
Denver Alfalfa, later National Afalfa, 76–77; see also Wilson, F. M.
description and use of crop, 76
description of mills, 77
Allen, John, xvii
Amache relocation camp, 160–162, 286
boost to Granada economy, 160
description, 161
farming, 161
local attitudes toward, 161
outside work for residents, 162
picture, 177
population, 161
Amache, Cheyenne princess & John Prowers's wife, 9
Ament family, 99
American Agriculture Movement (AAM), 215–218
farmers strike, 217
five-year reunion, 218
founding, 215
national publicity, 216
plan to save American agriculture, 215
tractorcade, picture, 237
Washington rally, 217
American Beef Packers, 231
American Beet Sugar, Rocky Ford plant, 25, 66, 89, 285, 295, 297

American Sugar Refining Company,
  sugar trust, 67–69
  break up of, 69
  control of industry in South Platte
    Valley, 67
  control of US sugar market, 67
  costs and benefits for South Platte
    Valley, 69
  local resistance to, 68
Amity Canal, 57, 61, 119, 227, 242
Amity Colony, 60–61
Arab oil boycott in 1970s, 210
Arapaho Indians 1, 41, 44
Arkansas River, 2, 39, 43, 122, 195
  flood in 1965, 195
  inconsistent flow, 43
  irrigation projects, 39, 41
  John Martin Reservoir, earlier Cadoa
    Dam, 119, 195
  Long expedition, xvi, 2
  low flow in 1930s, 119
  Pike expedition, 2
  Trail City, 7
Arkansas River Land and Canal
  Company, 44
Arkansas Valley, xv, 42, 122
  alfalfa, 76
  failure to attract meat packing plants,
    232
  irrigation projects, 41–47
  John Martin Reservoir, earlier Cadoa
    Dam, 195
  Listeria outbreak in 2011 damages
    cantaloupe market, 241
  loss of traffic along US50, 225
  sugar beet industry, 64–66, 69–70,
    124, 228
  water transfers, 222–223, 248–250
Arkansas Valley Correctional Facility,
  254

Arriba, 130, 215
Arriola, Hope, 265
Ashworth, William, 193
Aspen Ski Wear, 201
Astor, John Jacob, 2
Athearn. Robert, 21
Aughey, Samuel, 32
Aukland, William, 46
Ausmus, Glen, 313
author with mannequins of great aunts,
  picture, xii

B

Baca County, 31, 32, 37, 74, 121, 127, 141,
  145–146, 164, 170–171, 214, 243, 250,
  260, 298–299
  American Agriculture Movement
    (AAM), 215, 218
  broomcorn, 76, 146, 164
  Dust Bowl, 119, 139–159
  early cowboys, 5
  early mining ventures, 86
  early schools, 94
  emigration in 1930s, 144
  homesteaders 31, 36–37, 58
  indicators in 1930s, table, 157
  railroads, 58, 74, 96
  sugar beet cultivation in 1950s and
    60s, 194
  value of crops 1928–1940, chart, 157
  wheat acreage 1929–1940, chart, 156
  wheat, 146, 169–171
Baca Food and Fuel Cooperative, 218
Bailey, Nellie C., 93
Baker, Abner, 17, 44, 45, 277, 292
banking in 1930s, 128–132
  Emergency Banking Act of 1933, 130
  Lincoln County bank history, 130
  scrip issuance, 130
  state and national bank holidays, 130

Index

US bank conditions, 128
banking in 1970s and 80s, 218–221
  bank failures, 220
  Colorado National Bank adds to loan reserve, 220
  delinquent government farm loans, 221
  government actions to restore agricultural credit, 219, 221
  problem agricultural loans, 218
  regulatory pressure on banks, 220
barbed wire, 9, 13
Bates, Harry, 228
Baxter, A. H., 13
Bay Valley Foods, 258
beef boycott in 1970s, 211
Bell, Ham, 20
Bell, Thomas, 91
Bellus, Forest, 173
Bennett, Hugh, 185
Bent and St. Vrain, 2, 4
Bent County, 21, 47, 79, 96, 127, 139, 149, 161, 173, 226, 264
  alfalfa in early 1900s, 77
  businesses in 1928, 86, 91
  Fort Lyon Veterans Hospital, 127, 254, 258
  hog farms, 246
  Latino population, 107, 264
  original County, 9, 10, 32
    age-sex mix of population in early 1880s, 92
    Boggsville school in 1869, 94
    division into 6 counties, 18
    JJ ranch, 10
  population 1870–2020, chart, xxii
  rail connections in 1870s, 18
  selected economic statistics original Bent and Elbert Counties 1880, table, 50

Bent County Bank of Las Animas, 16, 294
Bent County Correctional Facility, 254
Bent, A. E., 285
Bent, Charles, 2–3
Bent, William, 2–5, 8–9
Bent's Fort, 2–4
  Big Timbers, 4
  business model, 3
  destruction of, 4
  dealing with Indians, 3, 4
  early attempt at irrigation, 41
  labor force, 3
  picture, 24
Bent County Stock Association, later Bent-Prowers Cattle and Horse Growers Association, 8
Bergland, Bob, 216, 217
Bernanke, Ben, 128
Betz, Ava, 29, 70, 93
Biggerstaff, Allan W., 196
Bijou Canal, 45, 68, 278
Bitner, Laurence "Bud", 215, 218
Black Kettle, Cheyenne leader, 41
Blizzard, George, 88
Boggs, William, 3
Bonnifield, Paul, 125, 139, 148, 150, 151
Bovina, 6, 140
Bowles, Joseph, 7
Bowman, Charles W., 21
Bracero program
  continuation after war, 164
  end of program, 189
  farmers' dependence on in 1960s, 190
  wartime, 164–165
Brandon, 170
Brannon, Charles F., 164
Brazell, Laebert, 192
Brisbin, James, 11
Bristol alfalfa mill, 77

Browne, William, 215
Browner, Ruth, 71
Brush, 19, 72, 201, 220, 224, 231, 254, 291–293, 318, 320
   Beet field workers and *colonia*, 72, 123
   economy slows in 1980s, 293
   electric plant, 224, 293
   High Plains Youth Facility, 254
   oil boom in 1950s, 197, 279, 292
   sugar factory, 47, 67–69, 279, 291–293
Brush, Jared, 10, 292
Bryan, William Jennings, 38
Buchanan, Lizzie Gordon, 33
Burgess, Phil, 316–317
Burk, Kinan, 218
Burke, Mark, 45
Burke, William C., 44
Burlington, 37, 58, 98, 181, 194, 199, 251, 256, 264, 293–294
   hog farm, 268–269, 294
   Interstate 70, 225, 294
   Kit Carson Correctional Facility, 251, 255–257, 294, 318
   Kit Carson Memorial Hospital, 199
Burlington Development and Improvement Company, 37
Burlington railroad, 17, 19, 21, 37, 277, 288, 290–293, 299
Burns, Ken, 150
Burns, Timothy, 35
Business Research Division of the University of Colorado Leeds School of Business, xiv, 314
Butler, William, 4

C

Caddoa Dam, 119, 127, 274; *see also* John Martin Reservoir
Cain, Mary, 93
Calhan Auction Market, 243
California gold discovery, 4
Campbell, H. W., system of dryland farming, 19, 63
Campo, 142, 215–218
Carr, Ralph, 160
Carter, Jimmy, 212, 217
Cather, Willa, 34
Cattle Kingdom, 4–14
   blizzards and "Big Die-Up", 14
   cowboys' work and life, 5
   end of open-range ranching, 12–14
   important eastern plains ranchers, 8–11; *see also* Iliff, Prowers
   legacy, 16
cattle ranching 1940–2015, 163, 166, 183, 190–191, 240, 243–244
   average value of beef cattle on US farms 1867–1900, chart, 25
   beef boycott in 1970s, 211
   feeding in 1950s and 60s, 167, 191
   price controls, 211
   South Platte Valley in 1990s and 2000s, 200, 231
cattle ranching in 1930s, 124–126, 141
   emergency financing for feed, 125
   Jones Connally Relief Bill, 125
   worsening range conditions, 125
cattle ranching in early 1900s, 78–80
   growth of feeding, 79–80
   use of beet plant bioproducts for feed, 79
   WWI boom, 80
Cech, Tom, 43–44
Center for the New West, 316
Che, Deborah, 253
Cheyenne County, 92, 102, 132, 140, 195, 252, 260
   land values in 1940s, 166
   wheat boom in 1940s, 169–170
   population projection, 313

Cheyenne Indians, 1, 9, 41, 44, 277
Cheyenne Wells, 118, 121, 169, 181, 260, 301
   dryland experiment station, 63
Chivington, 22, 59
Christensen, Mrs. Hans, 100
Civilian Conservation Corps (CCC), 117, 120, 143, 175
Civilian Works Administration (CWA), 145–146
Clark-Feather Manufacturing, 201
Cole, Erin, 148
Colo-Kan, Inc., 228
Colorado Canal and Twin Lakes Reservoir, 66, 222
Colorado Colony Company, 58
Colorado Department of Highways/Transportation, 121, 225
Colorado Division of Economic Development and Foreign Trade, 314
Colorado Gasohol, 218
Colorado Interstate Gas, 249
Colorado Milling and Elevator (CM&E), 189
Colorado National Bank, 220
Colorado Plant Food, 201
Colorado Rockies gold discovery, 4
Colorado State Board of Immigration, 31
Colorado State Demography Office, xiv, 262, 307
Colorado Territorial Board of Immigration, 31
Colorado Territory boundaries set, 2
Colorado Water Plan, 315
Colorado-Big Thompson project, 119, 195
Colt Production, 233
Comanche Indians, 1, 3
Comanche National Grassland, 149

Commodity Credit Corporation (CCC), 116
Compromise of 1850, 2
Conroy, Teressa, 319
Conservation Reserve Program (CRP)
   acreage enrolled in 2008, 240
   established in 1985, 214–215
   renewal in 1990s, 240
Cooke, Jay, 18
Cooley, Dale, 226
Coolidge, Calvin, 115
corn, 46, 48, 62, 64, 75, 112–113, 119, 123–124, 143, 212–213, 251, 300
   aquifer impact on, 191, 193–194
   drought resistant varieties, 64
   early settlers cultivation of, 35
   government corn-hog program, 120, 123
   price, 37, 111, 163, 166, 187, 210, 240, 244
Corrections Corporation of America (CCA), later CORECIVIC, 254
Cottrell, H. M., 63
Cronon, William, 4
Crowley Canning Company, 78
Crowley County, 102, 125, 200, 234, 246, 261–262, 310–311, 316, 318–319
   canning industry, 78
   irrigation, 46, 119, 126, 222–223, 248–250, 289
   population projections, 313
   prisons, 234, 254–255, 269, 311
   sugar factories, 66, 188, 258–259
Crowley County Correctional Facility, 255
Crowley County Historical Society, 78
Crowley, John, 64
Crowley-Kiowa-Lincoln Counties Cattlemen's Association, 183
Cunfer, Geoff, 63, 81, 150–151

D

dairy farming, 63, 77, 80
Darley, Ward, 69
Dary, David, 85
Davis, Horace, 58
Delgado, Luis, 101
Denney, C. L., 91
Denver Alfalfa, later National Alfalfa, 77, 285
Deutsch, Sarah, 103
Dillon, Joe, 8
Dingley Tariff of 1897, 65
Dinse, John, 215
direct basic employment by industry 2017, chart, 323
Drabenstott, Mark, 314, 317
Dunbar, Robert, 35, 37
Durrell, Glen, 59–60
Dust Bowl, 73, 115, 139–150, 168, 281, 286
  author's mother's memories of, xiii
  Baca County indicators in 1930s, table, 157
  Baca County soil condition survey, 149
  Baca County wheat acreage 1929–1940, chart, 156
  causes, 150–153
  CWA and WPA projects, 145–146
  dust storm in southeast Colorado, picture, 156
  emigration, 144
  government programs, 146, 149
  Jones-Connally Relief Bill, 125
  Ken Burns documentary, 150
  legacy, 153–154
  long-term changes in land use patterns, 150
  national media attention, 144–145
  rainfall in southeast Colorado 1930–1940, chart, 155
  The Future of the Great Plains, government report, 147
  The Plow that Broke the Plains, 145
  The Worst Hard Time, 141
  US counties with worst wind erosion 1934 and 1935, map, 155
  value of crops in Baca County 1928–1940, chart, 157
dust storms in 1950s, 181–186
  comparison with 1930s, 185
  damage to wheat crop, 182
  Dust Bowl tourism, 182
  government aid, 183–184
  measures of drought, 181
  role of soil conservation districts, 185
  Soil Bank, 183–184
  weather modification, 182
Dyer, E. F., 68

E

E.E. Sonnenberg and Sons Feed Lot, 191
Eads, 19, 181, 198, 200, 221, 252, 262, 301
Eckman, John, 36
economic base analysis, 307
economy 1990–2015, 250–258; *see also* Great Recession
  annual change in real nonfarm GDP, chart, 268
  Arkansas Valley economic slump, 256–258
  closure of Bent County Fort Lyon Veterans Hospital, 258
  closure of La Junta Bay Valley Foods factory, 258
  closure of Lamar Neoplan plant, 256–257
  cost-adjusted median family income by county, chart, 171
  cost of living indexes by county, chart, 271

Index

Great Recession, 239
hog farms, 246–248
Latino population, 263–266
oil and gas, 252
prisons, 253–256
renewable energy, 252–253
wage and salary employment 1990–2015, chart, 267
economy in 1930s, 113–115, 126–128; *see also* Great Depression, Dust Bowl
  Baca County indicators in 1930s, 157
  banking, 128–132; *see also* banking in 1930s
    banking statistics for eastern plains 1929–1940, table, 138
  employment change by subregion and in US, 1930–1940 chart, 138
  federal government growth in 1930s, chart, 135
  government response to Depression, 118
  job losses, 126
  manufacturing, 127
  railroads, 127
  recovery late in decade, 128
  worldwide depression, 113–114
  worst economic downturns since 1929, chart, 135
economy in 1940s, 159–162, 171–173
  banking, 173
  construction, 172
  employment by county,1940–1950, table, 179
  growth in labor force, 174
  incomes in 1949, 175
  manufacturing, 172
  median household income 1949, chart, 179
  nonfarm employment, 171
  railroads, 173

  US postwar boom, 171
  wartime government activities in region, 159–12
  wartime labor shortages, 163–164
  women enter labor force, 175
economy in 1950s and 60s, 195–202
  agribusiness, 201
  change in nonfarm employment by county 1950–1970, chart, 206
  early meat packing operations, economic development efforts, 200–202
  homebuilding, 199
  major employers close, 200
  national economic changes, 198–199
  oil boom 195–198
    production in Denver-Julesburg Basin,1950–1970, chart, 206
  population shifts to metro areas, 202–203
  services, 199–200
  smaller towns lose retail, 200
  US economy, 198
economy in 1970s and 80s, 223–233
  banking, 218–221; see also banking in 1920s and 1930s
  interstate highways, 225–227
  job growth and net migration, 1970–1990, chart, 238
  Limon travel center, 226
  meat packing plants, 230–232
  national recession and rebound in 1970s, 223
  national recession in early 80s, 224
  Neoplan bus plant in Lamar, 224, 232–233
  railroads reduce operations, 226–227
  real nonfarm earnings 1970–1990, chart, 237

slump in South Platte Valley in 1980s, 224
strong growth in early 70s, 223
sugar beet, 224, 227–230
women entering labor force, 234
economy in mid 2010s, 307–312
commuting, 310
direct basic employment by industry 2017, chart, 323
GDP by industry 2015–2017, chart, 324
government, 311
income shares from farms and transfers, chart, 324
investment and welfare income, 310
manufacturing, 311
multipliers, 312
retiree spending, 310
tourism, 311
economy in late 1800s and early 1900s, 85–91
automobile sales and service in 1920s, 90
businesses in Holyoke and Las Animas, 86–87
distribution of nonag workforce by industry, US and eastern plains, table, 105
electrification, 87
employment by industry, 1930, 88
manufacturing, 86, 88–89
population by county 1890–1930, table, 106
population change in irrigated and dryland counties 1890s through 1920s, chart, 106
railroads, 89–90
share of workforce in agriculture by county 1930, chart, 105
transformation to industrial economy, 85

women employed in service industries, 91
education and literacy, 93–95
contribution of education to economic growth, 94, 262–263
early schools in region, 94–95
education level of population, 95, 152, 203, 260–261, 317–318
high schools, 95
need for greater worker skills, 93–94
Latinos, 102, 264–266
literacy rates, 1900–30, 94
residents' investment in schooling, 94
school enrollments 1910–1930, 95
teacher qualifications in rural areas, 94
Egan, Timothy, 73, 141, 150, 185, 186
Eisenach, Marvin, 240
Eisenhower, Dwight, 225
Elbert County, 48, 80, 88, 121, 175, 198, 224, 245, 251–252, 261–262, 311–313
commuting, 234, 239, 259, 310
economic and demographic characteristics, 259–260
income and cost of living, 262
original County, 15, 31, 92, 95–96
population growth 1990–2015, 257, 259, 264
projected population, 313
selected economic characteristics, original Bent and Elbert Counties 1880, table, 50
Elbert town, 121
electric power, 87, 224, 281, 285, 295, 300
contribution to economic growth late 18th early 20th centuries, 87
early local utilities, 87
REA, 87, 118, 121, 167, 192
renewable energy, 252–253
Rush Creek windfarm, picture, 269

Elizabeth, 259
Emergency Agricultural Act of 1978, 221
Emergency Farm Mortgage Act of 1933, 116
Emmons, David, 32
Evans, Dick, 242
Ewegen, Bob, 202, 248

F

Farm Credit Administration (FCA), 131
farm depression of 1920s, 111–113
   cattle ranchers, 113
   falling prices after WWI, 111
   increased planting and debt,112
   pressures on sugar companies and beet growers, 112
Farmers and Merchants Bank of Limon, 130
Farmers Bank of Fleming, 130
Farmers Home Administration (FmHA), 219
Farmers State Bank of Bovina, 130
Farnham, Thomas, 3
Farr, Charles J., 5
Federal Aid Highway Act of 1956, 225
Federal Emergency Management Agency (FEMA), 243
Federal Emergency Relief Administration (FERA), 116, 145–146
First National Bank in Lamar, xiii
First National Bank of Brush, 220, 292
First National Bank of Eads, 220
First National Bank of Hugo, 130
First National Bank of La Junta, 16
First National Bank of Limon, 130
First National Bank of Springfield, 220
First National Bank of Stratton, 131
Flagler, 19
Fogel, Robert, 16
Ford, Henry, 61

foreign immigration 1880–1930, 97–103; *see also* German Russians, Mexicans
   foreign born population by country 1890–1930, table, 108
   German Russians, 71, 97–100
   immigration to US in late 1800s and early 1900s, 97
   influx to US in late 1800s and early 1900s, 97
   Japanese, 100
   Mexicans, 72, 100–103
Fort Lyon canal, 39, 44, 119, 242, 248–249
   financial problems in late 1800s, 44
   financial struggles in 1930s, 119
   Henry, T. C., 43–44
   limited water in 1930s, 119
   potential transfers in 2000s, 248–249
   Supreme Court gives farmers control, 44
Fort Lyon Veterans Hospital, 127, 254, 258, 295
Fort Lyon, military fort, 4, 294
Fort Morgan, 67, 96–97, 131, 162, 203, 217, 234, 252, 259, 274–275, 277–280
   arrival of railroads, 19, 21, 277
   Baker, Abner, 17, 45
   Bijou Ditch, 45, 68, 278
   Cargill, 232, 257, 276, 280, 293, 309
   early meat packing plants, 231–232
   economic slump in 1980s, 224, 232, 234, 279
   Great Western Sugar, 67–72, 229–230, 278–280
   irrigation, 278
   Latino population, 167, 190, 264–265
   layoffs at packing plant and closure of sugar factory in 1980s, 279
   Leprino Foods, 280, 309
   military fort 1866, 277

oil boom in 1950s, 197, 279
Western Sugar Cooperative, 230, 309
Fort Morgan canal, 45, 277–278
Fort Morgan Dressed Beef, 231
Fort Wise Treaty, 41
Fortier, Samuel, 43
Fosdick Irrigation Ditch, 41
Foutz, Alan, 240
Fowler, 164
Franke, Vernon, 213, 220
Frazier, Ian, 56
Fremont, John C., xvi
Frink, Maurice, 12
Frost, Reuben W., 182
Fuller, Angelina, 32
future challenges to region, 315–321

G

Gano, George, 169
Garver, Bruce, 20, 57
Garvey, Ray H., 169
Gausman, Claude, 153
GDP by industry 2015–2017, chart, 324
Genoa State Bank, 130
Gentz, John, 192
German Russians, 33, 71–72, 97–100, 101
  abandonment of field labor, 100
  knowledge of dryland farming, 64, 72, 98
  large families, 99
  origins in southern Russia, 97–98
  population in 1930, 100
  share of beet field workforce in 1909 and 1927, 100–101
  The Settlement in Kit Carson County, 98
GI bill, 174
Gilpin, William, xvii
Glasgow, Bert, 142
Goldin, Claudia, 94, 95, 102

Gonzales Daniel, 256
Goodnight, Charles, 6, 9, 10
Goodnight-Loving Trail, 6
Gordon, Arthur C, 44
Gordon, Robert, 87
Granada, 6, 19–20, 95–96, 102, 265, 274
  Alzada Lotz, 34
  Amache relocation camp, 160–161
  railroad, 6, 18, 20–21, 95
  ranked distressed in 2017, 256
Granada Fish Market, 162
Gray, Bill, 243
Great Depression, xiii, xvii, 74, 103, 111, 113–114, 139, 159, 171, 198, 252, 274–275; *see also* Economy in 1930s, Dust Bowl
  banking, 128–132, 173
  expanded government role in economy, 115
  impact on agriculture, 118–126
  impact on nonfarm economy, 126–128
  measures of severity, 113–114
  regional population loss, 115, 132–133
Greater Lamar Improvement Company (GLIC), 201
Great Plow-up, 140, 150
Great Western Sugar, 67–71, 89, 127, 189, 229–230, 279, 290, 293; *see also* Great Western United, HIRCO
  acquisition by Hunt brothers, 229
  bankruptcy, 229
  closure of Colorado factories and bankruptcy, 229–230
  description of Sterling factory, 70–71
  feed lots, 80
  irrigation projects, 46
  labor supply, 101, 199
  sale of Fort Morgan factory to Western Sugar Company in 1986, 230
  sugar trust, 67–70

White, William M. Jr.,"Billy", 189, 228
Great Western United, 189, 228-9
Greeley, Horace, 28, 277
Greever, William, 17, 19
Gregg, Josiah, 321
Gregory, James, 144
Gresham, Sir Thomas, 130
Griffin, Rip, 226

H

Hall, Larry, 213
Ham, A. B. "Bright", 79
Harper, Thomas, 298
Harris, Katherine, 28, 31, 33, 42
Harris, W. C., 79, 288
Hartman, xiii, 77
Harvey House restaurant, 128
Harvey, Robert, 162
Hasart, Jacob, 139
Haswell 22, 170, 302
Havemeyer, Henry O., 68
Helvetica Milk Condensing Company, 80, 285
Henderson, George, 97
Henderson, Jason, 227, 244, 314
Henderson, W.L., 68
Henry, Theodore C., 43-44
Hersperger, Tilghman P., 10
Herzog, Henry, 167
Hewes, Leslie, 152, 183
High Plains A&M, 249
High Plains Youth Facility, 254, 293
Hijar, Perfecto, 265
Hiltzik, Michael, 117
HIRCO, Hunt International Resources Corporation, 229-230
Hobbs, Greg, xvi
Holbrook Turkey Growers, 201
Holly, 6, 70, 95, 146, 170, 195, 301
  high school, 95
  sugar factory 66, 67, 70
Holly, Hiram, 11-12
Holly Sugar, 66-67, 70, 172, 188
Holmes, I. R., 284
Holyoke, 33, 202, 216, 264
  businesses in 1924, 86-87
  hog farm, 246
  Latino population, 264, 266
Holyoke Farmers State Bank, 220
homestead legislation, 28-29
  claims filed by McMillin family, 29-30
  Desert Land Act of 1877, 29
  Enlarged Homestead Act of 1909, 56
  Homestead Act of 1862, 28-30
  political issues, 28
  procedures for claiming land, 28-29
  Timber Culture Act of 1873, 29
homesteaders 1885-1900, 28-38; *see also* agriculture pre-1900
  available land west of hundredth meridian, 30
  corn's virtues and faults, 35
  drought in late 80s, 35-36
  farm depression in 90s, 37-38
  land promotion, 30
  numbers of farms and settlers, 31-32, 58
  rain follows the plow, the rain belt, 30-31
  relief efforts for central plains settlers, 38-39
  rise in farm populism, 37-38
  settlers' states of origin, 32
  social impact of drought failures, 37
  sod house in Morgan County, picture, 53
  transportation to new homes, 31; *see also* agriculature in early 1900s
homesteaders in early 1900s, 57-61

improved crop and livestock varieties, 64
land promotion, 57–58
numbers of new farms and people, 58
skills of settlers, 57
strategies to get land, 58
transformation of plains, 61
transportation to new homes, 58
Hoover, Herbert, 115
Hopkins, Tom, 74, 169
Hosokawa, Bill, 161
Howe, Charles, 223
Huddleston, C. C., 86, 96
Hughbank, J. D., 120
Hugo, 95, 130, 200
  CCC camp, 120, 121
  hospital, 200
  town in 1880, 95
  railroad, 17, 18, 21, 227, 273,
  rabbit drive, 120
  Spanish Flu, 111
Hunt brothers, Bunker and Douglas, 229
Hurt, Douglas, 116, 120, 139, 140, 154, 165, 167, 195, 225, 231

I

Iliff, John Wesley, 9–10, 12
incomes,
  adjusted for living costs 2013–17, 262
  comparison with US 1950s and 60s, 203
  cost-adjusted median family income by county, chart, 271
  Latino median incomes 2013–17, 265
  effect of low productivity jobs in region, 263
  median family incomes 1949, 175–176
  median family incomes 1969, 203
  median family incomes 2013–17, chart 271
  median family income in larger towns 1949–2015.chart 205
  median household income 1949, chart, 179
  productivity, relationship with, 262
  reasons for lagging growth in 1950s and 60s, 203
  shares in farm earnings and transfers 1969–2017, chart, 324
Interstate 70, 225–226, 251
  contribution to local economies, 251, 290, 296
  damage to Arkansas Valley towns, 225–226, 258, 280, 286
Interstate 80S, later I76, 225
Iowa Beef Processors (IBP), 232
irrigation, 38–48, 221–223, 248–250; see also Bijou and Fort Lyon Canals, Rocky Ford Ditch, Ogallala Aquifer
  Amity Canal, 119, 222, 242
  Bijou Canal, 45, 68, 278
  center pivots, 192
  Colorado Canal Company, 192
  Colorado Ground Water Management Act of 1965, 194
  early hopes for, 39
  Fort Lyon Canal, 39, 44, 119, 242, 248–249
  irrigated acreage 1940 and 1969, chart, 205
  irrigated farming in eastern Colorado 1890–1930, table, 51
  irrigated farmland 1920, map, 52
  Ogallala Aquifer, xv, 39, 193–195, 212, 247, 249–250, 300, 313, 315
  Prior Appropriation Doctrine, 41
  Riparian Doctrine, 39–40
  Rocky Ford Ditch, 45, 47, 119, 222, 248, 297

role of State Engineer, 194, 242, 247, 250
transfers of water rights 221–223, 248–250, 278, 295, 308, 325
use of ground water, 1959, 193
Water Rights Determination and Administration Act of 1969, 194
well use and regulation, 193

J

Jack Rabbits, 120
Jackson Reservoir, 46
Jacober, John, 98
Jarvis Conklin Company, 45
Jenkins, Alvin, 215, 218
Jensen Brothers, 241
JJ ranch, 10, 11, 13
John Martin Reservoir, 119, 182, 185, 242, 274, 295; *see also* Caddoa Dam
   dam construction, 173
   initial water delivery water, 195
Johnson, Ed, 103, 130
Johnson, Lyndon, 210
Johnson, Thomas, 275
Johnson, Vance, 63, 140, 166
Johnston, M. D., 33
Johnston, Mrs. J. M., author's great aunt, xii, 95
Jones-Connally Relief Bill, 125
Jones-Costigan Sugar Act, 124
Jordan, Terry, 12, 38
Julesburg, 95, 114, 246, 301
   boomtown in 1860s, 20
   early irrigation, 45–46
   railroad, 18–21, 273, 275, 290
   Roosevelt, Franklin, speech at, 116

K

Kansas Pacific railroad, 17–19, 21–22, 32, 95, 273, 281, 294

Karval, 10
Katz, Lawrence, 94–95, 102
Kendall, Charles, author's father, xiii, 130, 319
Kennedy, John F., 186
Kikuchi, Rose, cared for author as a child, 162
Kimmel, Roy, 147–148
Kiowa County, xv, 92, 125, 127, 132–133, 146, 171, 176, 182–183, 185, 191, 200, 219, 241, 252, 256, 260–262, 302, 316, 318–319
   CRP filings in 1980s, 214
   homesteaders in early 1900s, 59
   land values in late 1930s, 121
   large wheat growers in 1940s, 169–171
   Missouri Pacific railroad, 19, 21
   oil and gas activity in 1960s, 198
   population projection, 313
Kiowa Indians, 1, 3
Kit Carson Correctional Center, xiv, 254–255, 294
Kit Carson County, 32–33, 35–37, 73, 75, 80, 88, 113, 118, 122, 124, 132–133, 181, 185, 189, 193, 199, 212, 227, 250–252, 264, 293–294
   feed lots in 1940s, 167
   German Russian settlers, 33, 98
   hog farms, 246
   Interstate 70, 226, 311
   Latino population, 273
   population projection, 313
   prison, 251, 254–255, 256
   sugar beets, 194
Kit Carson town, 17–18, 21
Kit Carson, explorer and scout, 4
Klein, Murray, 20
Knearl, William, 292
Knowlton, Christopher, 5, 11, 13
Kobobel, Glen, 242

Kockhis, Jan, 241
Kraenzel, Frederick, 301
Kriss, John, 169, 186

L

La Junta, 78, 86, 88, 92, 96, 131, 150, 201, 203, 233, 273–276, 280–284
  canning industry, 78, 201
  closure of Bay Valley Foods, 258
  early electric power, 87
  economy diversifys in 1920s, 282
  Harvey House restaurant, 281
  high school, 95
  Kansas Pacific Railroad, 18, 281
  Latino population, 190, 265, 282
  New Mexico trade, 18
  Otero Junior College, 283
  Otero, Don Miguel Antonio, 22
  Santa Fe Railroad, 18–22, 89, 127, 173, 200, 243, 258, 273, 281–283
  wartime activity, 159–60
Lamar, xvii, 44, 87, 96, 118, 131–132, 146, 164, 173, 182, 195, 200–203, 216, 225, 254, 274–276, 284–287, 312, 328
  author on board of agricultural bank, xiii, 220
  author's boyhood home, xiii
  banking, 130–131, 319
  colonia, picture, 109
  dairy, 80
  Dust Bowl, 118–119, 142–147, 286
  early town, character of, 96
  economic development efforts, 201–202
  flour mill, 75, 86, 97, 170, 200, 285
  hog farm, 246, 248
  Interstate 70, impact of, 225, 286
  Lamar Junior College, later Community College, 286
  land boom in early 1900s, 32, 58–59, 96
  Latino population, 101–103, 265–266
  meat packing plant, attempted acquisition, 232
  National Alfalfa, Denver Alfalfa, 77, 172, 200, 285
  Neoplan, 224, 232–233, 250, 256–257, 276, 308, 319
  sugar plant, 66–67, 70
  wind farm, 252
Lamar Flour Mill, 75, 86, 97, 170, 200, 285
Lamar Heat, Light and Power Co., 87
Lamar National Bank, 131
Lamar, L. C. Q., 284
Las Animas, 2, 14, 35, 56, 92, 224, 273–274, 291, 294–296
  Bent County Correctional Facility, 254
  businesses listed, 85–86
  federal presence in 1930s, 274, 295
  Fort Lyon Veterans Hospital, 127, 258, 274, 295
  Kansas Pacific railroad, 18, 95, 294
  New Mexico trade, 21, 294
  proposed power plant, 224
  ranked distressed in 2017, 256
  Santa Fe railroad, 20–21, 95, 127, 295
  sugar factory, 66–67, 126
  West Las Animas, 9, 18, 20–21, 95, 295
Latham, Lester, 103
Latinos, 100–103, 263–266; *see also* Mexican
  Bracero program, 164–165, 189–190
  education, 102, 265
  efforts to improve migrant worker conditions in 1950s and 60s, 190
  incomes and poverty rates, 265
  Lamar *colonia*, picture, 109
  occupation mix, 265–266

population
- 1930–1970, 264
- 1970–1990, 234, 264
- 1990–2015, 263
- before 1930, 102
- by County 2015, table, 272
- Hispanic share of population 1970–2015, chart, 272
- Latino and non-Latino population, table, 272
- treatment of migrant workers in 1950s and 60s, 190

Lavender, David, 4
Lebsack Feed Yards, 191
Leroy, William, 86
Likes, Dr. L. E., 91
Limon, 19, 128, 130, 166, 173, 200, 216, 296–297, 318
- Interstate 70, 225–226, 296, 311
- Limon Correctional Facility, 251, 254, 291, 297
- railroads, 19, 21, 90, 127, 173, 227, 296
- Rip Griffin travel center, 226, 291, 296

Limon National Bank, 130
Limon State Bank, 130
Lincoln County, 92, 217, 226–227, 252, 296
- banks in County 1900–40, 130
- early ranches, 6, 10
- Interstate 70, 225–226, 291, 311
- population projection, 313
- prison, 254, 291, 297
- Rip Griffin Travel Center, 226, 296

Lincoln County Bank, 130
Lincoln State Bank in Arriba, 130
Lindstrom, Lorin, 62
Little Raven, Arapaho leader, 41
Logan County, 56, 75, 78, 100, 114, 123–124, 131–132, 176, 191, 224, 226, 231, 248, 252, 288–290, 308, 311
- German Russian population, 100
- homesteaders, 32–33
- hospital, 197, 200, 290
- irrigation, 41–43, 56, 195
- Sterling Correction Facility, 254, 291
- oil boom in 1950s, 196–197, 289–290
- population projection, 313
- sugar beets, 67–68, 70–71, 99, 165, 167

Logan town, previously Amen, 99
lone eagles, 316
Long, Major Stephen, xvi–xvii, xix, 2, 321
Longhorns, 6, 7, 10, 15
Lotz, Alzada, 33
Low, Sarah A., 319
Lucero, Chris, 266
Lutz, Johannes, 33

M

Macdonald, James, 10
Mackenzie, Murdo, 12
Mallet, Peter and Paul, 2
Manzanola Canning Company, 78, 203
map of eastern Colorado plains, xx
Markoff, Dena, 66
Martin, John, 121
Masterson, Bat, 284
Maxwell, Charles, 97, 285
May, author's Great Aunt, picture xiii, 95
May, William, 67, 69, 103
McDean, Harry, 152
McHendrie, A. W. 36, 41
McKeever, H. E., 159
McKenney, Harold, 174
McKinley, William, 38
McMath, Robert, 37
McMillan, Robert T, 144
McMillin family, 29
- Mary Craig, married Marsena, 93
- ranch, 29

Raymond, 125
McMurtry, Larry, 203
meat packing, 7, 17, 89, 224, 230, 232, 250–251, 286, 293, 295, 309
   beef boycott, 211–212
   Excel-Cargill, 232, 257, 276, 280, 291, 293
   Fort Mogan plant, 231, 234, 257, 276–277, 279–280
   migrant work force, 231, 234, 266
   Sterling plant, 232, 287, 291
Mencken, H. L., 144
Mercer, Lloyd, 17
Merino, 90
Merrill, George, 9
Merrill, Louise, 96
Messenger. Issac, 13
Mexicans; xv, 15, 79, 97, 100–103; *see also* Latinos
   Bracero program, 164–165, 189–190
   colonias, 101–102, picture 109, 314
   education, 102
   field workers, 72, 100–101, 194, 292
   population, 102–103
   resistance to, 103, 190
Michiner, George W., 87
Midway Homes, 201
Miller, Robert, 8
Miner, H. Craig, 169
Missouri Pacific railroad, 19, 21–22, 57, 76
Mohrland Brothers, 201, 233
Monahan, Doris, 114, 118
Moore, Judge R. H., 79
Morey, A, J., 69
Morey, Chester, 67, 69
Morgan Colorado Beef, 231
Morgan County, 175, 189, 191, 197, 240, 251, 253, 309
   alfalfa in early 1900s, 77
   Bijou canal, impact on growth, 45, 278
   German Russian population in 1930, 100
   irrigation, 45, 242–243, 278
   job losses in middle 1980s, 224
   Latino population, 234, 264, 266
   meat packing, 231–232, 234, 257, 279–280, 309
   oil and gas, 197, 252, 311
   population projection, 313
   sugar beets, 65, 67, 69, 71–72, 230
Morgan, Charles and Wendell, 34, 38
Motherhead, Harmon, 12
Mountain State Beet Growers Cooperative, 230
Mullen, J. K., 75, 97
Munsinger, 13

N

National Alfalfa; 77, 172, 200–201, 285–286; *see also* Denver Alfalfa
National Cattle Trail, 6
National Recovery Administration (NRA), 118
National Sugar Manufacturing Co, previously National Beet Sugar, 66
Neoplan, 202, 224, 233, 250, 276, 286–287, 308, 319
   boosts Lamar economy in 1980s, 224
   closure of Lamar plant 2005, 256–258
new counties, 22, 96, 262
New Deal, xvii, 5, 42, 115–121, 145–150, 168–169, 219, 299
   Agricultural Adjustment Act (AAA), 116–117
   Civilian Conservation Corps (CCC), 117, 120, 143, 175
   county agents, role of, 118
   President Roosevelt's speech on rasks for, 116

Resettlement Administration, xvii, 144–149
Rural Electrification Administration (REA), 87, 118, 192
soil conservation districta, 117–118, 146, 168, 185
Works Progress Administration (WPA), 70, 118, 146
NIBCO of Colorado, 201
Nichols Tillage Tools, 201
Nichols, Dean, 213
Niehaus, Fred, 129
Nikel, Henry, 132
Nixon, Richard, 209, 210–211
Nolan, John, 132
North Sterling Reservoir, 46
number of farms in eastern Colorado 1890–2010, chart, xxii
Nu-Way Cleaners, 143

O

Obmascik, Mark, 249
Ogallala Aquifer, xv, 39, 313, 315
   description, 193
   future depletion, 315
   irrigation from, 193, 212, 300
   long-term threats to, 250, 313, 315
   regulation of, 195, 250
oil and gas activity in central and southeast, 198
oil in Denver Julesburg Basin,195–198
   Biggerstaff, Allan W., 196
   impact on Sterling, 196–97
   Morgan County, 197
   production in Denver-Julesburg Basin, 1950–1970, chart, 206
   Washington County, 197
Oliver Manufacturing, 233
Olney Springs new prison in 1990s, 254
Oñate y Salazar, Juan de, 2

Opie, John, 187
Ordway, 19, 243
   new prison 1987, 254
Ortega, Jovita, 101
Osteen, Ike, 58, 94, 141, 143, 144
Ostwald, Fred, 99
Oswald, Joe, 22
Otero County, 48, 56, 88–90, 92, 148–149, 164, 173, 191, 200–201, 222, 225–226, 243, 251, 256, 258–262, 280–284, 297–298, 310
   early cowboys, 5
   irrigation, 39, 45–46, 48, 66, 92, 128, 222–223, 242, 248–250
   Latino population, 102, 264–265, 282
   melons and vegetables, 78, 94
   railroads, 20, 89; *see also* Santa Fe Railroad
   sugar beets, 66, 71–72, 227
Otero-Sellars, 22
Otero, Don Miguel Antonio, 22
Overland Trail, road ranchers, 5
Ovid, 165, 224, 299, 302
   colonia, 101
   feed lot, 80
   sugar factory, 69, 229
Owl Woman, William Bent's wife, 3
Oxnard brothers, 66

P

Padroni, 132, 196
Palmer Drought Severity Index, 181
Palmer, Minnie, 34
Paosour, E. C., Jr., 184
Parker, Dr. Leslie, 111
Patterson, Floyd, 142
Paulsen, Claus, 60
Pawnee Canal, 43
Payne Investment Company, 60
Payne, J. E., 13, 32

Peake, Ora Brooks, 7
Peetz, wind farm, 242
Penley, Gary, 88, 184
Peterson Canal and Reservoir Company, 45
Peterson, Peter, 45
Phillips County, 32, 36–37, 58, 74, 120–121, 123, 126, 171, 189, 202, 229, 251–252
   hog farm, 248
   irrigation, 189, 193, 212
   Latinos, 264
   population projection, 313
Phillips, Rufus, 8, 16, 88
Pike, Major Zebulon, 2
Pisani, Donald J., 43
Pletcher, Marvin, 250
Popper, Deborah and Frank, xvii
population, xviii
   1890, 92
   1890–2040, chart, 325
   1900–1930, 92, 113
   1940s, 174
   1950s & 1960s, 202
   1970s & 1980s, 234
   1990–2015, 258–259
   2015–2040, projection, 313
   age, xviii–ixx, 93, 174, 260, 303, 314
   baby boom, 174
   births and deaths by county 2015, chart, 270
   by county 1890–1930, table, 106
   by county, 1920s and 1930s, chart, 137
   by county 1940–1950, table, 178
   by county 1970–1990, table, 238
   change in irrigated and dryland counties 1890s through 1920s, chart, 106
   changes by subregion 1890–2040, chart, 325
   changes in sex mix 1880–1930, 92–93
   dependency ratios 2015, 261
   emigration by age in 1930s chart, 137
   foreign-born 1880–1930, table, 108
   Hispanic share 1970–2015, chart, 272
   in original Bent County 1870–2020, chart, xxii
   in selected smaller towns 1890–2010, charts, 304
   job growth and net migration, 1970–1990, chart, 238
   larger towns 1890–2010, chart, 305
   Latino, 102, 234, 259, 263–264
   Latino and non-Latino population, table, 272
   median age 1930–2010, chart, 270
   migration 1940–1950, chart, 178
   net migration 1940s, 1950s and 1960s, chart, 207
   projections by country, table, 326
   urban, rural-nonfarm and farm 1930–1980, chart, 207
Powell, John Wesley, 39
prisoners of war (POWs), 162, 165, 289, 292
prisons, 253–256, 258–260, 274, 287, 291, 294–295, 301, 311, 313, 318; *see also* economy, 1900–2015
   economic impact, 251, 253–254
   economics of, 255
   opposition to, 253, 255
   slowing inmate growth, 255–256
Pritchett, 142, 185
Proctor, 132
Production Credit Associations (PCAs), 116
Prowers County, xiii, 16, 21, 56, 76, 80, 89–90, 122, 132–133, 146, 170, 173–174, 182–183, 200, 215, 219, 225–226, 233, 240–241, 243, 248, 251–252, 256–259, 260, 262, 274, 284, 308, 311–312, 316

alfalfa milling, xiii, 77, 124, 200
Dust Bowl, 124, 126, 139, 146, 148, 152, 154
homeseaders, 29, 36, 60
irrigation, 39, 46, 222, 248
Latinos, 48, 102, 190, 264–265
Neoplan, 224, 233, 256–257
population projection, 313
ranching, 14, 16, 191, 211
sugar beets, 70, 72
Prowers, John Wesley, 8–10, 13, 38, 294
Pueblo West, attempt to purchase Amity rights, 1972, 222

Q

Quattlebaum, Gerald, 210

R

Ragan, Burt, 88
railroads, xvii, 16–22, 27, 93, 127, 173, 225–227; *see also* specific lines
  influence on early towns, 16–22, 95, 273, 316
  influence on early settlers, 31, 32, 58
  map of lines in late 1800s, 26
  ranching, 6, 7, 8, 19
  subsidies to, 16–17
rainbelt 30–31, 35–37, 278
Reconstruction Finance Corporation (RFC), 119, 129
Reifschneider, Sandy, 211
Republican Cattle Company, 88
Resettlement Administration (RA), xvii, 145, 147–149
Reyes, Jose, 103
Rialto Theatre in Haxtun, 203
Rice and Smith, filed plat for La Junta, 281
Richtofen, Baron von, 11
Riebsame, William E., 139

Riggs, Letha, 142
Riz, Florence, 71
road construction in 1930s, 121
Roaring Fork River, 119
Rock Island railroad, 19, 194, 293,
  financial problems in 1970s, 227
  land promotion, 58, 63
  Limon, 21, 127, 173, 296
Rocky Ford, 47, 87, 88, 92, 128, 224, 266, 274, 291, 297–298, 318, 320, 322
  melons and other vegetables, 47, 78, 201, 241–242, 297, 320,
  ranked as distressed in 2017, 256
  sugar factory, 47, 66, 69, 172, 188, 222, 228, 242, 297
Rocky Ford Ditch, 45, 47, 119, 222, 248, 297
Roosevelt, Franklin, 115, 116, 122, 130, 147, 160
Roosevelt, Theodore, 11
Rucker, Randal H., 184
RURAL COLORADO ECONOMIC RESILIENCY, 314, 319
Rural Electrification Administration (REA), 87, 119, 192
Rush Creek wind farm project, 252
  picture, 269
Russian Thistle, 100, 125
Rutheford, Turk, 142

S

Salazar, Ken, 321
Saloutos, Theodore, 150
Sand Creek Massacre, xiv, 4, 9
Santa Fe railroad, 17–22, 44, 66, 74, 75, 89, 95, 127–128, 160, 273, 284, 294, 297, 299, 308
  Amtrak designation, 227
  cattle shipping, 6

La Junta, 18, 19, 21, 127–128, 173, 200, 273, 280–282
Santa Fe Trail, 5, 85, 225
Schaeffer, Thomas, 35
Schafer, Conrad, 10
Scherler, Burl, 241
Schlebecker, John, 76
Schlosser, Eric, 255
Schreilber, Jodi, 260
Scott, C. B., 16
Scott, Marshall W., 59
Scott, P. G., 9
Seaboard Farms, 247, 264
Seckler's Feed Lots, 191
secession, proposed in 2013, 321
Sedgwick County, 8, 36, 38, 92, 113, 120–122, 126, 160, 165, 195, 224, 241, 260
  irrigation, 39, 45–46
  population projection, 313
Sedgwick town, 101, 302
Segura, Anna, 266
Segura, Roger (Rogelio), 266
Sheedy, W. A., 299
sheep ranching and feeding, 13, 15–16, 30, 38, 48, 78–80, 113, 295, 297
  feeding, 79–80, 167, 292
  slaughtering plants, 231, 293
Sheflin, Douglas, 118, 148, 154
Sheridan Lake, 19, 169
Sherow, James, 42–45, 47, 222, 267
Shroder, Derral, 218
Shroder, Gene, 217
Siefkas, Kim, 316
Silver, Mexican Sol, 3
Simla, 254
Simla State Bank, 121
Simpson, M. M., 119
Sindt, Ted, 115
Sizer, M. E., 47

Smith, Henry Nash, 30
Smith, Morgan, 222
Smoot-Hawley Tariff, 114, 123
Smythe, William Ellsworth, 39
Soil Bank, 183, 184, 186
Soil Conservation Districts, 117–118, 168, 185
Soil Erosion Service, 146
South Platte Ditch, 41
South Platte River, xvi, 2, 8, 10, 43, 119, 241, 242, 277
South Platte Valley, xviii, 42, 47, 48, 58, 65, 73, 76, 99, 100–101, 119, 162, 167, 174, 200, 203, 239, 251, 262, 264, 274, 277, 279, 301, 313
  irrigation, 39, 41–43, 46–48, 119, 193, 195, 241–242, 315, 322
  meat packing and cattle feeding, 167, 191, 231–232, 251, 257, 279, 322
  sugar beets, 46, 64–65, 67–73, 112, 119, 124, 127, 189, 224, 228–229, 230, 279, 288
Southeast Colorado Business Retention, Expansion & Attraction, 318
Southeast Colorado Enterprise Development, 318
Spanish Flu, 111
Splinter, WIlliam, 192
Springfield, 75, 87, 97, 114, 121, 132, 145, 162, 165, 181, 182, 184, 200, 216, 218, 220, 274, 291, 298–99
  Dust Bowl, 120–123, 132, 142–145, 168, 299
  rail, 74, 127, 140, 299
  wheat, 74, 141, 171–172
SS ranch, 10, 12
St. Vrain, Ceran, 2–4
Stafford, Archbishop, 224
Stagner, Bert and Mayme, 149

Index

Standard State Soil Conservation Districts Act of 1937, 117
Stanley, Henry M., 20
State Board of Immigration, 31, 57
Stegner, Wallace, 14
Stein, Ben, 114
Steinbeck, John, 144
Steinel, Alvin T., 12, 15
Stella, author's Great Aunt, picture, xii, 34, 93
Stenzel, Richard, 43
Sterling, 58, 87, 94, 96–97, 100, 114, 118–121, 127–128, 132, 182, 199, 203, 216, 224, 225, 233, 253, 259, 274–276, 287–291
    cattle feeding, 79–80, 191, 288, 290
    meat packing, 231–232, 290–292
    sugar beet factory, 67–72, 229, 288, 290
    oil, 196–197, 289
    prison, 254–255, 291
    rail, 19, 21, 90, 288, 290
Sterling Beef, 231, 290
Sterling Beef Company (SBC), previously Sterling Morgan Colorado Beef, 232
Sterling Ethanol, 253
Stiglitz, Joseph, 198
Stockgrowers Homestead Act of 1916, 56
Stockgrowers State Bank of Burlington, 129
Suetrak, 233
sugar beets, xiv, 55, 64–72, 76, 79, 86, 89, 112–113, 123–124, 127, 163, 167, 188–190, 201, 227–228, 230, 302, 309, 320; *see also* Great Western Sugar
    Arkansas Valley factories, 46–48, 66–67, 70, 89, 127, 172, 188–190, 200, 284–285, 295, 297–298
    cultivation in dryland counties, 194, 300
    economic and social impacts, 70, 72, 224
    Fort Morgan factory, 67–69, 229–230, 277, 280
    labor issues, 71–72, 98–103, 164–165, 189–190, 263
    Rocky Ford factory, 66, 172, 188, 222, 228, 297–298
    South Platte Valley factories, 46, 67–71, 89, 112, 189, 224, 228–230, 287–290, 291–292,
Sugar City beet sugar factory, picture, 84
sugar trust, 67–70
Sugar City, 46, 48, 66, 72, 172, 188, 256, 302
    beet sugar factory, picture, 84
Swanson, Terry, 241
Sweinhart, W. C., 163
Swink town, 66, 172, 188
Swink, George, 45, 47–48, 64, 66, 297
Syndicate Land and Irrigation Company, 32

T

Tanner, J. L., 5, 8
Tanner, Jack, 228
Taylor, Morris, 86
Taylor, Ralph, 18, 96
Territorial Board of Immigration, 31
Texas Fever, 6
The Future of the Great Plains, government report, 147, 150
The Plow that Broke the Plains, movie, 140, 145
Thornton, Dan, 182
Tomky, Chris, 246
Torizawa, Frank, 162
Torres, Daniel, 101
towns, see individual towns
    eastern plains towns 1880, table, 107

employment in larger towns, 1950–2015, chart, 305
histories of major towns, 276–300
median family income in larger towns 1949–2015, chart, 305
smaller towns, 300–303
towns before 1930, 95–97
town populations 1890–2010, charts, 304
towns with population > 1,000, population change 1890–1930, table, 107
tractors, 60–62, 163, 167, 210
tractorcade, 216–217
   picture, 237
Trail City, 6, 7
Turkey Red wheat, 73
Turner, Frederick Jackson, 37
Turner, Terry, 191
Twin Lakes Reservoir, 46, 66, 119, 126
Two Buttes Reservoir, 182

U

Union Bank of Yuma, 129
Union Pacific railroad, 11, 17–21, 68, 227, 277, 287, 290, 296
   land holdings, 29, 58
   land sale promotion, 11, 19, 58

V

Valdés, Dennis, 102
vegetables and fruits, 47, 64, 78, 163, 194, 223
   canning industry, 64, 78, 201, 278, 288, 297
   melon growing in Otero County, 47, 64, 78, 81, 189, 241, 297
Villa, Pancho, 101
Vivian, John, 164
Vona WPA project, 121
Vroman, John, 48

W

wage and price controls in 1970s, 211
Wagner, Lawrence, 167
Wagner, M. N., 34
Wallace, Henry, 115
Walsh, 142, 146, 190, 193–194, 215–216, 218
Walters, Lelia, 37
War Relocation Authority (WRA), 160, 162
Ward Laundry, 143
Washington County, xvii, 30, 57–58, 73–75, 80, 88, 96, 113, 115, 123, 126–127, 241, 251–252
   homesteaders, 28, 32–33
   oil boom in 1950s, 195, 197
   population projection, 313
weather, xvi
   average annual precipitation, map, xxi
   blizzards
      1880s, 14
      2000s, 243
   drought
      1885–1886, 14
      1930s, 115, 118–120, 122, 124, 126, 139–145
      1950s, 181–186
      1990s, 241
      2001–2002, 241–243
   Las Animas annual rainfall 1868–1890, chart, 25
   modification attempts in 1950s, 182
   precipitation by subregion 1929–1940, chart, 134
   rainfall in southeast Colorado 1930–1940, chart, 155
   wind erosion in 1930s, map, 155
Webb, Walter Prescott, xvi, 1, 2, 4, 11, 13, 16, 32, 322
Weiler, Stephan, 319

Wells, Henry, 32
Wessel, Thomas, 187
Western Canning, 201
Western Sugar Company, 230, 228, 280
Western Sugar Cooperative, 69, 230
Westkott, Jim, xiv
wheat, xviii, 72–75, 112, 114, 119, 142, 147, 153, 182, 185, 209–210, 212–213, 217, 240–241, 244, 299
   absentee ownership, suitcase farmers, 152, 169–170,
   boom in 1940s, 150, 168–171
   government programs, 73, 120, 122–123, 146–147, 163, 168, 185, 210, 215, 240, 244
   impact of WWI, 56, 73–74
   in 1930s, 123, 140–143
   price, 55, 111, 114–115, 141, 153, 163, 166, 187, 210, 213, 215, 240, 244
White Antelope, Cheyenne leader, 41
White, Gilbert, 150
White, Richard, 18
White, William M. Jr., "Billy", 189, 228–229
WHO Manufacturing, 201
Wiggins, 224, 231
Wilcox, Wallace, 32
Wiley, 72, 77, 146
Wiley, Clarence, 149
Willis, George W., 45
Wilson, F. M., Grandfather of author, xiii, 76–77
windmills, 38
Winter Livestock, 243
Wisdom Manufacturing, 233
Wishart, David, 30, 31, 37
Woodka, Chris, 166
Works Progress Administration (WPA), 70, 118, 146, 164
World War I, 56, 100
   labor shortages, 61, 100
   wheat growers, impact on, 73–74
World War II, 159–165
   Amache relocation camp, 160–162
   higher farm prices, 163
   labor shortages, 163–165,
Worster, Donald, 151
Wray, 166, 274, 301
Wray Milling Company, 75
Wright, Jerry, 218
Wunsch, Henry and Bill, 71

Y

Yuma County, xvii, 73–75, 80, 123–124, 126, 185, 231, 250–253, 315
   hog farms, 246–248
   homesteaders 31, 36, 58
   irrigation from Ogallala Aquifer, 193, 212, 250
   Latino population, 264–265
   population projection, 313
Yuma town, 74, 75, 165, 253, 274, 291, 299–300
   hog farm, 246–248, 300
   Introduction of electricity, 87, 300
   Latino population, 264–265

About the Author

WILSON "BILL" KENDALL IS AN EASTERN PLAINS native who grew up in Lamar where his family first settled in the 1880s. He studied economics at MIT and CU Boulder. His experience analyzing and interpreting economic developments in the state of Colorado includes a dozen years with the Governor's Budget Office and three decades as a partner and president of the Center for Business and Economic Forecasting, a consulting firm which specialized in the regional economy. Throughout his career he has been widely quoted on the Colorado economic issues and outlook in the local media.

www.ingramcontent.com/pod-product-compliance
Lightning Source LLC
Chambersburg PA
CBHW060228240426
43671CB00016B/2885